When most people think of Agatha Christie they think of murder mysteries—novels.

Most are unaware that she was also a prolific playwright. Here for the first time are eight of her outstanding plays in one volume.

"Ten Little Indians"—a quaint old nursery rhyme sets the scene for murder.

"Appointment with Death"—a devoted family shows its true colors in murder.

"The Hollow"—a weekend houseparty and the reunion of old lovers prove fatal.

"The Mousetrap"—an unknown killer stalks snowbound guests at an isolated inn.

"Witness for the Prosecution"—an act of kindness brings with it a charge of murder.

"Towards Zero"—if money is the root of all evil there are many motives for the murder of Lady Tressilian.

"Verdict"—the suicide of a hopeless invalid seems to be a shade too convenient for too many people.

"Go Back for Murder"—the daughter of a murderess tries desperately to undo the past.

Bantam Books by Agatha Christie
Ask your bookseller for the books you have missed

DEATH ON THE NILE
A HOLIDAY FOR MURDER
THE MYSTERIOUS AFFAIR AT STYLES
POIROT INVESTIGATES
POSTERN OF FATE
THE SECRET ADVERSARY
SLEEPING MURDERS

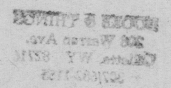

The Mousetrap
and
Other Plays

*

Agatha Christie

Introduction by Ira Levin

BANTAM BOOKS
TORONTO · LONDON · NEW YORK

THE MOUSETRAP AND OTHER PLAYS
*A Bantam Book / published by arrangement with
Dodd, Mead & Co.*

PRINTING HISTORY
*Dodd, Mead edition published November 1978
A Selection of Doubleday Book Club
Bantam edition / March 1981*

Cover painting by Tom Adams.

ISBN 0-553-13024-2

Published simultaneously in the United States and Canada

Bantam Books are published by Bantam Books, Inc. Its trademark, consisting of the words "Bantam Books" and the portrayal of a bantam, is Registered in U.S. Patent and Trademark Office and in other countries. Marca Registrada. Bantam Books, Inc., 666 Fifth Avenue, New York, New York 10103.

PRINTED IN THE UNITED STATES OF AMERICA

0 9 8 7 6 5 4 3 2 1

CONTENTS

Introduction   ix

Ten Little Indians   1

Appointment With Death   79

The Hollow   171

The Mousetrap   279

Witness for the Prosecution   359

Towards Zero   451

Verdict   531

Go Back for Murder   615

INTRODUCTION
by Ira Levin

An Agatha Christie is, of course, a mystery novel, cleanly written, masterfully surprising, and usually featuring Hercule Poirot or Miss Marple. One begins it, if one is sensible, around nine P.M., and some time after midnight one smites one's brow and says, "Of course! Why didn't I see it? It was staring me in the face!" One marvels awhile and falls into peaceful slumber. As the *New York Times* understated in a funeral piece on Dame Agatha, "She gave more pleasure than most other people who have written books."

There are about sixty Agatha Christies, which in a way is a pity, because their continuing popularity has overshadowed a second definition of the generic noun; for an Agatha Christie is also a mystery *play*, cleanly written, masterfully surprising, and *not* featuring Poirot or Miss Marple. It unfolds in two hours instead of four or five, and being both alive and more concentrated, produces a more intense pleasure. It runs for years, or in one instance forever.

There are about a dozen of these other Agatha Christies, and in them, if one knows the turf, is an accomplishment even more awe-inspiring than those sixty-odd novels. Other novelists, after all, have given us large numbers of first-rate mysteries; John Dickson Carr and George Simenon spring to mind. No playwright except Christie, however, has given us more than one great stage mystery. Check any critic's list of the ten or twelve masterworks in that trickiest and most demanding of genres and you'll find that each play—*Night Must Fall, Angel Street, The Bad Seed, Dial "M" for Murder, Sleuth,* and so on—is the work of a different hand. One real stunner per playwright seems to be all that's possible, and not for want of trying. The sole exception is Dame Agatha, who managed to write not one, not two, but three of the great stage mysteries: *Ten Little Indians, Witness for the Prosecu-*

tion, and *The Mousetrap*. When you have read them—all three are in this volume, along with five other Christie plays— perhaps you too will wonder that the second definition of an Agatha Christie isn't as widely known as the first.

Agatha Christie turned to playwriting in the midst of her novel-writing career for a reason that was, like the lady herself, both modest and astute. Other playwrights had adapted some of her novels to the stage; they had erred, she felt, in *following the books too closely*. A rare complaint for a novelist, believe me. But "a detective story is particularly unlike a play . . ." she explains in her autobiography. "It has such an intricate plot, and usually so many characters and false clues, that the thing is bound to be confusing and overladen. What was wanted was *simplification*."

And so, with *Ten Little Indians*, she decided to try the job herself. She proved to be instinctively theatrical, and ruthless as no other playwright would have dared be with her work. Three of the plays in this volume—*Appointment with Death*, *The Hollow*, and *Go Back for Murder*—are adapted from Poirot novels, but you won't find Poirot listed in the dramatis personae; Dame Agatha deemed him unnecessary. In *Appointment with Death* she found a new murderer among the principal characters; the novel's murderer becomes the play's comic relief. Two of the dead bodies of *Ten Little Indians* survive and find love in the stage version, and somehow do so without disturbing the pattern of that most dazzling of all Christie plots. (The novel, in its American editions, is called *And Then There Were None*, if you care to compare, and I hope you do.)

Nowhere is Agatha Christie's remarkable ingenuity more evident than in her adaptation of *Witness for the Prosecution*. The short story of the same title is seemingly perfect and complete, with a stunning final revelation that lifts the reader in his chair. Yet for the stage version Dame Agatha devised still another revelation beyond that one, an entirely plausible surprise that not only makes for an electrifying curtain but at the same time legitimizes what would otherwise have been a necessary deception in the list of characters. Again I hope you will read and compare, especially if you're an aspiring playwright.

Verdict is the only play in this volume not adapted from another Christie work. Dame Agatha considered it her best play except for *Witness for the Prosecution*; I would put it somewhat lower on the scale, but I am here to introduce, not argue.

The Mousetrap, based on a radio sketch to commemorate the eightieth birthday of Queen Mary, is the Christie play that is running forever. It opened in London in 1952 and has been wearing out actors, furniture, and theatrical records ever since. Cynics attribute its perpetual run to the smallness of the theater in which it plays, but that small theater was there long before 1952; why did none of its previous tenants become a tourist attraction as popular as Madame Tussaud's and the Tower of London? *The Mousetrap* is a superbly constructed mystery, irresistibly suspenseful from its very first moment, and therein lies the real reason for its enduring success.

Playwriting was, for Agatha Christie, a holiday from the book-a-year routine of her professional life. Reading her plays —more concise than the novels, richer than the short stories— can be the same sort of holiday for her readers. One word of advice to those not accustomed to reading plays: Don't worry too much about the chairs and tables. It rarely matters whether they're at stage right or stage left, or whether the doors are upstage or down. What does matter is the dialogue. Try to *hear* it, and try to hear the pauses too, that's where the shivers are.

I was fifteen when my parents took me to see the New York production of *Ten Little Indians*. As those figurines vanished one by one from the mantelpiece and the actors vanished one by one from the stage, I fell in love—with theater that grips and dazzles and surprises. I was already a would-be novelist, thanks in part to the other Agatha Christies; now I was a would-be playwright too. That 15-year-old boy and I are pleased to be introducing these plays to you.

Ira Levin

New York City
June, 1978

TEN LITTLE INDIANS

Program of the first performance of
"TEN LITTLE INDIANS" as produced at the
Broadhurst Theatre, New York, June 27, 1944.

Messers. Shubert and Albert deCourville
present
TEN LITTLE INDIANS
by
AGATHA CHRISTIE
Directed by Mr. deCourville
Scenery by Howard Bay

CAST
(In order of their appearance)

ROGERS	*Neil Fitzgerald*
MRS. ROGERS	*Georgia Harvey*
FRED NARRACOTT	*Patrick O'Connor*
VERA CLAYTHORNE	*Claudia Morgan*
PHILIP LOMBARD	*Michael Whalen*
ANTHONY MARSTON	*Anthony Kemble Cooper*
WILLIAM BLORE	*J. Pat O'Malley*
GENERAL MACKENZIE	*Nicholas Joy*
EMILY BRENT	*Estelle Winwood*
SIR LAWRENCE WARGRAVE	*Halliwell Hobbes*
DR. ARMSTRONG	*Harry Worth*

SCENE

*The scene of the play is in the living room of a house on
Indian Island, off the coast of Devon, England.*

ACT I. *A summer evening in August.*

ACT II.
SCENE I. *The following morning.*
SCENE II. *The same day—afternoon.*

ACT III.
SCENE I. *The same day—evening.*
SCENE II. *The following afternoon.*

Act One

SCENE: *The scene is the living room of the house on Indian Island. It is a very modern room, and luxuriously furnished. It is a bright sun-light evening. Nearly the whole of the back of the stage is a window looking directly out to sea. French doors are open in Center to balcony. It should give the impression of being like the deck of a liner almost overhanging the sea. There is a chair out Right on the balcony and the main approach to the house is presumed to be up steps on the Left side of the balcony. There is also presumed to be steps on the Right of the balcony, but these are not the direct way up from the landing stage, but are supposed to lead around the house and up behind it, since the house is supposed to be built against the side of a steep hill. The French doors are wide so that a good area of the balcony is shown.*

In the Left, near windows, is a door to dining room. Down stage Left is a door communicating with hall. Pull cord below this door.

Up Right is a door to study. Middle stage Right is fireplace. Over it hangs the reproduction of the "Ten Little Indians" nursery rhyme. On the mantelpiece are a group of ten china Indian figures. They are not spaced out, but clustered so that the exact number is not easily seen.

The room is barely furnished with modern furniture. Center are two sofas with space between. Chair and small table up Left. Club chair with tabouret Right and above it, down Left, where there is also a bookcase. There is a window seat up Right and cocktail cabinet below mantelpiece. Tabouret down Right. Before fireplace is a big white bearskin rug with a bear's head. There is an armchair and tabouret Right Center. A

3

*square ottoman at lower end of fireplace. A settee with
table Left of it in front of window Right at back.*

When Curtain rises, ROGERS *is busy putting final touches
to room. He is setting out bottle down Right.* ROGERS
*is a competent middle-aged man-servant. Not a butler,
but a house-parlourman. Quick and deft. Just a trifle
specious and shifty. There is a noise of* SEAGULLS.
Motor boat HORN *heard off.* MRS. ROGERS *enters from
dining room up Left. She is a thin, worried, frightened-
looking woman. Enter* NARRACOTT *at Center from Left.
He carries a market basket filled with packages.*

NARRACOTT. First lot to be arriving in Jim's boat. Another lot
not far behind. (*Crosses Left to her.*)

MRS. ROGERS. Good evening, Fred.

NARRACOTT. Good evening, Mrs. Rogers.

MRS. ROGERS. Is that the boat?

NARRACOTT. Yes.

MRS. ROGERS. Oh, dear, already? Have you remembered everything?

NARRACOTT. (*Giving her basket*) I think so. Lemons. Slip
soles. Cream. Eggs, tomatoes and butter. That's all,
wasn't it?

MRS. ROGERS. That's right. So much to do I don't know where
to start. No maids till the morning, and all these guests
arriving today.

ROGERS. (*At mantel*) Calm down, Ethel, everything's ship-
shape now. Looks nice, don't it, Fred?

NARRACOTT. Looks neat enough for me. Kind of bare, but rich
folks like places bare, it seems.

MRS. ROGERS. Rich folks is queer.

NARRACOTT. And he was a queer sort of gentleman as built
this place. Spent a wicked lot of money on it he did,
and then gets tired of it and puts the whole thing up
for sale.

MRS. ROGERS. Beats me why the Owens wanted to buy it,
living on an island.

ROGERS. Oh, come off it, Ethel, and take all that stuff out
into the kitchen. They'll be here any minute now.

MRS. ROGERS. Making that steep climb an excuse for a drink,
I suppose. Like some others I know.

(*Motor boat* HORN *heard off.*)

NARRACOTT. That be young Jim. I'll be getting along. There's two gentlemen arriving by car, I understand. (*Goes up to balcony.*)

MRS. ROGERS. (*Calling to him*) I shall want at least five loaves in the morning and eight pints of milk, remember.

NARRACOTT. Right.

(MRS. ROGERS *puts basket on floor up Left; exits to hall Left 1.*)

ROGERS. (*Breaks to Right of window*) Don't forget the oil for the engine, Fred. I ought to charge up tomorrow, or I'll have the lights running down.

NARRACOTT. (*Going off at Left*) 'Twas held up on railway. It's at the station now. I'll bring it across the first thing tomorrow.

ROGERS. And give a hand with the luggage, will you?

NARRACOTT. Right.

MRS. ROGERS. (*Enters with list*) I forgot to give you the list of guests, Tom.

ROGERS. Thanks, old girl. (*Looks reflectively at list*) H'mm, doesn't look a very classy lot to me. (*Refers to list*) Miss Claythorne. She'll probably be the secretary.

MRS. ROGERS. I don't hold much with secretaries. Worse than hospital nurses, and them giving themselves airs and graces and looking down on the servants.

ROGERS. Oh, stop grousing, Ethel, and cut along to that lovely up-to-date expensive kitchen of yours.

MRS. ROGERS. (*Picks up basket; going out Left 2*) Too many new-fangled gadgets for my fancy!

(VOICES *of* VERA *and* LOMBARD *heard outside.* ROGERS *stands at Center doors ready to receive them. He is now the well-trained, deferential manservant.* VERA *and* LOMBARD *enter from Left on balcony. She is a good-looking girl of twenty-five. He is an attractive, lean man of thirty-four, well-tanned, with a touch of the adventurer about him. He is already a good deal taken with* VERA.)

LOMBARD. (*Gazing round room, very interested*) So this is it!

VERA. How perfectly lovely!

ROGERS. Miss Claythorne!

VERA. You're—Rogers?

ROGERS. Yes. Good evening, Miss.

VERA. Good evening, Rogers. Will you bring up my luggage and Captain Lombard's?

ROGERS. Very good, Miss. (*He exits through Center windows to Left.*)

VERA. (*To* LOMBARD, *coming Right Center into room*) You've been here before?

LOMBARD. No—but I've heard a lot about the place.

VERA. From Mr. and Mrs. Owen?

LOMBARD. (*Crossing down Left*) No, old Johnny Brewer, a pal of mine, built this house—it's a sad and poignant story.

VERA. A love story?

LOMBARD. Yes, ma'am—the saddest of all. He was a wealthy old boy and fell in love with the famous Lily Logan— married her—bought the island and built this place for her.

VERA. Sounds most romantic.

LOMBARD. Poor Johnny! He thought by cutting her off from the rest of the world—without even a telephone as means of communication—he could hold her.

VERA. But of course the fair Lily tired of her ivory tower— and escaped?

LOMBARD. U'huh. Johnny went back to Wall Street, made a few more millions, and the place was sold.

VERA. And here we are. (*Moving as if to go out of door Left 1*) Well, I ought to find Mrs. Owen. The others will be up in a minute.

LOMBARD. (*Stopping her*) It would be very rude to leave me here all by myself.

VERA. Would it? Oh, well, I wonder where she is?

LOMBARD. She'll come along when she's ready. While we're waiting. (*Nodding towards cabinet down Right*) Do you think I could have a drink? I'm very dry. (*Goes below sofa to down Right and starts preparing drinks.*)

VERA. Of course you could.

LOMBARD. It's certainly warm after that steep climb. What's yours?

VERA. No, thanks, not for me— Not on duty. (*To behind chair, Right Center.*)

LOMBARD. A good secretary is never off duty.

VERA. Really. (*Looking around room*) This is exciting! (*Goes below sofa to up Center.*)

LOMBARD. What?

VERA. All this. The smell of the sea—the gulls—the beach and this lovely house. I am going to enjoy myself.

LOMBARD. (*Smiling. Coming to her*) I think you are. I think
we both are. (*Holding up drink*) Here's to you—you're
very lovely.

(ROGERS *enters Center from Left with two suitcases and
comes down Left Center.*)

VERA. (*To* ROGERS) Where is Mrs. Owen?

ROGERS. Mr. and Mrs. Owen won't be down from London
until tomorrow, Miss. I thought you knew.

VERA. Tomorrow—but—

ROGERS. I've got a list here of the guests expected, Miss, if
you would like to have it. The second boat load's just
arriving. (*Holds out list.*)

VERA. Thank you. (*Takes list.* ROGERS *goes into hall Left* 1)
How awful—I say you will be sweet and help me, won't
you?

LOMBARD. I won't move from your side.

VERA. Thank you. (*She reads list. They* BOTH *move down
Right*) It seems silly to have brought only us in the first
boat and all the rest in the second.

LOMBARD. That, I'm afraid, was design, not accident.

VERA. Design? What do you mean?

LOMBARD. I suggested to the boatman that there was no need
to wait for any more passengers. That and five shillings
soon started up the engine.

VERA. (*Laughing*) Oh, you shouldn't have done that!

LOMBARD. Well, they're not a very exciting lot, are they?

VERA. I thought the young man was rather nice-looking.

LOMBARD. Callow. Definitely callow. And very, very young.

VERA. I suppose you think a man in his thirties is more attractive.

LOMBARD. I don't think, my darling—I know.

(MARSTON *enters Center from Left. Good-looking young man
of twenty-three or so. Rich, spoiled—not very intelligent.*)

MARSTON. (*Coming down Right to them*) Wizard place
you've got here.

(*Prepares to greet* VERA *as his hostess.* LOMBARD *stands beside
her like a host.*)

VERA. (*Shakes hands*) I'm Mrs. Owen's secretary. Mrs. Owen
has been detained in London, I'm afraid, and won't be
down until tomorrow.

MARSTON. (*Vaguely*) Oh, too bad.

VERA. May I introduce Captain Lombard, Mr.—er—

MARSTON. Marston, Anthony Marston.

LOMBARD. Have a drink?

MARSTON. Oh, thank you.

(BLORE *comes up on balcony from Left. Middle-aged, thickset man. Is wearing rather loud clothes and is giving his impression of a South American gold magnate. His eyes dart about, making notes of everything.*)

LOMBARD. What will you have? Gin, whiskey, sherry—?

MARSTON. Whiskey, I think.

(*They go down Right to cabinet.*)

BLORE. (*Comes down to* VERA *at Right Center. Seizing* VERA's *hand and wringing it heartily*) Wonderful place you have here.

VERA. I'm Mrs. Owen's secretary. Mrs. Owen has been detained in London, I'm afraid, and won't be down until tomorrow.

LOMBARD. Say when!

MARSTON. Oh, wizard!

BLORE. How are you? (*Makes for cocktail cabinet.*)

LOMBARD. My name's Lombard. Have a drink, Mr.—

BLORE. Davis. Davis is the name.

LOMBARD. Mr. Davis—Mr. Marston!

(VERA *sits on Right sofa.*)

BLORE. How are you, Mr. Marston? Pleased to meet you. Thanks, Mr. Lombard. I don't mind if I do. Bit of a stiff climb up here. (*He goes up Center to balcony*) But whew! What a view and what a height! Reminds me of South Africa, this place. (*Comes down Center.*)

LOMBARD. (*Staring at him*) Does it? What part?

BLORE. Oh—er—Natal, Durban, you know.

LOMBARD. (*Crosses Center*) Really? (*Hands him drink*)

BLORE. Well, here's to temperance. Do you—er—know South Africa?

LOMBARD. Me? No.

BLORE. (*With renewed confidence*) That's where I come from. That's my Natal state—ha ha.

LOMBARD. Interesting country, I should think.

BLORE. Finest country in the world, sir. Gold, silver, dia-

monds, oranges, everything a man could want. Talk
about a land flowing with beer and skittles. (*Goes to
cocktail cabinet down Right.*)

(GENERAL MACKENZIE *arrives on balcony from Left. Upright
soldierly old man, with a gentle, tired face.*)

MACKENZIE. (*Hesitating courteously*) Er— How do you do?

(VERA *rises; meets him above sofa seat.*)

VERA. General MacKenzie, isn't it? I'm Mrs. Owen's secretary.
Mrs. Owen has been detained in London, I'm afraid,
and won't be down until tomorrow. Can I introduce
Captain Lombard—Mr. Marston and Mr.—

(MACKENZIE *crosses toward them.*)

BLORE. (*Approaching him*) Davis, Davis is the name. (*Shakes
hands.*)
LOMBARD. Whiskey and soda, sir?
MACKENZIE. Er-thanks. (*Goes down Right; studies* LOMBARD)
You in the service?
LOMBARD. Formerly in the King's African Rifles. Too tame for
me in peace time. I chucked it.
MACKENZIE. Pity. (*As* LOMBARD *pours out soda*) When.

(MISS EMILY BRENT *arrives Center from Left. She is a tall,
thin spinster, with a disagreeable, suspicious face.*)

EMILY. (*Sharply to* VERA) Where is Mrs. Owen? (*Puts case
on Left sofa.*)
VERA. Miss Brent, isn't it? I'm Mrs. Owen's secretary. Mrs.
Owen has been detained in London, I'm afraid.

(LOMBARD *to Right of* EMILY.)

LOMBARD *and* VERA. And won't be down until tomorrow.

(*They tail off, rather embarrassed.*)

EMILY. Indeed. Extraordinary. Did she miss the train?
VERA. I expect so. Won't you have something? May I intro-
duce Captain Lombard—General MacKenzie—Mr.
Marston. I think you all met on the boat. And Mr.—
BLORE. Davis, Davis is the name. May I take your case? (*Up
to* EMILY, *then goes behind her to Right.*)
LOMBARD. Do let me give you a drink? A dry Martini? A glass
of sherry? Whiskey and soda?

EMILY. (*Coldly*) I never touch alcohol.

LOMBARD. You never touched alcohol!

EMILY. (*She picks up case; goes below sofa to Left*) I suppose you know, young man, that you left us standing there on the wharf?

VERA. I'm afraid, Miss Brent, I was to blame for that. I wanted to—

EMILY. It seems to me most extraordinary that Mrs. Owen should not be here to receive her guests.

VERA. (*Smiling*) Perhaps she's the kind of person who just can't help missing trains.

BLORE. (*Laughs*) That's what I reckon she is.

EMILY. Not at all. Mrs. Owen isn't the least like that.

LOMBARD. (*Lightly*) Perhaps it was her husband's fault.

EMILY. (*Sharply*) She hasn't got a husband. (VERA *stares. Enter* ROGERS *Left 2.*) I should like to go to my room.

VERA. Of course. I'll take you there.

ROGERS. (*To* VERA) You'll find Mrs. Rogers upstairs, Miss. She will show you the room.

(*Exit* VERA *and* EMILY *Left 1.* ROGERS *exits Left 1.* WARGRAVE *enters Center from Left; comes Center.*)

LOMBARD. (*Comes forward*) I'm afraid our host and hostess haven't arrived, sir. My name's Lombard.

WARGRAVE. Mine's Wargrave. How do you do?

LOMBARD. How do you do? Have a drink, sir?

WARGRAVE. Yes, please. A whiskey.

BLORE. (*Crosses to* WARGRAVE) How are you? Davis, Davis is the name. (LOMBARD *gets his drink. Affably to* WARGRAVE) I say, wonderful place you've got here. Quite unique.

WARGRAVE. As you say— Quite unique.

BLORE. Your drink, sir.

(WARGRAVE *puts coat on sofa Left, takes his drink and sits up Left. Watches proceedings from there.*)

MARSTON. (*To* LOMBARD) Old Badger Berkely rolled up yet?

LOMBARD. Who did you say?

MARSTON. Badger Berkely. He roped me in for this show. When's he coming?

LOMBARD. I don't think he is coming. Nobody of the name of Berkely.

MARSTON. (*Jaw drops*) The dirty old double-crosser! He's let me down. Well, it's a pretty wizard island. Rather a wizard girl, that secretary. She ought to liven things up a bit. I say, old man, what about dressing for dinner if there's time?

LOMBARD. Let's go and explore.

MARSTON. Oh, wizard!

LOMBARD. Things are a bit at sixes and sevens with the Owens not turning up.

MARSTON. Tricky, what? I say, wizard place for a holiday, what?

(*Exit* MARSTON *and* LOMBARD *Left* 1. BLORE *wanders out on balcony, looks sharply into room and presently exits Right on balcony as* GENERAL MACKENZIE *and* WARGRAVE *talk.* WARGRAVE *continues to sit like a Buddha. He observes* MACKENZIE, *who is Right Center, standing looking rather lost, absent-mindedly pulling his moustache.* MACKENZIE *is carrying a shooting-stick. He looks at it wistfully, half opens and closes it.*)

WARGRAVE. Aren't you going to sit down?

MACKENZIE. Well, to tell you the truth, you seem to be in my chair.

WARGRAVE. I am sorry. I didn't realize you were one of the family.

MACKENZIE. Well, it's not that exactly. To tell you the truth, I've never been here before. But you see I live at the Benton Club—have for the last ten years. And my seat is just about there. Can't get used to sitting anywhere else.

WARGRAVE. It becomes a bit of a habit. (*He rises; breaks to Right.*)

MACKENZIE. Yes, it certainly does. Thank you—(*Sits up Left*) Well, it's not quite as good as the Club's but it's a nice chair. (*Confidentially*) To tell you the truth, I was a bit surprised when I got this invitation. Haven't had anything of the kind for well over four years. Very nice of them, I thought.

ROGERS. (*Enters Left* 1. *Picks up* WARGRAVE's *coat from sofa*) Can I have your keys, sir?

WARGRAVE. Is Lady Constance Culmington expected here, can you tell me? (*Gives him keys.*)

ROGERS. (*Surprised*) Lady Constance Culmington? I don't think so, sir. Unless she's coming down with Mr. and Mrs. Owen.

WARGRAVE. Oh.

ROGERS. Allow me, sir. (*Takes* GENERAL MACKENZIE's *coat*)
    Can I have your keys, sir?

MACKENZIE. (*Rising. Crossing down Left*) No, thanks. I'll
    unpack for myself.

ROGERS. Dinner is at eight o'clock, sir. Shall I show you to
    your room?

MACKENZIE. Please.

(MACKENZIE *goes to door Left* 1, *which* ROGERS *holds open
*   *for him.* WARGRAVE *follows more deliberately, looking
*   *around room in an unsatisfied fashion.* ROGERS *follows
*   *them out. Sound of SEAGULLS, then* DR. ARMSTRONG
*   *arrives upon balcony from Left, followed by* NARRACOTT
*   *carrying his suitcase.* ARMSTRONG *is a fussy, good-looking
*   *man of forty-four. He looks rather tired.*)

NARRACOTT. Here you are, sir. I'll call Rogers. (*Exits Left* 1.)

(ARMSTRONG *looks round; nods approval; looks out at sea.
*   *Then* NARRACOTT *returns.* ARMSTRONG *tips him.* NARRA-
*   *COTT *exits to Center Left.* ARMSTRONG *sits settee up
*   *Right.* BLORE *comes along balcony from Right; pauses at
*   *sight of* ARMSTRONG.)

BLORE. (*To above settee*) How are you? Davis. Davis is the
    name.

ARMSTRONG. Mine's Armstrong. (*Rises.*)

BLORE. Doctor Armstrong, I believe.

ARMSTRONG. Yes.

BLORE. Thought so. Never forget a face.

ARMSTRONG. Don't tell me I've forgotten one of my patients!

BLORE. No, no, nothing like that, but I once saw you in Court
    giving expert evidence.

ARMSTRONG. Oh, really? Are you interested in the Law?

BLORE. Well, you see, I'm from South Africa. Naturally, legal
    processes in this country are bound to interest a Colonial.

ARMSTRONG. Oh, yes, of course.

BLORE. (*Crossing down Right*) Have a drink?

ARMSTRONG. No, thanks. I never touch it.

BLORE. Do you mind if I do? Mine's empty.

ARMSTRONG. Not a bit.

BLORE. (*Pours himself a drink*) I've been having a look round
    the island. It's a wonderful place, isn't it?

ARMSTRONG. (*Crossing to Center*) Wonderful. I thought as I

was coming across the mainland what a haven of peace this was.

BLORE. (*Up to him, putting his face close to his*) Too peaceful for some, I daresay.

ARMSTRONG. (*Moves to Left*) Wonderfully restful. Wonderful for the nerves. I'm a nerve specialist, you know.

BLORE. Yes, I know that. Did you come down by train? (*Goes to him.*)

ARMSTRONG. (*Up Left to window*) No, I motored down. Dropped in on a patient on the way. Great improvement,—wonderful response.

BLORE. (*Up to him*) Best part of two hundred miles, isn't it? How long did it take you?

ARMSTRONG. (*To up Right Center*) I didn't hurry. I never hurry. Bad for the nerves. Some mannerless young fellow nearly drove me into the ditch near Amesbury. Shot past me at about eighty miles an hour. Disgraceful bit of driving. I'd like to have had his number.

BLORE. (*Comes to him*) Yes, and if only more people would take the numbers of these young road hogs.

ARMSTRONG. Yes. You must excuse me. I must have a word with Mr. Owen. (*He bustles out Left 1.*)

BLORE. (*Following down Left*) Oh, but—Mr. Owen isn't coming down—

(BLORE *rings bell below Left 1 door. Finishes drink; puts glass on Left sofa.* ROGERS *enters almost immediately Left 1.*)

ROGERS. You rang, sir?

BLORE. Yes, take my hat, will you? (*Hands him his cap*) What time's supper?

ROGERS. Dinner is at eight o'clock, sir. (*Pauses*) In a quarter of an hour. I think tonight dressing will be optional.

BLORE. (*Familiarly*) Got a good place, here.

ROGERS. (*Draws himself up rather stiffly*) Yes, thank you, sir.

BLORE. Been here long?

ROGERS. Just under a week, sir.

BLORE. Is that all? (*Pause*) So I don't suppose you know much about this crowd that's here?

ROGERS. No, sir.

BLORE. All old friends of the family?

ROGERS. I really couldn't say, sir.

BLORE. Oh, well— Oh, Rogers—

ROGERS. Yes, sir?

BLORE. Rogers, do you think you could put some sandwiches and a bottle of beer in my room at night? I get an 'el of an appetite with this sea air.

ROGERS. I'll see what I can do, sir.

BLORE. Rogers—I'll see you won't lose by it. Where's my room?

ROGERS. I'll show you, sir.

BLORE. (*As they go out*) Good. I can do with a wash and brush up straightaway. (*Exits Left 1 with* ROGERS.)

(*Enter* MRS. ROGERS *Left 2. She picks up glass from sofa and from table up Left and takes them down Right. Enter* ROGERS *with tray of eight glasses.*)

MRS. ROGERS. (*She takes glasses off tray and* ROGERS *puts on dirty ones*) Oh, there you are, Rogers. You ought to clear these dirty glasses. You're always leaving the dirty work to me. Here I am with a four-course dinner on my hands and no one to help me. You might come and give me a hand with the dishing up. (*To above Left sofa*) Who was it that you were talking to, by the way?

ROGERS. Davis, South African gentleman. No class if you ask me—and no money either.

MRS. ROGERS. (*Comes down Right of sofa to Center*) I don't like him—Don't like any of 'em much. More like that bunch we had in the boarding house, I'd say.

ROGERS. Davis gives out he's a millionaire or something. You should see his underwear! Cheap as they make 'em.

MRS. ROGERS. Well, as I said, it's not treating us right. All these visitors arriving today and the maids not coming till tomorrow. What do they think we are?

ROGERS. Now, then— Anyway, the money's good.

MRS. ROGERS. So it ought to be! Catch me going into service again unless the money was good.

ROGERS. (*To Center*) Well, it is good, so what are you going on about?

MRS. ROGERS. Well, I can tell you this, Rogers. I'm not staying any place where I'm put upon. Cooking's my business! I'm a good cook—

ROGERS. (*Placating her*) First rate, old girl.

MRS. ROGERS. But the kitchen's my place and housework's none of my business. All these guests! I've a good mind to put my hat and coat on and walk out now and go straight back to Plymouth.

ROGERS. (*Grinning*) You can't do that, old girl.

MRS. ROGERS. (*Belligerently*) Who says I can't? Why not, I should like to know?

ROGERS. Because you're on an island, old girl. Had you forgotten that?

MRS. ROGERS. Yes, and I don't know as I fancy being on an island.

ROGERS. Don't know that I do, either, come to that. No slipping down to a pub, or going to the pictures. Oh, well, it's double wages on account of the difficulties. And there's plenty of beer in the house.

MRS. ROGERS. That's all you ever think about—beer.

ROGERS. Now, now, stop your nagging. You get back to the kitchen or your dinner will be spoilt.

MRS. ROGERS. It'll be spoilt anyway, I expect. Everybody's going to be late. Wasted on them, anyway. Thank goodness, I didn't make a soufflé. (*Enter* VERA *Left 1.* MRS. ROGERS *goes to Left 2 door*) Oh, dinner won't be a minute, Miss. Just a question of dishing up. (*Exits Left 2.*)

VERA. (*To above Left sofa*) Is everything all right, Rogers? Can you manage between the two of you?

ROGERS. (*Crossing up Left*) Yes, thank you, Miss. The Missus talks a lot, but she gets it done. (*Exits Left 2.*)

(VERA *goes to Right window.* EMILY *enters Left 1, having changed.*)

VERA. What a lovely evening!

EMILY. Yes, indeed. The weather seems very settled. (*To Center window.*)

VERA. (*Comes down Right*) How plainly one can hear the sea.

EMILY. A pleasant sound. (*Comes down Center.*)

VERA. Hardly a breath of wind—and deliciously warm. Not like England at all.

EMILY. I should have thought you might feel a little uncomfortable in that dress.

VERA. (*Not taking the point*) Oh, no.

EMILY. (*Nastily*) It's rather tight, isn't it?

VERA. (*Good-humored*) Oh, I don't think so.

EMILY. (*Sits Left sofa; takes out gray knitting*) You'll excuse me, my dear, but you're a young girl and you've got your living to earn—

VERA. Yes?

EMILY. A well-bred woman doesn't like her secretary to appear flashy. It looks, you know, as though you were trying to attract the attention of the opposite sex.

VERA. (*Coming to Right Center*) And would you say I do attract them?

EMILY. That's beside the point. A girl who deliberately sets out to get the attention of men won't be likely to keep her job long.

VERA. (*Laughing at her*) Ah! Surely that depends on who she's working for?

EMILY. Really, Miss Claythorne!

VERA. Aren't you being a little unkind?

EMILY. (*Spitefully*) Young people nowadays behave in the most disgusting fashion.

VERA. Disgusting?

EMILY. (*Carried away*) Yes. Low-backed evening dresses. Lying half naked on beaches. All this so-called sun-bathing. An excuse for immodest conduct, nothing more. Familiarity! Christian names—drinking cocktails! And look at the young men nowadays. Decadent! Look at that young Marston. What good is he? And that Captain Lombard!

VERA. What do you object to in Captain Lombard? I should say he was a man who'd led a very varied and interesting life.

EMILY. The man's an adventurer. All this younger generation is no good—no good at all.

VERA. (*Breaks to Right*) You don't like youth—I see.

EMILY. (*Sharply*) What do you mean?

VERA. I was just remarking that you don't like young people.

EMILY. (*Rises; moves up Left*) And is there any reason why I should, pray?

VERA. Oh, no— (*Pauses*) but it seems to me that you must miss an awful lot.

EMILY. You're very impertinent.

VERA. (*Quietly*) I'm sorry, but that's just what I think.

EMILY. The world will never improve until we stamp out immodesty.

VERA. (*To herself*) Quite pathological. (*Goes down Right.*)

EMILY. (*Sharply*) What did you say?

VERA. Nothing.

(EMILY *sits up Left. Enter* ARMSTRONG *and* LOMBARD *Left 1, talking. They cross up Right.*)

L

LOMBARD. What about the old boy—

ARMSTRONG. He looks rather like a tortoise, don't you think so?

LOMBARD. All judges look like tortoises. They have that venomous way of darting their heads in and out. Mr. Justice Wargrave is no exception.

ARMSTRONG. I hadn't realized he was a judge.

LOMBARD. Oh, yes. (*Cheerfully*) He's probably been responsible for sending more innocent people to their death than anyone in England. (WARGRAVE *enters and looks at him*) Hello, you. (*To* VERA) Do you two know each other? Mr. Armstrong—Miss Claythorne. Armstrong and I have just decided that the old boy—

VERA. Yes, I heard you and so did he, I think.

(WARGRAVE *moves over to* EMILY. EMILY *rises as she sees* WARGRAVE *approaching*.)

EMILY. Oh, Sir Lawrence.

WARGRAVE. Miss Brent, isn't it?

EMILY. There's something I want to ask you. (EMILY *indicating she wants to talk to him on the balcony*) Will you come out here?

WARGRAVE. (*As they go*) A remarkably fine night! (*They go out Center.*)

(LOMBARD *up Center.* MARSTON *enters Left 1 with* BLORE. *They are in conversation.*)

MARSTON. Absolutely wizard car—a super-charged Sports Mulatti Carlotta. You don't see many of them on the road. I can get over a hundred out of her.

(VERA *sits on Right sofa.*)

BLORE. Did you come from London?

MARSTON. Yes, two hundred and eight miles and I did it in a bit over four hours. (ARMSTRONG *turns and looks at him*) Too many cars on the road, though, to keep it up. Touched ninety going over Salisbury Plain. Not too bad, eh?

ARMSTRONG. I think you passed me on the road.

MARSTON. Oh, yes?

ARMSTRONG. You nearly drove me into the ditch.

MARSTON. (*Unmoved*) Did I? Sorry. (*To above Left sofa.*)

ARMSTRONG. If I'd seen your number, I'd have reported you.

MARSTON. But you were footling along in the middle of the road.

ARMSTRONG. Footling? Me footling?

BLORE. (*To relieve atmosphere*) Oh, well, what about a drink?

MARSTON. Good idea. (*They move toward the drinks down Right*) Will you have one, Miss Claythorne?

(LOMBARD *drops down toward* VERA.)

VERA. No, thank you.

LOMBARD. (*Sitting beside* VERA *on sofa*) Good evening, Mrs. Owen.

VERA. Why Mrs. Owen?

LOMBARD. You'd make the most attractive wife for any wealthy business man.

VERA. Do you always flirt so outrageously?

LOMBARD. Always.

VERA. Oh! Well, now we know. (*She turns half away, smiling.*)

LOMBARD. Tell me, what's old Miss Brent talking to the Judge about? She tried to buttonhole him upstairs.

VERA. I don't know. Funny—she seemed so definite that there wasn't a Mr. Owen.

LOMBARD. You don't think that Mrs. Owen— I mean that there isn't—that they aren't—

VERA. What, married you mean?

(ROGERS *enters Left 2, switches on* LIGHTS, *draws curtains and exits to study up Right.* MARSTON *comes to Right end of Left sofa.* LOMBARD *rises to Left end sofa.*)

MARSTON. Damn shame we didn't know each other. I could have given you a lift down.

VERA. Yes, that would have been grand.

MARSTON. Like to show you what I can do across Salisbury Plain. Tell you what—maybe we can drive back together?

(*Enter* WARGRAVE *and* EMILY *Center.* MACKENZIE *enters; sits chair down Left.*)

VERA. (*Surprised*) But I— (*Rising.*)

MARSTON. But it seems damn silly. I've got an empty car.

LOMBARD. Yes, but she likes the way she's going back and—

VERA. (*Crosses to fireplace*) Look! Aren't they sweet? Those ten little china Indians. (MARSTON *and* LOMBARD *scowl at each other*) Oh, and there's the old nursery rhyme.

LOMBARD. What are you talking about? What figures? What nursery rhyme?

VERA. (*She points at the figures and rhyme—reading*) "Ten little Indian boys going out to dine
    One choked his little self and then there were nine—" (ROGERS *enters up Right and crosses Left.* VERA *continues reading nursery rhyme.* BLORE *crosses up to below her;* EMILY *to above her*)
"Nine little Indian boys sat up very late.
One overslept himself and then there were eight."

                (*Crosses Left.*)

BLORE.
    "Eight little Indian boys traveling in Devon.
    One got left behind and then there were seven—"

VOICE. (*Very slowly and clearly from off up Right*) Ladies and gentlemen, silence, please! (ALL *rise.* EVERYBODY *stops talking and stares round at each other, at the walls. As each name is mentioned that person reacts by a sudden movement or gesture*) You are charged with these indictments: that you did respectively and at divers times commit the following: Edward Armstrong, that you did cause the death of Louisa Mary Clees. William Henry Blore, that you brought about the death of James Stephen Lendor. Emily Caroline Brent, that you were responsible for the death of Beatrice Taylor. Vera Elizabeth Claythorne, that you killed Peter Ogilvie Hamilton. (VERA *sits Left sofa*) Philip Lombard, that you were guilty of the deaths of twenty-one men, members of an East African tribe. John Gordon MacKenzie, that you sent your wife's lover, Arthur Richmond, to his death. (MACKENZIE *sits down Left*) Anthony James Marston, that you were guilty of the murder of John and Lucy Combes. Thomas Rogers and Ethel Rogers, that you brought about the death of Jennifer Brady. Lawrence John Wargrave, that you were guilty of the murder of Edward Seton. Prisoners at the bar, have you anything to say in your defense?

(*There is a momentary paralyzed silence. Then there is a scream outside door Left 2.* LOMBARD *springs across the room to it. Indignant murmur breaks out as people recover from first shock. Door Left 2 opens to show* MRS. ROGERS *in a fallen heap.* MARSTON *springs across to*

LOMBARD. *They pick up* MRS. ROGERS *and carry her in to Right sofa.* ARMSTRONG *comes to her.*)

ARMSTRONG. It's nothing much. She's fainted, that's all. She'll be round in a minute. Get some brandy—
BLORE. Rogers, get some brandy.

(ROGERS, *shaking all over, goes out Left 2.*)

VERA. Who was that speaking? It sounded—
MACKENZIE. (*Above Left sofa. His hands shaking, pulling at his moustache*) What's going on here? What kind of practical joke was that?

(BLORE *wipes face with handkerchief.* WARGRAVE *stands in the middle of room near sofas, thoughtfully stroking chin, his eyes peering suspiciously from one to the other.*)

LOMBARD. Where the devil did that voice come from? (*They stare all round.* LOMBARD *goes into study up Right*) Here we are.
VOICE. You are charged with these indictments—
VERA. Turn it off! Turn it off! It's horrible!

(LOMBARD *switches it off.* MRS. ROGERS *groans.*)

ARMSTRONG. A disgraceful and heartless practical joke.
WARGRAVE. (*With significance*) So you think it's a joke, do you?
ARMSTRONG. What else could it be?

(EMILY *sits down Right.*)

WARGRAVE. (*With significance*) At the moment I'm not prepared to give an opinion.

(ROGERS *enters Left 2 with brandy and glass on tray. Puts it on table up Left.*)

MARSTON. Who the devil turned it on, though? And set it going?
WARGRAVE. We must enquire into that. (*He looks significantly at* ROGERS.)

(LOMBARD *enters up Right with record; puts it on chair Right Center.* MRS. ROGERS *begins to move and twist.*)

MRS. ROGERS. Oh, dear me! Oh, dear me!

(*The* OTHERS *move nearer, obscuring table where the brandy is. Attention is focused on* MRS. ROGERS.)

ROGERS. (*Above sofa*) Allow me, Madam. (*To* ARMSTRONG) Allow me, sir. If I speak to her— Ethel— Ethel— (*His tone is urgent and nervous*) It's all right. All right, do you hear? Pull yourself together.

(MRS. ROGERS *begins to gasp and moan. She tries to pull herself up. Her frightened eyes stare round the room.*)

ARMSTRONG. (*Taking wrist*) You'll be all right now, Mrs. Rogers. Just a nasty turn.

(BLORE *pours out brandy up Left.*)

MRS. ROGERS. Did I faint, sir?

ARMSTRONG. Yes.

MRS. ROGERS. It was the voice—the awful voice—like a judgment—

(ROGERS *makes anxious movement.* MRS. ROGERS' *eyelids flutter. She seems about to collapse again.*)

ARMSTRONG. Where's the brandy? (*They draw back a little, disclosing it.* BLORE *gives glass to* VERA, *who gives it to* ARMSTRONG. VERA *sits Left edge of sofa, holding cushion under* MRS. ROGERS' *head*) Drink this, Mrs. Rogers.

MRS. ROGERS. (*She gulps a little. Revives. She sits up again*) I'm all right now. I just—gave me a turn.

ROGERS. (*Quickly*) Of course it did. Gave me a turn too. Wicked lies it was! I'd like to know—

(WARGRAVE *at Center deliberately clears his throat. It stops* ROGERS, *who stares at him nervously.* WARGRAVE *clears his throat again, looking hard at* ROGERS.)

WARGRAVE. Who was it put that record on the gramophone? Was it you, Rogers?

ROGERS. I was just obeying orders, sir, that's all.

WARGRAVE. Whose orders?

ROGERS. Mr. Owen's.

WARGRAVE. Let me get this quite clear. Mr. Owen's orders were—what exactly?

ROGERS. I was to put on a record on the gramophone in the study. I'd find the records in the drawer in there. I was to start with that one, sir. I thought it was just to give you all some music.

WARGRAVE. (*Skeptically*) A very remarkable story.

ROGERS. (*Hysterically*) It's the truth, sir. Before Heaven, it's the truth. I didn't know what it was—not for a moment. It had a name on it. I thought it was just a piece of music.

(WARGRAVE *looks toward* LOMBARD, *who examines record*.)

WARGRAVE. Is there a title?

LOMBARD. (*Grinning*) A title? Yes, sir. It's entitled "Swan Song."

(*It amuses him, but some of the* OTHERS *react nervously*.)

MACKENZIE. The whole thing is preposterous—preposterous! Slinging accusations about like this. Something must be done about it. This fellow Owen, whoever he is— (*Moves up Left*.)

EMILY. That's just it. Who is he?

WARGRAVE. (*With authority*) That is exactly what we must go into very carefully. I should suggest that you get your wife to bed, Rogers. Then come back here.

ROGERS. Yes, sir.

ARMSTRONG. I'll give you a hand.

VERA. (*Rising*) Will she be all right, Doctor?

ARMSTRONG. Yes, quite all right.

(ARMSTRONG *and* ROGERS *help* MRS. ROGERS *up and take her out Left 1*.)

MARSTON. (*To* WARGRAVE) Don't know about you, sir, but I feel I need another drink.

WARGRAVE. I agree.

MARSTON. I'll get them. (*Goes down Right*.)

MACKENZIE. (*Muttering angrily*) Preposterous—that's what it is—preposterous. (*Sits up Left*.)

MARSTON. Whiskey for you, Sir Lawrence?

EMILY. (*Sits Right sofa*) I should like a glass of water, please.

VERA. Yes, I'll get it. I'll have a little whiskey too. (*Crosses down Right*.)

(VERA *takes glass of water to* EMILY, *then sits Right Center with her own drink. They sip drinks without speaking, but they eye each other.* ARMSTRONG *enters Left 1*.)

ARMSTRONG. She'll be all right. I've given her a sedative.

BLORE. (*Crosses down Left*) Now, then, Doctor, you'll want a drink after all this.

ARMSTRONG. No, thank you. I never touch it. (*Sits down Left.*)

BLORE. Oh, so you said. You have this one, General? (*Up Left to* MACKENZIE.)

(MARSTON *and* LOMBARD *refill their glasses.* ROGERS *enters Left 1.* WARGRAVE *takes charge.* ROGERS *stands near door Left 1. He is nervous.* EVERYONE *focuses attention on him.*)

WARGRAVE. (*Center above sofas*) Now, then, Rogers, we must get to the bottom of this. Tell us what you know about Mr. Owen.

ROGERS. He owns this place, sir.

WARGRAVE. I am aware of that fact. What I want you to tell me is what you yourself know about the man.

ROGERS. I can't say, sir. You see, I've never seen him.

(*Faint stir of interest.*)

MACKENZIE. What d'you mean, you've never seen him?

ROGERS. We've only been here just under a week, sir, my wife and I. We were engaged by letter through a registry office. The Regina, in Plymouth.

BLORE. That's a high-class firm. We can check on that.

WARGRAVE. Have you got the letter?

ROGERS. The letter engaging us? Yes, sir.

(*Hunts for it and hands it to* WARGRAVE, *who runs through it.*)

WARGRAVE. Go on with your story.

ROGERS. We arrived here like the letter said, on the 4th. Everything was in order, plenty of food in stock and everything very nice. Just needed dusting and that.

WARGRAVE. What next?

ROGERS. Nothing, sir. That is, we got orders to prepare the room for a house party—eight. Then yesterday, by the morning post, I received another letter saying Mr. and Mrs. Owen might be detained and, if so, we was to do the best we could, and it gave the instructions about dinner and putting on the gramophone record. Here it is, sir. (*Crosses to Center. Hands over letter. Retires up Center.*)

WARGRAVE. H'mm. Headed Ritz Hotel and typewritten.

(BLORE *steps up to him and takes letter out of his hands.*
MARSTON *to Left of* BLORE. MACKENZIE *rises; looks over*
WARGRAVE's *shoulder.*)

BLORE. Coronation machine Number 5. Quiet now. No de-
fects. Ensign paper—most common make. We shan't get
much out of this. We might try it for fingerprints, but
it's been handled too much.

LOMBARD. Quite the little detective.

(WARGRAVE *turns and looks at him sharply.* BLORE's *manner
has completely changed, so has his voice.* MACKENZIE
sits up Left again. LOMBARD *sits Left sofa.*)

MARSTON. (*Taking letter, moving down Right*) Got some
fancy Christian names, hasn't he? Ulick Norman Owen.
Quite a mouthful.

WARGRAVE. (*Takes letter from* MARSTON; *crosses Left below
sofa*) I am obliged to you, Mr. Marston. You have drawn
my attention to a curious and suggestive point. (*He
looks around in his court manner*) I think the time has
come for all of us to pool our information. It would be
well for everybody to come forward with all the information they have regarding our unknown host. We are
all his guests. I think it would be profitable if each one
of us were to explain exactly how that came about.

(*There is a pause.*)

EMILY. (*Rising*) There's something very peculiar about all
this. I received a letter with a signature that was not
very easy to read. It purported to be from a woman
whom I had met at a certain summer resort two or three
years ago. I took the name to be Ogden. I am quite
certain that I have never met or become friendly with
anyone of the name of Owen.

WARGRAVE. Have you got that letter, Miss Brent?

EMILY. Yes. I will fetch it for you. (*Goes out Left 1.*)

WARGRAVE. (*To Left of* VERA) Miss Claythorne?

VERA. (*Rises*) I never actually met Mrs. Owen. I wanted a
holiday post and I applied to a Secretarial Agency, Miss
Grenfell's in London. I was offered this post and accepted.

WARGRAVE. And you were never interviewed by your prospective employer?

VERA. No. This is the letter. (*Hands it to him. Sits again chair Right Center.*)

WARGRAVE. (*Reading*) "Indian Island, Sticklehaven, Devon. I have received your name from Miss Grenfell's Agency. I understand she knows you personally. I shall be glad to pay you the salary you ask, and shall expect you to take up your duties on August 8th. The train is the 12:10 from Paddington and you will be met at Oakbridge Station. I enclose five pounds for expenses.

Yours truly,
Una Nancy Owen."

(MARSTON *starts to go up Right*) Mr. Marston?

MARSTON. Don't actually know the Owens. Got a wire from a pal of mine, Badger Berkeley. Told me to roll up here. Surprised me a bit because I had an idea the old horse had gone to Norway. I haven't got the wire. (*To Right window.*)

WARGRAVE. Thank you. Doctor Armstrong?

ARMSTRONG. (*After a pause, rising and coming Left Center*) In the circumstances, I think I may admit that my visit here was professional. Mr. Owen wrote me that he was worried about his wife's health—her nerves, to be precise. He wanted a report without her being alarmed. He therefore suggested that my visit should be regarded as that of an ordinary guest.

WARGRAVE. You had no previous acquaintance with the family?

ARMSTRONG. No.

WARGRAVE. But you had no hesitation in obeying the summons?

ARMSTRONG. A colleague of mine was mentioned and a very handsome fee suggested. I was due for a holiday, anyway. (*Rises; crosses to Right to mantelpiece for cigarette.*)

WARGRAVE. (EMILY *re-enters and hands letter to* WARGRAVE, *who unfolds it and reads.* EMILY *sits down Left*) "Dear Miss Brent: I do hope you remember me. We were together at Bell Haven guest-house in August some years ago and we seemed to have so much in common. I am starting a guest-house of my own on an island off the coast of Devon. I think there is really an opening for a place where there is good plain English cooking, and a nice old-fashioned type of person. None of this nudity

and gramophones half the night. I shall be very glad if
you could see your way to spending your summer holiday on Indian Island—as my guest, of course. I suggest
August 8th, 12:40 from Paddington to Oakbridge.

> Yours sincerely,
> U.N."

H'm, yes, the signature is slightly ambiguous.

LOMBARD. (*Rises; crosses to* VERA. *Aside to her*) I like the
nudity touch!

WARGRAVE. (*To above sofas. Takes letter from pocket*) Here
is my own decoy letter. From an old friend of mine,
Lady Constance Culmington. She writes in her usual
vague, incoherent way, urges me to join her here and
refers to her host and hostess in the vaguest of terms.

(ARMSTRONG *Right of* WARGRAVE, MARSTON *to Right of* ARM-
STRONG *to look at letter.* MACKENZIE *to Left of* WAR-
GRAVE.)

LOMBARD. (*With sudden excitement, staring at* BLORE) Look
here, I've just thought of something—

WARGRAVE. In a minute.

LOMBARD. But I—

WARGRAVE. We will take one thing at a time, if you don't
mind, Captain Lombard. General MacKenzie?

(BLORE *sits Right end of Left sofa.*)

MACKENZIE. (*Rather incoherently, pulling at moustache*) Got
a letter—from this fellow Owen—thought I must have
met sometime at the Club—mentioned some old cronies
of mine who were to be here—hoped I'd excuse informal invitation. Haven't kept the letter, I'm afraid.
(*Sits up Left.*)

WARGRAVE. And you, Captain Lombard?

LOMBARD. Same sort of thing. Invitation mentioning mutual
friends. I haven't kept the letter either.

(*Pause.* WARGRAVE *turns his attention to* BLORE. *He looks at
him for some minutes. When he speaks, his voice is silky
and dangerous.*)

WARGRAVE. Just now we had a somewhat disturbing experience. An apparently disembodied voice spoke to us all
by name, uttering certain definite accusations against us.

We will deal with those accusations presently. At the moment I am interested in a minor point. Amongst the names received was that of William Henry Blore. But as far as we know, there is no one named Blore amongst us. The name of Davis was not mentioned. What have you to say about that, Mr. Davis?

BLORE. (*Rises*) Cat's out of the bag, it seems. I suppose I'd better admit my name isn't Davis.

WARGRAVE. You are William Henry Blore?

BLORE. That's right.

LOMBARD. (*To Right of* BLORE) I will add something to that. Not only are you here under a false name, Mr. Blore, but in addition I've noticed this evening that you're a first-class liar. You claim to have come from Natal, South Africa. I know South Africa and Natal well, and I'm prepared to swear that you've never set foot there in your life.

(ALL *turn toward* BLORE. ARMSTRONG *goes up to Right window.*)

BLORE. You gentlemen have got me wrong. I'm an ex-C. I. D. man.

LOMBARD. Oh, a copper!

BLORE. I've got my credentials and I can prove it. I run a detective agency in Plymouth. I was put onto this job.

WARGRAVE. By whom?

BLORE. Why, Mr. Owen. Sent a very nice money order for expenses, and said I was to join the house party, posing as a guest. He also sent a list of all your names and said I was to keep an eye on you all.

WARGRAVE. Any reason given?

BLORE. Said Mrs. Owen had got some valuable jewels. (*Pause*) Mrs. Owen, my foot! I don't believe there's any such person. (*Goes down Right to cabinet.*)

WARGRAVE. (*Sits Left sofa*) Your conclusions are, I think, justified. (*Looks down at letters*) Ulick Norman Owen. Una Nancy Owen. Each time, that is to say, U. N. Owen. Or, by a slight stretch of fancy, Unknown.

VERA. But it's fantastic! Mad!

WARGRAVE. (*Rises. Quietly*) Oh, yes, I've no doubt in my own mind that we have been invited here by a madman —probably a dangerous homicidal lunatic.

(There is an appalled silence.)

ROGERS. Oh, my gawd!

WARGRAVE. *(To back of Left sofa)* Whoever it is who has
    enticed us here, that person has taken the trouble to
    find out a great deal about us. *(Pause)* A very great deal.
    And out of his knowledge concerning us, he has made
    certain definite accusations.

BLORE. It's all very well to make accusations.

MACKENZIE. A pack of damn lies! Slander!

VERA. It's iniquitous! Wicked!   (EVERYBODY

ROGERS. A lie—a wicked lie—we never did,   *more or less*
    neither of us—   *speaks at once)*

MARSTON. Don't know what the damned
    fool was getting at—

WARGRAVE. *(Raises a hand for silence. Sits Left sofa)* I wish
    to say this. Our unknown friend accuses me of the
    murder of one Edward Seton. I remember Seton per-
    fectly well. He came up before me for trial in June, 1930.
    He was charged with the murder of an elderly woman.
    He was very ably defended and made a good impression
    on the jury in the witness box. Nevertheless, on the evi-
    dence he was certainly guilty. I summed up accordingly
    and the jury brought in a verdict of Guilty. In passing
    sentence of death, I fully concurred with this verdict.
    The appeal was lodged on the grounds of misdirection.
    The appeal was dismissed and the man was duly exe-
    cuted. *(Pause)* I wish to say before you all that my con-
    science is perfectly clear on the matter. I did my duty
    and nothing more. I passed sentence on a rightly con-
    victed murderer.

(There is a pause.)

ARMSTRONG. *(To above* WARGRAVE) Did you know Seton at
    all? I mean, personally.

WARGRAVE. *(Looks at him. He hesitates a moment)* I knew
    nothing of Seton previous to the trial.

LOMBARD. *(Low to* VERA) The old boy's lying. I'll swear he's
    lying.

*(*ARMSTRONG *to down Right.)*

MACKENZIE. *(Rises)* Fellow's a madman. Absolute madman.
    Got a bee in his bonnet. Got hold of the wrong end of

the stick all round. (*To* WARGRAVE) Best really to leave this sort of thing unanswered. However, feel I ought to say—no truth—no truth whatever in what he said about —er—young Arthur Richmond. Richmond was one of my officers. I sent him on reconnaisance in 1917. He was killed. Also like to say—resent very much—slur on my wife. Been dead a long time. Best woman in the world. Absolutely—Caesar's wife. (*He sits down again.*)

MARSTON. (*Right Center*) I've just been thinking—John and Lucy Combes. Must have been a couple of kids I ran over near Cambridge. Beastly bad luck.

WARGRAVE. (*Acidly*) For them or for you?

MARSTON. Well, I was thinking—for me—but, of course, you're right, sir. It was damned bad luck for them too. Of course, it was pure accident. They rushed out of some cottage or other. I had my license suspended for a year. Beastly nuisance.

ARMSTRONG. This speeding's all wrong—all wrong. Young men like you are a danger to the community.

MARSTON. (*Wanders to Right window; picks up his glass, which is half-full*) Well, I couldn't help it. Just an accident.

ROGERS. Might I say a word, sir?

LOMBARD. Go ahead, Rogers.

ROGERS. There was a mention, sir, of me and Mrs. Rogers, and of Miss Jennifer Brady. There isn't a word of truth in it. We were with Miss Brady when she died. She was always in poor health, sir, always from the time we came to her. There was a storm, sir, the night she died. The telephone was out of order. We couldn't get the doctor to her. I went for him, sir, on foot. But he got there too late. We'd done everything possible for her, sir. Devoted to her, we were. Anyone will tell you the same. There was never a word said against us. Never a word.

BLORE. (*In a bullying manner*) Came into a nice little something at her death, I suppose. Didn't you?

ROGERS. (*Crosses down Right to* BLORE. *Stiffly*) Miss Brady left us a legacy in recognition of our faithful service. And why not, I'd like to know?

LOMBARD. (*Right Center. With meaning*) What about yourself, Mr. Blore?

BLORE. What about me?

LOMBARD. Your name was on the list.

BLORE. I know, I know, Landor, you mean? That was the London & Commercial Bank robbery.

WARGRAVE. (*Crosses Right below sofa to mantelpiece. Lights pipe*) I remember the name, though it didn't come before me. Lander was convicted on your evidence. You were the police officer in charge of the case.

BLORE. (*Up to him*) I was, my Lud.

WARGRAVE. Landor got penal servitude for life and died in Dartmoor a year later. He was a delicate man.

BLORE. He was a crook. It was him put the nightwatchman out. The case was clear from the start.

WARGRAVE. (*Slowly*) You were complimented, I think, on your able handling of the case.

BLORE. I got my promotion. (*Pause*) I was only doing my duty.

LOMBARD. (*Sits Right sofa*) Convenient word—duty. (*There is a general suspicious movement.* VERA *rises, moves as if to cross Left, sees* EMILY, *turns. She sits again chair Right Center.* WARGRAVE *moves up to windowseat.* ARMSTRONG *to Center window*) What about you, Doctor?

ARMSTRONG. (*Shakes his head good-humoredly*) I'm at a loss to understand the matter. The name meant nothing to me—what was it? Close? Close? I really don't remember having a patient of that name—or its being connected with a death in any way. The thing's a complete mystery to me. Of course, it's a long time ago. (*Pause*) It might possibly be one of my operation cases in hospital. They come too late, so many of these people. Then, when the patient dies, it's always the surgeon's fault.

LOMBARD. And then it's better to take up nerve cases and give up surgery. Some, of course, give up drink.

ARMSTRONG. I protest. You've no right to insinuate such things. I never touch alcohol.

LOMBARD. My dear fellow, I never suggested you did. Anyway, Mr. Unknown is the only one who knows all the facts.

(WARGRAVE *to Left of* VERA. BLORE *to Right of her.*)

WARGRAVE. Miss Claythorne?

VERA. (*Starts. She has been sitting, staring in front of her. She speaks unemotionally and without feeling of any kind*) I was nursery governess to Peter Hamilton. We were in Cornwall for the summer. He was forbidden to swim out far. One day, when my attention was distracted, he started off—as soon as I saw what happened I swam after him. I couldn't get there in time—

WARGRAVE. Was there an inquest?

VERA. (*In the same dull voice*) Yes, I was exonerated by the Coroner. His mother didn't blame me, either.

WARGRAVE. Thank you. (*Crosses Left*) Miss Brent?

EMILY. I have nothing to say.

WARGRAVE. Nothing?

EMILY. Nothing.

WARGRAVE. You reserve your defense?

EMILY. (*Sharply*) There is no question of defense. I have always acted according to the dictates of my conscience. (*Rises; moves up Left.*)

(BLORE *to fireplace.*)

LOMBARD. What a law-abiding lot we seem to be! Myself excepted—

WARGRAVE. We are waiting for your story, Captain Lombard.

LOMBARD. I haven't got a story.

WARGRAVE. (*Sharply*) What do you mean?

LOMBARD. (*Grinning and apparently enjoying himself*) I'm sorry to disappoint all of you. It's just that I plead guilty. It's perfectly true. I left those natives alone in the bush. Matter of self-preservation.

(*His words cause a sensation.* VERA *looks at him unbelievingly.*)

MACKENZIE. (*Rises. Sternly*) You abandoned your men?

(EMILY *moves to window-seat up Right.*)

LOMBARD. (*Coolly*) Not quite the act of a pukka mahib, I'm afraid. But after all, self-preservation's a man's first duty. And natives don't mind dying, you know. They don't feel about it as Europeans do— (*To Right; sits fireplace fender.*)

(*There is a pause.* LOMBARD *looks around at* EVERYONE *with amusement.* WARGRAVE *clears throat disapprovingly.*)

WARGRAVE. Our inquiry rests there. (ROGERS *crossed to Left 1 door.*) Now, Rogers, who else is there on this island besides ourselves and you and your wife?

ROGERS. Nobody, sir. Nobody at all.

WARGRAVE. You're sure of that?

ROGERS. Quite sure, sir.

WARGRAVE. Thank you. (ROGERS *moves as if to go*) Don't go, Rogers. (*To* EVERYBODY) I am not yet clear as to the purpose of our unknown host in getting us to assemble here. But in my opinion he's not sane in the accepted sense of the word. He may be dangerous. In my opinion, it would be well for us to leave this place as soon as possible. I suggest that we leave tonight.

(*A chorus of "I agree," "Quite so," "Only thing to be done."*)

(*General agreement.* MACKENZIE *sits up Left.*)

ROGERS. I beg your pardon, sir, but there's no boat on the island.

WARGRAVE. No boat at all?

ROGERS. No, sir.

WARGRAVE. Why don't you telephone to the mainland?

ROGERS. There's no telephone. Fred Narracott, he comes over every morning, sir. He brings the milk and the bread and the post and the papers, and takes the orders.

MARSTON. (*Picks up drink from window-seat; crosses down Right to front of Right sofa. Raising his voice*) A bit unsporting, what? Ought to ferret out the mystery before we go. Whole thing's like a detective story. Positively thrilling.

WARGRAVE. (*Acidly*) At my time of life, I have no desire for thrills. (*Sits down Left.*)

(BLORE *to Left end sofa.* MARSTON *grins; stretches out his legs.*)

(WARN *Curtain.*)

MARSTON. The legal life's narrowing. I'm all for crime. (*Raises his glass*) Here's to it. (*Drinks it off at a gulp, appears to choke, gasps, has a violent convulsion and slips onto sofa. Glass falls from his hand.*)

ARMSTRONG. (*Runs over to him, bends down, feels pulse, raises eyelid*) My God, he's dead!

(MACKENZIE *to Left end sofa. The* OTHERS *can hardly take it in.* ARMSTRONG *sniffs lips, then sniffs glass. Nods.*)

MACKENZIE. Dead? D'you mean the fellow just choked and—died?

ARMSTRONG. You can call it choking if you like. He died of asphyxiation, right enough.

MACKENZIE. Never knew a man could die like that—just a choking fit.

EMILY. (*With meaning*) In the middle of life we are in death. (*She sounds inspired.*)

ARMSTRONG. A man doesn't die of a mere choking fit, General MacKenzie. Marston's death isn't what we call a natural death.

VERA. Was there something in the whiskey?

ARMSTRONG. Yes. By the smell of it, cyanide. Probably Potassium Cyanide. Acts pretty well instantaneously.

LOMBARD. Then he must have put the stuff in the glass himself.

BLORE. Suicide, eh? That's a rum go.

VERA. You'd never think he'd commit suicide. He was so alive. He was enjoying himself.

(EMILY *comes down and picks up remains of Indian from behind chair Right Center.*)

EMILY. Oh! Look—here's one of the little Indians off the mantelpiece—broken. (*Holds it up.*)

CURTAIN

Act Two

Scene I

The same. The following morning.

The windows are open and the room has been tidied. It is a fine morning. There are only eight Indians on the mantelpiece.

Suitcases are piled up on the balcony. ALL *are waiting for the boat to arrive.* MACKENZIE *is sitting up Left in his chair, looking definitely a little queer.* EMILY *is sitting Right Center, knitting, with her hat and coat on.* WARGRAVE *is sitting window-seat up Right, a little apart, and is thoughtful. His manner is judicial throughout scene.* VERA, *by window Center, is restless. She comes into the room as if to speak, no one takes any notice, goes down Left and sits.*

ARMSTRONG *and* BLORE *come up Right on balcony.*

ARMSTRONG. We've been up to the top. No sign of that boat yet.

VERA. It's very early still.

BLORE. Oh, I know. Still the fellow brings the milk and the bread and all that. I should have thought he'd have got here before this. (*Opens door Right 2 and looks in*) No sign of breakfast yet— Where's that fellow Rogers?

VERA. Oh, don't let's bother about breakfast—

WARGRAVE. How's the weather looking?

BLORE. (*To window Center*) The wind has freshened a bit. Rather a mackerel sky. Old boy in the train yesterday said we were due for dirty weather. Shouldn't wonder if he wasn't right—

ARMSTRONG. (*Up Center. Nervously*) I wish that boat would come. The sooner we get off this island the better. It's absurd not keeping a boat on the island.

BLORE. No proper harbor. If the wind comes to blow from the southeast, a boat would get dashed to pieces against the rocks.

EMILY. But a boat would always be able to make us from the mainland?

BLORE. (*To left of* EMILY) No, Miss Brent—that's just what it wouldn't.

EMILY. Do you mean we should be cut off from the land?

BLORE. Yes. Condensed milk, ryvita and tinned stuff till the gale had blown itself out. But you needn't worry. The sea's only a bit choppy.

EMILY. I think the pleasures of living on an island are rather overrated.

ARMSTRONG. (*Restless*) I wonder if that boat's coming. Annoying the way the house is built slap up against the cliff. You can't see the mainland until you've climbed to the top. (*To* BLORE) Shall we go up there again?

BLORE. (*Grinning*) It's no good, Doctor. A watched pot never boils. There wasn't a sign of a boat putting out when we were up there just now.

ARMSTRONG. (*To down Right*) What can this man Narracott be doing?

BLORE. (*Philosophically*) They're all like that in Devon. Never hurry themselves.

ARMSTRONG. And where's Rogers? He ought to be about.

BLORE. If you ask me, Master Rogers was pretty badly rattled last night.

ARMSTRONG. I know (*Shivers*) Ghastly—the whole thing.

BLORE. Got wind up properly. I'd take an even bet that he and his wife did do that old lady in.

WARGRAVE. (*Incredulous*) You really think so?

BLORE. Well, I never saw a man more scared. Guilty as hell, I should say.

ARMSTRONG. Fantastic—the whole thing—fantastic.

BLORE. I say, suppose he's hopped it?

ARMSTRONG. Who, Rogers? But there isn't any way he could. There's no boat on the island. You've just said so.

BLORE. Yes, but I've been thinking. We've only Rogers' word for that. Suppose there is one and he's nipped off in the first thing.

MACKENZIE. Oh! No. He wouldn't be allowed to leave the island. (*His tone is so strange they stare at him.*)

BLORE. Sleep well, General? (*Crosses Right of* MACKENZIE.)

MACKENZIE. I dreamed—yes, I dreamed—

BLORE. I don't wonder at that.

MACKENZIE. I dreamed of Lesley—my wife, you know.

BLORE. (*Embarrassed*) Oh—er—yes—I wish Narracott would come. (*Turns up to window.*)

MACKENZIE. Who is Narracott?

BLORE. The bloke who brought us over yesterday afternoon.

MACKENZIE. Was it only yesterday?

BLORE. (*Comes down Center. Determinedly cheerful*) Yes, I feel like that, too. Batty gramophone records—suicides— it's about all a man can stand. I shan't be sorry to see the back of Indian Island, I give you my word.

MACKENZIE. So you don't understand. How strange!

BLORE. What's that, General?

(MACKENZIE *nods his head gently.* BLORE *looks questioningly at* ARMSTRONG, *then taps his forehead significantly.*)

ARMSTRONG. I don't like the look of him.

BLORE. I reckon young Marston's suicide must have been a pretty bad shock to him. He looks years older.

ARMSTRONG. Where is that poor young fellow now?

BLORE. In the study—put him there myself.

VERA. Doctor Armstrong, I suppose it was suicide?

ARMSTRONG. (*Sharply*) What else could it be?

VERA. (*Rises; crosses to Right sofa; sits*) I don't know. But suicide— (*She shakes her head.*)

BLORE. (*Crosses to behind Left sofa*) You know I had a pretty funny feeling in the night. This Mr. Unknown Owen, suppose he's on the island. Rogers mayn't know. (*Pause*) Or he may have told him to say so. (*Watches* ARMSTRONG) Pretty nasty thought, isn't it?

ARMSTRONG. But would it have been possible for anyone to tamper with Marston's drink without our seeing him?

BLORE. Well, it was standing up there. Anyone could have slipped a dollop of cyanide in it if they'd wanted to.

ARMSTRONG. But that—

ROGERS. (*Comes running up from Right on balcony. He is out of breath. Comes straight to* ARMSTRONG) Oh, there you are, sir. I've been all over the place looking for you. Could you come up and have a look at my wife, sir?

ARMSTRONG. Yes, of course. (*Goes toward door Left 1*) Is she feeling under the weather still?

ROGERS. She's—she's— (*Swallows convulsively; exits Left 2.*)

ARMSTRONG. You won't leave the island without me?

(*They go out Left 1.*)

VERA. (*Rises; to Left of windows*) I wish the boat would come. I hate this place.

WARGRAVE. Yes. I think the sooner we can get in touch with the police the better.

VERA. The police?

WARGRAVE. The police have to be notified in a case of suicide, you know, Miss Claythorne.

VERA. Oh, yes—of course. (*Looks up Right toward the door of study and shivers.*)

BLORE. (*Opening door Left 2*) What's going on here? No sign of any breakfast.

VERA. Are you hungry, General? (MACKENZIE *does not answer. She speaks louder*) Feeling like breakfast?

MACKENZIE. (*Turns sharply*) Lesley—Lesley—my dear.

VERA. No,—I'm not—I'm Vera Claythorne.

MACKENZIE. (*Passes a hand over his eyes*) Of course. Forgive me. I took you for my wife.

VERA. Oh!

MACKENZIE. I was waiting for her, you see.

VERA. But I thought your wife was dead—long ago.

MACKENZIE. Yes. I thought so, too. But I was wrong. She's here. On this island.

LOMBARD. (*Comes in from hall Left 1*) Good morning.

(VERA *to above Left sofa.*)

BLORE. (*Coming to down Left*) Good morning, Captain Lombard.

LOMBARD. Good morning. Seem to have overslept myself. Boat here yet?

BLORE. No.

LOMBARD. Bit late, isn't it?

BLORE. Yes.

LOMBARD. (*To* VERA) Good morning. You and I could have had a swim before breakfast. Too bad all this.

VERA. Too bad you overslept yourself.

BLORE. You must have good nerves to sleep like that.

LOMBARD. Nothing makes me lose my sleep.

(VERA *to mantelpiece.*)

BLORE. Didn't dream of African natives, by any chance, did you?

LOMBARD. No. Did you dream of convicts on Dartmoor?

BLORE. (*Angrily*) Look here, I don't think that's funny, Captain Lombard.

LOMBARD. Well, you started it, you know. I'm hungry. What about breakfast? (*To Left sofa—sits.*)

BLORE. The whole domestic staff seems to have gone on strike.

LOMBARD. Oh, well, we can always forage for ourselves.

VERA. (*Examining Indian figures*) Hullo, that's strange.

LOMBARD. What is?

VERA. You remember we found one of these little fellows smashed last night?

LOMBARD. Yes— That ought to leave nine.

VERA. That ought to leave nine. I'm certain there were ten of them here when we arrived.

LOMBARD. Well?

VERA. There are only eight.

LOMBARD. (*Looking*) So there are. (*To mantelpiece.*)

(*They look at each other.*)

VERA. I think it's queer, don't you?

LOMBARD. Probably only were nine to begin with. We assumed there were ten because of the rhyme. (ARMSTRONG *enters Left 1. He is upset, but striving to appear calm. Shuts door and stands against it*) Hullo, Armstrong, what's the matter?

ARMSTRONG. Mrs. Rogers is dead.

(WARGRAVE *rises.*)

BLORE *and* VERA. No? How?

(VERA *to Right end Left sofa.*)

ARMSTRONG. Died in her sleep. Rogers thought she was still under the influence of the sleeping draught I gave her and came down without disturbing her. He lit the kitchen fire and did this room. Then, as she hadn't appeared, he went up, was alarmed by the look of her and went hunting for me. (*Pause*) She's been dead for about five hours, I should say. (*Sits down Left.* VERA *sits Left sofa.*)

BLORE. What was it? Heart?

ARMSTRONG. Impossible to say. It may have been.

BLORE. After all, she had a pretty bad shock last night.

ARMSTRONG. Yes.

WARGRAVE. (*Comes down to Left end of Right sofa*) She might have been poisoned, I suppose, Doctor?

ARMSTRONG. It is perfectly possible.

WARGRAVE. With the same stuff as young Marston?

ARMSTRONG. No, not cyanide. It would have to have been some narcotic or hypnotic. One of the barbiturates, or chloral. Something like that.

BLORE. You gave her some sleeping powders last night, didn't you?

ARMSTRONG. (*Rises, crossing to cabinet Right for drink of water*) Yes, I gave her a mild dose of Luminal.

BLORE. Didn't give her too much, did you?

ARMSTRONG. Certainly not. What do you mean?

BLORE. All right—no offense, no offense. I just thought that perhaps if she'd had a weak heart—

ARMSTRONG. The amount I gave her could not have hurt anyone.

LOMBARD. Then what exactly did happen?

ARMSTRONG. Impossible to say without an autopsy.

WARGRAVE. If, for instance, this death had occurred in the case of one of your private patients, what would have been your procedure?

ARMSTRONG. (*Crossing Left, sits down Left*) Without any previous knowledge of the woman's state of health, I could certainly not give a certificate.

VERA. She was a very nervous-looking creature. She had a bad fright last night. Perhaps it was heart failure.

ARMSTRONG. Her heart certainly failed to beat—but what caused it to fail?

EMILY. (*Firmly and with emphasis*) Conscience.

(*They all jump and look at her.* WARGRAVE *to Right.*)

ARMSTRONG. What exactly do you mean by that, Miss Brent?

EMILY. You all heard— She was accused, together with her husband, of having deliberately murdered her former employer—an old lady.

BLORE. And you believe that's true, Miss Brent?

EMILY. Certainly. You all saw her last night. She broke down completely and fainted. The shock of having her wickedness brought home to her was too much for her. She literally died of fear.

ARMSTRONG. (*Doubtfully*) It is a possible theory. One cannot adopt it without more exact knowledge of her state of health. If there was a latent cardiac weakness—

EMILY. Call it, if you prefer, An Act of God.

(EVERYONE *is shocked*.)

BLORE. Oh, no, Miss Brent. (*Moves up Left*.)

(LOMBARD *to window*.)

EMILY. (*Emphatically*) You regard it as impossible that a sinner should be struck down by the wrath of God? I do not.

WARGRAVE. (*Strokes his chin. His voice is ironic. Coming down Right*) My dear lady, in my experience of ill doing, Providence leaves the work of conviction and chastisement to us mortals—and the process is often fraught with difficulties. There are no short cuts.

BLORE. Let's be practical. What did the woman have to eat and drink last night after she went to bed?

ARMSTRONG. Nothing.

BLORE. Nothing at all? Not a cup of tea? Or a glass of water? I'll bet you she had a cup of tea. That sort always does.

ARMSTRONG. Rogers assures me she had nothing whatever.

BLORE. He might say so.

LOMBARD. So that's your idea?

BLORE. Well, why not? You all heard that accusation last night. What if it's true? Miss Brent thinks it is, for one. Rogers and his missus did the old lady in. They're feeling quite safe and happy about it—

VERA. Happy?

BLORE. (*Sits Left sofa*) Well—they know there's no immediate danger to them. Then, last night some lunatic goes and spills the beans. What happens? It's the woman cracks. Goes to pieces. Did you see him hanging round her when she was coming to? Not all husbandly solicitude? Not on your sweet life. He was like a cat on hot bricks. And that's the position. They've done a murder and got away with it. But if it's all going to be raked up again now, it's the woman will give the show away. She hadn't got the nerve to brazen it out. She's a living danger to her husband, that's what she is, and him— he's all right. He'll go on lying till the cows come home, but he can't be sure of her. So what does he do? He drops a nice little dollop of something into a nice cup of tea, and when she's had it, he washes up the cup and saucer and tells the doctor she ain't had nothing.

VERA. Oh, no. That's impossible. A man wouldn't do that— not to his wife. (*Rises; goes up Left.*)

BLORE. You'd be surprised, Miss Claythorne, what some husbands would do. (*Rises.*)

ROGERS. (*Enters Left 2. He is dead-white and speaks like an automaton, just the mask of the trained servant. To* VERA) Excuse me, Miss. I'm getting on with breakfast. I'm not much of a hand as a cook, I'm afraid. It's lunch that's worrying me. Would cold tongue and gelatine be satisfactory? And I could manage some fried potatoes. And then there's tinned fruit and cheese and biscuits.

VERA. That will be fine, Rogers.

BLORE. Lunch? Lunch? We shan't be here for lunch! And when the hell's that boat coming?

EMILY. Mr. Blore! (*Picks up her case and marches up to Right windowseat—sits.*)

BLORE. What?

ROGERS. (*Fatalistically*) You'll pardon me, sir, but the boat won't be coming.

BLORE. What?

ROGERS. Fred Narracott's always here before eight. (*Pause*) Is there anything else you require, Miss?

VERA. No, thank you, Rogers.

(ROGERS *goes out Left 2.*)

BLORE. And it's not Rogers! His wife lying dead upstairs and there he's cooking breakfast and calmly talking about lunch! Now he says the boat won't be coming. How the 'ell does he know?

EMILY. Mr. Blore!

BLORE. What?

VERA. (*Crossing down Left*) Oh, don't you see? He's dazed. He's just carrying on automatically as a good servant would. It's—it's pathetic, really.

BLORE. He's pulling a fast one, if you ask me.

WARGRAVE. The really significant thing is the failure of the boat to arrive. It means that we are being deliberately cut off from help.

MACKENZIE (*Rising*) Very little time. We mustn't waste it talking about things that don't matter.

(*He turns to window.* ALL *look at him dubiously before resuming.*)

LOMBARD. (*Down Right to* WARGRAVE) Why do you think Narracott hasn't turned up?

WARGRAVE. I think the ubiquitous Mr. Owen has given orders.

LOMBARD. You mean, told him it's a practical joke or something of that kind?

BLORE. He's never fallen for that, would he?

LOMBARD. Why not? Indian Island's got a reputation for people having crazy parties. This is just one more crazy idea, that's all. Narracott knows there's plenty of food and drink in the island. Probably thinks it's all a huge joke.

VERA. Couldn't we light a bonfire up on the top of the island? So that they'd see it?

LOMBARD. That's probably been provided against. All signals are to be ignored. We're cut off all right.

VERA. (*Impatiently*) But can't we do something?

LOMBARD. Oh, yes, we can do something. We can find the funny gentleman who's staged this little joke, Mr. Unknown Owen. I'll bet anything you like he's somewhere on the island, and the sooner we get hold of him the better. Because, in my opinion, he's mad as a hatter. And as dangerous as a rattlesnake.

WARGRAVE. Hardly a very good simile, Captain Lombard. The rattlesnake at least gives warning of its approach.

LOMBARD. Warning? My God, yes! (*Indicating nursery rhyme*) That's our warning. (*Reading*)

"Ten little Indian boys—"

There were ten of us after Narracott went, weren't there?

"Ten little Indian boys going out to dine;

One went and choked himself—"

Marston choked himself, didn't he? And then—

"Nine little Indians sat up very late.

One overslept himself"—overslept himself—

The last part fits Mrs. Rogers rather well, doesn't it?

VERA. You don't think—? Do you mean that he wants to kill us all?

LOMBARD. Yes, I think he does.

VERA. And each one fits with the rhyme!

ARMSTRONG. No, no, it's impossible. It's coincidence. It must be coincidence.

LOMBARD. Only eight little Indian boys here. I suppose that's coincidence too. What do you think, Blore?

BLORE. I don't like it.

ARMSTRONG. But there's nobody on the island.

BLORE. I'm not so sure of that.

ARMSTRONG. This is terrible.

MACKENZIE. None of us will ever leave this island.

BLORE. Can't somebody shut up Grandpa?

LOMBARD. Don't you agree with me, Sir Lawrence?

WARGRAVE. (Slowly) Up to a point—yes.

LOMBARD. Then the sooner we get to work the better. Come on, Armstrong. Come on, Blore. We'll make short work of it.

BLORE. I'm ready. Nobody's got a revolver, by any chance? I suppose that's too much to hope for.

LOMBARD. I've got one. (Takes it out of pocket.)

BLORE. (BLORE'S eyes open rather wide. An idea occurs to him—not a pleasant one) Always carry that about with you?

LOMBARD. Usually. I've been in some tight places, you know.

BLORE. Oh. Well, you've probably never been in a tighter place than you are today. If there's a homicidal maniac hiding on this island, he's probably got a whole arsenal on him—and he'll use it.

ARMSTRONG. You may be wrong there, Blore. Many homicidal maniacs are very quiet, unassuming people.

WARGRAVE. Delightful fellows!

ARMSTRONG. You'd never guess there was anything wrong with them.

BLORE. If Mr. Owen turns out to be one of that kind, we'll leave him to you, Doctor. Now, then, let's make a start. I suggest Captain Lombard searches the house while we do the island.

LOMBARD. Right. House ought to be easy. No sliding panels or secret doors. (Goes up Right toward study.)

BLORE. Mind he doesn't get you before you get him!

LOMBARD. Don't worry. But you two had better stick to-gether—Remember—"One got left behind."

BLORE. Come on, Armstrong.

(*They go along and out up Right.*)

WARGRAVE. (*Rises*) A very energetic young man, Captain Lombard.

VERA. (*To up Left*) Don't you think he's right? If someone is hiding on the island, they'll be bound to find him. It's practically bare rock.

WARGRAVE. I think this problem needs brains to solve it. Rather than brawn. (*Goes up Right on balcony.*)

VERA. Where are you going?

WARGRAVE. I'm going to sit in the sun—and think, my dear young lady. (*Goes up Right on balcony.*)

EMILY. Where did I put the skein of wool? (*Gets up and comes down Right.*)

VERA. Did you leave it upstairs? Shall I go and see if I can find it?

EMILY. No, I'll go. I know where it's likely to be. (*Goes out Left* 1.)

VERA. I'm glad Captain Lombard has got a revolver.

MACKENZIE. They're all wasting time—wasting time.

VERA. Do you think so?

MACKENZIE. Yes, it's much better to sit quietly—and wait.

VERA. Wait for what? (*Sits Left sofa.*)

MACKENZIE. For the end, of course. (*There is a pause. MACKENZIE rises, opens and shuts both doors Left*) I wish I could find Lesley.

VERA. Your wife?

MACKENZIE. (*Crosses up Right. Below Right sofa*) Yes. I wish you'd known her. She was so pretty. So gay—

VERA. Was she?

MACKENZIE. I loved her very much. Of course, I was a lot older than she was. She was only twenty-seven, you know. (*Pause*) Arthur Richmond was twenty-six. He was my A.D.C. (*Pause*) Lesley liked him. They used to talk of music and plays together, and she teased him and made fun of him. I was pleased. I thought she took a motherly interest in the boy. (*Suddenly to* VERA, *confidentially*) Damn fool, wasn't I? No fool like an old fool. (*A long pause*) Exactly like a book the way I found out. When I was out in France. She wrote to both of us, and she put the letters in the wrong envelope. (*He nods his head*) So I knew—

VERA. (*In pity*) Oh, no.

MACKENZIE. (*Sits Right sofa*) It's all right, my dear. It's a long time ago. But you see I loved her very much—and believed in her. I didn't say anything to him—I let it gather inside—here—(*Strikes chest*) a slow, murderous rage—Damned young hypocrite—I'd liked the boy—trusted him.

VERA. (*Trying to break spell*) I wonder what the others are doing?

MACKENZIE. I sent him to his death—

VERA. Oh—

MACKENZIE. It was quite easy. Mistakes were being made all the time. All anyone could say was that I'd lost my nerve a bit, made a blunder, sacrificed one of my best men. Yes, it was quite easy—(*Pause*) Lesley never knew. I never told her I'd found out. We went on as usual—but somehow nothing was quite real any more. She died of pneumonia. (*Pause*) She had a heartshaped face—and grey eyes—and brown hair that curled.

VERA. Oh, don't.

MACKENZIE. (*Rises*) Yes, I suppose in a way—it was murder. Curious, murder—and I've always been such a law-abiding man. It didn't feel like that at the time. "Serves him damn well right!" that's what I thought. But after—(*Pause*) Well, you know, don't you?

VERA. (*At a loss*) What do you mean?

MACKENZIE. (*Stares at her as though something puzzles him*) You don't seem to understand—I thought you would. I thought you'd be glad, too, that the end was coming—

VERA. (*Draws back, alarmed. Rises; backs down Left*) I—(*She eyes him warily.*)

MACKENZIE. (*Follows her—confidentially*) We're all going to die, you know.

VERA. (*Looking round for help*) I—I don't know.

MACKENZIE. (*Vaguely to* VERA) You're very young—you haven't got to that yet. The relief! The blessed relief when you know that you've done with it all, that you haven't got to carry the burden any longer. (*Moves up Right.*)

VERA. (*Follows him—moved*) General—

MACKENZIE. Don't talk to me that way. You don't understand. I want to sit here and wait—wait for Lesley to come for me. (*Goes out on balcony and draws up chair and sits. The back of his head down to shoulders is visible through window. His position does not change throughout scene.*)

VERA. (*Stares after him. Her composure breaks down. Sits Left sofa*) I'm frightened— Oh! I'm frightened—

(LOMBARD *comes in up Right.*)

LOMBARD. (*Crosses Left*) All correct. No secret passage—one corpse.

VERA. (*Tensely*) Don't!

LOMBARD. I say, you do look low. How about a drink to steady your nerves?

VERA. (*Rises, flaring up*) A drink! Two corpses in the house at nine o'clock in the morning and all you say, "Have a drink"! An old man going quite crackers—"Have a drink"! Ten people accused of murder—that's all right— just have a drink. Everything's fine so long as you have a drink.

LOMBARD. All right. All right.—Stay thirsty. (*Goes to Left 2 door.*)

VERA. Oh, you—you're nothing but a waster—an adventurer —you make me tired. (*Moves to fireplace.*)

LOMBARD (*Crossing to her*) I say, you are het up. What's the matter, my sweet?

VERA. I'm not your sweet.

LOMBARD. I'm sorry. I rather thought you were.

VERA. Well, you can think again.

LOMBARD. Come now—you know you don't really feel like that. We've got something in common, you and I. Rogues and murderers can't fall out. (*He takes her hand—she draws away.*)

VERA. Rogues and murderers—!

LOMBARD. Okay. You don't like the company of rogues and murderers—and you won't have a drink. I'll go and finish searching— (*Exits Left 1.*)

(EMILY *enters Left 1.* VERA *moves up to window.*)

EMILY. Unpleasant young man! I can't find it anywhere. (*Sees* VERA's *face*) Is anything the matter? (*To above Left sofa.*)

VERA. (*Low*) I'm worried about the General. He really is ill, I think.

EMILY. (*Looks from* VERA *to* MACKENZIE, *then goes out on balcony and stands behind him. In loud, cheerful voice, as though talking to an idiot child*) Looking out for the boat, General? (VERA *to down Left.* MACKENZIE *does not answer.* EMILY *waits a minute, then comes slowly in. Unctuously*) His sin has found him out.

VERA. (*Angrily*) Oh, don't.

EMILY. One must face facts.

VERA. Can any of us afford to throw stones?

EMILY. (*Comes down Center; sits Right sofa*) Even if his wife was no better than she should be—and she must have been a depraved woman—he had no right to take judgment into his own hands.

VERA. (*Coldly angry*) What about—Beatrice Taylor?

EMILY. Who?

VERA. That was the name, wasn't it? (*Looks at her challengingly.*)

EMILY. You are referring to that absurd accusation about myself?

VERA. Yes.

EMILY. Now that we are alone, I have no objection to telling you the facts of the case—Indeed I should like you to hear them. (VERA *sits Left sofa*) It was not a fit subject to discuss before gentlemen—so naturally I refused to say anything last night. That girl, Beatrice Taylor, was in my service. I was very much deceived in her. She had nice manners and was clean and willing. I was very pleased with her. Of course, all that was sheerest hypocrisy. She was a loose girl with no morals. Disgusting! It was some time before I found out that she was what they call "in trouble." (*Pause*) It was a great shock to me. Her parents were decent folks too, who had brought her up strictly. I'm glad to say they didn't condone her behavior.

VERA. What happened?

EMILY. (*Self-righteously*) Naturally, I refused to keep her an hour under my roof. No one shall ever say I condoned immorality.

VERA. Did she drown herself?

EMILY. Yes.

VERA. (*Rises to Left*) How old was she?

EMILY. Seventeen.

VERA. Only seventeen.

EMILY. (*With horrible fanaticism*) Quite old enough to know how to behave. I told her what a low depraved thing she was. I told her that she was beyond the pale and that no decent person would take her into their house. I told her that her child would be the child of sin and would be branded all its life—and that the man would naturally not dream of marrying her. I told her that I felt soiled by ever having had her under my roof—

VERA. (*Shuddering*) You told a girl of seventeen all that?

EMILY. Yes, I'm glad to say I broke her down utterly.

VERA. Poor little devil.

EMILY. I've no patience with this indulgence toward sin.

VERA. (*Moves up Left to above sofa*) And then, I suppose, you turned her out of the house?

EMILY. Of course.

VERA. And she didn't dare go home— (*Comes down Right to Center*) What did you feel like when you found she'd drowned herself?

EMILY. (*Puzzled*) Feel like?

VERA. Yes. Didn't you blame yourself?

EMILY. Certainly not. I had nothing with which to reproach myself.

VERA. I believe—I believe you really feel like that. That makes it even more horrible. (*Turns away to Right, then goes up to center windows.*)

EMILY. That girl's unbalanced. (*Opens bag and takes out a small Bible. Begins to read it in a low mutter*) "The heathen are sunk down in the pit that they made— (*Stops and nods her head*) In the net which they hid is their own foot taken." (ROGERS *enters Left 2.* EMILY *stops and smiles approvingly*) "The Lord is known by the judgment He executeth, the wicked is snared in the work of his own hand."

ROGERS. (*Looks doubtfully at* EMILY) Breakfast is ready.

EMILY. "The wicked shall be turned into hell." (*Turns head sharply*) Be quiet.

ROGERS. Do you know where the gentlemen are, Miss? Breakfast is ready. (*To above Left sofa.*)

VERA. Sir Lawrence Wargrave is sitting out there in the sun. Doctor Armstrong and Mr. Blore are searching the island. I should bother about them. (*She comes in.*)

(ROGERS *goes out to balcony.*)

EMILY. "Shall not the isles shake at the sound of the fall, when the wounded cry, when the slaughter is made in the midst of thee?"

VERA. (*To Left. Coldly. After waiting a minute or two*) Shall we go in?

EMILY. I don't feel like eating.

ROGERS. (*To* MACKENZIE) Breakfast is ready. (*Goes off Right on balcony.*)

EMILY. (*Opens Bible again*) "Then all the princes of the sea shall come down from their thrones, and lay away their robes, and put off their 'broidered garments." (*Enter* BLORE UP *Right*) "They shall clothe themselves with trembling, they shall sit upon the ground, and shall tremble at every moment, and be astonished at thee." (*Looks up and sees* BLORE, *but her eyes are almost unseeing.*)

BLORE (*Speaks readily, but watches her with a new interest*) Reading aloud, Miss Brent?

EMILY. It is my custom to read a portion of the Bible every day.

BLORE. Very good habit, I'm sure. (*To down Right.*)

(ARMSTRONG *comes Right along balcony and in.*)

VERA. What luck did you have?

ARMSTRONG. There's no cover in the island. No caves. No one could hide anywhere.

(WARN *Curtain.*)

BLORE. That's right. (LOMBARD *enters Left 2*) What about the house, Lombard?

LOMBARD. No one. I'll stake my life there's no one in the house but ourselves. I've been over it from attic to cellar.

(ROGERS *enters from balcony.* WARGRAVE *comes Right along balcony, slowly, and in to Right of window.*)

ROGERS. Breakfast is getting cold.

(EMILY *is still reading.*)

LOMBARD. (*Boisterously*) Breakfast! Come on, Blore. You've been yelping for breakfast ever since you got up. Let's eat, drink and be merry, for tomorrow we die. Or who knows, perhaps, even today!

(VERA *and* ARMSTRONG *cross to Left 2 door.*)

EMILY. (*Rises; drops knitting.* BLORE *picks it up*) You ought
    to be ashamed of such levity, Captain Lombard.
    (*Crosses Right.*)

LOMBARD. (*Still in the same vein, with determination*) Come
    on, General, can't have this. (*Calls*) Breakfast, I say,
    sir— (*Goes out on balcony to* MACKENZIE. *Stops—
    stoops—comes slowly back and stands in window. His
    face is stern and dangerous*) Good God! One got left
    behind—There's a knife in MacKenzie's back.

ARMSTRONG. (*Goes to him*) He's dead—he's dead.

BLORE. But he can't be— Who could have done it? There's
    only us on the island.

WARGRAVE. Exactly, my dear sir. Don't you realize that this
    clever and cunning criminal is always comfortably one
    stage ahead of us? That he knows exactly what we are
    going to do next, and makes his plans accordingly?
    There's only one place, you know, where a successful
    murderer could hide and have a reasonable chance of
    getting away with it.

BLORE. One place—where?

WARGRAVE. Here in this room—Mr. Owen is one of us!

CURTAIN

End of Scene 1

Scene II

*There is a storm; the room is much darker—the windows
closed and beating RAIN and WIND.*

    WARGRAVE *comes in from Left 2, followed by* BLORE.

BLORE. Sir Lawrence?

WARGRAVE. (*Center*) Well, Mr. Blore?

BLORE. I wanted to get you alone. (*Looks over shoulder at
    dining room*) You were right in what you said this
    morning. This damned murderer is one of us. And I
    think I know which one.

WARGRAVE. Really?

BLORE. Ever hear of the Lizzie Borden case? In America. Old couple killed with an axe in the middle of the morning. Only person who could have done it was the daughter, a respectable, middle-aged spinster. Incredible. So incredible that they acquitted her. But they never found any other explanation.

WARGRAVE. Then your answer to the problem is Miss Emily Brent?

BLORE. I tell you that woman is as mad as a hatter. Religious mad, I tell you—she's the one. And we must watch her.

WARGRAVE. Really? I had formed the impression that your suspicions were in a different quarter.

BLORE. Yes— But I've changed my mind, and I'll tell you for why—she's not scared and she's the only one who isn't. Why? Because she knows quite well she's in no danger—hush—

(WARGRAVE *goes up Right.* VERA *and* EMILY *enter from Left 2.* VERA *is carrying coffee tray.* EMILY *up Center.*)

VERA. We've made some coffee. (*She puts tray on tabouret Right Center.* BLORE *moves up to tabouret*) Brr—it's cold in here.

BLORE. You'd hardly believe it when you think what a beautiful day it was this morning.

VERA. Are Captain Lombard and Rogers still out?

BLORE. Yes. No boat will put out in this—and it couldn't land, anyway.

VERA. Miss Brent's. (*Hands coffee cup to* BLORE.)

(EMILY *comes down; sits Left Sofa.*)

WARGRAVE. Allow me. (*Takes cup and hands it to* EMILY.)

VERA. (*To* WARGRAVE) You were right to insist on our going to lunch—and drinking some brandy with it. I feel better.

WARGRAVE. (*Returns to coffee tray—takes his own coffee; stands by mantelpiece*) The court always adjourns for lunch.

VERA. All the same, it's a nightmare. It seems as though it can't be true. What—what are we going to do about it?

(BLORE *sits chair Right Center.*)

WARGRAVE. We must hold an informal court of inquiry. We may at least be able to eliminate some innocent people.

BLORE. You haven't got a hunch of any kind, have you, Miss Claythorne?

WARGRAVE. If Miss Claythorne suspects one of us three, that is rather an awkward question.

VERA. I'm sure it isn't any of you. If you ask me who I suspected, I'd say Doctor Armstrong.

BLORE. Armstrong?

VERA. Yes. Because, don't you see, he's had far and away the best chance to kill Mrs. Rogers. Terribly easy for him, as a doctor, to give her an overdose of sleeping stuff.

BLORE. That's true. But someone else gave her brandy, remember.

(EMILY *goes up Left and sits.*)

WARGRAVE. Her husband had a good opportunity of administering a drug.

BLORE. It isn't Rogers. He wouldn't have the brains to fix all this stunt—nor the money. Besides you can see he's scared stiff.

(ROGERS *and* LOMBARD, *in mackintoshes, come up Right on balcony and appear at window.* BLORE *goes and lets them in. As he opens the window, a swirl of loud WIND and RAIN comes in.* EMILY *half screams and turns around.*)

LOMBARD. My God, it's something like a storm.

EMILY. Oh, it's only you—

VERA. Who did you think it was? (*Pause*) Beatrice Taylor?

EMILY. (*Angrily*) Eh?

LOMBARD. Not a hope of rescue until this dies down. Is that coffee? Good. (*To* VERA) I'm taking to coffee now, you see.

VERA. (*Takes him a cup*) Such restraint in the face of danger is nothing short of heroic.

WARGRAVE. (*Crosses to down Left; sits*) I do not, of course, profess to be a weather prophet. But I should say that it is very unlikely that a boat could reach us, even if it knew of our plight, under twenty-four hours. Even if the wind drops, the sea has still to go down.

(LOMBARD *sits Left sofa.* ROGERS *pulls off his shoes.*)

VERA. You're awfully wet.

BLORE. Is anyone a swimmer? Would it be possible to swim to the mainland?

VERA. It's over a mile—and in this sea you'd be dashed on the rocks and drowned.

EMILY. (*Speaking like one in a trance*) Drowned—drowned —in the pond— (*Drops knitting.*)

WARGRAVE. (*Rising; startled, moves up to her*) I beg your pardon, Miss Brent. (*He picks it up for her.*)

BLORE. After dinner nap.

(*Another furious gust of WIND and RAIN.*)

VERA. It's terribly cold in here. (*To Right; sits on fender.*)

ROGERS. I could light the fire if you like, Miss?

VERA. That would be a good idea.

LOMBARD. (*Crossing Right*) Very sound scheme, Rogers. (*He sits on fender; puts on shoes.*)

ROGERS. (*Goes toward Left 1 door—is going through but comes back and asks*) Excuse me, but does anybody know what's become of the top bathroom curtain?

LOMBARD. Really, Rogers, are you going bats too?

BLORE. (*Blankly*) The bathroom curtain?

ROGERS. Yes, sir. Scarlet oilsilk. It's missing.

(*They look at each other.*)

LOMBARD. Anybody seen a scarlet oilsilk curtain? No good, I'm afraid, Rogers.

ROGERS. It doesn't matter, sir, only I just thought as it was odd.

LOMBARD. Everything on this island is odd.

ROGERS. I'll get some sticks and a few knobs of coal and get a nice fire going. (*Goes out Left 2.*)

VERA. I wonder if he would like some hot coffee. He's very wet. (*Runs out after him, calling "Rogers."*)

LOMBARD. What's become of Armstrong?

WARGRAVE. He went to his room to rest.

LOMBARD. Somebody's probably batted him one by now!

WARGRAVE. I expect he had the good sense to bolt his door.

BLORE. It won't be so easy now that we're all on our guard.
(*Lights cigarette at mantelpiece.*)

(*A rather unpleasant silence.*)

WARGRAVE. I advise you, Mr. Blore, not to be too confident. I should like shortly to propose certain measures of safety, which I think we should all adopt.

LOMBARD. Against whom?

WARGRAVE. (*Up Center*) Against each other. We are all in grave danger. Of the ten people who came to this island, three are definitely cleared. There are seven of us left—seven little Indian boys.

LOMBARD. One of whom is a bogus little Indian boy.

WARGRAVE. Exactly.

BLORE. (*To Right Center*) Well, in spite of what Miss Claythorne said just now, I'd say that you, Sir Lawrence, and Doctor Armstrong are above suspicion. He's a well-known doctor, and you're known all over England.

WARGRAVE. (*Interrupts him*) Mr. Blore, that proves nothing at all. Judges have gone mad before now. So have doctors. (*Pause*) So have policemen.

LOMBARD. Hear, hear. (VERA *enters Left 2*) Well, does he want some coffee?

VERA. (*Crossing Right to tabouret Right Center, lightly*) He'd rather make himself a nice cup of tea! What about Doctor Armstrong? Do you think we ought to take him up a cup?

WARGRAVE. I will take it up if you like.

LOMBARD. I'll take it. I want to change.

VERA. Yes, you ought to. You'll catch cold.

WARGRAVE. (*Smiling ironically*) I think Doctor Armstrong might prefer to see me. He might not admit you, Captain Lombard. He might be afraid of your revolver.

BLORE. Ah, that revolver. (*Meaningly*) I want a word with you about that—

VERA. (*To* LOMBARD) Do go and change.

(WARGRAVE *takes cup from her and, passing behind, goes out Left 2.*)

LOMBARD. (*Up Right Center to* BLORE) What were you going to say?

BLORE. I'd like to know why you brought a revolver down here on what's supposed to be a little social visit.

LOMBARD. You do, do you? (*After a momentary pause*) I've led a rather adventurous life. I've got into the habit of taking a revolver about with me. I've been in a bit of a jam once or twice. (*Smiles*) It's a pleasant feeling to have a gun handy. (*To* BLORE) Don't you agree?

(*Enter* ARMSTRONG *Left 1; stands down Left.*)

BLORE. We don't carry them. Now, then, I want the truth about this gun—

LOMBARD. What a damned suspicious fellow you are, Blore!

BLORE. I know a fishy story when I hear one.

ARMSTRONG. If it's about that revolver, I'd like to hear what you've got to say.

LOMBARD. (*Crossing down Left*) Oh, well, I got a letter, asking me to come here as the guest of Mr. and Mrs. Owen— It would be worth my while. The writer said that he had heard I'd got a reputation for being a good man in a tight place. There might be some danger, but I'd be all right if I kept my eyes open.

BLORE. I'd never have fallen for that.

LOMBARD. Well, I did. I was bored. God, how I was bored back in this tame country. It was an intriguing proposition, you must admit.

BLORE. Too vague for my liking.

LOMBARD. That was the whole charm. It aroused my curiosity.

BLORE. Curiosity killed the cat.

LOMBARD. (*Smiling*) Yes, quite.

VERA. Oh, do go and change, please!

LOMBARD. I'm going my sweet, I'm going. The maternal instinct I think it's called.

VERA. Don't be ridiculous—

(VERA, *up Left, collects* EMILY'S *cup; goes down Right with it.* LOMBARD *exits Left 1.*)

BLORE. (*Crosses down Left*) That's a tall story. If it's true, why didn't he tell it to us last night?

ARMSTRONG. He might have thought that this was exactly the emergency for which he had been prepared.

VERA. Perhaps it is.

ARMSTRONG. (*Crosses Right Center; puts down cup on tabouret and goes Right*) I hardly think so. It was just Mr. Owen's little bit of cheese to get him into the trap with the rest of us. He must have known him enough to rely on his curiosity.

BLORE. If it's true, he's a wrong 'un, that man. I wouldn't trust him a yard.

VERA. (*Up Center*) Are you such a good judge of truth?

(WARGRAVE *enters Left 1.*)

ARMSTRONG. (*With a sudden outburst*) We must get out of here—we must before it is too late. (*He is shaking violently.*)

(BLORE *sits down Left.*)

WARGRAVE. The one thing we must not do is to give away to nerves. (*Crosses Right above Left sofa.*)

ARMSTRONG. (*Sits on fender*) I'm sorry. (*Tries to smile*) Rather a case of "Physician, heal thyself." But I've been overworked lately and run down.

WARGRAVE. Sleeping badly?

ARMSTRONG. Yes. I keep dreaming— Hospital—operations— A knife at my throat— (*Shivers.*)

WARGRAVE. Real nightmares.

ARMSTRONG. Yes. (*Curiously*) Do you ever dream you're in court—sentencing a man to death?

WARGRAVE. (*Sits Left sofa; smiling*) Are you by any chance referring to a man called Edward Seton? I can assure you I should not lose any sleep over the death of Edward Seton. A particularly brutal and cold-blooded murderer. The jury liked him. They were inclined to let him off. I could see. However— (*With quiet ferocity*) I cooked Seton's goose.

(EVERYONE *gives a little shiver.*)

BLORE. Brr! Cold in here, isn't it? (*Rises; to Center.*)

VERA. (*Up Right of window*) I wish Rogers would hurry up.

BLORE. Yes, where is Rogers? He's been a long time.

VERA. He said he'd got to get some sticks.

BLORE. (*Struck by the word*) Sticks? Sticks? My God, sticks!

ARMSTRONG. My God! (*Rises, looking at mantelpiece.*)

BLORE. Is another one gone? Are there only six?

ARMSTRONG. (*Bewildered*) There are only five.

VERA. Five?

(*They stare at each other.*)

WARGRAVE. Rogers and Lombard? (*Rises.*)
VERA. (*With a cry*) Oh, no, not Philip!

(LOMBARD *enters Left 1; meets* BLORE *rushing out Left 1, calling "Rogers."*)

LOMBARD. Where the hell is Blore off to like a madman?
VERA. (*Running to him at Left Center*) Oh, Philip, I—
                                              (*WARN Curtain.*)
WARGRAVE. (*Up Right*) Have you seen Rogers?
LOMBARD. No, why should I?
ARMSTRONG. Two more Indians have gone.
LOMBARD. Two?
VERA. I thought it was you—

(BLORE *enters Left 1 looking pretty awful.*)

ARMSTRONG. Well, what is it?
BLORE. (*Only just able to speak. His voice quite unlike itself*) In the—scullery.
VERA. Is he—?
BLORE. Oh, yes, he's dead all right—
VERA. How?
BLORE. With an axe. Somebody must have come up behind him whilst he was bent over the wood box.
VERA. (*Wildly*) "One chopped himself in half—then there were six." (*She begins laughing hysterically.*)
LOMBARD. Stop it. Vera— Stop it! (*Sits her on Left sofa. Slaps her face. To the* OTHERS) She'll be all right. What next, boys? Bees? Do they keep bees on the island? (*They stare at him as if not understanding. He keeps his nonchalant manner up with a trace of effort. Down to Center*) Well, that's the next verse, isn't it?
  "Six little Indian boys playing with a hive;
    A bumble bee stung one, and then there were five."
  (*He moves around the room.*)
ARMSTRONG. My God! He's right. There are only five.
LOMBARD. A bumble bee stung one— We all look pretty spry, nothing wrong with any of us. (*His glance rests on* EMILY) My God, you don't think— (*He goes slowly over to her, bends down, touches her. He then picks up a hypodermic syringe, and turns to face the others*) A hypodermic syringe.

WARGRAVE. The modern bee-sting.

VERA. (*Stammering*) While she was sitting there—one of us—

WARGRAVE. One of us.

(*They look at each other.*)

ARMSTRONG. Which of us?

CURTAIN

Act Three

Scene I

Some hours later, the same night.

*The curtains are drawn and the room is lit by three
candles.* WARGRAVE, VERA, BLORE, LOMBARD *and* ARM-
STRONG, *who is dirty and unshaven, are sitting in silence.*
LOMBARD *sits chair Right Center,* ARMSTRONG *on Right
sofa,* WARGRAVE *Left sofa,* VERA *on fender,* BLORE *down
Left. From time to time they shoot quick, covert glances
at each other.* VERA *watches* ARMSTRONG; BLORE *watches*
LOMBARD; LOMBARD *watches* WARGRAVE; ARMSTRONG
watches BLORE *and* LOMBARD *alternately.* WARGRAVE
watches each in turn, but most often VERA *with a long,
speculative glance. There is silence for some few minutes. Then* LOMBARD *speaks suddenly in a loud, jeering
voice that makes them all jump.*

LOMBARD.
"Five little Indian boys sitting in a row,
    Watching each other and waiting for the blow."
New version up to date! (*He laughs discordantly.*)

ARMSTRONG. I hardly think this is a moment for factiousness.

LOMBARD. Have to relieve the gloom. (*Rises to above Right
sofa*) Damn that electric plant running down. Let's
play a nice round game. What about inventing one
called "Suspicions"? A suspects B., B. suspects C.—
and so on. Let's start with Blore. It's not hard to guess
whom Blore suspects. It sticks out a mile. I'm your
fancy, aren't I, Blore?

BLORE. I wouldn't say no to that.

59

LOMBARD. (*Crosses to Left a few steps*) You're quite wrong, you know. Abstract justice isn't my line. If I committed murder, there would have to be something in it for me.

BLORE. All I say is that you acted suspiciously from the start. You've told two different stories. You came here with a revolver. Now you say you've lost it.

LOMBARD. I have lost it.

BLORE. That's a likely story!

LOMBARD. What do you think I've done with it? I suggested myself that you should search me.

BLORE. Oh! You haven't got it on you. You're too clever for that. But you know where it is.

LOMBARD. You mean, I've cached it ready for the next time?

BLORE. I shouldn't be surprised.

LOMBARD. (*Crosses Right*) Why don't you use your brains, Blore? If I'd wanted to, I could have shot the lot of you by this time, pop, pop, pop, pop, pop.

BLORE. Yes, but that's not the big idea. (*Points to rhyme.*)

LOMBARD. (*Sits chair Right Center*) The crazy touch? My God, man, I'm sane enough!

BLORE. The doctor says there are some lunatics you'd never know were lunatics. (*Looks around at* EVERYONE) That's true enough, I'd say.

ARMSTRONG. (*Breaking out*) We—we shouldn't just sit here, doing nothing! There must be something—surely, surely, there is something that we can do? If we lit a bonfire—

BLORE. In this weather? (*Jerks his head towards window.*)

WARGRAVE. It is, I am afraid, a question of time and patience. The weather will clear. Then we can do something. Light a bonfire, heliograph, signal.

ARMSTRONG. (*Rises to up Right*) A question of time—time? (*Laughs in an unbalanced way*) We can't afford time. We shall all be dead.

WARGRAVE. I think the precautions we have now adopted will be adequate.

ARMSTRONG. I tell you—we shall all be dead. All but one— He'll think up something else—he's thinking now— (*Sits Right sofa again.*)

LOMBARD. Poor Louise—what was her name—Clees? Was it nerves that made you do her in, Doctor?

ARMSTRONG. (*Almost mechanically*) No, drink. I used to be a heavy drinker. God help me, I was drunk when I operated— Quite a simple operation. My hand shaking all over the place— (*Buries his face in his hands*) I can remember her now—a big, heavy, countrified woman. And I killed her!

LOMBARD. (*Rises; to Right above* VERA) So I was right—that's how it was?

ARMSTRONG. Sister knew, of course, but she was loyal to me—or to the Hospital. I gave up drink—gave it up altogether. I went in for a study of nervous diseases.

WARGRAVE. Very successfully. (*Rises; to up Center.*)

ARMSTRONG. One or two lucky shots. Good results with one or two important women. They talked to their friends. For the last year or two, I've been so busy I've hardly known which way to turn. I'd got to the top of the tree.

LOMBARD. Until Mr. Unknown Owen—and down will come cradle and doctor and all.

ARMSTRONG. (*Rises*) Will you stop your damnable sneering and joking?

WARGRAVE. (*Comes down Right between* ARMSTRONG *and* LOMBARD) Gentlemen, gentlemen, please. We can't afford to quarrel.

LOMBARD. That's okay by me. I apologize.

ARMSTRONG. It's this terrible inactivity that gets on my nerves. (*Sits Right sofa.*)

WARGRAVE. (*To Left sofa; sits*) We are adopting, I feel convinced, the only measures possible. So long as we remain together, all within sight of each other, a repetition of the tragedies that have occurred is—must be—impossible. We have all submitted to a search. Therefore, we know that no man is armed either with firearms or a knife. Nor has any man got cyanide or any drug about his person. If we remain, as I say, within sight of each other, nothing can happen.

ARMSTRONG. But we can't go on like this—we shall need food—sleep—

BLORE. That's what I say.

WARGRAVE. Obviously, the murderer's only chance is to get one of us detached from the rest. So long as we prevent that we are safe.

ARMSTRONG. Safe—?

LOMBARD. You're very silent, Vera?

VERA. There isn't anything to say— (*Pause.* WARGRAVE *rises; to up Center*) I wonder what the time is. It's this awful waiting—waiting for the hours to go by and yet feeling that they may be the last. What is the time?

LOMBARD. Half past eight.

VERA. Is that all?

LOMBARD. Pretty awful light, this. How are the candles holding out?

BLORE. There's a whole packet. Storm's dying down a bit, what do you think, sir? (*Rises; goes up to window.*)

WARGRAVE. Perhaps. We mustn't get too optimistic.

ARMSTRONG. The murderer's got everything on his side. Even the weather seems to be falling in with his plans.

(WARGRAVE *sits Left sofa. Long pause.*)

BLORE. (*Rising*) What about something to eat?

VERA. (*Rises. Crossing up Left*) If you like, I'll go out and open some tongue and make some coffee. But you four stay here. (*To* WARGRAVE) That's right, isn't it?

WARGRAVE. Not quite. You see, Miss Claythorne, it might be inadvisable to eat or drink something that you had prepared out of our sight.

VERA. Oh! (*Slowly*) You don't like me, do you?

WARGRAVE. It's not a question of likes or dislikes.

(VERA *sits down Left.*)

LOMBARD. There are very few tricks that will get past you, Sir Lawrence. You know, if you won't be offended at my saying so, you're my fancy.

WARGRAVE. (*Rises to Left, looking at him coldly through his spectacles in the best court manner*) This is hardly the moment, Captain Lombard, for any of us to indulge in the luxury of taking offence.

LOMBARD. (*Up Right Center*) I don't think it's Blore. (*To* BLORE) I may be wrong, but I can't feel you've got enough imagination for this job. All I can say is, if you are the criminal, I take my hat off to you for a damned fine actor.

BLORE. Thank you, for nothing. (*Sits Left sofa.*)

LOMBARD. (*Pause. Looks at* ARMSTRONG) I don't think it's the Doctor. I don't believe he's got the nerve. (*Looks at* VERA *down Left*) You've got plenty of nerve, Vera. On the other hand, you strike me as eminently sane. Therefore, you'd only do murder if you had a thoroughly good motive.

VERA. (*Sarcastically*) Thank you.

ARMSTRONG. (*Rises*) I've thought of something.

LOMBARD. Splendid. Animal, vegetable or mineral?

ARMSTRONG. That man (*Points to* BLORE) says he's a police officer. But we've no proof of that. He only said so after the gramophone record, when his name had been given. Before that he was pretending to be a South African millionaire. Perhaps the police officer is another impersonation. What do we know about him? Nothing at all.

LOMBARD. He's a policeman all right. Look at his feet.

BLORE. (*Rises and sits again*) That's enough from you, Mr. Lombard. (ARMSTRONG *sits chair Right Center*) Well, now we know where we are. By the way, Miss Claythorne suspects you, Doctor. Oh, yes, she does. Haven't you seen her shoot a dirty look from time to time? It all works out quite prettily. I suspect Sir Lawrence. Blore suspects me. Armstrong suspects Blore. (*To* WARGRAVE) What about you, sir?

WARGRAVE. Quite early in the day, I formed a certain conclusion. It seemed to me that everything that had occurred pointed quite unmistakably to one person. (*Pause. He looks straight ahead*) I am still of the same opinion. (*Above Left sofa*)

VERA. Which one?

WARGRAVE. Well—no, I think it would be inadvisable to mention that person's name at the present time.

LOMBARD. Inadvisable in the public interest?

WARGRAVE. Exactly.

(EVERYONE *looks at each other.*)

BLORE. What about the food idea?

ARMSTRONG. No, no, let's stay here. We're safe here.

VERA. I can't say I'm hungry.

LOMBARD. I'm not ravenous myself. You can go out and have a guzzle by yourself, Blore.

BLORE. Tell you what. Suppose I go and bring in a tin of biscuits? (*Rises to Left 2 door.*)

LOMBARD. Good idea.

(BLORE *starts to go.*)

LOMBARD. Oh, Blore.

BLORE. Eh?

LOMBARD. An unopened tin, Blore.

(BLORE *goes out; takes candle from bookcase. A pause.*
EVERYBODY *watches door. A gust of WIND—the cur-*
tains rattle. VERA *rises.* WARGRAVE *sits Left sofa.*)

LOMBARD. It's only the wind—making the curtains rattle.

VERA. (*Up Center*) I wonder what happened to the bathroom curtain? The one that Rogers missed.

LOMBARD. By the wildest stretch of imagination, I cannot see
what any homicidal maniac wants with a scarlet oilsilk
curtain.

VERA. Things seem to have been disappearing. Miss Brent
lost a skein of knitting wool.

LOMBARD. So the murderer, whoever he or she is, is a klepto-
maniac too.

VERA. How does it go? "Five little Indian boys—"

LOMBARD.

"Going in for law,
One got in Chancery—"

VERA. In chancery, but how could that apply? Unless, of
course— (*She looks at* WARGRAVE.)

WARGRAVE. Precisely, my dear young lady. That's why I'm
sitting right here.

LOMBARD. Ah! But I'm casting you for the role of murderer—
not victim.

WARGRAVE. The term can apply to a boxer.

LOMBARD. (*To* VERA) Maybe we'll start a free fight. That
seems to let you out, my dear.

VERA. That awful rhyme. It keeps going round and round in
my head. I think I'll remember it till I die. (*She realizes
what she has said and looks around at the* OTHERS.
Pause) Mr. Blore's a long time.

LOMBARD. I expect the big bad wolf has got him.

WARGRAVE. I have asked you once before to try and restrain
your rather peculiar sense of humor, Captain Lombard.

LOMBARD. Sorry, sir. It must be a form of nervousness.

(BLORE *enters Left 2 with a tin of biscuits.* VERA *to behind
chair Right Center.* WARGRAVE *rises to Left Center,
takes tin and opens it.*)

WARGRAVE. Put your hands up. Search him.

(ARMSTRONG *and* LOMBARD *cross to Left Center; search*
BLORE. ARMSTRONG *offers biscuits to* VERA.)

VERA. (*Sits Right Center*) No, thank you.

(BLORE *sits down Left.*)

LOMBARD. Come now—you've had no dinner. (*To above* VERA, *Right Center.*)

VERA. I couldn't eat anything.

LOMBARD. I warn you—Blore will wolf the lot.

BLORE. I don't see why you need be so funny about it. Starving ourselves won't do us any good. (*Sadly*) How are we off for cigarettes?

LOMBARD. (*Takes out his case and opens it; sighs ruefully*) I haven't got any.

ARMSTRONG. I've run out too.

WARGRAVE. Fortunately, I'm a pipe smoker.

VERA. (*Rousing herself. Crossing down Left*) I've got a whole box upstairs in my suitcase. I'll go get them. I could do with a cigarette myself. (*Pauses at door*) See that you all stay where you are. (*Goes out Left 1 carrying a candle from bookcase.*)

(WARGRAVE *to door, looking after her, leaving tin on sofa.*)

BLORE. (*Rises; fetches tin from sofa—eating solidly, up Left Center*) Not bad, these biscuits.

LOMBARD. What are they, cheese?

BLORE. Cheese and celery.

LOMBARD. That girl ought to have had some. (*To Left.*)

ARMSTRONG. Her nerves are in a bad state.

WARGRAVE. (*To above Left sofa*) I don't know that I'd agree with you there, Doctor. Miss Claythorne strikes me as a very cool and resourceful young lady—quite remarkably so.

LOMBARD. (*Up Left Center—looking curiously at* WARGRAVE) So that's your idea, is it? That she's the nigger in the woodpile?

ARMSTRONG. Hardly likely—a woman!

WARGRAVE. You and I, Doctor, see women from slightly different angles.

BLORE. (*Crossing down Right*) What does anyone say to a spot of whiskey?

LOMBARD. Good idea, providing we tackle an unopened bottle.

(*An appalling and blood-curdling SHRIEK of utter terror comes from overhead and a heavy THUD. All four men start up.* LOMBARD *and* BLORE *catch up candles.*

BLORE *takes candle from mantelpiece. All four rush to door Left 1 and out in this order:* LOMBARD, BLORE, ARMSTRONG *and* WARGRAVE—*the latter is slow getting under way, owing to age. Stage is quite dark as soon as* LOMBARD *and* BLORE *have gone through door and before* WARGRAVE *reaches door. Confused NOISES off. Then, on stage,* WARGRAVE's *voice calls out, "Who's that?" Sound of a SHOT. A confused moving about on the stage; voices off also; off faint—then come nearer. Left 2 door opens. Then door Left 1.* BLORE *heard swearing off. Also* ARMSTRONG's *voice.*)

VERA. (*Coming in Left 2, stumbling about*) Philip, Philip, where are you? I've lost you.

LOMBARD. (*Coming in Left 1*) Here I am.

VERA. Why can't we have some light? It's awful in the dark. You don't know where you are. You don't know where anyone is. (*Sits Left sofa.*)

LOMBARD. It's that damned draught on the stairs—blowing all the candles out. Here, I've got a lighter. (*Lights his and her candle. Sits Left sofa.*)

VERA. Where's Doctor Armstrong?

ARMSTRONG. (*From hall*) I'm hunting for the matches.

LOMBARD. Never mind matches—get some more candles.

VERA. I was horrified to death—it went right around my throat—

LOMBARD. What did?

VERA. The window was open in my room. It blew out the candle as I opened the door. And then a long strand of seaweed touched my throat. I thought, in the dark, that I was being strangled by a wet hand—

(*MURMUR off Left.*)

LOMBARD. I don't wonder you yelled.

VERA. Who hung that seaweed there?

LOMBARD. I don't know. But when I find out, he'll be sorry he was ever born.

(ARMSTRONG *comes quietly in from Left 1.*)

VERA. (*Sharply*) Who's that?   (*WARN Curtain.*)

ARMSTRONG. It's all right, Miss Claythorne. It's only me.

BLORE. (*In hall*) Here we are. (*A faint glow through door as he lights candles. He comes in carrying candle. Crosses Right*) Who fired that shot?

(VERA *rises; moves Left Center, turns and screams. Light reveals* WARGRAVE *set upright on window-seat, red oilsilk curtain draped around shoulders. Grey skein of wool plaited into wig on his head. In center of forehead is round dark mark with red trickling from it.* MEN *stand paralyzed.* VERA *screams.* ARMSTRONG *pulls himself together, waves* OTHERS *to stand back and goes over to* WARGRAVE. *Bends over him; straightens up.*)

ARMSTRONG. He's dead— Shot through the head—

VERA. (*Leans against window up Left*) One got in Chancery —and then there were four—

ARMSTRONG. Miss Claythorne.

LOMBARD. Vera.

VERA. You got me out of the way. You got me to go upstairs for cigarettes. You put that seaweed there— You did it all so that you could kill that helpless old man in the dark—you're mad—all of you—crazy. (*Her voice is low and full of horror*) That's why you wanted the red curtain and the knitting wool— It was all planned— long ago—for *that*— Oh, my God, let me out of here— (*She edges to the Left 1 door and rushes out, as—*

CURTAIN

(End of Scene I)

Scene II

The following morning.

It is brilliant sunshine. The room is as it was the night before.

BLORE, LOMBARD *and* VERA *are sitting on the Left sofa, backs to the audience, eating tinned tongue on tray.*

LOMBARD.

> Three little Indian boys,
> Sitting in a row.
> Thinking as they guzzle
> Who's next to go?

VERA. Oh, Philip!

BLORE. That's all right, Miss Claythorne. I don't mind joking on a full stomach.

VERA. I must say I was hungry. But all the same, I don't think I shall ever fancy tinned tongue again.

BLORE. I was wanting that meal! I feel a new man.

LOMBARD. We'd been nearly twenty-four hours without food. That does lower the morale.

VERA. Somehow, in the daylight, everything seems different.

LOMBARD. You mustn't forget there's a dangerous homicidal lunatic somewhere loose on this island.

VERA. Why is it one doesn't feel jittery about it any more?

LOMBARD. Because we know now, beyond any possible doubt, who it is, eh, Blore?

BLORE. That's right.

LOMBARD. It was the uncertainty before—looking at each other, wondering which.

VERA. I said all along it was Doctor Armstrong.

LOMBARD. You did, my sweet, you did. Until, of course, you went completely bats and suspected us all.

VERA. (*Rises to mantelpiece; takes three cigarettes out of box*) It seems rather silly in the light of day.

LOMBARD. Very silly.

BLORE. Allowing it is Armstrong, what's happened to him?

LOMBARD. We know what he wants us to think has happened to him.

VERA. (*Crosses Center; gives* BLORE *and* LOMBARD *cigarette*) What exactly did you find?

LOMBARD. One shoe—just one shoe—sitting prettily on the cliff edge. Inference—Doctor Armstrong has gone completely off his onion and committed suicide.

BLORE. (*Rises*) All very circumstantial—even to one little china Indian broken over there in the doorway.

VERA. I think that was rather overdoing it. A man wouldn't think of doing that if he was going to drown himself.

LOMBARD. Quite so. But we're fairly sure he didn't drown himself. But he had it make it appear as though he were the seventh victim all according to plan.

VERA. Supposing he really is dead?

LOMBARD. I'm a bit suspicious of death without bodies.

VERA. How extraordinary to think that there are five dead bodies in there, and here we've been eating tinned tongue.

LOMBARD. The delightful feminine disregard for facts—there are six dead bodies and they are not all in there.

BLORE. Oh, no, no. She's right. There are only five.

LOMBARD. What about Mrs. Rogers?

BLORE. I've counted her. She makes the fifth.

LOMBARD. (*Rises. A little exasperated*) Now look here: Marston, one. Mrs. Rogers, two. General MacKenzie, three. Rogers, four. Emily Brent, five, and Wargrave, six.

(VERA *takes tray to table up Left.*)

BLORE. (*Counting themselves*) Seven, eight, nine—Armstrong, ten. That's right, old man. Sorry. (*Sits Left sofa.*)

LOMBARD. (*Sits Left sofa*) Don't you think it would be an idea if we brought Mrs. Rogers downstairs and shoved her in the morgue, too?

BLORE. I'm a detective, not an undertaker.

VERA. (*Sits chair Right Center*) For Heaven's sake, stop talking about bodies. The point is Armstrong murdered them.

LOMBARD. We ought to have realized it was Armstrong straight away.

BLORE. How do you think Armstrong got hold of your revolver?

LOMBARD. Haven't the slightest idea.

VERA. Tell me exactly what happened in the night?

LOMBARD. Well, after you threw a fit of hysterics and locked yourself in your room, we all thought we'd better go to bed.

BLORE. So we all went to bed—and locked ourselves in our rooms.

LOMBARD. About an hour later, I heard someone pass my door. I came out and tapped on Blore's door. He was there all right. Then I went to Armstrong's room. It was empty. That's when I tapped on your door and told you to sit tight—whatever happened. Then I came down here. The window on the balcony was open—and my revolver was lying just beside it.

BLORE. But why the devil should Armstrong chuck that revolver away?

LOMBARD. Don't ask me—either an accident or he's crazy.

VERA. Where do you think he is?

LOMBARD. Lurking somewhere, waiting to have a crack at one of us.

VERA. We ought to search the house.

BLORE. What—and walk into an ambush?

VERA. (*Rises*) Oh—I never thought of that.

LOMBARD. Are you quite sure you heard no one moving about after we went out?

VERA. (*Above Right sofa*) Oh, I imagined all sorts of things—but nothing short of setting the house on fire would have got me to unlock my door.

LOMBARD. I see,—just thoroughly suspicious.

BLORE. (*Rises to Right*) What's the use of talking? What are we going to do?

LOMBARD. If you ask me—do nothing. Sit tight and take no risks.

BLORE. Look here, I want to go after that fellow.

LOMBARD. What a dog of the bulldog breed you are, Blore. By the way, between friends and without prejudice, you did go in for that little spot of perjury, didn't you?

(VERA *sits Left end Right sofa.*)

BLORE. (*Sits Right Center. Hesitating*) Well, I don't suppose it makes any odds now. Landor was innocent, all right. The gang squared me and between us we put him away for a stretch. Mind you, I wouldn't admit it now if it wasn't that—

LOMBARD. You think we're all in the same boat?

BLORE. Well, I couldn't admit it in front of Mr. Justice Wargrave, could I?

LOMBARD. No, hardly.

BLORE. (*Rises*) I say, that fellow Seton, do you think he was innocent?

LOMBARD. I'm quite sure of it. Wargrave had a reason for wanting him out of the way. Well, Blore, I'm delighted you've come off your virtuous perch. I hope you made a tidy bit out of it?

BLORE. (*Injured*) Nothing like what I ought to have done. They're a mean lot, that Benny gang. I got my promotion, though.

LOMBARD. And Landor got penal servitude and died in gaol.

BLORE. I couldn't tell he was going to die, could I?

LOMBARD. No, that was your bad luck.

BLORE. His, you mean.

LOMBARD. Yours, too. Because as a result of that fact you may get your life cut short unpleasantly soon.

BLORE. What? Me? By Armstrong? I'll watch it.

LOMBARD. You'll have to. Remember there are only three Indians there.

BLORE. Well, what about you?

LOMBARD. I shall be quite all right, thank you. I've been in tight places before and I've got out of them. And I mean to get out of this one. (*Pause*) Besides, I've got a revolver.

BLORE. (*Right end Right sofa*) Yes—that revolver. Now listen. You said you found it lying down there. What's to prove you haven't had it all the time?

LOMBARD. Same old gramophone record! No room in your head for more than one idea at a time, is there?

BLORE. No, but it's a good idea.

LOMBARD. And you're sticking to it.

BLORE. And I would have thought up a better story than that, if I were you.

LOMBARD. I only wanted something simple that a policeman could understand.

BLORE. What's wrong with the police?

LOMBARD. Nothing—now that you've left the Force.

BLORE. (*Above Right sofa*) Now look here, Captain Lombard, if you're an honest man, as you pretend—

LOMBARD. Oh, come, Blore, we're neither of us honest.

BLORE. If you're telling the truth for once, you ought to do the square thing and chuck that revolver down there.

LOMBARD. Don't be an ass.

BLORE. I've said I'll go through the house looking for Armstrong, haven't I? If I'm willing to do that, will you lend me that revolver?

LOMBARD. (*Rises to down Center*) No, I won't. That revolver's mine. It's my revolver and I'm sticking to it.

BLORE. (*Angrily*) Then do you know what I'm beginning to think?

LOMBARD. You're not beginning to think it, you square-headed flattie. You thought it last night, and now you've gone back to your original idea. I'm the one and only U. N. Unknown Owen. Is that it?

BLORE. I won't contradict you.

LOMBARD. Well, think what you damned well please. But I warn you—

VERA. (*Incisively*) I think you are both behaving like a pair of children.

(*They* BOTH *look at her rather sheepishly.*)

LOMBARD. Sorry, Teacher.

VERA. (*To* BLORE, *scornfully*) Of course, Captain Lombard isn't the unknown. The Unknown Owen is Armstrong—and I'll tell you one very good proof of it.

BLORE. Oh, what?

VERA. Think of the rhyme. "Four little Indian boys—going out to sea. A red herring swallowed one, and then there were three." Don't you see the subtlety of it? A red herring? That's Armstrong's pretended suicide, but it's only a red herring—so really he isn't dead!

BLORE. That's very ingenious.

VERA. To my mind, it's absolute proof. You see, it's all mad because *he's* mad. He takes a queer, childish, crazy pleasure in sticking to the rhyme and making everything happen in that way. Dressing up the Judge, killing Rogers when he was chopping sticks; using a hypodermic on Miss Brent, when he might just as well have drugged her. He's got to make it all fit in.

BLORE. And that might give us a pointer. Where do we go from here? (*Goes up to mantelpiece and reads*)
"Three little Indian boys walking in the Zoo.
A big bear hugged one and then there were two."
(*He laughs*) He'll have a job with that one. There's no Zoo on this island! (*His laughter is cut short as he sees the big bear rug on which he is standing. He edges off the rug and turns to* LOMBARD.)

BLORE. I say, Captain Lombard, what about a nice bottle of beer?

LOMBARD. Do stop thinking about your stomach, Blore. This craving for food and drink will be your undoing.

BLORE. But there's plenty of beer in the kitchen.

LOMBARD. Yes, and if anyone wanted to get rid of you, the first place they'd think of putting a lethal dose would be in a nice bottle of beer.

(*From outside comes the sound of a motor boat* HOOTER.)

BLORE. What's that? A boat! A boat!

(ALL *rush to balcony to Left.* BLORE *rushes out into balcony. There is a* SCREAM, *then a* CRASH *and* THUD.)

VERA. Oh, God! (*Puts hands over eyes.*)

(LOMBARD, *revolver in hand, rushes to window, looks out, then returns slowly to room.* VERA *sits down Left.*)

LOMBARD. Blore's got his.

VERA. How?

LOMBARD. A booby trap—all set—a wire across the door attached to something above.

VERA. Is he?

LOMBARD. Yes. Crushed. Head stove in. That great bronze bear holding a clock, from the landing.

VERA. A bear? Oh, how ghastly! It's this awful childishness!

LOMBARD. I know. God, what a fool Blore was!

VERA. And now there are two.

LOMBARD. (*To down Left*) Yes, and we'll have to be very careful of ourselves.

VERA. We shan't do it. He'll get us. We'll never get away from this island!

LOMBARD. Oh, yes, we will. I've never been beaten yet.

VERA. Don't you feel—that there's someone—now—in this room—watching us, watching and waiting?

LOMBARD. That's just nerves.

VERA. Then you do feel it?

LOMBARD. (*Fiercely*) No, I don't.

VERA. (*Rises, to Center*) Please, Philip, let's get out of this house—anywhere. Perhaps if that was a boat, they'll see us.

LOMBARD. All right. We'll go to the top of the island and wait for relief to come. It's sheer cliff on the far side and we can see if anyone approaches from the house.

VERA. Anything is better than staying here.

LOMBARD. Won't you be rather cold in that dress?

VERA. I'd be colder if I were dead.

LOMBARD. Perhaps you're right. (*Goes to window*) A quick reconnaissance.

VERA. Be careful, Philip—please! (*Follows him to window.*)

LOMBARD. I'm not Blore. There's no window directly above. (*He goes out on balcony and looks down. He is arrested by what he sees*) Hullo, there's something washed up on the rocks.

VERA. What? (*She joins him*) It looks like a body.

LOMBARD. (*In a strange new voice*) You'd better wait in there. I'm going to have a look.

(*He exits to Left on balcony.* VERA *back into room. Her face is full of conflicting emotions.*)

VERA. Armstrong—Armstrong's body—

LOMBARD. (*Comes in very slowly*) It's Armstrong drowned— Washed up at high water mark.

VERA. So there's no one on the island—no one at all, except us two.

LOMBARD. Yes, Vera. Now we know where we are.

VERA. Now we know where we are?

LOMBARD. A very pretty trick of yours, with that wire. Quite neat. Old Wargrave always knew you were dangerous.

VERA. You—

LOMBARD. So you did drown that kid after all.

VERA. I didn't! That's where you're wrong. Please believe me. Please listen to me!

LOMBARD. (*Crossing down Left*) I'm listening. You'd better make it a good story.

VERA. (*Above Right sofa*) It isn't a story. It's the truth. I didn't kill that child. It was someone else.

LOMBARD. Who?

VERA. A man. Peter's uncle. I was in love with him.

LOMBARD. This is getting quite interesting.

VERA. Don't sneer. It was hell. Absolute hell. Peter was born after his father's death. If he'd been a girl, Hugh would have got everything.

LOMBARD. Well known tale of the wicked uncle.

VERA. Yes—he was wicked—and I didn't know. He said he loved me, but that he was too poor to marry. There was a rock far out that Peter was always wanting to swim to. Of course, I wouldn't let him. It was dangerous. One day we were on the beach and I had to go back to the house for something I'd forgotten. When I got back to the rock, I looked down and saw Peter swimming out to the rock. I knew he hadn't a chance, the current had got him already. I flew towards the beach and Hugh tried to stop me. "Don't be a fool," he said. "I told the little ass he could do it."

LOMBARD. Go on. This is interesting.

VERA. I pushed past him—he tried to stop me, but I got away and rushed down. I plunged into the sea and swam after Peter. He'd gone before I could get to him.

LOMBARD. And everything went off well at the inquest. They

called you a plucky girl, and you kept discreetly quiet about Hugh's part in the business.

VERA. Do you think anyone would have believed me? Besides, I couldn't! I really was in love with him.

LOMBARD. Well, it's a pretty story. And then I suppose Hugh let you down?

VERA. Do you think I ever wanted to see him again?

LOMBARD. You certainly are an accomplished liar, Vera.

VERA. Can't you believe the truth when you hear it?

LOMBARD. Who set the trap that killed Blore? I didn't— and Armstrong's dead. I've broken most of the Commandments in my time—and I'm no saint. But there's one thing I won't stand for and that's murder.

VERA. You won't stand for murder. What about those natives you left to die in Africa?

LOMBARD. That's what's so damn funny—I didn't.

VERA. What do you mean?

LOMBARD. For once—just once, mark you, I played the hero. Risked my life to save the lives of my men. Left them my rifle and ammunition and all the food there was— and took a chance through the brush. By the most incredible luck it came off—but it wasn't in time to save them. And the rumor got around that I'd deliberately abandoned my men. There's life for you!

VERA. Do you expect me to believe that? Why, you actually admitted the whole thing.

LOMBARD. I know. I got such a kick out of watching their faces.

VERA. You can't fool me with a stupid lie like that.

LOMBARD. (Completely losing his temper) Blast you!

VERA. (To Right window) Why didn't I see it before? It's there in your face—the face of a killer—

LOMBARD. You can't fool me any longer.

VERA. Oh— (VERA sways forward as if fainting. LOMBARD runs to catch her. She wrests the revolver from him) Now!

LOMBARD. (Backing away down Left) You cunning little devil!

VERA. If you come on one step nearer, I'll shoot.

LOMBARD. You—young, lovely, and quite, quite mad.

(LOMBARD makes a movement to VERA. She shoots. He falls down Left. She goes over to him, her eyes full of hor-

ror, as she realizes what she has done. The revolver falls from her hand. Suddenly she hears a low LAUGH coming from the study door. She turns her head slowly in that direction. The laughter grows louder, the Right door slowly opens and WARGRAVE *enters. He carries a rope in his hand.*)

WARGRAVE. It's all come true. My Ten Little Indian plan— My rhyme—my rhyme—

VERA. Ah! (*Stifled scream.*)

WARGRAVE. (*Angrily*) Silence in Court! (*Looks around suspiciously*) If there is any more noise, I shall have the Court cleared. (*Down Right Center*) It's all right, my dear. It's all right. Don't be frightened. This is a Court of Justice. You'll get justice here. (*Crosses Left; locks doors Left 2 and Left 1.* VERA *to Right. Confidentially*) You thought I was a ghost. You thought I was dead. (*Above Right sofa*) Armstrong said I was dead. That was the clever part of my plan. Said we'd trap the murderer. We'd fix up my supposed death so I should be free to spy upon the guilty one. He thought it an excellent plan—came out that night to meet me by the cliff without suspicion. I sent him over with a push—so easily. He swallowed my red herring all right. (VERA *is petrified with horror. In a confidential manner*) You know, Vera Claythorne, all my life I've wanted to take life,—yes, to take life. I've had to get what enjoyment I could out of sentencing the guilty to death. (VERA *moves to revolver*) I always enjoyed that—but it wasn't enough. I wanted more— I wanted to do it myself with my own hands— (WARGRAVE *follows* VERA *to Left.* VERA *leans against Left 1 door. Suddenly curbs excitement and speaks with severe dignity*) But I'm a Judge of the High Court. I've got a sense of justice. (*As if listening to an echo*) As between our Sovereign Lord the King and the prisoner at the Bar—will true deliverance make— Guilty, my Lord. Yes. (*Nods head*) Guilty. You were all guilty, you know, but the Law couldn't touch you, so I had to take the Law into my own hands. (*Holds up hands in a frenzy of delight*) Into my own hands! Silence in the Court! (VERA *hammers on Left 1 door.* WARGRAVE *takes her arm and drags her to Right above Left sofa*) Anthony Marston first. Then Mrs. Rogers. Barbitone in the brandy. MacKenzie—stabbed.

Got Rogers with an axe when he was chopping sticks. Doped Emily Brent's coffee so she couldn't feel the hypodermic. Booby trap for Blore. (*Confidentially*) Blore was a fool. I always knew it would be easy to get Blore. Returning that revolver was a clever touch. Made the end interesting. I knew you two would suspect each other in the end. The question was, who'd win out? I banked on you, my dear. The female of the species. Besides, it's always more exciting to have a girl at the end. (*He steps onto sofa, and* VERA *falls to the ground*) Prisoner at the Bar, have you anything to say why sentence should not be passed on you? Vera Elizabeth Claythorne, I sentence you to death—

(*WARN Curtain.*)

VERA. (*With a sudden outcry*) Stop! Stop! I'm not guilty! I'm not guilty!

WARGRAVE. Ah, they all say that. Must plead not guilty. Unless, of course, you're going all out for a verdict of insanity. But you're not mad. (*Very reasonably*) I'm mad, but you're not.

VERA. But I *am* innocent!! I swear it! I never killed that child. I never wanted to kill him. You're a judge. You know when a person is guilty and when they're innocent. I swear I'm telling the truth.

WARGRAVE. So you didn't drown that boy after all? Very interesting. But it doesn't matter much now, does it?

VERA. What— (*Makes inarticulate sounds as the rope swings in front of her.*)

WARGRAVE. I can't spoil my lovely rhyme. My ten little Indian boys. You're the last one. One little Indian boy left all alone. He went and hanged himself. I must have my hanging—my hanging—

(LOMBARD *comes slowly to, picks up revolver and shoots.* WARGRAVE *falls back off the sofa.*)

VERA. Philip—Philip—

(BOTH *sit on floor in front of sofa.*)

LOMBARD. It's all right, darling. It's all right.

VERA. I thought you were dead. I thought I'd killed you.

LOMBARD. Thank God, women can't shoot straight. At least, not straight enough.

VERA. I shall never forget this.

LOMBARD. Oh, yes, you will. You know there's another end-
    ing to that Ten Little Indian rhyme:
        "One little Indian boy, left all alone,
            We got married—and then there were none!"

(Takes rope and puts his head in noose too. He kisses her.)

(There is the sound of a motor HOOTER.)

END OF PLAY

APPOINTMENT WITH DEATH

Produced at the Piccadilly Theatre, London, on the 31st March 1945, with the following cast of characters:

(in order of their appearance)

MRS. BOYNTON	*Mary Clare*
GINEVRA BOYNTON	*Deryn Kerbey*
LENNOX BOYNTON	*Ian Lubbock*
NADINE BOYNTON	*Beryl Machin*
LIFT BOY	*John Glennon*
ALDERMAN HIGGS	*Percy Walsh*
CLERK } BEDOUIN }	*Anthony Dorset*
LADY WESTHOLME	*Janet Burnell*
MISS PRYCE	*Joan Hickson*
DR. GERARD	*Gerard Hinze*
SARAH KING	*Carla Lehmann*
JEFFERSON COPE	*Alan Sedgwick*
RAYMOND BOYNTON	*John Wynn*
DRAGOMAN	*Harold Berens*
COLONEL CARBERY	*Owen Reynolds*
LADY VISITOR	*Cherry Herbert*
HOTEL VISITORS	{ *Corinne Whitehouse* { *Joseph Blanchard*

The play directed by TERENCE DE MARNEY

CHARACTERS

MRS. BOYNTON
GINEVRA BOYNTON, her stepdaughter
LENNOX BOYNTON, her elder stepson
NADINE BOYNTON, Lennox's wife
HOTEL CLERK
AN ITALIAN GIRL
ALDERMAN HIGGS
AN ARAB BOY
LADY WESTHOLME
MISS AMABEL PRYCE
DR. THEODORE GERARD
SARAH KING
JEFFERSON COPE
RAYMOND BOYNTON, Lennox's younger brother
A DRAGOMAN
COLONEL CARBERY

SYNOPSIS OF SCENES

ACT I
The lounge of the King Solomon Hotel, Jerusalem.
Afternoon

ACT II
SCENE 1   The Travellers' Camp at Petra. Early afternoon.
A week later
SCENE 2   The same, three hours later

ACT III
SCENE 1   The same, the following morning
SCENE 2   The same, the same afternoon

Time—the present

PRODUCTION NOTE

The effect of the lift ascending and descending can be easily obtained by having a gauze window in the lift door, behind which is a shutter which can be raised as the lift descends and lowered as the lift ascends. There should be a domed light which is always alight, suspended in the lift in sight of the audience.

Characters should wear semi-tropical clothes suitable to character and nationality. It will be found effective if all characters wear costume light in colour, except Mrs. Boynton who should dress throughout in unrelieved black. The Hotel Clerk wears a grey frock coat and tarboosh. The Dragoman wears a white Arab dress and red tarboosh in the hotel, but changes into brown garments for the camp scenes, as also does the Arab boy. Colonel Carbery wears the khaki uniform of the Palestine Police, i.e. tunic and shorts with a blue service peaked cap.

Act One

SCENE: *The lounge of the King Solomon Hotel, Jerusalem. Afternoon.*

Back c are three open arches, the centre one giving access to a terrace with a balcony rail with a wide expanse of blue sky beyond. An arch up R leads to the main entrance, and arches down R and up L lead to other parts of the hotel. There is a lift behind a sliding door down L. A quadrant counter for the reception clerk is up L. A small table stands c with five chairs around it. There is a low table with a chair above it, down R. Other small tables are set against the walls. On the terrace there are two chairs and a table with a sunshade.

When the CURTAIN *rises,* MRS. BOYNTON *is seated above the table c. She is a vast obese woman rather like an idol, with an expressionless face. She moves her head and eyes but not her body. A stick is beside her chair. Her family are grouped round her like courtiers round a queen.* GINEVRA BOYNTON, *her daughter, sits R of Mrs. Boynton. She is a pretty girl of nineteen with a lost, vacant expression. She sits staring into space: occasionally her lips move as though she is talking to herself. Her fingers are picking at a handkerchief which she is tearing in little bits. This is partly masked by the table.* NADINE BOYNTON, *the daughter-in-law, sits L of Mrs. Boynton. She is a quiet woman of twenty-eight. She is sewing.* LENNOX BOYNTON, *Mrs. Boynton's elder son and Nadine's husband, sits L of Nadine. He is holding a book upside down and appears to be reading. The* HOTEL CLERK *is behind his desk. A glamorous* ITALIAN GIRL *enters up R and crosses to the desk.*

GIRL. (*to the Clerk*) *La mia chiave, per favore.*

CLERK. (*puzzled*) I beg your pardon?

GIRL. (*emphasizing*) *Chiave.* Ah, you do not understand. My—key—please.

CLERK. Oh. Certainly, *signorina.* (*He hands her a key*)

GIRL. *Grazie, signor.* (*She moves towards the lift*)

(*The lift door opens.* ALDERMAN HIGGS *enters from the lift. He is a portly, middle-aged man and has a broad Lancashire accent. He stands aside to let the* GIRL *pass, half-raising his hat*)

(*She acknowledges Higgs' courtesy with a smile*) Signor.

(*The* GIRL *exits to the lift. The door closes and the lift ascends.* HIGGS *glances curiously at the Boyntons, as though slightly fascinated by their static quality, crosses hurriedly towards the arch up* R, *then stops, turns and moves to the desk*)

HIGGS. (*to the Clerk*) Any letters for me? Name of 'Iggs.

CLERK. Letters are at the concierge's office in the hall, sir.

HIGGS. Conciurge? Moost you call 'im by these fancy names? What's wrong with "porter"?

CLERK. (*indifferently*) Just as you please, sir.

HIGGS. Five quid a day you're charging me 'ere, and I don't think so mooch of this place. (*He looks around*) Give me the *Midland* at Manchester even if it 'asn't got so many fancy columns. (*He moves to the arch up* R, *then stops and returns a step or two*) See 'ere, if one of them Dragomen chaps turn oop from Cook's, askin' for me, you tell 'im to wait till I coom back. See?

(HIGGS *turns and exits up* R. *There is silence. You expect the* BOYNTONS *to speak, but they do not.* NADINE *drops her scissors. As she picks them up,* MRS. BOYNTON's *head turns to look at her, but she does not speak.* GINEVRA's *lips move. She smiles. Her fingers work. A faint whispering sound comes from her.* MRS. BOYNTON *transfers her attention to Ginevra, contemplates her in silence for a moment, then speaks in a deep voice*)

MRS. BOYNTON. Jinny!

(GINEVRA *starts, looks at Mrs. Boynton, opens her mouth to
speak but says nothing. The sound of a bus arriving outside and the murmur of native voices is heard off up* R.
MRS. BOYNTON *and* NADINE *look towards the arch up* R.
GINEVRA *and* LENNOX *have no reaction. An* ARAB BOY,
carrying some baggage, enters up R *and crosses to the
desk. He gets some directions from the* CLERK *and exits
with the baggage up* L. LADY WESTHOLME, MISS AMABEL
PRYCE *and* DR. GERARD *enter up* R *and cross to the desk.*
LADY WESTHOLME *is a large important-looking woman in
tweeds, very British and country.* MISS PRYCE *is a typical
spinster with a large terai hat and many bead chains and
scarves.* DR. GERARD *is a good-looking, middle-aged
Frenchman. He carries a newspaper*)

LADY WESTHOLME. (*announcing the fact*) I am Lady Westholme.

CLERK. (*indicating a pile of registration forms*) You will
register, please.

LADY WESTHOLME. You received my wire from Cairo?

CLERK. Certainly, Lady Westholme. Your rooms are reserved.
One-one-eight and one-one-nine on the second floor.

LADY WESTHOLME. I prefer the first floor.

CLERK. I am afraid we have nothing vacant on the first floor.

(*The* ARAB BOY *enters up* L)

LADY WESTHOLME. (*overpoweringly*) I have chosen to stay
here instead of at the High Commissioner's and I expect
to be treated properly. If there are no rooms vacant on
the first floor, somebody must be moved. You understand?

CLERK. (*defeated*) If your ladyship will go temporarily to the
second floor we will arrange something before tonight.
Can I have your passport, please? (*He indicates the
form*) Surname, Christian names and nationality, please.

(LADY WESTHOLME *fills up the form*)

LADY WESTHOLME. (*as she writes; loudly*) British.

GERARD. (*softly*) Very definitely.

CLERK. (*to the* ARAB BOY) Boy. (*He hands a key to the* ARAB
BOY)

(*The* ARAB BOY *moves to the lift.* LADY WESTHOLME *follows him.* MRS. BOYNTON *follows Lady Westholme with her eyes.* MISS PRYCE *struggles with her form*)

MISS PRYCE. Oh, dear, I *hope* I've filled this in right. I always find these forms so *confusing*.

GERARD. (*helping* MISS PRYCE) The nationality here. You, too, are British.

(*The* ARAB BOY *rings the lift bell and returns to the desk.* LADY WESTHOLME *waits impatiently*)

MISS PRYCE. Oh, well—yes, certainly—at least—really, you know—(*confidentially*) I'm *Welsh*—but still, it's all the *same.* (*She drops her handbag*)

GERARD. (*picking up the handbag*) Allow me.

MISS PRYCE. (*taking the bag*) Oh, thank you. (*To the Clerk*) Have you—is there—I believe you have a room booked for me—one with a view towards the Dead Sea, I asked for.

CLERK. The name?

MISS PRYCE. Oh, dear me—how stupid of me. Pryce. Miss Pryce. Miss Amabel Pryce.

(*The lift descends and the door opens.* LADY WESTHOLME *exits to the lift*)

CLERK. (*to the Arab Boy*) Number four-eighty-four. (*He hands him a key*)

(*The* ARAB BOY *moves to the lift.* MISS PRYCE *drops her handbag.* GERARD *picks up the bag*)

MISS PRYCE. So stupid of me. (*She takes the bag*) Thank you *so* much.

(*The* ARAB BOY *exits to the lift*)

(*She hurries to the lift*) Wait for me! Wait for me!

(MISS PRYCE *exits to the lift. The door closes and the lift ascends*)

GERARD. (*to the Clerk*) Dr. Theodore Gerard. (*He fills in a form*)

CLERK. Oh, yes, Doctor Gerard. Number one-eight-four. (*He hands him a key.*)

(GERARD *moves to the lift and waits.* GINEVRA *looks at Gerard. The lift descends and the door opens.* SARAH KING *enters from the lift. She is an attractive, decided looking girl of twenty-three. She passes Gerard, hesitates, then smiles at him.* GERARD *bows*)

GERARD. How do you do?

SARAH. I'm so pleased to see you. I never thanked you for helping me the other night at the station in Cairo.

GERARD. That was nothing—a pleasure. You are enjoying Jerusalem, Miss—er . . . ?

SARAH. King—Dr. Sarah King.

GERARD. (*gaily*) Ah, we are colleagues. (*He takes a card from his pocket and hands it to her*) Dr. Gerard.

SARAH. Colleagues? (*She looks at the card*) Dr. Theodore Gerard. Oh. (*Reverently*) Are you *the* Dr. Gerard? But yes, you must be.

GERARD. I am Dr. Theodore Gerard. So, as I say, we are colleagues.

SARAH. Yes, but you're distinguished and I am only starting.

GERARD. (*smiling*) Oh, well, I hope it will not be like your English proverb—wait a minute so that I get it right. (*Slowly*) "Doctors differ and patients die."

SARAH. Fancy you knowing that! Just as well we haven't any patients. Have you just come in on the afternoon train?

GERARD. Yes. With a very important English lady. (*He grimaces*) Lady Westholme. Since God is not in Jerusalem, she is forced to put up with the *King Solomon Hotel.*

SARAH. (*laughing*) Lady Westholme is a political big bug. In her own eyes at any rate. She's always heckling the Government about housing or equal pay for women. She was an under-secretary or something—but she lost her seat at the last election.

GERARD. Not the type that interests you?

SARAH. No—but—(*she drops her voice and draws Gerard up* L) there's someone over there who does. Don't look at once. It's an American family. They were on the train with me yesterday. I talked to the son.

(GERARD *looks at Lennox*)

Not that one—a younger one. He was rather nice. Extraordinary looking old woman, isn't she? Her family seem absolutely devoted to her.

GERARD. (*in a low voice*) Possibly because they know she will not long be with them. You recognized the signs?

SARAH. How long would you give her?

GERARD. Perhaps six months—who knows? You will have a drink?

SARAH. Not now. (*She glances at her watch*) I've got to call for a parcel at one of the shops. I must hurry. (*She gives him a friendly nod*) Another time.

(SARAH *crosses and exits quickly up* R. GERARD *looks after her a moment, then turns to the Clerk*)

GERARD. Cinzano à l'eau, please. (*He moves down* L, *then crosses slowly below the table* C *to* R, *glancing as he passes at the book Lennox is holding. He sits in the chair down* R, *and opens his newspaper, covertly studying the Boyntons*)

(*The* CLERK *claps his hands The* ARAB BOY *enters up* L. *The* CLERK *gives him Gerard's order. The* ARAB BOY *exits up* L. GINEVRA *raises her head and watches Gerard. Her fingers twist and tear her handkerchief*)

MRS. BOYNTON. (*her voice sudden and deep*) Ginevra, you're tired.

(GINEVRA *jumps*)

You'd better go and rest.

GINEVRA. I'm not tired, Mother. I'm not really.

MRS. BOYNTON. Yes, you are. I always know. I don't think— (*she pauses*) I don't think you'll be able to do any sightseeing tomorrow.

(*The lift door closes and the lift ascends*)

GINEVRA. Oh, but I shall. (*Vehemently*) I'm quite all right.

MRS. BOYNTON. No, you're not. (*With slow relish*) You're going to be ill.

GINEVRA. (*rising; hysterically*) I'm not. I'm not.

MRS. BOYNTON. Go up and lie down.

GINEVRA. I'm not going to be ill. I don't want to be ill.

MRS. BOYNTON. I always know.

NADINE. I'll come up with you, Jinny.

MRS. BOYNTON. No, let her go up alone.

GINEVRA. I want Nadine to come. (*Her handkerchief slips from her fingers to the floor*)

NADINE. (*putting her sewing on the table*) Then, of course, I will. (*She rises*)

MRS. BOYNTON. The child prefers to go by herself. (*She fixes Ginevra with her eye*) Don't you, Jinny?

GINEVRA. (*after a pause; mechanically*) Yes—I'd rather go alone. Thank you, Nadine. (*She crosses slowly to the lift*)

(MRS. BOYNTON *follows Ginevra with her eyes.* NADINE *resumes her seat and picks up her sewing. The lift descends and the door opens. The* ITALIAN GIRL *enters from the lift. She has changed into a very revealing sun-suit, and carries a magazine and an unlighted cigarette in a long holder.*

GINEVRA *passes the Girl, and exits into the lift. The door closes and the lift ascends. The* GIRL *goes to the* CLERK *who lights her cigarette for her*)

GIRL. (*to the Clerk*) I would like a Martini on the terrace, please. (*She goes on to the terrace and sits* R *of the table under the sunshade*)

(*The* ARAB BOY *enters up* L, *with Gerard's drink on a tray. He crosses above the table* C *and puts the glass on the table beside Gerard. He then returns to the desk, takes the Girl's order from the* CLERK *and exits up* L.

JEFFERSON COPE *enters breezily up* R. *He is about forty-five; a pleasant, normal, rather old-fashioned American*)

COPE. (*moving to* R *of the table* C) I was looking around for you all. (*He shakes hands all round, then stands* R *of the table*) How do you find yourself, Mrs. Boynton? Not too tired by the journey from Cairo?

MRS. BOYNTON. (*suddenly very gracious*) No, thank you. My health's never good, as you know . . .

COPE. Why, of course. (*Sympathetically*) Too bad, too bad.

MRS. BOYNTON. But I'm certainly no worse. (*She looks at* NADINE) Nadine takes good care of me, don't you, Nadine?

NADINE. (*without expression*) I do my best.

COPE. (*heartily*) Why, I bet you do. Well, Lennox, and what do you think of King David's city?

(LENNOX *continues to look at his book and does not answer*)

MRS. BOYNTON. Lennox!

LENNOX. (*as from very far away*) Sorry—what did you say, Cope?

COPE. (*crossing above the table to* LC) I asked what you thought of King David's city.

LENNOX. Oh—I don't know.

COPE. Find it kind of disappointing, do you? I'll confess it struck me that way at first. But perhaps you haven't been around much yet?

LENNOX. We can't do much because of mother.

MRS. BOYNTON. A couple of hours' sightseeing is about all I *can* do.

COPE. I think it's wonderful you manage to do all you do, Mrs. Boynton.

MRS. BOYNTON. I don't give in to my body. It's the mind that matters—(*with secret zest*) yes, the mind.

(RAYMOND BOYNTON *enters up* R *and moves to* R *of the table. He is a good-looking young man of twenty-four. He is smiling and looking happy. He carries a wrapped bottle of medicine*)

COPE. Hullo, Ray, caught sight of you just now as I came in— but you were too busy to see me. (*He laughs*)

MRS. BOYNTON. Busy? (*She turns her head slowly to look at Raymond*)

(RAYMOND'S *smile vanishes*)

Did you get my medicine at the chemist?

RAYMOND. Yes, Mother, here it is. (*He hands her the package, avoiding her eye*)

COPE. That was a nice-looking girl you were talking to, Ray.

MRS. BOYNTON. A girl? What girl? (*She puts the package on the table*)

RAYMOND. (*nervously*) She was on the train last night. I helped her with some of her cases—they were a bit heavy.

MRS. BOYNTON. (*intent on Raymond*) I see.

RAYMOND. (*turning desperately to Cope*) I suppose you've seen all there is to see by this time.

(*The* ARAB BOY *enters up* L. *He carries a tray with the* GIRL'S *drink. He goes on to the terrace, puts the glass on the table, then exits up* L)

COPE. Well, I hope to have done Jerusalem pretty thoroughly in another couple of days and then I'm going to have a look at Petra, the rose-red city of Petra—a most remarkable natural phenomenon, right off the beaten track.

MRS. BOYNTON. "A rose-red city—half as old as time."

RAYMOND. It sounds marvellous.

COPE. It's certainly worth seeing. (*He hesitates, moves* L, *then returns to* L *of Mrs. Boynton*) I wonder if I couldn't persuade some of you people to come along with me? I know *you* couldn't manage it, Mrs. Boynton, and naturally some of your family would want to remain with you—but if you were to divide forces, so to speak . . . (*He looks from one to the other of them, finally at Mrs. Boynton*)

MRS. BOYNTON. (*expressionless*) I don't think we'd care to divide up. We're a very united family. (*She pauses*) What do you say, children?

LENNOX ⎱ (*together*) ⎰ No, Mother.
RAYMOND ⎰ ⎱ Oh, no.

MRS. BOYNTON. You see. They won't leave me. What about you, Nadine? You didn't say anything.

NADINE. No, thank you, not unless Lennox cares about it.

MRS. BOYNTON. Well, Lennox, what about it? Why don't you and Nadine go? She seems to want to.

LENNOX. (*nervously*) I—well—no—I—I—think we'd better all stay together.

COPE. Well—you are a devoted family.

(COPE *exchanges a look and a smile with* RAYMOND, *and picks up a magazine from the table.*)

(SARAH *enters up* R. *She carries a small parcel. She goes on to the terrace and exits on it to* R. RAYMOND *watches Sarah.* MRS. BOYNTON *watches Raymond*)

MRS. BOYNTON. (*to Cope*) We keep ourselves to ourselves. (*To Raymond*) Is that the girl you were talking to outside?

RAYMOND. Yes—er—yes.

MRS. BOYNTON. Who is she?

RAYMOND. Her name is King. She's—she's a doctor.

MRS. BOYNTON. I see. One of those women doctors. (*Deliberately to him*) I don't think we'll have much to do with her, son. (*She rises*) Shall we go up now? (*She picks up the medicine*)

(NADINE *hastily puts her sewing together, rises, gets Mrs. Boynton's stick and hands it to her.* LENNOX *rises*)

(*To Cope*) I don't know what I should do without Nadine.

(COPE *moves to* R *of Mrs. Boynton and puts the magazine on the table* C. NADINE *is* L *of* MRS. BOYNTON)

She takes such good care of me. (*She moves towards the lift*)

(COPE, NADINE, LENNOX *and* RAYMOND *move with* MRS. BOYNTON *to the lift. It is a royal procession.* COPE *rings the lift bell.* GERARD *watches them*)

But it's dull for her sometimes. You ought to go sightseeing with Mr. Cope, Nadine.

COPE. (*to Nadine; eagerly*) I shall be only too delighted. Can't we fix up something definite?

NADINE. We'll see—tomorrow.

(*The lift descends and the door opens.* MRS. BOYNTON, NADINE, LENNOX *and* RAYMOND *exit to the lift. The door closes and the lift ascends.* COPE *wanders around for a moment then crosses to Gerard*)

COPE. Excuse me—but surely you're Dr. Theodore Gerard?

GERARD. Yes. (*He rises*) But I'm afraid . . .

COPE. Naturally you wouldn't remember me. But I had the pleasure of hearing you lecture at Harvard last year, and of being introduced to you afterwards. (*Modestly*) Oh, I was just one of fifty or so. A mighty interesting lecture it was, of course, on psychiatry.

GERARD. You are too kind.

COPE. Jerusalem certainly is full of celebrities. We must have a drink. What are you drinking?

GERARD. Thank you. *Cinzano à l'eau.*

COPE. (*as he crosses to the desk*) By the way, the name's Cope. (*To the Clerk*) A *Cinzano à l'eau* and a rye straight. (*He moves to* L *of the table* C)

(*The* CLERK *claps his hands. The* ARAB BOY *enters up* L, *takes the order from the* CLERK *for the drinks and exits up* L)

GERARD. (*moving to* R *of the table* C) Tell me, I am interested, is that a typical American family to whom you were talking?

COPE. Why, no, I wouldn't say it was exactly typical.

GERARD. They seem—a very devoted family.

COPE. You mean they all seem to revolve round the old lady? That's true enough. She's a very remarkable woman, you know.

GERARD. Indeed? Tell me something about her. (*He sits* R *of the table* C)

COPE. I've been having that family a good deal on my mind lately. You see, young Mrs. Boynton, Mrs. Lennox Boynton, is an old friend of mine.

GERARD. Ah, yes, that very charming young lady?

COPE. That's right—that's Nadine. I knew her before her marriage to Lennox Boynton. She was training in hospital to be a nurse. Then she went for a vacation to stay with the Boyntons—they were distant cousins—and she married Lennox.

GERARD. And the marriage—it has been a happy one?

COPE. (*after a pause; moving a little up* LC) I—I hardly know what to say about that.

GERARD. You are worried about something?

COPE. Yes. (*He moves above the chair* L *of the table* C *and leans on the back of it*) I'd value your opinion—that is, if you won't be bored?

GERARD. I shall not be bored. People are my speciality—always they interest me. Tell me about this Boynton family.

COPE. Well, the late Elmore Boynton was a very rich man. This Mrs. Boynton was his second wife.

GERARD. She is the stepmother, then?

COPE. Yes, but they were young children at the time of the marriage, and they've always looked upon her as their own mother. They're completely devoted to her, as you may have noticed.

GERARD. I noticed their—(*he pauses*) devotion—yes.

COPE. Elmore Boynton thought a lot of his second wife. When he died he left everything in her hands—she has an excellent head for business. Since his death she's devoted herself entirely to those children, and she's shut out the outside world altogether. I'm not sure, you know, that that is really a sound thing to do.

GERARD. Nothing could be more harmful to developing mentalities.

COPE. (*struck*) Well now, that's rather what I feel. In her devotion to them she's never let them make any outside contacts. Result is, they've grown up kind of—(*he pauses*) nervy. They can't make friends with strangers.

GERARD. Do they all live at home? Have the sons no professions? No careers?

COPE. No—there's plenty of money, you see.

GERARD. But they are dependent on their stepmother financially?

COPE. That's so. She's encouraged them to live at home and not go out and look for jobs.

(*The* ARAB BOY *enters up* L *with two drinks on a tray. He serves the drinks to Cope and Gerard, then exits up* L)

They don't play golf, they don't belong to any country clubs, they don't go around to dances, or meet other young people.

GERARD. What do they do, then?

COPE. Well, they just—sit around. You've seen them today.

GERARD. And you disapprove?

COPE. (*with heat*) No boy ought to keep on being tied to his mother's apron strings. He ought to strike out and be independent.

GERARD. And suppose that was impossible?

COPE. What do you mean—impossible?

GERARD. There are ways, Mr. Cope, of preventing a tree from growing.

COPE. (*staring*) They're a fine healthy well-grown lot.

GERARD. The mind can be stunted as well as the body.

COPE. The mind?

GERARD. I don't think you have quite grasped my point.

(COPE *stares at Gerard*)

But continue.

COPE. (*moving* LC) What I feel is that it's time Lennox Boynton stopped just sitting around twiddling his thumbs. How can a man who does that hope to keep a woman's respect.

GERARD. (*with a Gallic twinkle*) Aha—I see—you are thinking of his wife. (*He puts his glass on the table*)

COPE. I'm not ashamed of my feeling for that lady. I am very
deeply attached to her. All I want is her happiness. If
she were happy with Lennox, I'd sit right back and fade
right out of the picture.

GERARD. (*rising and moving to* R *of Cope*) Chivalry only lives
today in the American nation.

COPE. I don't mind your laughing at me, Dr. Gerard. I dare
say I sound romantic and old-fashioned, but that young
man riles me. Sitting there reading a book and taking no
notice of his wife or anybody else.

GERARD. (*moving above the table* C *to* R *of it*) But he was
not reading a book.

COPE. (*puzzled*) Not reading—but he had a book . . . (*He
puts his glass on the table*)

GERARD. He was holding that book upside down. Curious, is
it not? (*He sees Ginevra's torn handkerchief on the
floor*) And here is something else. (*He picks up the
handkerchief*) A handkerchief that has been torn to
pieces, so—by a girl's fingers.

COPE. (*moving below the table to* L *of Gerard*) But that's
—that's very extraordinary.

GERARD. Yes, it is extraordinary. (*He moves to the chair down*
R *and sits*) It is also very interesting.

COPE. Well, I've a great respect for maternal devotion, but I
think it can be carried too far. (*He moves* RC) I've got
to get down to the American Express before they close.
See you later.

GERARD. *A toute à l'heure.*

(COPE *exits up* R)

(*He looks at the handkerchief*) Maternal devotion? I
wonder.

(GINEVRA *enters up* L, *pauses, looks around, then comes
swiftly and romantically across to Gerard*)

GINEVRA. Please, please—I must speak to you.

(GERARD *looks at Ginevra in astonishment, then rises*)

GERARD. Miss Boynton?

GINEVRA. (*dramatically*) They're taking me away. They're
planning to kill me—or shut me up. (*She takes his arm
and shakes it vehemently*) You must help me—you *must*
help me. (*She stares pleadingly up at his face*)

GERARD. This is your handkerchief?

GINEVRA. Yes. (*She takes the handkerchief without interest*) Listen—I don't belong to them really. My name's not really Boynton at all. I'm—I'm—(*she draws herself up*) royal.

(GERARD *studies her attentively*)

GERARD. I see. Yes, I see.

GINEVRA. I knew I could trust you. There are enemies, you know, all round me. They try to poison my food—all sorts of things—they don't let me speak to anyone. If you could help me to escape . . . (*She starts and looks around*) They're coming. I'm spied on—all the time. (*She moves quickly up* L) They mustn't know I've spoken to you.

(GINEVRA *exits up* L)

GERARD. (*moving* C *and looking after her*) *Nom d'un nom d'un nom!*

(SARAH *enters on the terrace from* C *and comes into the room*)

SARAH. (*moving to* R *of Gerard*) Has something upset you, Dr. Gerard?

GERARD. Yes, I am upset. *Quelle histoire!* Royal blood, persecution, poison in the food, surrounded by enemies.

(*The lift descends and the door opens.* LADY WESTHOLME, MISS PRYCE *and the* DRAGOMAN *enter from the left.* LADY WESTHOLME *carries a copy of* "The Times" *and* MISS PRYCE *has her handbag*)

SARAH. But that . . . (*She breaks off and moves down* R)

(GERARD *moves down* RC)

LADY WESTHOLME. (*crossing to* L *of Gerard*) Ah—Dr. Gerard. I've been looking for you.

(*The* DRAGOMAN *moves to* L *of Lady Westholme.* MISS PRYCE *moves to the desk*)

The arrangements for our trip to Petra are quite complete. We start on Tuesday and spend the night at Amaan, then on to Petra the following day. The journey will be made in a first class touring car. (*She indicates the Dragoman*) This is our dragoman—Mahommed.

DRAGOMAN. My name not Mahommed, lady. My name Aissa.

LADY WESTHOLME. I always call dragomen Mahommed.

DRAGOMAN. I Christian dragoman. Name Aissa, all same Jesus.

LADY WESTHOLME. Most unsuitable. I shall call you Mahommed so please don't argue.

DRAGOMAN. As you like, lady. I always give satisfaction. (*He moves above Lady Westholme and stands between her and Gerard*) You see—(*he produces a handful of dirty and torn letters*) here are testimonials. Here one from English lady—Countess like you. Here one from very reverend clergyman—Bishop—wear gaiters and very funny hat. Here letter Miss Coralle Bell, lady who act and dance on stage. All say same thing—Aissa very clean —very religious—know all about Bible history . . .

LADY WESTHOLME. (*severely*) I hope you *are* clean. Those testimonials look *filthy* to me.

DRAGOMAN. No, no, lady—no filthy postcards. No hot stuff. All very Christian—like Aissa. (*He pats his chest*) Aissa very clean. Very hygiene.

(MISS PRYCE *moves down* LC)

LADY WESTHOLME. (*to Gerard*) As I was saying, we will start Tuesday. That will be four of us—Mahommed, you and I—and now who is the fourth?

(MISS PRYCE *moves to* L *of Lady Westholme and gives an apologetic little cough*)

Oh, yes, Miss Pryce, of course.

MISS PRYCE. So kind of you. Really, it will be a wonderful experience. Perhaps a little tiring.

LADY WESTHOLME. (*cutting her short*) I *never* feel fatigue.

MISS PRYCE. It really is wonderful—in spite of all you *do*.

LADY WESTHOLME. I have always found hard work a great stimulant.

(MISS PRYCE *moves and sits* L *of the table* C)

I was about to say, Dr. Gerard, that that will leave a vacant place in the car, since Mahommed, of course, will sit beside the driver.

DRAGOMAN. I stop car, turn round and tell you everything we see.

LADY WESTHOLME. That's what I'm afraid of.

(*The* DRAGOMAN *goes on to the terrace, tries to sell curios to the* ITALIAN GIRL, *fails, moves to the desk and has a word or two with the* CLERK)

It occurred to me that if you knew of anyone suitable it would reduce the *expense*. I abhor useless extravagance. (*She looks pointedly at Sarah*)

GERARD. Miss King? You were, I believe, expressing the wish to visit Petra. May I introduce Miss King—no, Dr. King —Lady Westholme.

(SARAH *moves to* R *of Gerard*)

LADY WESTHOLME. (*patronizingly*) I am always glad to meet a young woman who has set out to make a career for herself.

MISS PRYCE. Yes, women do such *wonderful* things nowadays.

LADY WESTHOLME. Don't be foolish, Miss Pryce. You had better go with Mahommed and buy that Keatings powder at the chemists. We shall probably need it.

DRAGOMAN. (*moving to* L *of Miss Pryce*) No, no—no bugs— no fleas. Everything very nice—very clean.

LADY WESTHOLME. Get the Keatings.

MISS PRYCE. (*rising*) Yes, yes, of course, Lady Westholme. (*She drops her bag*)

(*The* DRAGOMAN *picks up Miss Pryce's bag and returns it to her.* MISS PRYCE *moves to the arch up* R. *The* DRAGOMAN *follows her. She quickens her pace, protesting she does not want to buy anything until they end almost running off*)

DRAGOMAN. (*as they go*) I take you curio shop, too. Crosses, paper knives, inkstands, all made out of olive wood from Mount of Olives. Very nice souvenirs take home. All genuine—no rubbish.

(MISS PRYCE *and the* DRAGOMAN *exit up* R)

LADY WESTHOLME. She's a well-meaning creature, but of course not quite a sahib. Still, one mustn't let her *feel* that. I do so abhor snobbishness. Well, Miss King, I hope you *will* join us. But please do not bring a lot of baggage. We shall travel light.

SARAH. I shall have to think it over.

LADY WESTHOLME. (*graciously*) Discuss it with Dr. Gerard. (*To Gerard*) I think we shall be meeting again at the High Commissioner's at dinner tonight?

GERARD. I shall look forward to that pleasure.

(LADY WESTHOLME *crosses to the chair down* R, *sits and reads her paper.* GERARD *and* SARAH *move up* C *to the terrace*)

(*As they go*) Have you seen the view from the terrace— it is really very fine.

(GERARD *and* SARAH *exit on the terrace to* R. HIGGS *enters and crosses towards the lift*)

CLERK. (*to Higgs*) Excuse me, sir, but I am changing your room.

(HIGGS *stops and stands up* LC)

There was an unfortunate mistake . . .

HIGGS. What d'yer mean—mistake? Ah doesn't *want* ter change my room.

(*He moves above the table* C)

CLERK. Unfortunately we find that room was booked for Lady Westholme. We shall have to move you to the second floor.

HIGGS. Fer 'oo?

CLERK. Lady Westholme.

HIGGS. Lady Westholme! (*He chuckles*) That's a rum 'un. Lady Westholme! Where is she?

LADY WESTHOLME. (*rising and advancing on* HIGGS) I am Lady Westholme.

HIGGS. Oh! So *you're* Lady Westholme. Ah'm glad ter meet yer. (*He politely raises his hat*) Ah've been wantin' ter meet *you* for a long time.

LADY WESTHOLME. Meet me?

HIGGS. Aye, you.

LADY WESTHOLME. Meet me—what for?

HIGGS. My name's 'Iggs.

LADY WESTHOLME. 'Iggs?

HIGGS. No, not 'Iggs—'Iggs.

LADY WESTHOLME. Well?

HIGGS. 'Iggs—Halderman 'Iggs.

LADY WESTHOLME. Well?

HIGGS. (*chuckling*) Ah coom from Lancashire—same as you do—but I see yer doan't know 'oo I am.

LADY WESTHOLME. You've just told me, Alderman 'Iggs—Higgs.

HIGGS. Ah, but it doesn't mean nowt to yer?

LADY WESTHOLME. Ought it to?

HIGGS. Aybe, by gum, it ought. But if yer don't know *why*—I'm not goin' ter *tell* yer. And another thing—I'm not changing any rooms.

LADY WESTHOLME. But that room was reserved for *me*.

(*The lift door closes and the lift ascends*)

HIGGS. Do yer think I'm daft. Ah've been 'ere four days, and soon as *you* arrive ah've got the wrong room. But ah 'aven't—see? Now if you wanted my room special—and coom ter me in a friendly spirit—I doan't say I *would* of—but I *might* of—see? This may be *King Solomon 'Otel*, but you're not Queen of Sheba. (*He moves up* C)

(LADY WESTHOLME *decides to ignore Higgs and turns on the Clerk*)

LADY WESTHOLME. Unless I am moved down to the first floor by this evening I shall report the matter to the High Commissioner.

CLERK. But, your ladyship, I . . .

LADY WESTHOLME. I never argue.

(LADY WESTHOLME *turns and exits up* R)

HIGGS. (*to the Clerk*) And if you so much as shift a bluddy toothbrush from that room I won't pay a bluddy penny.

(HIGGS *exits on the terrace to* L. SARAH *and* GERARD *enter on the terrace from* R, *come into the room and stand* RC)

SARAH. (*as they enter*) I certainly would love to see Petra—and I definitely couldn't afford to go on my own.

(*The lift descends and the door opens.* RAYMOND *enters from the lift. The door closes and the lift ascends*)

GERARD. Then I think you will come?

(SARAH *turns and sees Raymond*)

SARAH. I—I'm not sure . . .

(GERARD *looks amused and exits up* R)

RAYMOND. (*agitated*) I—I *must* speak to you.

SARAH. (*moving to* R *of the table* C; *amused*) Well, why not?

RAYMOND. (*moving to* L *of the table* C) You don't understand. I'd like to tell you . . . (*He breaks off*)

SARAH. Is anything the matter?

RAYMOND. I came down to see if mother had left her spectacles on the table here. I—I mustn't be long.

SARAH. Is there such a hurry?

RAYMOND. You see, my mother—(*he pauses*) You don't know my mother.

SARAH. I caught a glimpse of her on the train last night, and I saw her sitting here this afternoon.

RAYMOND. You see—she's not very strong. She's got a bad heart. We—we have to take care of her.

SARAH. You seem a very devoted family.

RAYMOND. (*turning away* LC) Oh, yes, we are a very devoted family.

SARAH. Well, don't sound so depressed about it. I'm sure it's a very nice thing to be.

RAYMOND. (*moving to* L *of the table* C) Oh, how I wish . . . I can't say what I want to say. (*Desperately*) I've no time. And I may never have the chance of talking to you like this again.

SARAH. Why ever not? You're not leaving Jerusalem at once, are you?

RAYMOND. No, but—my mother doesn't like us talking to people outside the family.

SARAH. But how absurd.

RAYMOND. Yes, that's what it must seem like—just absurd.

SARAH. I'm sorry if I was rude. I know it's awfully difficult sometimes for parents to realize that their children are grown up—and, of course, if your mother isn't very strong . . . (*She hesitates*) But still, you know, it's a pity to give in. One must stand up for one's rights.

RAYMOND. You don't understand.

SARAH. Even if it seems unkind one must be free to live one's own life.

RAYMOND. Free? None of us will ever be free.

SARAH. What do you mean?

RAYMOND. We're not free.

SARAH. Why don't you leave home?

RAYMOND. Because I wouldn't know where to go or what to do. Oh, you don't understand. None of us has ever left home. We've never been to school, we've never had any friends. We've no money.

(*The lift descends and the door opens*)

SARAH. I suppose you could make some money.
RAYMOND. How?

(NADINE *enters from the lift. The door closes and the lift ascends.* SARAH *and* RAYMOND *watch* NADINE *as she moves* L *of Raymond*)

NADINE. Mother is asking for you, Ray.
RAYMOND. (*starting nervously*) I'll go.
NADINE. Won't you introduce me?
RAYMOND. (*to Sarah*) This is my sister-in-law—Nadine.
NADINE. (*to Sarah*) You were on the train last night, I think.
SARAH. Yes. (*to Raymond*) I was just going out for a stroll. Why don't you come?
RAYMOND. I—come with you?
NADINE. I think that's a very good idea, Ray.
RAYMOND. Oh. Yes, I'll come.

(SARAH *and* RAYMOND *exit up* R. COPE *enters up* R *and passes them as they go*)

COPE. (*crossing and standing down* R *of the table* C) Why, Nadine, all alone?
NADINE. (*moving below the table* C) I came down to fetch Mrs. Boynton's spectacles. (*She picks up the spectacles from the table* C) Here they are. (*She turns to go*)
COPE. Are you going up with them right away?
NADINE. (*turning to him*) Yes—Mrs. Boynton is waiting.
COPE. (*moving* R *of her*) I feel, you know, that you ought to think more of yourself. I don't think Mrs. Boynton always realizes . . . (*He breaks off*)
NADINE. (*with a queer smile*) What doesn't Mrs. Boynton always realize?
COPE. Well, that you have—lives of your own.
NADINE. (*bitterly*) Lives of our own!
COPE. (*anxiously*) You—you know what I mean?
NADINE. (*with sudden warmth*) You are such a nice person.

(The lift descends and the door opens)

COPE. You know there's nothing—at any time—that I wouldn't do for you. *(He takes her hand)*

   (LENNOX *enters from the lift and stands watching*)

   (He looks at Lennox, releases Nadine's hand and steps away from her. Hurriedly) Excuse me. I'll be going up to my room now.

(COPE *crosses and exits to the lift. The door closes and the lift ascends*)

LENNOX. *(moving to* L *of Nadine)* Nadine, why have you been so long? Where's Raymond? Mother's getting impatient.
NADINE. *(crossing below him to* LC*)* Is she?
LENNOX. Yes. *(Nervously)* Please, Nadine—come up to her.
NADINE. I'm coming.
LENNOX. But where's Ray?
NADINE. Ray has gone out for a walk.
LENNOX. *(astonished)* For a walk. By himself?
NADINE. No, with a girl.
LENNOX. With a *girl?*
NADINE. *(bitterly)* Does that surprise you so much? *(She moves to* L *of him)* Don't you remember how once you sneaked out of the house and went to Fountain Springs —to a roadhouse? Do you remember, Lennox?
LENNOX. Of course I do—but we *must* go up to mother.
NADINE. *(with sudden vehemence)* Lennox—let's go away.
LENNOX. What do you mean?
NADINE. I want to live my own life—our own lives—together.
LENNOX. I don't understand what you mean. *(He looks nervously towards the lift)* Mother will be getting so upset.
NADINE. Stop looking at that lift. Stop thinking about your mother. I want you to come away with *me.* It's not too late.
LENNOX. *(without looking at her; unhappy and frightened)* Please, Nadine. Don't let's talk like this. *(He crosses below her to* L*)* Must we go into it all again?
NADINE. *(following him)* Let's go away, Lennox, let's go away.
LENNOX. How can we? We've no money.

NADINE. You can earn money.

LENNOX. How can I earn money? I'm untrained—unqualified.

NADINE. I could earn enough for both of us.

LENNOX. (*his voice rising*) It's impossible—hopeless—(*his voice trails away*) hopeless.

NADINE. (*moving LC; bitterly*) It's our present life that is hopeless.

LENNOX. I don't know what you mean. Mother is very good to us. She gives us everything we want.

NADINE. Except liberty.

LENNOX. You must remember she's getting old and she's in bad health. When she dies father's money will come to us.

NADINE. (*desperately*) When she dies it may be too late.

LENNOX. Too late for what?

NADINE. Too late for happiness. (*Appealingly*) Lennox, I still love you. It's not too late. Won't you do what I ask?

LENNOX. I—I can't. It isn't possible.

(NADINE *draws away. Her manner changes back to its usual quiet reserve*)

NADINE. I see. So it's up to me. To do—what I want to do—with my own life. (*She goes on to the terrace*)

(LENNOX *follows Nadine and stands behind her.* LADY WESTHOLME *and the* DRAGOMAN *enter up* R. *He is thrusting curios upon her notice.* LADY WESTHOLME *moves down* C)

DRAGOMAN. (*moving to* R *of Lady Westholme*) No other dragoman got anything like these. Very special—I make for distinguished English lady very special price. The owner, he friend of mine. I get them very cheap.

LADY WESTHOLME. Now let us understand each other, Mahommed. (*Forcefully*) I don't buy rubbish.

DRAGOMAN. (*howling in anguish*) Rubbish? (*He holds up a long rusty nail*) The original nail from the toe of Balaam's ass.

(NADINE *moves along the terrace to* R *of it.* LENNOX *follows her*)

LADY WESTHOLME. I said *rubbish*. If I want to buy anything I will inform you of the fact and I will allow you a reasonable commission. The truth is that you have imposed upon tourists too much. I am *not* a tourist, and I have a very good sense of values.

DRAGOMAN. (*with a sudden ingratiating smile*) You very clever English high-up lady. Not want buy cheap junk. You want enjoy yourself, see sights. You like see Gilly-Gilly men? Bring chickens out of everywhere—(*he demonstrates on her*) out of sleeves, out of hat, out of shoes—everything. (*He twitches and lifts her skirt*)

LADY WESTHOLME. (*hitting him with her folded newspaper*) Certainly not. (*She crosses, sits in the chair down* R *and reads her paper*)

(*The* DRAGOMAN *crosses and exits up* L. SARAH *and* RAYMOND *enter up* R. RAYMOND *carries a small parcel*)

RAYMOND. (*as they enter*) There *is* a moon. I noticed it last night from the train.

(NADINE *turns from Lennox and stands with her back to him*)

SARAH. It really will be simply heavenly. That curly street and the gate where the donkeys were.

(LENNOX *moves to* C *of the terrace*)

RAYMOND. (*carelessly*) Hullo, Len. (*To Sarah*) This is my brother Lennox. (*He crosses to the lift*)

SARAH. (*hardly noticing Lennox*) How d'you do? (*She follows Raymond to the lift*)

(*The* ITALIAN GIRL *rises and exits on the terrace to* R)

Could we go to that courtyard place outside the mosque, or is it shut at night?

(RAYMOND *rings the lift bell*)

RAYMOND. We can easily find out.

SARAH. I must get my camera—you think there's enough light, still?

(*The lift descends and the door opens.* MRS. BOYNTON *enters from the lift, leaning on her stick.* RAYMOND *stands paralyzed.* SARAH *is taken aback*)

RAYMOND. I—I . . . (*He breaks off*)

SARAH. (*loudly and firmly*) Won't you introduce me to your mother?

MRS. BOYNTON. Where have you been, Raymond?

RAYMOND. I—went out . . .

SARAH. Won't you introduce me, Raymond?

RAYMOND. This is Miss King, Mother.

SARAH. How do you do?

MRS. BOYNTON. How do you do? You were wanting the lift? (*She moves aside*)

(SARAH *looks once at Raymond to see if he is resenting Mrs. Boynton's rudeness, then slowly exits to the lift.* RAYMOND *is staring at Mrs. Boynton. The door closes and the lift ascends*)

(*She crosses to the chair above the table* C) Who is that girl, Ray?

RAYMOND. I—I told you. Sarah King.

MRS. BOYNTON. Oh, yes, the girl you were talking to on the train last night. (*She sits*)

(RAYMOND *moves to* L *of Mrs. Boynton.* HIGGS *enters on the terrace from* L *and sits* R *of the table under the sunshade*)

Have you made plans to see her again?

(RAYMOND *stands like a prisoner in the dock and speaks like an automaton*)

RAYMOND. Yes, we were going out together after dinner.

MRS. BOYNTON. (*watching him*) I don't think, you know, she is quite our style. We'll keep ourselves to ourselves. That's the best way. (*She pauses*) You understand, Ray?

(NADINE *turns, moves in a little and watches.* LENNOX *relapses into complete vacancy*)

RAYMOND. (*automatically*) Yes.

MRS. BOYNTON. (*with authority*) So you won't be meeting her this evening.

RAYMOND. No—no . . .

MRS. BOYNTON. That's quite settled, isn't it?

RAYMOND. Yes.

MRS. BOYNTON. You'll have nothing more to do with that girl?

RAYMOND. No.

(*The lift descends and the door opens.* SARAH *enters from the lift and crosses to Raymond*)

SARAH. I forgot my parcel. Oh. You've got it in your hand.

(RAYMOND *looks down, stares at the parcel, then hands it to Sarah without looking at her*)

(*She turns to go. Cheerfully*) See you later.

MRS. BOYNTON. You'd better explain to Miss King, Raymond.

(SARAH *stops and turns*)

RAYMOND. (*with clenched hands; stiffly*) I'm so sorry, Miss King. I shan't be able to go out this evening.

(SARAH *gives a quick glance towards Mrs. Boynton*)

SARAH. (*belligerently*) Why not?

(RAYMOND *opens his mouth to speak, then shakes his head*)

MRS. BOYNTON. My son prefers to remain with his family.
SARAH. Can't your son speak for himself?
MRS. BOYNTON. Tell her, Son.
RAYMOND. I—I prefer to be with—with my family.
SARAH. (*angrily*) Really? What devotion! (*With a contemptuous glance at Raymond, she crosses below the table* C *to Lady Westholme*) Thank you for suggesting that I should come to Petra with your party, Lady Westholme. I should like to very much.
LADY WESTHOLME. Excellent.

(MRS. BOYNTON *turns her head and looks at Lady Westholme and Sarah. Her face shows no expression*)

On Tuesday, then, ten o'clock. So pleased you are joining us, Miss King.

(SARAH *crosses and exits quickly to the lift. The door closes and the lift ascends.* LADY WESTHOLME *rises and follows Sarah to the lift, but the door closes as she arrives. She angrily rings the bell.* MRS. BOYNTON *continues to observe Lady Westholme.* HIGGS *rises and moves to the desk*)

LENNOX. (*moving* LC) Do you want to go up now, Mother?
MRS. BOYNTON. What?
LENNOX. Do you want to go up now?

MRS. BOYNTON. Not just now. You and Ray go. I want my spectacles. You two go on. Nadine and I will follow.

(LENNOX *and* RAYMOND *move to the lift door. The lift descends and the door opens.* LADY WESTHOLME, LENNOX *and* RAYMOND *exit to the lift. The door closes and the lift ascends.* MRS. BOYNTON *smiles to herself, then turns her head and looks at Nadine*)

HIGGS. (*to the Clerk*) 'Ere! What floor's 'er ladyship goin' oop to?

CLERK. Second floor, sir.

HIGGS. Ho! And another thing. I'm goin' on this trip to Petra. There's room in the car?

CLERK. Yes, sir. I've a seat reserved for you.

HIGGS. Ho! And is 'er ladyship comin'?

CLERK. Yes, sir.

HIGGS Ho! Well, I'm not ridin' on t'roof, see.

(HIGGS *exits up* R)

MRS. BOYNTON. Nadine.

NADINE. (*moving to* R *of Mrs. Boynton*) Yes, Mother?

MRS. BOYNTON. My spectacles.

(*The lift descends and the door opens.* COPE *enters from the lift and goes to the desk*)

NADINE. (*holding out the spectacles*) They were on the table.

MRS. BOYNTON. Don't give them to me. Take them upstairs. And will you see that Jinny has some hot milk?

NADINE. She doesn't like hot milk.

MRS. BOYNTON. It's good for her. Go along, my dear. I'll just have a little talk with your friend Mr. Cope.

(NADINE *exits to the lift. The door closes and the lift ascends*)

COPE. (*moving* LC) Delighted, Mrs. Boynton.

MRS. BOYNTON. Such a good daughter to me—quite like a real daughter. I don't know what we should all do without Nadine.

COPE. Yes, indeed, I can quite appreciate how you rely upon her.

(*The* CLERK *exits up* L)

MRS. BOYNTON. We're a very devoted family.

COPE. I know—I know . . .

MRS. BOYNTON. (*looking sharply at him*) What's on your mind?

COPE. Why—nothing.

MRS. BOYNTON. Don't mind saying it.

COPE. Well—maybe you'll think it great cheek on my part . . .

MRS. BOYNTON. I like frankness.

COPE. Well, frankly, then, I just wondered . . . Oh, don't misunderstand me—I only meant that—well—one can shield people too much from the outside world.

MRS. BOYNTON. You mean—(*she smiles*) I'm too fond of my children?

COPE. Let's say—you're over-anxious about them. They— they've got to learn to stand on their own feet sometime, you know. (*He sits* L *of the table* C)

MRS. BOYNTON. You're probably quite right. That's partly, you know, why I brought them abroad. I didn't want them to become provincial. Travel, they say, broadens the mind.

COPE. Yes, indeed.

MRS. BOYNTON. It was very dull. (*Reminiscently*) Day after day—no savour to things. Yes, it was dull. (*She chuckles*) It's not dull here.

COPE. No, Jerusalem is a mighty interesting place.

MRS. BOYNTON. And I've been thinking of what you said earlier—about Petra.

COPE. Yes?

MRS. BOYNTON. I feel—the children ought to see Petra.

COPE. (*rising*) Why, that's grand. You'll do as I suggested, split up. Someone's got to stay and look after you, of course.

MRS. BOYNTON. No, I'm going to Petra, too.

COPE. Oh, but really, Mrs. Boynton, I don't think you realize the difficulties. It's right off the beaten track. Two long days motoring and the last stage is on horses or mules.

MRS. BOYNTON. I'm an old woman with many physical disabilities, but I don't allow that to interfere with my— (*she pauses*) pleasures. These things can be arranged— by the expenditure of money. The last stage can be done in a carrying chair with bearers or a kind of litter.

COPE. It sounds quite Biblical.

MRS. BOYNTON. Yes—quite Biblical.

COPE. But really, you know, I don't think you're wise. Your health isn't too good, you know. Your heart . . .

MRS. BOYNTON. I don't take my heart into account when I'm planning a pleasure party for other people. It's a bad plan to think too much of oneself. One should think of others. That's settled, then?

COPE. Well, I do really take my hat off to you, Mrs. Boynton. You're the most unselfish woman. Always thinking of the youngsters.

MRS. BOYNTON. It wouldn't be the same for them if I wasn't there. You'll travel with us?

COPE. Why, certainly, I shall be delighted.

MRS. BOYNTON. That will give Nadine great pleasure, I'm sure. You're very fond of Nadine, aren't you?

COPE. (*moving a little down L; embarrassed*) Well, I . . .

MRS. BOYNTON. You'll make the arrangements, won't you?

COPE. (*crossing up R*) Certainly. I'll go and make enquiries now.

COPE *exits* R. MRS. BOYNTON *is left alone. Presently she begins to laugh, a silent laugh that shakes her like a jelly. Her face is malevolent and full of glee as—*

the CURTAIN *falls*

Act Two

Scene I

SCENE: *The Travellers' Camp at Petra. Early afternoon, a week later.*

Fantastic scarlet rocks rise all round so that the stage has the appearance of an amphitheatre. On an upper level up R there is a path, masked by rocks, giving access to a cave. An exit RC leads to the sleeping tents. A slope of rock L leads to the path out of the camp. Down L is the entrance of a big marquee dining tent. A camp table and three chairs are set LC; there is a camp armchair with a tea chest behind it down L and a deck chair stands down R. On the rock up R, in front of the cave, are two camp stools.

When the CURTAIN *rises,* RAYMOND *is seated in the deck chair down R, lost in thought.* MRS. BOYNTON *is sitting on a stool outside the cave on the rock up R, her stick by her side, reading. She looks like a monstrous idol in a niche. The* DRAGOMAN *is standing* C, *looking benevolent.* LADY WESTHOLME, MISS PRYCE *and* GERARD *enter from the marquee L.* LADY WESTHOLME *picks up a "Baedaker" from the table* LC *and crosses to* RC. MISS PRYCE *stands* LC. GERARD *moves down L.*

DRAGOMAN. You had nice luncheon? You rested after big expedition this morning?

MISS PRYCE. Yes, thank you. It was most interesting.

DRAGOMAN. I tell you all about Babatesh architecture. I tell you ancient history. Very interesting place, Petra. I show you place high up there. Place of sacrifice.

111

LADY WESTHOLME. There is no need to hear it all over again. You were wrong on several points. I have just been checking up in *Baedaker*.

DRAGOMAN. No, no, lady. You not believe everything you read. You believe Aissa. Aissa educated Christian mission, learn speak truth. Everything I tell you truth and just like Holy Bible.

(SARAH *enters from the marquee, sees Raymond, turns abruptly back and goes inside again*)

LADY WESTHOLME. You were educated at a mission?

DRAGOMAN. Yes, lady, American Mission.

LADY WESTHOLME. Oh, American!

DRAGOMAN. I learn poetry—very beautiful. (*Rapidly, and with an indescribable intonation*) "Hail-to-the-blysprut Birtoneverwort."

GERARD. I beg your pardon?

DRAGOMAN. (*repeating*) "Hailtotheblysprut Birtoneverwort." (*He beams*)

MISS PRYCE. (*after a pause*) I *think* it's Shelley's "Skylark."

DRAGOMAN. (*beaming*) That's right, lady. Percy Bish Shelley. I know Willyam Wordwort, too. "I wonder lonely asaclout . . ."

GERARD. *Assez, assez.*

DRAGOMAN. I full of culture and higher education.

GERARD. Civilization has much to answer for.

LADY WESTHOLME. The thing, Mahommed, is not only to learn by heart, but to assimilate what you learn.

DRAGOMAN. You not call me Mahommed, lady. That Moslem name. You not like "Aissa," you call me Abraham. Like Father Abraham, I got clean bosom, very snowy. (*He opens his tunic*) Wear clean clothes every day.

GERARD. (*to Lady Westholme*) Which was more than Abraham did, I expect.

DRAGOMAN. (*moving close to Miss Pryce and displaying his chest*) All clean like Abraham's bosom.

MISS PRYCE. (*embarrassed*) Oh, yes, yes, very nice, I'm sure.

DRAGOMAN. What you like to do this afternoon? Another expedition or you like rest? Most of my ladies and gentlemen like rest on day when have done big expedition to place of sacrifice.

MISS PRYCE. It certainly was rather tiring. Such a very steep climb. But perhaps . . . (*She looks doubtfully at Lady Westholme*)

LADY WESTHOLME. I never feel fatigue. But I don't think another expedition. Perhaps a stroll later.

DRAGOMAN. You take nice walk-after-tea? I show you maiden hairyfern.

LADY WESTHOLME. Later. We'll let you know.

DRAGOMAN. Very good. (*He moves up* R) When you want Abraham, you just call Abraham. I come.

(*The* DRAGOMAN *exits up* R)

MISS PRYCE. He's really very obliging.

LADY WESTHOLME. He talks too much.

MISS PRYCE. I think, you know, that perhaps I shall lie down for a little. The sun is very hot.

LADY WESTHOLME. I shall go to my tent, but I shall not lie down. I shall write letters. (*She moves* R)

MISS PRYCE. (*crossing to* R) You have such wonderful energy, dear Lady Westholme.

LADY WESTHOLME. It's just a question of training.

(LADY WESTHOLME *and* MISS PRYCE *exit* R. GERARD *strolls to Raymond*)

GERARD. You reflect very earnestly upon something.

RAYMOND. I was thinking about our journey down here, it was like coming down into an illustration of Hell. Winding through those narrow gorges, I kept saying to myself, "Down into the valley of death"—(*he pauses*) "the valley of death . . ."

GERARD. So that is how you felt? But it was not death you found at the end of your journey.

RAYMOND. (*natural again*) No— it was a very pleasant camp, tents or caves to suit one's fancy, a really excellent dinner.

GERARD. And friendly faces to greet you.

RAYMOND. Yes, I—I remembered seeing you at the *King Solomon* and Cope had mentioned you to us.

GERARD. I really meant Miss King. She you already knew, did you not?

RAYMOND. (*upset*) Yes—yes, I suppose so. I wish she had come on the expedition this morning. She—she backed out very suddenly.

GERARD. (*moving* C) Young ladies change their minds. But she missed much of interest and scenery.

(SARAH *enters from the marquee. She carries a small metal case containing a hypodermic.* RAYMOND *rises and moves* RC)

SARAH. Dr. Gerard—one of the Bedouin . . . (*She pauses as Raymond moves towards them*)

GERARD. Yes?

SARAH. (*without looking at Raymond; brusquely*) One of the guides is ill, acute malaria. Have you got any quinine with you? Stupidly, I seem to have left mine in Jerusalem. I've got my hypodermic here—(*she indicates the case*) if you want to give it intravenously.

GERARD. I have a small medicine case of drugs with me. I will get it.

(GERARD *exits hurriedly* R. SARAH *moves above the table and puts her case on it.* RAYMOND *is in a pitiable state of nervousness*)

RAYMOND. Sarah. (*He pauses*)

(SARAH *ignores Raymond*)

(*He crosses to* R *of the table*) You despise me, don't you? I don't wonder. I despise myself.

SARAH. I really don't know what you are talking about.

RAYMOND. It was like a dream to arrive here—and find you. I thought at first you were a ghost—because I'd been thinking about you so much. (*He moves to* R *of her*) I love you. I want you to know that. It isn't me—the real man—who—who behaved so badly that day at the *King Solomon*. I can't answer for myself even now. (*He nervously clasps and unclasps his hands*) It's my nerves. I can't depend on them. If she tells me to do things, I have to do them—I can't help it. I know that I can never make you understand. It's courage I need—courage. And I haven't got it.

(GERARD *enters* R, *carrying his drug case. He pauses a moment and observes Sarah and Raymond.* RAYMOND *moves quickly away from Sarah, crosses and exits* R)

GERARD. (*crossing to the table*) I fear I interrupted something. (*He puts his case on the table and opens it*)

SARAH. (*trying to be matter of fact*) Nothing of any importance.

GERARD. Are you not being a little cruel to that young man?

SARAH. I can't stand a man who's tied to his mother's apron strings.

GERARD. Oh, la, la, so that is the trouble. (*He takes some quinine from his case and fills his own hypodermic syringe*) So you are, after all, just the English miss. And you call yourself a budding psychologist? Do you not recognize a psychological problem when you see one?

SARAH. Do you mean that old woman? (*She looks up towards Mrs. Boynton*) She's like some obscene Buddha—brooding over us all. Ugh! How they can all be devoted to her I can't imagine. It's thoroughly unhealthy. (*She sits* L *of the table*)

GERARD. You are wrong. They're not devoted to her. And she —she is not devoted to them. You have not been yourself since you have arrived here or you would have noticed many things.

SARAH. Travelling with Lady Westholme and Miss Pryce gets on my nerves.

GERARD. (*moving to* R *of the table*) Naturally. Lady Westholme is exactly fitted to the life she leads and enjoys it immensely. Miss Pryce is realizing the dream of a lifetime in travelling abroad. Both of them have got what they want, whereas you have not got what *you* want.

SARAH. What do I want?

GERARD. You want that young man who has just gone away.

SARAH. Really, Dr. Gerard, nothing of the kind.

GERARD. English miss.

SARAH. I'm not an English miss. (*She rises and moves down* L)

GERARD. But it is what you are. (*He moves to* R *of her*) You will talk learnedly of sex problems and sex life—but when it comes to a flesh and blood young man, you protest and blush just like your great-grandmother would have done. But come, let us be colleagues. Admittedly that young man is completely dominated by his mother—

she has, what I cannot but consider, a most unhealthy power over him. Do we rescue him or do we not?

SARAH. Can we?

GERARD. (*taking her hands for a moment*) I think perhaps you can. Now—where is this man?

SARAH. Through the marquee. I'll show you.

(SARAH *and* GERARD *exit to the marquee.* NADINE *enters from the slope* L. *She walks as though very tired. She moves to the table and looks at the open cases. The* ARAB BOY *enters* R, *carrying a tray*)

BOY. (*crossing to the table*) Good afternoon, ma'am.

NADINE. Hullo, Abdulla.

(*The* ARAB BOY *collects the dirty glasses from the table, crosses and exits* R. NADINE *picks the bottles out of* GERARD'S *case and puts them back, as though curious but only half aware of what she is doing.* COPE *strides on down the slope* L. NADINE *starts and moves from the table*)

COPE. So there you are. (*He crosses to* RC) You've been running away from me, Nadine.

NADINE. What makes you think that?

COPE. Nadine, things can't go on like this. I've got to talk to you.

NADINE. (*crossing to him*) Oh, please, Jeff, please.

COPE. (*turning her to face him*) No, listen. I've loved you for a long time. You know that. I want you to have some happiness in your life.

NADINE. Perhaps no-one is happy.

COPE. That's nonsense, dear, and you know it. You've been a loyal wife to Lennox—you've put up with an impossible life for his sake and you've never complained. But the time's come when you've got to think of *yourself*. I'm not expecting romantic devotion from you—but you do like me a little, don't you?

NADINE. I like you very much.

COPE. You're not doing Lennox any good by staying with him. Divorce him and marry me.

(SARAH *enters from the marquee*)

(*He moves* R) We might take a walk later—when the sun isn't so hot.

NADINE. Yes.

(COPE *exits* R. SARAH *looks at Nadine then sits* L *of the table*)

Miss King.

SARAH. Yes?

NADINE. May I say something to you?

SARAH. Why, of course.

NADINE. (*moving to* R *of the table*) I saw you talking to my brother-in-law just now.

SARAH. Really?

NADINE. Do help him if you can.

SARAH. What makes you think I can help him?

NADINE. If you can't help him, nobody can.

SARAH. He could help himself if he liked.

NADINE. That's where you're wrong. We're an odd family. He can't.

SARAH. You're a very devoted family—I know. Your mother-in-law told me so.

NADINE. No, we're not. That's the last thing we are.

(SARAH *looks in surprise at Nadine*)

(*She moves nearer to Sarah and lowers her voice*) Do you know what she—(*she gestures towards Mrs. Boynton*) was before my father-in-law married her?

SARAH. What was she?

NADINE. She was a wardress in a prison. (*She pauses*) My father-in-law was the governor. He was a widower with three young children, the youngest, Jinny, only six months old.

SARAH. (*looking at Mrs. Boynton*) Yes—I can see her as a wardress.

NADINE. It's what she still is—Lennox and Raymond and Jinny have been the prisoners. They've never known what it is to live outside the prison walls.

SARAH. Not even now—here—abroad?

NADINE. Yes. She's brought the prison walls with her. She's never allowed them to make friends—to have outside contacts—to have any ideas or interests of their own. It's all been done under the pretence of solicitude and devotion—but there's no devotion.

SARAH. What is there, then?

NADINE. Something that frightens me—something cruel—something that rejoices and gloats in its own power . . .

(MRS. BOYNTON *moves, puts down her book and peers forward*)

MRS. BOYNTON. (*calling*) Nadine. Come and help me.

NADINE. (*to Sarah; urgently*) I didn't understand when I married Lennox—I left things too late. I think he's beyond help. But it's different with Raymond. You could fight.

MRS. BOYNTON. (*calling*) Nadine.

NADINE. Coming, Mother. (*She goes up on the rock to Mrs. Boynton*)

(*The* ARAB BOY *enters from the marquee*)

BOY. (*to Sarah*) Selun, he very bad. You come, Miss Doctor.

SARAH. (*rising*) Very well.

(SARAH *and the* ARAB BOY *exit to the marquee.* RAYMOND *enters* R *and crosses to the table. He picks up a bottle that Nadine has left out of the case, at first casually, then with suddenly awakened attention. He stares down at it.* NADINE *helps* MRS. BOYNTON *to rise*)

RAYMOND. (*looking at the case*) Dr. Gerard's. (*He moves a step or two forward from the table, intent on the bottle in his hand*)

(MRS. BOYNTON *and* NADINE *move down* C)

MRS. BOYNTON. I think I'll sit here for a bit.

(RAYMOND, *startled, drops the bottle and turns*)

(*She indicates the chair* R *of the table*) There.

NADINE. Won't it be too hot for you in the sun?

MRS. BOYNTON. I don't mind the sun. It's really hotter up there among the rocks because of the refraction. This will do very well. (*She sits* R *of the table. To Raymond*) I saw you talking to that girl, Son.

RAYMOND. (*frightened*) I—I . . . (*with an effort*) Yes, I did speak to her. Why not?

MRS. BOYNTON. Why not, indeed. After all, you're young. You'd better go for a walk this afternoon.

RAYMOND. Go—for a walk? You—you want me to?

MRS. BOYNTON. Young people must enjoy themselves.

NADINE. Cat and mouse.

MRS. BOYNTON. That's an odd thing to say, Nadine.

NADINE. Is it?

MRS. BOYNTON. (*to Raymond*) Your friend went that way. (*She points with her stick to the marquee*)

(RAYMOND *exits doubtfully to the marquee.* NADINE *looks at Mrs. Boynton*)

(*She chuckles quietly*) Yes, young people must enjoy themselves—in their own way.

NADINE. (*crossing above Mrs. Boynton and standing above the table*) And old people in theirs.

MRS. BOYNTON. Now what do you mean by that, my dear?

NADINE. Just—cat and mouse.

MRS. BOYNTON. Very cryptic. You ought to go for a walk, Nadine, with that nice friend of yours—Mr. Cope.

NADINE. I suppose you saw us talking, too?

MRS. BOYNTON. Yes. He's very fond of you.

NADINE. (*moving L of the table*) I know.

MRS. BOYNTON. I'm afraid you don't get as much fun as you ought to get. It's a very dull life waiting on a sick old woman—and Lennox—he's changed a lot—yes, he's changed.

NADINE. (*moving down L*) He is not very happy.

MRS. BOYNTON. He ought to be—married to a charming and good-looking girl like you. I'm afraid sometimes, he doesn't appreciate you as much as he ought to do.

NADINE. You think Jefferson Cope appreciates me better?

MRS. BOYNTON. I think he's very much in love with you.

NADINE. And you want me to go away with him and leave Lennox—why?

MRS. BOYNTON. (*smoothly; with faint malicious amusement*) Really, Nadine, what words you put into my mouth— I've said nothing of the kind.

NADINE. It's what you mean, though. (*Slowly*) It was one of your reasons for coming here.

MRS. BOYNTON. You are talking very extravagantly, Nadine dear. Naturally I want you to be happy—but of course I am not urging you to leave your husband. That would be a very wrong thing to do.

(NADINE *stares at Mrs. Boynton in silence for a moment or two*)

NADINE. (*moving up* L *of the table*) Why do you hate us all so much?

MRS. BOYNTON. (*amused*) Really, my dear child!

NADINE. (*still staring at her*) You like hurting people—don't you? You like the sense of power. I've thought sometimes that it came from your having been a wardress—but I think I see further than that—it was what made you become a wardress.

(MRS. BOYNTON *smiles gently*)

There are a lot of people who can't stand that job—but you—(*she slows down, dropping truth after truth as she stares at Mrs. Boynton*) liked it. When you married, you missed it—but you found consolation in the children—three helpless children. You started on *them*.

MRS. BOYNTON. Dear me, what an imagination you have got, Nadine dear.

NADINE. You've never been physically cruel. It's been a mental sport. You've thwarted and tortured Jinny until she's gone nearly over the edge. You know only too well what you've done to Lennox—I can't reach him any more. He doesn't give you much sport nowadays, does he? But Raymond does. Raymond's still able to rebel. You can have some fun with Raymond, can't you?

MRS. BOYNTON. Such curious ideas you have, Nadine, haven't you?

NADINE. That's why you came abroad. You were bored, weren't you? You'd tamed your wild beasts. You'd got them jumping through hoops just as you told them to. It was dull for you. So you brought them abroad—hoping they would rebel—hoping they'd suffer and that you'd have some fresh fun hurting them, seeing them writhe and squirm. (*Sharply*) Haven't you any pity?

MRS. BOYNTON. (*turning an impassive face to her*) I don't know what you mean.

NADINE. (*crossing above the table to* RC) Why do you like hurting people? It seems so senseless.

MRS. BOYNTON. (*in a thick voice*) Does it?

NADINE. So it's true—you *are* like that.

MRS. BOYNTON. (*with infinite scorn*) You little fool.

NADINE. (*turning on her*) It's you who are the fool. Hasn't it ever occurred to you that what you're doing is *dangerous*?

MRS. BOYNTON. Dangerous?

NADINE. Yes, dangerous. You can drive people too far.

MRS. BOYNTON. I'm not afraid.

NADINE. You might—die.

MRS. BOYNTON. I'm not going to die for a long time to come, Nadine dear. I may not have good health, but I've great powers of enjoyment—(*she chuckles grimly*) great powers of enjoyment.

NADINE. I think you're mad.

MRS. BOYNTON. Not in the legal sense, my dear.

(GINEVRA *enters* R *and stands listening*)

You won't be able to get me certified. (*She looks at Nadine and laughs*) There's someone else who's likely to be certified before me.

NADINE. (*catching her breath*) You mean—Jinny?

MRS. BOYNTON. (*smoothly*) Poor child.

(GINEVRA *runs off* R)

NADINE. Dr. Gerard is very interested in Jinny's case.

MRS. BOYNTON. (*almost with a snarl*) It's nothing to do with him.

NADINE. He assures me that with treatment Jinny would become perfectly normal. I think we ought to get his advice.

MRS. BOYNTON. Jinny is under age—and what you think or don't think, Nadine, doesn't matter. I'm the one who decides.

NADINE. Yes—we're all in your power—but if Jinny gets worse . . .

MRS. BOYNTON. If Jinny gets violent—(*smoothly*) she will have, of course, to be restrained.

NADINE. Certified. Shut up. (*She shivers*) That's what you want to happen. I'm beginning to understand you—at last.

MRS. BOYNTON. My poor dear admirable daughter-in-law. And you don't know what to do about it.

NADINE. (*in a low voice*) Perhaps I do.

MRS. BOYNTON. Still going to remain devoted to Lennox however little he notices the fact? Jefferson Cope won't wait for ever, you know.

NADINE. (*crossing below the table to* L) As long as Lennox wants me I shall stay with him.

MRS. BOYNTON. Does Lennox want you very much?

(NADINE *winces*)

You must face facts, you know.

NADINE. What will you do if Raymond—escapes? (*She turns to her*)

MRS. BOYNTON. I can manage Raymond.

NADINE. Perhaps you won't be able to manage Sarah King. You may find that she's stronger than you are.

MRS. BOYNTON. She's a fool!

NADINE. Not Sarah.

MRS. BOYNTON. Have you been asking Lennox to go away with you lately? You haven't had much success with that idea of yours, have you?

(NADINE *turns away*)

Dear Lennox. He's always been such an obedient, devoted son. (*She laughs*)

(COPE *enters* R)

COPE. (*moving* RC) You sound in good spirits, Mrs. Boynton. That's fine. I was afraid, you know, that the journey here might knock you up completely.

MRS. BOYNTON. I'm enjoying myself here. I'm enjoying myself a good deal.

COPE. It's a wonderful place, it certainly is. (*To Nadine*) Are we going to have our walk? (*He looks at Mrs. Boynton*) But perhaps . . .

MRS. BOYNTON. Oh, don't mind leaving me. Nadine didn't go on the expedition this morning. She ought to have a little exercise.

COPE. You're always so considerate, Mrs. Boynton. (*To Nadine*) Shall we start? (*He crosses to the slope* L)

MRS. BOYNTON. (*to Nadine*) Just give me my medicine first, dear.

NADINE. I'll get it.

(NADINE *exits to the marquee*)

MRS. BOYNTON. A tired heart, you know. A tired heart. It has to be constantly stimulated. Never any good making a fuss. One must think of others—not oneself.

(NADINE *enters from the marquee, carrying a glass of medicine*)

NADINE. (*moving to Mrs. Boynton*) Here it is.

   (MRS. BOYNTON *takes the glass and drinks the medicine*)

MRS. BOYNTON. Isn't it rather stronger than usual? (*She puts the glass on the table*)
NADINE. I don't think so.
COPE. Shall we go now?
NADINE. (*moving to the slope* L) Yes, we'll go now.

   (COPE *exits up the slope*)

   (*She goes up the slope a few steps, then stops*) Good-bye, Mother.
MRS. BOYNTON. Good-bye.

(NADINE *exits up the slope.* MRS. BOYNTON *chuckles a little as she is left to herself. She examines the contents of Gerard's case, takes out a bottle or two and looks at them.* LENNOX *enters* R *and crosses toward the marquee. He has a book in his hand but walks like one in a dream*)

Lennox.

   (LENNOX *does not hear*)

(*Louder*) Lennox. Come here.

   (LENNOX *moves to* R *of Mrs. Boynton*)

What have you been doing, Son?

(LENNOX *acts throughout as though it took a long time for words to reach him*)

LENNOX. I've been reading.
MRS. BOYNTON. What have you been reading?
LENNOX. I can't remember. Was Nadine here?
MRS. BOYNTON. Yes, she's gone for a walk with Mr. Cope.
LENNOX. Oh.

   (MRS. BOYNTON *looks at Lennox for a moment or two*)

MRS. BOYNTON. Has it ever occurred to you that your wife's in love with Jefferson Cope.

LENNOX. (*rather quickly*) Nadine—in love with Cope?

MRS. BOYNTON. He's certainly in love with *her*. I think you ought to be prepared, Son, for the possibility that Nadine might—leave you.

LENNOX. Leave me—Nadine?

MRS. BOYNTON. He's a very charming man, you know, and they've always been great friends—and it's been a dull life for Nadine. I'm afraid you haven't been able to be much of a companion to her.

LENNOX. Nadine. I—I couldn't live without Nadine. (*He crosses down L*)

MRS. BOYNTON. I'm afraid you may have to live without her—whether you want to or not.

LENNOX. She said she might go . . . (*He breaks off*) She asked me . . . What did she ask me?

MRS. BOYNTON. How should I know?

LENNOX. I couldn't do it, though, could I? I mean—where should I go? How should I live?

MRS. BOYNTON. I'm afraid you could never support yourself, my poor boy.

(*LENNOX moves to L of the table. His manner is now definitely odd*)

LENNOX. It's you who are stopping me, isn't it? Can't you let me go? Please let me go.

MRS. BOYNTON. You can't go. (*She watches him closely*) You can't go, Lennox. You're no good. I'm afraid you're going to be very unhappy.

LENNOX. (*muttering*) Unhappy. (*He sits L of the table, his foot stepping on the bottle dropped by Raymond*)

MRS. BOYNTON. Pick that up.

(*LENNOX picks up the bottle and stares at it*)

It will be very quiet without Nadine—very quiet and very lonely.

LENNOX. There's something I could do—if I could only remember. (*He rises and looks at the bottle*) Something quite easy. (*He looks suddenly at Mrs. Boynton*) Are *you* my enemy?

MRS. BOYNTON. What a very odd thing to say, dear boy.

(*Voices are heard off R*)

Give me that bottle, it belongs in here.

(LENNOX *hands the bottle to Mrs. Boynton, then exits to the marquee.* MRS. BOYNTON *looks at the bottle and puts it on the table.* HIGGS *enters* R. MISS PRYCE *follows him on, catches her scarf on something and is held*)

MISS PRYCE. Oh dear.

HIGGS. Are ye fast? I mean, are yer stuck? (*He moves to Miss Pryce and detaches her*)

MISS PRYCE. Thank you so much. I'm quite loose now. (*She moves* RC)

(LADY WESTHOLME *enters* R)

LADY WESTHOLME. Now where is Mahommed? (*She crosses to the marquee*) That man is never about when one wants him.

(LADY WESTHOLME *exits to the marquee*)

HIGGS. (*crossing to* C) What is that lad's name? Mahommed or Abraham?

MISS PRYCE. Lady Westholme says she always calls her dragoman Mahommed.

HIGGS. What, even when it isn't 'is name?

MISS PRYCE. Apparently.

HIGGS. Well! I wonder they stand for it. Ah wouldn't.

MISS PRYCE. But then you're such a masterful man, Mr. Higgs.

HIGGS. Ay. Ah know my rights and I stand oop for 'em.

MISS PRYCE. I can see that.

HIGGS. And them as doan't is neither fish, flesh, fowl, nor good red 'errin'.

MISS PRYCE. And he's such a nice man—and *so clean.* (*Confidentially*) He changes his shirt every day.

HIGGS. 'E needs to in this climate. Eh, I wasn't 'alf in a muck sweat meself this morning.

MISS PRYCE. (*reprovingly*) *Mr.* Higgs!

HIGGS. Ah doan't 'old much with foreigners. I shared a cabin with one comin' over and one mornin' I caught 'im usin' my toothbrush.

MISS PRYCE. How revolting.

HIGGS. And d'yer know what 'e said? He said, "Ah thought it was a ship's toothbrush—for us all like." (*He laughs uproariously*)

(MISS PRYCE *winces*)

LADY WESTHOLME. (*off; calling*) Mahommed.
HIGGS. (*calling*) P'raps 'e's oop on second floor, Lady Breast-
bone.

(LADY WESTHOLME *appears at the entrance to the marquee*)

LADY WESTHOLME. (*furiously*) What did you say, Mr. Higgs?
HIGGS. Ah said p'raps 'e's oop on second floor, Lady Fishbone.
LADY WESTHOLME. You may find out to your cost, my good
man, that my name is Westholme.
HIGGS. Ay. An' 'is isn't Mahommed.

(LADY WESTHOLME *flounces back into the marquee and is
heard again calling defiantly*)

LADY WESTHOLME. (*off; calling*) Ma-hom-med.
HIGGS. (*chuckling*) Eh! That's a grand voice for electioneer-
ing. She wouldn't need loud-speaker van.
MISS PRYCE. You know, I think all the servants must be asleep.
LADY WESTHOLME. (*off; calling*) Mahommed.
HIGGS. (*chuckling*) Not after that.
MISS PRYCE. (*getting confidential again*) I do hope we're safe
here. Those servants look so wild and *fierce*. Suppose
they were to murder us all one night.
HIGGS. Ah could understand 'em murderin' 'er ladyship—but
what 'ave we done?
MISS PRYCE. They might rob us.
HIGGS. Well, they're doin' *that* already without murderin' us.
(*With maliciously assumed apprehension*) Of course,
they could kidnap us and 'old us to ransom.

(*The* DRAGOMAN *enters quietly* R)

MISS PRYCE. Kidnap us! How dreadful.
DRAGOMAN. (*moving suddenly between Miss Pryce and Higgs;
with a beaming smile*) You ready go nice walk, ladies
and gentlemen?
MISS PRYCE. (*startled*) Oh!
LADY WESTHOLME. (*off; calling*) Mahommed.

(LADY WESTHOLME *enters from the marquee*)

There you are. (*She moves below the table*) Didn't you
hear me calling?
DRAGOMAN. Abraham hear someone call *Mahommed*.
HIGGS. (*moving* LC; *to Lady Westholme*) And 'e put 'is tele-
scope to 'is blind ear.

(SARAH *and* RAYMOND *enter* R *and stand down* R. LADY WEST-
HOLME *ignores Higgs and crosses below him to* C)

LADY WESTHOLME. And *where* are all the servants?

DRAGOMAN. (*moving to* R *of Lady Westholme*) Bedouin all
sleep now. Later wake up, make dinner. But Abraham
Christian. Abraham understand Christian ladies and
gentlemen like afternoon instructive walk and then drink
afternoon tea. You come now?

HIGGS. Ay, we're coomin'. Coom on, ladies, and be kidnapped.

MISS PRYCE. *Mr. Higgs.* Don't say such dreadful things.

LADY WESTHOLME. (*crossing to* R) If you intend to accompany us, Mr. Higgs, I trust that you will curb your
facetiousness and allow those *better educated* than yourself to enjoy the archaeological and historical interests of
this place.

(LADY WESTHOLME *stalks out* R. MISS PRYCE *follows her off.*
HIGGS *stands for a moment, nonplussed, scratching his
head. He can think of no riposte. He chuckles and shakes
his head*)

HIGGS. Nay—she got me *that* time.

(HIGGS *exits* R. *The* DRAGOMAN *follows him off*)

SARAH. What a circus! Oof! I want a drink. (*To Raymond*)
Do you think you can find one?

(RAYMOND *crosses and exits to the marquee. There is a
silence during which* SARAH *crosses to* R *of Mrs. Boynton*)

This really is a fantastic place.

(MRS. BOYNTON *does not answer*)

(*She looks at Mrs. Boynton, smiles and shrugs her
shoulders*) Your son and I have had a very pleasant walk.

(MRS. BOYNTON *taps with her stick and does not answer.*
RAYMOND *enters from the marquee carrying a glass of
lime juice which he hands to Sarah*)

Thank you.

(SARAH *crosses and exits with the drink* R. RAYMOND *moves
a step or two after her*)

MRS. BOYNTON. Ray, my dear, it won't do.

RAYMOND. (*stopping* C *and turning*) What won't do?

MRS. BOYNTON. That girl. I encouraged you to go for a walk with her this afternoon against my better judgement— but I don't like her. I don't like the way she runs after you. I should just be barely civil to her and nothing more in future, if I were you.

RAYMOND. That's impossible.

MRS. BOYNTON. Oh, no, Raymond. You'll do what I say.

RAYMOND. (moving RC) I tell you it's impossible. Sarah and I are friends.

MRS. BOYNTON. (moving a little and fixing him with her eye) You won't be friends if I don't want you to be.

RAYMOND. But I shall—I must.

MRS. BOYNTON. You won't be friends if I don't want you to be.

RAYMOND. (crossing down L) You—you can't make me do things like that.

MRS. BOYNTON. Nonsense! You've always done what I wanted. (Firmly) You always will. You can't help yourself.

RAYMOND. But Sarah—it's different . . .

MRS. BOYNTON. It isn't different, Son. You've got to give up Sarah.

RAYMOND. No.

MRS. BOYNTON. You are going to give up Sarah.

RAYMOND. (moving to L of the table; his voice high and hysterical) No—no—I won't do it.

MRS. BOYNTON. I always know what's best for you. (Forcefully) You'll keep out of her way in future.

RAYMOND. No. I . . .

MRS. BOYNTON. You'll keep out of her way. You'll be rude to her.

RAYMOND. No . . .

MRS. BOYNTON. (with force) You'll do what I want.

RAYMOND. I—I . . .

MRS. BOYNTON. You'll do what I tell you.

RAYMOND. (after a pause; dully) Yes. Yes, I suppose so. (He sits L of the table)

(SARAH enters R)

MRS. BOYNTON. You'll avoid Sarah King.

RAYMOND. I'll avoid Sarah King.

MRS. BOYNTON. So that's settled. You understand? You're giving up Sarah King.

RAYMOND. I'm giving up Sarah King. (*He buries his face in his hands*)

SARAH. (*crossing and standing above the table*) Extraordinarily interesting. I'm glad I heard it. Cheer up, Ray—I'm not giving *you* up.

MRS. BOYNTON. Tell her to go away.

RAYMOND. I . . . Please go away.

SARAH. I'm not going.

MRS. BOYNTON. Tell her to leave you alone.

RAYMOND. I . . . You'd better—leave me alone.

SARAH. Your mother and I are going to have a talk.

RAYMOND. I . . . (*He looks at Mrs. Boynton*)

MRS. BOYNTON. Go away, Raymond.

SARAH. Yes, please go away, Ray.

(RAYMOND *rises and exits slowly to the marquee.* SARAH *and* MRS. BOYNTON *look at each other*)

What an extraordinary futile and silly old woman you are.

(MRS. BOYNTON *quivers*)

Yes, you didn't expect that. But it's true. (*She moves to* L *of the table*) You like to make yourself out a kind of ogre. Really, you're ludicrous—almost pathetic. Why don't you give up this silly sadistic business?

MRS. BOYNTON. How dare you speak to me like that?

SARAH. It's time someone did. It's time someone showed you what you really are. You've wanted to feel powerful, haven't you—you've enjoyed hurting and torturing people? It's made you feel grand and important. But you're only a petty little domestic tyrant. You've acquired a certain amount of hypnotic influence over your family. But the influence can be broken.

MRS. BOYNTON. Who's going to break it?

SARAH. I am.

MRS. BOYNTON. You think you'll get Raymond, do you? I know the sort of girl you are—man mad. Pretending to be professional and all the time running after some man or other.

SARAH. (*sitting* L *of the table; calmly*) Saying things like that won't upset me. I'm going to fight you, Mrs. Boynton.

MRS. BOYNTON. You'll lose.

SARAH. No, I shall win.

MRS. BOYNTON. You little fool. I've got Raymond—I've got all of them, like *that.* (*She makes a gesture with her thumb*)

(LENNOX *enters* R *and sits in the deck chair down* R)

SARAH. You really are quite incredible—like something in a medical textbook. I shall win all right. I've two strong weapons on my side.

MRS. BOYNTON. And what are they?

SARAH. Youth and sex.

MRS. BOYNTON. Aren't you ashamed to say a thing like that?

SARAH. I love Raymond. I'll fight for him with every weapon I've got.

MRS. BOYNTON. I'm stronger than you are. I've experience behind me—years of experience. (*With force*) I can do things to people's minds.

SARAH. Yes, you've got knowledge—a lot of evil knowledge. But you haven't got—very long to use it.

MRS. BOYNTON. What do you mean?

SARAH. There's something else on my side—time. (*She rises*)

MRS. BOYNTON. Time?

SARAH. I'm a doctor and I know what I'm talking about. (*Slowly*) You haven't got long to live. I give you—at the most—six months.

MRS. BOYNTON. (*badly shaken*) Six months? Rubbish!

SARAH. Ask Dr. Gerard if you don't believe me.

MRS. BOYNTON. (*stricken*) Six months . . .

SARAH. It's the truth. You've got an appointment—an appointment you'll have to keep—an appointment with death. When you're dead, your family will be free. So you see, death's on my side, as well as life.

MRS. BOYNTON. (*convulsed with rage*) Get out of my sight. Go away.

SARAH. Can't you stop hating? It's not too late for that.

MRS. BOYNTON. Get out! Get out! Get out! (*She strikes the table with her stick*)

(SARAH *looks at Mrs. Boynton, shakes her head, shrugs her shoulders and exits to the marquee.* COPE *and* NADINE *enter down the slope* L, COPE *leading*)

NADINE. (*as she enters*) It's too hot to walk far. (*She moves down* L)

(COPE *moves to the marquee entrance.* MRS. BOYNTON *says nothing. She sit glaring in front of her and shaking with rage*)

LENNOX. Nadine.

NADINE. Yes? (*She signs to Cope to go*)

        (COPE *exits to the marquee*)

LENNOX. (*rising*) Nadine.

(NADINE *crosses to Lennox.* MRS. BOYNTON *fumbles with the bottles on the table*)

Is it true—that you're going away with Cope?

NADINE. Yes.

(NADINE *looks at Lennox, then turns, crosses and exits to the marquee. There is a pause. The* ARAB BOY *enters from the marquee. He carries a tray with a cup and saucer on it*)

BOY. (*moving to Mrs. Boynton*) I bring you tea, lady, tea.

    (MRS. BOYNTON *strikes the table with her stick*)

(*He squeals, drops the tray on the ground and runs to the marquee entrance*) Allah Kerim! Very bad devil. Very bad devil . . .

(*The* ARAB BOY *runs into the marquee.* RAYMOND *enters from the marquee, looks at Mrs. Boynton then crosses to Lennox*)

LENNOX. (*quietly*) That's it. One of us has got to kill her.

MRS. BOYNTON		Raymond. Come and help me back up there.
	(*together*)	
LENNOX		One of us has got to kill her.

(RAYMOND *stares at Lennox, then crosses to* MRS. BOYNTON, *who rises.* RAYMOND *helps her up on the rock up* R *and settles her on the stool outside the cave.* LENNOX *stares out front.* RAYMOND *comes down and stands slightly behind Lennox*)

RAYMOND. What did you say?

             CURTAIN

Scene II

SCENE: *The same. Three hours later.*

When the CURTAIN *rises, it is just before sunset.* MRS.
BOYNTON *is seated at the mouth of the cave up* R, *but
the cave is now in very deep shadow.* GINEVRA *enters
cautiously from the marquee, hears voices off* R *and slips
back again. The* DRAGOMAN, HIGGS *and* LADY WESTHOLME
trail in R *in single file. They are tired, hot and cross.*
HIGGS *crosses and collapses into the chair* L *of the table.*
LADY WESTHOLME *crosses and sits in the chair* R *of the
table. The* DRAGOMAN *stands* C.

HIGGS. (*mopping his brow*) Well, I reckon we've earned our
supper. Ah reckon Miss Pryce knew what she was about,
turning back wi' headache. I'm fagged out, I am.

LADY WESTHOLME. I never feel fatigue.

HIGGS. I see—you're as strong as a horse.

DRAGOMAN. Yes. You very strong lady. You walk up, down
over—you just like goat.

LADY WESTHOLME. (*indignantly*) Mahommed!

HIGGS. (*laughing*) Aye, that's it, Abraham, like a goat.

(LADY WESTHOLME *freezes, and if looks could kill . . .*)

(*He mops his brow*) Eh, but I'm in muck sweat.

LADY WESTHOLME. (*at last finding her tongue again*) Your
sense of humour, Mr. Higgs, is only equalled by your
choice of epithet. "Muck sweat" is applied to *horses*.

HIGGS. Now I come to think of it, you look more like a horse
than a goat. (*To the Dragoman*) Bring a big bottle of
beer along to my tent, Abraham—aye, and take the same
along to 'er ladyship, and charge it oop ter me. That'll
show there's no ill feeling.

LADY WESTHOLME. Thank you—but I prefer a pot of tea.

DRAGOMAN. Too late make tea, lady. Supper now.

LADY WESTHOLME. Nonsense, there must be a kettle on the
boil.

DRAGOMAN. No, lady, kettle him not boil now.

HIGGS. (*rising*) That's the best o' beer, yer doan't 'ave ter boil it. Yer know, I doan't reckon much to this afternoon—why, we didn't see nowt.

DRAGOMAN. (*crossing to Higgs*) Oh, yes, please. You see maiden hairy-fern, all hang down.

HIGGS. Well, ah can see that hanging oop in me green-'ouse at 'ome. Ah doan't want to come abroad to 'eathen parts to see it 'angin' down.

DRAGOMAN. Very good, I get beer.

(*The* DRAGOMAN *crosses and exits to the marquee.* HIGGS *crosses to* RC)

HIGGS. (*looking up at Mrs. Boynton*) And I see we've got our 'eathen idol with us still. Sitting oop there for all the world like summat out of Old Testament. Moloch, was it, as they used to sacrifice children to? How their parents fell for it beats me. Ee, they moost 'ave been daft.

LADY WESTHOLME. It was an age of crude superstition. Nowadays . . .

HIGGS. Nowadays there's still sacrifices going on. I've kept my eyes open since I've been 'ere, and I tell you my 'eart bleeds for those kids of 'ers. That old image up there sees to it they're sacrificed all right. She's what them psycho-whatnots call a bluddy sadist.

LADY WESTHOLME. (*rising*) Mr. Higgs—oh!

(LADY WESTHOLME, *limping from a blistered foot, crosses and exits* R)

HIGGS. (*sniffing*) Ee, there's a champion smell of *animal* sacrifice. Now let's 'ope it won't be a burnt offerin'.

(HIGGS *exits* R. GINEVRA *enters cautiously from the marquee, and moves up* C. *She has a long sharp knife in her hand. She is taken unawares by hearing* GERARD's *voice off. She moves quickly to the table, conceals the knife under Gerard's medical case, then picks up Sarah's hypodermic case as though that had been her business at the table.* GERARD *enters from the marquee.* GINEVRA *moves quickly* C)

GERARD. (*noting her confusion*) What have you got there?
(*He crosses to* L *of Ginevra*)

GINEVRA. Nothing.

GERARD. Give that to me. (*He takes the case from her and opens it*) What have you done with the hypodermic?

GENEVRA. I don't know. I haven't touched it.

(GERARD *frowns, moves to the table, puts Sarah's case on it, then moves his own case preparatory to opening it and discovers the knife*)

GERARD. (*picking up the knife*) Aha! (*He moves down* R *of the table*)

(GINEVRA *springs forward and tries to take the knife from him*)

What is this?

GINEVRA. Give it me. I must have it.

GERARD. Where did you get it from?

GINEVRA. (*pointing to the marquee*) From in there. I want it—to defend myself—*against them.*

GERARD. Listen, *mon enfant*, you must give up all this make-believe. (*He puts the knife on the table*)

GINEVRA. You say that—but you know that it's true. (*She moves close to him*) You followed me here, didn't you? From Jerusalem. You're here to protect me. I know you are.

GERARD. (*taking her hands*) Listen, Ginevra, I want to help you . . .

GINEVRA. I knew—I knew. (*Sweetly*) You're in love with me, aren't you?

GERARD. I'm nearly old enough to be your father.

GINEVRA. But I like you very much. (*She smiles at him*) Dr. Gerard, I don't want to die. (*Angrily*) You must believe me—you must. (*Confidentially*) Listen, yesterday, they put poison in my food.

GERARD. (*firmly*) No, your food was quite all right.

GINEVRA. You—you do know that I don't really belong to them? You know that that's true. You can see, can't you, that I'm different?

GERARD. We would all like to be different.

GINEVRA. I can't tell you who I am. I promised. (*Grandly*) My lips are sealed.

GERARD. (*firmly*) You are Ginevra Boynton.

GINEVRA. I hate you. I hate you. (*She crosses to the chair R of the table, sits and cries*)

GERARD. (*moving behind her*) Don't you understand, Ginevra, that what you are doing is dangerous? The way of escape you have found for yourself is no real escape. You must face reality, not lose yourself in a world of fantasy.

GINEVRA. I thought you would help me to escape.

GERARD. That is what I want to do. (*He moves to L of the table*)

GINEVRA. You will take me away with you—to France—to Paris?

GERARD. I would like to take you to France. (*He sits L of the table*)

GINEVRA. You have a house there?

(GERARD *nods*)

A castle?

GERARD. (*with a smile*) No, a clinic.

GINEVRA. (*doubtfully*) Oh. (*With curiosity*) Should I like it there?

GERARD. Yes, you would do real things with your mind—and the unreal things would not be interesting any more.

GINEVRA. Real things. You wouldn't tell me that I am ill all the time?

GERARD. No, for you are not ill.

GINEVRA. (*with a gesture towards Mrs. Boynton*) She says I am ill. She—she wants me to be ill—she makes me ill. She says—she says—they are going to shut me up— (*her voice rises*) to shut me up. (*She rises and moves RC*)

GERARD. (*rising and moving above the table to C*) No, no, you must be calm.

GINEVRA. I want to come with you.

GERARD. I know.

GINEVRA. Why can't I? Because she won't let me go?

GERARD. For the moment, that is true.

GINEVRA. She won't let me go.

(GERARD *moves to Ginevra and puts a hand on her shoulder*)

GERARD. You must hold on, Jinny—hold on. Do you understand? It is just a question of waiting—perhaps not waiting very long.

GINEVRA. (*drawing away; emphatically*) When she is dead, I can go. That is what you mean, isn't it? When she is dead. When she is dead we can all go.

GERARD. Don't talk like that.

GINEVRA. Why not? (*She crosses to* L) *They* did.

GERARD. Who did?

(GINEVRA *looks at him sideways and laughs*)

GINEVRA. I heard them. They didn't know I was there. They said that she'd got to be killed—that it was the only way.

GERARD. (*crossing to her*) Who said that? (*He takes both her hands in his*)

GINEVRA. They said one of us would have to do it—for the sake of the others.

GERARD. Who said so?

GINEVRA. Lennox and Raymond.

GERARD. You're inventing again.

GINEVRA. No, this is really true.

GERARD. So you admit the other isn't?

GINEVRA. (*angrily*) I hate you. Let me go. Let me go.

(GINEVRA *twists away from him, runs across and exits* R. NADINE *enters* R *as Ginevra exits*)

NADINE. (*crossing to* C) What's the matter with Jinny?

(GERARD *picks up the knife and shows it to Nadine*)

What's that? A knife. That's bad—that's very bad.

GERARD. Yes, the case grows serious. (*He puts the knife on the table*)

NADINE. (*moving* LC) But it's not too late. She could have treatment.

GERARD. Yes, there is still time, but you understand—not much.

NADINE. (*crossing down* L) Do you believe in the Devil, Dr. Gerard?

GERARD. You mean, do I believe in Evil, positive Evil? Yes, I do.

NADINE. So do I.

(GERARD *and* NADINE *look up at Mrs. Boynton*)

GERARD. And we can do nothing.

NADINE. Don't be too sure of that.

(COPE *enters* R *and crosses to* C. *He looks radiant*)

COPE. Must be nearly supper time.

GERARD. Yes, I must go and wash. (*He picks up his case of drugs and crosses to* R)

COPE. It seems almost chilly after the heat of the afternoon.

GERARD. Yes, there is a sharp fall of temperature at sunset.

(GERARD *exits* R)

COPE. (*crossing to Nadine*) Hadn't I better get you a wrap, Nadine?

NADINE. No, thank you, it will be hot in the marquee. Jeff, I was just—talking about Jinny to Dr. Gerard.

COPE. (*his face becoming worried*) Oh—Jinny. I was talking to Dr. Gerard yesterday, and he was quite confident that by treatment in his sanatorium he could effect a perfect cure. It's a well-known place and bears the highest reputation. I said as much to Mrs. Boynton.

NADINE. So you talked to her about it. What did she say?

COPE. She said a mother's care was worth all the new-fangled doctors' cures put together.

NADINE. (*crossing to* RC) She isn't Jinny's mother.

COPE. Why, no, that's true. (*He moves* LC) But I know she's only anxious for Jinny's good.

NADINE. (*impatiently yet tenderly*) Oh, Jeff—the worst of a nice person like you—you're so—so trusting.

COPE. I trust in you.

NADINE. Don't.

COPE. You haven't—changed your mind?

NADINE. (*moving to him*) Why should you think I have? What's the good of staying with Lennox? I must start a new life—with you. (*She gives him her hand*)

COPE. It shall be a happy life, I promise you.

NADINE. Can anybody promise that?

(RAYMOND *enters* R, *moves to the deck chair down* R *and sits lost in a brown study*)

COPE. I feel I ought to speak to Lennox. I don't want to be anything but straightforward about this business.

NADINE. No, Jeff—please. No, I mean it.

DRAGOMAN. (*off; calling*) Dinner, him ready.

NADINE. You go on.

(COPE *hesitates then exits to the marquee.* LENNOX *enters* R
     and crosses to Nadine)

LENNOX. Nadine.

NADINE. Yes.

LENNOX. You took me by surprise this afternoon. Wait until
     we get back to Jerusalem. Things may be different then.

NADINE. (*turning to look at him*) Different? How should
     they be different?

(*The* DRAGOMAN *enters from the marquee. He holds a gong
     which he beats with enjoyment*)

DRAGOMAN. Dinner, him ready.

(NADINE *exits to the marquee.* LENNOX *follows her off. The*
     ARAB BOY *enters from the marquee. He has a tray of
     drinks which he puts on the table. He then exits to the
     marquee.* HIGGS *enters* R)

HIGGS. (*to the Dragoman*) Steady on, lad, we're not deaf.

DRAGOMAN. Dinner, him ready.

HIGGS. All right, we 'eard yer first time.

(LADY WESTHOLME *enters* R. *The* DRAGOMAN *crosses and ex-
     its* R)

LADY WESTHOLME. (*crossing and sitting* R *of the table*) Per-
     fectly barbarous! Really, natives are just like children.

HIGGS. (*moving above the table*) Aye, my kids at 'ome love
     bangin' gong. (*He pours drinks for Lady Westholme and
     himself*) 'Ave you got any kids, Lady Westholme?

LADY WESTHOLME. No.

HIGGS. Soom'ow I didn't think you 'ad. (*He sits* L *of the table*)

(GERARD *enters* R *and moves to Raymond*)

LADY WESTHOLME. Indeed!

(LADY WESTHOLME *and* HIGGS *sip their drinks*)

GERARD. (*to Raymond*) Lost in thought?

RAYMOND. I was thinking of our expedition this morning—to
     the place of sacrifice.

GERARD. Yes.

RAYMOND. You know, I think one can attach too much regard
     to life. Death isn't really as important as we make out.
     Sometimes, I think a sacrifice is really necessary.

GERARD. You mean—the sacrifice of human life?

RAYMOND. Yes.

GERARD. It is expedient that one man should die for the people? Is that your idea?

RAYMOND. Yes, there's a great truth there.

(*The* ARAB BOY *enters on to the rock from* R *and unsuccessfully tries to rouse Mrs. Boynton*)

GERARD. A man may lay down his life, that is one thing—to be forcibly deprived of it is another. I doubt if that has ever advanced human progress or human happiness.

RAYMOND. (*rising; excitedly*) I don't agree with you. It might be the only thing to do. There are deaths that would result only in good—deaths that would set people free— deaths that would save misery and disaster. The kind of death that would only mean advancing the clock a little. All that is needed is courage—yes, courage.

(*The* ARAB BOY *comes down to Gerard and whispers in his ear.* GERARD *and the* ARAB BOY *exit* R. *During the ensuing lines,* GERARD *enters on to the rock from* R *and bends over Mrs. Boynton.* LADY WESTHOLME *finishes her drink, rises and exits to the marquee.* LENNOX *enters* R *and moves to Raymond*)

HIGGS. (*to Raymond*) Courage is a funny thing, young man. There's men as'll face machine-guns and run from mother-in law.

(MISS PRYCE *enters* R)

MISS PRYCE. Oh, I do hope you haven't been waiting for me.

HIGGS. (*rising and placing a chair for Miss Pryce*) 'Ow's t'eadache? (*He pours a drink for Miss Pryce*)

MISS PRYCE. (*crossing and sitting* R *of the table*)Quite gone now, thank you.

HIGGS. Sorry you 'ad ter come back this afternoon. (*He resumes his seat*) But yer didn't miss mooch—except a bit of an argument with 'er 'oity-toityness and old father Abraham.

MISS PRYCE. Oh—what about?

HIGGS. Everything. And she was always right and he was always wrong.

MISS PRYCE. And do you agree, Mr. Higgs?

HIGGS. Ah doan't know. Ancient 'Istory isn't mooch in my line. I started at ten sixty-six and went t'other way.

(SARAH *enters* R, *crosses and stands above the table*)

SARAH. (*yawning*) Ooh—I've been asleep.

HIGGS. Pleasant dreams, I 'ope.

SARAH. No dreams at all.

HIGGS. Ah 'ad a peculiar dream once.

MISS PRYCE. Oh, do tell us, Mr. Higgs.

HIGGS. (*chuckling*) Ah dreamt there was three of me—and only one glass of beer.

MISS PRYCE. Oh, Mr. Higgs! Well, I really did have a peculiar dream once. I dreamed that I was going to tea with the Archbishop of Canterbury—so I took a ticket to Walham Green, of all places—and then I found I was in my night-dress.

(GERARD *comes down from the rock to Lennox*)

GERARD. Mr. Boynton. I fear I have some very bad news for you. Your mother—(*he pauses*) is dead.

CURTAIN

Act Three

Scene I

SCENE: *The same. The following morning.*

When the CURTAIN *rises, the* DRAGOMAN *is asleep in the chair* R *of the table. The* ARAB BOY *enters from the marquee, sweeping a small pile of rubbish before him with a long broom. He is not looking where he is going and the broom strikes the Dragoman's feet. The* DRAGOMAN *wakes with a yell and chases the* ARAB BOY *off* R. SARAH *and* RAYMOND *enter down the slope* L, *during this and watch with amusement. They move down* C *as the* DRAGOMAN *and the* ARAB BOY *exit to the marquee.*

RAYMOND. Is it true, Sarah? Is it really true? You *do* care for me?

SARAH. Idiot!

*(*RAYMOND *takes Sarah in his arms and they kiss)*

RAYMOND. *(crossing below the table)* The whole thing is like a dream. It seems rather awful in a way—so soon after last night.

SARAH. *(moving to* R *of him)* Don't be morbid. What's the good of hypocrisy?

RAYMOND. All the same, you know, Sarah, it's rather dreadful to be *glad* anyone is dead.

SARAH. Yes, I know. Your stepmother was not only an unpleasant woman, but a dangerous woman. It's a mercy she died as she did. Frankly, it's almost too good to be true.

RAYMOND. I know. I feel the same. It's like coming out of the shadow into sunlight. *(In a soft voice)* We're—free.

SARAH. It's terrible that one human being should have been able to acquire such power over others.

RAYMOND. We shouldn't have let it happen.

SARAH. My dear, you hadn't any choice. She started in on you as young children. Believe me, I do know what I'm talking about.

(*They lean on the downstage side of the table*)

RAYMOND. My learned physician.

SARAH. (*anxiously*) You don't mind my being a doctor, do you?

RAYMOND. Of course not, darling. Who am I to mind?

SARAH. Well, I rather imagined, you were going to be my husband—but, of course, you haven't really asked me.

RAYMOND. Sarah. (*He catches at her*)

(SARAH *eludes Raymond.* NADINE *and* LENNOX *enter* R. *They look quietly happy*)

NADINE. Oh, there you are, Sarah. I wanted to see you. I have been talking to Dr. Gerard about Ginevra.

SARAH. Yes?

NADINE. We are arranging for her to go into his clinic near Paris for treatment.

SARAH. Yes, indeed. Dr. Gerard is absolutely at the top of the tree as a psychiatrist. You couldn't have a better man. He's absolutely first class.

NADINE. He tells us that she will be absolutely all right—a perfectly normal girl.

SARAH. I think so, too. There's nothing fundamentally in the least wrong with Jinny. It was sheer escapism that was driving her into fantasy. But fortunately it's not too late.

NADINE. No, it's not too late. (*She looks up at the cave mouth*) The shadow's gone.

LENNOX. It's like waking up from a dream.

NADINE. One just doesn't believe it can be true.

RAYMOND. But it is. She can't harm us now. She can't stop us from doing what we want.

(SARAH *and* RAYMOND *move slowly up* C *during the following speech*)

(*Seriously*) Look here, Sarah, I've got to do something with my life. I've got to work at something—something that matters. And I don't even know what capabilities I've got—I don't know what I can do—I don't even know if I've got any brains at all.

(SARAH *and* RAYMOND *exit up* L)

LENNOX. (*catching Nadine's hand*) Nadine. You aren't going
   to leave me?

NADINE. You think not?

LENNOX. I shan't let you go.

NADINE. Why did you never say that before?

LENNOX. Why? Why? I can't imagine. (*He crosses to* L)
   What's been the matter with me? Why could I feel like
   I feel today? How did she do it? Why did she have that
   effect on me—on all of us? Just an ordinary, rather tyrannical old woman.

NADINE. No, Lennox, she was more than that. She had—
   (*gropingly*) *power*. There is such a thing as positive Evil.
   We've seen it in the world—working on nations. This
   was a small private instance that happened in a family—
   but it's the same thing—a lust for power, a delight in
   cruelty and torture . . . (*She breaks off*)

LENNOX. (*tenderly*) Nadine—my dear. It's all over. We've
   escaped.

NADINE. Yes, we've escaped. She can't harm us now.

(COLONEL CARBERY *enters on the rock from* R. *He is a tall,
middle-aged Englishman in uniform. He has a vacant
face and seems the huntin', shootin' and fishin' type, but
every now and then shows disturbing shrewdness. He is
carrying a small sheaf of papers. He examines the stools
on the rock, looks into the cave and makes some notes.
The* DRAGOMAN *enters from the marquee*)

DRAGOMAN. (*crossing to* LC) Good morning, sir and lady. I
   hope you sleep well in spite of sad and tragic occurrence.
   Very old lady, heat too much for her. You try not grieve
   too much. You have very fine funeral in Jerusalem—very
   nice cemetery there, very expensive. I take you to high
   class monumental shop, have very nice memorial. You
   have big stone angel with wings? Or big slab Jerusalem
   stone and very fine text from Bible. My friend he make
   you very special price if I ask him. He very big man—all
   best dead people go to him.

NADINE. (*indicating Carbery*) Who is that up there?

DRAGOMAN. That Colonel Carbery. Carbery Pasha. Big man
   Transjordania. He head of Transjordanian police.

(CARBERY *exits up* R)

NADINE. (*sharply*) Police.

DRAGOMAN. (*smiling*) I send policeman off last night—made report. Any death got to be reported.

LENNOX. Eh? Oh, yes, of course.

DRAGOMAN. So Carbery Pasha he come himself, arrange everything. (*He beams*) All ver' official and first class.

LENNOX. (*slowly*) I think—I ought to go and speak to him.

NADINE. Yes—yes. I'll come with you.

(LENNOX *and* NADINE *cross and exit* R. HIGGS *strolls on from the marquee*)

HIGGS. Ee, what's to do?

DRAGOMAN. Make arrangements take back old lady's body. Get horses for others. We leave camp this afternoon.

HIGGS. We do, do we? Ee, lad, I paid down me money for four days. I'll want a rebate on that.

DRAGOMAN. Very sad circumstances alter cases.

HIGGS. Ee, I've not noticed anybody looking sad.

(LADY WESTHOLME *and* MISS PRYCE *enter* R. LADY WESTHOLME *crosses to* C)

(*To Lady Westholme*) This chap says we're going back this afternoon.

DRAGOMAN. (*moving between Lady Westholme and Miss Pryce*) I take you two ladies and gentleman nice walk this morning. Show you interesting architecture and more maiden hairy-fern. You see best of Petra before you go back.

LADY WESTHOLME. I think it would be extremely *bad taste* to go on an expedition this morning.

DRAGOMAN. (*concerned*) Something you eat taste bad? You tell Abraham. Abraham scold cook.

HIGGS. No use kicking our heels here. Might as well do a bit of sightseeing. Coom on. (*He moves to* L *of Lady Westholme and takes her arm*)

(LADY WESTHOLME *jerks her arm away*)

You like your money's worth as well as another, I'll bet you do and all.

LADY WESTHOLME. Kindly allow me to know my own mind, Mr. Higgs.

DRAGOMAN. (*nudging Lady Westholme*) Very nice expedition——

(LADY WESTHOLME *glares at the Dragoman*)

—(*coaxingly*) Very antique. Two hundred B.C. before Christ.

LADY WESTHOLME. No, Mahommed.

DRAGOMAN. Very nice expedition. Not difficult climb. Not get tired at all.

LADY WESTHOLME. I am *never* tired.

HIGGS. Well, if you ask me, I think it's just ploom foolishness not to see all we can. We've paid our money, 'aven't we?

LADY WESTHOLME. Unfortunately, yes. But there are certain decencies to be respected, though I am sure that it's no good my attempting to explain them to *you*, Mr. Higgs.

HIGGS. You don't think I'd understand them? I would, though. All I say is, we've paid our money.

LADY WESTHOLME. (*crossing to the deck chair down* R) There is really no need to go into it again. (*She sits*)

HIGGS. It isn't that you liked the old woman. Coom to that, nobody did. I've not noticed any signs of grieving in her family. Coom into a bit of brass, they 'ave, by the look of them.

MISS PRYCE. I so often think these things are a merciful release.

HIGGS. You bet *they* see it that way. And why Lady W. here should be so cut up . . .

LADY WESTHOLME. Not at all. It is simply a question of not going off sightseeing just after a sudden and unexpected death. I have no feeling of *regret*. Mrs. Boynton was not even an acquaintance and I am strongly of the opinion that she *drank*.

MISS PRYCE. (*to Lady Westholme*) No, Arethusa. That is really a most *uncharitable* thing to say—and quite *untrue*.

LADY WESTHOLME. Don't be a fool, Amabel. I know alcohol when I see it.

HIGGS. So do I. (*Wistfully*) Ah wouldn't mind seein' some now—but I suppose it's a bit early.

MISS PRYCE. I feel strongly that one shouldn't speak evil of the dead. At any rate, my lips are sealed.

HIGGS. (*to the Dragoman*) Hi, Abraham, ah'm coomin' on expedition. (*He crosses to Miss Pryce*) You'd best come, too.

(MISS PRYCE *really wants to go, but has one eye on Lady Westholme*)

MISS PRYCE. Well, really—I hardly know—it seems . . .

DRAGOMAN. I take you very nice walk. See place where Nata-beans buried. Very *sad*—very *suitable*.

MISS PRYCE. A cemetery? I really think, Arethusa, *that* would be *quite* all right.

LADY WESTHOLME. *You* can do as you *please,* but I shall stay here.

HIGGS. (*to Miss Pryce*) Coom on then, lass.

MISS PRYCE. I hardly know . . .

(HIGGS *takes* MISS PRYCE *by the arm and leads her to the slope* L)

HIGGS. Ee—coom on. I'll look after yer. (*He stops on the slope and turns*) And look 'ere, Abraham, I don't want any maidenhair fern—'angin' *oop* or *down*.

(MISS PRYCE, HIGGS *and the* DRAGOMAN *exit up the slope* L. CARBERY *enters* R)

LADY WESTHOLME. Ah, Colonel Carbery, I wanted to speak to you.

CARBERY. (*moving* RC) Yes, Lady Westholme?

LADY WESTHOLME. I do hope you understand that there must be no *unpleasantness* about this business.

CARBERY. (*very vague*) Now what d'you mean by unpleasant-ness, Lady Westholme?

LADY WESTHOLME. I am speaking *diplomatically*. These people are Americans. Americans are very touchy and prone to take offence. They may resent any sign of officialdom.

CARBERY. (*mildly*) Well, you know, sudden death and all that—I have my duty to do.

LADY WESTHOLME. Quite. But the whole thing is perfectly straightforward. The heat here was intense yesterday. Radiation off these rocks. Old Mrs. Boynton was ob-viously in poor health. (*She lowers her voice*) Between ourselves, she *drank*.

CARBERY. Indeed? Do you happen to know that as a *fact*?

LADY WESTHOLME. I am positive of it.

CARBERY. But you've no evidence—eh?

LADY WESTHOLME. *I* don't *need* evidence.

CARBERY. Unfortunately, I do.

LADY WESTHOLME. A sudden heat stroke is not in the least surprising under the circumstances.

CARBERY. No, no. Perfectly natural thing to happen, I agree. (*He moves above the table.*)

LADY WESTHOLME. So we shan't be held up here?

CARBERY. No, no. I assure you, Lady Westholme. Horses will be along this afternoon, and arrangements made for re- moving the—er—body. We can all leave together.

(LENNOX *and* NADINE *enter* R)

Sit down, Mrs. Boynton. (*He indicates the chairs* R *of the table for Nadine and* L *of it for Lennox*)

(NADINE *sits* R *of the table,* LENNOX L *of it. There is a pause*)

(*He looks at Lady Westholme*) That's all right, then, Lady Westholme.

(LADY WESTHOLME *rises and stamps off* R)

(*He watches her go, smiling to himself*) Masterful woman. (*He sits above the table*) Thinks she runs the British Empire. (*His manner changes*) Now, Mr. Boyn- ton, I shall want a certain amount of details from you. (*He taps his papers*) Forms, you know. Curse of our age. Don't want to worry you more than we can help.

NADINE. Of course, we quite understand.

LENNOX. Yes, we understand.

CARBERY. Deceased's name and age?

LENNOX. Ada Caroline Boynton. She was sixty-two.

CARBERY. (*making notes*) And her health hadn't been too good, eh?

NADINE. She had congestive cardiac failure. We all knew that death might occur at any moment.

CARBERY. You put it quite professionally.

NADINE. I—I had a certain amount of nursing training before my marriage.

CARBERY. Oh, I see.

LENNOX. My mother was a sick woman—a very sick woman.

CARBERY. (*gently; with something significant in his voice*) Rather a strenuous trip, this, to bring a very sick woman, wasn't it?

NADINE. You didn't know my mother-in-law. She was a very determined woman. If she wanted to do a thing—(*she shrugs her shoulders*) well, she just did it. We had to give in.

CARBERY. I know, I know. Awfully obstinate, some of these old people. Just won't listen to reason. (*He pauses*) You did all you could to dissuade her, I suppose?

NADINE. (*quickly*) Of course.

CARBERY. Very distressing. (*He shoots a quick sideways glance at them*) I quite realize the—er—shock—and—er—grief —it must be to you.

LENNOX. It was a great shock, yes.

CARBERY. Quite, quite.

(*There is a pause*)

LENNOX. Is that all?

CARBERY. All?

NADINE. There are no further formalities to go through?

CARBERY. I'll fix up everything as far as I can. We've got to get back to civilization first. There will probably have to be an autopsy.

LENNOX. (*rising; sharply*) Is that necessary?

CARBERY. Well, under the circumstances—sudden death, you know. Not being attended by a doctor.

NADINE. But there are two doctors here in camp.

CARBERY. (*very vague*) Well, yes, that's true, of course.

NADINE. Surely one of them could certify the death?

CARBERY. (*rising and moving down* L) Well, I don't know— they weren't exactly attending her, were they?

NADINE. I believe Miss King did—talk to my mother-in-law about her state of health.

CARBERY. Did she now? Well, that might help. (*Sharply*) You don't like the idea of an autopsy?

LENNOX. Frankly, no. It—it would upset us all very much.

CARBERY. Of course I understand your feeling. Still—she was only your stepmother, wasn't she, Mr. Boynton?

LENNOX. No—yes . . .

NADINE. (*rising*) They were so young when their father remarried that it was like their own mother.

CARBERY. I see. I see.

NADINE. So you will do what you can?

CARBERY. I'll do what I can.

(LENNOX *and* NADINE *cross and exit* R)

(*He moves above the table, raises his eyebrows and purses his lips*) I wonder now. I wonder. Interestin'.

(RAYMOND *and* SARAH *enter quickly from the marquee, talking. They look happy and animated*)

Oh, Dr. King.

SARAH. (*moving to* L *of Carbery*) Yes?

CARBERY. Just wanted a word. (*He indicates the chair* L *of the table*)

(SARAH *sits* L *of the table*)

(*To Raymond*) About your mother's state of health, Mr. Boynton. Perhaps Dr. King could help us there.

RAYMOND. (*moving to* L *of Sarah*) In what way?

CARBERY. (*sitting above the table; to Sarah*) I understand that you had a talk with Mrs. Boynton on the subject of her health yesterday.

SARAH. Ye-es. It wasn't a consultation, though.

CARBERY. You mean she didn't call you in?

SARAH. No. (*She pauses. Embarrassed*) Actually, I spoke to her. I—I warned her.

CARBERY. Warned her?

SARAH. Oh—of the state of her health. I—I didn't think she took it seriously enough.

CARBERY. It was serious, then?

SARAH. Yes.

CARBERY. So you weren't surprised when she died?

SARAH. (*slowly*) No, I wasn't surprised—not really.

CARBERY. Excuse me, Dr. King, but what do you mean by "not really"?

SARAH. I just meant—that it came so soon after my warning her.

CARBERY. What did you warn her about—tell her not to overdo it—that sort of thing?

SARAH. (*after a pause*) Not quite. (*With a rush*) I told her I didn't think she had very long to live.

(CARBERY *whistles*)

CARBERY. Do you modern doctors usually say that sort of thing?

SARAH. No. It was—quite unprofessional.

CARBERY. But you had a reason, eh?

SARAH. I thought—she ought to know.

CARBERY. Well, of course, I'm no judge of medical etiquette, but . . .

(GERARD *enters quickly* R. *He is upset*)

GERARD. (*moving* RC) Colonel Carbery, can I speak to you?

CARBERY. (*rising; to Sarah and Raymond*) Would you mind?

(SARAH *rises and exits with* RAYMOND *to the marquee*)

(*He moves to* L *of Gerard*) Well, Dr. Gerard, what is it?

GERARD. It is my duty, clearly my duty, to put certain facts before you. (*He pauses*) I have with me a small travelling medicine case containing certain drugs.

CARBERY. Yes?

GERARD. This morning, on looking into it, I have discovered that one of the drugs is missing.

CARBERY. (*sharply*) What drug is it?

GERARD. Digitoxin.

CARBERY. Digitoxin is a heart poison, isn't it?

GERARD. Yes, it is obtained from *digitalis purpurea*, the common foxglove. It is official in France—though not in your British Pharmacopeia.

CARBERY. I see. (*He moves* L) What would be the effect, Dr. Gerard, of digitoxin administered to a human being? (*He moves to the table*)

GERARD. If a large dose—a lethal, not a therapeutic dose—if digitoxin were thrown suddenly on the circulation, say by intravenous injection—it would cause sudden death by palsy of the heart.

CARBERY. And Mrs. Boynton had a weak heart?

GERARD. Yes, as a matter of fact, she was actually taking medicine containing digitalin.

CARBERY. Then in that case the digitoxin wouldn't hurt her.

GERARD. Oh, my dear sir, that is the layman speaking. There is a difference, as I have said, between a lethal dose and a therapeutic dose. Besides, digitalin may be considered a cumulative drug.

CARBERY. That's interesting. (*He moves above the table*) What about post-mortem appearance?

GERARD. (*significantly*) The active principles of the digitalis may destroy life and leave no appreciable sign.

CARBERY. Then she may have died of the cumulative effects of digitalis legitimately given to her. By using the same drug, it means that it would be almost impossible to prove anything satisfactorily to a jury. Yes, somebody's been rather clever.

GERARD. You think that?

CARBERY. It's very possible. Rich old woman whom nobody loves. (*He pauses*) When did you last see this stuff of yours?

GERARD. Yesterday afternoon. I had my case here. (*He moves to R of the table*) I got out some quinine for one of the natives.

CARBERY. And you can swear that the digitoxin was there then?

GERARD. Yes. There were no gaps.

CARBERY. And this morning it was gone.

GERARD. Yes. You must have a search made. If it has been thrown away . . .

CARBERY. (*taking a small phial from his pocket*) Is this it?

GERARD. (*astonished*) Yes. Where did you find it?

(CARBERY *shakes his head at Gerard, goes to the marquee and calls*)

CARBERY. (*calling*) Mr. Boynton. (*He moves below the table*)

(RAYMOND *and* SARAH *enter from the marquee and move to L of Carbery*)

(*He hands the phial to Raymond*) Have you ever seen this before?

RAYMOND. (*wonderingly*) No.

CARBERY. And yet one of my Arab fellows found it in the pocket of the clothes you were wearing yesterday.

RAYMOND. (*utterly taken aback*) In my pocket?

CARBERY. (*his manner now quite different; no longer vague*) That's what I said.

RAYMOND. I simply don't understand what you are talking about. What is this thing?

CARBERY. It's got a label on it.

RAYMOND. (*reading*) "Digitoxin."

CARBERY. Digitoxin is a heart poison.

SARAH. What are you driving at, Colonel Carbery?

CARBERY. I'm just anxious to know how that phial of digitoxin got from Dr. Gerard's case into Mr. Boynton's pocket.

RAYMOND. I know nothing about it.

CARBERY. You deny taking it from Dr. Gerard's case?

RAYMOND. Certainly I do. I've never seen it before. (*He tips the phial*) Anyway, it's nearly empty.

GERARD. It was quite full—yesterday afternoon. (*He takes the phial from Raymond and moves C*)

RAYMOND. (*turning a startled face on Gerard*) You mean . . . ?

CARBERY. (*quickly*) Dr. King. Do you own a hypodermic syringe?

SARAH. Yes.

CARBERY. Where is it?

SARAH. In my tent. Shall I get it?

CARBERY. If you please.

(SARAH *crosses and exits* R)

RAYMOND. What you're suggesting is impossible—quite impossible.

CARBERY. I'm not aware that I've suggested anything.

RAYMOND. What sort of a fool do you take me for? The inference is perfectly plain. You think my mother was—(*he swallows*) poisoned?

CARBERY. I haven't said so.

RAYMOND. Then what do you mean?

CARBERY. I just want to know why Dr. Gerard's phial was in your pocket.

RAYMOND. It wasn't.

CARBERY. One of my fellows found it there.

RAYMOND. I tell you I never touched the . . . (*He stops, suddenly assailed by a sudden memory*)

CARBERY. Sure about that?

(SARAH *enters* R *and crosses to Carbery. She carries her hypodermic case*)

SARAH. Here you are. (*She hands the case to Carbery*)

CARBERY. Thank you, Dr. King. (*He opens the case, looks at Raymond, then at Sarah*)

SARAH. What . . . ?

(CARBERY *holds the case out*)

(*She sees the case is empty*) Empty?

CARBERY. Empty.

SARAH. But—how extraordinary. I'm sure I never . . . (*She stops, beginning to be frightened*)

GERARD. That is the hypodermic case you offered to me yesterday afternoon. You are sure it was in the case then?

SARAH. Yes.

CARBERY. (*crossing to Gerard*) Any idea when it was taken out, Gerard?

GERARD. (*upset*) I do not believe . . . (*He breaks off*)

CARBERY. Now what don't you believe?

GERARD. (*moving* RC) C'est impossible. C'est impossible.

SARAH. Jinny?

CARBERY. Jinny? Is that your sister, Mr. Boynton?

(RAYMOND *does not answer*)

Perhaps you would ask her to come here.

GERARD. (*sharply*) No.

CARBERY. (*turning a mildly surprised eye at him*) She may be able to clear up the matter. If you'd just fetch her, Mr. Boynton.

(RAYMOND *crosses and exits* R. CARBERY *crosses above the table to* L *of it*)

GERARD. You do not understand. You do not understand the very first principles. Listen, my dear sir, this girl will not be able to clear anything up.

CARBERY. But she handled this case—yesterday afternoon. (*He puts the case on the table*) That's right, isn't it? That's what's worrying you?

GERARD. Jinny couldn't possibly have used that hypodermic. It would be entirely out of character. I—ah, *mon Dieu*, how am I to make you understand?

CARBERY. (*sitting* L *of the table*) Just go on telling me.

GERARD. (*crossing and standing up* R *of the table*) Ginevra Boynton is at the moment in a highly abnormal mental condition. Dr. King will bear me out.

SARAH. (*moving* RC) Dr. Gerard is one of the greatest living authorities on this subject.

CARBERY. (*amiably*) I know. I know all about him.

(SARAH *moves to the deck chair down* R *and sits*)

GERARD. If Ginevra Boynton took that syringe from Dr. King's case, she certainly did not take it for the reason you are suggesting.

CARBERY. (*plaintively*) But I'm not suggesting anything. It's *you* people who are doing all the suggesting.

(RAYMOND *and* GINEVRA *enter* R. GINEVRA *crosses to* LC. CARBERY *rises and indicates the chair* R *of the table.* GINEVRA *thanks him with a little royal inclination of her head and sits* R *of the table*)

(*He resumes his seat*) Just want to ask you something, Miss Boynton. There's a hypodermic syringe missing from this case. Do you know anything about it?

GINEVRA. (*shaking her head*) No—oh, no.

CARBERY. Are you sure you didn't take it?

GINEVRA. Why should I take it?

CARBERY. Well—(*he smiles at her*) I'm asking *you*.

GINEVRA. (*leaning forward*) Are you on my side?

CARBERY. (*startled*) Eh, what's that?

GINEVRA. Or are you one of them?

(GERARD *makes a gesture of frustration*)

(*She turns swiftly and looks at Gerard*) Ask him. He knows. He came here—he followed me from Jerusalem—to protect me. To keep me safe from my enemies.

CARBERY. What enemies, Miss Boynton?

GINEGRA. I mustn't say. No, I mustn't say. It isn't safe.

CARBERY. What do you know about this hypodermic?

GINEVRA. I know who took it. (*She nods*)

CARBERY. Who?

GINEVRA. It was meant for *me*. They were going to kill me. After dark. I should have been asleep. I shouldn't have cried out. They knew, you see, that I'd not got the knife.

CARBERY. What knife?

GINEVRA. I stole a knife. He—(*she looks at Gerard*) took it away from me. I ought to have had it—to protect myself with. They were plotting to kill me.

GERARD. (*moving behind Ginevra and shaking her by the shoulders*) You must stop this play-acting—none of that that you please yourself by imagining is real. You know in your heart that it is not real.

GINEVRA. It's true—it's all true.

GERARD. (*kneeling by her*) No, it is not true. Listen, Ginevra, your mother is dead and you will lead a new life. You must come out of this world of shadows and fancies. You are free now—free.

GINEVRA. (*rising*) Mother is dead—I am free—free. (*She crosses to* RC) Mother is dead. (*She turns suddenly to* Carbery) Did I kill her?

GERARD. (*rising and moving up* C) Ah! *Mon Dieu!*

SARAH. (*rising; fiercely*) Of course you didn't kill her.

GINEVRA. (*turning a mad lovely smile on Sarah*) How do you know?

(GINEVRA *exits* R)

SARAH. (*After a moment's stunned pause*) She doesn't know what she's saying.

CARBERY. (*rising*) The question seems to be, did she know what she was doing.

SARAH. She didn't do anything. (*She moves* RC)

CARBERY. I wonder.

(LENNOX *and* NADINE *enter* R. *Their faces are anxious*)

NADINE. (*moving* RC) What have you been doing to Jinny? She said—she said . . .

CARBERY. What did she say, Mrs. Boynton?

NADINE. She said, "They think I killed mother". She was smiling. Oh!

GERARD. It all fits in. It is the instinct to dramatize herself. You have given her a new role, that is all.

NADINE. (*crossing to* R *of the table*) You don't understand, Colonel Carbery. My sister-in-law is not well. She is suffering from a kind of nervous breakdown. It's all so fantastic. Just because my mother-in-law unfortunately died . . .

CARBERY. Unfortunately?

NADINE. What do you mean?

CARBERY. It was, if you'll excuse me for saying it, not such a very unfortunate death for all of you, was it?

LENNOX. (*crossing to* R *of Nadine*) What are you hinting at? What are you trying to say?

CARBERY. We'd better have it quite clear. (*He pauses, moves down* LC *a little then speaks in a dry official voice*) Cases of sudden death, Mr. Boynton, are always investigated if there has been no physician attending the deceased who can give a death certificate. There will have to be an inquest on Mrs. Boynton. The object of that inquest will be to determine how the deceased came to her death. There are several possibilities. First, there is death from natural causes—well, that's perfectly possible. Mrs. Boynton was suffering from a heart complaint. But, there are other possibilities. There's accidental death. She was taking digitalin. Could she have taken by some mistake— an overdose. (*He pauses*) Or could she have been given —(*significantly*) by mistake, an overdose.

NADINE. I . . .

CARBERY. I understand, Mrs. Boynton, that it was you who habitually administered digitalin to your mother-in-law.

NADINE. Yes.

CARBERY. Is there any possibility that you might have given her an overdose?

NADINE. No. (*Clearly*) Neither by accident nor, Colonel Carbery, by intention.

CARBERY. Come come, now, I never suggested that.

NADINE. It is what you meant.

CARBERY. I was just considering the possibilities of accident. (*He crosses to* LC) So we come to the third possibility. (*Sharply*) Murder. Yes, just that, murder. And we have got certain evidence to support that view. First, the digitoxin that disappeared from Dr. Gerard's case and reappeared in Raymond Boynton's pocket.

(GERARD *moves to* L *of the table*)

RAYMOND. I tell you I know nothing about that—nothing.

CARBERY. Secondly, the hypodermic needle that is missing from Dr. King's case.

SARAH. (*crossing to* R) If Ginevra took it, it was play-acting, nothing more.

CARBERY. (*to Lennox*) And thirdly, Mr. Boynton, we come to *you*.

LENNOX (*starting*) To me?

SARAH. One of your Arab fellows has found something else, I suppose?

CARBERY. One of my Arab fellows—as you put it, Dr. King— *saw* something else.

LENNOX. Saw?

CARBERY. Yes. Yesterday afternoon most people were out walking or else resting from a walk, Mr. Boynton. There was no-one, or you thought there was no-one about. You went up to your mother as she was sitting up there. (*He nods towards the cave*) You took her hand and bent over her wrist. I don't know exactly what you did, Mr. Boynton, and my Arab fellow couldn't see what you did, but your mother cried out.

LENNOX. (*agitated*) I can explain. I—she—her bracelet had come undone. She asked me to fasten it. I did. But I was clumsy—I caught the flesh of her wrist in the hinge at the back. That's what made her cry out.

CARBERY. I see. That's your story.

LENNOX. It's the truth.

NADINE. I know that bracelet. It was tight fitting. It wasn't at all easy to fasten.

(CARBERY *nods quietly*)

LENNOX. (*shrilly*) What do you think I did?

CARBERY. I was wondering whether you gave her a rapid injection. (*To Gerard*) Death would result, I think you said, very quickly from rapid palsy of the heart.

GERARD. That is correct.

CARBERY. She would cry out and try to rise—and that would be all.

GERARD. That would be all.

LENNOX. It's not true. You can't prove it.

CARBERY. There is a mark out her wrist. It is the mark of a hypodermic needle—not a mark caused by the hinge of a bracelet. I don't like murder, Mr. Boynton.

LENNOX. She wasn't murdered.

CARBERY. I think she was.

SARAH. It's fantastic. You built up all this from what a few Arabs have pretended to find or to see. They're probably lying.

CARBERY. My men don't lie to me, Dr. King. They've found what they say they've found where they said they found it. And they've seen what they said they've seen. And they've heard what they've said they heard. (*He pauses*)

GERARD. Heard?

CARBERY. (*crossing down* L *and turning*) Yes—heard. Don't you remember? "One of us has got to kill her."

CURTAIN

Scene II

SCENE: *The same. The same afternoon.*

When the CURTAIN *rises, the four Boyntons are sitting on the rock up* R, *which is now in shadow. They are quite still and are lost in a stupor of despair.* NADINE *and* GINEVRA *are seated on stools with their backs to the audience.* LENNOX *is leaning on the rock* L *of the cave mouth.* RAYMOND *is seated half way up the steps.* SARAH *is pacing up and down* RC. *Her hands are clenched and she is obviously fighting misery and doubt.* COPE *enters down the slope* L. *He is fatigued and despondent. He looks at the group on the rock then moves.* C.

SARAH. Have you got a cigarette?

COPE. (*moving to Sarah*) Why certainly. (*He proffers his case*)

SARAH. (*taking a cigarette*) Thanks.

COPE. (*lighting her cigarette*) I suppose we shall be leaving before long.

SARAH. (*crossing and sitting* R *of the table*) I suppose so. I wish we had never come here.

COPE. (*crossing and sitting* L *of the table*) Amen to that. I'm the kind of guy who's born to be a stooge. As soon as the old lady went west I knew my number was up. Why the heck did she have to die just then? Now—well, Nadine will never leave her husband now. She'll stand by him now, whatever he's done.

SARAH. (*sharply*) Do you think *he*—did it?

COPE. Lennox is a queer guy. I've never been able to size him up properly. You'd say, to look at him, that he wouldn't have the guts to do anything violent—but, well, you never know what a man's like underneath. I'd still like to think that the old lady died a natural death. After all, she *was* a very sick woman.

SARAH. (*rising and looking up at the Boyntons*) Look at them.

COPE. (*staring up at the Boyntons*) You mean—they don't think so? (*He rises and moves to* L *of her*) It—yes, it sort of gets you, the way they sit there, not saying anything. Almost Wagnerian, isn't it? The twilight of the gods. Symbolical in a way, sitting in that shadow.

SARAH. *Her* shadow.

COPE. Yes—yes, I see what you mean.

SARAH. (*crossing down* L; *desperately*) She's got them still. Her death hasn't set them free after all.

COPE. (*shaking his head*) I guess this has been a very trying day for all of us. Oh, well, I guess I might as well let Abraham show me where the Natabeans are buried.

(COPE *crosses and exits* R. GERARD *enters down* R)

SARAH. (*crossing to Gerard*) When we get back to civilization, what will happen?

GERARD. It will depend largely on the result of the autopsy.

SARAH. There's a very strong chance that it won't be conclusive.

GERARD. I know.

SARAH. (*desperately*) Why can't we *do* something?

GERARD. What do you want to do?

SARAH. That's easy. I want Raymond. It was a battle between me and that old she-devil. This morning I thought I'd won. Now—look at them.

(GERARD *looks up at the Boyntons, then studies Sarah*)

GERARD. (*after a pause*) Do you think he killed her?

SARAH. (*fiercely*) No. (*She crosses to* L *of the table*)

GERARD. You don't *think* so, but you're not *sure*.

SARAH. I *am* sure.

GERARD. One of them killed her.

SARAH. Not Raymond.

GERARD. (*shrugging his shoulders*) *Efin*, you are a woman. (*He crosses to* R *of the table*)

SARAH. It's not that. (*With courage*) Oh, well, perhaps it is. But they didn't plan to kill her. (*She moves down* L) They may have *thought* of killing her, but it's not the same thing. We all—think of things.

GERARD. Very true. All the same, one of them did more than think.

SARAH. Yes.

GERARD. The question is, which of them? One can make out a case against any one of them. Raymond actually had the digitoxin in his possession.

SARAH. (*moving and sitting* L *of the table*) That's a point in his favour. If he had used it he wouldn't be so idiotic as to leave the bottle in his pocket.

GERARD. I don't know. He may have been quite confident that her death would be attributed to natural causes—as it would have been but for my discovery of the missing phial.

SARAH. It wasn't Raymond. I watched his face when Colonel Carbery produced that bottle.

GERARD. *Eh bien!* (*He sits* R *of the table*) Then there is Nadine Boynton. She has plenty of nerve and efficiency, that quiet young woman. Nothing easier for her than to administer a lethal dose of digitoxin in Mrs. Boynton's medicine. Then she slips the bottle in Raymond's pocket.

SARAH. You are making her out a revolting character.

GERARD. Women are unscrupulous. She plants suspicion against her brother-in-law in order to be sure that no suspicion falls on her husband.

SARAH. Suspicion did fall on him.

GERARD. Yes. Is his story of the bracelet true? Myself I do not believe it.

SARAH. (*rising*) What you mean is that you don't want it to be your precious Jinny.

GERARD. (*rising; excitably*) Of course it was not Jinny. I tell you it is psychologically impossible.

SARAH. (*crossing to* R) You Frenchmen! It is not at all psychologically impossible that Jinny should kill someone— and you know it.

GERARD. (*following her; excitedly*) Yes, but not in that way. If she killed, she would kill flamboyantly, spectacularly. With the knife—that, yes, I can imagine it. But she would have to *dramatize* her act.

SARAH. Couldn't it be someone outside altogether?

GERARD. (*moving* LC) It would be pleasant to think so—but you know only too well that what you say is unsound. After all, who is there? The good Jefferson Cope. But the death of the tyrannical old woman deprives him of the lady of his affection.

SARAH. Oh, it isn't Jefferson Cope. As you say, he's no motive. Nor have the others. But there's you—and there's me. You know, Dr. Gerard, I had a motive—and it is my syringe that is missing.

GERARD. And the digitoxin is mine. All the same we did not kill her.

SARAH. That's what you say.

GERARD. We are doctors. We save life—we do not take it.

SARAH. "Doctors differ—and patients die." What years ago it seems when you said that to me in Jerusalem.

GERARD. Courage, *mon enfant*. And if I can help, remember that we are colleagues.

(GERARD *exits to the marquee*, SARAH *moves towards the rock up* R)

SARAH. Raymond. (*She moves nearer. Imperiously*) Raymond.

(RAYMOND *turns his head and looks at Sarah*)

Come down here.

(RAYMOND *rises, but does not come down. His manner is apathetic and he does not look at Sarah*)

RAYMOND. Yes, Sarah?

SARAH. Why don't you stay down here and—talk to me? Why do you all sit up there by that cave?

RAYMOND. It seems—the right place for us.

(SARAH *reaches up and takes Raymond's hand*)

SARAH. I never heard such nonsense.

RAYMOND. (*sighing*) You don't understand. (*He turns away*)

SARAH. Raymond—(*she goes up to him*) do you think I believe you killed her? I don't. I don't.

RAYMOND. One of us killed her.

SARAH. You don't even know that.

RAYMOND. Yes, I do. (*Thoughtfully*) We all know.

SARAH. But *you* didn't kill her. You yourself didn't kill her.

RAYMOND. No, I didn't kill her. (*He looks at the others*)

SARAH. Well then, that's all that *matters*. Surely you see that?

RAYMOND. No, it's you who don't see. I suggested killing her. One of us acted on that suggestion. I don't know which of us. I don't want to know. But there it is. We're all in it together.

SARAH. You won't even fight?

RAYMOND. (*turning and smiling at her*) There's no-one to fight. Don't you understand, Sarah? One can't fight the dead. (*He sits on the steps*)

SARAH. (*moving down* C) Oh, what shall I do?

LADY WESTHOLME. (*off* L) I can only tell you, Colonel Carbery, that I shall take it up with the Foreign Office.

(SARAH *moves wearily to* R *of the table and sits.* LADY WEST-HOLME *and* CARBERY *enter from the marquee. They cross* C, CARBERY L *of* LADY WESTHOLME)

CARBERY. This is my territory, Lady Westholme, and I am responsible for its administration. To put it plainly, an old woman has been cold-bloodedly murdered, and you are suggesting that I should refrain from enquiring into the matter.

LADY WESTHOLME. There are wider diplomatic considerations to be observed. The whole thing must be dropped.

CARBERY. I don't take my orders from you, Lady Westholme.

LADY WESTHOLME. I assure you that I shall pull strings—and that I can pull strings. Once I get to a telegraph office.

CARBERY. You will get to a telegraph office tomorrow, and you can send wires to the Prime Minister, the Foreign Secre-

tary and the President of the United States and play cats'
cradle with the Minister of Agriculture and Fisheries if it
pleases you. In the meantime, I run my own show.

LADY WESTHOLME. You will find, Colonel Carbery, that I am
more influential than you think.

(LADY WESTHOLME *exits angrily* R)

CARBERY. Phew! What a tartar! (*He moves down above the
table*) The worst of it is—(*he smiles ruefully at Sarah*)
the damn woman's quite right.

SARAH. What do you mean?

CARBERY. The whole thing will have to be dropped.

SARAH. Why?

CARBERY. Because there's no evidence. One of 'em did it, all
right, but as the evidence lies there's no earthly chance
of proving which one. Oh, that's a very common state of
affairs in police work. Knowledge without proof. And in
this case the Westholme woman is quite right—there is
an international aspect. Can't bring an accusation against
an American subject unless you've got sufficient evidence.
We haven't.

SARAH. (*slowly*) So the whole thing will be dropped.

CARBERY. Yes. There'll be an inquest and all that. But the
result's a foregone conclusion. They'll go scot free. (*He
gives her a quick glance*) That please you?

SARAH. I don't know.

CARBERY. (*moving to* L *of the table*) Well—(*he jerks his
thumb towards the Boyntons*) it ought to please *them*.

SARAH. Ought it?

CARBERY. Don't you think so?

SARAH. (*rising and moving* RC; *explosively*) No, no, no!

CARBERY. You're very emphatic, Miss King.

SARAH. Don't you see—it's the most awful thing that could
happen to them? They don't know *themselves* which one
of them it was—and now they'll never know.

CARBERY. May have been all in it together. (*He sits* L *of the
table*)

SARAH. No, they weren't. That's just the awful part of it.
Three of them are innocent—but they're all four of them
in the shadow together— and now they'll never get out
of the shadow.

CARBERY. Yes, that's the worst of the verdict not proven. The
innocent suffer. (*He coughs*) You've got—a special interest, I gather.

SARAH. Yes.

CARBERY. I'm sorry. I wish I could help you.

SARAH. You see—he won't fight for himself.

CARBERY. So you've got to fight for him.

SARAH. (*moving to* R *of the table*) Yes—it began when she was alive. I fought her. I thought I'd win, too. This morning I thought I had won. But now—they're back again—back in her shadow. That's where she sat, you know. In the mouth of the cave there—like an obscene old idol. Gloating in her own power and her cruelty. I feel as though she's sitting there now, holding them still, laughing because she's got them where she wants them, knowing that they'll never escape her now. (*She speaks up to the cave*) Yes, you've won, you old devil. You've proved that death is stronger than life. It oughtn't to be —it oughtn't to be. (*She breaks down and sinks on to the chair* R *of the table*)

(*There is a pause.* CARBERY *realizes there is nothing he can do, rises and exits to the marquee.* HIGGS *enters from the marquee*)

HIGGS. Aye, but it's warm. (*He crosses to* C)

(*The* DRAGOMAN *enters down the slope* L)

DRAGOMAN. Horses coming over pass. Be here in a few moments.

HIGGS. Then hurry oop and get some beer—ah'm in a muck sweat again.

(*The* DRAGOMAN *exits to the marquee.* MISS PRYCE *enters down the slope.*)

MISS PRYCE. What a wonderful place this is.

SARAH. I think it's a damnable place.

MISS PRYCE. (*crossing to* RC) Oh, really—Miss King . . .

SARAH. Sorry.

MISS PRYCE. Oh, I quite understand. Such tragic associations. And then, of course, you are so young.

(MISS PRYCE *exits* R)

SARAH. (*bitterly*) Yes, I'm young. What's the good of being young? It ought to be some good. Youth means strength. It means life. Life ought to be stronger than death.

HIGGS. (*seriously*) So it is, lass. Make no mistake about that.

SARAH. It isn't. (*She indicates the Boyntons*) Look at them. Sitting in the shadow of death.

HIGGS. (*considering them*) Aye! They look as though they'd been given a life sentence.

SARAH. That's just what they have been given. (*She rises*) Of course. *That's* it. (*She crosses to* RC) That's what *she* wanted.

HIGGS. What's oop?

SARAH. (*laughing wildly*) I think I've got a touch of the sun. But the sun lets in light, doesn't it?

HIGGS. (*crossing to the marquee and calling*) Hey, Doctor, here's a patient for you out here.

(GERARD *enters from the marquee.* HIGGS *jerks his thumb at Sarah and exits to the marquee*)

GERARD. (*moving* LC) Are you ill?

SARAH. (*moving to* R *of Gerard*) No, I'm not ill. Listen, Dr. Gerard. I know who killed Mrs. Boynton. I know it quite certainly—(*she touches her forehead*) here. What I must do—what you must help me to do—is to get proof.

GERARD. You know which of them killed her?

SARAH. None of them killed her.

(GERARD *is about to interrupt*)

Wait. I know what you are going to say—that they themselves think so. That's what she wanted.

GERARD. *Comment?*

SARAH. Listen. Yesterday I lost my temper—I told her what was the truth, that she couldn't live long. I told her that when she died, they'd be free. You know what she was like—the lust for power and cruelty had grown—she wasn't quite sane, was she?

GERARD. She was a sadist—yes. She specialized in mental cruelty.

SARAH. She couldn't bear what I told her, she couldn't face the thought of their being free—and happy. And she saw a way to keep them in prison for ever.

GERARD. *Mon Dieu*, you mean . . .

SARAH. Yes, don't you see? She took the digitoxin from your case. She took my syringe. She slipped the empty bottle into Raymond's pocket, and she asked Lennox to fasten her bracelet and then cried out when she knew someone was watching them. It was clever—damnably clever— just enough supicion against each of them. Not enough to convict one but enough to keep them believing all their lives that one of them *had* killed her.

GERARD. And then she committed suicide. Yes, she had the courage for that.

SARAH. She'd got *guts* all right. And hate.

GERARD. (*crossing to* R *as he works it out*) After filling the syringe she slipped the empty bottle into Raymond's pocket—yes, she could have done that as he was helping her up to the cave. Then later she called Lennox, pretended her bracelet was undone. Yes, that too. But she made no attempt to incriminate Nadine or Jinny.

SARAH. Nadine would come under suspicion because of always giving her medicine, and she could pretty well trust Jinny to incriminate herself with her wild talk.

GERARD. (*crossing to* L *of Sarah*) That is true. And then, at the last, when there is no-one to see, she plunges the needle into her wrist—so—and dies. But no, that will not do—for in that case what happened to the hypodermic needle? It would have been found by the body. There would have been only a minute or two—not time enough for her to get up and hide it. There is a flaw there.

SARAH. (*moving up* C) I tell you I know what happened. She's laughing at me—somewhere—now, taunting me because I can't prove it—to *him*.

GERARD. (*following Sarah*) That is all you are thinking of—to prove it to Raymond? And you think he will not believe you without proof.

SARAH. Do you?

GERARD. No.

SARAH. Then I must get proof. I must. I must. Oh, God, I *must*.

(*The jingle of harness is heard off* L. MISS PRYCE *enters* R, *crosses to the slope* L *and looks off*)

GERARD. You do well to invoke God. It is a miracle you need. (*He crosses and sits on the case down.*)

SARAH. Miracles don't happen, and there's no time—no time.

MISS PRYCE. (*turning and moving* LC) Were you talking about *miracles*?

SARAH. (*bitterly*) I was saying that miracles don't happen.

MISS PRYCE. Oh, but they do. A friend of mine had the most wonderful results from a bottle of water from Lourdes—really quite *remarkable*.

SARAH. (*to herself*) I must go on fighting. I won't give in.

MISS PRYCE. The doctors were really quite astonished. They said . . . (*She breaks off*) Is anything the matter, dear?

SARAH. Yes, that she-devil, Mrs. Boynton.

MISS PRYCE. (*shocked*) Oh, really, Miss King, I don't think . . . After all, we must remember she is *dead*.

SARAH. *De mortuis.*

MISS PRYCE. Quite—quite.

SARAH. Death doesn't make people good who have been wicked.

MISS PRYCE. Wicked is rather a *strong* word, dear. I always feel people who take drugs are to be pitied rather than blamed.

SARAH. I know what I'm talking about and . . . (*She stops*) What did you say? Mrs. Boynton didn't take drugs.

MISS PRYCE. (*confused*) Oh, really, I never meant—I mean, I thought you, being a doctor, had probably noticed the signs. I'm sure *I* don't want to say anything against the poor old woman.

SARAH. Mrs. Boynton didn't take drugs. Why do you think she did?

MISS PRYCE. Oh, but I'm afraid she was a drug addict, my dear. Lady Westholme goes about saying she *drank*, which of course wasn't so at all, but I haven't liked to contradict her because saying that anyone is a *dope fiend* is *worse*.

SARAH. (*slowly but excited*) Why do you think Mrs. Boynton was a dope fiend?

MISS PRYCE. I should not dream of saying.

(*The* DRAGOMAN *enters down the slope* L)

There is such a thing as Christian charity.

DRAGOMAN. Abraham good Christian dragoman. All my ladies and gentleman say Abraham first-class Christian dragoman. You come now, ladies, horses all ready.

(SARAH *seizes* MISS PRYCE *by the arm and sits her in the chair* R *of the table*)

SARAH. You don't leave here until you tell me why you think Mrs. Boynton took drugs. You can't just hint things like that out of your imagination.

MASS PRYCE. (*indignantly*) Not at all. It was not imagination. I saw her . . . (*She stops*)

SARAH. You saw what?

DRAGOMAN. You come now.

SARAH. (*sharply*) Shut up, Abraham.

(*The* DRAGOMAN *exits to the marquee*)

MISS PRYCE. (*upset and rather on her dignity*) Really, I did not want to mention the occurrence, it seems so unkind. But since you have accused me of imagining—well, it was yesterday afternoon.

SARAH. Yes?

MISS PRYCE. I came out of my tent—at least, not right out—I just pushed back the flap and tried to remember where I had left my book. Was it in the marquee, I said to myself, or was it in the deck chair.

SARAH. Yes—yes.

MISS PRYCE. And then I noticed Mrs. Boynton. She was sitting up there quite alone and she rolled up her sleeve and injected the dope into her arm, looking about her first, you know, in a most *guilty* manner.

(GERARD *rises and exchanges glances with* SARAH)

SARAH. You're quite sure? What happened then?

MISS PRYCE. My dear, it was quite like a *novel*. She unscrewed the knob of her stick and put the hypodermic needle inside. So of course, I knew then that it was *drugs*—not *drink* as Lady Westholme said.

(CARBERY *and* LADY WESTHOLME *enter* R. CARBERY *beckons to the Boyntons.* NADINE *and* GINEVRA *rise and group with* RAYMOND *and* LENNOX *at the foot of the rock up* R)

CARBERY. (*moving* RC) Miss King—Pryce. We're starting.

SARAH. (*crossing to* L *of Carbery*) Colonel Carbery, Miss Pryce has something to tell you.

(MISS PRYCE *rises*)

When she was alone in camp yesterday, she saw Mrs. Boynton inject something into her own arm.

CARBERY. What's that?

(NADINE *and* LENNOX *move down* R)

SARAH. (*to Miss Pryce*) That's quite true, isn't it?

MISS PRYCE. Yes, indeed.

SARAH. After that Mrs. Boynton concealed the hypodermic needle in her stick, the head of which unscrews.

CARBERY. (*calling sharply*) Aissa.

(*The* DRAGOMAN *enters from the marquee*)

(*To the Dragoman*) *Tal a hinna. Fee bataga.*

(*The* DRAGOMAN *exits to the marquee*)

SARAH. (*to Raymond*) Oh, Ray!

(RAYMOND *moves to* L *of Sarah*)

We've found out the truth.

(*The* DRAGOMAN *enters from the marquee with Mrs. Boynton's stick. He crosses to* CARBERY *who takes the stick, unscrews the knob and produces the hypodermic needle, handling it carefully with his handkerchief*)

She did it *herself*. (*She catches Raymond's arm excitedly*) Do you understand? She did it herself.

CARBERY. Well, that seems to clinch matters. There will be traces of digitoxin in the barrel, and in all probability deceased's fingerprints. That, and Miss Pryce's evidence, seems conclusive. Mrs. Boynton took her own life.

RAYMOND. Sarah!

SARAH. (*half crying*) Miracles do happen. Darling Miss Pryce, you're better than any Lourdes water.

CARBERY. Well, we must be getting along. The plane is waiting at Ain Musa. (*He moves up* C)

(*The* ARAB BOY *enters from the marquee. He carries a cablegram which he hands to Carbery*)

GINEVRA. (*moving to Gerard*) Dr. Gerard—I—I did invent those things. Sometimes—(*confusedly*) I really thought they were true. You will help me, won't you?

GERARD. Yes, *cherie*, I will help you.

CARBERY. (*handing the cablegram to Lady Westholme*) Lady Westholme, there's a cable they brought along for you.

(LADY WESTHOLME *opens the cable; reads it.* HIGGS *enters from the marquee*)

LADY WESTHOLME. Dear me. Sir Eric Hartly-Witherspoon is dead.

HIGGS. So's Queen Anne.

LADY WESTHOLME. (*radiant*) This is *most* important. I must return to England at once.

CARBERY. A near relation?

LADY WESTHOLME. No relation at all. Sir Eric was Member
for Market Spotsbury. (*Pronounced Spurry*) That means
a by-election. I am the prospective Conservative candidate and I may say that when I get into the House
again . . .

HIGGS. Yer seem mighty sure about it.

LADY WESTHOLME. Market Spotsbury has *always* returned a
Conservative.

HIGGS. Aye—but times is changin' and "always" 'as a 'abit of
becomin' "never no more". 'Oo's yer opponent?

LADY WESTHOLME. I believe some Independent candidate.

HIGGS. What's 'is name?

LADY WESTHOLME. (*nonplussed*) I've no idea. Probably someone *quite* unimportant.

HIGGS. Ah'll tell yer 'is name—it's Alderman 'Iggs—and if I
can keep you out of the first floor in Jerusalem—by gum
—I'll keep yer out of the ground floor in Westminster.

CURTAIN

THE HOLLOW

Presented by Peter Saunders at the Fortune Theatre, London, W.C.2, on June 7th, 1951, with the following cast of characters—

(in the order of their appearance)

HENRIETTA ANGKATELL	*Beryl Baxter*
SIR HENRY ANGKATELL, K.C.B.	*George Thorpe*
LADY ANGKATELL	*Jeanne de Casalis*
MIDGE HARVEY	*Jessica Spencer*
GUDGEON	*A. J. Brown*
EDWARD ANGKATELL	*Colin Douglas*
DORIS	*Patricia Jones*
GERDA CRISTOW	*Joan Newell*
JOHN CRISTOW, M.D., F.R.C.P.	*Ernest Clark*
VERONICA CRAYE	*Dianne Foster*
INSPECTOR COLQUHOUN, C.I.D.	*Martin Wyldeck*
DETECTIVE SERGEANT PENNY	*Shaw Taylor*

The play directed by HUBERT GREGG

The play was subsequently transferred to the Ambassador's Theatre

SYNOPSIS OF SCENES

The action of the play passes in the garden room of Sir Henry Angkatell's house, The Hollow, about eighteen miles from London

ACT I   A Friday afternoon in early September

ACT II   SCENE 1 Saturday morning
               SCENE 2 Later the same day

ACT III   The following Monday morning

The lights are lowered during Act III to denote the passing of one hour

TIME: The present

Act One

SCENE: *The garden room of* SIR HENRY ANGKATELL'S
*house, The Hollow, about eighteen miles from London.
A Friday afternoon in early September.*

*It is an informal room, but furnished with taste. Back
C., up three steps, there are french windows opening on
to a terrace with a low wall at the far side. Beyond the
wall there is a view of the wooded hillside on which the
house is built. There are smaller french windows, up one
step, C. of the wall R., leading to the garden and giving
a view of dense shrubbery. A door down L. leads to the
other parts of the house. There is a large alcove in the
back wall L. of the french windows. The entrance to this
is arched and a heavy curtain in the archway closes it off
from the rest of the room. The back wall of the alcove
is fitted with well-filled, built-in bookshelves and furnished with a small table on which stands a silver bowl
of roses. A piece of statuary can be supposed to stand
in the alcove though not visible to the audience. The
fireplace is C. of the wall L. and there are well-filled,
built-in bookshelves in the walls R. of the french windows
up C. and below the french windows R. There is a small
writing table down R., on which stands a small table-
lamp and a telephone. A small chair is set at the table
and a waste-paper basket stands below it. Above the
writing table there is a pedestal on which stands a piece
of abstract statuary. There is a table with a table-lamp on
it below the bookshelves up R. A small table with a radio
receiver stands above the fireplace. There is an armchair
up L.C., and a comfortable sofa R.C. Below the sofa
stands a small, circular coffee table. A pouffe near the
hearth completes the furniture. The room is carpeted and
gay curtains hang at the windows. In addition to the
table-lamps, the room is lit at night by an electric candle-*

lamp wall-bracket L. *of the french windows up* C., *and small electric candle-lamps on the mantelpiece. One or two miniatures decorate the walls, and over the mantelpiece there is a fine picture depicting the idyllic scene of a Georgian house with columns, set in woodlands. The light switch and bell-push are in the wall below the fireplace. There is also a switch controlling the light in the alcove,* R. *of the arch. Two wall vases, filled with flowers, decorate the side walls of the french windows up* C.

When the CURTAIN *rises, it is a fine afternoon and all the french windows stand open.* SIR HENRY ANGKATELL, K.C.B., *a distinguished-looking, elderly man, is seated at the right end of the sofa, reading "The Times".* HENRI-ETTA ANGKATELL *is on the terrace outside the french windows up* C., *standing at a tall sculptor's stand, modelling in clay. She is a handsome young woman of about thirty-three, dressed in good country tweeds and over them a painter's overall. She advances and retreats towards her creation once or twice then enters up* C. *and moves to the coffee table below the sofa. There is a smear of clay on her nose and she is frowning.*

HENRIETTA. (*as she enters*) Damn and damn and damn!

SIR HENRY. (*looking up*) Not going well?

HENRIETTA. (*taking a cigarette from the box on the coffee table*) What misery it is to be a sculptor.

SIR HENRY. It must be. I always thought you had to have models for this sort of thing.

HENRIETTA. It's an abstract piece I'm modelling, darling.

SIR HENRY. What— (*he points with distaste to the piece of modern sculpture on the pedestal* R.) like that?

HENRIETTA. (*crossing to the mantelpiece*) Anything interesting in The Times? (*She lights her cigarette with the table lighter on the mantelpiece.*)

SIR HENRY. Lots of people dead. (*He looks at* HENRIETTA.) You've got clay on your nose.

HENRIETTA. What?

SIR HENRY. Clay—on your *nose.*

HENRIETTA. (*looking in the mirror on the mantelpiece; vaguely*) Oh, so I have. (*She rubs her nose, then her forehead, turns and moves* L.C.)

SIR HENRY. Now it's all over your face.

HENRIETTA. (*moving up* C.; *exasperated*) Does it matter, darling?

SIR HENRY. Evidently not.

(HENRIETTA *goes on to the terrace up* C. *and resumes work.* LADY ANGKATELL *enters* R. *She is a very charming and aristocratic-looking woman aged about sixty, completely vague, but with a lot of personality. She is apparently in the middle of a conversation.*)

LADY ANGKATELL. (*crossing above the sofa to the fireplace*) Oh dear, oh dear! If it isn't one thing it's another. Did I leave a mole-trap in here? (*She picks up the mole-trap from the mantelpiece and eases* C.) Ah yes—there it is. The worst of moles is—you never know where they are going to pop up next. People are quite right when they say that nature in the mild is seldom raw. (*She crosses below the sofa to* R.) Don't you think I'm right, Henry?

SIR HENRY. I couldn't say, my dear, unless I know what you're talking about.

LADY ANGKATELL. I'm going to pursue them quite ruthlessly— I really am.

(*Her voice dies away as she exits* R.)

HENRIETTA. (*looking in through the french window up* C.) What did Lucy say?

SIR HENRY. Nothing much. Just being Lucyish. I say, it's half past six.

HENRIETTA. I'll have to stop and clean myself up. They're all coming by car, I suppose? (*She drapes a damp cloth over her work.*)

SIR HENRY. All except Midge. She's coming by Green Line bus. Ought to be here by now.

HENRIETTA. Darling Midge. She is nice. Heaps nicer than any of us, don't you think? (*She pushes the stand out of sight* R. *of the terrace.*)

SIR HENRY. I must have notice of that question.

HENRIETTA. (*moving* C.; *laughing*) Well, less eccentric, anyway. There's something very sane about Midge. (*She rubs her hands on her overall.*)

SIR HENRY. (*indignantly*) I'm perfectly sane, thank you.

HENRIETTA. (*removing her overall and looking at* SIR HENRY) Ye-es—perhaps *you* are. (*She puts her overall over the back of the armchair* L.C.)

SIR HENRY. (*smiling*) As sane as anyone can be that has to live with Lucy, bless her heart. (*He laughs.*)

(HENRIETTA *laughs, crosses to the mantelpiece and puts her cigarette ash in the ashtray.*)

(*He puts his newspaper on the coffee table. Worried.*) You know, Henrietta, I'm getting worried about Lucy.

HENRIETTA. Worried? Why?

SIR HENRY. Lucy doesn't realize there are certain things she can't do.

HENRIETTA. (*looking in the mirror*) I don't think I quite know what you mean. (*She pats her hair.*)

SIR HENRY. She's always got away with things. I don't suppose any other woman in the world could have flouted the traditions of Government House as she did. (*He takes his pipe from his pocket.*) Most Governors' wives have to toe the line of convention. But not Lucy! Oh dear me, no! She played merry hell with precedence at dinner parties—and that, my dear Henrietta, is the blackest of crimes.

(HENRIETTA *turns.*)

(*He pats his pockets, feeling for his tobacco pouch.*) She put deadly enemies next to each other. She ran riot over the colour question. And instead of setting everyone at loggerheads, I'm damned if she didn't get away with it.

(HENRIETTA *picks up the tobacco jar from the mantelpiece, crosses and hands it to* SIR HENRY.)

Oh, thank you. It's that trick of hers—always smiling at people and looking so sweet and helpless. Servants are the same—she gives them any amount of trouble and they simply adore her.

HENRIETTA. I know what you mean. (*She sits on the sofa at the left end.*) Things you wouldn't stand from anyone else, you feel they are quite all right if Lucy does them. What is it? Charm? Hypnotism?

SIR HENRY. (*filling his pipe*) I don't know. She's always been the same from a girl. But you know, Henrietta, it's growing on her. She doesn't seem to realize there *are* limits. I really believe Lucy would feel she could get away with *murder*.

HENRIETTA. (*rising and picking up the piece of clay from the carpet*) Darling Henry, you and Lucy are angels letting me make my messes here—treading clay into your carpet. (*She crosses and puts the piece of clay in the waste-paper basket down* R.) When I had that fire at my studio, I thought it was the end of everything— it was sweet of you to let me move in on you.

SIR HENRY. My dear, we're proud of you. Why, I've just been reading a whole article about you and your show in *The Times*.

HENRIETTA. (*crossing to the coffee table and picking up "The Times"*) Where?

SIR HENRY. Top of the page. There, I believe. Of course, I don't profess to know much about it myself.

HENRIETTA. (*reading*) "The most significant piece of the year." Oh, what gup! I must go and wash.

(*She drops the paper on the sofa, crosses, picks up her overall and exits hurriedly* L. SIR HENRY *rises, puts the papers and tobacco on the coffee table, takes the clay from the table to the waste-paper basket, moves to the drinks table, and picks up the matches.* MIDGE HARVEY *enters up* C. *from* L. *She is small, neatly dressed but obviously badly off. She is a warm-hearted, practical and very nice young woman, a little younger than* HENRIETTA. *She carries a suitcase.*)

MIDGE. (*as she enters*) Hullo, Cousin Henry.

SIR HENRY. (*turning*) Midge! (*He moves to* R. *of her, takes the suitcase from her, and kisses her.*) Nice to see you.

MIDGE. Nice to see *you*.

SIR HENRY. How are you?

MIDGE. Terribly well.

SIR HENRY. Not been overworking you in that damned dress shop of yours?

MIDGE. (*moving down* C.) Business is pretty slack at the moment, or I shouldn't have got the weekend off. The bus was absolutely crowded; I've never known it go so slowly. (*She sits on the sofa, puts her bag and gloves beside her and looks towards the window* R.) It's heaven to be here. Who's coming this weekend?

SIR HENRY. (*putting the suitcase on the floor* R. *of the armchair* L.C.) Nobody much. The Cristows. You know them, of course.

MIDGE. The Harley Street doctor with a rather dim wife?

SIR HENRY. That's right. Nobody else. Oh yes—(*he strikes a match*) Edward, of course.

MIDGE. (*turning to face* SIR HENRY; *suddenly stricken by the sound of the name*) Edward!

SIR HENRY. (*lighting his pipe*) Quite a job to get Edward away from Ainswick these days.

MIDGE. (*rising*) Ainswick! Lovely, lovely Ainswick! (*She crosses to the fireplace and gazes up at the picture above it.*)

SIR HENRY. (*moving down* C.) Yes, it's a beautiful place.

MIDGE. (*feelingly*) It's the most beautiful place in the world.

SIR HENRY. (*putting the matchbox on the coffee table*) Had some happy times there, eh? (*He eases to* R. *of the armchair* L.C.)

MIDGE. (*turning*) All the happy times I've ever had were there.

(LADY ANGKATELL *enters* R. *She carries a large empty flowerpot.*)

LADY ANGKATELL. (*as she enters*) Would you believe it, (*she crosses above the sofa to* R. *of* SIR HENRY) they've been at it again. They've pushed up a whole row of lovely little lobelias. Ah well, as long as the weather keeps fine . . .

SIR HENRY. Here's Midge.

LADY ANGKATELL. Where? (*She crosses to* MIDGE *and kisses her.*) Oh, darling Midge, I didn't see you, dear. (*To* SIR HENRY. *Confidentially.*) That would help, wouldn't it? What were you both doing when I came in?

SIR HENRY. Talking Ainswick.

LADY ANGKATELL. (*sitting in the armchair* L.C.; *with a sudden change of manner*) Ainswick!

SIR HENRY. (*patting* LADY ANGKATELL'S *shoulder*) There, there, Lucy.

(*A little disturbed, he crosses and exits* L.)

MIDGE. (*indicating the flower-pot; surprised*) Now why did you bring that in here, darling?

LADY ANGKATELL. I can't begin to think. Take it away.

(MIDGE *takes the flower-pot from* LADY ANGKATELL, *crosses, goes on to the terrace up* C. *and puts the flower-pot on the ground out of sight.*)

Thank you, darling. As I was saying, at any rate the weather's all right. That's *something*. Because if a lot of discordant personalities are boxed up indoors ... (*She looks around.*) Where are you?

(MIDGE *moves to* R. *of the armchair* L.C.)

Ah, there you are. It makes things ten times worse. Don't you agree?

MIDGE. Makes what worse?

LADY ANGKATELL. One can play games, of course—but that would be like last year when I shall never forgive myself about poor Gerda—and the worst of it is that she really is so nice. It's odd that anyone as nice as Gerda should be so devoid of any kind of intelligence. If that is what they mean by the law of compensation I don't think it's at all fair.

MIDGE. What are you talking about, Lucy?

LADY ANGKATELL. This weekend, darling. (*She takes hold of* MIDGE'S *left hand.*) It's such a relief to talk it over with you, Midge dear, you're so practical.

MIDGE. Yes, but what *are* we talking over?

LADY ANGKATELL. John, of course, is delightful, with that dynamic personality that all really successful doctors seem to have. But as for Gerda, ah well, we must all be very, very kind.

MIDGE. (*crossing to the fireplace*) Come now, Gerda Cristow isn't as bad as all that.

LADY ANGKATELL. Darling. Those eyes. Like a puzzled cow. And she never seems to understand a word one says to her.

MIDGE. I don't suppose she understands a word *you* say—and I don't know that I blame her. Your mind goes so fast, Lucy, that to keep pace with it, your conversation has to take the most astonishing leaps—with all the connecting links left out. (*She sits on the pouffe.*)

LADY ANGKATELL. Like monkeys. Fortunately Henrietta is here. She was wonderful last Spring when we played limericks or anagrams—one of those things—we had all finished when we suddenly discovered that poor Gerda hadn't even started. She didn't even know what the game *was*. It was dreadful, wasn't it, Midge?

MIDGE. Why anyone ever comes to stay with the Angkatells, I don't know. What with the brainwork and the round games and your peculiar style of conversation, Lucy.

LADY ANGKATELL. I suppose we must be rather trying. (*She rises, moves to the coffee table and picks up the tobacco jar.*) The poor dear looked so bewildered; and John looked so impatient. (*She crosses to the fireplace.*) It was then that I was grateful to Henrietta. (*She puts the jar on the mantelpiece, turns and moves* C.) She turned to Gerda and asked for the pattern of the knitted pullover she was wearing—a dreadful affair in pea green —with little bobbles and pom-poms and things—oh, sordid—but Gerda brightened up at once and looked so pleased. The worst of it is Henrietta had to buy some wool and knit one.

MIDGE. And was it very terrible?

LADY ANGKATELL. Oh, it was ghastly. No—on Henrietta it looked quite charming—which is what I mean when I say that the world is so very very sad. One simply doesn't know *why* . . .

MIDGE. Woah! Don't start rambling again, darling. Let's stick to the weekend.

(LADY ANGKATELL *sits on the sofa.*)

I don't see where the worry is. If you manage to keep off round games, and try to be coherent when you're talking to Gerda, and put Henrietta on duty to tide over the awkward moments, where's the difficulty?

LADY ANGKATELL. It would all be perfectly all right if only Edward weren't coming.

MIDGE. (*reacting at the name*) Edward? (*She rises and turns to the fireplace.*) Yes, of course. What on earth made you ask Edward for the weekend, Lucy?

LADY ANGKATELL. I didn't ask him. He wired to know if we could have him. You know how sensitive Edward is. If I'd wired back "No", he would never have asked himself again. Edward's like that.

MIDGE. Yes.

LADY ANGKATELL. Dear Edward. If only Henrietta would make up her mind to marry him.

(MIDGE *turns and faces* LADY ANGKATELL.)

She really is quite fond of him. If only they could have been alone this weekend without the Cristows. As it is, John has the most unfortunate effect on Edward. John becomes so much *more* so, and Edward so much *less* so. If you know what I mean.

(MIDGE *nods.*)

But I do feel that it's all going to be terribly difficult. (*She picks up the "Daily Graphic."*)

(GUDGEON, *the butler, enters* L. *He is in all respects the perfect butler.*)

GUDGEON. (*announcing*) Mr. Edward.

(EDWARD ANGKATELL *enters* L. *He is a tall, slightly stooping man, between thirty-five and forty-five, with a pleasant smile and a diffident manner. He is a bookish man and wears well-cut but rather shabby tweeds.* GUDGEON *exits* L.)

LADY ANGKATELL. (*rising and crossing to* EDWARD) Edward. (*She kisses him.*) We were just saying how nice it was of you to come.

EDWARD. Lucy, Lucy. How nice of you to *let* me come. (*He turns to* MIDGE. *Pleased and surprised.*) Why—it's little Midge. (*He talks throughout to* MIDGE *with indulgent affection as to a child.*) You look very grown up.

MIDGE. (*with slight acidity*) I've been grown up for quite a few years now.

EDWARD. I suppose you have. I haven't noticed it.

MIDGE. I know.

EDWARD. At Ainswick, you see, time stands still.

(LADY ANGKATELL *turns with a brusque movement, puts the newspaper on the coffee table, then moves to the drinks table, picks up the book from it and puts it in the bookshelves over the drinks table.*)

I always remember you as you used to be in the holidays when Uncle Hugh was alive. (*He turns to* LADY ANGKATELL.) I wish you'd come more often to Ainswick, Lucy. It's looking so beautiful just now.

LADY ANGKATELL. Is it, darling?

(GUDGEON *enters* L.)

GUDGEON. Excuse me, m'lady, but Mrs. Medway would like to see you a moment. It's about the savoury for dinner.

LADY ANGKATELL. Chicken livers. (*She crosses to* R. *of* GUDGEON.) Butchers have no conscience about chicken livers. Don't tell me they haven't arrived.

GUDGEON. They have arrived, m'lady, but Mrs. Medway is a little dubious . . .

(LADY ANGKATELL *crosses and exits* L. GUDGEON *follows her off, closing the door behind him.*)

EDWARD. (*taking his cigarette case from his pocket*) I some-times wonder whether Lucy minds very much about Ainswick.

MIDGE. In what way?

EDWARD. Well, it was her home. (*He takes a cigarette from his case.*)

MIDGE. May I?

EDWARD. (*offering the case to her*) Yes, of course.

(MIDGE *takes a cigarette.*)

If she'd been born a boy it would have gone to her in-stead of to me. I wonder if she resents it? (*He replaces the case in his pocket and takes out his lighter.*)

MIDGE. Not in the sense you mean. After all, you're an Angkatell and that's all that matters. The Angkatells stick together. They even marry their cousins.

EDWARD. Yes, but she does care very much about Ainswick.

MIDGE. Oh yes. Lucy cares more about Ainswick than any-thing in the world. (*She looks up at the picture over the mantelpiece.*) That picture up there is the dominating note of this house. (*She turns to* EDWARD.) But if you think Lucy resents *you*, you're wrong, Edward.

EDWARD. (*lighting* MIDGE's *cigarette*) I never quite understand Lucy. (*He turns, moves to* L. *of the sofa and lights his own cigarette.*) She's got the most extraordinary charm.

MIDGE. Lucy is the most adorable creature I know—and the most maddening.

(HENRIETTA *enters* L. *and closes the door behind her. She has tidied herself.*)

HENRIETTA. Hullo, Edward.

EDWARD. Henrietta, lovely to see you.

HENRIETTA. (*crossing to* L. *of* EDWARD) How's Ainswick?

EDWARD. It's looking beautiful just now.

HENRIETTA. (*turning to* MIDGE). Hullo, Midge darling. How are you?

EDWARD. (*offering* HENRIETTA *a cigarette*) You ought to come, Henrietta.

HENRIETTA. (*taking a cigarette*) Yes, I know I ought—what fun we all had there as children.

(LADY ANGKATELL *enters* L. *She carries a large lobster on a short length of string.*)

LADY ANGKATELL. (*crossing to* R. *of the coffee table*) Tradespeople are just like gardeners. They take advantage of your not knowing. Don't you agree, Edward? When you want them to mass in big clumps—they start fiddling about with . . . (*She suddenly becomes conscious of the lobster.*) Now what is that?

EDWARD. It looks to me like a lobster.

LADY ANGKATELL. It is a lobster. Where did I get it? How did I come by it?

HENRIETTA. I should think you got it off the kitchen table.

LADY ANGKATELL. (*holding the lobster against the back of the sofa*) Oh! I remember. I thought a cushion this colour would look nice here. What do you feel about it?

HENRIETTA. No!

LADY ANGKATELL. No. Well it was just a little thought.

(GUDGEON *enters* L. *and crosses to* LADY ANGKATELL. *He carries a salver.*)

GUDGEON. (*impassively*) Excuse me, m'lady, Mrs. Medway says, may she have the lobster.

(LADY ANGKATELL *puts the lobster on the salver.*)

Thank you, m'lady.

(*He turns, crosses and exits* L. *They all laugh.*)

LADY ANGKATELL. Gudgeon is wonderful. (*She sits on the sofa.*) He always appears at the right moment.

HENRIETTA. (*aside*) Could I have a light, Midge?

EDWARD. (*moving to* LADY ANGKATELL *and offering her a cigarette*) How's the sculpture, Henrietta?

LADY ANGKATELL. You know I don't smoke, dear.

(MIDGE *picks up the table lighter from the mantelpiece.*)

HENRIETTA. Getting along. I've finished the big wooden figure for the International Group. Would you like to see it?

EDWARD. Yes.

HENRIETTA. It's concealed in what I believe the house agent who sold Henry this house calls the "breakfast nook."

(MIDGE *lights* HENRIETTA'S *cigarette then replaces the lighter on the mantelpiece.*)

LADY ANGKATELL. Thank heavens that's something I have *never* had—my breakfast in a nook.

(*They all laugh.* HENRIETTA *moves to the alcove up* L., *draws back the curtain, switches on the light, then moves up* C. EDWARD *leads* MIDGE *to the alcove and stands* R. *of her as they both look off* L.)

HENRIETTA. It's called The Worshipper.
EDWARD. (*impressed*) That's a very powerful figure. Beautiful graining. What wood is it?
HENRIETTA. Pearwood.
EDWARD. (*slowly*) It's—an uncomfortable sort of thing.
MIDGE. (*nervously*) It's horrible.
EDWARD. That heavy forward slant of the neck and shoulders —the submission. The fanaticism of the face—the eyes —she's blind? (*He turns to face* HENRIETTA.)
HENRIETTA. Yes.
EDWARD. What's she looking at—with her blind eyes?
HENRIETTA. (*turning away*) I don't know. Her God, I suppose.
LADY ANGKATELL. (*softly*) Poor Henrietta.
HENRIETTA. (*moving to* R. *of the armchair* L.C.) What did you say, Lucy?

(EDWARD *crosses to the fireplace and flicks his ash into it.*)

LADY ANGKATELL. (*rising*) Nothing. (*She moves to* R. *of the sofa and glances off* R.) Ah look, chaffinches. Sweet. One ought to look at birds through glasses, on tops of trees, oughtn't one? (*She turns.*) Are there still herons at Ainswick, Edward?
EDWARD. Ah, yes—down by the river.
LADY ANGKATELL. (*softly*) Down by the river—ah dear.

(*Her voice fades away as she exits* R.)

EDWARD. Why did she say "Poor Henrietta?"

(MIDGE *closes the alcove curtain, switches off the light, crosses above the sofa to* R. *of it, then sits on it at the right end.*)

HENRIETTA. Lucy isn't blind.
EDWARD. (*stubbing out his cigarette in the ashtray on the*

mantelpiece) Shall we go for a walk, Henrietta? (*He moves* L.C.) I'd like to stretch my legs after that drive.

HENRIETTA. I'd love to. (*She moves to the coffee table and stubs out her cigarette in the ashtray on it.*) I've been modelling most of the day. Coming, Midge?

MIDGE. No, thank you.

(EDWARD *moves slowly up* C.)

I'll stay here and help Lucy with the Cristows when they arrive.

EDWARD. (*stopping and turning; sharply*) Cristow? Is he coming?

HENRIETTA. Yes.

EDWARD. I wish I'd known.

HENRIETTA. (*belligerently*) Why?

EDWARD. (*very quietly*) I could have come—some other weekend.

(*There is a pause, then* HENRIETTA *and* EDWARD *exit up* C. *to* L. MIDGE *watches them go, her face revealing her hopeless love for* EDWARD. LADY ANGKATELL *enters* R. *and moves above the* R. *end of the sofa.*)

LADY ANGKATELL. (*whispering*) Have Henrietta and Edward gone for a walk?

MIDGE. Yes.

LADY ANGKATELL. Does Edward know about the Cristows?

MIDGE. Yes.

LADY ANGKATELL. Was it all right?

MIDGE. Not noticeably.

LADY ANGKATELL. (*moving to the french windows* R.) Oh dear. I knew this weekend was going to be awkward.

(MIDGE *rises, stubs out her cigarette in the ashtray on the coffee table, picks up her handbag and gloves and moves to* LADY ANGKATELL.)

MIDGE. Let's go round the garden, Lucy. What's on in the flower world at the moment? I'm such a hopeless cockney nowadays. Most dahlias?

LADY ANGKATELL. Yes. Handsome—in a rather dull way. And so full of earwigs. Mind you, I'm told earwigs are very good mothers, not that it makes one *like* them any better.

(LADY ANGKATELL *and* MIDGE *exit* R. DORIS, *the maid, enters* L. *and holds the door open. She looks slightly half-witted and is terrified of* GUDGEON. GUDGEON *enters* L. *and crosses to the drinks table. He carries a tray of drinks, a bowl of olives and a tea-cloth.* DORIS *closes the door, moves* L.C. *and stands gaping.*)

GUDGEON. (*putting the tray on the drinks table*) Well, fold the papers, Doris, the way I showed you. (*He starts to polish the glasses.*)

DORIS. (*moving hastily to* L. *of the coffee table*) Yes, Mr. Gudgeon. (*She picks up "The Times" and folds it.*) Her ladyship is bats, isn't she, Mr. Gudgeon?

GUDGEON. (*turning*) Certainly not. Her ladyship has a very keen intellect. She speaks five foreign languages, and has been all over the world with Sir Henry. Sir Henry was Governor of one of the principal provinces in India. He would have been the next Viceroy most probably if it hadn't been for that terrible Labour Government doing away with the Empire.

DORIS. (*putting the newspaper on the* L. *arm of the sofa*) My dad's Labour.

(*There is a pause as* GUDGEON *looks almost pityingly at* DORIS.)

(*She takes a step back. Apologetically.*) Oh, I'm sorry, Mr. Gudgeon.

GUDGEON. (*tolerantly*) You can't help your parents, Doris.

DORIS. (*humbly*) I know they're not class.

GUDGEON. (*patronizingly*) You are coming along quite nicely —(*he turns to the drinks table and continues polishing the glasses*) although it's not what any of us have been used to. Gamekeeper's daughter, or Head Groom's daughter, a young girl who knows her manners, and has been brought up right.

(DORIS *picks up the "Daily Graphic" and folds it.*)

That's what I like to train.

DORIS. (*putting all the papers together tidily on the coffee table*) Sorry, Mr. Gudgeon. (*She crosses to the writing table, picks up the ashtray from it, returns to the coffee table and empties the ashtray she is carrying into that on the coffee table.*)

GUDGEON. Ah well, it seems those days are gone for ever.

DORIS. (*replacing the ashtray on the writing table*) Miss Simmonds is always down on me, too.

GUDGEON. She's doing it for your own good, Doris. She's training you.

DORIS. (*picking up the ashtray from the coffee table, crossing to the fireplace and emptying the ashtray into the one on the mantelpiece*) Shan't get more money, shall I, when I'm trained? (*She replaces the ashtray on the coffee table.*)

GUDGEON. Not much, I'm afraid.

DORIS. (*crossing to the fireplace*) Doesn't seem worth being trained then, does it? (*She picks up the full ashtray from the mantelpiece.*)

GUDGEON. I'm afraid you may be right, my girl.

(DORIS *is about to empty the ashtray into the fire.*)

Ah!

(DORIS *turns guiltily, and puts the ashtray on the mantelpiece.*)

The trouble is there are no proper *employers* nowadays. Nobody who knows what's what. Those who have the money to employ servants don't appreciate what a good servant is.

DORIS. (*moving to the armchair* L.C.) My dad says I ought to call myself a domestic help. (*She tidies the cushion on the armchair.*)

GUDGEON. (*moving above the sofa*) That's about all you are. (*He leans over the back of the sofa and tidies the cushions.*) Let me tell you, my girl, you're very lucky to be in a household where wine glasses are used in the proper way, and where the master and mistress appreciate highly technical skill. (*He moves to the chair down* R. *and tidies the cushion.*) There aren't many employers left who'd even notice if you went the wrong way round the table.

DORIS. (*moving to the fireplace*) I still think her ladyship does funny things. (*She picks up the full ashtray from the mantelpiece.*) Picking up that lobster now.

GUDGEON. (*crossing below the sofa to* R. *of the armchair* L.C.) Her ladyship is somewhat forgetful, not to say absent-minded, but in this house I see to it that everything possible is done to spare her ladyship trouble and annoyance.

(*The sound of a motor-car horn is heard off.*)

(*He crosses to the drinks table, picks up the tea-cloth, then crosses to* L.C. *and picks up* MIDGE'S *suitcase.*) That will be Dr. and Mrs. Cristow. Go upstairs and be ready to help Simmonds with the unpacking.

DORIS. (*moving to the door* L. *and opening it*) Yes, Mr. Gudgeon. (*She starts to exit.*)

GUDGEON. (*reprovingly*) Ah-ah!

DORIS. (*with a step back*) Oh! (*She holds the door open.*)

GUDGEON. (*crossing to the door* L.) Thank you.

(*A clock strikes seven. He exits* L. DORIS *follows him off, leaving the door open.*)

(*After the fourth stroke. Off* L.) Good evening, sir.

JOHN. (*off* L.) Good evening, Gudgeon. How are you?

GUDGEON. (*off* L.) Good evening, madam. Very well, thank you, sir.

GERDA. (*off* L.) Good evening, Gudgeon.

(GUDGEON *enters* L. *and ushers in* JOHN *and* GERDA CRISTOW. JOHN *is a good-looking man of thirty-eight with a dynamic personality, but is somewhat brusque in manner.* GERDA *is timid and rather stupid. She carries an arty leather handbag.*)

GUDGEON. (*as he enters*) Will you come through, madam.

GERDA. (*crossing to* L.C.) Very warm, still.

GUDGEON. Still very warm, madam. I hope you had a pleasant drive down.

(JOHN *crosses to* C.)

GERDA. Yes, thank you.

GUDGEON. (*closing the door*) I think her ladyship is in the garden, sir. (*He crosses to* R.) I'll inform her that you've arrived.

JOHN. Thank you, Gudgeon.

(GUDGEON *exits* R.)

(*He goes out on to the terrace up* C. *and looks off* L.) Mm, wonderful to get out of town into this.

GERDA. (*easing to* R. *of the armchair* L.C.; *flatly*) Yes, it's very nice.

JOHN. God, I hate being penned up in London. Sitting in that blasted consulting room, listening to whining women. How I hate sick people!

GERDA. Oh, John, you don't mean that.

JOHN. I loathe illness.

GERDA. If you hated sick people, you wouldn't be a doctor, would you, dear?

JOHN. (*moving above the sofa*) A man doesn't become a doctor because he has a partiality for sick people. It's the disease that's interesting, not the patient. (*He crosses to* R., *and studies the pieces of sculpture on the pedestal.*) You have odd ideas, Gerda.

GERDA. But you do like curing people.

JOHN. (*turning*) I don't cure them. (*He moves and sits on the sofa at the right end.*) Just hand out faith, hope and probably a laxative. Oh, good Lord, I'm tired.

GERDA. (*moving below the sofa*) John, you work too hard. You're so unselfish. (*She sits on the sofa at the left end of it.*) I'm always telling the children how a doctor's life is almost a dedication. I'm so proud of the way you give all your time and all your energy and never spare yourself.

JOHN. Oh, for heaven's sake, Gerda. You don't know in the least what you're talking about. Don't you realize I enjoy my profession? It's damned interesting and I make a lot of money.

GERDA. It's not the money you do it for, dear. Look how interested you are in your hospital work. It's to relieve pain and suffering.

JOHN. Pain is a biological necessity and suffering will always be with us. It's the techniques of medicine that interest me.

GERDA. And—people suffering.

JOHN. (*rising and moving above the sofa*) Oh, for God's sake . . . (*He breaks off, suddenly ashamed.*) I'm sorry, Gerda. I didn't mean to shout at you. (*He takes a cigarette case from his pocket.*) I'm afraid I've been terribly nervy and bad-tempered lately. I'm—I'm sorry.

GERDA. It's quite all right, dear. *I* understand.

(*There is a pause as* JOHN *moves below the armchair* L.C. *and takes a cigarette out of his case.*)

JOHN. You know, Gerda, if you weren't so patient, so long-suffering, it would be better. Why don't you turn on me sometimes, swear at me, give as good as you get? Oh, don't look so shocked. It would be better if you did. No man likes being drowned in treacle. (*He shuts his cigarette case with a snap and replaces it in his pocket.*)

GERDA. You're tired, John.

JOHN. (*sitting in the armchair* L.C.; *sombrely*) Yes, I'm tired. (*He leans back and closes his eyes.*)

GERDA. You need a holiday.

JOHN. (*dreamily*) I'd like to go to the South of France—the Mediterranean—the sun, the mimosa in flower . . .

GERDA. (*rising and crossing to* R. *of* JOHN) Why shouldn't we go, then? (*Doubtfully.*) Oh, I don't quite know how we should manage about the children; of course, Terence is at school all day, but he's so rude to Mademoiselle. She really has very little authority even over Zena. No, I don't think I should be very happy. Of course, they could go to Elsie at Bexhill. Or perhaps Mary Foley would take them . . .

JOHN. (*opening his eyes; vaguely*) 'M, what were you saying?

GERDA. The children.

JOHN. What about them?

GERDA. I was wondering how we could manage about them if we went to the South of France.

JOHN. (*taking his lighter from his pocket*) Why should we go to the South of France, what are you talking about? (*He lights his cigarette.*)

GERDA. Because you said—you—would—like to.

JOHN. Oh that! I was day-dreaming.

GERDA. (*crossing above the armchair* L.C. *to* L. *of it*) I don't see why we couldn't manage it—only it's a little worrying if one feels that the person left in charge isn't really reliable, and I do sometimes feel . . .

JOHN. (*rising and crossing below the sofa to* R.) You never stop worrying about something or other. For heaven's sake let's relax and enjoy this weekend. At least you have a respite from domestic bothers.

GERDA. Yes, I know.

JOHN. (*moving above the sofa*) Wonderful people—the Angkatells. I always find them an absolute tonic.

GERDA. Yes.

JOHN. (*moving on the terrace up* C.) I wonder where they all are? (*He glances off* L.)

GERDA. (*sitting in the armchair* L.C.) Will Henrietta be here?

JOHN. (*turning*) Yes, she's here.

GERDA. Oh, I'm so glad. I do like Henrietta.

JOHN. (*rather shortly*) Henrietta's all right.

GERDA. I wonder if she's finished that statuette she was doing of me?

JOHN. (*moving above the* L. *end of the sofa; sharply*) I don't know why she asked you to sit for her. Most extraordinary.

(GERDA *flinches at his tone and look.*)

(*He crosses to* R.) I always think it's rather a good thing if people are around to meet their guests.

(*He exits* R. GERDA *rises, crosses below the sofa to* R., *looks off, turns, looks* L., *hesitates, fidgets with her handbag, then gives a nervous cough and crosses to* L.C.)

EDWARD. (*off up* C.) And this winter I'm going to cut down that avenue of trees so that we can have a better view of the lake.

(HENRIETTA *and* EDWARD *enter up* C. *from* L. GERDA *turns.* EDWARD *eases to* L. *of the sofa.*)

HENRIETTA. (*as she enters*) I think it's a very good idea, Edward. Hullo, Gerda, how are you? You know Edward Angkatell, don't you? (*She eases above the* R. *end of the sofa.*)

EDWARD. How d'you do, Mrs. Cristow?

GERDA. How do you do? (*She drops one glove and picks it up.*)

(EDWARD *bends to pick up the glove but* GERDA *forestalls him.*)

HENRIETTA. Where's John?

(EDWARD *turns and looks at* HENRIETTA.)

GERDA. He just went out into the garden to see if he could find Lady Angkatell.

HENRIETTA. (*moving to the french window* R. *and glancing off*) It's an impossible garden to find anyone in, all woods and shrubs.

GERDA. But soon there'll be such lovely autumn tints.

HENRIETTA. (*turning*) Yes. (*She turns and gazes out of the window.*)

EDWARD. (*crossing to the door* L.) You'll forgive me if I go and change.

(*He exits* L. GERDA *starts to follow him but stops as* HENRIETTA *speaks.*)

HENRIETTA. Autumn takes one back—one keeps saying, "Don't you remember?"

(GERDA, *strung up and obviously miserable, moves to the armchair* L.C.)

(*She turns suddenly, looks at* GERDA *and her face softens.*) Shall we go and look for the others, too?

GERDA. (*about to sit in the armchair*) No, please—I mean— (*she rises*) yes, that would be very nice.

HENRIETTA. (*moving below the sofa; vigorously*) Gerda! Why do you come down here when you hate it so much?

GERDA. But I don't.

HENRIETTA. (*kneeling with one knee on the sofa*) Yes you do.

GERDA. I don't really. It's delightful to get down here into the country and Lady Angkatell is always so kind.

HENRIETTA. Lucy? (*She sits on the sofa at the right end of it.*) Lucy's not a bit kind. She has good manners and she knows how to be gracious. But I always think she's rather a cruel person, perhaps because she isn't quite human. She doesn't know what it is to feel and think like ordinary people. And you *are* hating it here, Gerda, you know you are.

GERDA. (*easing to* L. *of the sofa*) Well, you see, John likes it.

HENRIETTA. Oh, John likes it all right. But you could let him come by himself.

GERDA. He wouldn't do that. He wouldn't enjoy himself here without me. He is so unselfish. He thinks it does me good to get down into the country. (*She moves below the* L. *end of the sofa.*) But I'm glad you're here though—it makes it so much better.

HENRIETTA. Does it? I'm glad.

GERDA. (*sitting on the sofa at the left end of it; in a burst of confidence*) You see, I don't really like being away from home. There is so much to do before I leave, and John is so impatient. Even now I'm not sure I turned the bathroom taps off properly, and there was a note I meant to leave for the laundry. And you know, Henrietta, I don't really trust the children's French governess—when I'm not there they never do anything she tells them. Oh well, it's only for two days.

HENRIETTA. Two days of hell—cheerfully endured for John's sake.

GERDA. You must think I'm very ungrateful—when everybody is so kind. My breakfast brought up to my room and the housemaids so beautifully trained—but I do sometimes feel . . .

HENRIETTA. I know. They snatch away one's clothes and put them where you can't find them, and always lay out the dress and shoes you don't want to wear. One has to be strong-minded.

GERDA. Oh, I'm afraid I'm never strong-minded.

HENRIETTA. How's the knitting?

GERDA. I've taken up leathercraft. (*She holds up her handbag.*) I made this handbag.

HENRIETTA. Did you? (*She rises, crosses to the alcove and opens the curtains.*) That reminds me, I've something for you.

(*She switches on the light and exits. She re-enters immediately carrying a small plaster statuette. She switches off the alcove light, closes the curtain and moves to the armchair* L.C.)

GERDA. (*rising and crossing to* HENRIETTA) Henrietta! The statuette you were doing of me?

(HENRIETTA *gives* GERDA *the statuette.*)

Oh, it's lovely.

HENRIETTA. I'm glad you like it.

GERDA. (*moving below the* L. *end of the sofa*) I do, I like it very much.

JOHN. (*off* R.) I say, Sir Henry, your gardener has really made a wonderful job of those roses.

(LADY ANGKATELL, JOHN, MIDGE *and* SIR HENRY *enter* R.)

SIR HENRY. (*as he enters*) The soil here is pretty good for roses.

JOHN. (*crossing above the sofa to* L. *of it*) Hello, Henrietta.

HENRIETTA. Hello, John.

LADY ANGKATELL. (*moving below the sofa*) How very nice to see you, Gerda.

SIR HENRY. (*moving above the sofa*) How are you, Mrs. Cristow?

LADY ANGKATELL (*to* GERDA) You haven't been here for so long. You know my cousin, Midge Harvey? (*She sits on the sofa.*)

MIDGE. (*moving to the writing table*) Yes, we met last year. (*She puts her bag on the writing table.*)

(HENRIETTA *moves to the fireplace, takes a cigarette from the box on the mantelpiece and lights it with the table lighter.*)

GERDA. (*turning and moving to* R. *of* JOHN) John, look what Henrietta's just given me. (*She hands the statuette to him.*)

JOHN. (*to* HENRIETTA) Why—what on earth made you do this?

GERDA. Oh, John, it's very pretty.

JOHN. (*crossing down* L., *turning and facing* HENRIETTA) Really, Henrietta.

SIR HENRY. (*tactfully interposing*) Mrs. Cristow, I must tell you about our latest excitement. You know the cottage at the end of this lane? It's been taken by a well-known film star, and all the locals are simply goggling.

GERDA. Oh yes, of course—they will be.

MIDGE. Is she very glamorous?

SIR HENRY. Well, I haven't seen her yet, though I believe she's in residence. What's her name now?

MIDGE. Hedy Lamarr?

SIR HENRY. No. Who's that girl with her hair over her eyes?

MIDGE. Veronica Lake.

SIR HENRY. No.

MIDGE. Lauren Bacall.

SIR HENRY. No.

LADY ANGKATELL. Nazimova—no. We'd better ask Gudgeon. He'll know.

SIR HENRY. We saw her in that film—you remember, that tough chap—plays gangsters, and they flew to the Pacific and then flew back again, and there was a particularly horrible child . . .

MIDGE. *San Francisco Story?*

SIR HENRY. Yes.

MIDGE. Veronica Craye.

(JOHN *drops the statuette.* GERDA *moves quickly down* L. *with a cry and picks up the statuette. It is not broken.*)

HENRIETTA. John! (*She watches him with sharpened interest.*)

GERDA ⎫   ⎧ Oh, John, my statuette.
JOHN ⎬ (*together*).   ⎨ I'm sorry.
SIR HENRY ⎭   ⎩ That's it. Blonde with a husky voice.

LADY ANGKATELL. (*rising and crossing to* R. *of* GERDA) Would you like to see your room, Gerda?

GERDA. Oh—yes, perhaps I'd better go and unpack.

LADY ANGKATELL. (*crossing below* GERDA *to the door* L.) Simmonds will have done that. But if you'd like to come up . . . ?

MIDGE. (*crossing to* L.) I'll come with you. Where am I, Lucy? In the Blue Room?

LADY ANGKATELL. Yes, and I've put Edward in the Hermit, and I've put the rest . . .

(*Her voice dies away as she exits* L. GERDA *and* MIDGE *follow her off.* JOHN *stands in a daze.*)

SIR HENRY. Where is Edward? Has he put his car away, I wonder? There's room in the end garage.

(*He exits up* C. *to* L. HENRIETTA *moves to* JOHN *and gives him her cigarette. Now that they are alone her voice holds a new intimacy.*)

HENRIETTA. Is there anything the matter, darling?

JOHN. (*crossing to the sofa*) M'm? I was—thinking—remembering. I'm sorry. (*He sits on the sofa at the left end, and faces* R.)

HENRIETTA. (*easing to the fireplace*) There's an atmosphere of remembering about this place. (*She turns and looks at the picture over the mantelpiece.*) I've been remembering, too.

JOHN. Have you? (*Disinterested.*) Remembering what?

HENRIETTA. (*turning; bitterly*) The time when I was a long-legged lanky girl with untidy hair—a happy girl with no idea of the things that life could do to her. (*She turns to face the fire*) Going back . . .

JOHN. (*dreamily*) Why should one want to go back—suddenly? Why do things you haven't thought of for years suddenly spring into your mind?

HENRIETTA. (*turning*) What things, John?

JOHN. (*dreamily*) Blue sea—the smell of mimosa . . .

HENRIETTA. When?

JOHN. Ten years ago.

HENRIETTA. (*crossing to* L. *of the sofa*) And you'd like—to go back?

JOHN. I don't know—I'm so tired.

(HENRIETTA, *from behind, lays a hand on* JOHN's *shoulder*.)

    (*He holds her hand but still stares dreamily* R.) What would I do without you?

HENRIETTA. Get along quite well, I expect.

JOHN. Why should things come back into your mind—things that are over and done with?

HENRIETTA. (*crossing above the sofa to* R. *of it*) Perhaps because they are *not* really over and done with.

JOHN. Not aften ten years? Heaven knows how long since I thought about it. But lately—even when I'm walking round the wards, it comes into my mind and it's as vivid as a picture. (*He pauses. With sudden energy.*) And now, on top of it all, she's here, just a few yards down the lane.

HENRIETTA. (*moving below the* R. *end of the sofa*) Veronica Craye, you mean?

JOHN. Yes. I was engaged to her once—ten years ago.

HENRIETTA. (*sitting on the sofa at the right end of it*) I—see.

JOHN. Crazy young fool! I was mad about her. She was just starting in pictures then. I'd qualified about a year before. I'd had a wonderful chance—to work under Radley. D. H. Radley, you know, *the* authority on cortex of degeneration.

HENRIETTA. What happened?

JOHN. What I might have guessed would happen. Veronica got her chance to go to Hollywood. Well, naturally, she took it. But she assumed, without making any bones about it, that I'd give up everything and go with her. (*He laughs.*) No idea how important my profession was to me. I can hear her now. "Oh, there's absolutely no need for you to go on doctoring—*I* shall be making heaps of money." (*He gives his cigarette to* HENRIETTA.) I tried to explain it all to her. Radley—what a wonderful opportunity it was to work under him. Do you know what she said? "What, that comic little old man?" I told her that that comic little old man had done some of the most remarkable work of our generation—that his experiments might revolutionize the treatment of Rigg's Disease. But of course that was a waste of time. She'd never even heard of Rigg's Disease.

HENRIETTA. Very few people have. I hadn't till you told me about it and I read it up.

(JOHN *rises, moves up* C., *goes on to the terrace and stands facing* L.)

JOHN. She said who cared about a lot of obscure diseases anyway. California was a wonderful climate—it would be fun for me to see the world. She'd hate to go there without me. Miss Craye was the complete egoist—never thought of anyone but herself.

HENRIETTA. You're rather by way of being an egoist too, John.

JOHN. (*turning to face* HENRIETTA) I saw her point of view. Why couldn't she see mine?

HENRIETTA. What did you suggest?

JOHN. (*moving to the sofa and leaning over the back of it*) I told her I loved her. I begged her to turn down the Hollywood offer and marry me there and then.

HENRIETTA. And what did she say to that?

JOHN. (*bitterly*) She was just—amused.

HENRIETTA. And so?

JOHN. (*moving down* R.) Well, there was only one thing to be done—break it off. I did. It wasn't easy. All that was when we were in the South of France. (*He crosses to the coffee table, picks up a magazine, then crosses and stands below the armchair* L.C.) I broke with Veronica, and came back to London to work under Radley. (*During the following speeches he occasionally glances idly at the magazine.*)

HENRIETTA. And then you married Gerda?

JOHN. The following year. Yes.

HENRIETTA. Why?

JOHN. Why?

HENRIETTA. Yes. Was it because you wanted someone as different as possible from Veronica Craye?

JOHN. Yes, I suppose that was it. (*He sits in the armchair* L.C.) I didn't want a raving beauty as a wife. I didn't want a damned egoist out to grab everything she could get. I wanted safety and peace and devotion, and all the quiet enduring things of life. I wanted someone who'd take her ideas from *me*.

HENRIETTA. Well, you certainly got what you wanted. None could be more devoted to you than Gerda.

JOHN. That's the irony of it. I picked Gerda for just the qualities she has, and now half the time I snap her head off because of them. How was I to know how irritating devotion can be?

HENRIETTA. (*rising and stubbing out her cigarette in the ashtray on the coffee table*) And what about Gerda? Is she satisfied?

JOHN. Oh, Gerda's all right. She's quite happy.

HENRIETTA. Is she?

JOHN. Oh, yes. She spends her life fussing about the house and the children. That's all she thinks about. She's the most incompetent housekeeper and the most injudicious mother that you can imagine. Still, it keeps her occupied.

HENRIETTA. (*crossing to* R. *of* JOHN) How horribly cruel you are, John.

JOHN. (*surprised*) Me?

HENRIETTA. Do you never see or feel anything except from your own point of view? Why do you bring Gerda down here for weekends when you know it's misery for her?

JOHN. Nonsense! Does her a world of good to get away. It makes a break for her.

HENRIETTA. Sometimes, John, I really hate you.

JOHN. (*startled*) Henrietta. (*He rises.*) Darling—don't say that. You know it's only you who makes life possible for me.

HENRIETTA. I wonder. (*She puts up a hand to touch him lovingly, then checks herself.*)

(JOHN *kisses her, then crosses and puts the magazine on the coffee table.*)

JOHN. Who's the Edward Angkatell?

HENRIETTA. A second cousin of mine—and of Henry's.

JOHN. Have I met him?

HENRIETTA. Twice.

JOHN. I don't remember. (*He perches himself on the left arm of the sofa.*) Is he in love with you, Henrietta?

HENRIETTA. Yes.

JOHN. Well, you watch your step. You're mine, you know.

(HENRIETTA *looks at him in silence.*)

And look here, what do you mean by doing that absurd statuette of Gerda? Hardly up to your standard, is it?

HENRIETTA. It's technically quite good craftsmanship—a straightforward portrait statuette. It pleased Gerda.

JOHN. Oh, Gerda!

HENRIETTA. It was made to please her.

JOHN. Gerda doesn't know the difference between a work of art and a coloured photograph. What about your pear-wood figure for the International Group? Have you finished that?

HENRIETTA. Yes.

JOHN. Let's have a look at it.

(HENRIETTA *moves unwillingly to the alcove, opens the curtain, switches on the light, then stands* L. *of the arch and watches* JOHN's *face.* JOHN *rises, crosses to the alcove and stands in the arch looking off* L.)

I say, that's rather good. Why, what on earth . . . ? (*Angrily.*) So *that's* why you wanted Gerda to sit for you. How dare you!

HENRIETTA. (*thoughtfully*) I wondered if you'd see it.

JOHN. See it? Of course I see it.

HENRIETTA. The face isn't Gerda's.

JOHN. No, it's the neck—the shoulders—the whole attitude.

(*The daylight starts to fade and continues to do so steadily until the end of the Act.*)

HENRIETTA. Yes, that's what I wanted.

JOHN. *How could you do a thing like that?* It's indefensible.

HENRIETTA. You don't understand, John. You don't know what it is to want something—to look at it day after day—that line of neck—the muscle—the angle of the head—that heaviness under the jaw. I've been looking at them, wanting them, every time I saw Gerda. In the end—I just had to have them.

JOHN. Utterly unscrupulous.

HENRIETTA. Yes—I suppose you could call it that.

JOHN. (*uneasily*) That's a terrifying thing you've made, Henrietta. What's she looking at—who is it there, in front of her?

HENRIETTA. I don't know, John. I think—it might be *you.*

(EDWARD *enters* L. *He now wears dinner clothes.*)

You remember Edward—John.

JOHN. (*tersely*) Of course.

EDWARD. (*moving below the armchair* L.C.) Looking at Henrietta's latest masterpiece?

JOHN. (*without looking at* EDWARD) Yes. (*He crosses to the fireplace.*) Yes, I was.

EDWARD. What do you think of it?

JOHN. (*with his back to* EDWARD) I'm not really qualified to judge. (*He takes a cigarette from his case.*)

EDWARD. Powerful!

JOHN. 'M?

EDWARD. I said it's powerful.

JOHN. Yes.

HENRIETTA. (*switching off the light and closing the alcove curtain*) I must go and change.

EDWARD. Still lots of time. (*He crosses to the drinks table*) Can I get you a drink, Cristow?

JOHN. No, thank you. (*He taps his cigarette on his case.*)

EDWARD. (*moving to the french window* R.) Quite a mild evening.

(*He glances at* HENRIETTA *and* JOHN, *then exits* R.)

HENRIETTA. (*moving* C.) You were very rude, John.

JOHN. (*turning*) I've no time for that sort of person.

HENRIETTA. Edward's a dear.

JOHN. Possibly. (*He lights his cigarette.*) I don't like him. I think he is quite ineffectual.

HENRIETTA. You know, sometimes, John, I'm afraid for you.

JOHN. Afraid for me? What do you mean?

HENRIETTA. It's dangerous to be as oblivious as you are.

JOHN. Oblivious?

HENRIETTA. You never see or know anything that people are feeling about you.

JOHN. I should have said the opposite.

HENRIETTA. You see what you're looking *at*—yes. You're like a searchlight. A powerful beam turned on to the one spot where your interest is, but behind it, and each side of it, darkness.

JOHN. Henrietta, darling, what is all this?

HENRIETTA. I tell you, it's *dangerous*. You assume everybody likes you—(*she moves in to* R. *of* JOHN) Lucy and Gerda, Henry, Midge and Edward.

(JOHN *puts his cigarette in the ashtray on the mantelpiece.*)

Do you know at all what they feel about you?

JOHN. (*smiling*) And Henrietta? What does she feel? At least—(*he catches her hand and draws her to him*) I'm sure of you.

HENRIETTA. You can be sure of no-one in this world, John.

(JOHN *kisses her. As she gives to him helplessly, he releases her, smiles, turns, picks up his cigarette and moves to the door* L. EDWARD. *enters* R. JOHN *gives* EDWARD *a cynical look then exits* L.)

(*She turns to* EDWARD.) Get me a drink, would you, Edward, before I go. (*She turns, looks in the mirror on the mantelpiece and touches up her lipstick with her handkerchief.*)

EDWARD. (*moving to the drinks table*) Sherry?

HENRIETTA. Please.

EDWARD. (*pouring out two sherries*) I wish you'd come to Ainswick more often, Henrietta. It's a long time now.

HENRIETTA. I know. One gets tangled up in things.

EDWARD. Is that the real reason?

HENRIETTA. Not quite.

EDWARD. You can tell me, Henrietta.

HENRIETTA. (*turning; feelingly*) You are a dear, Edward. I'm very fond of you.

EDWARD. (*crossing to* R. *of* HENRIETTA *with the drinks*) Why don't you come to Ainswick? (*He hands a drink to her.*)

HENRIETTA. Because—one can't go back.

EDWARD. You used to be happy there, in the old days.

HENRIETTA. Yes, happy in the loveliest way of all—when one doesn't know one is happy.

EDWARD. (*raising his glass*) To Ainswick.

HENRIETTA. (*raising her glass*) Ainswick.

(*They both laugh, then sip their drinks.*)

Is it the same, Edward? Or has it changed? Things do change.

EDWARD. I don't change.

HENRIETTA. No, darling Edward. You're always the same.

EDWARD. Same old stick-in-the-mud.

HENRIETTA. (*crossing below* EDWARD *to the sofa*) Don't say that. (*She sits on the sofa at the left end.*)

EDWARD. It's true. I've never been very good at—doing things.

HENRIETTA. I think perhaps you're wise not to do things.

EDWARD. That's an odd thing for you to say, Henrietta. You who've been so successful.

HENRIETTA. Sculpture isn't a thing you set out to do and succeed in. It's something that gets *at* you—and haunts you—so that, in the end, you just have to make terms with it. And then—for a while—you get some peace.

EDWARD. Do you want to be peaceful, Henrietta?

HENRIETTA. Sometimes I think I want to be peaceful more than anything in the world.

EDWARD. (*crossing to* L. *of the sofa*) You could be peaceful at Ainswick. (*He puts his hand on* HENRIETTA'S *shoulder.*) I think you could be happy there. Even—even if you had to put up with me. (*He crosses and sits on the sofa at the right end of it.*) What about it, Henrietta? Won't you come to Ainswick and make it your home? It's always been there, you know, waiting for you.

HENRIETTA. Edward, I wish I weren't so very fond of you. It makes it so much more difficult to go on saying no.

EDWARD. It is no, then?

HENRIETTA. (*putting her glass on the coffee table*) I'm sorry.

EDWARD. You've said no before, but this time—(*he rises*) well, I thought it might be different. When we walked in the woods your face was so young and happy, (*he moves to the window* R.) almost as it used to be. Talking about Ainswick, thinking about Ainswick. Don't you see what that means, Henrietta?

HENRIETTA. Edward, we've been living this afternoon in the past.

EDWARD. (*moving to* R. *of the sofa*) The past is sometimes a very good place to live.

HENRIETTA. One can't go back. That's the one thing you can't do—go back.

(*There is a pause.* EDWARD *moves above the sofa to* L. *of it and looks towards the door* L.)

EDWARD. (*quietly*) What you really mean is that you won't marry me because of John Cristow. (*He pauses, then turns.*) That's it, isn't it? If there were no John Cristow in the world you would marry me.

HENRIETTA. I can't imagine a world in which there was no John Cristow.

(SIR HENRY *enters* L. *He now wears dinner clothes.* HENRI-
    ETTA *rises.*)

SIR HENRY. (*switching on the wall-bracket and mantelpiece
    lights by the switch below the fireplace*) Hurry up,
    Henrietta. It's nearly dinner time.

HENRIETTA. (*crossing to the door* L.) I'll be quick as a flash.

(*She exits hurriedly* L. EDWARD *sits on the sofa at the left
    end of it.*)

SIR HENRY. (*crossing to the drinks table*) Have you got a
    drink, Edward? (*He switches on the table-lamp on the
    drinks table.*)

EDWARD. Thank you, yes.

SIR HENRY. (*mixing cocktails*) Haven't seen much of you
    since Lucy and I settled down at The Hollow.

EDWARD. No. How does it affect you both—laying aside the
    cares of state?

SIR HENRY. I sometimes think, Edward, that you've been the
    wisest of the family.

EDWARD. That's an original point of view. I always regard
    myself as a walking example of how to fail in life.

SIR HENRY. Oh no, it's a question of the right values. To look
    after one's estate and to read and care for one's books—

(MIDGE *enters* L. *She wears an evening frock.* EDWARD *rises.*)

    —not to compete in the struggle for material achieve-
    ment . . . (*He turns to* MIDGE.) Hullo, there—that's a
    pretty frock.

MIDGE. (*moving* L.C. *and turning completely around, show-
    ing off her frock*) One of my perks from the shop.

EDWARD. You can't really like working in a shop, Midge.

MIDGE. (*crossing to the drinks table*) Who said I like it?
    (*She picks up the bowl of olives.*)

EDWARD. (*resuming his seat on the sofa*) Then why do it?

MIDGE. What do you suggest I should live on? Beautiful
    thoughts?

EDWARD. (*shocked*) But, my dear girl, if I'd had any idea you
    were hard up . . .

SIR HENRY. Save your breath, Edward. She's obstinate. Re-
    fused an allowance and won't come and live with us,
    though we've begged her to. I can't think of anything
    nicer than having young Midge about the house.

EDWARD. Why don't you, Midge?

MIDGE. (*moving* R. *of the sofa then below it*) I have ideas. (*She offers the olives to* EDWARD.) Poor, proud and prejudiced—

(EDWARD *shakes his head, refusing the olives.*)

—that's me.

(LADY ANGKATELL *enters* L. *She wears an evening gown.* EDWARD *rises.*)

They're badgering me, Lucy.

LADY ANGKATELL. (*crossing to the armchair* L.C.) Are they, darling? (*She sits.*)

EDWARD. I don't like the idea of her working in that dress shop.

MIDGE. (*crossing to* LADY ANGKATELL) Well, find me a better job. (*She offers the olives to her.*)

(LADY ANGKATELL *takes an olive.* MIDGE *moves to the fireplace and puts the dish on the mantelpiece.*)

EDWARD. There surely must be something . . .

MIDGE. I've no particular qualifications, remember. Just a pleasant manner and the ability to keep my temper when I'm shouted at.

EDWARD. Do you mean to say the customers are rude to you?

MIDGE. Abominably rude, sometimes. (*She sits on the pouffe.*) It's their privilege.

EDWARD. (*crossing to the fireplace; horrified*) But, my dear girl, that's all wrong. (*He puts his glass on the mantelpiece.*) If I'd only known. . .

(*He takes his case from his pocket and offers* MIDGE *a cigarette.*)

MIDGE. (*taking a cigarette*) How should you know? Your world and mine are so far apart.

(EDWARD *lights* MIDGE's *cigarette.*)

I'm only half an Angkatell. The other half's just plain business girl, with unemployment always lurking round the corner in spite of the politicians' brave words.

SIR HENRY. (*crossing to* MIDGE *with two drinks*) You be a good girl and drink that. (*He hands one drink to her.*)

What's rubbed your fur up the wrong way, kitten? (*He offers the other drink to* LADY ANGKATELL.)

LADY ANGKATELL. (*to* SIR HENRY) Sherry for me, dear.

(SIR HENRY *moves to drinks table.*)

Edward does have that effect sometimes.

(GERDA *enters* L. *She wears an evening frock.*)

GERDA. (*crossing to* R. *of* LADY ANGKATELL) I'm so sorry if I'm late.

LADY ANGKATELL. (*holding* GERDA's *hand*) But you're not at all late, my dear.

MIDGE. We've just come down.

SIR HENRY. What will you have, Mrs. Cristow—sherry—gin?

(JOHN *enters* L. *He wears dinner clothes.*)

GERDA (*crossing to* L. *of the drinks table*) Oh—thank you, gin and something, please.

JOHN. Am I the last? (*He crosses down* R.)

LADY ANGKATELL. Henrietta isn't down yet.

(SIR HENRY *crosses with a drink to* LADY ANGKATELL *and hands it to her, then returns to the drinks table and pours a drink for* GERDA. *The conversations overlap in a hubbub of talk.*)

EDWARD. Yes, it's one of your perks, didn't you say, Midge?

LADY ANGKATELL. Perks? Do you mean to say you get them for nothing? Henry, darling, do you know that this child gets . . .

GERDA. (*crossing to* R.) This is very nice.

JOHN. It will go straight to your head, if you are not careful.

(VERONICA CRAYE *enters on the terrace up* C. *fom* L. *and stands posed in the french windows. She is a very beautiful woman and knows it. She wears a resplendent evening gown and carries an evening bag. Her appearance causes a sensation.* JOHN *stares at her like a man dazed.* MIDGE *and* LADY ANGKATELL *rise. They all turn and stare at* VERONICA.)

VERONICA. (*moving to* R. *of* LADY ANGKATELL) You must forgive me—for bursting in upon you this way. I'm your
neighbour, Lady Angkatell—from that ridiculous cottage, Dovecotes—and the most awful thing has happened. (*She moves* C. *and dominates the scene*.) Not a
single match in the house and my lighter won't work.
So what could I do? I just came along to beg help from
my only neighbour within miles.

LADY ANGKATELL. Why, of course. How awkward for you.

VERONICA. (*turning* R. *and affecting to see* JOHN *quite suddenly*) Why, surely—John! Why, it's John Cristow.
(*She crosses to* L. *of* JOHN *and takes hold of both his
hands*.) Now isn't that amazing? I haven't seen you
for years and years and years. And suddenly—to find
you—here. This is just the most wonderful surprise.
(*To* LADY ANGKATELL.) John's an old friend of mine.
(*She retains hold of* JOHN'S *left hand*.) Why, John's
the first man I ever loved.

SIR HENRY. (*moving above the sofa with two drinks*) Sherry?
Or dry Martini?

VERONICA. No, no, thank you.

(JOHN *takes a sherry from* SIR HENRY.)

LADY ANGKATELL. (*resuming her seat in the armchair* L.C.)
Midge dear, ring the bell.

(MIDGE *moves below the fireplace and presses the bell-push*.)

VERONICA. I hope you don't think it's just too awful of me
butting in like this.

LADY ANGKATELL. Not at all.

SIR HENRY. (*moving up* C.) We are honoured. (*He indicates*
MIDGE.) My cousin, Miss Harvey. Edward Angkatell.
(*He looks towards* GERDA.) Er . . .

(GERDA *eases down* R. *of* JOHN.)

JOHN. And this is my wife, Veronica.

VERONICA. (*crossing below* JOHN *to* L. *of* GERDA *and taking
her by the hand*) Oh, but how lovely to meet you.

(GUDGEON *enters* L.)

GUDGEON. You rang, m'lady?

LADY ANGKATELL. A dozen boxes of matches, please, Gudgeon.

(GUDGEON *is momentarily taken aback, but regains his normal impassivity immediately and exits* L.)

SIR HENRY. And how do you like living at Dovecotes?

VERONICA. (*turning*) I adore it. (*She crosses up stage to* L. *of the sofa and looks off* R.) I think it's so wonderful to be right in the heart of the country—these lovely English woods—and yet to be quite near London.

SIR HENRY. You've no idea what a thrill you've caused in the neighbourhood. But you must be used to that sort of thing.

VERONICA. Well, I've signed a few autograph books, (*she eases below the* L. *end of the sofa*) but what I like about it here is that one isn't in a village, and there's no-one to stare or gape. (*She sits on the sofa at the left end.*) I just appreciate the peacefulness of it all.

(GUDGEON *enters* L. *He carries a packet of a dozen boxes of matches on a salver.*)

LADY ANGKATELL. (*indicating* VERONICA) For madam.

(GUDGEON *crosses to* VERONICA.)

VERONICA. (*taking the matches*) Oh dear, Lady Angkatell— I can't really accept . . .

LADY ANGKATELL. Please. It's nothing at all.

VERONICA. Well, I do appreciate your kindness.

(GUDGEON *crosses and exits* L.)

John, do you live in this neighbourhood too?

JOHN. No—no, I live in London. I'm just down here for the weekend.

VERONICA. Oh, I just can't get over meeting you again after all these years.

(HENRIETTA *enters* L. *and moves to* L. *of* LADY ANGKATELL. *She wears an evening frock.*)

(*She glances at* HENRIETTA *and rises.*) Now—I must get back—carrying my spoils with me. John, will you see me down the lane?

(LADY ANGKATELL *rises.*)

JOHN. Yes, of course.

VERONICA. (*crossing to* R. *of* LADY ANGKATELL.) And thank you a thousand times. (*She smiles at* SIR HENRY *and* EDWARD *but ignores the ladies.*) You've all been very kind.

(JOHN *moves to the drinks table and puts his glass on it.*)

LADY ANGKATELL. Not at all.

VERONICA. (*crossing above the sofa to* JOHN) Now, John, you must tell me all you've been doing in the years and years since I've seen you.

(GUDGEON *enters* L.)

GUDGEON. Dinner is served, m'lady.

(*He exits* L.)

VERONICA. Oh, I mustn't take you away just as dinner is ready.

SIR HENRY. Won't you stay and dine with us?

VERONICA. No, no, no. I couldn't dream of it. John, can't you come over after dinner? I'm just dying to hear all your news. I'll be expecting you. (*She goes up the steps, turns and stands in the french window up* C.) And thank you all—so much.

(*She exits up* C. *to* L. JOHN *stands* R. *of the french window up* C. *and looks after her.* LADY ANGKATELL *hands her glass to* EDWARD, *who puts it on the mantelpiece.* MIDGE *puts her glass on the mantelpiece, moves to the door* L. *and opens it.* JOHN *goes on to the terrace.*)

LADY ANGKATELL. What a beautiful performance! Shall we go in to dinner? (*She crosses to the door* L.)

(SIR HENRY *crosses to the door* L. *A hubbub of conversation breaks out and the following speeches overlap as the exits are made.*)

I remember seeing that girl in a film. She was wearing a sari very low down.

(*She exits* L.)

EDWARD. I've seen her too, but I can't remember the name of the film.

MIDGE. *San Francisco Story*—it must be. It was revived two months ago.

(*She exits* L.)

EDWARD. Which theatre? Did you see *San Francisco Story?*

SIR HENRY. She must have changed her hair. She had it flowing down her back. Mrs. Cristow, what do you think of our film star?

(GERDA *crosses to the door* L.)

GERDA. She's very nice, very nice indeed, really.

(*She exits* L.)

EDWARD. Yes, she is. Isn't she, Henry?

SIR HENRY. Not so tall as I should have thought, seeing her on the films.

(*He exits* L.)

EDWARD. No, I agree, but they are very different in real life.

(*He exits* L. *The conversation continues off stage.* JOHN, *oblivious of everything else, stands on the terrace looking off* L. HENRIETTA *moves to the door* L. *and turns.*)

HENRIETTA. Are you coming, John?

JOHN. H'm? Oh yes—yes, of course.

HENRIETTA *exits* L. JOHN *crosses to the door* L. *and follows her off as*—

the CURTAIN *falls*

Act Two

Scene I

SCENE: *The same. Saturday morning.*

> When the CURTAIN *rises it is a fine morning. The clock is striking eleven. The french windows are open and music is coming softly from the radio. The tune is "I cried for you."* JOHN *enters briskly* L. *He is humming, looks happy and good-tempered. He moves to* L.C., *checks his watch with the clock on the mantelpiece, goes on to the terrace up* C., *takes a cigarette from his case and lights it.* GUDGEON *enters* L. *He carries a salver with a note on it.*

GUDGEON. (*moving* L.C.) A note for you, sir.

JOHN. (*moving to* R. *of* GUDGEON; *surprised*) For me? (*He takes the note.*)

GUDGEON. They are waiting for an answer, sir.

JOHN. It looks as though it's going to be a fine day, Gudgeon.

GUDGEON. Yes, sir. There was quite a haze over the downs early this morning.

> (JOHN *reads the note and frowns angrily.*)

JOHN. There's no answer, Gudgeon.

GUDGEON. (*turning and crossing to the door* L.) Very good, sir.

JOHN. Where is everybody?

GUDGEON. (*stopping and turning*) Her ladyship has gone down to the farm, sir. The gentlemen have gone out shooting, and I believe Miss Harvey and Miss Henrietta are in the garden.

JOHN. Thank you, Gudgeon.

(GUDGEON *exits* L. JOHN *moves on to the terrace up* C., *re-reads the note, utters an angry ejaculation, crumples the note and puts it in his pocket.* MIDGE *enters* R. *She carries an armful of dahlias and loose leaves.*)

MIDGE. (*crossing to* L. *of the coffee table*) Good morning. (*She kneels, takes the vase from the coffee table and starts filling it with the dahlias.*)

JOHN. Good morning.

MIDGE. Gerda up yet?

JOHN. No, she had breakfast in bed. She had a headache. I told her to lie in for once.

MIDGE. I meant to spend the whole morning in bed, but it was so lovely outside that I couldn't.

JOHN. Where's Henrietta?

MIDGE. I don't know. She was with me just now. She may be in the rose garden.

(JOHN *exits up* C. *to* R. LADY ANGKATELL *enters* L. *She carries a basket of eggs.*)

LADY ANGKATELL. Music? (*She moves to the radio.*) Oh no, dear, oh no—no. (*She switches off the radio.*) *Stop!* We can't be swinging so early in the day.

MIDGE. I wish you'd do these dahlias, Lucy. They defeat me.

LADY ANGKATELL. (*crossing to the drinks table*) Do they, darling? (*She puts the basket on the floor* L. *of the drinks table.*) What a shame—never mind. (*She moves dreamily to the writing table.*) Now then, what did I want? Ah, I know. (*She lifts the telephone receiver.*) Now let me see—ah yes, this thing. (*She cradles the receiver first in one arm and then in the other.*)

(MIDGE *stares amazed at* LADY ANGKATELL.)

(*With satisfaction.*) Ah! I see what it is. (*She replaces the receiver.*)

MIDGE. What *are* you doing, Lucy?

LADY ANGKATELL. Doing?

MIDGE. You seemed to be having a kind of game with the telephone receiver.

LADY ANGKATELL. Oh, that was Mrs. Bagshaw's baby. (*She looks at* MIDGE.) You've got the wrong vase, darling.

MIDGE. (*rising*) What did you say?

LADY ANGKATELL. I said you'd got the wrong vase. It's the white vase for dahlias.

MIDGE. No, I meant what did you say about somebody's baby?

LADY ANGKATELL. Oh, that was the telephone receiver, my pet.

MIDGE. (*moving to the drinks table*) I don't wonder that Gerda Cristow nearly has a nervous breakdown every time you talk to her. (*She picks up the white vase and jug of water from the drinks table, moves and puts them on the coffee table*.) What has Mrs. Bagshaw's baby got to do with the telephone receiver? (*She pours some water into the vase and fills it with the dahlias, during the ensuing speeches*.)

LADY ANGKATELL. She seemed to be holding it—the baby I mean—upside down. So I was trying this way and that way. And of course I see what it is—she's left-handed. That's why it looked all wrong. Is John Cristow down yet?

MIDGE. Yes, he went into the garden to look for Henrietta.

LADY ANGKATELL. (*sitting on the sofa at the right end of it*) Oh! Do you think that was very wise of him?

MIDGE. What do you mean?

LADY ANGKATELL. Well, I don't want to say anything . . .

MIDGE. Come on, Lucy. Give.

LADY ANGKATELL. Well, you know, darling, that I don't sleep very well. And when I can't sleep I'm inclined to prowl around the house.

MIDGE. I know, half the guests think it's burglars, the other half think it's ghosts.

LADY ANGKATELL. Well, I happened to be looking through the passage window. John was just coming back to the house, and it was close on three o'clock.

(*There is a pause.* MIDGE *and* LADY ANGKATELL *look at each other.*)

MIDGE. (*picking up the jug and vase of dahlias and crossing with them to the drinks table*) Even for old friends who have a lot to say to each other, three in the morning is a little excessive. (*She puts the jug and vase on the drinks table*.) One wonders what Gerda thinks about it.

LADY ANGKATELL. One wonders if Gerda thinks.

MIDGE. (*easing above the sofa*) Even the meekest of wives may turn.

LADY ANGKATELL. I don't think Henrietta was sleeping very well either last night. The light was on in her room, and I thought I saw her curtains move.

MIDGE. Really, John is a *fool*.

LADY ANGKATELL. He's a man who's always taken risks—and usually got away with them.

MIDGE. One day he'll go too far. This was a bit blatant, even for him.

LADY ANGKATELL. My dear child, he couldn't help himself. That woman just sailed in last night and—grabbed him. I must say I admired her performance. It was so beautifully timed and planned.

MIDGE. Do you think it was planned?

LADY ANGKATELL. (*rising*) Well, darling, come, come. (*She smiles, picks up the* Daily Mirror *and crosses to the fireplace.*)

MIDGE. You may say, in your detached way, she gave a beautiful performance—but it remains to be seen whether Gerda and Henrietta agree with you.

(SIR HENRY *enters* L. *He carries two revolvers.*)

SIR HENRY. (*crossing to* R.) Just going to have a little practice down at the targets. Like to come along and try your hand, Midge?

MIDGE. I've never shot with a pistol or a revolver in my life. I shall probably drill a hole in you, Cousin Henry.

SIR HENRY. I'll take jolly good care that you don't.

MIDGE. Well, it would be nice to think that I might some day be able to turn the tables on a burglar.

SIR HENRY. Every woman ought to learn to shoot with a revolver.

LADY ANGKATELL. (*moving and sitting in the armchair* L.C.) Now you're on Henry's hobby. He has a whole collection of pistols and revolvers, including a lovely pair of French duelling pistols. (*She starts to read the paper.*)

MIDGE. Don't you have to have licences for them?

SIR HENRY. Of course.

MIDGE. Have you ever had a burglar?

SIR HENRY. Not yet, but we live in hopes. If he does come, Lucy will probably shoot him dead.

MIDGE. (*surprised*) Lucy?

SIR HENRY. Lucy's a far better shot than I am. Lucy always gets her man.

MIDGE. I shall be simply terrified.

(*She exits* R. SIR HENRY *follows her off.* HENRIETTA *enters up* C. *from* L.)

HENRIETTA. (*easing above the sofa*) Hullo, are the Angkatells
     going to exterminate each other?
LADY ANGKATELL. They've gone down to the targets. Why
     don't you join them, Henrietta?
HENRIETTA. Yes, I will. I was rather good last Spring. Are
     you going, Lucy?
LADY ANGKATELL. Yes. No. I must do something about my
     eggs first. (*She looks around.*)
HENRIETTA. Eggs?
LADY ANGKATELL. Yes, they are over there in the basket,
     darling.

(HENRIETTA *moves to the drinks table, picks up the basket
     of eggs and takes it to* LADY ANGKATELL.)

     Oh! Thank you, my pet. (*She puts the basket on the
     floor* R. *of her chair, then resumes reading.*)
HENRIETTA. (*moving down* C.) Where's Edward?
LADY ANGKATELL. I think he took his gun and went up to the
     woods. Henry was going with him—but someone came
     to see him about something.
HENRIETTA. I see. (*She stands lost in thought.*)

(*Two revolver shots are heard off* R.)

LADY ANGKATELL. Doing any work this morning?
HENRIETTA. (*sitting on the sofa*) No. It's gone stale on me.

(*A revolver shot is heard off* R.)

LADY ANGKATELL. I think it's so clever of you, darling—
     doing all these odd abstract things.
HENRIETTA. I thought you didn't like them, Lucy.
LADY ANGKATELL. No, I've always thought them rather silly.
     But I think it's so clever of you to know they're not.

(GERDA *enters hurriedly* L. *She looks alarmed.*)

GERDA. I heard shots—quite near the house.
LADY ANGKATELL. Nothing, darling—Henry—target practice
     —they've got targets in what used to be the bowling
     alley.
HENRIETTA. (*rising*) Come and have a try, Gerda.
GERDA. Is it difficult? (*She crosses to* HENRIETTA.)
HENRIETTA. No, of course not. You just close your eyes and
     press the trigger and the bullet goes somewhere.

(*Two shots are heard off* R. HENRIETTA *and* GERDA *exit* R. *A shot is heard off* R. LADY ANGKATELL *rises, crosses to the coffee table, puts the newspaper on it, and picks up the vase and odd leaves. Two shots are heard off* R. LADY ANGKATELL *crosses to the waste-paper basket, drops the leaves in it, then moves to the drinks table and puts the vase on it. Two shots are heard off* R. JOHN *enters up* C. *from* R. *He is smoking a cigarette.*)

JOHN. Has the war started?

LADY ANGKATELL. Yes, dear—no, dear. Henry. Target practice.

JOHN. He's very keen. I remember.

LADY ANGKATELL. Why don't you join them?

JOHN. (*crossing to the fireplace*) I ought to write some letters. (*He stubs out his cigarette in the ashtray on the mantelpiece.*) I wonder if you'd mind if I wrote them in here?

LADY ANGKATELL. (*easing above the sofa*) Of course. You'll find stamps in the little drawer. If you put the letters on the hall table, Gudgeon will see that they go.

JOHN. This is the best run house in England.

LADY ANGKATELL. Bless you, darling. Now let me see—(*she looks around*) where did I lay my eggs? Ah, there, by the chair. (*She picks up the basket of eggs and moves to the door* L.)

JOHN. I didn't quite understand what you meant.

(LADY ANGKATELL *exits* L. JOHN *crosses to the writing table, and takes a note from his pocket. He reads it, then crumples it and throws it into the waste-paper basket. He sits, sighs heavily and starts to write.* VERONICA *enters up* C. *from* L. *She carries a large, very flamboyant, red suède handbag.*)

VERONICA. (*standing at the french window up* C.; *imperiously*) John.

JOHN. (*turning; startled*) Veronica. (*He rises.*)

VERONICA. (*moving down* C.) I sent you a note asking you to come over at once. Didn't you get it?

JOHN. (*pleasantly, but with reserve*) Yes, I got it.

VERONICA. Well, why didn't you come? I've been waiting.

JOHN. I'm afraid it wasn't convenient for me to come over this morning.

VERONICA. (*crossing to* L. *of* JOHN) Can I have a cigarette, please?

JOHN. Yes, of course. (*He offers her a cigarette from his case.*)

(*Before he can give her a light,* VERONICA *takes her own lighter from her handbag and lights the cigarette herself.*)

VERONICA. I sent for you because we've got to talk. We've got to make arrangements. For our future, I mean.

JOHN. Have we a future?

VERONICA. Of course we've got a future. We've wasted ten years. There's no need to waste any more time. (*She sits on the sofa, centre of it, and puts her handbag on the right end of the sofa.*)

JOHN. (*easing to* R. *of the sofa*) I'm sorry, Veronica. I'm afraid you've got this worked out the wrong way. I've— enjoyed meeting you again very much, but you know we don't really belong together—we're worlds apart.

VERONICA. Nonsense, John. I love you and you love me. We've always loved each other. You were very obstinate in the past. But never mind that now.

(JOHN *crosses above the sofa to* L. *of it.*)

Look, our lives needn't clash. I don't mean to go back to the States for quite a while. When I've finished the picture I'm working on now, I'm going to play a straight part on the London stage. I've got a new play— Elderton's written it for me. It'll be a terrific success.

JOHN. (*politely*) I'm sure it will.

VERONICA. (*condescendingly*) And you can go on being a doctor. You're quite well known, they tell me.

JOHN. (*moving down* L.C.; *irritably*) I am a fairly well-known consultant on certain diseases—if it interests you—but I imagine it doesn't.

VERONICA. What I mean is we can both get on with our own jobs. It couldn't have worked out better.

JOHN. (*surveying her dispassionately*) You really are the most interesting character. Don't you realize that I'm a married man—I have children?

VERONICA. (*rising and crossing to* R. *of* JOHN) Well, I'm married myself at the moment. But these things are easily arranged. A good lawyer can fix anything. (*Softly.*) I always did mean to marry you, darling. I can't think why I have this terrible passion for you—(*she puts her arms around* JOHN's *neck*) but there it is.

JOHN. (*shaking her off; brusquely*) I'm sorry, Veronica. (*He moves to the fireplace.*) It's out of the question.

VERONICA. But I tell you a good lawyer can easily fix ...

JOHN. No good lawyer is going to fix anything. Your life and mine have nothing in common.

VERONICA. (*moving to R. of JOHN and facing him*) Not after last night?

JOHN. You're not a child, Veronica. You've had two husbands and, I've no doubt, a good many lovers. What does "last night" mean exactly? Nothing at all, and you know it.

VERONICA. If you'd seen your face, yesterday evening—when I came through that window—we might have been back in the South of France all those years ago.

JOHN. I was back in the South of France. (*Gently.*) Try to understand, Veronica. You came to me last night straight out of the past. I'd been thinking about you. Wondering whether I'd been as wise a young man as I'd thought myself—or whether I'd simply been a coward. And suddenly—there you were—like a dream come to life. But you were a dream. Today I'm back in the present, a man ten years older. (*He crosses to L. of the sofa.*) A man you don't know and probably wouldn't like very much if you did know him.

VERONICA. Are you telling me that you prefer your wife to me?

JOHN. Yes—yes, I am. (*He sits on the sofa at the left end of it.*) I've suddenly realized how very much fonder I am of her than I knew. When I got back to this house last night—or in the early hours of the morning—I suddenly saw how stupidly I'd risked losing everything in the world I need. Fortunately, Gerda was asleep. She'd no idea what time I got back. She believes I left you quite early.

VERONICA. Your wife must be a very credulous woman.

JOHN. She loves me—and she trusts me.

VERONICA. She's a fool! (*She crosses to L. of the sofa.*) And anyway I don't believe a word of what you say. You love me.

JOHN. I'm sorry, Veronica.

VERONICA. (*breaking down C.; incredulously*) You *don't* love me?

JOHN. I've been perfectly frank with you. You are a very

beautiful and very seductive woman, Veronica—(*he rises
and moves up* R. *of the sofa*) but I don't love you.

VERONICA. (*furiously*) You *belong* to me, John. (*She moves
below the sofa.*) You always have. Ever since I got to
England, I've been thinking about you, planning how
best to meet you again. (*She kneels on the sofa.*) Why
do you think I took this idiotic cottage down here?
Simply because I found out that you often came down
for weekends with the Angkatells.

JOHN. So it *was* all planned last night. (*He crosses above the
sofa to* R. *of the armchair* L.C.) I noticed your lighter
was working this morning.

VERONICA. (*rising and turning*) You belong to me.

JOHN. (*coldly angry*) I don't belong to anyone. Where do you
get this idea that you can own another human being?
I loved you once and I wanted you to marry me and
share my life. (*He moves to the fireplace and stands with
his back to it.*) You wouldn't.

VERONICA. My life and my career were much more important
than yours. Anyone can be a doctor. (*She stubs out
her cigarette in the ashtray on the coffee table.*)

JOHN. Are you really quite as important as you think?

VERONICA. (*crossing to* R. *of* JOHN) If I'm not right at the
top yet, I will be.

JOHN. I wonder. I rather doubt it. There's something lacking
in you, Veronica—what is it? Warmth—generosity—
you give nothing. You take—take—take all the time.

VERONICA. (*speaking in a low voice convulsed with rage*) You
turned me down ten years ago. You've turned me down
today. My God, I'll make you suffer for it!

JOHN. I'm sorry if I've hurt you, Veronica. You're very lovely,
my dear, and I once cared for you very much. Can't we
leave it at that?

VERONICA. No. (*She crosses to the french windows up* C.,
turns and stands in the window.) You be careful of yourself, John Cristow. I hate you more than I ever thought
it possible to hate anyone.

JOHN. (*annoyed*) Oh!

VERONICA. And don't fool yourself that I believe you're turning me down because of your *wife*. It's that other woman.

JOHN. What other woman?

VERONICA. The one who came through that door last night
and stood looking at you. If I can't have you, nobody
else shall have you, John. Understand that.

(*She exits angrily up* C. *to* L., *leaving her handbag on the sofa.* JOHN *stands looking after her for a moment, then crosses to the writing table, picks up the letter he has been writing, tears it up and puts it in the waste-paper basket.* GUDGEON *enters* R., *crosses to* L. *of the sofa, turns and sees* JOHN.)

GUDGEON. I beg your pardon, sir, do you know where her ladyship is?

JOHN. They're all down in the target alley, I believe.

GUDGEON. They finished shooting some time ago, sir.

(JOHN *takes* VERONICA's *note from his pocket, screws it up, drops it in the direction of the waste-paper basket but it misses and falls alongside.*)

JOHN. (*moving to the bookshelves above the drinks table*) Then they must be in the garden somewhere.

(GUDGEON *crosses below the sofa, picks up the crumpled note, puts it in the waste-paper basket, then picks up the waste-paper basket, crosses and exits* L. JOHN *selects a book from the bookshelves, moves above the sofa and glances at the opening pages. There is a noise off from the* L. *end of the terrace up* C. JOHN *drops the book on the sofa, goes on to the terrace, faces* L., *and gives a sudden start of alarm.*)

Why! What are you doing? Put that down. Why you . . .

(*The sound of a revolver shot is heard up* C. JOHN *staggers down the steps, tries to cross to the door* L., *then collapses on the floor down* L.C. *A revolver is tossed on to the terrace up* C. *from* L. *There is a pause, then* GERDA *enters quickly down* L. *She carries her leathercraft bag. She runs to* L. *of* JOHN.)

GERDA. John—oh, John! (*She crosses up* C., *goes on to the terrace, picks up the revolver, looks off* L., *then stands at the top of the steps, facing front.*)

(GUDGEON *enters hurriedly* L. *A moment later* SIR HENRY *enters* R. *He is followed on by* MIDGE.)

SIR HENRY. (*crossing to* R. *of* JOHN) What's happened?

(GUDGEON *moves to* L. *of* JOHN.)

Cristow! Cristow! Good God, what's happened? (*He kneels beside* JOHN.)

MIDGE. (*moving above the sofa*) Gerda—John—what is it?

GUDGEON. (*kneeling* L. *of* JOHN) Dr. Cristow, sir—what is it?

SIR HENRY. (*raising* JOHN'S *head and shoulders*) He's been wounded. (*He feels* JOHN'S *heart.*)

(JOHN *is still breathing.* GUDGEON *rises and eases* L.)

GUDGEON. Wounded? How did it happen?

SIR HENRY. Ring for a doctor, Gudgeon.

(GUDGEON *crosses to the writing table and lifts the telephone receiver.*)

MIDGE. Is he dead?

SIR HENRY. No.

(LADY ANGKATELL *enters* L. HENRIETTA *enters* R.)

HENRIETTA. I heard—a shot. (*She kneels down* R. *of* JOHN.) John—John.

(EDWARD *enters up* C. *from* L. *and stands* R. *of the french windows.* JOHN *opens his eyes and looks at* HENRIETTA.)

JOHN. (*trying to raise himself; in a loud urgent voice*) Henrietta— Henrietta . . . (*He collapses.*)

(SIR HENRY *feels* JOHN'S *heart, then looks at* HENRIETTA *and* GERDA.)

GERDA. (*moving below the armchair* L.C.; *hysterically*) He's dead—he's dead. John's dead.

(HENRIETTA *moves to* R. *of* GERDA *and takes the revolver from her.* LADY ANGKATELL *moves to* L. *of* GERDA *and puts her arms around her.*)

John's dead.

(*The* CURTAIN *begins to fall.*)

GUDGEON. (*into the telephone*) Get me Dr. Murdock.

CURTAIN

Scene II

SCENE: *The same. Later the same day.*

When the CURTAIN *rises, the weather has changed, the wind is rising and the sky is overcast. The windows are closed with the exception of the right side of the french windows up* C. LADY ANGKATELL *is seated on the sofa at the right end, knitting.* MIDGE *is seated on the chair down* R. EDWARD *is seated in the armchair* L.C., *doing "The Times" crossword.* HENRIETTA *is standing on the terrace up* C. *After a while* HENRIETTA *moves down* C. *She pauses as the clock strikes two, then paces below the sofa to* R. *and gazes out of the window* R.

LADY ANGKATELL. I knew the weather was too good to last. I wish I knew what to do about meals. This Inspector person and the other one—does one send them something on a tray? Or do they have a meal with us later?

(HENRIETTA *turns.*)

The police aren't at all as they are in books. This Inspector Colquhoun, for instance, well he's a *gentleman.* I know one mustn't say that these days—it annoys people—but he is. (*She pauses.*)

(HENRIETTA *crosses above the sofa to* L.)

(*Suddenly.*) St. Albans!

(EDWARD *and* HENRIETTA *look at* LADY ANGKATELL *in surprise.*)

HENRIETTA. What about St. Albans? (*She moves to the alcove.*)

LADY ANGKATELL. No, no, Hendon. The police college. Quite unlike our local Inspector Jackson, who is very nice, but such a heavy accent, and such a heavy moustache.

(HENRIETTA *opens the curtain of the alcove, switches on the light and stands* R. *of the arch, looking off* L. *at the statue.*)

MIDGE. Why did they send someone down from Scotland
     Yard? I thought the local people always dealt with things
     first.
EDWARD. This is the Metropolitan area.
MIDGE. Oh, I see.

(HENRIETTA *moves to the fireplace, leaving the alcove curtain
     open and light on.*)

LADY ANGKATELL. I don't think his wife looks after him
     properly. I imagine she's the kind of woman that's al-
     ways cleaning the house, and doesn't bother to cook.
EDWARD. Inspector Colquhoun?
LADY ANGKATELL. No, no, dear. Inspector Jackson. I shouldn't
     think Colquhoun was married. Not yet. He's quite
     attractive.
HENRIETTA. They're a long time in with Henry.
LADY ANGKATELL. The worst of murder is it does upset the
     servants so.

     (HENRIETTA *crosses above the sofa to the window* R.)

     We were to have duck for lunch. Still, cold duck can
     be quite nice. I suppose one couldn't sit down and have
     a little bit, could one? (*She pauses.*) No.
MIDGE. It was. all horrible. (*She shivers.*) It's dreadful having
     to sit in here.
LADY ANGKATELL. Well, darling, we've got to sit in here. There
     is nowhere else to sit.

(HENRIETTA *turns and crosses below the sofa to the fireplace.*)

     First they turn us out of here and take photographs,
     then they herd us back in here and make the dining-
     room their headquarters, and now this Inspector Colqu-
     houn is in the study with Henry.

(*There is a pause.* HENRIETTA *turns and faces the fireplace.*)

     What does one do about Gerda, do you think? Some-
     thing on a tray? A little strong soup, perhaps?
MIDGE. (*rising and moving to the window* R.; *vehemently*)
     Really, Lucy, you're quite inhuman. (*She gazes out of
     the window.*)
LADY ANGKATELL. (*surprised*) Darling, it's all very upsetting,
     but one has to go on with meals and things. Excitement
     even makes one rather hungry—rather sick, too.

MIDGE. Yes, I know. That's just what one does feel.

LADY ANGKATELL. Reading about murders in newspapers gives one no idea how trying they can be. I feel as though I'd walked about fifteen miles. Just think, we'll be in the *News of the World* next week—perhaps even tomorrow.

EDWARD. I never see the *News of the World*.

LADY ANGKATELL. Don't you? Oh, I always do. We pretend to get it for the servants, but Gudgeon is very understanding. He doesn't take it to the servants' hall before the evening. You should read it, Edward. You'd be amazed at the number of old Colonels who make improper advances to nursemaids.

(GUDGEON *enters* L. *He carries a tray of coffee and sandwiches.*)

Ah! (*She moves along the sofa and sits centre of it.*)

GUDGEON. (*crossing to the coffee table*) Shall I take something in to the study to Sir Henry and the police officer?

LADY ANGKATELL. Yes, yes, thank you, Gudgeon. I'm a little worried about Mrs. Cristow.

GUDGEON. Simmonds has already taken her up some tea, and some thin bread and butter and a boiled egg, m'lady. (*He turns and crosses to the door* L.)

LADY ANGKATELL. Thank you, Gudgeon. I had forgotten about the eggs, Gudgeon. I meant to do something about them.

GUDGEON. (*stopping and turning*) I have already attended to that, m'lady. (*With a trace of emphasis.*) *Quite* satisfactorily, I think. You need have no further anxiety.

(*He exits* L.)

LADY ANGKATELL. I don't know what I should do without him. These substantial sandwiches are just what is needed—not as heartless as a sit-down meal, and yet . . .

MIDGE. (*starting to cry; hysterically*) Oh, Lucy—don't!

(LADY ANGKATELL *looks surprised.* EDWARD *rises, crosses to the drinks table, puts his paper and pencil on it, then moves to* MIDGE *and puts an arm around her as she sobs unrestrainedly.*)

EDWARD. Midge . . .

LADY ANGKATELL. Poor dear. It's all been too much for her.

EDWARD. Don't worry, Midge. It's all right. Come and sit down. (*He leads her to the sofa and sits her at the right end of it.*)

MIDGE. I'm sorry to be such a fool.

EDWARD. We understand.

MIDGE. I've lost my handkerchief.

(LADY ANGKATELL *pours out four cups of coffee.*)

EDWARD. (*handing* MIDGE *his handkerchief*) Here—have mine.

MIDGE. Thank you.

EDWARD. (*moving to the coffee table*) And have some coffee.

MIDGE. No, I don't want anything.

EDWARD. Yes, you do. (*He hands* MIDGE *a cup of coffee.*) Come on now—drink this. It'll make you feel better.

LADY ANGKATELL. Some coffee, Henrietta?

HENRIETTA. Yes, thank you. Shouldn't one of us go up to Gerda?

(EDWARD *picks up a cup of coffee and crosses with it to* HENRIETTA.)

LADY ANGKATELL. My dear child, one doesn't know what to think.

(EDWARD *moves to the coffee table, picks up a cup of coffee for himself and eases up* C.)

One doesn't even know what her reactions *are*. How would one feel if one had just killed one's husband? One simply doesn't know.

HENRIETTA. Aren't we assuming rather too readily that Gerda *has* killed her husband?

(*There is an awkward pause.* EDWARD *looks at* LADY ANGKATELL *and shifts uneasily.* LADY ANGKATELL *looks searchingly at* HENRIETTA, *trying to make up her mind about something.*)

EDWARD. Well, we found her standing over his body with the revolver in her hand. I imagined there was no question about it.

HENRIETTA. We haven't heard yet what she has to say.

EDWARD. It seems self-evident to me.

(HENRIETTA *moves up* C. *and goes on to the terrace.*)

LADY ANGKATELL. Mind you, she had every provocation. John behaved in a most barefaced manner. After all, there are ways of doing these things. Being unfaithful, I mean.

(GERDA *enters* L. *She is very shaky and incoherent. She carries her leathercraft bag.*)

GERDA. (*looking around apologetically*) I—I really couldn't lie down any longer. I felt—so restless.

LADY ANGKATELL. (*rising and moving to* GERDA) No, of course not. (*She leads her to the sofa and sits her at the left end of it.*) Come and sit here, my dear. (*She moves above the sofa.*) Midge, that little cushion.

(MIDGE *rises, puts her cup on the writing table, then takes the cushion from the chair down* R. *and hands it to* LADY ANGKATELL.)

(*To* GERDA.) Put your feet up. (*She puts the cushion behind* GERDA'S *head.*) We were just about to have some sandwiches. Would you like one?

GERDA. No, no, thank you. I—I am only just beginning to realize it. I haven't been able to feel—I still can't feel—that John is really *dead*. That I shall never see him again. Who could possibly have killed him?

(*They all look embarrassed.* SIR HENRY *enters* L. *He is followed on by* INSPECTOR COLQUHOUN, *who is a thoughtful quiet man with charm and a sense of humour. His personality is sympathetic. He must not be played as a comedy part.* SIR HENRY *has a filled pipe in his hand.*)

SIR HENRY. (*moving to the fireplace*) Inspector Colquhoun would like to talk to Gerda, my dear. (*He turns.*) Could you take him up and . . . (*He sees* GERDA *and breaks off.*)

LADY ANGKATELL. This is Mrs. Cristow, Mr. Colquhoun.

(*The* INSPECTOR *crosses to* L. *of the sofa.*)

GERDA. (*nervously*) Yes—yes—I—you want to talk to me? About John's death?

INSPECTOR. I don't want to distress you, Mrs. Cristow, but I would like to ask you a few questions. You're not bound to answer them unlesss you wish to do so, and you are entitled, if you like, to have your solicitor present before you say anything at all.

SIR HENRY. That is what I should advise, Gerda.

GERDA. (*putting her feet to the ground and sitting up*) A solicitor? But why a solicitor? A solicitor wouldn't know anything about John's death.

INSPECTOR. Any statement you choose to make . . .

GERDA. I want to tell you. It's all so bewildering—like a bad dream. I haven't been able to cry, even. I just don't feel anything at all.

SIR HENRY. It's the shock.

GERDA. You see, it all happened so suddenly. I'd gone back to the house. I was just coming downstairs to fetch my leathercraft bag, and I heard a shot—came in here and there was John—lying all twisted up—and blood—blood . . .

(MIDGE *moves to the chair down* R. *and sits*)

INSPECTOR. What time was this, Mrs. Cristow?

(LADY ANGKATELL *and* MIDGE *exchange looks.*)

GERDA. I don't know. It might have been twelve o'clock—or half past.

INSPECTOR. Where had you been before you came downstairs?

GERDA. In my room.

INSPECTOR. Had you just got up?

GERDA. No. I'd been up for about three-quarters of an hour. I'd been outside. Sir Henry was very kindly teaching me how to shoot—but I did it so badly I couldn't hit the target at all.

(LADY ANGKATELL *and* MIDGE *exchange looks.*)

Then I walked round a little—for exercise—came back to the house for my leatherwork bag, went upstairs, came down and then—as I told you—I heard a shot and came in here—and there was John dead.

HENRIETTA. (*coming down the steps up* C.) Dying. (*She moves to the drinks table, puts down her cup, takes a cigarette from the box on the table and lights it from the one she is smoking.*)

(*They all look at* HENRIETTA.)

GERDA. I thought he was dead. There was the blood and the revolver. I picked it up . . .

INSPECTOR. Why did you pick it up, Mrs. Cristow?

(*There is a tense pause. All look at the* INSPECTOR.)

GERDA. I don't know.

INSPECTOR. You shouldn't have touched it, you know.

GERDA. Shouldn't I?

(MIDGE *takes a cigarette from the case in her bag.*)

INSPECTOR. And then what happened?

GERDA. Then the others all came in and I said, "John's dead—somebody's killed John." But who could have killed him? Who could possibly have wanted to kill him?

(SIR HENRY *strikes a match suddenly and lights his pipe.* EDWARD *looks at him for a moment.*)

John was the best of men, so good, so kind. He did everything for everyone. He sacrificed himself. Why, his patients all adored him. It must have been some sort of accident, it must—it must.

MIDGE. Couldn't it have been suicide?

(MIDGE *feels in her bag for her lighter.*)

INSPECTOR. No. (*He crosses below the sofa to* R. *of it.*) The shot was fired from at least four feet away.

GERDA. But it must have been an accident.

INSPECTOR. It wasn't an accident, Mrs. Cristow. (*He takes his lighter from his pocket and lights* MIDGE's *cigarette.*) There was no disagreement between you?

GERDA. Between John and me? No.

(MIDGE *rises and crosses above the sofa to the steps up* C.)

INSPECTOR. Are you sure of that?

GERDA. He was a little annoyed with me when we drove down here. I change gear so badly. I—I don't know how it is, whenever I'm in the car with him, I never seem to do anything right. I get nervous.

INSPECTOR. There was no serious disagreement? No—quarrel?

GERDA. Quarrel? Between John and me? No, Inspector. No, John and I never quarrelled. He was so good, so kind. (*She starts to cry.*) I shall never see him again.

(MIDGE *moves to* L. *of the sofa.*)

LADY ANGKATELL		(*To* GERDA.) Darling. (*She turns to* MIDGE.) Midge, dear.
MIDGE	(*together*).	(*Moving to* GERDA *and helping her to rise.*) I'll take her up, Lucy.
INSPECTOR		That's all, Mrs. Cristow.
GERDA		If I could go back to my room—please.

(*The* INSPECTOR *nods and moves up* R.)

MIDGE. Yes. Come and have a rest. You'll feel better.

LADY ANGKATELL. Tell Simmonds—a hot-water bottle.

(MIDGE *leads* GERDA *to the door* L. *and they exit together.*)

(*To the* INSPECTOR.) She adored him.

INSPECTOR. Just so. (*He moves down* R.) Now, I should like to talk to you all, one at a time. Perhaps, Lady Angkatell, you wouldn't mind . . . ?

LADY ANGKATELL. (*delighted*) Oh no, of course not, Inspector. I want to do everything I can to help you. (*She eases to* L. *of the sofa.*) I feel that we must all be very very co-operative.

INSPECTOR. That's certainly what we should like.

LADY ANGKATELL. (*confidentially*) Actually, this is my first murder.

INSPECTOR. Indeed?

LADY ANGKATELL. Yes, an old story to you, of course. I suppose you're always rushing here and there, arresting people, sending out flying squads?

INSPECTOR. We're not quite so dynamic as all that.

SIR HENRY. My wife is very fond of going to the pictures, Inspector.

INSPECTOR. I'm afraid in real life it's much more boring than on the screen. (*He crosses below* LADY ANGKATELL *to* L.C.) We just go on asking people a lot of rather dull questions.

LADY ANGKATELL. (*radiantly*) And now you want to ask *me* a lot of questions. Well, I shall do everything I can to help you. As long as you don't ask me what time anything was, or where I was, or what I was doing. Because that's something I never remember—even when I was quite tiny.

SIR HENRY. Don't discourage the Inspector too much, my dear. (*He moves to the door* L. *and opens it.*) May I come along, too?

INSPECTOR. I should be pleased, Sir Henry.

SIR HENRY. My wife's remarks are sometimes rather hard to follow. I can act as interpreter.

(LADY ANGKATELL *crosses and exits* L. *The* INSPECTOR *and* SIR HENRY *follow her off.* HENRIETTA *moves on to the terrace up* C. *and stands in the window.* EDWARD *watches her in silence for a few moments. She pays no attention to him.*)

EDWARD. It's not so warm as yesterday.

HENRIETTA. No, no—it's cold—autumn chill.

EDWARD. You'd better come in—you'll catch cold.

HENRIETTA. I think I'll go for a walk.

EDWARD. I shouldn't.

HENRIETTA. Why?

EDWARD. (*crossing to the fireplace and putting his cup and saucer on the mantelpiece*) Well, for one thing it's going to rain—and another—they might think it odd.

HENRIETTA. You think a policeman would plod after me through the woods?

EDWARD. I really don't know. One can't tell what they're thinking—the whole thing *seems* obvious.

HENRIETTA. Gerda, you mean?

EDWARD. After all, who else is there?

HENRIETTA. (*moving to* R. *of the armchair* L.C.) Who else had a motive to kill John Cristow?

EDWARD. Yes.

HENRIETTA. Did Gerda have a motive?

EDWARD. If she found out a few things—after all, last night . . . (*He breaks off.*)

HENRIETTA. John and Veronica Craye, you mean?

EDWARD. (*slightly embarrassed*) Well, yes. (*Impatiently.*) He must have been crazy.

HENRIETTA. He was. Adolescent passion unresolved and kept in cold storage and then suddenly released. (*She crosses to the coffee table and stubs out her cigarette in the ashtray.*) He was crazy all right.

EDWARD. She's a remarkably good-looking woman in a rather hard obvious sort of way. But I can't see anything to lose your head about.

HENRIETTA. I don't suppose John could—this morning.

EDWARD. (*turning to face the fire*) It's an unsavoury business.

HENRIETTA. Yes. (*She crosses to R. of the sofa.*) I think I will go for a walk.

EDWARD. Then I'll come with you.

HENRIETTA. I'd rather be alone.

EDWARD. (*moving below the sofa*) I'm coming with you.

HENRIETTA. Don't you understand? I want to be alone—with my dead.

EDWARD. I'm sorry. (*He pauses.*) Henrietta, I haven't said anything—I thought you'd rather I didn't. But you do know, don't you, how sorry I am?

HENRIETTA. Sorry? (*With a bitter smile.*) That John Cristow's dead?

EDWARD. (*taken aback*) I meant—sorry for you. I know it's been a great shock.

HENRIETTA. (*bitterly*) Shock? Oh, but I'm tough, Edward. I can stand shocks. Was it a shock to you? (*She crosses above the sofa to L. of it.*) I wonder what you felt when you saw him lying there? Glad, I suppose. (*Accusingly.*) Were you glad?

EDWARD. Of course I wasn't glad. Cristow and I had nothing in common, but . . .

HENRIETTA. You had me in common. You were both fond of me, weren't you? But it didn't make a bond between you—quite the opposite.

EDWARD. Henrietta—don't speak so bitterly. I do feel for you in your loss—your grief.

HENRIETTA. (*sombrely*) Is it grief?

EDWARD. What do you mean?

HENRIETTA. (*to herself*) So quick. (*She crosses to the fire-place.*) It can happen so quickly. One moment living—breathing—and—the next—dead—gone—emptiness. Oh, the emptiness. And here we are eating sandwiches and drinking coffee, and calling ourselves alive. And John, who was more alive than any of us, is dead. (*She moves C.*) I say the word, you know, over and over again to myself. Dead—dead—dead—dead—dead.

EDWARD. (*moving in to* HENRIETTA *and taking her by the shoulders*) Henrietta. Henrietta, stop it—stop!

HENRIETTA. (*regaining control of herself; quietly*) Didn't you know I'd feel like this? What did you think? That I'd sit crying gently into a nice little pocket handkerchief while you held my hand? That it would all be a great shock for me, but that presently I'd begin to get over it?

(EDWARD *drops his arms.*)

And you'd comfort me very nicely? You are nice, Edward—(*she crosses below him and sits on the sofa at the left end of it*) but it's not enough.

EDWARD. (*deeply hurt*) Yes, I've always known that.

HENRIETTA. What do you think it's been like here today? With John dead and nobody caring but me and Gerda. With you glad, and Midge upset, and Henry worried, and Lucy enjoying, in a delicate sort of way, the *News of the World* come from print into real life. Can't you see how like a fantastic nightmare it is?

EDWARD. (*moving up* R.) Yes, I see.

HENRIETTA. At this moment nothing seems real to me but John. I know—I'm being a brute to you, Edward, but I can't help it, I can't help resenting that John who was so alive is dead . . . (*She breaks off.*)

EDWARD. And that I—(*he turns above the sofa*) who am half dead, am alive?

HENRIETTA. (*rising quickly and turning to face* EDWARD) I didn't mean that, Edward.

EDWARD. I think you did, Henrietta.

(HENRIETTA *makes a hopeless gesture, turns and exits* R., *leaving the window open.* EDWARD *looks after her like a man in a dream.* MIDGE *enters* L.)

MIDGE. (*moving* L.C.) Brrrr! It's cold in here.

EDWARD. (*absently*) Yes.

MIDGE. Where's everybody?

EDWARD. I don't know.

MIDGE. (*moving up* C.) Is something wrong? (*She closes the french windows up* C., *then crosses and closes the window* R.) Do we want the windows open? Edward—(*she touches his hand*) you're icy cold. (*She takes his hand and leads him to the fireplace.*) Come over here and I'll light a fire. (*She takes a box of matches from the mantelpiece, kneels and lights the fire.*)

EDWARD. (*moving to the armchair* L.C.; *deeply moved*) You're a dear child, Midge. (*He sits.*)

MIDGE. No, not a child. Do you still have fir cones at Ainswick?

EDWARD. Oh yes, there's always a basket of them beside the fire.

MIDGE. Dear Ainswick.

EDWARD. (*looking towards the french windows* R.) One shouldn't have to live there alone.

MIDGE. Did Henrietta go out?

EDWARD. Yes.

MIDGE. What an odd thing to do. It's raining.

EDWARD. She was upset. Did you know that she and John Cristow . . . ?

MIDGE. Were having an affair? (*She rises and replaces the matches on the mantelpiece.*) Yes, of course.

EDWARD. Everybody knew, I suppose.

MIDGE. (*turning*) Everybody except Gerda.

EDWARD. Damn him!

MIDGE. (*moving to* EDWARD *and kneeling down* L. *of him*) Darling—don't. (*She holds his arm.*)

EDWARD. Even dead—he's got her.

MIDGE. Don't, Edward—please.

EDWARD. She's changed so much—since those days at Ainswick.

MIDGE. We've all changed.

EDWARD. I haven't. I've just stayed still.

MIDGE. What about me?

EDWARD. You haven't changed.

MIDGE. (*releasing his arm and looking away; bitterly*) How do you know? You never look at me.

(EDWARD *is startled. He takes her face in his left hand.*)

I'm a woman, Edward.

(GUDGEON *enters* L. MIDGE *rises.*)

GUDGEON. The Inspector would like to see you in the dining-room, sir.

EDWARD. (*rising*) Oh yes, certainly.

(*He exits* L. GUDGEON *closes the door after him.* MIDGE *moves above the armchair* L.C. *to* R. *of it. During the ensuing dialogue,* GUDGEON *collects the tray from the coffee table, gets the coffee cups and saucers and puts them on it.*)

MIDGE. Is Mrs. Cristow still resting?

GUDGEON. As far as I know, miss, yes. Dr. Murdock left her

some tablets and Simmonds has instructions to administer one every two hours.

MIDGE. Would you like one of us to go up to her?

GUDGEON. I hardly think that necessary, miss. Simmonds is quite reliable.

MIDGE. I'm sure she is.

GUDGEON. (*moving to the door* L.) Thank you, miss. Thank you.

(*He exits* L. *taking the tray and coffee cups with him.* MIDGE *closes the door behind him.* HENRIETTA *enters the terrace up* C. *from* L. *and taps on the window.* MIDGE *runs up* C., *lets* HENRIETTA *in, then closes the window behind her.*)

MIDGE. How you startled me. (*She nods* R.) I expected you to come in that way.

HENRIETTA. (*crossing to the fire*) I've been walking round and round the house. I'm glad you lit a fire.

MIDGE. (*moving to* L. *of the sofa; accusingly*) What did you do to Edward?

HENRIETTA. (*absently*) Edward?

MIDGE. Yes, when I came in just now, he was looking dreadful—so cold and grey.

HENRIETTA. (*turning*) Midge—Midge, if you care so much for Edward, why don't you do something about him?

MIDGE. Do something? What do you mean?

HENRIETTA. (*impatiently*) I don't know. Stand on a table and shout. Draw attention to yourself. Don't you know that's the only hope with a man like Edward?

MIDGE. (*sitting on the sofa at the left end of it*) I don't think Edward will ever care for anyone but you, Henrietta.

HENRIETTA. Then it's very unintelligent of him.

MIDGE. Perhaps—but there it is.

HENRIETTA. He doesn't even know what I'm like. He just goes on caring for his idea of what I once was. Today— I hate Edward.

MIDGE. You *can't* hate Edward. *Nobody* could hate Edward.

HENRIETTA. I can.

MIDGE. But why?

HENRIETTA. Because he reminds me of a lot of things I'd like to forget.

MIDGE. What things?

HENRIETTA. Ainswick.

MIDGE. Ainswick? You want to forget Ainswick?

HENRIETTA. Yes, yes. I was happy at Ainswick. (*She moves L.C.*) Don't you understand that I can't bear just now to be reminded of a time when I was happy?

(LADY ANGKATELL *enters* L. MIDGE *rises*.)

(*Abruptly*.) I shall never go back to Ainswick.

(*She moves to the door* L., *ignores* LADY ANGKATELL *and exits*.)

LADY ANGKATELL. What did she say?

MIDGE. (*crossing to* R.) She said she would never go back to Ainswick.

LADY ANGKATELL. (*closing the door*) Oh, I think she will, darling.

MIDGE. You mean she'll—marry Edward?

LADY ANGKATELL. Yes. (*She crosses to the drinks table, picks up the box of chocolates, then moves to* L. *of* MIDGE.) I think so. (*Cheerfully*.) Now that John Cristow's out of the way. Oh yes, I think she'll marry Edward. Everything's working out quite for the best, isn't it?

MIDGE. Perhaps John Cristow wouldn't think so.

LADY ANGKATELL. No, well I wasn't thinking of him.

(*The* INSPECTOR *enters* L. *He is followed on by* DETECTIVE SERGEANT PENNY. *The* SERGEANT *is in plain clothes. He carries a notebook to which he frequently refers, and in which he makes further notes*.)

INSPECTOR. Is Miss Angkatell about?

MIDGE. She went upstairs to change, I think. Shall I fetch her?

LADY ANGKATELL. (*crossing to* L.) No, no, I'll go. I want to see how Gerda is. (*She offers the chocolates to the* IN-SPECTOR.) Sweetie? Soft centres.

INSPECTOR. No, thank you.

LADY ANGKATELL. (*Offering the sweets to the* SERGEANT) There's a jelly baby there.

SERGEANT. No, thank you.

(LADY ANGKATELL *exits* L. *The* SERGEANT *closes the door*.)

INSPECTOR. (*crossing to* L. *of the sofa*) You're Miss Harvey, aren't you?

MIDGE. Yes. Margerie Harvey.

INSPECTOR. You don't live here? (*He indicates the sofa.*) Do sit down.

MIDGE. No, I live at twenty-seven Strathmere Mansions, W—two.

INSPECTOR. But you are a relation?

MIDGE. (*sitting on the sofa at the right end of it*) My mother was Lady Angkatell's first cousin.

INSPECTOR. And where were you when the shot was fired?

MIDGE. In the garden.

INSPECTOR. You were all rather scattered, weren't you? (*He crosses above the sofa to* R. *of it.*) Lady Angkatell had just come in from the farm. Mr. Angkatell down from the woods. You from the garden, Mrs. Cristow from her bedroom, Sir Henry from the target alley. And Miss Angkatell?

MIDGE. She'd been in the garden somewhere.

INSPECTOR. (*crossing above the sofa to* L. *of it*) You quite boxed the compass between you all. Now, Miss Harvey, I'd like you to describe what you saw when you came in here, very carefully.

MIDGE. (*pointing* L.C.) John Cristow was lying there. There was blood—Mrs. Cristow was standing with the—revolver in her hand.

INSPECTOR. And you thought she had shot him?

MIDGE. Well, frankly, yes, I did.

INSPECTOR. You had no doubt about it?

MIDGE. No, not then.

INSPECTOR. (*quickly*) But you have now. Why?

MIDGE. I suppose because I realized that I simply jumped to conclusions.

INSPECTOR. Why were you so sure she had shot him?

MIDGE. Because she had the revolver in her hand, I suppose.

INSPECTOR. But you must have thought she had some reason for shooting him. (*He looks keenly at her.*)

MIDGE. (*looking troubled*) I . . .

INSPECTOR. Well, Miss Harvey?

MIDGE. I don't know of any reason.

INSPECTOR. In fact, as far as you know, they were a very devoted couple?

MIDGE. Oh yes, they were.

INSPECTOR. I see. (*He crosses below the sofa to* R. *of it.*) Let's get on. What happened next?

MIDGE. I think—yes, Sir Henry went and knelt down by
him. He said he wasn't dead. He told Gudgeon to telephone for the doctor.

INSPECTOR. Gudgeon? That's the butler. So he was there too.

MIDGE. Yes, he was. Gudgeon went to the telephone and
just then John Cristow opened his eyes. I think he tried
to struggle up. And then—then he died. It was horrible.

INSPECTOR. And that's all?

MIDGE. Yes.

INSPECTOR. (moving up R.) He didn't say anything at all
before he died?

MIDGE. I think he said "Henrietta."

INSPECTOR. (turning) He said "Henrietta."

MIDGE. She—(agitatedly) she was just opposite him when
he opened his eyes. He was looking right at her. (She
looks at the INSPECTOR as if in explanation.)

INSPECTOR. I see. That's all for now, thank you, Miss Harvey.

MIDGE. (rising and crossing to the door L.) Well, I'd better
go and find Henrietta. Lady Angkatell is so very vague,
you know. She usually forgets what she went to do.

(The SERGEANT opens the door. MIDGE exits L. and the SER-
GEANT closes the door behind her.)

INSPECTOR. (thoughtfully) Lady Angkatell is so very vague.

SERGEANT. (crossing to C.) She's bats, if you ask me.

(The INSPECTOR holds out his hand and the SERGEANT gives
him his notebook.)

INSPECTOR. I wonder. I wonder. (He flicks over the pages of
the notebook.) Interesting discrepancies. Lady Angkatell says, (he reads) "He murmured something before
he died, but she couldn't catch what it was."

SERGEANT. Perhaps she's deaf.

INSPECTOR. Oh no, I don't think she is. According to Sir
Henry, John Cristow said "Henrietta" in a loud voice.
When I put it to her—but not before—Miss Harvey
says the same thing. Edward Angkatell says Cristow
died without saying a word. Gudgeon does not precisely
recollect. (He moves below the sofa.) They all know
something, Penny, but they're not telling us. (He sits
on the sofa at the right end of it.)

SERGEANT. We'll get round to it. (He crosses to the IN-

SPECTOR.) Think the wife did shoot him? (*He takes his notebook from the* INSPECTOR, *then eases to* R. *of the sofa.*)

INSPECTOR. Wives so often have excellent reasons for shooting their husbands that one tends to suspect them automatically.

SERGEANT. It's clear enough that all the others think she did it.

INSPECTOR. Or do they probably all *want* to think she did it?

SERGEANT. Meaning exactly?

INSPECTOR. There's an atmosphere of family solidarity in this house. They're all blood relations. Mrs. Cristow's the only outsider. Yes, I think they'd be glad to be sure she did it.

SERGEANT. (*crossing above the sofa to* C.) But you're not so sure?

INSPECTOR. Actually anyone could have shot him. There are no alibis in this case. (*He rises and stands* R. *of the sofa.*) No times or places to check. Just look at the entrances and exits. You could shoot him from the terrace, pop round the house and—(*he indicates the window* R.) in by this window. Or through the front door and hall and in by that door, and if you say you've come from the farm or the kitchen garden or from shooting in the woods, nobody can check that statement. (*He looks through the window* R.) There are shrubs and undergrowth right up to the house. You could play hide-and-seek there for hours. (*He moves above the sofa.*) The revolver was one of those used for target practice. Anyone could have picked it up and they'd all handled it, though the only clear prints on it are those of Mrs. Cristow and Henrietta Angkatell. (*He moves* L. *of the sofa.*) It all boils down really to what sort of a man John Cristow was. (*He moves below the sofa.*) If you know all about a man, you can guess who would have wanted to murder him.

SERGEANT. We'll pick up all that in London, in Harley Street. Secretary, servants.

INSPECTOR. (*sitting on the sofa at the left end of it*) Any luck with the servants here?

SERGEANT. Not yet. They're the starchy kind. There's no kitchenmaid unfortunately. I always had a success with kitchenmaids. (*He moves above the armchair* L.C. *to the fireplace.*) There's a daily girl as underhousemaid I've got hopes of. I'd like to put in a little more work on her now, sir, if you don't want me.

(*The* INSPECTOR *nods. The* SERGEANT *grins and exits* L. *The* INSPECTOR *rises, moves to the window* R., *looks out for a moment, then turns, moves up* C. *and goes out on to the terrace. After a few moments he moves to the sofa and sits on it at the left end. He becomes aware of something under the cushion behind him, moves the cushion and picks up* VERONICA's *red handbag. He opens the bag, looks into it and shows considerable surprise. He closes the bag, rises, moves to* L. *of the sofa and weighs the bag in his hand. As he does so voices are heard off* L. *He immediately replaces the bag on the sofa and covers it with the cushion.*)

MIDGE. (*off* L.) Oh, there you are, Henrietta. The Inspector would like to see you.

HENRIETTA. (*off* L.) Thank you, Midge. Lucy's just told me. I'm going in to see him now.

MIDGE. (*off* L.) Oh good. I thought she might forget.

(*The* INSPECTOR *crosses to* R. *of the sofa.* HENRIETTA *enters* L.)

HENRIETTA. (*closing the door*) You wanted to see me? (*She crosses to the sofa and sits on it at the left end.*)

INSPECTOR. Yes, Miss Angkatell. You're a relation as well, aren't you?

HENRIETTA. Yes, we're all cousins. It's rather confusing because Lady Angkatell married her second cousin and is actually an Angkatell herself.

INSPECTOR. Just a family party—with the exception of Dr. and Mrs. Cristow?

HENRIETTA. Yes.

INSPECTOR. (*moving up* R.) Will you give me your account of what happened?

HENRIETTA. I was in the flower garden. (*She points* R.) It's through there. Not very far from the house. I heard the shot and realized it came from the house and not from the target alley down below. I thought that was strange, so I came in.

INSPECTOR. By which window?

HENRIETTA. (*pointing* R.) That one.

INSPECTOR. Will you describe what you saw?

HENRIETTA. Sir Henry and Gudgeon, the butler, were bending over John Cristow. Mrs. Cristow was beside them. She had the revolver in her hand.

INSPECTOR. (*moving to* R. *of the sofa*) And you concluded that she had shot him?

HENRIETTA. Why should I think so?

INSPECTOR. Didn't you, in fact, think so?

HENRIETTA. No, I didn't.

INSPECTOR. What did you think, then?

HENRIETTA. I don't think I thought at all. It was all rather unexpected. Sir Henry told Gudgeon to call the doctor and he went over to the phone.

INSPECTOR. Who else was in the room?

HENRIETTA. Everybody, I think. No—Edward came in after I did.

INSPECTOR. Which way?

HENRIETTA. By the terrace.

INSPECTOR. And then?

HENRIETTA. And then—John died.

INSPECTOR. Was he conscious before he died?

HENRIETTA. Oh yes, he opened his eyes.

INSPECTOR. Did he say anything?

HENRIETTA. (*after a pause*) He said "Henrietta."

INSPECTOR. You knew him well?

HENRIETTA. Very well indeed.

INSPECTOR. He didn't say anything else?

HENRIETTA. No.

INSPECTOR. (*crossing above the sofa to* L. *of it*) What happened next?

HENRIETTA. Let me see—oh yes, Gerda cried out. She was swaying, and waving the revolver about. I thought it might go off. I went and took it from her and tried to get her on to the sofa.

INSPECTOR. (*crossing to the fireplace*) Were you particularly a friend of Dr. Cristow or of Mrs. Cristow?

HENRIETTA. That's a rather difficult question to answer.

INSPECTOR. (*sympathetically and gently*) Is it, Miss Angkatell?

HENRIETTA. (*resolutely*) Well, I'll take a short cut. I was John Cristow's mistress. That's what you wanted to know, isn't it?

INSPECTOR. (*crossing to* HENRIETTA) Thank you, Miss Angkatell. (*He takes a cigarette case from his pocket and offers a cigarette to* HENRIETTA. *Gently.*) I'm afraid we have to know all the facts.

HENRIETTA. (*taking a cigarette; in a dry voice*) If this particular fact has no bearing on the case, and I don't see how it can have, is there any necessity to make it public? Not only for my sake. It would give Mrs. Cristow a good deal of unnecessary pain.

INSPECTOR. (*lighting* HENRIETTA's *cigarette*) Mrs. Cristow had no idea of the relationship between you and her husband?

HENRIETTA. None.

INSPECTOR. Are you sure of that?

HENRIETTA. Absolutely.

INSPECTOR. (*crossing above the sofa to* R. *of it*) How long had you and Dr. Cristow been lovers?

HENRIETTA. I became his mistress six months ago. I did not say we were lovers.

INSPECTOR. (*looking at her with quickened interest*) I'm not sure that I know what you mean, Miss Angkatell.

HENRIETTA. I think you will know if you think about it.

INSPECTOR. There was no question of a divorce?

HENRIETTA. Certainly not. That's what I've been trying to explain. John Cristow had had affairs with other women. I was only one of—a procession. I don't think he really cared for any woman except his wife. But she wasn't the kind of woman he could talk to about his work. He was doing research on an obscure disease.

(*The* INSPECTOR *sits on the sofa at the right end of it.*)

He was a very brilliant man, and his research work was the real passion of his life. He got into the habit of coming into my studio and talking to me about it. Actually it was a good deal above my head, but I got some books on the subject and read it up, so that I could understand better. And my questions, even if they weren't very technical, helped him to formulate his own ideas. (*She speaks naturally, as to a friend.*) And then—suddenly—I got between John and what he was thinking about. I began to affect him as a woman. He didn't want to fall in love with me—he'd been in love when he was a young man, and it had left him afraid of going through it again. No, he just wanted an affair, like other affairs he had. I think he thought that if he had an affair with me, he'd get me out of his system and not be distracted from his work any more.

INSPECTOR. And was that satisfactory to you?

HENRIETTA. No, no, of course not. But it had to do. I loved John Cristow, and I was content that he should have what he wanted.

INSPECTOR. I see. It was like that.

HENRIETTA. I've been forgetting that you're a policeman.

INSPECTOR. Policemen are quite like other men. We hear a good deal that isn't strictly relevant—perhaps it's because we're impersonal—like priests.

HENRIETTA. Yes, yes, I suppose you must learn a good deal about the human heart. (*She rises and flicks her cigarette ash into the ashtray on the coffee table. The following sentence does not ring quite true.*) So now you understand why John said "Henrietta" just before he died.

(*The* SERGEANT *enters* L.)

INSPECTOR. It's a small point, Miss Angkatell—(*he rises and stands* R. *of the sofa*) but why did you take the revolver away from Mrs. Cristow?

HENRIETTA. I told you. I thought she was going to faint.

INSPECTOR. It was one of the revolvers used earlier for target practice. The only clear prints on it are Mrs. Cristow's and naturally—yours. (*He pauses.*) It would have been better if nobody had touched it.

HENRIETTA. One doesn't realize these things at the time. Is that all, Inspector?

INSPECTOR. Yes, thank you, Miss Angkatell, that's all for the present.

(*The* SERGEANT *opens the door.* HENRIETTA *crosses and exits* L. *The* SERGEANT *closes the door behind her.*)

SERGEANT. Get anything useful out of her?

INSPECTOR. She was Cristow's mistress. She told me that accounts for his saying "Henrietta" before he died.

SERGEANT. (*crossing to* L. *of the sofa*) That seems fair enough.

INSPECTOR. If it's true.

SERGEANT. What other reason could he have for saying her name?

INSPECTOR. It could have been—an accusation.

SERGEANT. You mean she might have done him in?

INSPECTOR. (*crossing to the fireplace*) It's possible.

SERGEANT. My money's on the wife. If Mrs. Cristow had found out about her husband and this Henrietta, it gives us what we want—a motive.

INSPECTOR. Henrietta Angkatell says she didn't know.

SERGEANT. You can't be sure of that. Somebody tipped Mrs. Cristow off as like as not.

INSPECTOR. (*moving to the alcove and looking off at the statue*) She couldn't have hidden her feelings for long. She's not that kind of woman.

SERGEANT. What about the others? They're in the clear, I suppose?

INSPECTOR. There doesn't seem any reason why any of them should have wanted John Cristow dead. (*He turns and crosses above the sofa to the writing table.*) But there's a good deal we don't know yet. They're all watchful and cagey about what they say.

SERGEANT. I can't see how Sir Henry or Lady Angkatell could have any reason for wanting Cristow out of the way.

INSPECTOR. Nor the little girl—Miss Harvey. But remember that statement of Edward Angkatell's: "Did John Cristow say anything before he died? Nothing at all." A flat denial, that of what we know to be true. Both Sir Henry and Miss Harvey say that John Cristow said "Henrietta" in quite a loud voice.

SERGEANT. You think Edward Angkatell's sweet on this Henrietta woman?

INSPECTOR. That is my idea.

SERGEANT. And was doing his best not to get her mixed up in it.

INSPECTOR. Exactly.

SERGEANT. Yes—it certainly looks like it.

INSPECTOR. (*easing below the sofa*) And granting that, Penny, it gives us another suspect.

SERGEANT. Edward Angkatell?

INSPECTOR. (*sitting on the sofa at the right end of it*) Yes. He's the nervous sort. If he cared very much for Henrietta and discovered that she was John Cristow's mistress, he's just the quiet type that goes off half-cocked when everybody least expects it.

SERGEANT. Hoped he's get her when the other man was out of the way?

INSPECTOR. We've both known cases like that.

SERGEANT. (*moving up* C.) So in your opinion it's between the three of them, Henrietta Angkatell, Edward Angkatell and the wife?

INSPECTOR. Oh, I've got a very open mind about it, Penny—a very open mind. (*He takes* VERONICA'S *handbag from under the cushion and holds it up.*) Just tell me what you make of this?

SERGEANT. (*moving to* L. *of the sofa*) Lady's handbag.

INSPECTOR. Undoubtedly.

SERGEANT. We went over it when we did this room. (*He consults his notebook.*) Two pounds ten shillings in notes, seven shillings in cash, the usual lipstick, powder compact and rouge. Silver cigarette lighter. Lace handkerchief unmarked. All very Ritzy. Belongs to one of the ladies, I suppose, I couldn't say which.

(*The* INSPECTOR *rises with the bag in his hand, crosses to the fireplace and presses the bell-push.*)

I didn't go into the matter as I didn't think it important.

INSPECTOR. You think it belongs to one of the ladies in this house?

SERGEANT. (*moving up* L.C.) I assumed so. Have you any reason for thinking otherwise?

INSPECTOR. Only aesthetic sense. (*He crosses to* L. *of the sofa.*) Not in good enough taste for Lady Angkatell. Too expensive for little Miss Harvey. Far too fashionable for Mrs. Cristow. Too flamboyant for Henrietta Angkatell. It doesn't seem to me to belong to this household at all. (*He looks at the bag.*) I find it—very intriguing.

SERGEANT. (*easing to the fireplace*) I daresay I can find out who it does belong to. But as I say, the contents being nothing out of the ordinary . . .

INSPECTOR. Are you quite sure you've mentioned all its contents?

SERGEANT. I think so, sir.

(GUDGEON *enters* L.)

GUDGEON. You rang, sir?

INSPECTOR. Yes. Can you tell me to whom this bag belongs?

GUDGEON. (*crossing to* L. *of the* INSPECTOR) I'm afraid not, sir. I don't recollect ever having seen it before. I could ask her ladyship's own maid, sir. She would probably know better than I should.

INSPECTOR. Thank you.

(GUDGEON *turns, moves to the door down* L., *then hesitates and turns.*)

GUDGEON. It just occurred to me, sir, if I might make a suggestion?

INSPECTOR. By all means.

GUDGEON. (*moving* L.C.) It might possibly be the property of Miss Veronica Craye.

SERGEANT. (*moving to* L. *of* GUDGEON) Veronica Craye? The film star? Is she in this part of the world?

GUDGEON. (*giving the* SERGEANT *a dirty look; to the* IN-SPECTOR) She occupies the cottage a hundred yards up the lane. Dovecotes, it's called.

INSPECTOR. Has Miss Craye been here?

GUDGEON. She was here yesterday evening, sir.

INSPECTOR. And she was carrying this bag?

GUDGEON. No, sir. She was in evening dress and was carrying a white diamanté bag. But I think it possible Miss Craye was here earlier this morning for a short time.

INSPECTOR. When?

GUDGEON. About midday, sir.

INSPECTOR. You saw her?

GUDGEON. I didn't see her myself, sir.

SERGEANT. Well, who did?

GUDGEON. (*with an angry glance at the* SERGEANT) The underhousemaid observed her from one of the bedroom windows, sir. The girl is an ardent movie fan. She was quite thrilled.

SERGEANT. I'll have a word with that girl.

(*He exits* L.)

INSPECTOR. Lady Angkatell didn't mention that Miss Craye had been here this morning.

GUDGEON. I don't think her ladyship was aware of Miss Craye's visit.

INSPECTOR. Who did she come to see, then?

GUDGEON. As to that, sir, I couldn't say.

(*The* INSPECTOR *crosses above the sofa to* R. *of it.*)

H'm! (*He coughs.*)

INSPECTOR. (*turning to* GUDGEON) Yes?

GUDGEON. A note was brought over from Dovecotes for Dr. Cristow earlier in the morning. Dr. Cristow said there was no answer.

INSPECTOR. I see. What happened to that note?

GUDGEON. I think I could produce it for you, sir. I picked up some crumpled paper by the waste-paper basket.

INSPECTOR. Thank you, Gudgeon—I should be extremely obliged if you will bring it to me at once.

GUDGEON. (*turning and crossing to the door* L.) Very good, sir.

INSPECTOR. I gather Dr. Cristow knew Miss Craye?

GUDGEON. It would seem so, sir. He went over to see her last night—after dinner. (*He waits expectantly.*)

INSPECTOR. When did he return?

GUDGEON. As to that, sir, I could not say. Acting on Sir Henry's instructions I left the side door unfastened when I retired to bed at twelve-fifteen A.M.

(*The* INSPECTOR *puts the bag on the writing table.*)

Up to that time Dr. Cristow had not returned.

(VERONICA *enters up* C. *from* L.)

VERONICA. I've just heard the news. It's awful—just awful. (*She moves above the sofa.*) Are you . . . ?

INSPECTOR. I'm Inspector Colquhoun of Scotland Yard.

VERONICA. Then John *was* murdered?

(GUDGEON *exits abruptly* L.)

INSPECTOR. Oh yes, Miss Craye, he was murdered.

VERONICA. So you know who I am? (*She moves below the left end of the sofa.*)

INSPECTOR. I'm very fond of a good film.

VERONICA. How charming of you. (*She sits on the sofa at the left end of it.*) I'm over in England to make a picture.

INSPECTOR. (*crossing below the sofa to* L.C.) Dr. Cristow was a friend of yours?

VERONICA. I hadn't seen him for years. I came over last night to borrow some matches—and the first person I saw when I came into the room was John Cristow.

INSPECTOR. Were you pleased to see him?

VERONICA. I was very pleased. It's always nice to meet an old friend.

INSPECTOR. He called on you yesterday evening, I believe?

VERONICA. Yes, I asked him to come over after dinner if he could manage it. We had a delightful talk about old times and old friends.

INSPECTOR. (*crossing to the fireplace*) What time did he leave?

VERONICA. I've really no idea. We talked for quite a while.

INSPECTOR. About old times?

VERONICA. Yes, of course a lot had happened to us both.

(*The* INSPECTOR *moves up* C. *and closes the window.*)

He'd done very well in his profession, I understand. And he'd married since I knew him.

INSPECTOR. (*easing up* R.) You didn't know his wife?

VERONICA. No, no, he introduced us here last night. I gathered from what he—well, didn't exactly say, but hinted at— that his married life wasn't awfully happy.

INSPECTOR. Oh, really.

VERONICA. I think his wife was one of those dim ineffectual women who are inclined to be jealous.

INSPECTOR. (*moving to* R. *of the sofa*) Had she any cause for jealousy?

VERONICA. Oh, don't ask me. I just thought there might have been a little trouble lately. Jealousy does make people do such dreadful things.

INSPECTOR. You think he was shot by his wife?

VERONICA. Oh, I don't really know anything about it. It was my maid—she told me that his wife had actually been found standing over him with the revolver still in her hand. But of course the wildest stories do get around in the country.

INSPECTOR. (*easing above the writing table*) This one happens to be quite true.

VERONICA. Oh, I suppose his wife found out about him and the sculptress woman.

(*The* SERGEANT *enters* L. *He carries the crumpled note.*)

INSPECTOR. Excuse me.

(*The* SERGEANT *crosses below the coffee table to the* IN- SPECTOR *and hands him the crumpled note.*)

VERONICA. Of course.

SERGEANT (*aside to the* INSPECTOR) He got back at three
o'clock. (*He moves up* R.)

VERONICA. I really just came over to—to . . .

INSPECTOR. (*picking up the handbag*) To get your bag perhaps? It *is* your bag?

VERONICA. (*disconcerted*) Oh yes. (*She rises.*) Thank you.

INSPECTOR. Just a moment.

(VERONICA *resumes her seat on the sofa.*)

(*He refers to the note, then crosses below the sofa to*
L.C.) Dr. Cristow returned to this house at three a.m.
this morning. Isn't that rather an unconventional hour?

VERONICA. We were talking about old times.

INSPECTOR. So you said.

VERONICA. It must have been much later than I thought.

INSPECTOR. Was that the last time you saw Dr. Cristow?

VERONICA. (*quickly*) Yes.

INSPECTOR. Are you quite sure, Miss Craye?

VERONICA. Of course I'm sure.

INSPECTOR. What about this bag of yours?

VERONICA. Oh, I must have left that last night, when I came
to get the matches.

INSPECTOR. Rather large and heavy for an evening bag. (*He
pauses.*) I think you left it here this morning.

VERONICA. And what makes you think that?

INSPECTOR. (*moving to the fireplace and putting the bag
on the mantelpiece*) Partly this note of yours. (*He
smooths out the note and reads it.*) "Please come over
this morning. I must see you, Veronica." A little curt,
Miss Craye. Dr. Cristow, I believe, said there was no
answer. He didn't come to you—so you came here to
see him, didn't you?

VERONICA. (*rising and moving to the armchair* L.C.; *with a
change of manner*) How wonderful you are! You seem
to know *everything*.

INSPECTOR. Not quite everything. What happened when you
came here? Did you quarrel?

VERONICA. We-ell—you couldn't call it a *quarrel* exactly. (*She
sighs and sits in the armchair* L.C.) Poor John.

INSPECTOR. Why poor John?

VERONICA. I didn't want to tell you. It didn't seem *fair*.

INSPECTOR. Yes?

VERONICA. John went mad—quite mad. He'd been in love with me years ago. He—he wanted to leave his wife and children—he wanted me to get a divorce and marry him. It's really quite frightening to think one can have such an effect on a man.

INSPECTOR. It must be. Very sudden and unexpected.

VERONICA. I know. Almost unbelievable. But it's possible, you know, never to forget—to wait and hope and plan. There are men like that.

INSPECTOR. (*watching her closely and moving above the armchair to* R. *of it*) And women.

VERONICA. Yes—yes—I suppose so. Well, that's how he was. I pretended at first not to take him seriously. I told him he was mad. He'd said something of the kind last night. That's why I sent him that note. I couldn't leave things like that. I came over to make him realize that what he suggested was impossible. But he wouldn't listen to what I had to say. And now—he's dead. I feel dreadful.

(*The* SERGEANT *clears his throat.*)

INSPECTOR. Yes, Sergeant?

SERGEANT. (*easing above the sofa; to* VERONICA) I understand from information received that as you left by that window you were heard to say—(*he refers to his notebook*) "I hate you more than I ever thought it possible to hate anyone."

VERONICA. I'm sure I *never* said that. What have you been listening to? Servants' talk?

SERGEANT. One of your fans, Miss Craye, was hanging around hoping to get your autograph. (*Significantly.*) She heard a great deal of what went on in this room.

VERONICA. (*rising; angrily*) All a pack of lies. (*To the* IN-SPECTOR.) Can I have my bag, please?

INSPECTOR. (*crossing to the fireplace*) Certainly, Miss Craye. (*He picks up the bag.*) But I'm afraid I shall have to keep the gun.

VERONICA. Gun?

(*The* INSPECTOR *takes a handkerchief from his pocket, puts it round his hand, opens the bag and takes out a revolver.*)

INSPECTOR. Didn't you know there was a gun in your bag?

SERGEANT. (*with a step towards the* INSPECTOR) But . . .

(*The* INSPECTOR *quells the* SERGEANT *with a glance.*)

VERONICA. There wasn't a gun. It's not mine. I don't know anything about a gun.

INSPECTOR. (*examining the revolver*) Thirty-eight Smith and Wesson—the same calibre as the bullet that killed John Cristow.

VERONICA. (*angrily*) Don't you think you can frame me! (*She moves to the* INSPECTOR) I'll see my attorney. I'll . . . How dare you!

INSPECTOR. (*holding out the bag*) Here's your bag, Miss Craye.

(VERONICA *snatches the bag from him. She looks both angry and frightened.*)

VERONICA. I won't say another word.

INSPECTOR. Very wise.

(VERONICA *turns, glares at the* SERGEANT, *then exits hurriedly up* C. *to* L. *The* INSPECTOR *looks after her, twisting the revolver which he holds carefully in the handkerchief.*)

SERGEANT. (*easing to* R. *of the armchair* L.C.) But, sir, I . . .

INSPECTOR. But me no buts, Penny. Things are not what they seem, and all the rest of it. (*He moves to the armchair* L.C. *and sits slowly in it.*)

(*The* SERGEANT *opens his mouth to protest.*)

(*He silences the* SERGEANT *with a gesture.*) I know—I know. Now I wonder . . . ?

CURTAIN

Act Three

SCENE: *The same. The following Monday morning.*

When the CURTAIN rises, it is a fine morning, the french windows are open and a small fire burns in the grate. GUDGEON ushers in the INSPECTOR and the SERGEANT L.

GUDGEON. I will inform Sir Henry you are here, sir.

(*He exits L.*)

SERGEANT. (*glancing at the drinks table*) Nice flowers. (*He moves to the fireplace.*)

INSPECTOR. (*moving up C. and standing in the french windows*) Yes.

SERGEANT. (*turning and looking at the picture over the mantelpiece*) I rather like this picture. Nice house. I wonder whose it is?

INSPECTOR. That's Lady Angkatell's old home.

SERGEANT. Is it now? All sold up like everything else nowadays?

INSPECTOR. No, it belongs to Edward Angkatell. Entailed, you see.

SERGEANT. (*turning*) Why not to Sir Henry? He's got the title.

INSPECTOR. No. He's a K.C.B. He was only a second cousin.

SERGEANT. You seem to know all about the family.

INSPECTOR. (*moving down R.*) I've taken the trouble to find out all I could. I thought it might have a bearing on the case.

SERGEANT. I don't quite see how. (*He eases L.C.*) Anyway, we're getting places at last—or aren't we?

INSPECTOR. Aren't we is probably right.

(DORIS *enters up* C. *from* L.)

DORIS. (*standing in the french windows*) Ssh!

SERGEANT. Hullo.

DORIS. (*moving* C.; *conspiratorially*) I come round this way because I didn't want Mr. Gudgeon to spot me. They say out there it's common to have anything to do with the police, but what I say is let justice be done.

SERGEANT. That's the spirit, my girl. And who says it's common to have anything to do with the police?

DORIS. (*turning to the* SERGEANT) Mrs. Medway—the cook. She said it was bad enough anyway to have police in the house and a thing that had never happened to her before and she was afraid she wasn't going to have a light hand with her pastry. (*She pauses for breath.*) And if it wasn't for her ladyship she'd give in her notice, but she couldn't leave her ladyship in the lurch. (*She crosses to* L. *of the sofa. To the* INSPECTOR.) All potty about her ladyship they are.

SERGEANT. Well, come to the part about justice being done.

DORIS. (*turning and crossing to* R. *of the* SERGEANT) It's what I seen with my own eyes.

SERGEANT. And very nice eyes they are, too.

DORIS. (*nudging the* SERGEANT) Oh, go on! Well, Saturday afternoon it was—the very day of the murder. I went to shut the bedroom windows because it looked like rain, and I happened to glance over the banisters, and what did I see?

SERGEANT. Well—what did you see?

DORIS. I saw Mr. Gudgeon standing in the front hall with a revolver in his hand and he looked ever so peculiar. Gave me quite a turn it did.

INSPECTOR. Gudgeon?

DORIS. (*moving to* L. *of the sofa*) Yes, sir. And it come to me as perhaps *he* was the murderer.

INSPECTOR. Gudgeon!

DORIS. (*crossing below the sofa to* L. *of the* INSPECTOR) And I hope I've done right in coming to you, but what they'll say to me in the servants' hall I don't know, but what I felt was—let——

SERGEANT	} (*together*). {	(*Moving below the sofa.*) Justice be done.
DORIS		—justice be done.

SERGEANT. You did quite right, my girl.

DORIS. And what I feel is . . . (*She breaks off and listens.*) Someone's coming. (*She moves quickly up* c.) I must hop it. I'm supposed to be counting the laundry.

(*She exits up* c. *to* L.)

SERGEANT. (*moving up* c. *and looking after* DORIS) That's a useful girl. She's the one who was hanging about for Miss Craye's autograph.

(SIR HENRY *enters* L.)

INSPECTOR. Good morning, Sir Henry.

SIR HENRY. (*crossing to* L. *of the sofa*) Good morning, Inspector.

SERGEANT. Good morning, sir.

(SIR HENRY *nods to the* SERGEANT.)

SIR HENRY. (*to the* INSPECTOR) You wanted to see me?

INSPECTOR. (*crossing to* L.C.) Yes, Sir Henry. We wanted some further information.

SIR HENRY. Yes?

INSPECTOR. Sir Henry, you have a considerable collection of firearms, mostly pistols and revolvers. I wanted to know if any of them are missing.

SIR HENRY. (*sitting on the sofa at the left end of it*) I don't quite understand. I have already told you that I took two revolvers and one pistol down to the target alley on Saturday morning, and that I subsequently found that one of them, a thirty-eight Smith and Wesson, was missing. I identified this missing revolver as the one that Mrs. Cristow was holding just after the murder.

INSPECTOR. That is quite correct, Sir Henry. According to Mrs. Cristow's statement, she picked it up from the floor by her husband's body. We assumed, perhaps naturally, that *that* was the gun with which Dr. Cristow was shot.

SIR HENRY. Do you mean—it *wasn't?*

INSPECTOR. We have now received the report of our ballistics expert. Sir Henry, the bullet that killed Dr. Cristow was *not* fired from that gun.

SIR HENRY. You astound me.

INSPECTOR. Yes, it's extremely odd. The bullet was of the right calibre, but that was definitely not the gun used.

SIR HENRY. But may I ask, Inspector, why you should assume that the murder weapon came from my collection?

INSPECTOR. I don't assume it, Sir Henry—but I must check up before looking elsewhere.

SIR HENRY. (*rising and crossing to* L.) Yes, I see that. Well, I can tell you what you want to know in a very few moments.

(*He exits* L.)

SERGEANT. He doesn't know anything.

INSPECTOR. (*moving up* C.) So it seems. (*He goes on to the terrace and stands looking off* L.)

SERGEANT. What time's the inquest?

INSPECTOR. Twelve o'clock. There's plenty of time.

SERGEANT. Just routine evidence and an adjournment. It's all fixed up with the Coroner, I suppose?

(MIDGE *enters* L. *She wears her hat and coat, and carries her handbag, gloves and suitcase.*)

INSPECTOR. (*turning*) Are you leaving, Miss Harvey?

MIDGE. (*crossing to* C.) I have to get up to town immediately after the inquest.

INSPECTOR. (*moving to* R. *of* MIDGE) I'm afraid I must ask you not to leave here today.

MIDGE. But that's very awkward. You see, I work in a dress shop. And if I'm not back by two-thirty there'll be an awful to-do.

INSPECTOR. I'm sorry, Miss Harvey. You can say you are acting on police instructions.

MIDGE. That won't go down very well, I can tell you. (*She crosses below the sofa to the writing table, puts her handbag and gloves on it and stands the case on the floor above the writing table.*) Oh well, I suppose I'd better ring up now and get it over. (*She lifts the telephone receiver. Into the telephone.*) Hello . . .

(*The voice of the* OPERATOR *is reasonably audible.*)

OPERATOR. Number please.

MIDGE. Regent four-six-nine-two, please.

OPERATOR. What is your number?

MIDGE. Dowfield two-two-one.

(*The* INSPECTOR *eases to* L. *of the sofa and looks at the* SERGEANT.)

OPERATOR. Dowfield two-two-one. There's a twenty-minute delay on the line.

MIDGE. Oh!

OPERATOR. Shall I keep the call in?

MIDGE. Yes, keep the call in, please. You'll ring me?

OPERATOR. Yes.

MIDGE. Thank you. (*She replaces the receiver.*)

(SIR HENRY *enters* L.)

SIR HENRY. Do you mind leaving us, Midge?

MIDGE. Of course—but I'm expecting a call. (*She picks up her suitcase and crosses to* L.)

SIR HENRY. I'll give you a hail when it comes through, unless they forget all about it.

(MIDGE *exits* L. SIR HENRY *closes the door behind her.*)

(*He crosses to* L. *of the* INSPECTOR.) A second thirty-eight Smith and Wesson exhibit in a brown leather holster is missing from my study.

INSPECTOR. (*taking a revolver from his pocket*) Would it be this gun, Sir Henry?

(SIR HENRY, *surprised, takes the revolver from the* INSPECTOR *and carefully examines it.*)

SIR HENRY. Yes—yes, this is it. Where did you find it?

INSPECTOR. That doesn't matter for the moment. But the shot that killed Dr. Cristow was fired from that gun. May I speak to your butler, Sir Henry? (*He holds out his hand for the revolver.*)

SIR HENRY. (*handing the revolver to the* INSPECTOR) Of course. (*He turns, crosses to the fireplace and presses the bell-push.*) Do you want to speak to him in here?

INSPECTOR. (*putting the revolver in his pocket*) If you please, Sir Henry.

SIR HENRY. Do you want me to go away or to remain? I should prefer to remain. Gudgeon is a very old and valued servant.

INSPECTOR. I would prefer you to be here, Sir Henry.

(GUDGEON *enters* L.)

GUDGEON. You rang, Sir Henry?

SIR HENRY. Yes, Gudgeon. (*He indicates the* INSPECTOR.)

(GUDGEON *looks politely at the* INSPECTOR.)

INSPECTOR. Gudgeon, have you lately had a pistol or a revolver in your possession?

(SIR HENRY *sits in the armchair* L.C.)

GUDGEON. (*crossing to* L. *of the* INSPECTOR; *imperturbably*) I don't think so, sir. I don't own any firearms.

SERGEANT. (*reading from his notebook*) "I happened to glance over the banisters and I saw Mr. Gudgeon standing in the front hall with a revolver—

(GUDGEON *reacts by clenching his fists.*)

—in his hand and he looked ever so peculiar . . ."

(*The* INSPECTOR *looks at the* SERGEANT, *who breaks off abruptly.*)

GUDGEON. That is quite correct, sir. I'm sorry it slipped my memory.

INSPECTOR. Perhaps you will tell us exactly what occurred.

GUDGEON. Certainly, sir. It was about one o'clock on Saturday. Normally of course I should have been bringing in luncheon, but owing to a murder having taken place a short time before, household routine was disorganized. As I was passing through the front hall, I noticed one of Sir Henry's pistols, a small Derringer it was, sir, lying on the oak chest there. I didn't think it should be left lying about, so I picked it up and subsequently took it to the master's study and put it back in its proper place. I may add, sir, that I have no recollection of having looked peculiar.

INSPECTOR. (*moving to* R. *of the sofa*) You say you put the gun in Sir Henry's study? (*He moves below the sofa and faces up stage.*) Is it there now?

GUDGEON. To the best of my belief, sir. I can easily ascertain.

INSPECTOR. (*moving to* L. *of the sofa and taking the revolver from his pocket*) It wasn't—this gun?

GUDGEON. (*moving in to* L. *of the* INSPECTOR *and looking at the revolver*) Oh no, sir. That's a thirty-eight Smith and Wesson—this was a small pistol—a Derringer.

INSPECTOR. You seem to know a good deal about firearms.

GUDGEON. I served in the nineteen-fourteen-eighteen war, sir.

INSPECTOR. (*turning and moving down* R.) And you say you

found this Derringer pistol—on the oak chest in the hall?

GUDGEON. Yes, sir.

(LADY ANGKATELL *enters up* C. *from* L. *The* INSPECTOR *eases above the* R. *end of the sofa.*)

LADY ANGKATELL. (*moving* C.) How nice to see you, Mr. Colquhoun. What is all this about a pistol and Gudgeon? I found that child Doris in floods of tears. The girl was quite right to say what she saw if she thought she saw it. I find right and wrong bewildering myself—easy when wrong is pleasant and right is unpleasant—but confusing the other way about, if you know what I mean. And what have you been telling them about this pistol, Gudgeon?

GUDGEON. (*respectfully but emphatically*) I found the pistol in the hall, m'lady. I have no idea who put it there. I picked it up and put it back in its proper place. That is what I have told the Inspector and he quite understands.

LADY ANGKATELL. (*gently shaking her head at* GUDGEON) You shouldn't have done that, Gudgeon. I'll talk to the Inspector myself.

GUDGEON. But . . .

LADY ANGKATELL. I appreciate your motives, Gudgeon. I know you always try to save us trouble and annoyance. (*Firmly.*) That will do now.

(GUDGEON *hesitates, throws a quick glance at* SIR HENRY, *then bows and exits* L. SIR HENRY *looks very grave.*)

(*She crosses to the sofa, sits and smiles disarmingly at the* INSPECTOR.)

That was really very charming of Gudgeon. Quite feudal, if you know what I mean. Yes, feudal is the right word.

INSPECTOR. Am I to understand, Lady Angkatell, that you yourself have some further knowledge about the matter?

LADY ANGKATELL. Of course. Gudgeon didn't find the gun in the hall at all. He found it when he took the eggs out.

INSPECTOR. The eggs?

LADY ANGKATELL. Yes, out of the basket. (*She seems to think all is now explained.*)

SIR HENRY. You must tell us a little more, my dear. Inspector Colquhoun and I are still at sea.

LADY ANGKATELL. Oh! The gun, you see, was *in* the basket—

(SIR HENRY *rises*.)

—*under* the eggs.

INSPECTOR. What basket? And what eggs, Lady Angkatell?

LADY ANGKATELL. The basket I took down to the farm. The gun was in it and I put the eggs in on top of the gun and forgot about it. When we found poor John Cristow shot in here, it was such a shock that I let go the basket and Gudgeon caught it just in time—because of the eggs.

(SIR HENRY *moves slowly to the fireplace*.)

Later I asked him about writing the date on the eggs— so that one shouldn't eat the fresh ones before the old ones—and he said all that had already been attended to—and I remember now he was rather emphatic about it. He found the gun, you see, and put it back in Henry's study. Very nice and loyal of him—but also very foolish, because, of course, Inspector, the truth is what you want to hear, isn't it?

INSPECTOR. (*crossing above the sofa to* C.; *grimly*) The truth is what I mean to get.

LADY ANGKATELL. *Of course*. It's all so sad, all this hounding people.

(*The* INSPECTOR *moves to* L. *of the sofa*.)

I don't suppose whoever it was that shot John Cristow really *meant* to shoot him—

(*The* INSPECTOR *and the* SERGEANT *look at each other*.)

—not seriously I mean. If it was Gerda, I'm quite sure she didn't. In fact, I'm rather surprised she didn't miss— it's the sort of thing one would expect of her.

(*The* INSPECTOR *crosses above the sofa to* R.)

If she did shoot him, she's probably dreadfully sorry about it now. It's bad enough for children having their father murdered, without having their mother hanged for it. (*Accusingly*.) I sometimes wonder if you policemen *think* of these things.

INSPECTOR. (*crossing below the sofa to* L. *of it; taken aback*) We are not contemplating making an arrest just at present, Lady Angkatell.

LADY ANGKATELL. (*with a dazzling smile*) Well, that's sensible. But I have always felt that you are a very sensible
man, Mr. Colquhoun.

INSPECTOR. Er—thank you, Lady Angkatell. (*He breaks up*
C. *and turns.*) Now I want to get this clear. (*He moves
down* L.C.) You had been shooting with this revolver?

LADY ANGKATELL. Pistol.

INSPECTOR. Ah yes, so Gudgeon said. You had been shooting
with it at the targets?

LADY ANGKATELL. Oh, no, no. I took it out of Henry's study
before I went to the farm.

INSPECTOR. (*looking at* SIR HENRY *and then at the armchair*
L.C.) May I?

(SIR HENRY *nods*)

(*He sits.*) Why, Lady Angkatell?

LADY ANGKATELL. (*with unexpected triumph*) I knew you'd
ask me that. And of course there must be some answer.
(*She looks at* SIR HENRY.) Mustn't there, Henry?

SIR HENRY. I should certainly have thought so, my dear.

LADY ANGKATELL. Yes, obviously I must have had *some* idea
in my head when I took that little Derringer and put it
in my egg basket. (*She looks hopefully at* SIR HENRY.)
I wonder what it could have been?

SIR HENRY. My wife is extremely absent-minded, Inspector.

INSPECTOR. So it seems.

LADY ANGKATELL. Why should I have taken that pistol?

INSPECTOR. (*rising and breaking up* C.) I haven't the faintest
idea, Lady Angkatell.

LADY ANGKATELL. (*rising*) I came in *here*—this being your
study, Henry—with the window there and the fireplace
here. I had been talking to Simmonds about pillow
cases—let's hang on to pillow cases—and I distinctly
remember crossing—(*she moves to the writing table*)
over to the fireplace—and thinking we must get a new
poker—the curate, not the rector—(*she looks at the*
INSPECTOR) you're probably too young to know what
that means.

(*The* INSPECTOR *and the* SERGEANT *look at each other.*)

And I remember opening the drawer and taking out the
Derringer—it was a nice handy little gun—I've always
liked it—and dropping it in the egg basket. And then

I . . . No, there were so many things in my head—
(*she eases to the sofa and sits*) what with bindweed in
the border—and hoping Mrs. Medway would make a
really rich Nigger in his Shirt.

SERGEANT. (*unable to contain himself*) A Nigger in his Shirt?

LADY ANGKATELL. Yes, chocolate, eggs and cream. John Cristow loved a really rich sweet.

INSPECTOR. (*moving to* L. *of the sofa*) Did you load the
pistol?

LADY ANGKATELL. (*thoughtfully*) Ah, did I? Really, it's too
ridiculous that I can't remember. But I should think I
must have, don't you, Inspector?

INSPECTOR. I think I'll have a few more words with Gudgeon.
(*He turns and crosses to the door* L.) When you re-
member a little more, perhaps you'll let me know, Lady
Angkatell?

(*The* SERGEANT *crosses to the door* L.)

LADY ANGKATELL. Of course. Things come back to one quite
suddenly sometimes, don't they?

INSPECTOR. Yes.

(*He exits* L. *The* SERGEANT *follows him off. The clock strikes
eleven.*)

SIR HENRY. (*crossing to* L. *of the sofa*) Why did you take
the pistol, Lucy?

LADY ANGKATELL. I'm really not quite sure, Henry—I suppose
I had some vague idea about an accident.

SIR HENRY. Accident?

LADY ANGKATELL. Yes, all those roots of tree sticking up—
so easy to trip over one. I've always thought that an
accident would be the simplest way to do a thing of
that kind. One would be dreadfully sorry, of course,
and blame oneself . . . (*Her voice trails off.*)

SIR HENRY. Who was to have had the accident?

LADY ANGKATELL. John Cristow, of course.

SIR HENRY. (*sitting* L. *of her on the sofa*) Good God, Lucy!

(LADY ANGKATELL'S *manner suddenly changes. All the vague-
ness goes and she is almost fanatical.*)

LADY ANGKATELL. Oh, Henry, I've been so dreadfully worried.
About Ainswick.

SIR HENRY. I see. So it was Ainswick. You've always cared too much about Ainswick, Lucy.

LADY ANGKATELL. You and Edward are the last of the Angkatells. Unless Edward marries, the whole thing will die out—and he's so obstinate—that long head of his, just like my father. I felt that if only John were out of the way, Henrietta would marry Edward—she's really quite fond of him—and when a person's dead, you do forget. So, it all came to that—get rid of John Cristow.

SIR HENRY. (*aghast*) Lucy! It was you . . .

LADY ANGKATELL. (*her elusive self again*) Darling, darling, you don't imagine for a moment that I shot John? (*She laughs, rises, crosses to the fireplace and picks up the box of chocolates from the mantelpiece.*) I did have that silly idea about an accident. But then I remembered that he was our guest. (*She eases* C.) One doesn't ask someone to be a guest and then get behind a bush and have a pop at them. (*She moves above the sofa and leans over the back of it.*) So you mustn't worry, Henry, any more.

SIR HENRY. (*hoarsely*) I always worry about you, Lucy.

LADY ANGKATELL. (*taking a chocolate from the box*) There's no need to, dear. (*She holds up the chocolate.*) Look what's coming. Open.

(SIR HENRY *opens his mouth.*)

(*She pops the chocolate into* SIR HENRY'S *mouth.*) There! John has been got rid of without our having to do anything about it. It reminds me of that man in Bombay who was so rude to me at a dinner party. (*She crosses to the window* R.) Do you remember? Three days later he was run over by a tram.

(*She exits* R. *The telephone rings.* SIR HENRY *rises, moves to the telephone and lifts the receiver.*)

OPERATOR. Your Regent call, sir.

SIR HENRY. (*into the telephone*) Hullo—yes—Regent call?

(MIDGE *enters* L.)

MIDGE. For me?

SIR HENRY. Yes.

(MIDGE *crosses to the telephone and takes the receiver from* SIR HENRY, *who exits* R.)

MIDGE. (*into the telephone*) Hullo. Is that Madame?

VOICE. No, it's Vera.

MIDGE. Can I speak to Madame herself?

VOICE. Hold on, will you.

(*There is a short pause, then another* VOICE *is heard through the telephone.*)

VOICE. 'Allo. This is Madame Henri speaking.

MIDGE. It's Miss Harvey.

VOICE. Why are you not 'ere? You are coming back this afternoon, yes?

MIDGE. No, no, I'm afraid I can't come back this afternoon.

(EDWARD *enters up* C. *from* L. *and moves to* L.C.)

VOICE. Oh, always these excuses.

MIDGE. No, no, it's not an excuse.

(EDWARD *asks by a gesture whether she minds him staying.*)

(*She puts her hand over the mouthpiece. To* EDWARD.) No—no, don't go. It's only my shop.

VOICE. What is it then?

MIDGE. (*into the telephone*) There's been an accident.

(EDWARD *picks up a magazine from the coffee table, then sits on the sofa at the left end of it.*)

VOICE. An accident? Don't tell me these lies. Don't make these excuses.

MIDGE. No, I'm not telling you lies or making excuses. I can't come back today. I'm not allowed to leave. It's the police.

VOICE. The police?

MIDGE. Yes, the police.

VOICE. What 'ave you done?

MIDGE. It's not my fault. One can't help these things.

VOICE. Where are you?

MIDGE. I'm at Dowfield.

VOICE. Where there is a murder?

MIDGE. Yes, you read about it in the paper?

VOICE. Of course. This is most inconvenient. What do you think my customers will say when they know you are mixed up in a murder?

MIDGE. It's hardly my fault.

VOICE. It's all most upsetting.

MIDGE. Murder is.

VOICE. It's very exciting for you. Very nice for you to be in the limelight.

MIDGE. I think you are being rather unjust.

VOICE. If you do not return today, you will not 'ave any job. There are plenty of girls who would be 'appy to 'ave it.

MIDGE. Please don't say such things. I'm very sorry.

VOICE. You will return tomorrow or don't dare to show your face again.

(MIDGE *replaces the receiver. She is near to tears.*)

EDWARD. Who was that?

MIDGE. My employer.

EDWARD. You should have told her to go to hell.

MIDGE. And get myself fired?

EDWARD. I can't bear to hear you so—subservient.

MIDGE. You don't understand what you're talking about. (*She moves above the sofa.*) To show an independent spirit one needs an independent income.

EDWARD. My God, Midge, there are other jobs—interesting jobs.

MIDGE. Yes—you read advertisements asking for them every day in *The Times*.

EDWARD. Yes.

MIDGE. (*moving up* C.) Sometimes, Edward, you make me lose my temper. What do you know about jobs? Getting them and keeping them? This job, as it happens, is fairly well paid, with reasonable hours.

EDWARD. Oh, money!

MIDGE. (*moving to* L. *of the sofa*) Yes, money. That's what I use to live on. I've got to have a job that *keeps* me, do you understand?

EDWARD. Henry and Lucy would . . .

MIDGE. We've been into that before. Of course they would. (*She crosses to the fireplace.*) It's no good, Edward. You're an Angkatell and Henry and Lucy are Angkatells, but I'm only half an Angkatell. My father was a plain little business man—honest and hardworking and probably not very clever. It's from him I get the feeling I don't like to accept favours. When his business failed, his creditors got paid twenty shillings in the pound. I'm like him. I mind about money and about debts. Don't you see, Edward, it's all right for you and Lucy. Lucy would have any of her friends to stay indefinitely and never think about it twice—and she could go and live on her friends if necessary. There would be no feeling of obligation. But I'm different.

EDWARD. (*rising*) You dear ridiculous child. (*He puts the magazine on the coffee table.*)

MIDGE. I may be ridiculous but *I am not a child.*

EDWARD. (*crossing to the fireplace and standing above* MIDGE) But it's all wrong that you should have to put up with rudeness and insolence. My God, Midge, I'd like to take you out of it all—carry you off to Ainswick.

MIDGE. (*furiously and half crying*) Why do you say these stupid things? You don't mean them. (*She sits on the pouffe.*) Do you think it makes life any easier when I'm being bullied and shouted at to remember that there are places like Ainswick in the world? Do you think I'm grateful to you for standing there and babbling about how much you'd like to take me out of it all? It sounds so charming and means absolutely nothing.

EDWARD. Midge!

MIDGE. Don't you know I'd sell my soul to be at Ainswick now, this minute? I love Ainswick so much I can hardly bear to think of it. You're cruel, Edward, saying nice things you don't mean.

EDWARD. But I do mean them. (*He eases* C., *turns and faces* MIDGE.) Come on, Midge. We'll drive to Ainswick now in my car.

MIDGE. Edward!

EDWARD. (*drawing* MIDGE *to her feet*) Come on, Midge. We're going to Ainswick. Shall we? What about it, eh?

MIDGE. (*laughing a little hysterically*) I've called your bluff, haven't I?

EDWARD. It isn't bluff.

MIDGE. (*patting* EDWARD's *arm then crossing to* L. *of the sofa*) Calm down, Edward. In any case, the police would stop us.

EDWARD. Yes, I suppose they would.

MIDGE. (*sitting on the sofa at the left end of it; gently*) All right, Edward, I'm sorry I shouted at you.

EDWARD. (*quietly*) You really love Ainswick, don't you?

MIDGE. I'm resigned to not going there, but don't rub it in.

EDWARD. I can see it wouldn't do to rush off there this moment—(*he moves to* L. *of the sofa*) but I'm suggesting that you come to Ainswick for good.

MIDGE. For good?

EDWARD. I'm suggesting that you marry me, Midge.

MIDGE. Marry . . . ?

EDWARD. I'm not a very romantic proposition. I'm a dull dog. I read what I expect you would think are dull books, and I write a few dull articles and potter about the estate. But we've known each other a long time—and perhaps Ainswick would make up for me. Will you come, Midge?

MIDGE. *Marry* you? (*She rises.*)

EDWARD. Can you bear the idea?

MIDGE. (*kneeling at the left end of the sofa and leaning over the end of it towards* EDWARD; *incoherently*) Edward, oh, Edward—you offer me heaven like—like something on a plate.

(EDWARD *takes her hands and kisses them.* LADY ANGKATELL *enters* R.)

LADY ANGKATELL. (*as she enters*) What I feel about rhododendrons is that unless you mass them in big clumps you don't get . . .

MIDGE. (*rising and turning to* LADY ANGKATELL) Edward and I are going to be married.

LADY ANGKATELL. (*dumbfounded*) Married? You and Edward? But, Midge, I never dre . . . (*She recovers herself, moves to* MIDGE, *kisses her, then holds out her hand to* EDWARD.) Oh, darling, I'm so happy. (*She shakes* EDWARD's *hand and her face lights up.*) I am so delighted. You'll stay on here and give up that horrid shop. You can be married from here—Henry can give you away.

MIDGE. Darling Lucy, I'd love to be married from here.

LADY ANGKATELL. (*sitting on the sofa at the right end of it.*) Off-white satin, and an ivory prayer book—no bouquet. Bridesmaids?

MIDGE. Oh no, I don't want any fuss.

EDWARD. Just a very quiet wedding, Lucy.

LADY ANGKATELL. Yes, I know exactly what you mean, darling. Unless one carefully chooses them, bridesmaids never match properly—there's nearly always one plain one who ruins the whole effect—usually the bridegroom's sister. And children—children are the worst of all. They step on the train, they howl for Nannie. I never feel a bride can go up the aisle in a proper frame of mind while she's so uncertain what's happening behind her.

MIDGE. I don't need to have anything behind me, not even a train. I can be married in a coat and skirt.

LADY ANGKATELL. (*rising and crossing* L.C.) Oh no, Midge —that's too much like a widow. Off-white satin and I shall take you to Mireille.

MIDGE. I can't possibly afford Mireille.

LADY ANGKATELL. Darling, Henry and I will give you your trousseau.

MIDGE. (*crossing to* LADY ANGKATELL *and kissing her*) Darling. (*She turns, crosses to* EDWARD *and holds his hands.*)

LADY ANGKATELL. Dear Midge, dear Edward! I do hope that band on Henry's trousers won't be too tight. I'd like him to enjoy himself. As for me, I shall wear . . . (*She closes her eyes.*)

MIDGE. Yes, Lucy?

LADY ANGKATELL. Hydrangea blue—and silver fox. That's settled. What a pity John Cristow's dead. Really quite unnecessary after all. But what an exciting weekend. (*She moves to* L. *of* MIDGE *and* EDWARD.) First a murder, then a marriage, then this, then that.

(*The* INSPECTOR *and the* SERGEANT *enter* L.)

(*She turns.*) Come in—come in. These young people have just got engaged to be married.

INSPECTOR. (*easing* L.C.) Indeed. My congratulations.

EDWARD. Thank you very much.

LADY ANGKATELL. (*crossing to the door* L.) I suppose I ought to get ready for the inquest. I am *so* looking forward to it. I've never been to an inquest before.

(*She exits* L. *The* SERGEANT *closes the door.* EDWARD *and* MIDGE *cross and exit* R.)

SERGEANT. (*crossing to* R.) You may say what you like, she's a queer one. (*He nods towards the window* R.) And what about those two? So it was *her* he was keen on, and not the other one.

INSPECTOR. So it seems now.

SERGEANT. Well, that about washes him out. Who have we got left?

INSPECTOR. We've only got Gudgeon's word for it that the gun in Lady Angkatell's basket is what he says it was. It's still wide open. You know, we've forgotten one thing, Penny—the holster.

SERGEANT. Holster?

INSPECTOR. Sir Henry told us that the gun was originally in a brown leather holster. Where's the holster?

(SIR HENRY *enters* L.)

SIR HENRY. I suppose we ought to be starting—(*he crosses to the windows* R.) but everyone seems to have disappeared for some extraordinary reason. (*He looks out of the window and calls.*) Edward. Midge.

(LADY ANGKATELL *enters* L. *She wears her hat and coat. She carries a prayer book and one white glove and one grey glove.*)

LADY ANGKATELL. (*moving* L.C.) How do I look? Is this the sort of thing one wears?

SIR HENRY. (*turning and moving to* R. *of the sofa*) You don't need a prayer book, my dear.

LADY ANGKATELL. But I thought one swore things.

INSPECTOR. Evidence isn't usually taken on oath in a Coroner's court, Lady Angkatell. In any case, the proceedings will be purely formal today. (*He crosses to the door* L.)

(*The* SERGEANT *crosses to the door* L.)

Well, if you'll excuse me, we'll both be getting on our way.

(*He exits* L. *The* SERGEANT *follows him off.*)

LADY ANGKATELL. (*easing to the fireplace*) You and I and Gerda can go in the Daimler, and Edward can take Midge and Henrietta.

SIR HENRY. (*moving* C.) Where's Gerda?

LADY ANGKATELL. Henrietta is with her.

(EDWARD *and* MIDGE *enter* R. MIDGE *picks up her bag and gloves from the writing table, and moves below the sofa.* EDWARD *crosses above the sofa to* R. *of* SIR HENRY.)

SIR HENRY. Well, what's this I hear about you two? (*He shakes hands with* EDWARD.) Isn't this wonderful news? (*He crosses to* L. *of* MIDGE *and kisses her.*)

EDWARD. Thank you, Henry.

MIDGE. Thank you, Cousin Henry.

LADY ANGKATELL. (*looking at her gloves*) Now what made me take one white glove and one grey glove? How very odd.

(*She exits* L.)

EDWARD. (*moving up* C.) I'll get my car round.

(*He exits up* C. *to* L.)

MIDGE. (*sitting on the sofa*) Are you really pleased?

SIR HENRY. It's the best news I've heard for a long time. You don't know what it'll mean to Lucy. She's got Ainswick on the brain, as you know.

MIDGE. She wanted Edward to marry Henrietta. (*Troubled.*) Will she mind that it's me?

SIR HENRY. Of course not. She only wanted Edward to marry. If you want my opinion, you'll make him a far better wife than Henrietta.

MIDGE. It's always been Henrietta with Edward.

SIR HENRY. (*crossing to the fireplace*) Well, don't you let those police fellows hear you say so. (*He fills his cigarette case from the box on the mantelpiece.*) Best thing in the world from that point of view that he's got engaged to you. Takes suspicion right off him.

MIDGE. (*rising*) Suspicion? Off Edward?

SIR HENRY. (*turning*) Counting Gerda out of it, I should say he was suspect number one. To put it bluntly, he loathed John Cristow's guts.

MIDGE. (*crossing to* C. *then moving up* L.) I remember— the evening after the murder—so that's why . . . (*Her face grows desperately unhappy.*)

(HENRIETTA *enters* L.)

HENRIETTA. Oh, Henry, I'm taking Gerda with me. (*She crosses to the drinks table and picks up her gloves and bag.*) She is in rather a nervous state—and I think that one of Lucy's conversations would just about finish her. We're starting now.

SIR HENRY. (*moving to the door* L.) Yes, we ought to be starting too.

(*He exits* L., *leaving the door open.*)

(*Off; calling.*) Are you ready, Lucy?

HENRIETTA. (*putting on her gloves*) Congratulations, Midge. Did you stand on a table and shout at him?

MIDGE. (*solemnly*) I rather think I did.

HENRIETTA. I told you that was what Edward needed.

MIDGE. (*moving to the radio*) I don't think Edward will ever *really* love anyone but you.

HENRIETTA. Oh, don't be absurd, Midge.

MIDGE. I'm not absurd. It's the sort of thing one—knows.

HENRIETTA. Edward wouldn't ask you to marry him unless he wanted to.

MIDGE. (*switching on the radio*) He may have thought it—wise.

HENRIETTA. What do you mean?

GERDA. (*off L.; calling*) Henrietta.

HENRIETTA. (*crossing to the door L.*) I'm coming, Gerda.

(*She exits L. The radio warms up and music is heard. The tune is "La Fille aux Cheveux de Lin." MIDGE moves to the fireplace, puts her gloves on the mantelpiece and looks in the mirror. EDWARD enters up C. from L.*)

EDWARD. (*moving L.C.*) The car's outside.

MIDGE. (*turning*) If you don't mind, I'll go with Lucy.

EDWARD. But why . . . ?

MIDGE. She loses things—and flutters—I'll be useful. (*She moves down L.*)

EDWARD. (*hurt*) Midge, is anything the matter? What is it?

MIDGE. (*crossing to R.*) Never mind now. We must get to the inquest.

EDWARD. Something *is* the matter.

MIDGE. Don't—don't bother me.

EDWARD. Midge, have you changed your mind? Did I—rush you into things just now? (*He moves below the sofa.*) You don't want to marry me after all?

MIDGE. No, no—we must keep on with it now. Until all this is over.

EDWARD. What do you mean?

MIDGE. As things are—it's better you should be engaged to me. Later, we can break it off. (*She turns her back to him.*)

(EDWARD *looks stunned for a moment, then controls himself and speaks in a monotone.*)

EDWARD. I see—even for Ainswick—you can't go through with it.

MIDGE. (*turning*) It wouldn't work, Edward.

EDWARD. No, I suppose you are right. (*He turns and faces up* L.) You'd better go. The others will be waiting.

MIDGE. Aren't you . . . ?

EDWARD. I'll be along. I'm used to driving alone.

(MIDGE *exits up* C. *to* L. EDWARD *crosses and exits* L. *After a few moments, he re-enters. He carries a revolver. He closes the door, crosses to the radio and switches it off, moves to the fireplace, picks up* MIDGE's *gloves from the mantelpiece and puts them in his pocket. He then moves* L.C. *and opens the revolver to see if it is loaded. As he snaps the revolver shut,* MIDGE *enters up* C. *from* L.)

MIDGE. Edward—are you still here?

EDWARD. (*striving to appear natural*) Why, Midge, you startled me.

MIDGE. (*moving above the sofa*) I came back for my gloves. (*She leans over the back of the sofa and looks under the cushions.*) I left them somewhere. (*She looks towards the mantelpiece and sees the revolver in* EDWARD's *hand.*) Edward, what are you doing with that revolver?

EDWARD. I thought I might have a shot or two down at the targets.

MIDGE. At the targets? But there's the inquest.

EDWARD. The inquest, yes, of course. I forgot.

MIDGE. (*with a step towards him*) Edward—what is it? (*She moves in to* R. *of him.*) My God! (*She snatches the gun from him, crosses to the mantelpiece.*) Give me that revolver—you must be mad. (*She puts the revolver on the upstage end of the mantelpiece.*)

(EDWARD *sits in the armchair* L.C.)

(*She turns.*) How could you? (*She kneels down* L. *of* EDWARD.) But why, Edward, but why? Because of Henrietta?

EDWARD. (*surprised*) Henrietta? No. That's all over now.

MIDGE. Why—tell me why?

EDWARD. It's all so hopeless.

MIDGE. Tell me, darling. Make me understand.

EDWARD. I'm no good, Midge. Never any good. It's men like
Cristow—they're successful—women admire them. But
I . . . Even for Ainswick you couldn't bring yourself
to marry me.

MIDGE. You thought I was marrying you for Ainswick?

EDWARD. Heaven on a plate—but you couldn't face the prospect of having me thrown in.

MIDGE. That's not true, that's not true. Oh, you fool! Don't
you understand? It was you I wanted, not Ainswick. I
adore you—I've always adored you. I've loved you ever
since I can remember. I've been sick with love for you
sometimes.

EDWARD. You love *me?*

MIDGE. Of course I love you, you darling idiot. When you
asked me to marry you I was in heaven.

EDWARD. But then why . . . ?

MIDGE. I was a fool. I got it into my head you were doing
it because of the police.

EDWARD. The police?

MIDGE. I thought—perhaps—you'd killed John Cristow.

EDWARD. I . . . ?

MIDGE. For Henrietta—and I thought you'd got engaged to
me to throw them off the scent. Oh, I must have been
crazy. (*She rises.*)

EDWARD. (*rising*) I can't say I'm sorry that Cristow is dead—
(*he crosses to the fireplace*) but I should never have
dreamed of killing him.

MIDGE. (*moving in to* R. *of him*) I know. I'm a fool. (*She
lays her head on his chest.*) But I was so jealous of
Henrietta.

EDWARD. (*putting his arms around her*) You needn't be,
Midge. It was Henrietta, the girl, I loved. But that day
you lit the fire for me, I realized Henrietta the woman
was a stranger I didn't know. When you asked me to
look at you, I saw you for the first time, not Midge the
little girl, but Midge the woman—warm and alive.

MIDGE. Oh, Edward.

EDWARD. Midge, don't ever leave me again.

MIDGE. Never. I promise you never.

(*The sound of a motor horn is heard up* C.)

Heavens, Edward, we must go. They're waiting. What
did I come back for? Gloves!

(EDWARD *takes* MIDGE's *gloves from his pocket and holds them out to her.*)

Oh, darling!

(*She takes the gloves from him, turns and exits up* C. *to* L. EDWARD *follows her off. The lights fade to a black-out, during which the alcove curtain is closed. There is a pause of six seconds then the lights come up. One hour is presumed to have elapsed, during which the weather has turned stormy and the sky is overcast.* GERDA *and* HENRIETTA *enter up* C. *from* L. HENRIETTA *is supporting* GERDA. *They both carry handbags.*)

HENRIETTA. (*as she enters*) We've beaten the storm. Good heavens, it's as dark as night in here. (*As she passes the drinks table she switches on the lamp.*) Are you all right? Sure? (*She leads* GERDA *to the sofa.*) Come over here and put your feet up. (*She puts her handbag on the writing table.*)

(GERDA *sits on the sofa at the left end of it.* HENRIETTA *moves to the drinks table.*)

GERDA. I'm so sorry to give so much trouble. I can't think why I felt faint.

HENRIETTA. (*pouring out a brandy and water*) Anyone might, it was very stuffy in that place.

GERDA. I hope I gave my evidence all right. I get so confused.

HENRIETTA. You did very well indeed.

GERDA. The Coroner was so very kind. Oh dear, I'm so glad it's all over. If only my head didn't ache so.

HENRIETTA. (*picking up the drink and moving below the sofa*) You need a drink. (*She holds out the glass to* GERDA.)

GERDA. Oh no, thank you, not for me.

HENRIETTA. Well, *I* need one. You'd much better have one too.

GERDA. No—really.

(HENRIETTA *moves to the drinks table, takes a sip from the glass, then stands it on the table.*)

What I would love—but perhaps it would be giving a lot of trouble . . .

HENRIETTA. (*moving to* R. *of the sofa*) Get the idea of giving trouble out of your head, Gerda. What would you like so much?

GERDA. I'd love some tea—a nice cup of hot tea.

HENRIETTA. (*crossing to* L.C.) Of course.

GERDA. But it is a trouble. The servants . . .

HENRIETTA. (*crossing to the fireplace*) That's all right. (*She stretches out a hand towards the bell-push, then stops.*) Oh, I forgot, Gudgeon's at the inquest.

GERDA. It doesn't matter.

HENRIETTA. I'll go down to the kitchen and ask Mrs. Medway.

GERDA. She might not like being asked.

HENRIETTA. She won't mind. She mightn't have liked answering a bell.

GERDA. You're very good to me.

(HENRIETTA *exits* L. *There is a flash of lightning followed by a peal of thunder.* GERDA *rises, startled, crosses to the windows* R., *glances out, moves up* C., *then turns, moves* L.C. *and looks horror-struck at the spot where* JOHN *died. She catches her breath, crosses to the sofa, sits and starts to cry quietly.*)

(HENRIETTA *enters* L.)

Oh, John—John—I can't bear it.

HENRIETTA. The kettle's on—only be a moment. (*She crosses to* L. *of the sofa. Gently.*) Oh—Gerda, don't cry. It's all over now.

GERDA. But what shall I do? What can I do without John?

HENRIETTA. There are the children.

GERDA. I know, I know. But John always decided everything.

HENRIETTA. I know. (*She hesitates a moment, then moves above the sofa, puts her hand on* GERDA's *shoulders, and draws her back on the sofa.*) There's just one thing, Gerda. (*She pauses.*) What did you do with the holster?

GERDA. (*staring front*) Holster?

HENRIETTA. The second revolver, the one you took from Henry's study, was in a holster. What have you done with the holster?

GERDA. (*repeating the word with an appearance of stupidity*) Holster?

HENRIETTA. (*urgently*) You must tell me. Apart from that everything's all right. There's nothing else that can possibly give you away. They may suspect—but they

can't prove anything. But that holster's dangerous. Have
you still got it?

(GERDA *slowly nods her head.*)

Where is it?

GERDA. I cut it up in pieces and put it in my leathercraft bag.

HENRIETTA. (*moving to the drinks table and picking up the
leathercraft bag*) In this?

(GERDA *turns and nods.*)

(*She moves to the writing table, switches on the table-
lamp, then takes some pieces of brown leather out of
the leathercraft bag.*) I'll take them and get rid of them.
(*She puts them in her own handbag.*) Quite a clever
idea of yours.

(GERDA, *for the first time, speaks in a high, excited voice and
shows that she is not quite sane.*)

GERDA. I'm not so stupid as people think. When did you
know that I shot John?

HENRIETTA. (*putting the bags on the writing table*) I've
always known. (*She moves to* R. *of the sofa.*) When
John said "Henrietta" to me just before he died, I knew
what he meant. I always knew what John wanted. He
wanted me to protect you—to keep you out of it somehow. He loved you very much. He loved you better
than he knew.

GERDA. (*weeping*) Oh, John—John.

HENRIETTA. (*sitting* R. *of* GERDA *on the sofa*) I know, my
dear. I know. (*She puts her arm around* GERDA.)

GERDA. But you can't know. It was all a lie—everything. I
had to kill him. I'd adored him so. I worshipped him. I
thought he was everything that was noble and fine. He
wasn't any of those things.

HENRIETTA. He was a man—not a god.

GERDA. (*fiercely*) It was all a lie. The night when that woman
came here—that film woman. I saw his face as he looked
at her. And after dinner he went over to see her. He
didn't come back. I went up to bed, but I couldn't sleep.
Hour after hour—he didn't come. At last I got up and
put on a coat and my shoes and I crept downstairs and
through the side door. I went along the lane to her
cottage. The curtains were drawn at the front but I

went round to the back. They weren't drawn there because I crept up to the window and looked in. (*Her voice rises hysterically.*) I looked in.

(*There is a flash of lightning and a distant peal of thunder.*)

HENRIETTA. (*rising*) Gerda!

GERDA. I saw them—that woman and John. (*She pauses.*) I saw them. (*She pauses.*) I'd believed in John—completely—utterly—and it was all a lie. I was left with nothing—nothing. (*She suddenly resumes a quiet conversational tone.*) You do see, don't you, Henrietta, that I had to kill him? (*She pauses.*) Is that tea coming? I do so want a cup of tea.

HENRIETTA. (*moving above the right end of the sofa*) In a moment. Go on telling me, Gerda.

GERDA. (*cunningly*) They always said I was stupid when I was a child—stupid and slow. They used to say, "Don't let Gerda do it, Gerda will take all day." And sometimes, "Gerda never seems to take in anything you say to her." Didn't they see, all of them, that that made me more stupid and slower still? And then you know—I found a way. I used to pretend to be stupider than I was. I'd stare as though I didn't understand. But inside, sometimes, I laughed. Because often I knew more than they thought.

HENRIETTA. (*moving to L. of the sofa*) I see—yes, I see.

GERDA. John didn't mind my being stupid—not at first. He used to tell me not to worry—to leave everything to him. Only when he was very busy he got impatient. And sometimes I used to think I couldn't do anything right. Then I'd remember how clever he was—and how good. Only—after all, he wasn't—so I had to kill him.

HENRIETTA. Go on.

GERDA. I knew I must be careful because the police are very clever. I read in a detective story that they could tell which revolver a bullet had been fired from. So I took a second revolver from Henry's study and I shot John with that, and dropped the other by him. Then I ran round the house, in at the front door and through that door and over to John and picked the revolver up. I thought, you see, that first they'd think I had done it, and then they'd find that it wasn't the right revolver and so I'd be cleared. And then I meant to put the revolver that had shot him into that film woman's house and they'd think that *she'd* done it. Only she left her bag—so it was easier still. I slipped it into that later in the day. I can't think why they haven't arrested her. (*Her voice rises.*) They should have. (*Hysterically.*) It was because of her I had to kill John.

HENRIETTA. (*moving below the left end of the sofa*) You wiped your fingerprints off the second revolver you shot him with?

GERDA. Of course. I'm cleverer than people think. I got rid of the revolver. (*She frowns.*) But I did forget about the holster.

HENRIETTA. Don't worry about that. I've got it now. I think you're quite safe, Gerda. (*She sits* L. *of* GERDA *on the sofa.*) You must go away and live in the country quietly somewhere—and forget.

GERDA. (*unhappily*) Yes, yes, I suppose I must. I don't know what to do. I don't really know where to go. I can't make up my mind—John always decided everything. My head aches.

HENRIETTA. (*rising*) I'll go and get the tea.

(*She crosses and exits* L. GERDA *looks cunningly towards the door* L., *rises, moves to the drinks table, takes a small poison bottle out of her handbag and stretches out her hand towards* HENRIETTA'S *glass. She pauses, takes a handkerchief from her handbag and lifts the glass with it.* HENRIETTA *re-enters quietly* L. *She carries a tray of tea.* GERDA, *with her back to* HENRIETTA, *is unaware of the entry. As* HENRIETTA *watches,* GERDA *tips the contents of the poison bottle into* HENRIETTA'S *glass, then replaces the bottle and handkerchief in her handbag.* HENRIETTA *quietly exits.* GERDA *turns, moves below the sofa and sits.* HENRIETTA *re-enters, crosses to the coffee table and puts the tray on it.*)

Here's your tea, Gerda.

GERDA. Thank you so much, Henrietta.

HENRIETTA. (*moving to the drinks table*) Now, where's my drink? (*She picks up her glass.*)

GERDA. (*pouring milk into the cup*) This is just what I wanted. You are very good to me, Henrietta.

HENRIETTA. (*moving slowly down* R.) Shall I have this? Or shall I have a cup of tea with you?

GERDA. (*pouring the tea; cunningly*) You don't really like tea, do you, Henrietta?

HENRIETTA. (*sharply*) I think, *today*, I prefer it. (*She puts her glass on the coffee table and crosses to the door* L.) I'll go and get another cup.

(*She exits* L. GERDA *frowns with annoyance, and rises. She looks around, sees the revolver on the mantelpiece, glances at the door* L., *then runs to the mantelpiece and picks up the revolver. She examines it, notes that it is loaded, nods with satisfaction and utters a little sob. The* INSPECTOR *enters down* R.)

INSPECTOR. What are you doing with that gun, Mrs. Cristow?

GERDA. (*turning; startled*) Oh, Inspector, how you startled me. (*She puts her hand over her heart.*) My heart—my heart isn't strong, you know.

INSPECTOR. (*crossing to* R. *of* GERDA) What were you doing with that gun?

GERDA. I found it—here.

INSPECTOR. (*taking the revolver from* GERDA) You know all about loading a gun, don't you? (*He unloads it, puts the cartridges in one pocket and the revolver in another.*)

GERDA. Sir Henry very kindly showed me. Is—is the inquest over?

INSPECTOR. Yes.

GERDA. And the verdict?

INSPECTOR. It was adjourned.

GERDA. That's not right. They should have said it was wilful murder and that she did it.

INSPECTOR. She?

GERDA. That actress. That Veronica Craye. If they adjourn things, she'll get away—she'll go back to America.

INSPECTOR. Veronica Craye didn't shoot your husband, Mrs. Cristow.

GERDA. She did. She did. Of course she did.

INSPECTOR. No. The gun wasn't in her bag when we first searched this room. It was put there afterwards. (*He pauses.*) We often know quite well who's guilty of crime, Mrs. Cristow—(*he looks meaningly at her*) but we can't always get sufficient evidence.

(GERDA, *terrified, steps back, stumbles and collapses on to the pouffe.*)

GERDA. (*wildly*) Oh, John—John—where are you? I want you, John.

INSPECTOR. Mrs. Cristow—Mrs. Cristow—don't—don't, please.

(GERDA *sobs hysterically. The* INSPECTOR *crosses to the coffee table, picks up* HENRIETTA'S *glass, sniffs it, takes it to* GERDA *and hands it to her.* GERDA, *not noticing what it is, drinks the contents of the glass. After a few moments, she rises, staggers and crosses below the sofa. As she starts to fall the* INSPECTOR *crosses to her and lowers her on to the sofa.* HENRIETTA *enters* L. *She carries a cup and saucer. She crosses hurriedly to* L. *of the sofa, kneeling and putting the cup and saucer on the coffee table, as the* INSPECTOR *takes the empty glass from* GERDA.)

HENRIETTA. Gerda, Gerda. (*She sees the glass. To the* IN-SPECTOR.) Did you—did you give her *that?*

INSPECTOR. Why, what was in it?

HENRIETTA. She put something in it—out of her bag.

(*The* INSPECTOR *picks up* GERDA'S *handbag, opens it and takes out the poison bottle.*)

INSPECTOR. (*reading the label*) I wonder how she got hold of that? (*He feels* GERDA'S *pulse then shakes his head.*) So—she's killed herself.

HENRIETTA. (*rising and crossing to* R.) No, it was meant for me.

INSPECTOR. For *you,* why?

HENRIETTA. Because I—I knew—something. (*She crosses above the sofa to the back of the armchair* C.)

INSPECTOR. You knew she'd killed her husband? Oh yes, *I* knew that too. We get to know people in our job. You're not the killer type. She was.

HENRIETTA. (*breaking to the fireplace*) She loved John Cris-tow—too much.

INSPECTOR. The worshipper—that was the name of the statue, wasn't it? What happens next for you?

HENRIETTA. John told me once that if he were dead, the first thing I'd do would be to model a figure of grief It's odd, but that's exactly what I'm going to do.

(*The* INSPECTOR *moves to the writing table.* LADY ANGKATELL *enters up* C. *from* L. *She looks radiant.*)

LADY ANGKATELL. (*moving down* C.) It was a wonderfu inquest.

(*The* INSPECTOR *lifts the telephone receiver.*)

Exactly as they describe it in books, and . . . (*She sees* GERDA.) Has—has Gerda . . . ?

(*The* INSPECTOR *looks at her in silence.* HENRIETTA *puts her hands to her eyes to hide her tears.*)

(*She nods her head.*) How very very fortunate . . .

INSPECTOR. (*into the telephone*) Get me the police station, will you?

HENRIETTA *starts to sob as—*

the CURTAIN *falls*

THE MOUSETRAP

Presented by Peter Saunders at the Ambassadors Theatre, London, W.C.2, on 25th November 1952, with the following cast of characters:

(in the order of their appearance)

MOLLIE RALSTON	*Sheila Sim*
GILES RALSTON	*John Paul*
CHRISTOPHER WREN	*Allan McClelland*
MRS. BOYLE	*Mignon O'Doherty*
MAJOR METCALF	*Aubrey Dexter*
MISS CASEWELL	*Jessica Spencer*
MR. PARAVICINI	*Martin Miller*
DETECTIVE SERGEANT TROTTER	*Richard Attenborough*

The play produced by Peter Cotes
Décor by Roger Furse

SYNOPSIS OF SCENES

ACT I

SCENE 1   The Great Hall at Monkswell Manor. Late afternoon
SCENE 2   The same. The following day after lunch

ACT II

The same. Ten minutes later

Time: *the present*

Act One

Scene I

SCENE: *The Great Hall at Monkswell Manor. Late afternoon.*

The house looks not so much a period piece but a house which has been lived in by generations of the same family with dwindling resources. There are tall windows up C; *a big arched opening up* R *leading to the entrance hall, the front door and the kitchen; and an arched opening* L *leading upstairs to the bedrooms. Up* L *leading off the stairs is the door to the library; down* L *is the door to the drawing-room; and down* R *the door (opening on stage) to the dining-room.* R *is an open fireplace and beneath the window up* C *a window seat and a radiator.*

The hall is furnished as a lounge. There is some good old oak, including a large refectory table by the window up C, *an oak chest in the entrance hall up* R, *and a stool on the stairs* L. *The curtains and the upholstered furniture—a sofa* LC, *an armchair* C, *a large leather armchair* R, *and a small Victorian armchair down* R—*are shabby and old-fashioned. There is a combined desk and bookcase* L, *with a radio and telephone on it and a chair beside it. There is another chair up* RC *by the window, a Canterbury containing newspapers and magazines above the fireplace and a small half circular card table behind the sofa. There are two wall brackets over the fireplace which are worked together; and a wall bracket on the* L *wall, one* L *of the library door and one in the entrance hall, which are also worked together. There are double switches* L *of the arch up* R, *and on the downstage side of the door down* L, *and a single switch on the upstage side of the door down* R. *A table lamp stands on the sofa table.*

Before the CURTAIN *rises the House Lights fade to a complete* BLACK-OUT *and the music of "Three Blind Mice" is heard.*

When the CURTAIN *rises the stage is in complete darkness. The music fades giving place to a shrill whistle of the same tune, "Three Blind Mice." A woman's piercing scream is heard then a mixture of male and female voices saying: "My God, what's that?" "Went that way!" "Oh, my God!" Then a police whistle sounds, followed by several other police whistles, all of which fade to silence.*

VOICE ON THE RADIO. . . . and according to Scotland Yard, the crime took place at twenty-four Culver Street, Paddington.

The LIGHTS *come up, revealing the Hall at Monkswell Manor. It is late afternoon, and almost dark. Snow can be seen falling heavily through the windows up* C. *There is a fire burning. A freshly-painted sign board is standing on its side on the stairs against the archway* L; *it has on it in large letters:* MONKWELL MANOR GUEST HOUSE.

The murdered woman was a Mrs. Maureen Lyon. In connexion with the murder, the police are anxious to interview a man seen in the vicinity, wearing a dark overcoat, light scarf, and a soft felt hat.

(MOLLIE RALSTON *enters through the arch up* R. *She is a tall, pretty young woman with an ingenuous air, in her twenties. She puts down her handbag and gloves on the armchair* C *then crosses to the radio and switches it off during the next speech. She places a small parcel in the desk cupboard*)

Motorists are warned against ice-bound roads. The heavy snow is expected to continue, and throughout the country there will be a certain freezing, particularly at points on the north and north-east coast of Scotland.

MOLLIE. (*calling*) Mrs. Barlow! Mrs. Barlow! (*Receiving no reply she crosses to the armchair* C, *picks up her handbag and one glove and then goes out through the arch up* R. *She removes her overcoat and then returns*) Brr! It's cold. (*She goes to the wall switch above the door down* R *and switches on the wall brackets over the fire-place. She moves up to the window, feels the radiator and draws the curtains. Then she moves down to the sofa table and switches on the table lamp. She looks round and notices the large sign board lying on its side on the stairs. She picks it up and places it against the wall* L *of the window alcove. She steps back, nodding her head*) It really does look nice—oh! (*She notices that there is no "S" on the sign*) How stupid of Giles. (*She looks at her watch then at the clock*) Gosh!

(MOLLIE *hurries off up the stairs* L. GILES *enters from the front door* R. *He is a rather arrogant but attractive young man in his twenties. He stamps his feet to shake off the snow, opens the oak chest and puts inside a big paper carrier he has been carrying. He takes off his overcoat, hat and scarf, moves down and throws them on the armchair* C. *Then he goes to the fire and warms his hands*)

GILES. (*calling*) Mollie? Mollie? Mollie? Where are you?

(MOLLIE *enters from the arch* L)

MOLLIE. (*cheerfully*) Doing all the work, you brute. (*She crosses to Giles*)

GILES. Oh, there you are—leave it all to me. Shall I stoke the Aga?

MOLLIE. Done.

GILES. (*kissing her*) Hullo, sweetheart. Your nose is cold.

MOLLIE. I've just come in. (*She crosses to the fire*)

GILES. Why? Where have you been? Surely you've not been out in this weather?

MOLLIE. I had to go down to the village for some stuff I'd forgotten. Did you get the chicken netting?

GILES. It wasn't the right kind. (*He sits on the left arm of the armchair* C) I went on to another dump but that wasn't any good either. Practically a whole day wasted. My God, I'm half frozen. Car was skidding like anything. The snow's coming down thick. What do you bet we're not snowed up tomorrow?

MOLLIE. Oh dear, I do hope not. (*She crosses to the radiator and feels it*) If only the pipes don't freeze.

GILES. (*rising and moving up to Mollie*) We'll have to keep the central heating well stoked up. (*He feels the radiator*) H'm, not too good—I wish they'd send the coke along. We've not got any too much.

MOLLIE. (*moving down to the sofa and sitting*) Oh! I do so want everything to go well at first. First impressions are so important.

GILES. (*moving down to R of the sofa*) Is everything ready? Nobody's arrived yet, I suppose?

MOLLIE. No, thank goodness. I think everything's in order. Mrs. Barlow's hooked it early. Afraid of the weather, I suppose.

GILES. What a nuisance these daily women are. That leaves everything on your shoulders.

MOLLIE. *And* yours! This is a partnership.

GILES. (*crossing to the fire*) So long as you don't ask me to cook.

MOLLIE. (*rising*) No, no, that's my department. Anyway, we've got lots of tins in case we are snowed up. (*Crossing to Giles*) Oh, Giles, do you think it's going to be all right?

GILES. Got cold feet, have you? Are you sorry now we didn't sell the place when your aunt left it to you, instead of having this mad idea of running it as a guest house?

MOLLIE. No, I'm not. I love it. And talking of a guest house. Just look at *that!* (*She indicates the sign board in an accusing manner*)

GILES. (*complacently*) Pretty good, what? (*He crosses to L of the sign board*)

MOLLIE. It's a disaster! Don't you see? You've left out the "S". Monkwell instead of Monkswell.

GILES. Good Lord, so I did. However did I come to do that? But it doesn't really matter, does it? Monkwell is as good a name.

MOLLIE. You're in disgrace. (*She crosses to the desk*) Go and stoke up the central heating.

GILES. Across that icy yard! Ugh! Shall I bank it up for the night now?

MOLLIE. No, you don't do that until ten or eleven o'clock at night.

GILES. How appalling!

MOLLIE. Hurry up. Someone may arrive at any minute now.

GILES. You've got all the rooms worked out?

MOLLIE. Yes. (*She sits at the desk and picks up a paper from it*) Mrs. Boyle, Front Fourposter Room. Major Metcalf, Blue Room. Miss Casewell, East Room. Mr. Wren, Oak Room.

GILES. (*crossing to* R *of the sofa table*) I wonder what all these people will be like. Oughtn't we to have got rent in advance?

MOLLIE. Oh no, I don't think so.

GILES. We're rather mugs at this game.

MOLLIE. They bring luggage. If they don't pay we hang on to their luggage. It's quite simple.

GILES. I can't help thinking we ought to have taken a correspondence course in hotel keeping. We're sure to get had in some way. Their luggage might be just bricks wrapped up in newspaper and where should we be then?

MOLLIE. They all wrote from very good addresses.

GILES. That's what servants with forged references do. Some of these people may be criminals hiding from the police. (*He moves up to the sign board and picks it up*)

MOLLIE. I don't care what they are so long as they pay us seven guineas every week.

GILES. You're such a wonderful woman of business, Mollie.

(GILES *exits through the arch up* R, *carrying the sign board.* MOLLIE *switches on the radio*)

VOICE ON THE RADIO. And according to Scotland Yard, the crime took place at twenty-four Culver Street, Paddington. The murdered woman was a Mrs. Maureen Lyon. In connexion with the murder, the police—

(MOLLIE *rises and crosses to the armchair* C)

—are anxious to interview a man seen in the vicinity, wearing a dark overcoat—

(MOLLIE *picks up Giles' overcoat*)

—light scarf—

(MOLLIE *picks up his scarf*)

—and a soft felt hat.

(MOLLIE *picks up his hat and exits through the arch up* R)

Motorists are warned against ice-bound roads.

(*The door bell rings*)

The heavy snow is expected to continue, and throughout the country . . .

(MOLLIE *enters, crosses to the desk, switches off the radio and hurries off through the arch up* R)

MOLLIE. (*off*) How do you do?
CHRISTOPHER. (*off*) Thanks so much.

(CHRISTOPHER WREN *enters through the arch up* R *with a suitcase which he places* R *of the refectory table. He is a rather wild-looking neurotic young man. His hair is long and untidy and he wears a woven artistic tie. He has a confiding, almost childish manner.* MOLLIE *enters and moves up* C)

Weather is simply awful. My taxi gave up at your gate. (*He crosses and places his hat on the sofa table*) Wouldn't attempt the drive. No sporting instinct. (*Moving up to Mollie*) Are you Mrs. Ralston? How delightful! My name's Wren.
MOLLIE. How do you do, Mr. Wren?
CHRISTOPHER. You know you're not at all as I'd pictured you. I've been thinking of you as a retired General's widow, Indian Army. I thought you'd be terrifically grim and Memsahibish, and that the whole place would be simply crammed with Benares brass. Instead, it's heavenly (*crossing below the sofa to* L *of the sofa table*)—quite heavenly. Lovely proportions. (*Pointing at the desk*) That's a fake! (*Pointing at the sofa table*) Ah, but this table's genuine. I'm simply going to love this place. (*He moves below the armchair* C) Have you got any wax flowers or birds of Paradise?
MOLLIE. I'm afraid not.
CHRISTOPHER. What a pity! Well, what about a sideboard? A purple plummy mahogany sideboard with great solid carved fruits on it?
MOLLIE. Yes, we have—in the dining-room. (*She glances at the door down* R)
CHRISTOPHER. (*following her glance*) In here? (*He moves down* R *and opens the door*) I must see it.

(CHRISTOPHER *exits into the dining-room and* MOLLIE *follows him.* GILES *enters through the archway up* R. *He looks round and examines the suitcase. Hearing voices from the dining-room,* GILES *exits up* R)

MOLLIE. (*off*) Do come and warm yourself.

(MOLLIE *enters from the dining-room, followed by* CHRIS-
TOPHER. MOLLIE *moves* C)

CHRISTOPHER. (*as he enters*) Absolutely perfect. Real bed-
rock respectability. But why do away with a centre
mahogany table? (*Looking off* R) Little tables just spoil
the effect.

(GILES *enters up* R *and stands* L *of the large armchair* R)

MOLLIE. We thought guests would prefer them—this is my
husband.

CHRISTOPHER. (*moving up to Giles and shaking hands with
him*) How do you do? Terrible weather, isn't it? Takes
one back to Dickens and Scrooge and that irritating
Tiny Tim. So bogus. (*He turns towards the fire*) Of
course, Mrs. Ralston, you're absolutely right about the
little tables. I was being carried away by my feeling for
period. If you had a mahogany dining-table, you'd have
to have the right family round it. (*He turns to Giles*)
Stern handsome father with a beard, prolific, faded
mother, eleven children of assorted ages, a grim governess, and somebody called "poor Harriet," the poor
relation who acts as general dogsbody and is very, *very*
grateful for being given a good home!

GILES. (*disliking him*) I'll take your suitcase upstairs for
you. (*He picks up the suitcase. To Mollie*) Oak Room,
did you say?

MOLLIE. Yes.

CHRISTOPHER. I do hope that it's got a fourposter with little
chintz roses?

GILES. It hasn't.

(GILES *exits* L *up the stairs with the suitcase*)

CHRISTOPHER. I don't believe your husband is going to like
me. (*Moving a few paces towards Mollie*) How long
have you been married? Are you very much in love?

MOLLIE. (*coldly*) We've been married just a year. (*Moving
towards the stairs* L) Perhaps you'd like to go up and
see your room?

CHRISTOPHER. Ticked off! (*He moves above the sofa table*)
But I do so like knowing all about people. I mean, I
think people are so madly interesting. Don't you?

MOLLIE. Well, I suppose some are and (*turning to Christopher*) some are not.

CHRISTOPHER. No, I don't agree. They're *all* interesting, because you never really know what anyone is like—or what they are really thinking. For instance, *you* don't know what *I'm* thinking about now, do you? (*He smiles as at some secret joke*)

MOLLIE. Not in the least. (*She moves down to the sofa table and takes a cigarette from the box*) Cigarette?

CHRISTOPHER. No, thank you. (*Moving to* R *of Mollie*) You see? The only people who really know what other people are like are artists—and they don't know why they know it! But if they're portrait painters (*he moves* C) it comes out—(*he sits on the right arm of the sofa*) on the canvas.

MOLLIE. Are you a painter? (*She lights her cigarette*)

CHRISTOPHER. No, I'm an architect. My parents, you know, baptized me Christopher, in the hope that I would be an architect. Christopher Wren! (*He laughs*) As good as halfway home. Actually, of course, everyone laughs about it and makes jokes about St. Paul's. However— who knows?—I may yet have the last laugh.

(GILES *enters from the archway up* L *and crosses to the arch up* R)

Chris Wren's Prefab Nests may yet go down in history! (*To Giles*) I'm going to like it here. I find your wife *most* sympathetic.

GILES. (*coldly*) Indeed.

CHRISTOPHER. (*turning to look at Mollie*) And really very beautiful.

MOLLIE. Oh, don't be absurd.

(GILES *leans on the back of the large armchair*)

CHRISTOPHER. There, isn't that like an Englishwoman? Compliments always embarrass them. European women take compliments as a matter of course, but Englishwomen have all the feminine spirit crushed out of them by their husbands. (*He turns and looks at Giles*) There's something very boorish about English husbands.

MOLLIE. (*hastily*) Come up and see your room. (*She crosses to the arch up* L)

CHRISTOPHER. Shall I?

MOLLIE. (*to Giles*) Could you stoke up the hot water boiler?

(MOLLIE *and* CHRISTOPHER *exit up the stairs* L. GILES *scowls and crosses to* C. *The door bell peals. There is a pause then it peals several times impatiently.* GILES *exits hurriedly up* R *to the front door. The sound of wind and snow is heard for a moment or two*)

MRS. BOYLE. (*off*) This is Monkswell Manor, I presume?

GILES. (*off*) Yes . . .

(MRS. BOYLE *enters through the archway up* R, *carrying a suitcase, some magazines and her gloves. She is a large, imposing woman in a very bad temper*)

MRS. BOYLE. I am Mrs. Boyle. (*She puts down the suitcase*)

GILES. I'm Giles Ralston. Come in to the fire, Mrs. Boyle, and get warm.

(MRS. BOYLE *moves down to the fire*)

Awful weather, isn't it? Is this your only luggage?

MRS. BOYLE. A Major—Metcalf, is it?—is seeing to it.

GILES. I'll leave the door for him.

(GILES *goes out to the front door*)

MRS. BOYLE. The taxi wouldn't risk coming up the drive.

(GILES *returns and comes down to* L *of Mrs. Boyle*)

It stopped at the gate. We had to share a taxi from the station—and there was great difficulty in getting *that*. (*Accusingly*) Nothing ordered to meet us, it seems.

GILES. I'm so sorry. We didn't know what train you would be coming by, you see, otherwise of course, we'd have seen that someone was—er—standing by.

MRS. BOYLE. All trains should have been met.

GILES. Let me take your coat.

(MRS. BOYLE *hands Giles her gloves and magazines. She stands by the fire warming her hands*)

My wife will be here in a moment. I'll just go along and give Metcalf a hand with the bags.

(GILES *exits up* R *to the front door*)

MRS. BOYLE. (*moving up to the arch as Giles goes*) The drive might at least have been cleared of snow. (*After his exit*) Most offhand and casual, I must say. (*She moves down to the fire and looks round her disapprovingly*)

(MOLLIE *hurries in from the stairs* L, *a little breathless*)

MOLLIE. I'm so sorry I . . .
MRS. BOYLE. Mrs. Ralston?
MOLLIE. Yes . . . . (*She crosses to Mrs. Boyle, half puts out her hand, then draws it back, uncertain of what guest house proprietors are supposed to do*)

(MRS. BOYLE *surveys Mollie with displeasure*)

MRS. BOYLE. You're very young.
MOLLIE. Young?
MRS. BOYLE. To be running an establishment of this kind. You can't have had much experience.
MOLLIE. (*backing away*) There has to be a beginning for everything, hasn't there?
MRS. BOYLE. I see. Quite inexperienced. (*She looks round*) An old old house. I hope you haven't got dry rot. (*She sniffs suspiciously*)
MOLLIE. (*indignantly*) Certainly not!
MRS. BOYLE. A lot of people don't know they have got dry rot until it's too late to do anything about it.
MOLLIE. The house is in perfect condition.
MRS. BOYLE. H'm—it could do with a coat of paint. You know, you've got worm in this oak.
GILES. (*off*) This way, Major.

(GILES *and* MAJOR METCALF *enter up* R. *Major Metcalf is a middle-aged, square-shouldered man, very military in manner and bearing.* GILES *moves up* C. MAJOR METCALF *puts down a suitcase he is carrying and moves above the armchair* C; MOLLIE *moves up to meet him*)

This is my wife.
MAJOR METCALF. (*shaking hands with Mollie*) How d'you do? Absolute blizzard outside. Thought at one time we shouldn't make it. (*He sees Mrs. Boyle*) Oh, I beg your pardon. (*He removes his hat*)

(MRS. BOYLE *exits down* R)

If it goes on like this I should say you'll have five or six feet of snow by morning. (*He crosses to the fire*) Not seen anything like it since I was on leave in nineteen-forty.

GILES. I'll take these up. (*Picking up the cases. To Mollie*) Which rooms did you say? Blue Room and the Rose Room?

MOLLIE. No—I put Mr. Wren in the Rose Room. He liked the fourposter so much. So it's Mrs. Boyle in the Oak Room and Major Metcalf in the Blue Room.

GILES. (*authoritatively*) Major? (*He moves* L *towards the stairs*)

MAJOR METCALF. (*instinctively the soldier*) Sir!

(MAJOR METCALF *follows* GILES *and they exit up the stairs* L. MRS. BOYLE *enters down* R *and moves up to the fireplace*)

MRS. BOYLE. Do you have much servant difficulty here?

MOLLIE. We have quite a good local woman who comes in from the village.

MRS. BOYLE. And what indoor staff?

MOLLIE. No indoor staff. Just us. (*She moves down to* L *of the armchair* C)

MRS. BOYLE. In-deed. I understood this was a guest house in full running order.

MOLLIE. We're only just starting.

MRS. BOYLE. I would have said that a proper staff of servants was essential before opening this kind of establishment. I consider your advertisement was most misleading. May I ask if I am the only guest—with Major Metcalf, that is?

MOLLIE. Oh no, there are several here.

MRS. BOYLE. This weather, too. A blizzard (*she turns to the fire*)—no less—all very unfortunate.

MOLLIE. But we couldn't very well foresee the weather!

(CHRISTOPHER WREN *enters quietly from the stairs* L *and comes up behind Mollie*)

CHRISTOPHER. (*singing*)
    "The North Wind doth blow
      And it will bring snow
    And what will the robin do then, poor thing?"

I adore nursery rhymes, don't you? Always so tragic and *macabre*. That's why children like them.

MOLLIE. May I introduce. Mr. Wren—Mrs. Boyle.

(CHRISTOPHER *bows*)

MRS. BOYLE. (*coldly*) How d'you do?

CHRISTOPHER. This is a *very* beautiful house. Don't you think so?

MRS. BOYLE. I have come to the time of life when the amenities of an establishment are more important than its appearance.

(CHRISTOPHER *backs away up* R. GILES *enters from the stairs* L *and stands below the arch*)

If I had not believed this was a running concern I should never have come here. I understand it was *fully* equipped with every home comfort.

GILES. There is no obligation for you to remain here if you are not satisfied, Mrs. Boyle.

MRS. BOYLE. (*crossing to* R *of the sofa*) No, indeed, I should not think of doing so.

GILES. If there has been any misapprehension it would perhaps be better if you went elsewhere. I could ring up for the taxi to return. The roads are not yet blocked.

(CHRISTOPHER *moves down and sits in the armchair* C)

We have had so many applications for rooms that we shall be able to fill your place quite easily. In any case we are raising our terms next month.

MRS. BOYLE. I am certainly not going to leave before I have tried what the place is like. You needn't think you can turn me out now.

(GILES *moves down* L)

Perhaps you will take me up to my bedroom, Mrs. Ralston? (*She moves majestically towards the staircase* L)

MOLLIE. Certainly, Mrs. Boyle. (*She follows Mrs. Boyle. To Giles, softly, as she passes him*) Darling, you were wonderful . . .

(MRS. BOYLE *and* MOLLIE *exit* L *up the stairs*)

CHRISTOPHER. (*rising; childishly*) I think that's a perfectly horrible woman. I don't like her at all. I'd love to see you turn her out into the snow. Serve her right.

GILES. It's a pleasure I've got to forgo, I'm afraid.

(*The door bell peals*)

Lord, there's another of them.

(GILES *goes out to the front door*)

(*Off*) Come in—come in.

(CHRISTOPHER *moves to the sofa and sits.* MISS CASEWELL *enters up* R. *She is a young woman of a manly type, and carries a case. She has a long dark coat, a light scarf and no hat.* GILES *enters*)

MISS CASEWELL. (*in a deep, manly voice*) Afraid my car's bogged about half a mile down the road—ran into a drift.

GILES. Let me take this. (*He takes her case and puts it* R *of the refectory table*) Any more stuff in the car?

MISS CASEWELL. (*moving down to the fire*) No, I travel light.

(GILES *moves above the armchair* C)

Ha, glad to see you've got a good fire. (*She straddles in front of it in a manly fashion*)

GILES. Er—Mr. Wren—Miss ——?

MISS CASEWELL. Casewell. (*She nods to Christopher*)

GILES. My wife will be down in a minute.

MISS CASEWELL. No hurry. (*She takes off her overcoat*) Got to get myself thawed out. Looks as though you're going to be snowed up here. (*Taking an evening paper from her overcoat pocket*) Weather forecast says heavy falls expected. Motorists warned, etcetera. Hope you've got plenty of provisions in.

GILES. Oh yes. My wife's an excellent manager. Anyway, we can always eat our hens.

MISS CASEWELL. Before we start eating each other, eh?

(*She laughs stridently and throws the overcoat at* GILES, *who catches it. She sits in the armchair* C)

CHRISTOPHER. (*rising and crossing to the fire*) Any news in the paper—apart from the weather?

MISS CASEWELL. Usual political crisis. Oh yes, and a rather juicy murder!

CHRISTOPHER. A murder? (*Turning to Miss Casewell*) Oh, I *like* murder!

MISS CASEWELL. (*handing him the paper*) They seem to think it was a homicidal maniac. Strangled a woman somewhere near Paddington. Sex maniac, I suppose. (*She looks at Giles*)

(GILES *crosses to* L *of the sofa table*)

CHRISTOPHER. Doesn't say much, does it? (*He sits in the small armchair* R *and reads*) "The police are anxious to interview a man seen in the vicinity of Culver Street at the time. Medium height, wearing darkish overcoat, lightish scarf and soft felt hat. Police messages to this effect have been broadcast throughout the day."

MISS CASEWELL. Useful description. Fit pretty well anyone, wouldn't it?

CHRISTOPHER. When it says that the police are anxious to interview someone, is that a polite way of hinting that he's the murderer?

MISS CASEWELL. Could be.

GILES. Who was the woman who was murdered?

CHRISTOPHER. Mrs. Lyon. Mrs. Maureen Lyon.

GILES. Young or old?

CHRISTOPHER. It doesn't say. It doesn't seem to have been robbery . . .

MISS CASEWELL. (*to Giles*) I told you—sex maniac.

(MOLLIE *comes down the stairs and crosses to Miss Casewell*)

GILES. Here's Miss Casewell, Mollie. My wife.

MISS CASEWELL. (*rising*) How d'you do? (*She shakes hands with Mollie vigorously*)

(GILES *picks up her case*)

MOLLIE. It's an awful night. Would you like to come up to your room? The water's hot if you'd like a bath.

MISS CASEWELL. You're right, I would.

(MOLLIE *and* MISS CASEWELL *exit to the stairs* L. GILES *follows them, carrying the case. Left alone,* CHRISTOPHER *rises and makes an exploration. He opens the door down* L, *peeps in and then exits. A moment or two later he reappears on the stairs L. He crosses to the arch up R and looks off. He sings "Little Jack Horner" and chuckles to himself, giving the impression of being slightly unhinged mentally. He moves behind the refectory table.* GILES *and* MOLLIE *enter from the stairs L, talking.* CHRISTOPHER *hides behind the curtain.* MOLLIE *moves above the armchair C and* GILES *moves to the R end of the refectory table*)

MOLLIE. I must hurry out to the kitchen and get on with things. Major Metcalf is very nice. He won't be difficult. It's Mrs. Boyle really frightens me. We *must* have a nice dinner. I was thinking of opening two tins of minced beef and cereal and a tin of peas, and mashing the potatoes. And there's stewed figs and custard. Do you think that will be all right?

GILES. Oh—I should think so. Not—not very original, perhaps.

CHRISTOPHER. (*coming from behind the curtains and moving between Giles and Mollie*) Do let me help. I adore cooking. Why not an omelette? You've got eggs, haven't you?

MOLLIE. Oh yes, we've got plenty of eggs. We keep lots of fowls. They don't lay as well as they should but we've put down a lot of eggs.

(GILES *breaks away* L)

CHRISTOPHER. And if you've got a bottle of cheap, any type wine, you could add it to the—"minced beef and cereals," did you say? Give it a Continental flavour. Show me where the kitchen is and what you've got, and I daresay I shall have an inspiration.

MOLLIE. Come on.

(MOLLIE *and* CHRISTOPHER *exit through the archway R to the kitchen.* GILES *frowns, ejaculates something uncomplimentary to Christopher and crosses to the small armchair down R. He picks up the newspaper and stands reading it with deep attention. He jumps as* MOLLIE *returns to the room and speaks*)

Isn't he sweet? (*She moves above the sofa table*) He's put on an apron and he's getting all the things together. He says leave it all to him and don't come back for

half an hour. If our guests want to do the cooking themselves, it will save a lot of trouble.

GILES. Why on earth did you give him the best room?

MOLLIE. I told you, he liked the fourposter.

GILES. He liked the pretty fourposter. Twerp!

MOLLIE. Giles!

GILES. I've got no use for that kind. (*Significantly*) You
didn't handle his suitcase, I did.

MOLLIE. Had it got bricks in it? (*She crosses to the armchair
c and sits*)

GILES. It was no weight at all. If you ask me there was *nothing* inside it. He's probably one of those young men
who go about bilking hotel keepers.

MOLLIE. I don't believe it. I like him. (*She pauses*) I think
Miss Casewell's rather peculiar, don't you?

GILES. Terrible female—if she *is* a female.

MOLLIE. It seems very hard that all our guests should be
either unpleasant or odd. Anyway, I think Major Metcalf's all right, don't you?

GILES. Probably drinks!

MOLLIE. Oh, do you think so?

GILES. No, I don't. I was just feeling rather depressed. Well,
at any rate, we know the worst now. They've all arrived.

(*The door bell rings*)

MOLLIE. Who can that be?

GILES. Probably the Culver Street murderer.

MOLLIE. (*rising*) Don't!

(GILES *exits up* R *to the front door.* MOLLIE *crosses to the
fire*)

GILES. (*off*) Oh.

(MR. PARAVICINI *staggers in up* R, *carrying a small bag. He is
foreign and dark and elderly with a rather flamboyant
moustache. He is a slightly taller edition of Hercule
Poirot, which may give a wrong impression to the audience. He wears a heavy fur-lined overcoat. He leans on
the* L *side of the arch and puts down the bag.* GILES
enters)

PARAVICINI. A thousand pardons. I am—where am I?

GILES. This is Monkswell Manor Guest House.

PARAVICINI. But what stupendous good fortune! Madame! (*He moves down to Mollie, takes her hand and kisses it*)

(GILES *crosses above the armchair* C)

What an answer to prayer. A guest house—and a charming hostess. My Rolls Royce, alas, has run into a snow-drift. Blinding snow everywhere. I do not know where I am. Perhaps, I think to myself, I shall freeze to death. And then I take a little bag, I stagger through the snow, I see before me big iron gates. A habitation! I am saved. Twice I fall into the snow as I come up your drive, but at last I arrive and immediately—(*he looks round*) despair turns to joy. (*Changing his manner*) You can let me have a room—yes?

GILES. Oh yes . . .

MOLLIE. It's rather a small one, I'm afraid.

PARAVICINI. Naturally—naturally—you have other guests.

MOLLIE. We've only just opened this place as a guest house today, and so we're—we're rather new at it.

PARAVICINI (*leering at Mollie*) Charming—charming . . .

GILES. What about your luggage?

PARAVICINI. That is of no consequence. I have locked the car securely.

GILES. But wouldn't it be better to get it in?

PARAVICINI. No, no. (*He moves up to* R *of Giles*) I can assure you on such a night as this, there will be no thieves abroad. And for me, my wants are very simple. I have all I need—here—in this little bag. Yes, all that I need.

MOLLIE. You'd better get thoroughly warm.

(PARAVICINI *crosses to the fire*)

I'll see about your room. (*She moves to the armchair* C) I'm afraid it's rather a cold room because it faces north, but all the others are occupied.

PARAVICINI. You have several guests, then?

MOLLIE. There's Mrs. Boyle and Major Metcalf and Miss Casewell and a young man called Christopher Wren—and now—you.

PARAVICINI. Yes—the unexpected guest. The guest that you did not invite. The guest who just arrived—from no-where—out of the storm. It sounds quite dramatic, does it not? Who am I? You do not know. Where do I come from? You do not know. Me, I am the man of mystery. (*He laughs*)

(MOLLIE *laughs and looks at* GILES, *who grins feebly.* PARA-
VICINI *nods his head at Mollie in high good humour*)

But now, I tell you this. I complete the picture. From
now on there will be no more arrivals. And no de-
partures either. By tomorrow—perhaps even already—
we are cut off from civilization. No butcher, no baker,
no milkman, no postman, no daily papers—nobody and
nothing but ourselves. That is admirable. It could not
suit me better. My name, by the way, is Paravicini. (*He
moves down to the small armchair* R)

(GILES *moves to* L *of Mollie*)

PARAVICINI. Mr. and Mrs. Ralston? (*He nods his head as they
agree. He looks round him and moves up to* R *of Mollie*)
And this—is Monkswell Manor Guest House, you said?
Good. Monkswell Manor Guest House. (*He laughs*)
Perfect. (*He laughs*) Perfect. (*He laughs and crosses to
the fireplace*)

MOLLIE *looks at* GILES *and they look at Paravicini uneasily
as—*

the CURTAIN *falls*

Scene II

SCENE: *The same. The following afternoon.*

When the CURTAIN *rises it is not snowing, but snow
can be seen banked high against the window.* MAJOR
METCALF *is seated on the sofa reading a book, and* MRS.
BOYLE *is sitting in the large armchair* R *in front of the
fire, writing on a pad on her knee.*

MRS. BOYLE. I consider it *most* dishonest not to have told
me they were only just starting this place.
MAJOR METCALF. Well, everything's got to have a beginning,
you know. Excellent breakfast this morning. Good coffee. Scrambled eggs, homemade marmalade. And all
nicely served, too. Little woman does it all herself.
MRS. BOYLE. Amateurs—there should be a proper staff.

MAJOR METCALF. Excellent lunch, too.

MRS. BOYLE. Cornbeef.

MAJOR METCALF. But very well disguised cornbeef. Red wine in it. Mrs. Ralston promised to make a pie for us tonight.

MRS. BOYLE. (*rising and crossing to the radiator*) These radiators are not really hot. I shall speak about it.

MAJOR METCALF. Very comfortable beds, too. At least mine was. Hope yours was, too.

MRS. BOYLE. It was quite adequate. (*She returns to the large armchair* R *and sits*) I don't quite see why the best bed-room should have been given to that *very* peculiar young man.

MAJOR METCALF. Got here ahead of us. First come, first served.

MRS. BOYLE. From the advertisement I got *quite* a different impression of what this place would be like. A comfortable writing-room, and a much larger place altogether —with bridge and other amenities.

MAJOR METCALF. Regular old tabbies' delight.

MRS. BOYLE. I beg your pardon.

MAJOR METCALF. Er—I mean, yes, I quite see what you mean.

(CHRISTOPHER *enters* L *from the stairs unnoticed*)

MRS. BOYLE. No, indeed, I shan't stay here long.

CHRISTOPHER. (*laughing*) No. No, I don't suppose you will.

(CHRISTOPHER *exits into the library up* L)

MRS. BOYLE. Really that is a very peculiar young man. Unbalanced mentally, I shouldn't wonder.

MAJOR METCALF. Think he's escaped from a lunatic asylum?

MRS. BOYLE. I shouldn't be at all surprised.

(MOLLIE *enters through the archway up* R)

MOLLIE. (*calling upstairs*) Giles?

GILES. (*off*) Yes?

MOLLIE. Can you shovel the snow away again from the back door?

GILES. (*off*) Coming.

(MOLLIE *disappears through the arch*)

MAJOR METCALF. I'll give you a hand, what? (*He rises and crosses up* R *the arch*) Good exercise. Must have exercise.

(MAJOR METCALF *exits.* GILES *enters from the stairs, crosses and exits up* R. MOLLIE *returns, carrying a duster and a vacuum cleaner, crosses the Hall and runs upstairs. She collides with* MISS CASEWELL *who is coming down the stairs*)

MOLLIE. Sorry!

MISS CASEWELL. That's all right.

(MOLLIE *exits.* MISS CASEWELL *comes slowly* C)

MRS. BOYLE. Really! What an incredible young woman. Doesn't she know anything about housework? Carrying a carpet sweeper through the front hall. Aren't there any back stairs?

MISS CASEWELL. (*taking a cigarette from a packet in her handbag*) Oh yes—nice stairs. (*She crosses to the fire*) Very convenient if there was a fire. (*She lights the cigarette*)

MRS. BOYLE. Then why not use them? Anyway, all the housework should have been done in the morning before lunch.

MISS CASEWELL. I gather our hostess had to cook the lunch.

MRS. BOYLE. All very haphazard and amateurish. There should be a proper staff.

MISS CASEWELL. Not very easy to get nowadays, is it?

MRS. BOYLE. No, indeed the lower classes seem to have no idea of their responsibilities.

MISS CASEWELL. Poor old lower classes. Got the bit between their teeth, haven't they?

MRS. BOYLE. (*frostily*) I gather you are a Socialist.

MISS CASEWELL. Oh, I wouldn't say that. I'm not a Red—just pale pink. (*She moves to the sofa and sits on the right arm*) But I don't take much interest in politics—I live abroad.

MRS. BOYLE. I suppose conditions are much easier abroad.

MISS CASEWELL. I don't have to cook and clean—as I gather most people have to do in this country.

MRS. BOYLE. This country has gone sadly downhill. Not what it used to be. I sold my house last year. Everything was too difficult.

MISS CASEWELL. Hotels and guest houses are easier.

MRS. BOYLE. They certainly solve some of one's problems. Are you over in England for long?

MISS CASEWELL. Depends. I've got some business to see to. When it's done—I shall go back.

MRS. BOYLE. To France?

MISS CASEWELL. No.

MRS. BOYLE. Italy?

MISS CASEWELL. No. (*She grins*)

(MRS. BOYLE *looks at her inquiringly but* MISS CASEWELL *does not respond.* MRS. BOYLE *starts writing.* MISS CASEWELL *grins as she looks at her, crosses to the radio, turns it on at first softly, then increases the volume*)

MRS. BOYLE. (*annoyed, as she is writing*) Would you mind not having that on quite so loud! I always find the radio rather distracting when one is trying to write letters.

MISS CASEWELL. Do you?

MRS. BOYLE. If you don't particularly want to listen just now . . .

MISS CASEWELL. It's my favourite music. There's a writing table in there. (*She nods towards the library door up* L)

MRS. BOYLE. I know. But it's much warmer here.

MISS CASEWELL. Much warmer, I agree. (*She dances to the music*)

(MRS. BOYLE, *after a moment's glare, rises and exits into the library up* L. MISS CASEWELL *grins, moves to the sofa table, and stubs out her cigarette. She moves up stage and picks up a magazine from the refectory table*)

Bloody old bitch. (*She moves to the large armchair and sits*)

(CHRISTOPHER *enters from the library up* L *and moves down* L)

CHRISTOPHER. Oh!

MISS CASEWELL. Hullo.

CHRISTOPHER. (*gesturing back to the library*) Wherever I go that woman seems to hunt me down—and then she glares at me—positively glares.

MISS CASEWELL. (*indicating the radio*) Turn it down a bit.

(CHRISTOPHER *turns the radio down until it is playing quite softly*)

CHRISTOPHER. Is that all right?

MISS CASEWELL. Oh yes, it's served its purpose.

CHRISTOPHER. What purpose?

MISS CASEWELL. Tactics, boy.

(CHRISTOPHER *looks puzzled.* MISS CASEWELL *indicates the library*)

CHRISTOPHER. Oh, you mean *her.*

MISS CASEWELL. She'd pinched the best chair. I've got it now.

CHRISTOPHER. You drove her out. I'm glad. I'm very glad. I don't like her a bit. (*Crossing quickly to Miss Casewell*) Let's think of things we can do to annoy her, shall we? I wish she'd go away from here.

MISS CASEWELL. In this? Not a hope.

CHRISTOPHER. But when the snow melts.

MISS CASEWELL. Oh, when the snow melts lots of things may have happened.

CHRISTOPHER. Yes—yes—that's true. (*He goes to the window*) Snow's rather lovely, isn't it? So peaceful—and pure . . . It makes one forget things.

MISS CASEWELL. It doesn't make me forget.

CHRISTOPHER. How fierce you sound.

MISS CASEWELL. I was thinking.

CHRISTOPHER. What sort of thinking? (*He sits on the window seat*)

MISS CASEWELL. Ice on a bedroom jug, chilblains, raw and bleeding—one thin ragged blanket—a child shivering with cold and fear.

CHRISTOPHER. My dear, it sounds too, too grim—what is it? A novel?

MISS CASEWELL. You didn't know I was a writer, did you?

CHRISTOPHER. Are you? (*He rises and moves down to her*)

MISS CASEWELL. Sorry to disappoint you. Actually I'm not. (*She puts the magazine up in front of her face*)

(CHRISTOPHER *looks at her doubtfully, then crosses* L., *turns up the radio very loud and exits into the drawing-room. The telephone rings.* MOLLIE *runs down the stairs, duster in hand, and goes to the telephone*)

MOLLIE. (*picking up the receiver*) Yes? (*She turns off the radio*) Yes—this is Monkswell Manor Guest House . . . What? . . . No, I'm afraid Mr. Ralston can't come to the telephone just now. This is Mrs. Ralston speaking. Who . . . The Berkshire Police . . . ?

(MISS CASEWELL *lowers her magazine*)

Oh yes, yes, Superintendent Hogben, I'm afraid that's impossible. He'd never get here. We're snowed up. Completely snowed up. The roads are impassable . . .

(MISS CASEWELL *rises and crosses to the arch up* L)

Nothing can get through . . . Yes . . . Very well . . . But what . . . Hullo—hullo . . . (*She replaces the receiver*)

(GILES *enters up* R *wearing an overcoat. He removes the overcoat and hangs it up in the hall*)

GILES. Mollie, do you know where there's another spade?

MOLLIE. (*moving up* C) Giles, the police have just rung up.

MISS CASEWELL. Trouble with police, eh? Serving liquor without a licence?

(MISS CASEWELL *exits* L *up the stairs*)

MOLLIE. They're sending out an inspector or a sergeant or something.

GILES. (*moving to* R *of Mollie*) But he'll never get here.

MOLLIE. That's what I told them. But they seemed quite confident that he would.

GILES. Nonsense. Even a jeep couldn't get through today. Anyway, what's it all about?

MOLLIE. That's what I asked. But he wouldn't say. Just said I was to impress on my husband to listen very carefully to what Sergeant Trotter, I think it was, had to say, and to follow his instructions implicitly. Isn't it extraordinary?

GILES. (*moving down to the fire*) What on earth do you think we've done?

MOLLIE. (*moving to* L *of Giles*) Do you think it's those nylons from Gibraltar?

GILES. I did remember to get the wireless licence, didn't I?

MOLLIE. Yes, it's in the kitchen dresser.

GILES. I had rather a near shave with the car the other day but it was entirely the other fellow's fault.

MOLLIE. We must have done something . . .

GILES. (*kneeling and putting a log on the fire*) Probably something to do with running this place. I expect we've ignored some tinpot regulation of some Ministry or other. You practically can't avoid it, nowadays. (*He rises and faces Mollie*)

MOLLIE. Oh dear, I wish we'd never started this place. We're going to be snowed up for days, and everyone is cross, and we shall go through all our reserve of tins.

GILES. Cheer up, darling, (*he takes Mollie in his arms*) everything's going all right at the moment. I've filled up all the coalscuttles, and brought in the wood, and stoked the Aga and done the hens. I'll go and do the boiler next, and chop some kindling . . . (*He breaks off*) You know, Mollie, (*he moves slowly up to* R *of the refectory table*) come to think of it, it must be something pretty serious to send a police sergeant trekking out in all this. It must be something really urgent . . .

(GILES *and* MOLLIE *look at each other uneasily.* MRS. BOYLE *enters from the library up* L.)

MRS. BOYLE. (*coming to* L *of the refectory table*) Ah, there you are, Mr. Ralston. Do you know the central heating in the library is practically stone cold?

GILES. Sorry, Mrs. Boyle, we're a bit short of coke and . . .

MRS. BOYLE. I am paying seven guineas a week here—seven guineas, and I do not want to freeze.

GILES. I'll go and stoke it up.

(GILES *exits by the archway up* R. MOLLIE *follows him to the arch*)

MRS. BOYLE. Mrs. Ralston, if you don't mind my saying so, that is a very extraordinary young man you have staying here. His manners—and his ties—and does he ever brush his hair?

MOLLIE. He's an extremely brilliant young architect.

MRS. BOYLE. I beg your pardon?

MOLLIE. Christopher Wren is an architect . . .

MRS. BOYLE. My dear young woman. I have naturally heard of Sir Christopher Wren. (*She crosses to the fire*) Of course, he was an architect. He built St. Paul's. You young people seem to think that no-one is educated but yourselves.

MOLLIE. I meant *this* Wren. His name is Christopher. His parents called him that because they hoped he'd be an architect. (*She crosses to the sofa table and takes a cigarette from the box*) And he is—or nearly one—so it turned out all right.

MRS. BOYLE. Humph. Sounds a fishy story to me. (*She sits in the large armchair*) I should make some inquiries about him if I were you. What do you know of him?

MOLLIE. Just as much as I know about you, Mrs. Boyle—which is that you are both paying us seven guineas a week. (*She lights her cigarette*) That is really all I need to know, isn't it? And all that concerns me. It doesn't matter to me whether I like my guests, or whether (*meaningly*) I don't.

MRS. BOYLE. You are young and inexperienced and should welcome advice from someone more knowledgeable than yourself. And what about this foreigner?

MOLLIE. What about him?

MRS. BOYLE. You weren't expecting him, were you?

MOLLIE. To turn away a *bona fide* traveller is against the law, Mrs. Boyle. *You* should know that.

MRS. BOYLE. Why do you say that?

MOLLIE. (*moving down* C) Weren't you a magistrate, sitting on the bench, Mrs. Boyle?

MRS. BOYLE. All I say is that this Paravicini, or whatever he calls himself, seems to me . . .

(PARAVICINI *enters softly from the stairs* L)

PARAVICINI. Beware, dear lady. You talk of the devil and there he is. Ha, ha.

(MRS. BOYLE *jumps*)

MRS. BOYLE. I didn't hear you come in.

(MOLLIE *moves behind the sofa table*)

PARAVICINI. I came in on tiptoe—like this. (*He demonstrates, moving down* C) Nobody ever hears me if I do not want them to. I find that very amusing.

MRS. BOYLE. Indeed?

PARAVICINI. (*sitting in the armchair* C) Now there was a young lady . . .

MRS. BOYLE. (*rising*) Well, I must get on with my letters. I'll see if it's a little warmer in the drawing-room.

(MRS. BOYLE *exits to the drawing-room down* L. MOLLIE *follows her to the door*)

PARAVICINI. My charming hostess looks upset. What is it, dear lady? (*He leers at her*)

MOLLIE. Everything's rather difficult this morning. Because of the snow.

PARAVICINI. Yes. Snow makes things difficult, does it not? (*He rises*) Or else it makes them easy. (*He moves up to the refectory table and sits*) Yes—very easy.

MOLLIE. I don't know what you mean.

PARAVICINI. No, there is quite a lot you do not know. I think, for one thing, that you do not know very much about running a guest house.

MOLLIE. (*moving to L of the sofa table and stubbing out her cigarette*) I daresay we don't. But we mean to make a go of it.

PARAVICINI. Bravo—bravo! (*He claps his hands and rises*)

MOLLIE. I'm not such a very bad cook . . .

PARAVICINI. (*leering*) You are without doubt an enchanting cook. (*He moves behind the sofa table and takes Mollie's hand*)

(MOLLIE *draws it away and moves below to sofa down* C)

May I give you a little word of warning. Mrs. Ralston? (*Moving below the sofa*) You and your husband must not be too trusting, you know. Have you references with these guests of yours?

MOLLIE. Is that usual? (*She turns to Paravicini*) I always thought people just—just *came*?

PARAVICINI. It is advisable to know a little about the people who sleep under your roof. Take, for example, myself. I turn up saying that my car is overturned in a snow-drift. What do you know of me? Nothing at all! I may be a thief, a robber, (*he moves slowly towards Mollie*) a fugitive from justice—a madman—even—a murderer.

MOLLIE. (*backing away*) Oh!

PARAVICINI. You see! And perhaps you know just as little of your other guests.

MOLLIE. Well, as far as Mrs. Boyle goes . . .

(MRS. BOYLE *enters from the drawing-room.* MOLLIE *moves up* C *to the refectory table*)

MRS. BOYLE. The drawing-room is far too cold to sit in. I shall write my letters in here. (*She crosses to the large armchair*)

PARAVICINI. Allow me to poke the fire for you. (*He moves* R *and does so*)

(MAJOR METCALF *enters up* R *through the archway*)

MAJOR METCALF. (*to Mollie; with old-fashioned modesty*) Mrs. Ralston, is your husband about? I'm afraid the pipes of the—er—the downstairs cloakroom are frozen.

MOLLIE. Oh dear. What an awful day. First the police and then the pipes. (*She moves to the arch up* R)

(PARAVICINI *drops the poker with a clatter.* MAJOR METCALF *stands as though paralysed*)

MRS. BOYLE. (*startled*) Police?

MAJOR METCALF. (*loudly, as if incredulous*) Police, did you say? (*He moves to the* L *end of the refectory table*)

MOLLIE. They rang up. Just now. To say they're sending a sergeant out here. (*She looks at the snow*) But I don't think he'll ever get here.

(GILES *enters from the archway up* R *with a basket of logs*)

GILES. The ruddy coke's more than half stones. And the price . . . Hullo, is anything the matter?

MAJOR METCALF. I hear the police are on their way here. Why?

GILES. Oh, that's all right. No-one can get through in this. Why, the drifts must be five feet deep. The roads are all banked up. Nobody will get here today. (*He takes the logs to the fireplace*) Excuse me, Mr. Paravicini. May I put these down?

(PARAVICINI *moves down stage of the fireplace. There are three sharp taps on the window as* SERGEANT TROTTER *presses his face to the pane and peers in.* MOLLIE *gives a cry and points.* GILES *crosses and throws open the window.* SERGEANT TROTTER *is on skis and is a cheerful, commonplace young man with a slight cockney accent*)

TROTTER. Are you Mr. Ralston?

GILES. Yes.

TROTTER. Thank you, sir. Detective Sergeant Trotter. Berkshire Police. Can I get these skis off and stow them somewhere?

GILES. (*pointing* R) Go round that way to the front door. I'll meet you.

TROTTER. Thank you, sir.

(GILES *leaves the window open and exits to the front door up* R)

MRS. BOYLE. I suppose that's what we pay our police force for, nowadays, to go round enjoying themselves at winter sports.

(MOLLIE *crosses below the refectory table to the window*)

PARAVICINI. (*moving up to* C *of the refectory table; in a fierce whisper to Mollie*) Why did you send for the police, Mrs. Ralston?
MOLLIE. But I didn't. (*She shuts the window*)

(CHRISTOPHER *enters from the drawing-room* L *and comes to* L *of the sofa*. PARAVICINI *moves to the* R *end of the refectory table*)

CHRISTOPHER. Who's that man? Where did he come from? He passed the drawing-room window on skis. All over snow and looking terribly hearty.
MRS. BOYLE. You may believe it or not, but the man is a policeman. A policeman—ski-ing!

(GILES *and* TROTTER *enter from the front door*. TROTTER *has removed his skis and is carrying them*)

GILES. (*moving* R *of the arch up* R) Er—this is Detective Sergeant Trotter.
TROTTER. (*moving to* L *of the large armchair*) Good afternoon.
MRS. BOYLE. You can't be a sergeant. You're too young.
TROTTER. I'm not quite as young as I look, madam.
CHRISTOPHER. But terribly hearty.
GILES. We'll stow your skis away under the stairs.

(GILES *and* TROTTER *exit through the archway up* R)

MAJOR METCALF. Excuse me, Mrs. Ralston, but may I use your telephone?
MOLLIE. Of course, Major Metcalf.

(MAJOR METCALF *goes to the telephone and dials*)

CHRISTOPHER. (*sitting at the* R *end of the sofa*) He's very attractive, don't you think so? I always think that policemen are very attractive.
MRS. BOYLE. No brains. You can see that at a glance.
MAJOR METCALF. (*into the telephone*) Hullo! Hullo! . . . (*To Mollie*) Mrs. Ralston, this telephone is dead—quite dead.

MOLLIE. It was all right about half an hour ago.

MAJOR METCALF. The line's gone with the weight of the snow, I suppose.

CHRISTOPHER. (*laughing hysterically*) So we're quite cut off now. Quite cut off. That's funny, isn't it?

MAJOR METCALF. (*moving to L of sofa*) I don't see anything to laugh at.

MRS. BOYLE. No, indeed.

CHRISTOPHER. Ah, it's a private joke of my own. Hist, the sleuth is returning.

(TROTTER *enters from the archway up* R, *followed by* GILES. TROTTER *moves down* C *while* GILES *crosses to* L *of the sofa table*)

TROTTER. (*taking out his notebook*) Now we can get to business, Mr. Ralston. Mrs. Ralston?

(MOLLIE *moves down* C)

GILES. Do you want to see us alone? If so, we can go into the library. (*He points towards the library door up* L)

TROTTER. (*turning his back to the audience*) It's not necessary, sir. It'll save time if everybody's present. If I might sit at this table? (*He moves up to the* R *end of the refectory table*)

PARAVICINI. I beg your pardon. (*He moves behind the table to the* L *end*)

TROTTER. Thank you. (*He settles himself in a judicial manner* C *behind the refectory table*)

MOLLIE. Oh, do hurry up and tell us. (*She moves up the* R *end of the refectory table*) What have we done?

TROTTER. (*surprised*) Done? Oh, it's nothing of *that* kind, Mrs. Ralston. It's something quite different. It's more a matter of police protection, if you understand me.

MOLLIE. Police protection?

TROTTER. It relates to the death of Mrs. Lyon—Mrs. Maureen Lyon of twenty-four Culver Street, London, West two, who was murdered yesterday, the fifteenth instant. You may have heard or read about the case?

MOLLIE. Yes. I heard it on the wireless. The woman who was strangled?

TROTTER. That's right, madam. (*To Giles*) The first thing I want to know is if you were acquainted with this Mrs. Lyon.

GILES. Never heard of her.

(MOLLIE *shakes her head*)

TROTTER. You mayn't have known of her under the name of Lyon. Lyon wasn't her real name. She had a police record and her fingerprints were on file so we were able to identify her without difficulty. Her real name was Maureen Stanning. Her husband was a farmer, John Stanning, who resided at Longridge Farm not very far from here.

GILES. Longridge Farm! Wasn't that where those children . . . ?

TROTTER. Yes, the Longridge Farm case.

(MISS CASEWELL *enters from the stairs* L)

MISS CASEWELL. Three children . . . (*She crosses to the armchair down* R *and sits*)

(*Everyone watches her*)

TROTTER. That's right, miss. The Corrigans. Two boys and a girl. Brought before the court as in need of care and protection. A home was found for them with Mr. and Mrs. Stanning at Longridge Farm. One of the children subsequently died as the result of criminal neglect and persistent ill-treatment. Case made a bit of a sensation at the time.

MOLLIE. (*very much shaken*) It was horrible.

TROTTER. The Stannings were sentenced to terms of imprisonment. Stanning died in prison. Mrs. Stanning served her sentence and was duly released. Yesterday, as I say, she was found strangled at twenty-four Culver Street.

MOLLIE. Who did it?

TROTTER. I'm coming to that, madam. A notebook was picked up near the scene of the crime. In that notebook was written two addresses. One was twenty-four Culver Street. The other (*he pauses*) was Monkswell Manor.

GILES. What?

TROTTER. Yes, sir.

(*During the next speech* PARAVICINI *moves slowly* L *to the stairs and leans on the upstage side of the arch*)

That's why Superintendent Hogben, on receiving this information from Scotland Yard, thought it imperative for me to come out here and find out if you knew of any connexion between this house, or anyone in this house, and the Longridge Farm case.

GILES. (*moving to the L end of the refectory table*) There's nothing—absolutely nothing. It must be a coincidence.

TROTTER. Superintendent Hogben doesn't think it is a co-incidence, sir.

(MAJOR METCALF *turns and looks at Trotter. During the next speeches he takes out his pipe and fills it*)

He'd have come himself if it had been in any way possible. Under the weather conditions, and as I can ski, he sent me with instructions to get full particulars of everyone in the house, to report back to him by phone, and to take what measures I thought fit to ensure the safety of the household.

GILES. Safety? What danger does he think we're in? Good Lord, he's not suggesting that somebody is going to be killed here?

TROTTER. I don't want to frighten any of the ladies—but frankly, yes, that is the idea.

GILES. But—why?

TROTTER. That's what I'm here to find out.

GILES. But the whole thing's crazy!

TROTTER. Yes, sir. It's because it's crazy that it's dangerous.

MRS. BOYLE. Nonsense!

MISS CASEWELL. I must say it seems a bit far-fetched.

CHRISTOPHER. I think it's wonderful. (*He turns and looks at Major Metcalf*)

(MAJOR METCALF *lights his pipe*)

MOLLIE. Is there something that you haven't told us, Sergeant?

TROTTER. Yes, Mrs. Ralston. Below the two addresses was written "Three Blind Mice." And on the dead woman's body was a paper with "This is the First" written on it, and below the words, a drawing of three little mice and a bar of music. The music was the tune of the nursery rhyme *Three Blind Mice*. You know how it goes. (*He sings*) "Three Blind Mice . . ."

MOLLIE. (*singing*) "Three Blind Mice,
                    See how they run,
                    They all ran after the farmer's wife . . ."
Oh, it's horrible.

GILES. There were three children and one died?

TROTTER. Yes, the youngest, a boy of eleven.

GILES. What happened to the other two?

TROTTER. The girl was adopted by someone. We haven't been able to trace her present whereabouts. The elder boy would now be about twenty-two. Deserted from the Army and has not been heard of since. According to the Army psychologist, was definitely schizophrenic. (*Explaining*) A bit queer in the head, that's to say.

MOLLIE. They think that it was he who killed Mrs. Lyon— Mrs. Stanning? (*She moves down to the armchair* c)

TROTTER. Yes.

MOLLIE. And that he's a homicidal maniac (*she sits*) and that he will turn up here and try to kill someone—but why?

TROTTER. That's what I've got to find out from you. As the Superintendent sees it, there must be some connexion. (*To Giles*) Now you state, sir, that you yourself have never had any connexion with the Longridge Farm case?

GILES. No.

TROTTER. And the same goes for you, madam?

MOLLIE. (*not at ease*) I—no—I mean—no connexion.

TROTTER. What about servants?

(MRS. BOYLE *registers disapproval*)

MOLLIE. We haven't got any servants. (*She rises and moves up* R *to the arch*) That reminds me. Would you mind, Sergeant Trotter, if I went to the kitchen? I'll be there if you want me.

TROTTER. That's quite all right, Mrs. Ralston.

(MOLLIE *exits by the archway up* R. GILES *crosses up* R *to the arch, but he is stopped as* TROTTER *speaks*)

Now can I have all your names, please?

MRS. BOYLE. This is quite ridiculous. We are merely staying in a kind of hotel. We only arrived yesterday. We've nothing to do with this place.

TROTTER. You'd planned to come here in advance, though. You'd booked your rooms here ahead.

MRS. BOYLE. Well, yes. All except Mr. ——? (*She looks at Paravicini*)

PARAVICINI. Paravicini. (*He moves to the* L *end of the refectory table*) My car overturned in a snowdrift.

TROTTER. I see. What I'm getting at is that anyone who's been following you around might know very well that you were coming here. Now, there's just one thing I want to know and I want to know it quick. Which one of you is it that has some connexion with that business at Longridge Farm?

(*There is a dead silence*)

You're not being very sensible, you know. One of you is in danger—deadly danger. I've got to know which one that is.

(*There is another silence*)

All right, I'll ask you one by one. (*To Paravicini*) You, first, since you seem to have arrived here more or less by accident, Mr. Pari——?

PARAVICINI. Para—Paravicini. But, my dear Inspector, I know nothing, but nothing of what you have been talking about. I am a stranger in this country. I know nothing of these local affairs of bygone years.

TROTTER. (*rising and moving down to* L *of Mrs. Boyle*) Mrs. ——?

MRS. BOYLE. Boyle. I don't see—really I consider it an impertinence . . . Why on earth should I have anything to do with such—this distressing business?

(MAJOR METCALF *looks sharply at her*)

TROTTER. (*looking at Miss Casewell*) Miss——?

MISS CASEWELL. (*slowly*) Casewell. Leslie Casewell. I never heard of Longridge Farm, and I know nothing about it.

TROTTER. (*moving to* R *of the sofa; to Major Metcalf*) You, sir?

MAJOR METCALF. Metcalf—Major. Read about the case in the papers at the time. I was stationed at Edinburgh then. No personal knowledge.

TROTTER. (*to Christopher*) And you?

CHRISTOPHER. Christopher Wren. I was a mere child at the time. I don't remember even hearing about it.

TROTTER. (*moving behind the sofa table*) And that's all you have to say—any of you?

(*There is a silence*)

(*Moving* C) Well, if one of you gets murdered, you'll have yourself to blame. Now then, Mr. Ralston, can I have a look round the house?

(TROTTER *exits up* R *with* GILES. PARAVICINI *sits at the window seat*)

CHRISTOPHER. (*rising*) My dears, how melodramatic. He's very attractive, isn't he? (*He moves up to the refectory table*) I do admire the police. So stern and hardboiled. Quite a thrill, this whole business. *Three Blind Mice.* How does the tune go? (*He whistles or hums it*)

MRS. BOYLE. Really, Mr. Wren!

CHRISTOPHER. Don't you like it? (*He moves to* L *of Mrs. Boyle*) But it's a signature tune—the signature of the murderer. Just fancy what a kick he must be getting out of it.

MRS. BOYLE. Melodramatic rubbish. I don't believe a word of it.

CHRISTOPHER. (*stalking behind her*) But just wait, Mrs. Boyle. Till I creep up behind you, and you feel my hands on your throat.

MRS. BOYLE. Stop . . . (*She rises*)

MAJOR METCALF. That'll do, Christopher. It's a poor joke, anyway. In fact, it's not a joke at all.

CHRISTOPHER. Oh, but it *is*! (*He moves above the armchair* C) That's just what it is. A madman's joke. That's just what makes it so deliciously *macabre*. (*He moves up* R *to the archway, looks round and giggles*) If you could just see your faces!

(CHRISTOPHER *exits through the archway*)

MRS. BOYLE. (*moving up* R *to the arch*) A singularly ill-mannered and neurotic young man.

(MOLLIE *enters from the dining-room down* R *and stands by the door*)

MOLLIE. Where's Giles?

MISS CASEWELL. Taking our policeman on a conducted tour of the house.

MRS. BOYLE. (*moving down to the large armchair*) Your friend, the architect, has been behaving in a most abnormal manner.

MAJOR METCALF. Young fellows seem nervy nowadays. Daresay he'll grow out of it.

MRS. BOYLE. (*sitting*) Nerves? I've no patience with people who say they have nerves. I haven't any nerves.

(MISS CASEWELL *rises and crosses to the stairs* L)

MAJOR METCALF. No? Perhaps that's just as well for you, Mrs. Boyle.

MRS. BOYLE. What do you mean?

MAJOR METCALF. (*moving to* L *of the armchair* C) I think you were actually one of the magistrates on the Bench at the time. In fact, you were responsible for sending those three children to Longridge Farm.

MRS. BOYLE. Really, Major Metcalf. I can hardly be held responsible. We had reports from welfare workers. The farm people seemed very nice and were most anxious to have the children. It seemed most satisfactory. Eggs and fresh milk and a healthy out-of-doors life.

MAJOR METCALF. Kicks, blows, starvation, and a thoroughly vicious couple.

MRS. BOYLE. But how was I to know? They were very civilly spoken.

MOLLIE. Yes, I was right. (*She moves up* C *and stares at Mrs. Boyle*) It was you . . .

(MAJOR METCALF *looks sharply at Mollie*)

MRS. BOYLE. One tries to do a public duty and all one gets is abuse.

(PARAVICINI *laughs heartily*)

PARAVICINI. You must forgive me, but indeed I find all this most amusing. I enjoy myself greatly.

(*Still laughing,* PARAVICINI *exits down* L *to the drawing-room.* MOLLIE *moves to* R *of the sofa*)

MRS. BOYLE. I never did like that man!

MISS CASEWELL. (*moving to* L *of the sofa table*) Where did he come from last night? (*She takes a cigarette from the box*)

MOLLIE. I don't know.

MISS CASEWELL. Looks a bit of a spiv to me. Makes his face up, too. Rouge and powder. Disgusting. He must be quite old, too. (*She lights the cigarette*)

MOLLIE. And yet he skips about as though he were quite young.

MAJOR METCALF. You'll be wanting more wood. I'll get it.

(MAJOR METCALF *exits up* R)

MOLLIE. It's almost dark and yet it's only four in the afternoon. I'll turn the lights on. (*She moves down* R *and switches on the wall brackets over the fireplace*) That's better.

(*There is a pause.* MRS. BOYLE *glances uncomfortably first at* MOLLIE *and then at* MISS CASEWELL, *who are both watching her*)

MRS. BOYLE. (*assembling her writing things*) Now where did I leave my pen? (*She rises and crosses* L)

(MRS. BOYLE *exits up* L *to the library. There is the sound of a piano being played from the drawing-room—the tune of "Three Blind Mice" picked out with one finger*)

MOLLIE. (*moving up to the window to close the curtains*) What a horrid little tune that is.

MISS CASEWELL. Don't you like it? Reminds you of your childhood perhaps—an unhappy childhood?

MOLLIE. I was very happy as a child. (*She moves round to* C *of the refectory table*)

MISS CASEWELL. You were lucky.

MOLLIE. Weren't you happy?

MISS CASEWELL. (*crossing to the fire*) No.

MOLLIE. I'm sorry.

MISS CASEWELL. But all that's a long time ago. One gets over things.

MOLLIE. I suppose so.

MISS CASEWELL. Or doesn't one? Damned hard to say.

MOLLIE. They say that what happened when you're a child matters more than anything else.

MISS CASEWELL. They say—they say. Who says?

MOLLIE. Psychologists.

MISS CASEWELL. All humbug. Just a damned lot of nonsense. I've no use for psychologists and psychiatrists.

MOLLIE. (*moving down below the sofa*) I've never really had much to do with them.

MISS CASEWELL. A good thing for you you haven't. It's all a lot of hooey—the whole thing. Life's what you make of it. Go straight ahead—don't look back.

MOLLIE. One can't always help looking back.

MISS CASEWELL. Nonsense. It's a question of will power.

MOLLIE. Perhaps.

MISS CASEWELL. (*forcefully*) I *know*. (*She moves down* C)

MOLLIE. I expect you're right . . . (*She sighs*) But sometimes things happen—to make you remember . . .

MISS CASEWELL. Don't give in. Turn your back on them.

MOLLIE. Is that really the right way? I wonder. Perhaps that's all wrong. Perhaps one ought really to face them.

MISS CASEWELL. Depends what you're talking about.

MOLLIE. (*with a slight laugh*) Sometimes, I hardly know what I am talking about. (*She sits on the sofa*)

MISS CASEWELL. (*moving to Mollie*) Nothing from the past is going to affect me—except in the way I want it to.

(GILES *and* TROTTER *enter from the stairs* L)

TROTTER. Well, everything's all right upstairs. (*He looks at the open dining-room door, crosses and exits into the dining-room. He reappears in the archway up* R)

(MISS CASEWELL *exits into the dining-room, leaving the door open.* MOLLIE *rises and begins to tidy up, rearranging the cushions, then moves up to the curtains.* GILES *moves up to* L *of Mollie.* TROTTER *crosses down* L)

(*Opening the door down* L) What's in here, drawing-room?

(*The sound of the piano is heard much louder while the door is open.* TROTTER *exits into the drawing-room and shuts the door. Presently he reappears at the door up* L)

MRS. BOYLE. (*off*) Would you mind shutting that door. This place is full of draughts.

TROTTER. Sorry, madam, but I've got to get the lay of the land.

(TROTTER *closes the door and exits up the stairs.* MOLLIE *moves above the armchair* C)

GILES. (*coming down to* L *of Mollie*) Mollie, what's all this . . . ?

(TROTTER *reappears down the stairs*)

TROTTER. Well, that completes the tour. Nothing suspicious. I think I'll make my report now to Superintendent Hogben. (*He goes to the telephone*)

MOLLIE. (*moving to* L *of the refectory table*) But you can't telephone. The line's dead . . .

TROTTER. (*swinging round sharply*) What? (*He picks up the receiver*) Since when?

MOLLIE. Major Metcalf tried it just after you arrived.

TROTTER. But it was all right earlier. Superintendent Hogben got through all right.

MOLLIE. Oh yes. I suppose, since then, the lines are down with the snow.

TROTTER. I wonder. It may have been *cut*. (*He puts the receiver down and turns to them*)

GILES. Cut? But who could cut it?

TROTTER. Mr. Ralston . . . Just how much do you know about these people who are staying in your guest house?

GILES. I—we—we don't really know anything about them.

TROTTER. Ah. (*He moves above the sofa table*)

GILES. (*moving to* R *of Trotter*) Mrs. Boyle wrote from a Bournemouth hotel, Major Metcalf from an address in— where was it?

MOLLIE. Leamington. (*She moves to* L *of Trotter*)

GILES. Wren wrote from Hampstead and the Casewell woman from a private hotel in Kensington. Paravicini, as we've told you, turned up out of the blue last night. Still, I suppose they've all got ration books—that sort of thing.

TROTTER. I shall go into all that, of course. But there's not much reliance to be placed on that sort of evidence.

MOLLIE. But even if this—this maniac is trying to get here and kill us all—or one of us, we're quite safe now. Because of the snow. No-one can get here till it melts.

TROTTER. Unless he's here already.

GILES. Here already?

TROTTER. Why not, Mr. Ralston? All these people arrived here yesterday evening. Some hours after the murder of Mrs. Stanning. Plenty of time to get here.

GILES. But except for Mr. Paravicini, they'd all booked beforehand.

TROTTER. Well, why not? These crimes were planned.

GILES. Crimes? There's only been one crime. In Culver Street. Why are you sure there will be another here?

TROTTER. That it will happen here, no—I hope to prevent that. That it will be attempted, yes.

GILES. (*crossing to the fire*) I can't believe it. It's so fantastic.

TROTTER. It isn't fantastic. It's just facts.

MOLLIE. You've got a description of what this—man looked
like in London?

TROTTER. Medium height, indeterminate build, darkish overcoat, soft felt hat, face hidden by a muffler. Spoke in a
whisper. (*He crosses to L of the armchair C. He pauses*)
There are three darkish overcoats hanging up in the
hall now. One of them is yours, Mr. Ralston . . . There
are three lightish felt hats . . .

(GILES *starts to move towards the arch up R but he stops
when Mollie speaks*)

MOLLIE. I still can't believe it.

TROTTER. You see? It's this telephone wire that worries me.
If it's been cut . . . (*He crosses to the phone, bends
down and studies the wire*)

MOLLIE. I must go and get on with the vegetables.

(MOLLIE *exits through the archway up R. GILES picks up
Mollie's glove from the armchair C and holds it absently, smoothing it out. He extracts a London bus
ticket from the glove—stares at it—then after Mollie—
then back to the ticket*)

TROTTER. Is there an extension?

(GILES *frowns at the bus ticket, and does not answer*)

GILES. I beg your pardon. Did you say something?

TROTTER. Yes, Mr. Ralston, I said "Is there an extension?"
(*He crosses to C*)

GILES. Yes, up in our bedroom.

TROTTER. Go and try it up there for me, will you?

(GILES *exits to the stairs, carrying the glove and bus ticket
and looking dazed. TROTTER continues to trace the wire
to the window. He pulls back the curtain and opens the
window, trying to follow the wire. He crosses to the arch
up R, goes out and returns with a torch. He moves to
the window, jumps out and bends down, looking, then
disappears out of sight. It is practically dark. MRS. BOYLE
enters from the library up L, shivers and notices the open
window*)

MRS. BOYLE. (*moving to the window*) Who's left this window open? (*She shuts the window and closes the cur-*

*tain, then moves to the fire and puts another log on it.
She crosses to the radio and turns it on. She moves up
to the refectory table, picks up a magazine and looks at
it)*

(There is a music programme on the radio. MRS. BOYLE
*frowns, moves to the radio and tunes in to a different
programme)*

VOICE ON THE RADIO. . . . to understand what I may term as
the mechanics of fear, you have to study the precise
effect produced on the human mind. Imagine, for instance, that you are alone in a room. It is late in the
afternoon. A door opens softly behind you . . .

*(The door down R opens. The tune of "Three Blind Mice"
is heard whistled.* MRS. BOYLE *turns with a start)*

MRS. BOYLE. *(with relief)* Oh, it's you. I can't find any programme worth listening to. *(She moves to the radio and
tunes in to the music programme)*

*(A hand shows through the open doorway and clicks the light
switch. The lights suddenly go out)*

Here—what are you doing? Why did you turn out the
light?

*(The radio is at full volume, and through it are heard gurgles
and a scuffle.* MRS. BOYLE's *body falls.* MOLLIE *enters by
the archway up R and stands perplexed)*

MOLLIE. Why is it all dark? What a noise!

*She switches on the light at the switch up R and crosses to
the radio to turn it down. Then she sees Mrs. Boyle
lying strangled in front of the sofa and screams as—*

the CURTAIN *quickly falls*

Act Two

SCENE: *The same. Ten minutes later.*

When the CURTAIN *rises, Mrs. Boyle's body has been removed and everyone is assembled in the room.* TROTTER *is in charge and is sitting on the upstage side of the refectory table.* MOLLIE *is standing at the R end of the refectory table. The others are all sitting;* MAJOR METCALF *in the large armchair R,* CHRISTOPHER *in the dark chair,* GILES *on the stairs L,* MISS CASEWELL *at the R end of the sofa, and* PARAVICINI *at the L end.*

TROTTER. Now, Mrs. Ralston, try and think—*think* . . .

MOLLIE. (*at breaking point*) I can't think. My head's numbed.

TROTTER. Mrs. Boyle had only just been killed when you got to her. You came from the kitchen. Are you sure you didn't see or hear anybody as you came along the hallway?

MOLLIE. No—no, I don't think so. Just the radio blaring out in here. I couldn't think who'd turned it on so loud. I wouldn't hear anything else with that, would I?

TROTTER. That was clearly the murderer's idea—or (*meaningly*) murderess.

MOLLIE. How could I hear anything else?

TROTTER. You might have done. If the murderer had left the Hall that way (*he points* L) he might have heard you coming from the kitchen. He might have slipped up the back stairs—or into the dining-room . . .

MOLLIE. I think—I'm not sure—I heard a door creak—and shut—just as I came out of the kitchen.

TROTTER. Which door?

MOLLIE. I don't know.

TROTTER. Think, Mrs. Ralston—try and *think*. Upstairs? Downstairs? Close at hand? Right? Left?

321

MOLLIE. (*tearful*) I don't know, I tell you. I'm not even sure I heard anything. (*She moves down to the arm-chair c and sits*)

GILES. (*rising and moving to L of the refectory table; angrily*) Can't you stop bullying her? Can't you see she's all in?

TROTTER. (*sharply*) We're investigating a murder, Mr. Ralston. Up to now, nobody has taken this thing seriously. Mrs. Boyle didn't. She held out on me with information. You all held out on me. Well, Mrs. Boyle is dead. Unless we get to the bottom of this—and quickly, mind—there may be another death.

GILES. Another? Nonsense. Why?

TROTTER. (*gravely*) Because there were *three* little blind mice.

GILES. A death for each of them? But there would have to be some connexion—I mean another connexion—with the Longridge Farm business.

TROTTER. Yes, there would have to be that.

GILES. But why another death *here*?

TROTTER. Because there were only two addresses in the note-book we found. Now, at twenty-four Culver Street there was only one possible victim. She's dead. But here at Monkswell Manor there is a wider field. (*He looks round the circle meaningly*)

MISS CASEWELL. Nonsense. Surely it would be a most unlikely coincidence that there should be *two* people brought here by chance, both of them with a share in the Long-ridge Farm case?

TROTTER. Given certain circumstances, it wouldn't be so much of a coincidence. Think it out, Miss Casewell. (*He rises*) Now I want to get down quite clearly where everyone was when Mrs. Boyle was killed. I've already got Mrs. Ralston's statement. You were in the kitchen preparing vegetables. You came out of the kitchen, along the passage, through the swing door into the hall and in here. (*He points to the archway R*) The radio was blaring, but the light was switched off, and the hall was dark. You switched the light on, saw Mrs. Boyle, and screamed.

MOLLIE. Yes. I screamed and screamed. And at last—people came.

TROTTER. (*moving down to L of Mollie*) Yes. As you say, people came—a lot of people from different directions—all arriving more or less at once. (*He pauses, moves down*

c *and turns his back to the audience*) Now then, when
I got out of that window (*he points*) to trace the telephone wire, *you*, Mr. Ralston, went upstairs to the room
you and Mrs. Ralston occupy, to try the extension telephone. (*Moving up* c) Where were you when Mrs.
Ralston screamed?

GILES. I was still up in the bedroom. The extension telephone
was dead, too. I looked out of the window to see if I
could see any sign of the wires being cut there, but I
couldn't. Just after I closed the window again, I heard
Mollie scream and I rushed down.

TROTTER. (*leaning on the refectory table*) Those simple actions took you rather a long time, didn't they, Mr.
Ralston?

GILES. I don't think so. (*He moves away to the stairs*)

TROTTER. I should say you definitely—took your time over
them.

GILES. I was thinking about something.

TROTTER. Very well. Now then, Mr. Wren, I'll have your
account of where you were.

CHRISTOPHER. (*rising and moving to* L *of Trotter*) I'd been
in the kitchen, seeing if there was anything I could do
to help Mrs. Ralston. I adore cooking. After that I went
upstairs to my bedroom.

TROTTER. Why?

CHRISTOPHER. It's quite a natural thing to go to one's bedroom, don't you think? I mean—one does want to be
alone *sometimes*.

TROTTER. You went to your bedroom because you wanted
to be alone?

CHRISTOPHER. And I wanted to brush my hair—and—er—
tidy up.

TROTTER. (*looking hard at Christopher's dishevelled hair*)
You wanted to brush your hair?

CHRISTOPHER. Anyway, that's where I was!

(GILES *moves down* L *to the door*)

TROTTER. And you heard Mrs. Ralston scream?

CHRISTOPHER. Yes.

TROTTER. And you came down?

CHRISTOPHER. Yes.

TROTTER. Curious that you and Mr. Ralston didn't meet on
the stairs.

(CHRISTOPHER *and* GILES *look at each other*)

CHRISTOPHER. I came down by the back stairs. They're nearer to my room.

TROTTER. Did you go to your room by the back stairs, or did you come through here?

CHRISTOPHER. I went up by the back stairs, too. (*He moves to the desk chair and sits*)

TROTTER. I see. (*He moves to* R *of the sofa table*) Mr. Paravicini?

PARAVICINI. I have told you. (*He rises and moves to* L *of the sofa*) I was playing the piano in the drawing-room —through there, Inspector. (*He gestures* L)

TROTTER. I'm not an Inspector—just a Sergeant, Mr. Paravicini. Did anybody hear you playing the piano?

PARAVICINI. (*smiling*) I do not expect so. I was playing very, very softly—with one finger—so.

MOLLIE. You were playing *Three Blind Mice*.

TROTTER. (*sharply*) Is that so?

PARAVICINI. Yes. It is a very catchy little tune. It is—how shall I say?—a haunting little tune? Don't you all agree?

MOLLIE. I think it's horrible.

PARAVICINI. And yet—it runs in people's heads. Someone was whistling it, too.

TROTTER. Whistling it? Where?

PARAVICINI. I am not sure. Perhaps in the front hall—perhaps on the stairs—perhaps even upstairs in a bedroom.

TROTTER. Who was whistling *Three Blind Mice?*

(*There is no answer*)

Are you making this up, Mr. Paravicini?

PARAVICINI. No, no, Inspector—I beg your pardon—Sergeant, I would not do a thing like that.

TROTTER. Well, go on, you were playing the piano.

PARAVICINI. (*holding out a finger*) With one finger—so . . . And then I hear the radio—playing very loud—someone is shouting on it. It offended my ears. And after that—suddenly—I hear Mrs. Ralston scream. (*He sits at the* L *end of the sofa*)

TROTTER. (*moving up to* C *of the refectory table; gesturing with his fingers*) Mr. Ralston upstairs. Mr. Wren upstairs. Mr. Paravicini in drawing-room. Miss Casewell?

MISS CASEWELL. I was writing letters in the library.

TROTTER. Could you hear what was going on in here?

MISS CASEWELL. No, I didn't hear anything until Mrs. Ralston screamed.

TROTTER. And what did you do then?

MISS CASEWELL. I came in here.

TROTTER. At once?

MISS CASEWELL. I—think so.

TROTTER. You say you were writing letters when you heard Mrs. Ralston scream?

MISS CASEWELL. Yes.

TROTTER. And got up from the writing table hurriedly and came in here?

MISS CASEWELL. Yes.

TROTTER. And yet there doesn't seem to be any unfinished letter on the writing desk in the library.

MISS CASEWELL. (*rising*) I brought it with me. (*She opens her handbag, takes out a letter, moves up to L of Trotter and hands it to him*)

TROTTER. (*looking at it and handing it back*) Dearest Jessie— h'm—a friend of yours, or a relation?

MISS CASEWELL. That's none of your damned business. (*She turns away*)

TROTTER. Perhaps not. (*He moves round the R end of the refectory table to behind it* C) You know if I were to hear someone screaming blue murder when I was writing a letter, I don't believe I'd take the time to pick up my unfinished letter, fold it and put it in my handbag before going to see what was the matter.

MISS CASEWELL. You wouldn't? How interesting. (*She moves up the stairs and sits on the stool*)

TROTTER. (*moving to L of Major Metcalf*) Now, Major Metcalf, what about you? You say you were in the cellar. Why?

MAJOR METCALF. (*pleasantly*) Looking around. Just looking around. I looked into that cupboard place under the stairs near the kitchen. Lot of junk and sports tackle. And I noticed there was another door inside it, and I opened it and saw a flight of steps. I was curious and I went down. Nice cellars you've got.

MOLLIE. Glad you like them.

MAJOR METCALF. Not at all. Crypt of an old monastery, I should say. Probably why this place is called "Monkswell."

TROTTER. We're not engaged in antiquarian research, Major
Metcalf. We're investigating a murder. Mrs. Ralston
has told us that she heard a door shut with a faint
creak. (*He moves to* R *of the sofa*) That particular door
shuts with a creak. It could be, you know, that after
killing Mrs. Boyle, the murderer heard Mrs. Ralston
(*moving to* L *of the armchair* C) coming from the
kitchen and slipped into the cupboard pulling the door
to after him.

MAJOR METCALF. A lot of things could be.

(MOLLIE *rises, moves down to the small armchair and sits.
There is a pause*)

CHRISTOPHER. (*rising*) There would be fingerprints on the
inside of the cupboard.

MAJOR METCALF. Mine are there all right. But most criminals are careful to wear gloves, aren't they?

TROTTER. It's usual. But all criminals slip up sooner or later.

PARAVICINI. I wonder, Sergeant, if that's really true?

GILES. (*moving to* L *of Trotter*) Look here, aren't we wasting
time? There's one person who . . .

TROTTER. Please, Mr. Ralston, I'm in charge of this investigation.

GILES. Oh, very well, but . . .

(GILES *exits by the door down* L)

TROTTER. (*calling authoritatively*) Mr. Ralston!

(GILES *re-enters grudgingly and stands by the door*)

Thank you. (*Moving behind the refectory table*) We've
got to establish opportunity, you know, as well as motive. And now let me tell you this—you *all* had opportunity.

(*There are several murmured protests*)

(*He holds up his hand*) There are two staircases—anyone could go up by one and come down by the other.
Anyone could go down to the cellars by the door near
the kitchen and come up by a flight of steps that leads
up through a trap-door to the foot of the stairs over
there. (*He points off* R) The vital fact was that every
one of you was *alone* at the time the murder was
committed.

GILES. But look here, Sergeant, you speak as though we were all under suspicion. That's absurd!

TROTTER. In a murder case, everyone is under suspicion.

GILES. But you know pretty well who killed that woman in Culver Street. You think it's the eldest of those three children at the farm. A mentally abnormal young man who is now twenty-three years of age. Well, damn it all, there's only one person here who fits the bill. (*He points to Christopher and moves slightly towards him*)

CHRISTOPHER. It's not true—it's not true! You're all against me. Everyone's always been against me. You're going to frame me for a murder. It's persecution, (*crossing to* L *of Major Metcalf*) that's what it is—persecution.

(GILES *follows him but pauses at the* L *end of the refectory table*)

MAJOR METCALF. (*rising; kindly*) Steady, lad, steady. (*He pats Christopher on the shoulder, then he takes out his pipe*)

MOLLIE. (*rising and moving up to* L *of Christopher*) It's all right, Chris. Nobody's against you. (*To Trotter*) Tell him it's all right.

TROTTER. (*looking at Giles; stolidly*) We don't frame people.

MOLLIE. (*to Trotter*) Tell him you're not going to arrest him.

TROTTER. (*moving to* L *of Mollie; stolidly*) I'm not arresting anyone. To do that, I've got to have evidence. I haven't got any evidence—yet.

(CHRISTOPHER *moves to the fire*)

GILES. I think you're crazy, Mollie. (*Moving up* C. *To Trotter*) And you, too! There's just one person who fits the bill and, if only as a safety measure, he ought to be put under arrest. It's only fair to the rest of us.

MOLLIE. Wait, Giles, wait. Sergeant Trotter, can I—can I speak to you a minute?

TROTTER. Certainly, Mrs. Ralston. Will the rest of you go into the dining-room, please.

(*The others rise and move down* R *to the door: first* MISS CASEWELL, *then* MR. PARAVICINI, *protesting, followed by* CHRISTOPHER *and* MAJOR METCALF, *who pauses to light his pipe.* MAJOR METCALF *becomes aware of being stared at. They all exit*)

GILES. I'm staying.

MOLLIE. No, Giles, you, too, please.

GILES. (*furious*) I'm staying. I don't know what's come over you, Mollie.

MOLLIE. Please.

(GILES *exits after the others down* R, *leaving the door open.* MOLLIE *shuts it.* TROTTER *moves to the arch up* R)

TROTTER. Yes, Mrs. Ralston, (*moving above the armchair* C) what is it you want to say to me?

MOLLIE. (*moving up to* L *of Trotter*) Sergeant Trotter, you think that this—(*she moves below the sofa*) this crazy killer must be the—eldest of those three boys at the Farm—but you don't know that, do you?

TROTTER. We don't actually know a thing. All we've got so far is that the woman who joined with her husband in ill-treating and starving those children, has been killed, and that the woman magistrate who was responsible for placing them there has been killed. (*He moves down to* R *of the sofa*) The telephone wire that links me with police headquarters has been cut . . .

MOLLIE. You don't even know that. It may have been just the snow.

TROTTER. No, Mrs. Ralston, the line was deliberately cut. It was cut just outside by the front door. I found the place.

MOLLIE. (*shaken*) I see.

TROTTER. Sit down, Mrs. Ralston.

MOLLIE. (*sitting on the sofa*) But, all the same, you don't know . . .

TROTTER. (*moving in a circle* L *above the sofa and then* R *below it*) I'm going by probability. It all points one way; mental instability, childish mentality, desertion from the Army and the psychiatrist's report.

MOLLIE. Oh I know, and therefore it all seems to point to Christopher. But I don't believe it is Christopher. There must be other possibilities.

TROTTER. (R *of the sofa; turning to her*) Such as?

MOLLIE. (*hesitating*) Well—hadn't those children any relations at all?

TROTTER. The mother was a drunk. She died soon after the children were taken away from her.

MOLLIE. What about their father?

TROTTER. He was an Army sergeant, serving abroad. If he's alive, he's probably discharged from the Army by now.

MOLLIE. You don't know where he is now?

TROTTER. We've no information. To trace him may take some time, but I can assure you, Mrs. Ralston, that the police take every eventuality into account.

MOLLIE. But you don't know where he may be at this minute, and if the son is mentally unstable, the father may have been unstable, too.

TROTTER. Well, it's a possibility.

MOLLIE. If he came home, after being a prisoner with the Japs, perhaps, and having suffered terribly—if he came home and found his wife dead and that his children had gone through some terrible experience, and one of them had died through it, he might go off his head a bit and want—revenge!

TROTTER. That's only surmise.

MOLLIE. But it's possible?

TROTTER. Oh yes, Mrs. Ralston, it's quite possible.

MOLLIE. So the murderer may be middle-aged, or even old. (*She pauses*) When I said the police had rung up, Major Metcalf was frightfully upset. He really was. I saw his face.

TROTTER. (*considering*) Major Metcalf? (*He moves to the armchair* C *and sits*)

MOLLIE. Middle-aged. A soldier. He seems quite nice and perfectly normal—but it mightn't show, might it?

TROTTER. No, often it doesn't show at all.

MOLLIE. (*rising and moving to* L *of Trotter*) So, it's not only Christopher who's a suspect. There's Major Metcalf as well.

TROTTER. Any other suggestions?

MOLLIE. Well, Mr. Paravicini did drop the poker when I said the police had rung up.

TROTTER. Mr. Paravicini. (*He appears to consider*)

MOLLIE. I know he seems quite old—and foreign and everything, but he mightn't really be as old as he looks. He moves like a much younger man, and he's definitely got make-up on his face. Miss Casewell noticed it, too. He might be—oh, I know it sounds very melodramatic—but he might be *disguised*.

TROTTER. You're very anxious, aren't you, that it shouldn't be young Mr. Wren?

MOLLIE. (*moving to the fire*) He seems so—helpless, somehow. (*Turning to Trotter*) And so unhappy.

TROTTER. Mrs. Ralston, let me tell you something. I've had

all possibilities in mind ever since the beginning. The boy Georgie, the father—and someone else. There was a sister, you remember.

MOLLIE. Oh—the sister?

TROTTER. (*rising and moving to Mollie*) It could have been a woman who killed Maureen Lyon. A woman. (*Moving* C) The muffler pulled up and the man's felt hat pulled well down, and the killer whispered, you know. It's the voice that gives the sex away. (*He moves above the sofa table*) Yes, it might have been a woman.

MOLLIE. Miss Casewell?

TROTTER. (*moving to the stairs*) She looks a bit old for the part. (*He moves up the stairs, opens the library door, looks in, then shuts the door*) Oh yes, Mrs. Ralston, there's a very wide field. (*He comes down the stairs*) There's yourself, for instance.

MOLLIE. Me?

TROTTER. You're about the right age.

(MOLLIE *is about to protest*)

(*Checking her*) No, no. Whatever you tell me about yourself, I've got no means of checking it at this moment, remember. And then there's your husband.

MOLLIE. Giles, how ridiculous!

TROTTER. (*crossing slowly to* L *of Mollie*) He and Christopher Wren are much of an age. Say, your husband looks older than his years, and Christopher Wren looks younger. Actual age is very hard to tell. How much do you know about your husband, Mrs. Ralston?

MOLLIE. How much do I know about Giles? Oh, don't be silly.

TROTTER. You've been married—how long?

MOLLIE. Just a year.

TROTTER. And you met him—where?

MOLLIE. At a dance in London. We went in a party.

TROTTER. Did you meet his people?

MOLLIE. He hasn't any people. They're all dead.

TROTTER. (*significantly*) They're all dead?

MOLLIE. Yes—but, oh you make it sound all wrong. His father was a barrister and his mother died when he was a baby.

TROTTER. You're only telling me what *he* told you.

MOLLIE. Yes—but . . . (*She turns away*)

TROTTER. You don't know it of your own knowledge.

MOLLIE. (*turning back quickly*) It's outrageous that . . .

TROTTER. You'd be surprised, Mrs. Ralston, if you knew how many cases rather like yours we get. Especially since the war. Homes broken up and families dead. Fellow says he's been in the Air Force, or just finished his Army training. Parents killed—no relations. There aren't any backgrounds nowadays and young people settle their own affairs—they meet and marry. It's parents and relatives who used to make the enquiries before they consented to an engagement. That's all done away with. Girl just marries her man. Sometimes she doesn't find out for a year or two that he's an absconding bank clerk, or an Army deserter or something equally undesirable. How long had you known Giles Ralston when you married him?

MOLLIE. Just three weeks. But . . .

TROTTER. And you don't know anything about him?

MOLLIE. That's not true. I know everything about him! I know exactly the sort of person he is. He's *Giles*. (*Turning to the fire*) And it's absolutely absurd to suggest that he's some horrible crazy homicidal maniac. Why, he wasn't even in London yesterday when the murder took place.

TROTTER. Where was he? Here?

MOLLIE. He went across country to a sale to get some wire netting for our chickens.

TROTTER. Bring it back with him? (*He crosses to the desk*)

MOLLIE. No, it turned out to be the wrong kind.

TROTTER. Only thirty miles from London, aren't you? Oh, you got an ABC? (*He picks up the ABC and reads it*) Only an hour by train—a little longer by car.

MOLLIE. (*stamping her foot with temper*) I tell you Giles wasn't in London.

TROTTER. Just a minute, Mrs. Ralston. (*He crosses to the front hall, and comes back carrying a darkish overcoat. Moving to L of Mollie*) This your husband's coat?

(MOLLIE *looks at the coat*)

MOLLIE. (*suspiciously*) Yes.

(TROTTER *takes out a folded evening paper from the pocket*)

TROTTER. *Evening News.* Yesterday's. Sold on the streets about three-thirty yesterday afternoon.

MOLLIE. I don't believe it!

TROTTER. Don't you? (*He moves up* R *to the arch with the coat*) Don't you?

(TROTTER *exits through the archway up* R *with the overcoat.* MOLLIE *sits in the small armchair down* R, *staring at the evening paper. The door down* R *slowly opens.* CHRISTOPHER *peeps in through the door, sees that Mollie is alone and enters*)

CHRISTOPHER. Mollie!

(MOLLIE *jumps up and hides the newspaper under the cushion in the armchair* C)

MOLLIE. Oh, you startled me! (*She moves* L *of the armchair* C)
CHRISTOPHER. Where is he? (*Moving to* R *of Mollie*) Where has he gone?
MOLLIE. Who?
CHRISTOPHER. The sergeant.
MOLLIE. Oh, he went out that way.
CHRISTOPHER. If only I could get away. Somehow—some way. Is there anywhere I could hide—in the house?
MOLLIE. Hide?
CHRISTOPHER. Yes—from *him*.
MOLLIE. Why?
CHRISTOPHER. But, darling, they're all so frightfully against me. They're going to say I committed these murders—particularly your husband. (*He moves to* R *of the sofa*)
MOLLIE. Never mind him. (*She moves a step to* R *of Christopher*) Listen, Christopher, you can't go on—running away from things—all your life.
CHRISTOPHER. Why do you say that?
MOLLIE. Well, it's true, isn't it?
CHRISTOPHER. (*hopelessly*) Oh yes, it's quite true. (*He sits at the* L *end of the sofa*)
MOLLIE. (*sitting at the* R *end of the sofa; affectionately*) You've got to grow up some time, Chris.
CHRISTOPHER. I wish I hadn't.
MOLLIE. Your name isn't really Christopher Wren, is it?
CHRISTOPHER. No.
MOLLIE. And you're not really training to be an architect?
CHRISTOPHER. No.
MOLLIE. Why did you . . . ?

CHRISTOPHER. Call myself Christopher Wren? It just amused
me. And then they used to laugh at me at school and
call me little Christopher Robin. Robin—Wren—asso-
ciation of ideas. It was hell being at school.

MOLLIE. What's your real name?

CHRISTOPHER. We needn't go into that. I ran away whilst I
was doing my Army service. It was all so beastly—I
hated it.

(MOLLIE *has a sudden wave of unease, which* CHRISTOPHER
notices. She rises and moves to R *of the sofa*)

(*Rising and moving down* L.) Yes, I'm just like the unknown murderer.

(MOLLIE *moves up to* L *of the refectory table, and turns away
from him*)

I told you I was the one the specification fitted. You
see, my mother—my mother . . . (*He moves up to* L
of the sofa table)

MOLLIE. Yes, your mother?

CHRISTOPHER. Everything would be all right if she hadn't
died. She would have taken care of me—and looked
after me . . .

MOLLIE. You can't go on being looked after all your life.
Things happen to you. And you've got to bear them—
you've got to go on just as usual.

CHRISTOPHER. One can't do that.

MOLLIE. Yes, one can.

CHRISTOPHER. You mean—you have? (*He moves up to* L *of
Mollie*)

MOLLIE. (*facing Christopher*) Yes.

CHRISTOPHER. What was it? Something very bad?

MOLLIE. Something I've never forgotten.

CHRISTOPHER. Was it to do with Giles?

MOLLIE. No, it was long before I met Giles.

CHRISTOPHER. You must have been very young. Almost a
child.

MOLLIE. Perhaps that's why it was so—awful. It was horrible—horrible . . . I try to put it out of my mind. I
never try to think about it.

CHRISTOPHER. So—you're running away, too. Running away
from things—instead of facing them?

MOLLIE. Yes—perhaps, in a way, I am.

(*There is a silence*)

Considering that I never saw you until yesterday, we seem to know each other rather well.

CHRISTOPHER. Yes, it's odd, isn't it?

MOLLIE. I don't know. I suppose there's a sort of—sympathy between us.

CHRISTOPHER. Anyway, you think I ought to stick it out.

MOLLIE. Well, frankly, what else can you do?

CHRISTOPHER. I might pinch the sergeant's skis. I can ski quite well.

MOLLIE. That would be frightfully stupid. It would be almost like admitting you're guilty.

CHRISTOPHER. Sergeant Trotter thinks I'm guilty.

MOLLIE. No, he doesn't. At least—I don't know what he thinks. (*She moves down to the armchair* C, *pulls out the evening paper from under the cushion and stares at it. Suddenly, with passion*) I hate him—I hate him— I hate him . . .

CHRISTOPHER. (*startled*) Who?

MOLLIE. Sergeant Trotter. He puts things into your head. Things that aren't true, that can't possibly be true.

CHRISTOPHER. What is all this?

MOLLIE. I don't believe it—I won't believe it . . .

CHRISTOPHER. What won't you believe? (*He moves slowly to Mollie, puts his hands on her shoulders and turns her round to face him*) Come on—out with it!

MOLLIE. (*showing the paper*) You see that?

CHRISTOPHER. Yes.

MOLLIE. What is it? Yesterday's evening paper—a London paper. And it was in Giles' pocket. But Giles didn't go to London yesterday.

CHRISTOPHER. Well, if he was here all day . . .

MOLLIE. But he wasn't. He went off in the car to look for chicken wire, but he couldn't find any.

CHRISTOPHER. Well, that's all right. (*Moving* LC) Probably he did go up to London after all.

MOLLIE. Then why shouldn't he tell me he did? Why pretend he'd been driving all round the countryside?

CHRISTOPHER. Perhaps, with the news of this murder . . .

MOLLIE. He didn't know about the murder. Or did he? Did he? (*She moves to the fire*)

CHRISTOPHER. Good Lord, Mollie. Surely you don't think— the Sergeant doesn't think . . .

(*During the next speech* MOLLIE *crosses slowly up stage to*
L *of the sofa.* CHRISTOPHER *silently drops the paper on
the sofa*)

MOLLIE. I don't know what the Sergeant thinks. And he can
make you think things about people. You ask yourself
questions and you begin to doubt. You feel that somebody you love and know well might be—a stranger.
(*Whispering*) That's what happens in a nightmare.
You're somewhere in the middle of friends and then
you suddenly look at their faces and they're not your
friends any longer—they're different people—just pretending. Perhaps you can't trust anybody—perhaps
everybody's a stranger. (*She puts her hands to her face*)

(CHRISTOPHER *moves to the* L *end of the sofa, kneels on it
and takes her hands away from her face.* GILES *enters
from the dining-room down* R, *but stops when he sees
them.* MOLLIE *backs away, and* CHRISTOPHER *sits on the
sofa*)

GILES. (*at the door*) I seem to be interrupting something.

MOLLIE. No, we were—just talking. I must go to the kitchen
—there's the pie and potatoes—and I must do—do the
spinach. (*She moves* R *above the armchair* C)

CHRISTOPHER. (*rising and moving* C) I'll come and give you
a hand.

GILES. (*moving up to the fire*) No, you won't.

MOLLIE. Giles.

GILES. *Tête-à-têtes* aren't very healthy things at present. You
keep out of the kitchen and keep away from my wife.

CHRISTOPHER. But really, look here . . .

GILES. (*furious*) You keep away from my wife, Wren. She's
not going to be the next victim.

CHRISTOPHER. So that's what you think about me.

GILES. I've already said so, haven't I? There's a killer loose
in this house—and it seems to me you fit the bill.

CHRISTOPHER. I'm not the only one to fit the bill.

GILES. I don't see who else does.

CHRISTOPHER. How blind are you—or do you just pretend
to be blind?

GILES. I tell you I'm worrying about my wife's safety.

CHRISTOPHER. So am I. I'm not going to leave you here alone
with her. (*He moves up to* L *of Mollie*)

GILES. (*moving up to* R *of Mollie*) What the hell . . . ?

MOLLIE. Please go, Chris.

CHRISTOPHER. I'm not going.

MOLLIE. Please go, Christopher. Please. I mean it ...

CHRISTOPHER. (*moving* R) I shan't be far away.

(*Unwillingly* CHRISTOPHER *exits through the arch up* R. MOLLIE *crosses to the desk chair, and* GILES *follows her*)

GILES. What is all this? Mollie, you must be crazy. Perfectly prepared to shut yourself up in the kitchen with a homicidal maniac.

MOLLIE. He isn't.

GILES. You've only got to look at him to see he's barmy.

MOLLIE. He isn't. He's just unhappy. I tell you, Giles, he isn't dangerous. I'd know if he was dangerous. And anyway, I can look after myself.

GILES. That's what Mrs. Boyle said!

MOLLIE. Oh, Giles—don't. (*She moves down* L)

GILES. (*moving down to* R *of Mollie*) Look here, what is there between you and that wretched boy?

MOLLIE. What do you mean by between us? I'm sorry for him—that's all.

GILES. Perhaps you'd met him before. Perhaps you suggested to him to come here and that you'd both pretend to meet for the first time. All cooked up between you, was it?

MOLLIE. Giles, have you gone out of your mind? How dare you suggest these things?

GILES. (*moving up to* C *of the refectory table*) Rather odd, isn't it, that he should come and stay at an out-of-the-way place like this?

MOLLIE. No odder than that Miss Casewell and Major Metcalf and Mrs. Boyle should.

GILES. I read once in a paper that these homicidal cases were able to attract women. Looks as though it were true. (*He moves down* C) Where did you first know him? How long has this been going on?

MOLLIE. You're being absolutely ridiculous. (*She moves* R *slightly*) I never set eyes on Christopher Wren until he arrived yesterday.

GILES. That's what you say. Perhaps you've been running up to London to meet him on the sly.

MOLLIE. You know perfectly well that I haven't been up to London for weeks.

GILES. (*in a peculiar tone*) You haven't been up to London for weeks. Is—that—so?

MOLLIE. What on earth do you mean? It's quite true.

GILES. Is it? Then what's this? (*He takes out Mollie's glove from his pocket and draws out of it the bus ticket*)

(MOLLIE *starts*)

This is one of the gloves you were wearing yesterday. You dropped it. I picked it up this afternoon when I was talking to Sergeant Trotter. You see what's inside it—a London bus ticket!

MOLLIE. (*looking guilty*) Oh—that . . .

GILES. (*turning away* RC) So it seems that you didn't only go to the village yesterday, you went to London as well.

MOLLIE. All right, I went to . . .

GILES. Whilst I was safely away racing round the country-side.

MOLLIE. (*with emphasis*) Whilst you were racing round the countryside . . .

GILES. Come on now—admit it. You went to London.

MOLLIE. All right. (*She moves* C *below the sofa*) I went to London. So did you!

GILES. What?

MOLLIE. So did you. You brought back an evening paper. (*She picks up the paper from the sofa*)

GILES. Where did you get hold of that?

MOLLIE. It was in your overcoat pocket.

GILES. Anyone could have put it in there.

MOLLIE. Did they? No, you were in London.

GILES. All right. Yes, I was in London. I didn't go to meet a woman there.

MOLLIE. (*in horror; whispering*) Didn't you—are you sure you didn't?

GILES. Eh? What d'you mean? (*He comes nearer to her*)

(MOLLIE *recoils, backing away down* L)

MOLLIE. Go away. Don't come near me.

GILES. (*following her*) What's the matter?

MOLLIE. Don't touch me.

GILES. Did you go to London yesterday to meet Christopher Wren?

MOLLIE. Don't be a fool. Of course I didn't.

GILES. Then why did you go?

(MOLLIE *changes her manner. She smiles in a dreamy fashion*)

MOLLIE. I—shan't tell you that. Perhaps—now—I've forgotten why I went . . . (*She crosses towards the archway up* R)

GILES. (*moving to* L *of Mollie*) Mollie, what's come over you? You're different all of a sudden. I feel as though I don't know you any more.

MOLLIE. Perhaps you never did know me. We've been married how long—a year? But you don't really know anything about me. What I'd done or thought or felt or suffered before you knew me.

GILES. Mollie, you're crazy . . .

MOLLIE. All right then, I'm crazy! Why not? Perhaps it's fun to be crazy!

GILES. (*angrily*) What the hell are you . . . ?

(MR. PARAVICINI *enters from the archway up* R. *He moves between them*)

PARAVICINI. Now, now. I do hope you young people are not both saying a little more than you mean. One is so apt to in these lovers' quarrels.

GILES. "Lovers' quarrels"! That's good. (*He moves to* L *of the refectory table*)

PARAVICINI. (*moving down to the small armchair* R) Quite so. Quite so. I know just how you feel. I have been through all this myself when I was a younger man. *Jeunesse—jeunesse*—as the poet says. Not been married long, I imagine?

GILES. (*crossing to the fire*) It's no business of yours, Mr. Paravicini . . .

PARAVICINI. (*moving down* C) No, no, no business at all. But I just came in to say that the Sergeant cannot find his skis and I'm afraid he is very annoyed.

MOLLIE. (*moving to* R *of the sofa table*) Christopher!

GILES. What's that?

PARAVICINI. (*moving to face Giles*) He wants to know if you have by any chance moved them, Mr. Ralston.

GILES. No, of course not.

(SERGEANT TROTTER *enters from the archway up* R *looking red and annoyed*)

TROTTER. Mr. Ralston—Mrs. Ralston, have you removed my skis from the cupboard back there where we put them?

GILES. Certainly not.

TROTTER. Somebody's taken them.

PARAVICINI. (*moving to R of Trotter*) What made you happen to look for them?

TROTTER. The snow is still lying. I need help here, reinforcements. I was going to ski over to the police station at Market Hampton to report on the situation.

PARAVICINI. And now you can't—dear, dear . . . Somebody's seen to it that you certainly shan't do that. But there could be another reason, couldn't there?

TROTTER. Yes, what?

PARAVICINI. Somebody may want to get away.

GILES. (*moving to R of Mollie; to her*) What did you mean when you said "Christopher" just now?

MOLLIE. Nothing.

PARAVICINI. (*chuckling*) So our young architect has hooked it, has he? Very, very interesting.

TROTTER. Is this true, Mrs. Ralston? (*He moves to C of the refectory table*)

(CHRISTOPHER *enters from the stairs L and comes to L of the sofa*)

MOLLIE. (*moving slightly L*) Oh, thank goodness. You haven't gone, after all.

TROTTER. (*crossing to R of Christopher*) Did you take my skis, Mr. Wren?

CHRISTOPHER. (*surprised*) Your skis, Sergeant? No, why should I?

TROTTER. Mrs. Ralston seemed to think . . . (*He looks at Mollie*)

MOLLIE. Mr. Wren is very fond of ski-ing. I thought he might have taken them just to—get a little exercise.

GILES. Exercise? (*He moves up to C of the refectory table*)

TROTTER. Now, listen, you people. This is a serious matter. Somebody has removed my only chance of communication with the outside world. I want everybody here—at once.

PARAVICINI. I think Miss Casewell has gone upstairs.

MOLLIE. I'll get her.

(MOLLIE *exits up the stairs.* TROTTER *moves to* L *of the arch up* L)

PARAVICINI. (*moving down* R) I left Major Metcalf in the dining-room. (*He opens the door down* R *and looks in*) Major Metcalf! He's not there now.

GILES. I'll try and find him.

(GILES *exits up* R. MOLLIE *and* MISS CASEWELL *enter from the stairs.* MOLLIE *moves to* R *of the refectory table and* MISS CASEWELL *to* L *of it.* MAJOR METCALF *enters up* L *from the library*)

MAJOR METCALF. Hullo, wanting me?

TROTTER. It's a question of my skis.

MAJOR METCALF. Skis? (*He moves to* L *of the sofa*)

PARAVICINI. (*moving to the archway up* R *and calling*) Mr. Ralston!

(GILES *enters up* R *and stands below the arch.* PARAVICINI *returns and sits in the small armchair down* R)

TROTTER. Did either of you two remove a pair of skis from the cupboard near the kitchen door?

MISS CASEWELL. Good Lord, no. Why should I?

MAJOR METCALF. And *I* didn't touch 'em.

TROTTER. Nevertheless they are gone. (*To Miss Casewell*) Which way did you go to your room?

MISS CASEWELL. By the back stairs.

TROTTER. Then you passed the cupboard door.

MISS CASEWELL. If you say so—I've no idea where your skis are.

TROTTER. (*to Major Metcalf*) You were actually *in* that cupboard today.

MAJOR METCALF. Yes, I was.

TROTTER. At the time Mrs. Boyle was killed.

MAJOR METCALF. At the time Mrs. Boyle was killed I'd gone down to the cellar.

TROTTER. Were the skis in the cupboard when you passed through?

MAJOR METCALF. I haven't the least idea.

TROTTER. Didn't you see them there?

MAJOR METCALF. Can't remember.

TROTTER. You must remember if those skis were there then?

MAJOR METCALF. No good shouting at me, young fellow. I wasn't thinking about any damned skis. I was interested in the cellars. (*He moves to the sofa and sits*) Architecture of this place is very interesting. I opened the other door and I went on down. So I can't tell you whether the skis were there or not.

TROTTER. (*moving down to* L *of the sofa*) You realize that you, yourself, had an excellent opportunity of taking them?

MAJOR METCALF. Yes, yes, I grant you that. If I wanted to, that is.

TROTTER. The question is, where are they now?

MAJOR METCALF. Ought to be able to find them if we all set to. Not a case of "Hunt the Thimble." Whacking great things, skis. Supposing we all set to. (*He rises and crosses* R *towards the door*)

TROTTER. Not quite so fast, Major Metcalf. That may be, you know, what we are meant to do.

MAJOR METCALF. Eh, I don't get you?

TROTTER. I'm in the position now where I've got to put myself in the place of a crazy cunning brain. I've got to ask myself what he wants us to do and what he, himself, is planning to do next. I've got to try and keep just one step ahead of him. Because, if I don't, there's going to be another death.

MISS CASEWELL. You still don't believe that?

TROTTER. Yes, Miss Casewell. I do. Three blind mice. Two mice cancelled out—a third mouse still to be dealt with. (*Moving down* C, *with his back to the audience*) There are six of you here listening to me. One of you's a killer!

(*There is a pause. They are all affected and look uneasily at one another*)

One of you's a killer. (*He moves to the fire*) I don't know which yet, but I shall. And another of you is the killer's prospective victim. That's the person I'm speaking to. (*He crosses to Mollie*) Mrs. Boyle held out on me—Mrs. Boyle is dead. (*He moves up* C) You—whoever you are—are holding out on me. Well—don't. Because you're in danger. Nobody who's killed twice is going to hesitate to kill a third time. (*He moves to* R *of Major Metcalf*) And as it is, I don't know which of you it is who needs protection.

(*There is a pause*)

(*Crossing down* c *and turning his back to the audience*)
Come on, now, anybody here who has anything, however slight, to reproach themselves for in that bygone
business, had better come out with it.

(*There is a pause*)

All right—you won't. I'll get the killer—I've no doubt
of that—but it may be too late for one of you. (*He
moves up to* c *of the refectory table*) And I'll tell you
another thing. The killer's enjoying this. Yes, he's enjoying himself a good deal . . .

(*There is a pause*)

(*He moves round the* R *end of the refectory table to
behind it. He opens the* R *curtain, looks out and then
sits at the* R *end of the window seat*) All right—you
can go.

(MAJOR METCALF *exits into the dining-room down* R. CHRIS-
TOPHER *exits up the stairs* L. MISS CASEWELL *crosses to
the fire and leans on the mantelpiece.* GILES *moves* C *and
MOLLIE follows;* GILES *stops and turns* R. MOLLIE *turns
her back on him and moves behind the armchair* C.
PARAVICINI *rises and moves to* R *of Mollie*)

PARAVICINI. Talking of chicken, dear lady, have you ever
tried chicken's livers served on toast that has been
thickly smeared with *foie gras*, with a very thin rasher
of bacon just touched with a *soupçon* of fresh mustard?
I will come with you to the kitchen and we will see what
we can concoct together. A charming occupation.

(PARAVICINI *takes Mollie's right arm and starts to move up* R)

GILES. (*taking Mollie's left arm*) I'm helping my wife, Paravicini.

(MOLLIE *throws off Giles' arm*)

PARAVICINI. Your husband is afraid for you. Quite natural
under the circumstances. He doesn't fancy your being
alone with me.

(MOLLIE *throws off Paravicini's arm*)

It is my sadistic tendencies he fears—not my dishonourable ones. (*He leers*) Alas, what an inconvenience the husband always is. (*He kisses her fingers*) A *riverderla* . . .

MOLLIE. I'm sure Giles doesn't think . . .

PARAVICINI. He is very wise. Take no chances. (*He moves down to* R *of the armchair* C) Can I prove to you or to him or to our dogged Sergeant that I am *not* a homicidal maniac? So difficult to prove a negative. And suppose that instead I am really . . . (*He hums the tune of "Three Blind Mice"*)

MOLLIE. Oh don't. (*She moves to the back of the armchair* C)

PARAVICINI. But such a gay little tune? Don't you think? She cut off their tails with a carving knife—snick, snick, snick—delicious. Just what a child would adore. Cruel little things, children. (*Leaning forward*) Some of them never grow up.

(MOLLIE *gives a frightened cry*)

GILES. (*moving to* R *of the refectory table*) Stop frightening my wife at once.

MOLLIE. It's silly of me. But you see—I found her. Her face was all purple. I can't forget it . . .

PARAVICINI. I know. It's difficult to forget things, isn't it. You aren't really the forgetting kind.

MOLLIE. (*incoherently*) I must go—the food—dinner—prepare the spinach—and the potatoes all going to pieces—please, Giles.

(GILES *and* MOLLIE *exit through the archway up* R. PARAVICINI *leans on the* L *side of the arch and looks after them, grinning.* MISS CASEWELL *stands by the fireplace, lost in thought*)

TROTTER. (*rising and crossing to* L *of Paravicini*) What did you say to the lady upset her, sir?

PARAVICINI. Me, Sergeant? Oh, just a little innocent fun. I've always been fond of a little joke.

TROTTER. There's nice fun—and there's fun that's not so nice.

PARAVICINI. (*moving down* C) Now I do wonder what you mean by that, Sergeant?

TROTTER. I've been doing a little wondering about you, sir.

PARAVICINI. Indeed?

TROTTER. I've been wondering about that car of yours, and how it happened to overturn in a snowdrift (*he pauses and draws the* R *curtain*) so conveniently.

PARAVICINI. Inconveniently, you mean, don't you, Sergeant?

TROTTER. (*moving down to* R *of Paravicini*) That rather depends on the way you're looking at it. Just where were you bound for, by the way, when you had this—accident?

PARAVICINI. Oh—I was on my way to see a friend.

TROTTER. In this neighbourhood?

PARAVICINI. Not so very far from here.

TROTTER. And what was the name and address of this friend?

PARAVICINI. Now really, Sergeant Trotter, does that matter now? I mean, it has nothing to do with this predicament, has it? (*He sits at the* L *end of the sofa*)

TROTTER. We always like the fullest information. What did you say this friend's name was?

PARAVICINI. I didn't say. (*He takes a cigar from a case in his pocket*)

TROTTER. No, you didn't say. And it seems you're not going to say. (*He sits on the right arm of the sofa*) Now that's very interesting.

PARAVICINI. But there might be—so many reasons. An *amour* —discretion. These jealous husbands. (*He pierces the cigar*)

TROTTER. Rather old to be running around with the ladies at your time of life, aren't you?

PARAVICINI. My dear Sergeant, I am not, perhaps, quite so old as I look.

TROTTER. That's just what I've been thinking, sir.

PARAVICINI. What? (*He lights the cigar*)

TROTTER. That you may not be as old as you—try to look. There's a lot of people trying to look younger than they are. If somebody goes about trying to look older— well, it does make one ask oneself why.

PARAVICINI. Having asked questions of so many people—you ask questions of yourself as well? Isn't that overdoing things?

TROTTER. I might get an answer from myself—I don't get many from you.

PARAVICINI. Well, well—try again—that is, if you have any more questions to ask.

TROTTER. One or two. Where were you coming from last night?

PARAVICINI. That is simple—from London.

TROTTER. What address in London?

PARAVICINI. I always stay at the Ritz Hotel.

TROTTER. Very nice, too, I'm sure. What is your permanent address?

PARAVICINI. I dislike permanency.

TROTTER. What's your business or profession?

PARAVICINI. I play the markets.

TROTTER. Stockbroker?

PARAVICINI. No, no, you misunderstand me.

TROTTER. Enjoying this little game, aren't you? Sure of yourself, too. But I shouldn't be too sure. You're mixed up in a murder case, and don't you forget it. Murder isn't just fun and games.

PARAVICINI. Not even this murder? (*He gives a little giggle, and looks sideways at Trotter*) Dear me, you're very serious, Sergeant Trotter. I always have thought policemen have no sense of humour. (*He rises and moves to* L *of the sofa*) Is the inquisition over—for the moment?

TROTTER. For the moment—yes.

PARAVICINI. Thank you so much. I shall go and look for your skis in the drawing-room. Just in case someone has hidden them in the grand piano.

(PARAVICINI *exits down* L. TROTTER *looks after him, frowning, moves down to the door and opens it.* MISS CASEWELL *crosses quietly towards the stairs* L. TROTTER *shuts the door*)

TROTTER. (*without turning his head*) Just a minute, please.

MISS CASEWELL. (*pausing at the stairs*) Were you speaking to me?

TROTTER. Yes. (*Crossing to the armchair* C) Perhaps you'd come and sit down. (*He arranges the armchair for her*)

(MISS CASEWELL *looks at him warily and crosses below the sofa*)

MISS CASEWELL. Well, what do you want?

TROTTER. You may have heard some of the questions I was asking Mr. Paravicini?

MISS CASEWELL. I heard them.

TROTTER. (*moving to the* R *end of the sofa*) I'd like to have a little information from you.

MISS CASEWELL. (*moving to the armchair* C *and sitting*) What do you want to know?

TROTTER. Full name, please.

MISS CASEWELL. Leslie Margaret (*she pauses*) Katherine Casewell.

TROTTER. (*with just a nuance of something different*) Katherine . . .

MISS CASEWELL. I spell it with a "K."

TROTTER. Quite so. Address?

MISS CASEWELL. Villa Mariposa, Pine d'or, Majorca.

TROTTER. That's in Italy?

MISS CASEWELL. It's an island—a Spanish island.

TROTTER. I see. And your address in England?

MISS CASEWELL. Care of Morgan's Bank, Leadenhall Street.

TROTTER. No other English address?

MISS CASEWELL. No.

TROTTER. How long have you been in England?

MISS CASEWELL. A week.

TROTTER. And you have been staying since your arrival . . . ?

MISS CASEWELL. At the Ledbury Hotel, Knightsbridge.

TROTTER. (*sitting at the* R *end of the sofa*) What brought you to Monkswell Manor, Miss Casewell?

MISS CASEWELL. I wanted somewhere quiet—in the country.

TROTTER. How long did you—or do you—propose to remain here? (*He starts twirling his hair with his right hand*)

MISS CASEWELL. Until I've finished what I came here to do. (*She notices the twirling*)

(TROTTER *looks up startled by a force in her words. She stares at him*)

TROTTER. And what was that?

(*There is a pause*)

And what was that? (*He stops twirling his hair*)

MISS CASEWELL. (*with a puzzled frown*) Eh?

TROTTER. What was it you came here to do?

MISS CASEWELL. I beg your pardon. I was thinking of something else.

TROTTER. (*rising and moving to* L *of Miss Casewell*) You haven't answered my question.

MISS CASEWELL. I really don't see, you know, why I should. It's a matter that concerns me alone. A strictly private affair.

TROTTER. All the same, Miss Casewell . . .

MISS CASEWELL. (*rising and moving to the fire*) No, I don't think we'll argue about it.

TROTTER. (*following her*) Would you mind telling me your age?

MISS CASEWELL. Not in the least. It's on my passport. I am twenty-four.

TROTTER. Twenty-four?

MISS CASEWELL. You were thinking I look older. That is quite true.

TROTTER. Is there anyone in this country who can—vouch for you?

MISS CASEWELL. My bank will reassure you as to my financial position. I can also refer you to a solicitor—a very discreet man. I am not in a position to offer you a social reference. I have lived most of my life abroad.

TROTTER. In Majorca?

MISS CASEWELL. In Majorca—and other places.

TROTTER. Were you born abroad?

MISS CASEWELL. No, I left England when I was thirteen.

(*There is a pause, with a feeling of tension in it*)

TROTTER. You know, Miss Casewell, I can't quite make you out. (*He backs away* L *slightly*)

MISS CASEWELL. Does it matter?

TROTTER. I don't know. (*He sits in the armchair* C) What are you doing here?

MISS CASEWELL. It seems to worry you.

TROTTER. It does worry me . . . (*He stares at her*) You went abroad when you were thirteen?

MISS CASEWELL. Twelve—thirteen—thereabouts.

TROTTER. Was your name Casewell then?

MISS CASEWELL. It's my name now.

TROTTER. What was your name then? Come on—tell me.

MISS CASEWELL. What are you trying to prove? (*She loses her calm*)

TROTTER. I want to know what your name was when you left England?

MISS CASEWELL. It's a long time ago. I've forgotten.

TROTTER. There are things one doesn't forget.

MISS CASEWELL. Possibly.

TROTTER. Unhappiness—despair . . .

MISS CASEWELL. I daresay . . .

TROTTER. What's your real name?

MISS CASEWELL. I told you—Leslie Margaret Katherine Case-
well. (*She sits in the small armchair down* R)
TROTTER. (*rising*) Katherine . . . ? (*He stands over her*)
What the hell are you doing here?
MISS CASEWELL. I . . . Oh God . . . (*She rises, moves* C, *and
drops on the sofa. She cries, rocking herself to and fro*)
I wish to God I'd never come here.

(TROTTER, *startled, moves to* R *of the sofa.* CHRISTOPHER
enters from the door down L)

CHRISTOPHER. (*coming to* L *of the sofa*) I always thought the
police weren't allowed to give people the third degree.
TROTTER. I have merely been interrogating Miss Casewell.
CHRISTOPHER. You seem to have upset her. (*To Miss Casewell*) What did he do?
MISS CASEWELL. No, it's nothing. It's just—all this—murder
—it's so horrible. (*She rises and faces Trotter*) It came
over me suddenly. I'll go up to my room.

(MISS CASEWELL *exits up the stairs* L)

TROTTER. (*moving to the stairs and looking up after her*)
It's impossible . . . I can't believe it . . .
CHRISTOPHER. (*moving up and leaning over the desk chair*)
What can't you believe? Six impossible things before
breakfast like the Red Queen?
TROTTER. Oh yes. It's rather like that.
CHRISTOPHER. Dear me—you look as though you'd seen a
ghost.
TROTTER. (*resuming his usual manner*) I've seen something
I ought to have seen before. (*He moves* C) Blind as a
bat, I've been. But I think now we may be able to get
somewhere.
CHRISTOPHER. (*impertinently*) The police have a clue.
TROTTER. (*moving* R *of the sofa table; with a hint of menace*)
Yes, Mr. Wren—at last the police *have* a clue. I want
everyone assembled in here again. Do you know where
they are?
CHRISTOPHER. (*moving to* L *of Trotter*) Giles and Mollie are
in the kitchen. I have been helping Major Metcalf to
look for your skis. We've looked in the most entertain-
ing places—but all to no avail. I don't know where
Paravicini is.

TROTTER. I'll get him. (*He moves down* L *to the door*) You get the others.

(CHRISTOPHER *exits up* R)

(*Opening the door*) Mr. Paravicini. (*Moving below the sofa*) Mr. Paravicini. (*Returning to the door and shouting*) Paravicini! (*He moves up to* C *of the refectory table*)

(PARAVICINI *enters gaily down* L)

PARAVICINI. Yes, Sergeant? (*He moves to the desk chair*) What can I do for you? Little Bo Policeman has lost his skis and doesn't know where to find them. Leave them alone, and they'll come home, dragging a murderer behind them. (*He moves down* L)

(MAJOR METCALF *enters through the arch up* R. GILES *and* MOLLIE *enter up* R, *with* CHRISTOPHER)

MAJOR METCALF. What is all this? (*He moves down to the fire*)

TROTTER. Sit down, Major, Mrs. Ralston . . .

(*No-one sits.* MOLLIE *moves above the armchair* C, GILES *moves to* R *of the refectory table and* CHRISTOPHER *stands between them*)

MOLLIE. *Must* I come now? It's very inconvenient.

TROTTER. There are more important things than meals, Mrs. Ralston. Mrs. Boyle, for instance, won't want another meal.

MAJOR METCALF. That's a very tactless way of putting things, Sergeant.

TROTTER. I'm sorry, but I want co-operation and I intend to get it. Mr. Ralston, will you go and ask Miss Casewell to come down again? She went up in her room. Tell her it will only be for a few minutes.

(GILE *exits to the stairs* L)

MOLLIE. (*moving to* R *of the refectory table*) Have your skis been found, Sergeant?

TROTTER. No, Mrs. Ralston, but I may say I have a very shrewd suspicion of who took them, and of why they were taken. I won't say any more at the present moment.

PARAVICINI. Please don't. (*He moves up to the desk chair*) I always think explanations should be kept to the very end. That exciting last chapter, you know.

TROTTER. (*reprovingly*) This isn't a game, sir.

CHRISTOPHER. Isn't it? Now there I think you are wrong. I think it *is* a game—to somebody.

PARAVICINI. You think the murderer is enjoying himself. Maybe—maybe. (*He sits in the desk chair*)

(GILES *and* MISS CASEWELL, *now quite composed, enter from the stairs* L)

MISS CASEWELL. What is happening?

TROTTER. Sit down, Miss Casewell, Mrs. Ralston ...

(MISS CASEWELL *sits on the right arm of the sofa,* MOLLIE *moves down and sits in the armchair* C. GILES *remains standing at the bottom of the stairs*)

(*Officially*) Will you all pay attention, please? (*He sits* C *on the refectory table*) You may remember that after the murder of Mrs. Boyle, I took statements from you all. Those statements related to your positions at the time the murder was committed. These statements were as follows: (*he consults his notebook*) Mrs. Ralston in the kitchen, Mr. Paravicini playing the piano in the drawing-room, Mr. Ralston in his bedroom. Mr. Wren ditto. Miss Casewell in the library. Major Metcalf (*he pauses and looks at Major Metcalf*) in the cellar.

MAJOR METCALF. Correct.

TROTTER. Those were the statements you made. I had no means of checking these statements. They may be true—they may not. To put it quite clearly, five of those statements are true, but one is false—which one? (*He pauses while he looks from one to the other*) Five of you were speaking the truth, one of you was lying. I have a plan that may help me to discover the liar. And if I discover that one of you lied to me—then I know who the murderer is.

MISS CASEWELL. Not necessarily. Someone may have lied—for some other reason.

TROTTER. I rather doubt that.

GILES. But what's the idea? You've just said you had no means of checking these statements.

TROTTER. No, but supposing everyone was to go through these actions a second time.

PARAVICINI. (*sighing*) Ah, that old chestnut. Reconstruction of the crime.

GILES. That's a foreign idea.

TROTTER. Not a reconstruction of the *crime*, Mr. Paravicini. A reconstruction of the movements of apparently innocent persons.

MAJOR METCALF. And what do you expect to learn from that?

TROTTER. You will forgive me if I don't make that clear just at the moment.

GILES. You want—a repeat performance?

TROTTER. Yes, Mr. Ralston, I do.

MOLLIE. It's a trap.

TROTTER. What do you mean, it's a trap?

MOLLIE. It is a trap. I know it is.

TROTTER. I only want people to do exactly what they did before.

CHRISTOPHER. (*also suspicious*) But I don't see—I simply can't see—what you can possibly hope to find out by just making people do the things they did before. I think it's just nonsense.

TROTTER. Do you, Mr. Wren?

MOLLIE. Well, you can count me out. I'm too busy in the kitchen. (*She rises and moves up* R)

TROTTER. I can't count anybody out. (*He rises and looks round at them*) One might almost believe that you're *all* guilty by the looks of you. Why are you all so unwilling?

GILES. Of course, what you say goes, Sergeant. We'll all co-operate. Eh, Mollie?

MOLLIE. (*unwilling*) Very well.

GILES. Wren?

(CHRISTOPHER *nods*)

Miss Casewell?

MISS CASEWELL. Yes.

GILES. Paravicini?

PARAVICINI. (*throwing up his hands*) Oh yes, I consent.

GILES. Metcalf?

MAJOR METCALF. (*slowly*) Yes.

GILES. Are we all to do exactly what we did before?

TROTTER. The same actions will be performed, yes.

PARAVICINI. (*rising*) Then I will return to the piano in the drawing-room. Once again I will pick out with one finger the signature tune of a murderer. (*He sings, ges-*

turing with his finger) Tum, dum, dum—dum dum
dum . . . (*He moves down* L)

TROTTER. (*moving down* C) Not quite so fast, Mr. Paravicini.
(*To Mollie*) Do you play the piano, Mrs. Ralston?

MOLLIE. Yes, I do.

TROTTER. And you know the tune of *Three Blind Mice?*

MOLLIE. Don't we all know it?

TROTTER. Then you could pick it out on the piano with one
finger just as Mr. Paravicini did.

(MOLLIE *nods*)

Good. Please go into the drawing-room, sit at the piano,
and be ready to play when I give you the signal.

(MOLLIE *crosses* L *below the sofa*)

PARAVICINI. But, Sergeant, I understood that we were each to
repeat our former roles.

TROTTER. The same actions will be performed, *but not necessarily by the same people*. Thank you, Mrs. Ralston.

(PARAVICINI *opens the door down* L. MOLLIE *exits*)

GILES. I don't see the point.

TROTTER. (*moving up to* C *of the refectory table*) There is
a point. It is a means of checking up on the original
statements, and maybe *one* statement in particular. Now
then, will you all pay attention, please. I will assign
each of you your new stations. Mr. Wren, will you
kindly go to the kitchen. Just keep an eye on Mrs. Ralston's dinner for her. You're very fond of cooking, I
believe.

(CHRISTOPHER *exits up* R)

Mr. Paravicini, will you go up to Mr. Wren's room.
By the back stairs is the most convenient way. Major
Metcalf, will you go up to Mr. Ralston's room and
examine the telephone there. Miss Casewell, would you
mind going down to the cellars? Mr. Wren will show
you the way. Unfortunately, I need someone to re-
produce my own actions. I am sorry to ask it of you,
Mr. Ralston, but would you go out by that window
and follow the telephone wire round to near the front
door. Rather a chilly job—but you're probably the
toughest person here.

MAJOR METCALF. And what are you going to do?

TROTTER. (*crossing to the radio and switching it on and off*) I am enacting the part of Mrs. Boyle.

MAJOR METCALF. Taking a bit of a risk, aren't you?

TROTTER. (*reeling against the desk*) You will all stay in your places and remain there until you hear me call you.

(MISS CASEWELL *rises and exits up* R. GILES *moves behind the refectory table and opens the* R *curtain.* MAJOR METCALF *exits up* L. TROTTER *nods to Paravicini to leave*)

PARAVICINI. (*shrugging his shoulders*) Parlour games!

(PARAVICINI *exits up* R)

GILES. No objection to my wearing a coat?

TROTTER. I should advise it, sir.

(GILES *fetches his overcoat from the front hall, puts it on and returns to the window.* TROTTER *moves* C *below the refectory table and writes in his notebook*)

Take my torch, sir. It's behind the curtain.

(GILES *climbs out through the window and exits.* TROTTER *crosses to the library door up* L *and exits. After a short pause he re-enters, switches off the library light, goes up to the window, shuts it and closes the curtain. He crosses to the fire and sinks into the large armchair. After a pause he rises and goes to the door down* L)

(*Calling*) Mrs. Ralston, count twenty and then begin to play.

(TROTTER *shuts the door down* L, *moves to the stairs and looks off. "Three Blind Mice" is heard being played on the piano. After a pause, he moves down* R *and switches off the* R *wall brackets, then moves up* R *and switches off the* L *wall brackets. He moves quickly down to the table lamp and switches it on, then crosses down* L *to the door*)

(*Calling*) Mrs. Ralston! Mrs. Ralston!

(MOLLIE *enters down* L *and moves below the sofa*)

MOLLIE. Yes, what is it?

(TROTTER *shuts the door down* L *and leans against the downstage side of the door reveal*)

You're looking very pleased with yourself. Have you got what you wanted?

TROTTER. I've got exactly what I wanted.

MOLLIE. You know who the murderer is?

TROTTER. Yes, I know.

MOLLIE. Which of them?

TROTTER. *You* ought to know, Mrs. Ralston.

MOLLIE. I?

TROTTER. Yes, you've been extraordinarily foolish, you know. You've run a very good chance of being killed by holding out on me. As a result, you've been in serious danger more than once.

MOLLIE. I don't know what you mean.

TROTTER. (*moving slowly above the sofa table to* R *of the sofa; still quite natural and friendly*) Come now, Mrs. Ralston. We policemen aren't quite so dumb as you think. All along I've realized that you had first-hand knowledge of the Longridge Farm affair. You knew Mrs. Boyle was the magistrate concerned. In fact, you knew all about it. Why didn't you speak up and say so?

MOLLIE. (*very much affected*) I don't understand. I wanted to forget—forget. (*She sits at the* L *end of the sofa*)

TROTTER. Your maiden name was Waring?

MOLLIE. Yes.

TROTTER. Miss Waring. You taught school—in the school where those children went.

MOLLIE. Yes.

TROTTER. It's true, isn't it, that Jimmy, the child who died, managed to get a letter posted to you? (*He sits at the* R *end of the sofa*) The letter begged for help—help from his kind young teacher. You never answered that letter.

MOLLIE. I couldn't. I never got it.

TROTTER. You just—didn't bother.

MOLLIE. That's not true. I was ill. I went down with pneumonia that very day. The letter was put aside with others. It was weeks afterwards that I found it with a lot of other letters. And by then that poor child was dead . . . (*Her eyes close*) Dead—dead . . . Waiting for me to do something—hoping—gradually losing hope . . . Oh, it's haunted me ever since . . . If only I hadn't been ill—if only I'd known . . . Oh, it's monstrous that such things should happen.

TROTTER. (*his voice suddenly thick*) Yes, it's monstrous. (*He takes a revolver out of his pocket*)

MOLLIE. I thought the police didn't carry revolvers . . . (*She suddenly sees* TROTTER's *face, and gasps in horror*)

TROTTER. The police don't . . . I'm not a policeman, Mrs. Ralston. You thought I was a policeman because I rang up from a call box and said I was speaking from police headquarters and that Sergeant Trotter was on his way. I cut the telephone wires before I came to the front door. You know who I am, Mrs. Ralston? I'm Georgie— I'm Jimmy's brother, Georgie.

MOLLIE. Oh. (*She looks round her wildly*)

TROTTER. (*rising*) You'd better not scream, Mrs. Ralston— because if you do I shall fire this revolver . . . I'd like to talk to you a little. (*He turns away*) I said I'd like to talk to you a little. Jimmy died. (*His manner becomes very simple and childlike*) That nasty cruel woman killed him. They put her in prison. Prison wasn't bad enough for her. I said I'd kill her one day . . . I did, too. In the fog. It was great fun. I hope Jimmy knows. "I'll kill them all when I've grown up." That's what I said to myself. Because grown-ups can do anything they like. (*Gaily*) I'm going to kill you in a minute.

MOLLIE. You'd better not. (*She tries very hard to be persuasive*) You'll never get safely away, you know.

TROTTER. (*pettishly*) Someone's hidden my skis! I can't find them. But it doesn't matter. I don't really mind if I get away or not. I'm tired. It's all been such fun. Watching you all. And pretending to be a policeman.

MOLLIE. That revolver will make a lot of noise.

TROTTER. It will rather. Much better to do it the usual way, and take you by the neck. (*He slowly approaches her, whistling "Three Blind Mice"*) The last little mouse in the trap. (*He drops the revolver on the sofa, and leans over her with his left hand on her mouth and his right hand on her neck*)

(MISS CASEWELL *and* MAJOR METCALF *appear in the arch up* R)

MISS CASEWELL. Georgie, Georgie, you know me, don't you? Don't you remember the farm, Georgie? The animals, that fat old pig, and the day the bull chased us across the field. And the dogs. (*She crosses to* L *of the sofa table*)

TROTTER. Dogs?

MISS CASEWELL. Yes, Spot and Plain.

TROTTER. Kathy?

MISS CASEWELL. Yes, Kathy—you remember me now, don't you?

TROTTER. Kathy, it is you. What are you doing here? (*He rises and moves to* R *of the sofa table*)

MISS CASEWELL. I came to England to find you. I didn't recognize you until you twirled your hair the way you always used to do.

(TROTTER *twirls his hair*)

Yes, you always did it. Georgie, come with me. (*Firmly*) You're coming with me.

TROTTER. Where are we going?

MISS CASEWELL. (*gently, as if to a child*) It's all right, Georgie. I'm taking you somewhere where they will look after you, and see that you won't do any more harm.

(MISS CASEWELL *exits up the stairs, leading* TROTTER *by the hand.* MAJOR METCALF *switches on the lights, crosses to the stairs, and looks up*)

MAJOR METCALF. (*calling*) Ralston! Ralston!

(MAJOR METCALF *exits up the stairs.* GILES *enters from the arch up* R. *He rushes over to Mollie on the sofa, sits and takes her in his arms, placing the revolver on the sofa table*)

GILES. Mollie, Mollie, are you all right? Darling, darling.

MOLLIE. Oh, Giles.

GILES. Whoever would have dreamt it was Trotter?

MOLLIE. He's mad, quite mad.

GILES. Yes, but you . . .

MOLLIE. I was mixed up in it all, I taught in the school. It wasn't my fault—but he thought I could have saved that child.

GILES. You should have told me.

MOLLIE. I wanted to forget.

(MAJOR METCALF *enters from the stairs and comes to* C)

MAJOR METCALF. Everything's under control. He will be unconscious soon with a sedative—his sister's looking after him. Poor fellow's as mad as a hatter, of course. I've had my suspicions of him all along.

MOLLIE. You did? Didn't you believe he was a policeman?

MAJOR METCALF. I knew he wasn't a policeman. You see, Mrs. Ralston, I'm a policeman.

MOLLIE. You?

MAJOR METCALF. As soon as we got hold of that notebook with "Monkswell Manor" written in it, we saw it was vital to have someone on the spot. When it was put to him, Major Metcalf agreed to let me take his place. I couldn't understand it when Trotter turned up. (*He sees the revolver on the sofa table and picks it up*)

MOLLIE. And Casewell is his sister?

MAJOR METCALF. Yes, it seems she recognized him just before this last business. Didn't know what to do, but fortunately came to me about it, just in time. Well, it's started to thaw, help should be here pretty soon. (*Moving up to the arch* R) Oh, by the way, Mrs. Ralston, I'll remove those skis. I hid them on top of the fourposter.

(MAJOR METCALF *exits up* R)

MOLLIE. And I thought it was Paravicini.

GILES. I gather they'll examine that car of his rather carefully. I shouldn't be surprised if they found a thousand or so Swiss watches in the spare wheel. Yes, that's his line of business, nasty little bit of goods. Mollie, I believe you thought I was . . .

MOLLIE. Giles, what were you doing in London yesterday?

GILES. Darling, I was buying you an anniversary present. We've been married just a year today.

MOLLIE. Oh. That's what I went to London for, and I didn't want you to know.

GILES. No.

(MOLLIE *rises, goes to the desk cupboard, and takes out the parcel.* GILES *rises and goes to* R *of the sofa table*)

MOLLIE. (*handing him the parcel*) They're cigars. I do hope they're all right.

GILES. (*unwrapping the parcel*) Oh, darling, how sweet of you. They're splendid.

MOLLIE. You will smoke them?

GILES. (*heroically*) I'll smoke them.

MOLLIE. What's my present?

GILES. Oh yes, I forgot all about your present. (*He rushes up to the chest in the entrance hall, takes out the hat-box and returns. Proudly*) It's a hat.

MOLLIE. (*taken aback*) A hat? But I practically never wear one.

GILES. Just for best.

MOLLIE. (*lifting out the hat*) Oh, how lovely, darling.

GILES. Put it on.

MOLLIE. Later, when my hair's done properly.

GILES. It is all right, isn't it? The girl in the shop said it was the last thing in hats.

(MOLLIE *puts the hat on.* GILES *moves below the desk.* MAJOR METCALF *rushes in up* R)

MAJOR METCALF. Mrs. Ralston! Mrs. Ralston! There's a terrible smell of burning coming from the kitchen.

(MOLLIE *rushes up* R *towards the kitchen*)

MOLLIE. (*wailing*) Oh, my pie!

QUICK CURTAIN

WITNESS FOR THE
PROSECUTION

WITNESS FOR THE PROSECUTION

Produced by Peter Saunders at The Winter Garden Theatre, London, on the 28th October 1953, with the following cast of characters:

(in the order of their appearance)

GRETA, typist to Sir Wilfrid	*Rosalie Westwater*
CARTER, Sir Wilfrid's Chief Clerk	*Walter Horsbrugh*
MR. MAYHEW, a solicitor	*Milton Rosmer*
LEONARD VOLE	*Derek Blomfield*
SIR WILFRED ROBARTS, Q.C.	*David Horne*
INSPECTOR HEARNE	*David Raven*
PLAIN-CLOTHES DETECTIVE	*Kenn Kennedy*
ROMAINE	*Patricia Jessel*
CLERK OF THE COURT	*Philip Holles*
MR. JUSTICE WAINWRIGHT	*Percy Marmont*
ALDERMAN	*Walter Horsbrugh*
MR. MYERS, Q.C.	*D. A. Clarke-Smith*
COURT USHER	*Nicolas Tannar*
COURT STENOGRAPHER	*John Bryning*
WARDER	*Denzil Ellis*
THE JUDGE'S CLERK	*Muir Little*
1ST BARRISTER	*George Dudley*
2ND BARRISTER	*Jack Bulloch*
3RD BARRISTER	*Lionel Gadsden*
4TH BARRISTER	*John Farries Moss*
5TH BARRISTER	*Richard Coke*
6TH BARRISTER	*Agnes Fraser*
1ST MEMBER OF THE JURY	*Lauderdale Beckett*
2ND MEMBER OF THE JURY	*Iris Fraser Foss*
3RD MEMBER OF THE JURY	*Kenn Kennedy*
A POLICEMAN	*David Homewood*
DR. WYATT, a police surgeon	*Graham Stuart*
JANET MACKENZIE	*Jean Stuart*
MR. CLEGG, a laboratory assistant	*Peter Franklin*
THE OTHER WOMAN	*Rosemary Wallace*

The play directed by Wallace Douglas

Décor by Michael Weight

Suggestions for reducing the cast to ten men and five
women will be found on page 364.

SYNOPSIS OF SCENES

ACT ONE

The Chambers of Sir Wilfrid Robarts, Q.C. Afternoon

ACT TWO

The Central Criminal Court, London—better known as
the Old Bailey. Six weeks later. Morning.

ACT THREE

SCENE I. The chambers of Sir Wilfrid Robarts, Q.C. The
same evening.

SCENE II: The Old Bailey. The next morning.

During Act Three, Scene II, the lights are lowered to
denote the passing of one hour.

Copy of program for the first performance of WITNESS
FOR THE PROSECUTION as produced at Henry Miller's
Theatre, New York, December 16, 1954.

Gilbert Miller and Peter Saunders
present

WITNESS FOR THE PROSECUTION

A Murder Mystery by
Agatha Christie

Production directed by Robert Lewis with

Francis L. Sullivan
Ernest Clark
Patricia Jessel
Gene Lyons
Una O'Connor
Robin Craven
Horace Braham

Production designed by Raymond Sovey

Costumes supervised by Kathryn Miller

CAST

(In order of appearance)

CARTER	Gordon Nelson
GRETA	Mary Barclay
SIR WILFRID ROBARTS, Q.C.	Francis L. Sullivan
MR. MAYHEW	Robin Craven
LEONARD VOLE	Gene Lyons
INSPECTOR HEARNE	Claude Horton
PLAIN CLOTHES DETECTIVE	Ralph Leonard
ROMAINE	Patricia Jessel
THIRD JUROR	Dolores Rashid
SECOND JUROR	Andrew George
FOREMAN OF THE JURY	Jack Bittner
COURT USHER	Arthur Oshlag
CLERK OF THE COURT	Ronald Dawson
MR. MYERS, Q.C.	Ernest Clark
MR. JUSTICE WAINWRIGHT	Horace Braham
ALDERMAN	R. Cobden-Smith
JUDGE'S CLERK	Harold Webster

COURT STENOGRAPHER	*W. H. Thomas*
WARDER	*Ralph Roberts*
BARRISTER	*Henry Craig Neslo*
BARRISTER	*Brace Conning*
BARRISTER	*Ruth Greene*
BARRISTER	*Albert Richards*
BARRISTER	*Franklyn Monroe*
BARRISTER	*Sam Kramer*
POLICEMAN	*Bryan Herbert*
DR. WYATT	*Guy Spaull*
JANET MACKENZIE	*Una O'Connor*
MR. CLEGG	*Michael McAloney*
THE OTHER WOMAN	*Dawn Steinkamp*

SYNOPSIS OF SCENES

ACT ONE

The chambers of Sir Wilfrid Robarts, Q.C., in London.
Late afternoon.

ACT TWO

The Central Criminal Court (The Old Bailey) in London.
Morning. Six weeks later.

ACT THREE

SCENE I: The chambers of Sir Wilfrid Robarts, Q.C., in London. The same evening.

SCENE II: The Old Bailey. The next morning.

(The lights will be lowered during this scene to denote
the passing of one hour.)

TIME: The present.
Production stage manager, JOHN EFFRAT

AUTHOR'S NOTE

I have great faith in the ingenuity of amateurs and repertory companies to derive means of reducing the very large cast of *Witness for the Prosecution* in order to make it possible to perform, and my suggested means of reducing the cast is probably only one of many.

As there are a large number of non-speaking parts, it may well be that local amateurs can be used, or members of the audience be invited on to the stage, and I believe that this would be greatly to the benefit of the play rather than lose the spectacle of a lot of people in the court scene.

Although Greta never appears at the same time as "The Other Woman," i.e. the strawberry blonde in the final scene, this part should *not* be doubled, as the audience will think it is "plot"—which, of course, it isn't.

The play has given me enormous enjoyment in writing, and I do hope that the repertory companies who do it will derive the same pleasure from it. Good luck.

AGATHA CHRISTIE

CARTER	Can double the Judge
INSPECTOR HEARNE	Can double Policeman at end of last act
PLAIN-CLOTHES DETECTIVE	Can be doubled by Warder
CLERK OF THE COURT	This part can be combined with Court Usher
ALDERMAN	Can be dispensed with
COURT STENOGRAPHER	Can be dispensed with
JUDGE'S CLERK	Can be dispensed with
SIX BARRISTERS	Four can be dispensed with
THREE MEMBERS OF THE JURY	These can be dispensed with and the "taking of the oath" and "returning the verdict" can be done by a voice "off"
MR. MYERS, Q.C.	Can double plain-clothes Detective

Act One

SCENE: *The chambers of Sir Wilfrid Robarts, Q.C.*

The scene is Sir Wilfrid's private office. It is a narrow room with the door L. *and a window* R. *The window has a deep built-in window seat and overlooks a tall plain brick wall. There is a fireplace* C. *of the back wall, flanked by bookcases filled with heavy legal volumes. There is a desk* R.C. *with a swivel chair* R. *of it and a leather-covered upright chair* L. *of it. A second upright chair stands against the bookcases* L. *of the fireplace. In the corner up* R. *is a tall reading desk, and in the corner up* L. *are some coat-hooks attached to the wall. At night the room is lit by electric candle-lamp wall-brackets* R. *and* L. *of the fireplace and an angle-poise lamp on the desk. The light switch is below the door* L. *There is a bell push* L. *of the fireplace. The desk has a telephone on it and is littered with legal documents. There are the usual deed-boxes and there is a litter of documents on the window seat.*

When the Curtain rises it is afternoon and there is sunshine streaming in through the window R. *The office is empty.* GRETA, *Sir Wilfrid's typist, enters immediately. She is an adenoidal girl with a good opinion of herself. She crosses to the fireplace, doing a "square dance" step, and takes a paper from a box-file on the mantelpiece.* CARTER, *the Chief Clerk, enters. He carries some letters.* GRETA *turns, sees* CARTER, *crosses and quietly exits.* CARTER *crosses to the desk and puts the letters on it. The* TELEPHONE *rings.* CARTER *lifts the receiver.*

CARTER. (*Into the telephone.*) Sir Wilfrid Robart's Chambers . . . Oh, it's you, Charles . . . No, Sir Wilfrid's in court . . . Won't be back just yet . . . Yes, Shuttleworth Case . . . What—with Myers for the prosecution and

Banter trying it? . . . He's been giving judgment for close on two hours already . . . No, not an earthly this evening. We're full up. Can give you an appointment tomorrow . . . No, couldn't possibly. I'm expecting Mayhew, of Mayhew and Brinskill you know, any minute now . . . Well, so long. (*He replaces the receiver and sorts the documents on the desk.*)

GRETA. (*Enters. She is painting her nails.*) Shall I make the tea, Mr. Carter?

CARTER. (*Looking at his watch*) It's hardly time yet, Greta.

GRETA. It is by my watch.

CARTER. Then your watch is wrong.

GRETA. (*Crossing to* C.) I put it right by the radio.

CARTER. Then the radio must be wrong.

GRETA. (*Shocked.*) Oh, not the radio, Mr. Carter. That *couldn't* be wrong.

CARTER. This watch was my father's. It never gains nor loses. They don't make watches like that nowadays. (*He shakes his head, then suddenly changes his manner and picks up one of the typewritten papers.*) Really, your typing. Always mistakes. (*He crosses to* R. *of* GRETA.) You've left out a word.

GRETA. Oh, well—just one word. Anyone might do that.

CARTER. The word you have left out is the word *not*. The omission of it entirely alters the sense.

GRETA. Oh, does it? That's rather funny when you come to think of it. (*She giggles.*)

CARTER. It is not in the least funny. (*He tears the letter in half and hands the piece to her.*) Do it again. You may remember I told you last week about the celebrated case of Bryant and Horsfall. Case of a will and a trust fund, and entirely owing to a piece of careless copying by a clerk . . .

GRETA. (*Interrupting*) The wrong wife got the money, I remember.

CARTER. A woman divorced fifteen years previously. Absolutely contrary to the intention of the testator, as his lordship himself admitted. But the wording had to stand. They couldn't do anything about it. (*He crosses above the desk to* R. *of it.*)

GRETA. I think *that's* rather funny, too. (*She giggles.*)

CARTER. Counsel's Chambers are no place to be funny in. The Law, Greta, is a serious business and should be treated accordingly.

GRETA. You wouldn't think so—to hear some of the jokes Judges make.

CARTER. That kind of joke is the prerogative of the Bench.

GRETA. And I'm always reading in the paper about "laughter in Court."

CARTER. If that's not caused by one of the Judge's remarks you'll find he'll soon threaten to have the Court cleared.

GRETA. (*Crossing to the door*) Mean old thing. (*She turns and crosses to* L. *of the desk.*) Do you know what I read the other day, Mr. Carter? (*Sententiously.*) "The Law's an Ass." I'm not being rude. It's a quotation.

CARTER. (*Coldly.*) A quotation of a facetious nature. Not meant to be taken seriously. (*He looks at his watch.*) You can make the tea—(*He pauses, waiting for the exact second.*)—now, Greta.

GRETA. (*Gladly.*) Oh, thank you, Mr. Carter. (*She crosses quickly to the door.*)

CARTER. Mr. Mayhew, of Mayhew and Brinskill, will be here shortly. A Mr. Leonard Vole is also expected. They may come together or separately.

GRETA. (*Excitedly.*) Leonard Vole? (*She crosses to the desk.*) Why, that's the name—it was in the paper . . .

CARTER. (*Repressively.*) The tea, Greta.

GRETA. Asked to communicate with the police as he might be able to give them useful information.

CARTER. (*Raising his voice*) Tea!

GRETA. (*Crossing to the door and turning*) It was only last . . .

(CARTER *glowers at* GRETA.)

The tea, Mr. Carter. (GRETA, *abashed but unsatisfied, exits.*)

CARTER. (*Continues his arrangement of the papers, muttering to himself.*) These girls. Sensational—inaccurate—I don't know what the Temple's coming to. (*He examines a typewritten document, makes an angry sound, picks up a pen and makes a correction.*)

GRETA. (*Enters. Announcing*) Mr. Mayhew.

(MR. MAYHEW *and* LEONARD VOLE *enter.* MAYHEW *is a typical middle-aged solicitor, shrewd and rather dry and precise in manner.* LEONARD *is a likeable, friendly young man, about twenty-seven. He is looking faintly worried.* MAYHEW *carries a brief-case.*)

MAYHEW. (*Giving his hat to* GRETA) Sit down, Mr. Vole. (*He crosses and stands above the desk.*) Good afternoon, Carter. (*He puts his brief-case on the desk.*)

(GRETA *takes* LEONARD'S *hat and hangs both on the pegs above the door. She then exits, staring at* LEONARD *over her shoulder.*)

CARTER. Good afternoon, Mr. Mayhew. Sir Wilfrid shouldn't be long, sir, although you never can tell with Mr. Justice Banter. I'll go straight over to the Robing Room and tell him that you're here! (*He hesitates.*) with . . . (*He crosses below the desk to* R. *of* LEONARD.)

MAYHEW. With Mr. Leonard Vole. Thank you, Carter. I'm afraid our appointment was at rather short notice. But in this case time is—er—rather urgent.

(CARTER *crosses to the door.*)

How's the lumbago?

CARTER. (*Turning*) I only feel it when the wind is in the East. Thank you for remembering, Mr. Mayhew. (CARTER *exits hurriedly.*)

(MAYHEW *sits* L. *of the desk.* LEONARD *prowls uneasily.*)

MAYHEW. Sit down, Mr. Vole.

LEONARD. Thanks—I'd rather walk about. I—this sort of thing makes you feel a bit jumpy. (*He crosses down* L.)

MAYHEW. Yes, yes, very probably . . .

GRETA. (*Enters. She speaks to* MAYHEW, *but stares with fascinated interest at* LEONARD.) Would you care for a cup of tea, Mr. Mayhew? I've just made it.

LEONARD. (*Appreciatively.*) Thanks, I don't mind if I . . .

MAYHEW. (*Interrupting; decisively.*) No, thank you.

(GRETA *turns to exit.*)

LEONARD. (*To* GRETA.) Sorry. (*He smiles at her.*)

(GRETA *smiles at* LEONARD *and exits. There is a pause.*)

(*He crosses up* R. *Abruptly and with a rather likeable air of bewilderment.*) What I mean is, I can't believe it's *me* this is happening to. I keep thinking—perhaps it's all a dream and I'll wake up presently.

MAYHEW. Yes, I suppose one might feel like that.

LEONARD. (*Moving to* R. *of the desk*) What I mean is—well, it seems so silly.

MAYHEW. (*Sharply.*) Silly, Mr. Vole?

LEONARD. Well, yes. I mean I've always been a friendly sort of chap—get on with people and all that. I mean, I'm not the sort of fellow that does—well, anything violent. (*He pauses.*) But I suppose it will be—all right, won't it? I mean you don't get convicted for things you haven't done in this country, do you?

MAYHEW. Our English judicial system is, in my opinion, the finest in the world.

LEONARD. (*Is not much comforted. Crossing above the desk to* L.) Of course there was that case of—what was his name—Adolf Beck. I read about it only the other day. After he'd been in prison for years, they found out it was another chap called Smith. They gave him a free pardon then. That's a thing that seems odd to me— giving you a "pardon" for something you haven't done.

MAYHEW. It is the necessary legal term.

LEONARD. (*Bringing the chair from* L. *of the fireplace and setting it* C.) Well, it doesn't seem right to me.

MAYHEW. The important thing was that Beck was set at liberty.

LEONARD. Yes, it was all right for him. But if it had been murder now— (*He sits astride the chair* C.) if it had been murder it would have been too late. He would have been hanged.

MAYHEW. (*Dry but kindly.*) Now, Mr. Vole, there is really no need to take a—er—morbid point of view.

LEONARD. (*Rather pathetically.*) I'm sorry, sir. But you see, in a way, I'm rather getting the wind up.

MAYHEW. Well, try and keep calm. Sir Wilfrid Robarts will be here presently and I want you to tell your story to him exactly as you told it to me.

LEONARD. Yes, sir.

MAYHEW. But meantime perhaps we might fill out a little more of the detail—er—background. You are at present, I understand, out of a job?

LEONARD. (*Embarrassed.*) Yes, but I've got a few pounds put by. It's not much, but if you can see your way . . .

MAYHEW. (*Upset.*) Oh, I'm not thinking of—er—legal fees. It's just the—er—pictures I'm trying to get clear. Your surroundings and—er—circumstances. How long have you been unemployed?

LEONARD. (*Answers everything readily, with an engaging friendliness.*) About a couple of months.

MAYHEW. What were you doing before that?

LEONARD. I was in a motor servicing firm—kind of mechanic, that's what I was.

MAYHEW. How long had you worked there?

LEONARD. Oh, about three months.

MAYHEW. (*Sharply.*) Were you discharged?

LEONARD. No, I quit. Had words with the foreman. Proper old b— (*He breaks off.*) That is, he was a mean sort of chap, always picking on you.

MAYHEW. Hm! And before that?

LEONARD. I worked in a petrol station, but things got a bit awkward and I left.

MAYHEW. Awkward? In what way?

LEONARD. (*Embarrassed.*) Well—the boss's daughter—she was only a kid, but she took a—well, a sort of fancy to me—and there was nothing there shouldn't have been between us, but the old man got a bit fed up and said I'd better go. He was quite nice about it and gave me a good chit. (*He rises and suddenly grins.*) Before *that*, I was selling egg beaters on commission. (*He replaces the chair* L. *of the fireplace.*)

MAYHEW. Indeed.

LEONARD. (*Crossing and standing above the desk; boyishly.*) And a rotten job they were, too. I could have invented a better egg beater myself. (*Catching* MAYHEW's *mood*) You're thinking I'm a bit of a drifter, sir. It's true in a way—but I'm not really like that. Doing my army service unsettled me a bit—that and being abroad. I was in Germany. It was fine there. That's where I met my wife. She's an actress. Since I've come back to this country I can't seem somehow to settle down properly. I don't know really just what I want to do—I like working on cars best and thinking out new gadgets for them. That's interesting, that is. And you see . . .

(SIR WILFRID ROBARTS, Q.C., *enters. He is followed on by* CARTER. SIR WILFRID *is wearing his* Q.C.'s *jacket and bands and carries his wig and gown.* CARTER *carries* SIR WILFRID'S *ordinary jacket and bow tie.*)

SIR WILFRID. Hullo, John.

MAYHEW. (*Rising*) Ah, Wilfrid.

SIR WILFRID. (*Handing the wig and gown to* CARTER) Carter told you I was in Court? Banter really surpassed himself. (*He looks at* LEONARD.) And this is Mr.—er—Vole? (*He crosses to* L. *of* LEONARD.)

MAYHEW. This is Leonard Vole.

LEONARD. How do you do, sir?

(MAYHEW *moves to the fireplace.*)

SIR WILFRID. How do you do, Vole? Won't you sit down?

(LEONARD *sits* L. *of the desk.*)

How's the family, John? (*He crosses to* CARTER.)

(CARTER *assists* SIR WILFRID *to change his jacket and remove his bands.*)

MAYHEW. Molly's got a touch of this twenty-four hour flu.

SIR WILFRID. Too bad!

MAYHEW. Yes, damnable. Did you win your case, Wilfrid?

SIR WILFRID. Yes, I'm glad to say.

MAYHEW. It always gives you satisfaction to beat Myers, doesn't it?

SIR WILFRID. It gives me satisfaction to beat anyone.

MAYHEW. But especially Myers.

SIR WILFRID. (*Taking the bow tie from* CARTER) Especially Myers. (*He crosses to the mirror* R.) He's an irritating —gentleman. (*He puts on his bow tie.*) He always seems to bring out the worst in me.

MAYHEW. That would appear to be mutual. You irritate him because you hardly ever let him finish a sentence.

(CARTER *exits, taking the wig, gown, jacket and bands with him.*)

SIR WILFRID. He irritates me because of that mannerism of his. (*He turns and stands* R. *of the desk.*) It's this— (*He clears his throat and adjusts an imaginary wig.*) that drives me to distraction, and he will call me Ro-barts—Ro-barts. But he's a very able advocate, if only he'd remember not to ask leading questions when he knows damn well he shouldn't. But let's get down to business.

MAYHEW. (*Moving above the desk*) Yes, I brought Vole here, because I am anxious for you to hear his story

exactly as he told it to me. (*He takes some typewritten
papers from his brief-case.*) There is some urgency in
the matter, it seems. (*He hands the papers to* SIR WIL-
FRID.)

SIR WILFRID. Oh?

LEONARD. My wife thinks I'm going to be arrested. (*He looks
embarrassed.*) She's much cleverer than I am—so she
may be right.

SIR WILFRID. Arrested for what?

LEONARD. (*Still more embarrassed.*) Well—for murder.

(SIR WILFRID *perches himself on the down* R. *corner of the
desk.*)

MAYHEW. (*Crossing to* C.) It's the case of Miss Emily
French. You've probably seen the reports in the Press?

(SIR WILFRID *nods.*)

She was a maiden lady, living alone but for an elderly
housekeeper, in a house at Hampstead. On the night of
October the fourteenth her housekeeper returned at
eleven o'clock to find that apparently the place had
been broken into, and that her mistress had been
coshed on the back of the head and killed. (*To*
LEONARD.) That is right?

LEONARD. That's right. It's quite an ordinary sort of thing
to happen nowadays. And then, the other day, the
papers said that the police were anxious to interview a
Mr. Leonard Vole, who had visited Miss French earlier
on the evening in question, as they thought he might be
able to give them useful information. So of course I
went along to the police station and they asked me a
lot of questions.

SIR WILFRID. (*Sharply.*) Did they caution you?

LEONARD. (*Vaguely.*) I don't quite know. I mean they said
would I like to make a statement and they'd write it
down, and it might be used in Court. Is that cautioning
me?

(SIR WILFRID *exchanges a glance with* MAYHEW, *and speaks
more to him than to* LEONARD.)

SIR WILFRID. (*Rising*) Oh well, can't be helped now. (*He
crosses above the desk to* L.)

LEONARD. Anyway, it sounded damned silly to me. I told them all I could and they were very polite and seemed quite satisfied and all that. When I got home and told Romaine about it—my wife that is—well, she got the wind up. She seemed to think that they—well—that they'd got hold of the idea that I might have done it.

(SIR WILFRID *moves the chair from* L. *of the fireplace to* C. *for* MAYHEW, *who sits.*)

So I thought perhaps I ought to get hold of a solicitor— (*To* MAYHEW.) so I came along to you. I thought you'd be able to tell me what I ought to do about it. (*He looks anxiously from one to the other.*)

SIR WILFRID. (*Moving down* L.) You knew Miss French well?

(LEONARD *rises, but* SIR WILFRID *motions him to sit.*)

LEONARD. Oh yes, she'd been frightfully kind to me. (*He resumes his seat.*) Actually it was a bit of a bore sometimes—she positively fussed over me, but she meant it very well, and when I saw in the paper that she'd been killed I was awfully upset, because, you see, I'd really got fond of her.

MAYHEW. Tell Sir Wilfrid, just as you told me, how it was you came to make Miss French's acquaintance.

LEONARD. (*Turning obediently to* SIR WILFRID) Well, it was one day in Oxford Street. I saw an old lady crossing the road carrying a lot of parcels and in the middle of the street she dropped them, tried to get hold of them again and found a bus was almost on top of her.

(SIR WILFRID *crosses slowly below the others to* R. *of desk.*)

Just managed to get to the curb safely. Well, I recovered her parcels from the street, wiped some of the mud off them as best I could, tied up one again that had burst open with string and generally soothed the old dear down. You know the sort of thing.

SIR WILFRID. And she was grateful?

LEONARD. Oh yes, she seemed very grateful. Thanked me a lot and all that. Anyone would think I'd saved her life instead of her parcels.

SIR WILFRID. There was actually no question of your having saved her life? (*He takes a packet of cigarettes from the desk drawer.*)

LEONARD. Oh, no. Nothing heroic. I never expected to see her again.

SIR WILFRID. Cigarette?

LEONARD. No, thanks, sir, never do. But by an extraordinary coincidence, two days later I happened to be sitting behind her in the theatre. She looked round and recognized me and we began to talk, and in the end she asked me to come and see her.

SIR WILFRID. And you went?

LEONARD. Yes. She'd urged me to name a day specially and it seemed rather churlish to refuse. So I said I'd go on the following Saturday.

SIR WILFRID. And you went to her house at . . . (*He looks at one of the papers.*)

MAYHEW. Hampstead.

LEONARD. Yes.

SIR WILFRID. What did you know about her when you first went to the house? (*He perches himself on the down R. corner of the desk.*)

LEONARD. Well, nothing really but what she'd told me, that she lived alone and hadn't very many friends. Something of that kind.

SIR WILFRID. She lived with only a housekeeper?

LEONARD. That's right. She had eight cats, though. Eight of them. The house was beautifully furnished and all that, but it smelt a bit of cat.

SIR WILFRID. (*Rising and moving above the desk*) Had you reason to believe she was well off?

LEONARD. Well, she talked as though she was.

SIR WILFRID. And you yourself? (*He crosses and stands up L. of LEONARD.*)

LEONARD. (*Cheerfully.*) Oh, I'm practically stony broke and have been for a long time.

SIR WILFRID. Unfortunate.

LEONARD. Yes, it is rather. Oh, you mean people will say I was sucking up to her for her money?

SIR WILFRID. (*Disarmed.*) I shouldn't have put it quite like that, but in essence, yes, that is possibly what people might say.

LEONARD. It isn't really true, you know. As a matter of fact, I was sorry for her. I thought she was lonely. I was brought up by an old aunt, my Aunt Betsy, and I like old ladies.

SIR WILFRID. You say old ladies. Do you know what age Miss French was?

LEONARD. Well, I didn't know, but I read it in the paper after she was murdered. She was fifty-six.

SIR WILFRID. Fifty-six. You consider that old, Mr. Vole, but I should doubt if Miss Emily French considered herself old.

LEONARD. But you can't call it a chicken, can you?

SIR WILFRID. (*Crossing above the desk and sitting* R. *of it*) Well, let us get on. You went to see Miss French fairly frequently?

LEONARD. Yes, I should say once, twice a week perhaps.

SIR WILFRID. Did you take your wife with you?

LEONARD. (*Slightly embarrassed.*) No, no, I didn't.

SIR WILFRID. Why didn't you?

LEONARD. Well—well, frankly, I don't think it would have gone down very well if I had.

SIR WILFRID. Do you mean with your wife or with Miss French?

LEONARD. Oh, with Miss French. (*He hesitates.*)

MAYHEW. Go on, go on.

LEONARD. You see, she got rather fond of me.

SIR WILFRID. You mean, she fell in love with you?

LEONARD. (*Horrified.*) Oh, good Lord, no, nothing of that kind. Just sort of pampered me and spoiled me, that sort of thing.

SIR WILFRID. (*After a short pause.*) You see, Mr. Vole, I have no doubt part of the police case against you, if there *is* a case against you which as yet we have no definite reason to suppose, will be why did you, young, good-looking, married, devote so much of your time to an elderly woman with whom you could hardly have very much in common?

LEONARD. (*Gloomily.*) Yes, I know they'll say I was after her for her money. And in a way perhaps that's true. But only in a way.

SIR WILFRID. (*Slightly disarmed.*) Well, at least you're frank, Mr. Vole. Can you explain a little more clearly?

LEONARD. (*Rising and moving to the fireplace*) Well, she made no secret of the fact that she was rolling in money. As I told you, Romaine and I—that's my wife—are pretty hard up. (*He moves and stands above his chair.*) I'll admit that I did hope that if I was really in a tight place she'd lend me some money. I'm being honest about it.

SIR WILFRID. Did you ask her for a loan?

LEONARD. No, I didn't. I mean, things weren't desperate. (*He becomes suddenly rather more serious as though he realized the gravity of that.*) Of course I can see—it does look rather bad for me. (*He resumes his seat.*)

SIR WILFRID. Miss French knew you were a married man?

LEONARD. Oh, yes.

SIR WILFRID. But she didn't suggest that you should bring your wife to see her?

LEONARD. (*Slightly embarrassed.*) No. She—well, she seemed to take it for granted my wife and I didn't get on.

SIR WILFRID. Did you deliberately give her that impression?

LEONARD. No, I didn't. Indeed I didn't. But she seemed to—well, assume it, and I thought perhaps if I kept dragging Romaine into it she'd, well, lose interest in me. I didn't want exactly to cadge money from her, but I'd invented a gadget for a car—a really good idea it is—and if I could have persuaded her to finance that, well, I mean it would have been *her* money, and it might have brought her in a lot. Oh, it's very difficult to explain—but I wasn't sponging on her. Sir Wilfrid, really I wasn't.

SIR WILFRID. What sums of money did you obtain at any time from Miss French?

LEONARD. None. None at all.

SIR WILFRID. Tell me something about the housekeeper.

LEONARD. Janet MacKenzie? She was a regular old tryant, you know, Janet was. Fairly bullied poor Miss French. Looked after her very well and all that, but the poor old dear couldn't call her soul her own when Janet was about. (*Thoughtfully.*) Janet didn't like me at all.

SIR WILFRID. Why didn't she like you?

LEONARD. Oh, jealous, I expect. I don't think she liked my helping Miss French with her business affairs.

SIR WILFRID. Oh, so you helped Miss French with her business affairs?

LEONARD. Yes. She was worried about some of her investments and things, and she found it a bit difficult to fill up forms and all that sort of thing. Yes, I helped her with a lot of things like that.

SIR WILFRID. Now, Mr. Vole, I'm going to ask you a very serious question. And it's one to which it's vital I should have a truthful answer. You were in low water financially, you had the handling of this lady's affairs. Now did you at any time convert to your own use the securities that you handled?

(LEONARD *is about to repudiate this hotly.*)

Now, wait a minute, Mr. Vole, before you answer. Because, you see, there are two points of view. Either we can make a feature of your probity and honesty or, if you swindled the woman in any way, then we must take the line that you had no motive for murder, since you had already a profitable source of income. You can see that there are advantages in either point of view. What I want is the truth. Take your time if you like before you reply.

LEONARD. I assure you, Sir Wilfrid, that I played dead straight and you won't find anything to the contrary. Dead straight.

SIR WILFRID. Thank you, Mr. Vole. You relieve my mind very much. I pay you the compliment of believing that you are far too intelligent to lie over such a vital matter. And we now come to October the . . . (*He hesitates.*)

MAYHEW. The fourteenth.

SIR WILFRID. Fourteenth. (*He rises.*) Did Miss French ask you to go and see her that night?

LEONARD. No, she didn't, as a matter of fact. But I'd come across a new kind of gadget and I thought she'd like it. So I slipped up there that evening and got there about a quarter to eight. It was Janet MacKenzie's night out and I knew she'd be alone and might be rather lonely.

SIR WILFRID. It was Janet MacKenzie's night out and you knew that fact.

LEONARD. (*Cheerfully.*) Oh yes, I knew Janet always went out on a Friday.

SIR WILFRID. That's not quite so good.

LEONARD. Why not? It seems very natural that I should choose that evening to go and see her.

SIR WILFRID. Please go on, Mr. Vole.

LEONARD. Well, I got there at a quarter to eight. She'd finished her supper but I had a cup of coffee with her and we played a game of Double Demon. Then at nine o'clock I said good night to her and went home.

(SIR WILFRID *crosses below the* OTHERS *to* L.)

MAYHEW. You told me the housekeeper said she came home that evening earlier than usual.

LEONARD. Yes, the police told me she came back for something she'd forgotten and she heard—or she says she heard—somebody talking with Miss French. Well, whoever it was, it wasn't me.

SIR WILFRID. Can you prove that, Mr. Vole?

LEONARD. Yes, of course I can prove it. I was at home again with my wife by then. That's what the police kept asking me. Where was I at nine-thirty. Well, I mean some days one wouldn't know where one was. As it happens I can remember quite well that I'd gone straight home to Romaine and we hadn't gone out again.

SIR WILFRID. (*Crossing up* C.) You live in a flat?

LEONARD. Yes. We've got a tiny maisonette over a shop behind Euston Station.

SIR WILFRID. (*Standing up* L. *of* LEONARD) Did anybody see you returning to the flat?

LEONARD. I don't suppose so. Why should they?

SIR WILFRID. It might be an advantage if they had.

LEONARD. But surely you don't think—I mean if she were really killed at half past nine my wife's evidence is all I need, isn't it?

(SIR WILFRID *and* MAYHEW *look at each other.* SIR WILFRID *crosses and stands* L.)

MAYHEW. And your wife will say definitely that you were at home at that time?

LEONARD. Of course she will.

MAYHEW. (*Rising and moving to the fireplace*) You are very fond of your wife and your wife is very fond of you?

LEONARD. (*His face softening*) Romaine is absolutely devoted to me. She's the most devoted wife any man could have.

MAYHEW. I see. You are happily married.

LEONARD. Couldn't be happier. Romaine's wonderful, absolutely wonderful. I'd like you to know her, Mr. Mayhew.

(*There is a KNOCK at the door.*)

SIR WILFRID. (*Calling*) Come in.

GRETA. (*Enters. She carries an evening paper.*) The evening paper, Sir Wilfrid. (*She points to a paragraph as she hands the paper to him.*)

SIR WILFRID. Thank you, Greta.

GRETA. Would you like a cup of tea, sir?

SIR WILFRID. No, thank you. Oh, would you like a cup, Vole?

LEONARD. No thank you, sir.

SIR WILFRID. No, thank you, Greta. (*He crosses below the* OTHERS *to* R. *of the desk*)

(GRETA *exits.*)

MAYHEW. I think it would be advisable for us to have a meeting with your wife.

LEONARD. You mean have a regular round-table conference?

(SIR WILFRID *sits* R. *of the desk.*)

MAYHEW. I wonder, Mr. Vole, if you are taking this business quite seriously enough?

LEONARD. (*Nervously.*) I am. I am, really, but it seems— well, I mean it seems so much like a bad dream. I mean that it should be happening to me. Murder. It's a thing you read about in books or newspapers, but you can't believe it's a thing that could ever happen to you, or touch you in any way. I suppose that's why I keep trying to make a joke of it, but it isn't a joke, really.

MAYHEW. No, I'm afraid it's not a joke.

LEONARD. But I mean it's all right, isn't it? Because I mean if they think Miss French was killed at half past nine and I was at home with Romaine . . .

MAYHEW. How did you go home? By bus or underground?

LEONARD. I walked. It took me about twenty-five minutes, but it was a fine night—a bit windy.

MAYHEW. Did you see anyone you knew on the way?

LEONARD. No, but does it matter? I mean Romaine . . .

SIR WILFRID. The evidence of a devoted wife unsupported by any other evidence may not be completely convincing, Mr. Vole.

LEONARD. You mean, they'd think Romaine would tell a lie on my account?

SIR WILFRID. It has been known, Mr. Vole.

LEONARD. Oh, I'm sure she would, too, only in this case I mean she won't be telling a lie. I mean it really is so. You do believe me, don't you?

SIR WILFRID. Yes, I believe you, Mr. Vole, but it's not me you will have to convince. You are aware, are you not, that Miss French left a will leaving you all her money?

LEONARD. (*Absolutely flabbergasted.*) Left all her money to me? You're joking!

(MAYHEW *resumes his seat* C.)

SIR WILFRID. I'm not joking. It's in tonight's evening paper. (*He hands the paper across the desk.*)

LEONARD. (*Reads the paragraph.*) Well, I can hardly believe it.

SIR WILFRID. You knew nothing about it?

LEONARD. Absolutely nothing. She never said a word. (*He hands the paper to* MAYHEW.)

MAYHEW. You're quite sure of that, Mr. Vole?

LEONARD. Absolutely sure. I'm very grateful to her—yet in a way I rather wish now that she hadn't. I mean it—it's a bit unfortunate as things are, isn't it, sir?

SIR WILFRID. It supplies you with a very adequate motive. That is, if you knew about it, which you say you didn't. Miss French never talked to you about making a will?

LEONARD. She said to Janet once, "You're afraid I shall make my will again," but that was nothing to do with me. I mean, it was just a bit of a dust-up between them. (*His manner changes.*) Do you really think they're going to arrest me?

SIR WILFRID. I think you must prepare yourself, Mr. Vole, for that eventuality.

LEONARD. (*Rising*) You—you will do the best you can for me, won't you, sir?

SIR WILFRID. (*With friendliness.*) You may rest assured, my dear Mr. Vole, that I will do everything in my power to help you. Don't worry. Leave everything in my hands.

LEONARD. You'll look after Romaine, won't you? I mean, she'll be in an awful state—it will be terrible for her.

SIR WILFRID. Don't worry, my boy. Don't worry.

LEONARD. (*Resuming his seat; to* MAYHEW) Then the money side, too. That worries me. I've got a few quid, but it's not much. Perhaps I oughtn't to have asked you to do anything for me.

MAYHEW. I think we shall be able to put up adequate defence. The Court provides for these cases you know.

LEONARD. (*Rising and moving above the desk*) I can't believe it. I can't believe that I, Leonard Vole, may be standing in a dock saying "Not guilty." People staring at me. (*He shakes himself as though it were a bad dream then turns to* MAYHEW.) I can't see why they

don't think it was a burglar. I mean, apparently the
window was forced and smashed and a lot of things were
strewn around, so the papers said. (*He resumes his
seat.*) I mean, it seems much more probable.

MAYHEW. The police must have some good reason for not
thinking that it was a burglary.

LEONARD. Well, it seems to me . . .

(CARTER *enters.*)

SIR WILFRID. Yes, Carter?

CARTER. (*Crossing above the desk*) Excuse me, sir, there
are two gentlemen here asking to see Mr. Vole.

SIR WILFRID. The police?

CARTER. Yes, sir.

(MAYHEW *rises.*)

SIR WILFRID. (*Rising and crossing to the door*) All right,
John, I'll go and talk to them.

(SIR WILFRID *exits and* CARTER *follows him off.*)

LEONARD. My God! Is this—it?

MAYHEW. I'm afraid it may be, my boy. Now take it easy.
Don't lose heart. (*He pats* LEONARD *on the shoulder.*)
Make no further statement—leave it all to us. (*He re-
places his chair* L. *of the fireplace.*)

LEONARD. But how did they know I'm here?

MAYHEW. It seems probable that they have had a man
watching you.

LEONARD. (*Still unable to believe it.*) Then they really do
suspect me.

(SIR WILFRID, DETECTIVE INSPECTOR HEARNE *and a plainclothes*
DETECTIVE *enter. The* INSPECTOR *is a tall, good-looking
officer.*)

INSPECTOR. (*As he enters; to* SIR WILFRID) I'm sorry to
trouble you, sir.

SIR WILFRID. (*Standing up* L.) This is Mr. Vole.

(LEONARD *rises.*)

INSPECTOR. (*Crossing to* LEONARD) Is your name Leonard
Vole?

LEONARD. Yes.

INSPECTOR. I am Detective Inspector Hearne. I have here a warrant for your arrest on the charge of murdering Emily French on October fourteenth last. I must warn you that anything you say may be taken down and used in evidence.

LEONARD. O.K. (*He looks nervously at* SIR WILFRID *then crosses and takes his hat from the hooks up* L.) I'm ready.

MAYHEW. (*Moving to* L. *of the* INSPECTOR) Good afternoon, Inspector Hearne. My name is Mayhew. I am representing Mr. Vole.

INSPECTOR. Good afternoon, Mr. Mayhew. That's quite all right. We'll take him along and charge him now.

(LEONARD *and the* DETECTIVE *exit.*)

(*He crosses to* SIR WILFRID. *To* MAYHEW.) Very seasonable weather we're having just now. Quite a nip of frost last night. We'll be seeing you later, sir, I expect. (*He crosses to the door.*) Hope we haven't inconvenienced you, Sir Wilfrid.

SIR WILFRID. I am never inconvenienced.

(*The* INSPECTOR *laughs politely and exits.*)

(*He closes the door.*) I must say, John, that that young man is in a worse mess than he seems to think.

MAYHEW. He certainly is. How does he strike you?

SIR WILFRID. (*Crossing to* L. *of* MAYHEW) Extraordinarily naïve. Yet in some ways quite shrewd. Intelligent, I should say. But he certainly doesn't realize the danger of his position.

MAYHEW. Do you think he did it?

SIR WILFRID. I've no idea. On the whole, I should say *not.* (*Sharply.*) You agree?

MAYHEW. (*Taking his pipe from his pocket*) I agree.

(SIR WILFRID *takes the tobacco jar from the mantelpiece and hands it to* MAYHEW, *who crosses, stands above the desk and fills his pipe.*)

SIR WILFRID. Oh well, he seems to have impressed both of us favourably. I can't think why. I never heard a weaker story. God knows what we're going to do with it. The only evidence in his favour seems to be his wife's— and who's going to believe a wife?

MAYHEW. (*With dry humour.*) It has been known to happen.

SIR WILFRID. She's a foreigner, too. Nine out of the twelve in a jury box believe a foreigner is lying anyway. She'll be emotional and upset, and won't understand what the prosecuting counsel says to her. Still, we shall have to interview her. You'll see, she'll have hysterics all over my Chambers.

MAYHEW. Perhaps you'd prefer not to accept the brief.

SIR WILFRID. Who says I won't accept it? Just because I point out that the boy has an absolute tomfool story to tell.

MAYHEW. (*Crossing and handing the tobacco jar to* SIR WILFRID) But a true one.

SIR WILFRID. (*Replacing the jar on the mantelpiece*) It must be a true one. It couldn't be so idiotic if it wasn't true. Put all the facts down in black and white and the whole thing is utterly damning.

(MAYHEW *feels in his pockets for matches.*)

And yet, when you talk to the boy, and he blurts out these damning facts, you realize that the whole thing could happen just as he said. Damn it, I had the equivalent of an Aunt Betsy myself. I loved her dearly.

MAYHEW. He's got a good personality, I think. Sympathetic.

SIR WILFRID. (*Taking a matchbox from his pocket and handing it to* MAYHEW) Yes, he ought to go down well with the jury. That cuts no ice with the Judge, though. And he's the simple sort of chap who may get rattled easily in the box.

(MAYHEW *finds that the box is empty and throws it in the waste-paper basket.*)

A lot depends on this girl.

(*There is a KNOCK at the door.*)

(*He calls.*) Come in.

(GRETA *enters. She is excited and a little scared. She closes the door.*)

Yes, Greta, what is it?

GRETA. (*In a whisper.*) Mrs. Leonard Vole is here.

MAYHEW. Mrs. Vole.

SIR WILFRID. Come here. You saw that young man? He's been arrested for murder.

GRETA. (*Crossing to* L. *of* SIR WILFRID) I know. Isn't it exciting?

SIR WILFRID. Do you think he did it?

GRETA. Oh no, sir, I'm sure he didn't.

SIR WILFRID. Oh, why not?

GRETA. He's far too nice.

SIR WILFRID. (*To* MAYHEW) That makes three of us. (*To* GRETA.) Bring Mrs. Vole in.

(GRETA *crosses and exits*.)

And we're probably three credulous fools—(*He crosses to the chair* L. *of the desk*.) taken in by a young man with a pleasing personality. (*He sets the chair in readiness for* ROMAINE.)

CARTER. (*Enters and stands to one side. Announcing*) Mrs. Vole.

(ROMAINE *enters. She is a foreign woman of great personality, but very quiet. Her voice has a strangely ironic inflection*.)

MAYHEW. (*Crossing to* R. *of* ROMAINE) My dear Mrs. Vole. (*He goes towards her with a great air of sympathy, but is slightly rebuffed by her personality*.)

(CARTER *exits, closing the door behind him*.)

ROMAINE. Ah! You are Mr. Mayhew.

MAYHEW. Yes. This is Sir Wilfrid Robarts, who has agreed to handle your husband's case for him.

ROMAINE. (*Crossing to* C.) How do you do, Sir Wilfrid?

SIR WILFRID. How do you do?

ROMAINE. I have just come from your office, Mr. Mayhew. They told me you were here with my husband.

SIR WILFRID. Quite, quite.

ROMAINE. Just as I arrived I thought I saw Leonard getting into a car. There were two men with him.

SIR WILFRID. Now, my dear Mrs. Vole, you must not upset yourself.

(ROMAINE *is not in the least upset*.)

(*He is slightly disconcerted*.) Won't you sit down, here?

ROMAINE. Thank you. (*She sits in the chair* L. *of the desk*.)

SIR WILFRID. (*Moving above the desk to* R. *of it*) There is nothing to be alarmed about as yet, and you must not give way. (*He moves below the desk.*)

ROMAINE. (*After a pause.*) Oh, no, I shall not give way.

SIR WILFRID. Then let me tell you that, as perhaps you already suspect, your husband has just been arrested.

ROMAINE. For the murder of Miss Emily French?

SIR WILFRID. I'm afraid so, yes. But please don't be upset.

ROMAINE. You keep saying that, Sir Wilfrid, but I am not upset.

SIR WILFRID. No. No, I see you have great fortitude.

ROMAINE. You can call it that if you like.

SIR WILFRID. The great thing is to be calm and to tackle all this sensibly.

ROMAINE. That suits me very well. But you must not hide anything from me, Sir Wilfrid. You must not try and spare me. I want to know everything. (*With a slightly different inflection.*) I want to know—the worst.

SIR WILFRID. Splendid. Splendid. That's the right way to tackle things. (*He moves to* R. *of the desk.*) Now, dear lady, we're not going to give way to alarm or despondency, we're going to look at things in a sensible and straightforward manner. (*He sits* R. *of the desk.*) Your husband became friendly with Miss French about six weeks ago. You were—er—aware of that friendship?

ROMAINE. He told me that he had rescued an old lady and her parcels one day in the middle of a crowded street. He told me that she had asked him to go and see her.

SIR WILFRID. All very natural, I think. And your husband did go and see her.

ROMAINE. Yes.

SIR WILFRID. And they became great friends.

ROMAINE. Evidently.

SIR WILFRID. There was no question of your accompanying your husband on any occasion?

ROMAINE. Leonard thought it better not.

SIR WILFRID. (*Shooting a keen glance at her*) He thought it better not. Yes. Just between ourselves, why did he think it better not?

ROMAINE. He thought Miss French would prefer it that way.

SIR WILFRID. (*A little nervously and sliding off the subject.*) Yes, yes, quite. Well, we can go into that some other time. Your husband, then, became friends with Miss French, he did her various little services, she was a lonely old woman with time on her hands and she found your husband's companionship congenial to her.

ROMAINE. Leonard can be very charming.

SIR WILFRID. Yes, I'm sure he can. He felt, no doubt, it was a kindly action on his part to go and cheer up the old lady.

ROMAINE. I daresay.

SIR WILFRID. You yourself did not object at all to your husband's friendship with this old lady?

ROMAINE. I do not think I objected, no.

SIR WILFRID. You have, of course, perfect trust in your husband, Mrs. Vole. Knowing him as well as you do . . .

ROMAINE. Yes, I know Leonard very well.

SIR WILFRID. I can't tell you how much I admire your calm and your courage, Mrs. Vole. Knowing as I do how devoted you are to him . . .

ROMAINE. So you know how devoted I am to him?

SIR WILFRID. Of course.

ROMAINE. But excuse me, I am a foreigner. I do not always know your English terms. But is there not a saying about knowing something of your own knowledge? You do not know that I am devoted to Leonard, of your own knowledge, do you, Sir Wilfrid? (*She smiles.*)

SIR WILFRID. (*Slightly disconcerted.*) No, no, that is of course true. But your husband told me.

ROMAINE. Leonard told you how devoted I was to him?

SIR WILFRID. Indeed, he spoke of your devotion in the most moving terms.

ROMAINE. Men, I often think, are very stupid.

SIR WILFRID. I beg your pardon?

ROMAINE. It does not matter. Please go on.

SIR WILFRID. (*Rising and crossing above the desk to* C.) This Miss French was a woman of some considerable wealth. She had no near relations. Like many eccentric elderly ladies she was fond of making wills. She had made several wills in her lifetime. Shortly after meeting your husband she made a fresh will. After some small bequests she left the whole of her fortune to your husband.

ROMAINE. Yes.

SIR WILFRID. You know that?

ROMAINE. I read it in the paper this evening.

SIR WILFRID. Quite, quite. Before reading it in the paper, you had no idea of the fact? Your husband had no idea of it?

ROMAINE. (*After a pause.*) Is that what he told you?

SIR WILFRID. Yes. You don't suggest anything different?

ROMAINE. No. Oh, no. I do not suggest anything.

SIR WILFRID. (*Crossing above the desk to R. of it and sitting*) There seems to be no doubt that Miss French looked upon your husband rather in the light of a son, or perhaps a very favourite nephew.

ROMAINE. (*With distinct irony.*) You think Miss French looked upon Leonard as a son?

SIR WILFRID. (*Flustered.*) Yes, I think so. Definitely I think so. I think that could be regarded as quite natural, quite normal under the circumstances.

ROMAINE. What hypocrites you are in this country.

(MAYHEW *sits on the chair L. of the fireplace.*)

SIR WILFRID. My dear Mrs. Vole!

ROMAINE. I shock you? I am so sorry.

SIR WILFRID. Of course, of course. You have a continental way of looking at these things. But I assure you, dear Mrs. Vole, that is *not* the line to take. It would be most unwise to suggest in any way that Miss French had—er—any—er—feelings for Leonard Vole other than those of a—of a mother or—shall we say—an aunt.

ROMAINE. Oh, by all means let us say an aunt, if you think it best.

SIR WILFRID. One has to think of the effect on the jury of all these things, Mrs. Vole.

ROMAINE. Yes. I also wish to do that. I have been thinking of that a good deal.

SIR WILFRID. Quite so. We must work together. Now we come to the evening of October fourteenth. That is just over a week ago. You remember that evening?

ROMAINE. I remember it very well.

SIR WILFRID. Leonard Vole called on Miss French that evening. The housekeeper, Janet MacKenzie, was out. Mr. Vole played a game of Double Demon with Miss French and finally took leave of her about nine o'clock. He returned home on foot, he tells me, arriving at approximately twenty-five minutes past nine. (*He looks interrogatively at her.*)

(ROMAINE *rises and moves to the fireplace.* SIR WILFRID *and* MAYHEW *rise.*)

ROMAINE. (*Without expression; thoughtfully.*) Twenty-five
past nine.

SIR WILFRID. At half past nine the housekeeper returned to
the house to get something she had forgotten. Passing
the sitting-room door she heard Miss French's voice in
conversation with a man. She assumed that the man
with Miss French was Leonard Vole, and Inspector
Hearne says that it is this statement of hers which has
led to your husband's arrest. Mr. Vole, however, tells
me that he has an absolute alibi for that time, since he
was at home with you at nine-thirty.

(*There is a pause.* ROMAINE *does not speak although* SIR
WILFRID *looks at her.*)

That is so, is it not? He was with you at nine-thirty?

(SIR WILFRID *and* MAYHEW *look at* ROMAINE).

ROMAINE. That is what Leonard says? That he was home
with me at nine-thirty?

SIR WILFRID. (*Sharply*) Isn't it true?

(*There is a long silence.*)

ROMAINE. (*Moving to the chair* L. *of the desk; presently.*)
But of course. (*She sits.*)

SIR WILFRID. (*Sighs with relief and resumes his seat* R. *of
the desk.*) Possibly the police have already questioned
you on that point?

ROMAINE. Oh yes, they came to see me yesterday evening.

SIR WILFRID. And you said . . .

ROMAINE. (*As though repeating something that she has
learned by rote*) I said Leonard came in at nine-twenty-
five that night and did not go out again.

MAYHEW. (*A little uneasily.*) You said . . . ? Oh! (*He sits
on the chair* L. *of the fireplace.*)

ROMAINE. That was right, was it not?

SIR WILFRID. What do you mean by that, Mrs. Vole?

ROMAINE. (*Sweetly.*) That is what Leonard wants me to say,
is it not?

SIR WILFRID. It's the truth. You said so just now.

ROMAINE. I have to understand—to be sure. If I say yes, it is
so, Leonard was with me in the flat at nine-thirty—will
they acquit him?

(SIR WILFRID *and* MAYHEW *are puzzled by* ROMAINE'S *manner.*)

Will they let him go?

MAYHEW. (*Rising and crossing to* L. *of her*) If you are both speaking the truth then they will—er—have to acquit him.

ROMAINE. But when I said—that—to the police, I do not think they believed me. (*She is not distressed; instead she seems faintly satisfied.*)

SIR WILFRID. What makes you think they did not believe you?

ROMAINE. (*With sudden malice.*) Perhaps I did not say it very well?

(SIR WILFRID *and* MAYHEW *exchange glances.* MAYHEW *resumes his seat.* ROMAINE'S *cool, impudent glance meets* SIR WILFRID'S. *There is a definite antagonism between them.*)

SIR WILFRID. (*Changing his manner*) You know, Mrs. Vole, I don't quite understand your attitude in all this.

ROMAINE. So you don't understand? Well, perhaps it is difficult.

SIR WILFRID. Perhaps your husband's position is not quite clear to you?

ROMAINE. I have already said that I want to understand fully just how black the case against—my husband is. I say to the police, Leonard was at home with me at nine-thirty —and they do not believe me. But perhaps there is someone who saw him leave Miss French's house, or who saw him in the street on his way home? (*She looks sharply and rather slyly from one to the other.*)

(SIR WILFRID *looks enquiringly at* MAYHEW.)

MAYHEW. (*Rising and moving* C.; *reluctantly*) Your husband cannot think of, or remember, anything helpful of that kind.

ROMAINE. So it will be only his word—and mine. (*With intensity.*) And mine. (*She rises abruptly.*) Thank you, that is what I wanted to know. (*She crosses to* L.)

MAYHEW. But, Mrs. Vole, please don't go. There is a lot more to be discussed.

ROMAINE. Not by me.

SIR WILFRID. Why not, Mrs. Vole?

ROMAINE. I shall have to swear, shall I not, to speak the truth and all the truth and nothing but the truth? (*She seems amused.*)

SIR WILFRID. That is the oath you take.

ROMAINE. (*Crossing and standing above the chair* L. *of the desk; now openly mocking*) And suppose that then, when you ask me—(*She imitates a man's voice.*) "When did Leonard Vole come that night?" I should say . . .

SIR WILFRID. Well?

ROMAINE. There are so many things I could say.

SIR WILFRID. Mrs. Vole, do you love your husband?

ROMAINE. (*Shifting her mocking glance to* MAYHEW) Leonard says I do.

MAYHEW. Leonard Vole believes so.

ROMAINE. But Leonard is not very clever.

SIR WILFRID. You are aware, Mrs. Vole, that you cannot by law be called to give testimony damaging to your husband?

ROMAINE. How very convenient.

SIR WILFRID. And your husband can . . .

ROMAINE. (*Interrupting*) He is not my husband.

SIR WILFRID. What?

ROMAINE. Leonard Vole is not my husband. He went through a form of marriage with me in Berlin. He got me out of the Russian zone and brought me to this country. I did not tell him, but I had a husband living at the time.

SIR WILFRID. He got you out of the Russian sector and safely to this country? You should be very grateful to him. (*Sharply.*) Are you?

ROMAINE. One can get tired of gratitude.

SIR WILFRID. Has Leonard Vole ever injured you in any way?

ROMAINE. (*Scornfully*) Leonard? Injured me? He worships the ground I walk on.

SIR WILFRID. And you?

(*Again there is a duel of eyes between them, then she laughs and turns away.*)

ROMAINE. You want to know too much. (*She crosses to the door.*)

MAYHEW. I think we must be quite clear about this. Your statements have been somewhat ambiguous. What exactly happened on the evening of October fourteenth?

ROMAINE. (*In a monotonous voice*) Leonard came in at twenty-five minutes past nine and did not go out again. I have given him an alibi, have I not?

SIR WILFRID. (*Rising*) You have. (*He crosses to her.*) Mrs. Vole . . . (*He catches her eye and pauses.*)

ROMAINE. Yes?

SIR WILFRID. You're a very remarkable woman, Mrs. Vole.

ROMAINE. And you are satisfied, I hope? (ROMAINE *exits.*)

SIR WILFRID. I'm damned if I'm satisfied.

MAYHEW. Nor I.

SIR WILFRID. She's up to something, that woman—but what? I don't like it, John.

MAYHEW. She certainly hasn't had hysterics all over the place.

SIR WILFRID. Cool as a cucumber.

MAYHEW. (*Sitting on the chair* L. *of the desk*) What's going to happen if we put her into the witness box?

SIR WILFRID. (*Crossing to* C.) God knows!

MAYHEW. The prosecution would break her down in no time, especially if it were Myers.

SIR WILFRID. If it's not the Attorney-General, it probably will be.

MAYHEW. Then what's your line of attack?

SIR WILFRID. The usual. Keep interrupting—as many objections as possible.

MAYHEW. What beats me is that young Vole is convinced of her devotion.

SIR WILFRID. Don't put your trust in that. Any woman can fool a man if she wants to and if he's in love with her.

MAYHEW. He's in love with her all right. And trusts her completely.

SIR WILFRID. More fool he. Never trust a woman.

CURTAIN

Act Two

SCENE: *The Central Criminal Court, London—better known as the Old Bailey. Six weeks later. Morning.*

The section of the Court Room seen has a tall rostrum, the bench, running from down R. *to up* C. *On it are the armchairs and desks for the Judge, his Clerk and the Alderman. Access to the bench is by a door in the up* R. *corner and by steps up* R. *from the floor of the court. On the wall over the Judge's chair are the Royal Arms and the Sword of Justice. Below the bench are small desks and chairs for the Clerk of the Court and the Court Stenographer. There is a small stool* R. *of the desks for the Usher. The witness box is immediately below the up* C. *end of the bench. Up* C. *is a door leading to the Barristers' robing room and up* L.C. *are glass-panelled double doors leading to a corridor and other parts of the building. Up* L.C., *between the doors, are two pews for the Barristers. Below the pews is a table with three chairs and a stool. The dock is* L. *and is entered by a door in the* L. *wall and a gate in the up-stage rail. There are chairs in the dock for Leonard and the Warder. The jury box is down* R., *only the back of the three end seats being visible to the audience.*

When the Curtain rises, the Court has opened. The Judge, MR. JUSTICE WAINWRIGHT, *is seated* R. *of him and the* ALDERMAN *is seated* L. *of the Judge. The* CLERK OF THE COURT *and the* STENOGRAPHER *are in their seats below the bench.* MR. MYERS, Q.C., *for the Prosecution, is seated* R. *of the front row of Barristers with his* ASSISTANT L. *of him.* SIR WILFRID, *for the Defence, is seated* L. *of the front row of Barristers with his* ASSISTANT R. *of him. Four* BARRISTERS, *one a woman, are seated in the back row of the Barristers' seats.* LEONARD *is standing in the dock with the* WARDER *beside him.* DR. WYATT *is seated on the stool* R. *of the table. The* INSPECTOR *is seated on the chair above the* R. *end of the table.* MAYHEW *is seated* L. *of the table. A* POLICEMAN *stands at the double doors. Three* MEMBERS *of the* JURY *are seen, the first a man, the* FOREMAN, *the second a* WOMAN *and the third a* MAN. *The* USHER *is administering the oath to the* WOMAN JUROR *who is standing.*

WOMAN JUROR. (*Holding the Bible and oath card*) . . . lady the Queen and the prisoner at the Bar whom I shall have in charge, and a true verdict give according to the evidence. (*She hands the Bible and oath card to the* USHER, *then sits.*)

(*The* USHER *gives the Bible and oath card to the* FOREMAN.)

FOREMAN. (*Rising*) I swear by Almighty God that I will well and truly try and true deliverance make between our sovereign lady the Queen and the prisoner at the Bar whom I have in charge, and a true verdict give according to the evidence. (*He hands the Bible and oath card to the* USHER, *then sits.*)

(*The* USHER *puts the Bible and card on the ledge of the jury box, then sits on his stool down* R.)

CLERK. (*Rising*) Leonard Vole, you are charged on indictment for that you on the fourteenth day of October in the County of London murdered Emily Jane French. How say you, Leonard Vole, are you guilty or not guilty?
LEONARD. Not guilty.
CLERK. Members of the Jury, the prisoner stands indicted for that he on the fourteenth day of October murdered Emily Jane French. To this indictment he has pleaded not guilty, and it is your charge to say, having heard the evidence, whether he be guilty or not. (*He motions to* LEONARD *to sit, then resumes his own seat.*)

(LEONARD *and the* WARDER *sit.* MYERS *rises.*)

JUDGE. One moment, Mr. Myers.

(MYERS *bows to the* JUDGE *and resumes his seat.*)

(*He turns to the jury.*) Members of the Jury, the proper time for me to sum up the evidence to you, and instruct you as to the law, is after you have heard all the evidence. But because there has been a considerable amount of publicity about this case in the Press, I would just like to say this to you now. By the oath which each of you has just taken you swore to try this case on the evidence. That means on the evidence that you are now going to hear and see. It does not mean that you are to consider also anything you have heard or read before taking your oaths. You must shut out from your minds everything except what will take place in this Court. You must not let anything else influence your minds in favour of or against the prisoner. I am quite sure that you will do your duty conscientiously in the way that I have indicated. Yes, Mr. Myers.

(MYERS *rises, clears his throat and adjusts his wig in the manner taken off by* SIR WILFRID *in the previous scene.*)

MYERS. May it please you, my lord. Members of the Jury, I appear in this case with my learned friend Mr. Barton for the prosecution, and my learned friends Sir Wilfrid Robarts and Mr. Brogan-Moore appear for the defence. This is a case of murder. The facts are simple and up to a certain point are not in dispute. You will hear how the prisoner, a young and, you may think, a not unattractive man, made the acquaintance of Miss Emily French, a woman of fifty-six. How he was treated by her with kindness and even with affection. The nature of that affection you will have to decide for yourselves. Dr. Wyatt will tell you that in his opinion death occurred at some time between nine-thirty and ten on the night of the fourteenth of October last. You will hear the evidence of Janet MacKenzie, who was Miss French's faithful and devoted housekeeper. The fourteenth of October—it was a Friday—was Janet MacKenzie's night out, but on this occasion she happened to return for a few minutes at nine twenty-five. She let herself in with a key and upon going upstairs to her room she passed the door of the sitting-room. She will tell you that in the sitting-room she heard the voices of Miss French and of the prisoner, Leonard Vole.

LEONARD. (*Rising*) That's not true. It wasn't me.

(*The* WARDER *restrains* LEONARD *and makes him resume his seat.*)

MYERS. Janet MacKenzie was surprised, since as far as she knew, Miss French had not expected Leonard Vole to call that evening. However, she went out again and when she returned finally at eleven she found Miss Emily French murdered, the room in disorder, a window smashed and the curtains blowing wildly. Horror-stricken, Janet MacKenzie immediately rang up the police. I should tell you that the prisoner was arrested on the twentieth of October. It is the case for the prosecution that Miss Emily Jane French was murdered between nine-thirty and ten p.m. on the evening of the fourteenth of October, by a blow from a cosh and that the blow was struck by the prisoner. I will now call Inspector Hearne.

(*The* INSPECTOR *rises. He holds a file of papers which he refers to often during the scene. He hands a typewritten sheet to the* CLERK *and another to the* STENOGRAPHER. *He then enters the witness box. The* CLERK *hands the sheet to the* JUDGE. *The* USHER *rises, crosses and stands by the witness box. The* INSPECTOR *picks up the oath card and Bible from the ledge of the box.*)

INSPECTOR. I swear by Almighty God that the evidence that I shall give shall be the truth, the whole truth and nothing but the truth. Robert Hearne, Detective Inspector, Criminal Investigation Department, New Scotland Yard. (*He puts the Bible and oath card on the ledge of the box.*)

(*The* USHER *crosses and sits on his stool.*)

MYERS. Now, Inspector Hearne, on the evening of the fourteenth October last were you on duty when you received an emergency call?
INSPECTOR. Yes, sir.
MYERS. What did you do?
INSPECTOR. With Sergeant Randell I proceeded to twenty-three Ashburn Grove. I was admitted to the house and established that the occupant, whom I later ascertained was Miss Emily French, was dead. She was lying on her face, and had received severe injuries to the back of

her head. An attempt had been made to force one of the windows with some implement that might have been a chisel. The window had been broken near the catch. There was glass strewn about the floor, and I also later found fragments of glass on the ground outside the window.

MYERS. Is there any particular significance in finding glass both inside and outside the window?

INSPECTOR. The glass outside was not consistent with the window having been forced from outside.

MYERS. You mean that if it had been forced from the inside there had been an attempt to make it look as though it had been done from the outside?

SIR WILFRID. (Rising) I object. My learned friend is putting words into the witness's mouth. He really must observe the rules of evidence. (He resumes his seat.)

MYERS. (To the INSPECTOR.) You have been engaged on several cases of burglary and housebreaking?

INSPECTOR. Yes, sir.

MYERS. And in your experience when a window is forced from the outside, where is the glass?

INSPECTOR. On the inside.

MYERS. In any other case where the windows have been forced from the outside, have you found glass on the outside of the window some distance below, on the ground?

INSPECTOR. No.

MYERS. No. Will you go on?

INSPECTOR. A search was made, photographs were taken, the place was fingerprinted.

MYERS. What fingerprints did you discover?

INSPECTOR. Those of Miss Emily French herself, those of Janet MacKenzie and some which proved later to be those of the prisoner, Leonard Vole.

MYERS. No others?

INSPECTOR. No others.

MYERS. Did you subsequently have an interview with Mr. Leonard Vole?

INSPECTOR. Yes, sir. Janet MacKenzie was not able to give me his address, but as a result of a broadcast and a newspaper appeal, Mr. Leonard Vole came and saw me.

MYERS. And on October the twentieth, when arrested, what did the prisoner say?

INSPECTOR. He replied. "O. K. I'm ready."

MYERS. Now, Inspector, you say the room had the appearance of a robbery having been committed?

SIR WILFRID. (*Rising*) That is just what the Inspector did not say. (*To the* JUDGE.) If your lordship remembers, that was a suggestion made by my friend—and quite improperly made—to which I objected.

JUDGE. You are quite right, Sir Wilfrid.

(MYERS *sits.*)

At the same time, I'm not sure that the Inspector is not entitled to give evidence of any facts which might tend to prove that the disorder of the room was not the work of a person who broke in from outside for the purpose of robbery.

SIR WILFRID. My lord, may I respectfully agree with what your lordship has said. Facts, yes. But not the mere expression of opinion without even the facts on which it is based. (*He sits.*)

MYERS. (*Rising*) Perhaps, my lord, if I phrased my question in this way my friend would be satisfied. Inspector, could you say from what you saw whether there had or had not been a bona fide breaking in from outside the house?

SIR WILFRID. (*Rising*) My lord, I really must continue my objection. My learned friend is again seeking to obtain an opinion from this witness. (*He sits.*)

JUDGE. Yes. Mr. Myers, I think you will have to do a little better than that.

MYERS. Inspector, did you find anything inconsistent with a breaking in from outside?

INSPECTOR. Only the glass, sir.

MYERS. Nothing else?

INSPECTOR. No, sir, there was nothing else.

JUDGE. We all seem to have drawn a blank there, Mr. Myers.

MYERS. Was Miss French wearing jewellery of any value?

INSPECTOR. She was wearing a diamond brooch, two diamond rings, value of about nine hundred pounds.

MYERS. And these were left untouched?

INSPECTOR. Yes, sir.

MYERS. Was in fact anything taken?

INSPECTOR. According to Janet MacKenzie, nothing was missing.

MYERS. In your experience, when anyone breaks into a house do they leave without taking anything?

INSPECTOR. Not unless they're interrupted, sir.

MYERS. But in this case it does not seem as if the burglar *was* interrupted.

INSPECTOR. No, sir.

MYERS. Do you produce a jacket, Inspector?

INSPECTOR. Yes, sir.

(*The USHER rises, crosses to the table, picks up the jacket and hands it to the INSPECTOR.*)

MYERS. Is that it?

INSPECTOR. Yes, sir. (*He returns the jacket to the USHER.*)

(*The USHER replaces the jacket on the table.*)

MYERS. From where did you get it?

INSPECTOR. I found it at the prisoner's flat some time after he was arrested, and later handed it to Mr. Clegg at the lab to test for possible bloodstains.

MYERS. Lastly, Inspector, do you produce the will of Miss French?

(*The USHER picks up the will from the table and hands it to the INSPECTOR.*)

INSPECTOR. I do, sir.

MYERS. Dated October the eighth?

INSPECTOR. Yes, sir. (*He returns the will to the USHER.*)

(*The USHER replaces the will on the table, crosses and resumes his seat.*)

MYERS. After certain bequests, the residue is left to the prisoner?

INSPECTOR. That's right, sir.

MYERS. And what is the net value of that estate?

INSPECTOR. It will be, as far as can be ascertained at the moment, about eighty-five thousand pounds.

(*MYERS resumes his seat. SIR WILFRID rises.*)

SIR WILFRID. You say that the only fingerprints you found in the room were those of Miss French herself, the prisoner Leonard Vole and Janet MacKenzie. In your experience, when a burglar breaks in does he usually leave fingerprints or does he wear gloves?

INSPECTOR. He wears gloves.

SIR WILFRID. Invariably?

INSPECTOR. Almost invariably.

SIR WILFRID. So the absence of fingerprints in a case of robbery would hardly surprise you?

INSPECTOR. No, sir.

SIR WILFRID. Now, these chisel marks on the window. Were they on the inside or the outside of the casement?

INSPECTOR. On the outside, sir.

SIR WILFRID. Isn't that consistent—and only consistent— with a breaking in from the outside?

INSPECTOR. He could have gone out of the house afterwards to have done that, sir, or he could have made those marks from the inside.

SIR WILFRID. From the inside, Inspector? Now how could he have possibly done that?

INSPECTOR. There are two windows together there. Both are casements, and with their catches adjacent. It would have been easy for anyone in the room to open one window, lean out, and force the catch of the other.

SIR WILFRID. Tell me, did you find any chisel near the premises, or at the prisoner's flat?

INSPECTOR. Yes, sir. At the prisoner's flat.

SIR WILFRID. Oh?

INSPECTOR. But it didn't fit the marks on the window.

SIR WILFRID. It was a windy night, was it not, on October fourteenth?

INSPECTOR. I really can't remember, sir. (*He refers to his notes.*)

SIR WILFRID. According to my learned friend, Janet MacKenzie said that the curtains were blowing. Perhaps you noticed that fact yourself?

INSPECTOR. Well, yes, sir, they did blow about.

SIR WILFRID. Indicating that it was a windy night. I suggest that if a burglar had forced the window from the outside and then swung it back, some of the loose glass might easily have fallen down *outside* the window, the window having been blown back violently by the wind. That is possible, is it not?

INSPECTOR. Yes, sir.

SIR WILFRID. Crimes of violence, as we all have been unhappily aware, have been much on the increase lately. You would agree to that, would you not?

INSPECTOR. It's been a little above normal, sir.

SIR WILFRID. Let us take the case that some young thugs had broken in, who meant to attack Miss French and steal; it is possible that if one of them coshed her and found that she was dead, they might give way to panic and leave without taking anything? Or they might even have been looking for money and would be afraid to touch anything in the nature of jewellery?

MYERS. (*Rising*) I submit that it is impossible for Inspector Hearne to guess at what went on in the minds of some *entirely* hypothetical young criminals who may not even exist. (*He sits.*)

SIR WILFRID. The prisoner came forward of his own accord and gave his statement quite willingly?

INSPECTOR. That is so.

SIR WILFRID. Is it the case that at all times the prisoner has protested his innocence?

INSPECTOR. Yes, sir.

SIR WILFRID. (*Indicating the knife on the table*) Inspector Hearne, will you kindly examine that knife?

(*The* USHER *rises, crosses, picks up the knife and hands it to the* INSPECTOR.)

You have seen that knife before?

INSPECTOR. I may have.

SIR WILFRID. This is the knife taken from the kitchen table in Leonard Vole's flat and which was brought to your attention by the prisoner's wife on the occasion of your first interview with her.

MYERS. (*Rising*) My lord, to save the time of the Court, may I say that we accept this knife as being a knife in the possession of Leonard Vole and shown to the Inspector by Mrs. Vole. (*He sits.*)

SIR WILFRID. That is correct, Inspector?

INSPECTOR. Yes, sir.

SIR WILFRID. It is what is known, I believe, as a French vegetable knife?

INSPECTOR. I believe so, sir.

SIR WILFRID. Just test the edge of the knife with your finger— carefully.

(*The* INSPECTOR *tests the knife edge.*)

You agree that the cutting edge and the point are razor sharp?

INSPECTOR. Yes, sir.

SIR WILFRID. And if you were cutting—say, ham—carving it, that is, and your hand slipped with this knife, it would be capable of inflicting a very nasty cut, and one which would bleed profusely?

MYERS. (*Rising*) I object. That is a matter of opinion, and medical opinion at that. (*He sits.*)

(*The* USHER *takes the knife from the* INSPECTOR, *puts it on the table, crosses and resumes his seat.*)

SIR WILFRID. I withdraw the question. I will ask you instead, Inspector, if the prisoner, when questioned by you as to the stains on the sleeve of his jacket, drew your attention to a recently healed scar on his wrist, and stated that it had been caused by a household knife when he was slicing ham?

INSPECTOR. That is what he said.

SIR WILFRID. And you were told the same thing by the prisoner's wife?

INSPECTOR. The first time. Afterwards . . .

SIR WILFRID. (*Sharply*) A simple yes or no, please. Did the prisoner's wife show you this knife, and tell you that her husband had cut his wrist with it slicing ham?

INSPECTOR. Yes, she did.

(SIR WILFRID *resumes his seat.*)

MYERS. (*Rising*) What first drew your attention to that jacket, Inspector?

INSPECTOR. The sleeve appeared to have been recently washed.

MYERS. And you're told this story about an accident with a kitchen knife?

INSPECTOR. Yes, sir.

MYERS. And your attention was drawn to a scar on the prisoner's wrist?

INSPECTOR. Yes, sir.

MYERS. Granted that the scar was made by this particular knife, there was nothing to show whether it was an accident or done deliberately?

SIR WILFRID. (*Rising*) Really, my lord, if my learned friend is going to answer his own questions, the presence of the witness seems to be superfluous. (*He sits.*)

MYERS. (*Resignedly*) I withdraw the question. Thank you, Inspector.

(*The* INSPECTOR *stands down, crosses and exits up* L. *The* POLICEMAN *closes the door behind him.*)

Dr. Wyatt.

(DR. WYATT *rises and enters the box. He carries some notes. The* USHER *rises, crosses, hands the Bible to him and holds up the oath card.*)

WYATT. I swear by Almighty God that the evidence that I shall give shall be the truth, the whole truth and nothing but the truth.

(*The* USHER *puts the Bible and oath card on the ledge of the witness box, crosses and resumes his seat.*)

MYERS. You are Dr. Wyatt?
WYATT. Yes.
MYERS. You are a police surgeon attached to the Hampstead Division?
WYATT. Yes.
MYERS. Dr. Wyatt, will you kindly tell the Jury what you know regarding the death of Miss Emily French?
WYATT. (*Reading from his notes*) At eleven p.m. on October fourteenth, I saw the dead body of the woman who subsequently proved to be Miss French. By examination of the body I was of the opinion that the death had resulted from a blow on the head, delivered from an object such as a cosh. Death would have been practically instantaneous. From the temperature of the body and other factors, I placed the time of death at not less than an hour previously and not more than, say, an hour and a half. That is to say between the hours of nine-thirty and ten p.m.
MYERS. Had Miss French struggled with her adversary at all?
WYATT. There was no evidence that she had done so. I should say, on the contrary, that she had been taken quite unprepared.

(MYERS *resumes his seat.*)

SIR WILFRID. (*Rising*) Doctor, where exactly on the head had this blow been struck? There was only one blow, was there not?
WYATT. Only one. On the left side at the asterion.
SIR WILFRID. I beg your pardon? Where?

WYATT. The asterion. The junction of the parietal, occipital and temple bones.

SIR WILFRID. Oh, yes. And in layman's language, where is that?

WYATT. Behind the left ear.

SIR WILFRID. Would that indicate that the blow had been struck by a left-handed person?

WYATT. It's difficult to say. The blow appeared to have been struck directly from behind, because the bruising ran perpendicularly. I should say it is really impossible to say whether it was delivered by a right- or left-handed man.

SIR WILFRID. We don't know yet that it was a *man*, Doctor. But will you agree, from the position of the blow, that if anything it is more likely to have been delivered by a left-handed person?

WYATT. That is possibly so. But I would prefer to say that it is uncertain.

SIR WILFRID. At the moment the blow was struck, would blood have been likely to have got on to the hand or arm that struck the blow?

WYATT. Yes, certainly.

SIR WILFRID. And only on that hand or arm?

WYATT. Probably only on that hand and arm, but it's difficult to be dogmatic.

SIR WILFRID. Quite so, Doctor Wyatt. Now, would great strength have been needed to strike such a blow?

WYATT. No. From the position of the wound no great strength would have been needed.

SIR WILFRID. It would not necessarily be a man who had struck the blow. A woman could have done so equally well?

WYATT. Certainly.

SIR WILFRID. Thank you. (*He sits.*)

MYERS. (*Rising*) Thank you, Doctor. (*To the* USHER.) Call Janet MacKenzie.

(WYATT *stands down, crosses and exits up* L. *The* POLICEMAN *opens the door. The* USHER *rises and crosses to* C.)

USHER. Janet MacKenzie.
POLICEMAN. (*Calling*) Janet MacKenzie.

(JANET MACKENZIE *enters up* L. *She is a tall, dour-looking Scotswoman. Her face is set in a grim line. Whenever she looks at* LEONARD, *she does so with loathing. The* POLICEMAN *closes the door.* JANET *crosses and enters the witness box. The* USHER *moves and stands beside the witness box.* JANET *picks up the Bible in her left hand.*)

USHER. Other hand, please. (*He holds out the oath card.*)

JANET. (*Puts the Bible into her right hand.*) I swear by Almighty God that the evidence that I shall give shall be the truth, the whole truth and nothing but the truth. (*She hands the Bible to the* USHER.)

(*The* USHER *puts the Bible and oath card on the ledge of the witness box, crosses and resumes his seat.*)

MYERS. Your name is Janet MacKenzie?

JANET. Aye—that's my name.

MYERS. You were companion housekeeper to the late Miss Emily French?

JANET. I was her housekeeper. I've no opinion of companions, poor feckless bodies, afraid to do a bit of honest domestic work.

MYERS. Quite so, quite so, I meant only that you were held in esteem and affection by Miss French, and were on friendly terms together. Not quite those of mistress and servant.

JANET. (*To the* JUDGE.) Twenty years I've been with her and looked after her. She knew me and she trusted me, and many's the time I've prevented her doing a foolish action!

JUDGE. Miss MacKenzie, would you please address your remarks to the Jury.

MYERS. What sort of a person was Miss French?

JANET. She was a warm-hearted body—too warmhearted at times, I'm thinking. A wee bit impulsive too. There were times when she'd have no sense at all. She was easily flattered, you see.

MYERS. When did you first see the prisoner, Leonard Vole?

JANET. He came to the house, I mind, at the end of August.

MYERS. How often did he come to the house?

JANET. To begin with once a week, but later it was oftener. Two and even three times he'd come. He'd sit there flattering her, telling her how young she looked and noticing any new clothes she was wearing.

MYERS. (*Rather hastily*) Quite, quite. Now will you tell the Jury in your own words, Miss MacKenzie, about the events of October the fourteenth.

JANET. It was a Friday and my night out. I was going round to see some friends of mine in Glenister Road, which is not above three minutes' walk. I left the house at half past seven. I'd promised to take my friend the pattern of a knitted cardigan that she'd admired. When I got there I found I'd left it behind, so after supper I said I'd slip back to the house at twenty-five past nine. I let myself in with my key and went upstairs to my room. As I passed the sitting-room door I heard the prisoner in there talking to Miss French.

MYERS. You were sure it was the prisoner you heard?

JANET. Aye, I know his voice well enough. With him calling so often. An agreeable voice it was, I'll not say it wasn't. Talking and laughing they were. But it was no business of mine so I went up and fetched the pattern, came down and let myself out and went back to my friend.

MYERS. Now I want these times very exact. You say that you re-entered the house at twenty-five past nine.

JANET. Aye. It was just after twenty past nine when I left Clenister Road.

MYERS. How do you know that, Miss MacKenzie?

JANET. By the clock on my friend's mantelpiece, and I compared it with my watch and the time was the same.

MYERS. You say it takes three or four minutes to walk to the house, so that you entered the house at twenty-five minutes past nine, and you were there . . .

JANET. I was there under ten minutes. It took me a few minutes to search for the pattern as I wasna' sure where I'd left it.

MYERS. And what did you do next?

JANET. I went back to my friend in Glenister Road. She was delighted with the pattern, simply delighted. I stayed there until twenty to eleven, then I said good night to them and came home. I went into the sitting-room then to see if the mistress wanted anything before she went to bed.

MYERS. What did you see?

JANET. She was there on the floor, poor body, her head beaten in. And all the drawers of the bureau out on the ground, everything tossed hither and thither, the broken vase on the floor and the curtains flying in the wind.

MYERS. What did you do?

JANET. I rang the police.

MYERS. Did you really think that a burglary had occurred?

SIR WILFRID. (*Jumping up*) Really, my lord, I must protest. (*He sits.*)

JUDGE. I will not allow that question to be answered, Mr. Myers. It should not have been put to the witness.

MYERS. Then let me ask you this, Miss MacKenzie. What did you do after you had telephoned the police?

JANET. I searched the house.

MYERS. What for?

JANET. For an intruder.

MYERS. Did you find one?

JANET. I did not. Nor any signs of disturbance save in the sitting-room.

MYERS. How much did you know about the prisoner, Leonard Vole?

JANET. I knew that he needed money.

MYERS. Did he ask Miss French for money?

JANET. He was too clever for that.

MYERS. Did he help Miss French with her business affairs—with her income tax returns, for instance?

JANET. Aye—not that there was any need of it.

MYERS. What do you mean by not any need of it?

JANET. Miss French had a good, clear head for business.

MYERS. Were you aware of what arrangements Miss French had made for the disposal of her money in the event of her death?

JANET. She'd make a will as the fancy took her. She was a rich woman and she had a lot of money to leave and no near relatives. "It must go where it can do the most good," she would say. Once it was to orphans she left it, and once to an old people's home, and another time a dispensary for cats and dogs, but it always came to the same in the end. She'd quarrel with the people and then she'd come home and tear up the will and make a new one.

MYERS. Do you know when she made her last will?

JANET. She made it on October the eighth. I heard her speaking to Mr. Stokes, the lawyer. Saying he was to come tomorrow, she was making a new will. He was there at the time—the prisoner, I mean, kind of protesting, saying, "No, no."

(LEONARD *hastily scribbles a note.*)

And the mistress said, "But I want to, my dear boy. I want to. Remember that day I was nearly run over by a bus. It might happen any time."

(LEONARD *leans over the dock and hands the note to* MAYHEW, *who passes it to* SIR WILFRID.)

MYERS. Do you know when your mistress made a will previous to that one?

JANET. In the spring it was.

MYERS. Were you aware, Miss MacKenzie, that Leonard Vole was a married man?

JANET. No, indeed. Neither was the mistress.

SIR WILFRID. (*Rising*) I object. What Miss French knew or did not know is pure conjecture on Janet MacKenzie's part. (*He sits.*)

MYERS. Let us put it this way: You formed the opinion that Miss French thought Leonard Vole a single man? Have you any facts to support that opinion?

JANET. There was the books she ordered from the library. There was the *Life of Baroness Vurdett Coutts* and one about Disraeli and his wife. Both of them about women who'd married men years younger than themselves. I knew what she was thinking.

JUDGE. I'm afraid we cannot admit that.

JANET. Why?

JUDGE. Members of the Jury, it is possible for a woman to read the life of Disraeli without contemplating marriage with a man younger than herself.

MYERS. Did Mr. Vole ever mention a wife?

JANET. Never.

MYERS. Thank you. (*He sits.*)

SIR WILFRID. (*Rises. Gently and kindly*) I think we all appreciate how very devoted to your mistress you were.

JANET. Aye—I was.

SIR WILFRID. You had great influence over her?

JANET. Aye—maybe.

SIR WILFRID. In the last will Miss French made—that is to say the one made last spring, Miss French left almost the whole of her fortune to you. Were you aware of that fact?

JANET. She told me so. "All crooks, these charities," she said. "Expenses here and expenses there and the money not going to the object you give it for. I've left it to you, Janet, and maybe you can do what you think's right and good with it."

SIR WILFRID. That was an expression of great trust on her part. In her present will, I understand, she had merely left you an annuity. The principal beneficiary is the prisoner, Leonard Vole.

JANET. It will be wicked injustice if he ever touches a penny of that money.

SIR WILFRID. Miss French, you say, had not many friends and acquaintances. Now why was that?

JANET. She didn't go out much.

SIR WILFRID. When Miss French struck up this friendship with Leonard Vole it made you very sore and angry, didn't it?

JANET. I didn't like seeing my dear lady imposed upon.

SIR WILFRID. But you have admitted that Mr. Vole did not impose upon her. Perhaps you mean that you didn't like to see someone else supplanting you as an influence on Miss French?

JANET. She leaned on him a good deal. Far more than was safe, I thought.

SIR WILFRID. Far more than you personally liked?

JANET. Of course. I've said so. But it was of her good I was thinking.

SIR WILFRID. So the prisoner had a great influence over Miss French, and she had a great affection for him?

JANET. That was what it had come to.

SIR WILFRID. So that if the prisoner had ever asked her for money, she would almost certainly have given him some, would she not?

JANET. I have not said that.

SIR WILFRID. But he never received any money from her?

JANET. That may not have been for want of trying.

SIR WILFRID. Returning to the night of October the fourteenth, you say you heard the prisoner and Miss French talking together. What did you hear him say?

JANET. I didn't hear what they actually said.

SIR WILFRID. You mean you only heard the voices—the murmur of voices?

JANET. They were laughing.

SIR WILFRID. You heard a man's voice and a woman's and they were laughing. Is that right?

JANET. Aye.

SIR WILFRID. I suggest that is exactly what you did hear. A man's voice and a woman's voice laughing. You didn't hear what was said. What makes you say that the man's voice was Leonard Vole's?

JANET. I know his voice well enough.

SIR WILFRID. The door was closed, was it not?

JANET. Aye. It was closed.

SIR WILFRID. You heard a murmur of voices through a closed door and you swear that one of the voices was that of Leonard Vole. I suggest that is mere prejudice on your part.

JANET. It was Leonard Vole.

SIR WILFRID. As I understand it you passed the door twice, once going to your room, and once going out?

JANET. That is so.

SIR WILFRID. You were no doubt in a hurry to get your pattern and return to your friend?

JANET. I was in no particular hurry. I had the whole evening.

SIR WILFRID. What I am suggesting is that on both occasions you walked quickly past that door.

JANET. I was there long enough to hear what I heard.

SIR WILFRID. Come, Miss MacKenzie, I'm sure you don't wish to suggest to the Jury that you were eavesdropping.

JANET. I was doing no such thing. I've better things to do with my time.

SIR WILFRID. Exactly. You are registered, of course, under the National Health Insurance?

JANET. That's so. Four and sixpence I have to pay out every week. It's a terrible lot of money for a working woman to pay.

SIR WILFRID. Yes, yes, many people feel that. I think, Miss MacKenzie, that you recently applied for a national hearing apparatus?

JANET. Six months ago I applied for it and not got it yet.

SIR WILFRID. So your hearing isn't very good, is that right? (*He lowers his voice.*) When I say to you, Miss Mac-Kenzie, that you could not possibly recognize a voice through a closed door, what do you answer? (*He pauses.*) Can you tell me what I said?

JANET. I can no' hear anyone if they mumble.

SIR WILFRID. In fact you didn't hear what I said, although I am only a few feet from you in an open court. Yet you say that behind a closed door with two people talking in an ordinary conversational tone, you definitely recognized the voice of Leonard Vole as you swept past that door on two occasions.

JANET. It was him, I tell you. It was him.

SIR WILFRID. What you mean is you want it to be him. You have a preconceived notion.

JANET. Who else could it have been?

SIR WILFRID. Exactly. Who else could it have been? That was the way your mind worked. Now tell me, Miss Mac-Kenzie, was Miss French sometimes lonely all by herself in the evening?

JANET. No, she was not lonely. She had books from the library.

SIR WILFRID. She listened to the wireless, perhaps?

JANET. Aye, she listened to the wireless.

SIR WILFRID. She was fond of a talk on it, perhaps, or of a good play?

JANET. Yes, she liked a good play.

SIR WILFRID. Wasn't it possible that on that evening when you returned home and passed the door, that what you really heard was the wireless switched on and a man and woman's voice, and laughter? There was a play called *Lover's Leap* on the wireless that night.

JANET. It was not the wireless.

SIR WILFRID. Oh, why not?

JANET. The wireless was away being repaired that week.

SIR WILFRID. (*Slightly taken aback.*) It must have upset you very much, Miss MacKenzie, if you really thought Miss French intended to marry the prisoner.

JANET. Naturally it would upset me. It was a *daft* thing to do.

SIR WILFRID. For one thing, *if* Miss French had married the prisoner it's quite possible, isn't it, that he might have persuaded her to dismiss you?

JANET. She'd never have done that, after all these years.

SIR WILFRID. But you never know what anyone will do, do you? Not if they're strongly influenced by anyone.

JANET. He would have used his influence, oh yes, he would have done his best to make her get rid of me.

SIR WILFRID. I see. You felt the prisoner was a very real menace to your present way of life at the time.

JANET. He'd have changed everything.

SIR WILFRID. Yes, very upsetting. No wonder you feel so bitterly against the prisoner. (*He sits.*)

MYERS. (*Rising*) My learned friend has been at great pains to extract from you an admission of vindictiveness towards the prisoner . . .

SIR WILFRID. (*Without rising, and audibly for the benefit of the Jury*) A painless extraction—quite painless.

MYERS. (*Ignoring him*) Did you really believe your mistress might have married the prisoner?

JANET. Indeed I did. I've just said so.

MYERS. Yes, indeed you have. In your view had the prisoner such an influence over Miss French that he could have persuaded her to dismiss you?

JANET. I'd like to have seen him try. He'd not have succeeded.

MYERS. Had the prisoner ever shown any dislike of you in any way?

JANET. No, he had his manners.

MYERS. Just one more question. You say you recognized Leonard Vole's voice through that closed door. Will you tell the jury how you knew it was his?

JANET. You know a person's voice without hearing exactly what they are saying.

MYERS. Thank you, Miss MacKenzie.

JANET. (*To the* JUDGE) Good morning. (*She stands down and crosses to the door up* L.)

MYERS. Call Thomas Clegg.

(*The* POLICEMAN *opens the door.*)

USHER. (*Rising and crossing to* C.) Thomas Clegg.

POLICEMAN. (*Calling*) Thomas Clegg.

(JANET *exits.* THOMAS CLEGG *enters up* L. *He carries a notebook. The* POLICEMAN *closes the door. The* USHER *moves to the witness box and picks up the Bible and oath card.* CLEGG *crosses and enters the witness box and takes the Bible from the* USHER.)

CLEGG. (*Saying the oath by heart*) I swear by Almighty God that the evidence that I shall give shall be the truth, the whole truth and nothing but the truth. (*He puts the Bible on the ledge of the witness box.*)

(*The* USHER *puts the oath card on the ledge of the witness box, crosses and resumes his seat.*)

MYERS. You are Thomas Clegg?

CLEGG. Yes, sir.

MYERS. You are an assistant in the forensic laboratory at New Scotland Yard?

CLEGG. I am.

MYERS. (*Indicating the jacket on the table*) Do you recognize that coat?

(*The* USHER *rises, crosses to the table and picks up the jacket.*)

CLEGG. Yes. It was given to me by Inspector Hearne and tested by me for traces of blood.

(*The* USHER *hands the coat up to* CLEGG, *who brushes it aside. The* USHER *replaces the jacket on the table, crosses and resumes his seat.*)

MYERS. Will you tell me your findings?

CLEGG. The coat sleeves had been washed, though not properly pressed afterwards, but by certain tests I am able to state that there are traces of blood on the cuffs.

MYERS. Is this blood of a special group or type?

CLEGG. Yes. (*He refers to his notebook.*) It is of the type O.

MYERS. Were you also given a sample of blood to test?

CLEGG. I was given a sample labelled "Blood of Miss Emily French." The blood group was of the same type—O.

(MYERS RESUMES *his seat.*)

SIR WILFRID. (*Rising*) You say there were traces of blood on both cuffs?

CLEGG. That is right.

SIR WILFRID. I suggest that there were traces of blood on only one cuff—the left one.

CLEGG. (*Looking at his notebook*) Yes. I am sorry, I made a mistake. It was only the left cuff.

SIR WILFRID. And it was only the left sleeve that had been washed?

CLEGG. Yes, that is so.

SIR WILFRID. Are you aware that the prisoner had told the police that he had cut his wrist, and that that blood was on the cuff of this coat?

CLEGG. So I understand.

(SIR WILFRID *takes a certificate from his* ASSISTANT.)

SIR WILFRID. I have here a certificate stating that Leonard Vole
is a blood donor at the North London Hospital, and that
his blood group is O. That is the same blood group, is
it not?

CLEGG. Yes.

SIR WILFRID. So the blood might equally well have come from
a cut on the prisoner's wrist?

CLEGG. That is so.

(SIR WILFRID *resumes his seat.*)

MYERS. (*Rising*) Blood group O is a very common one, is it
not?

CLEGG. O? Oh, yes. At least forty-two per cent of people are
in blood group O.

MYERS. Call Romaine Heilger.

(CLEGG *stands down and crosses to the door up* L.)

USHER. (*Rising and crossing to* C.) Romaine Heilger.

POLICEMAN. (*Opens the door. Calling*) Romaine Heilger.

(CLEGG *exits.* ROMAINE *enters up* L. *There is a general buzz
of conversation in the Court as she crosses to the witness
box. The* POLICEMAN *closes the door. The* USHER *moves
to the witness box and picks up the Bible and oath
card.*)

USHER. Silence! (*He hands the Bible to* ROMAINE *and holds
up the card.*)

ROMAINE. I swear by Almighty God that the evidence that
I shall give shall be the truth, the whole truth and nothing but the truth.

(*The* USHER *replaces the Bible and oath card on the ledge
of the witness box, crosses and resumes his seat.*)

MYERS. Your name is Romaine Heilger?

ROMAINE. Yes.

MYERS. You have been living as the wife of the prisoner,
Leonard Vole?

ROMAINE. Yes.

MYERS. Are you actually his wife?

ROMAINE. I went through a form of marriage with him in
Berlin. My former husband is still alive, so the marriage
is not . . . (*She breaks off.*)

MYERS. Not valid.

SIR WILFRID. (*Rising*) My lord, I have the most serious objection to this witness giving evidence at all. We have
the undeniable fact of marriage between this witness
and the prisoner, and no proof whatsoever of this so-
called previous marriage.

MYERS. If my friend had not abandoned his customary
patience, and had waited for one more question, your
lordship would have been spared this further interruption.

(SIR WILFRID *resumes his seat.*)

(*He picks up a document.*) Mrs. Heilger, is this a certificate of a marriage between yourself and Otto Gerthe
Heilger on the eighteenth of April, nineteen forty-six,
in Leipzig?

(*The* USHER *rises, takes the certificate from* MYERS *and takes
it to* ROMAINE.)

ROMAINE. It is.

JUDGE. I should like to see that certificate.

(*The* USHER *gives the certificate to the* CLERK, *who hands
it to the* JUDGE.)

It will be exhibit number four, I think.

MYERS. I believe it will be, my lord.

JUDGE. (*After examining the document.*) I think, Sir Wilfrid, this witness is competent to give evidence. (*He
hands the certificate to the* CLERK.)

(*The* CLERK *gives the certificate to the* USHER, *who hands it
to* MAYHEW. *The* USHER *then crosses and resumes his
seat.* MAYHEW *shows the certificate to* SIR WILFRID.)

MYERS. In any event, Mrs. Heilger, are you willing to give
evidence against the man you have been calling your
husband?

ROMAINE. I'm quite willing.

(LEONARD *rises, followed by the* WARDER.)

LEONARD. Romaine! What are you doing here?—what are
you saying?

JUDGE. I must have silence. As your counsel will tell you; Vole, you will very shortly have an opportunity of speaking in your own defence.

(LEONARD *and the* WARDER *resume their seats.*)

MYERS. (*To* ROMAINE.) Will you tell me in your own words what happened on the evening of October the fourteenth.

ROMAINE. I was at home all the evening.

MYERS. And Leonard Vole?

ROMAINE. Leonard went out at half past seven.

MYERS. When did he return?

ROMAINE. At ten minutes past ten.

(LEONARD *rises, followed by the* WARDER.)

LEONARD. That's not true. You know it's not true. It was about twenty-five past nine when I came home.

(MAYHEW *rises, turns to* LEONARD *and whispers to him to be quiet.*)

Who's been making you say this? I don't understand. (*He shrinks back and puts his hands to his face. Half whispering.*) I—I don't understand. (*He resumes his seat.*)

(MAYHEW *and the* WARDER *sit.*)

MYERS. Leonard Vole returned, you say, at ten minutes past ten? And what happened next?

ROMAINE. He was breathing hard, very excited. He threw off his coat and examined the sleeves. Then he told me to wash the cuffs. They had blood on them.

MYERS. Did he speak about the blood?

ROMAINE. He said, "Dammit, there's blood on them."

MYERS. What did you say?

ROMAINE. I said, "What have you done?"

MYERS. What did the prisoner say to that?

ROMAINE. He said, "I've killed her."

LEONARD. (*Rising; frenzied.*) It's not true, I tell you. It's not true.

(*The* WARDER *rises and restrains* LEONARD.)

JUDGE. Please control yourself.

LEONARD. Not a word of this is true. (*He resumes his seat.*)

(*The* WARDER *remains standing.*)

JUDGE. (*To* ROMAINE) You know what you're saying, Mrs. Heilger?

ROMAINE. I am to speak the truth, am I not?

MYERS. The prisoner said, "I have killed her." Did you know to whom he referred?

ROMAINE. Yes, I knew. It was the old woman he had been going to see so often.

MYERS. What happened next?

ROMAINE. He told me that I was to say he had been at home with me all that evening, especially he said I was to say he was at home at half past nine. I said to him, "Do the police know you've killed her?" And he said, "No, they will think it's a burglary. But anyway, remember I was at home with you at half past nine."

MYERS. And you were subsequently interrogated by the police?

ROMAINE. Yes.

MYERS. Did they ask you if Leonard Vole was at home with you at half past nine?

ROMAINE. Yes.

MYERS. What did you answer to that?

ROMAINE. I said that he was.

MYERS. But you have changed your story now. Why?

ROMAINE. (*With sudden passion.*) Because it is murder. I cannot go on lying to save him. I am grateful to him, yes. He married me and brought me to this country. What he has asked me to do always I have done it because I was grateful.

MYERS. Because you loved him?

ROMAINE. No, I never loved him.

LEONARD. Romaine!

ROMAINE. I never loved him.

MYERS. You were grateful to the prisoner. He brought you to this country. He asked you to give him an alibi and at first you consented, but later you felt that what he had asked you to do was wrong?

ROMAINE. Yes, that is it exactly.

MYERS. Why did you feel it was wrong?

ROMAINE. When it is murder. I cannot come into Court

and lie and say that he was there with me at the time
it was done. I cannot do it. I cannot *do* it.

MYERS. So what did you do?

ROMAINE. I did not know what to do. I do not know your
country and I am afraid of the police. So I write a
letter to my ambassador, and I say that I do not wish to
tell any more lies. I wish to speak the truth.

MYERS. That *is* the truth—that Leonard Vole returned that
night at ten minutes past ten. That he had blood on the
sleeves of his coat, that he said to you, "I have killed
her." That is the truth before God?

ROMAINE. That is the truth.

(MYERS *resumes his seat.*)

SIR WILFRID. (*Rising*) When the prisoner went through this
form of marriage with you, was he aware that your first
husband was still alive?

ROMAINE. No.

SIR WILFRID. He acted in good faith?

ROMAINE. Yes.

SIR WILFRID. And you were very grateful to him?

ROMAINE. I was grateful to him, yes.

SIR WILFRID. You've shown your gratitude by coming here
and testifying against him.

ROMAINE. I have to speak the truth.

SIR WILFRID. (*Savagely.*) Is it the truth?

ROMAINE. Yes.

SIR WILFRID. I suggest to you that on the night of October
the fourteenth Leonard Vole was at home with you at
nine-thirty, the time that the murder was committed. I
suggest to you that this whole story of yours is a wicked
fabrication, that you have for some reason a grudge
against the prisoner, and that this is your way of expressing it.

ROMAINE. No.

SIR WILFRID. You realize that you are on oath?

ROMAINE. Yes.

SIR WILFRID. I warn you, Mrs. Heilger, that if you care nothing for the prisoner, be careful on your own account.
The penalty for perjury is heavy.

MYERS. (*Rising and interposing*) Really, my lord. I don't
know whether these theatrical outbursts are for the
benefit of the Jury, but I do most respectfully submit

that there is nothing to suggest that this witness has spoken anything but the truth.

JUDGE. Mr. Myers. This is a capital charge, and within the bounds of reason I would like the defence to have every latitude. Yes, Sir Wilfrid.

(MYERS *resumes his seat.*)

SIR WILFRID. Now then. You have said—that there was blood on both cuffs?

ROMAINE. Yes.

SIR WILFRID. *Both* cuffs?

ROMAINE. I have told you, that is what Leonard said.

SIR WILFRID. No, Mrs. Heilger, you said, "He told me to wash the cuffs. They had blood on them."

JUDGE. That is precisely my note, Sir Wilfrid.

SIR WILFRID. Thank you, my lord. (*To* ROMAINE.) What you were saying is that you had washed both cuffs.

MYERS. (*Rising*) It is my friend's turn to be inaccurate now, my lord. Nowhere has this witness said she washed both cuffs, or indeed that she washed even one. (*He sits.*)

SIR WILFRID. My friend is right. Well, Mrs. Heilger, did you wash the sleeves?

ROMAINE. I remember now. It was only one sleeve that I washed.

SIR WILFRID. Thank you. Perhaps your memory as to other parts of your story is equally untrustworthy. I think your original story to the police was that the blood on the jacket came from a cut caused while carving ham?

ROMAINE. I said so, yes. But it was not true.

SIR WILFRID. Why did you lie?

ROMAINE. I said what Leonard told me to say.

SIR WILFRID. Even going so far as to produce the actual knife with which he was cutting the ham?

ROMAINE. When Leonard found he had blood on him, he cut himself to make it seem the blood was his.

LEONARD. (*Rising*) I never did.

SIR WILFRID. (*Silencing* LEONARD) Please, please.

(LEONARD *resumes his seat.*)

(*To* ROMAINE.) So you admit that your original story to the police was all lies? You seem to be a very good liar.

ROMAINE. Leonard told me what to say.

SIR WILFRID. The question is whether you were lying then
or whether you are lying *now*. If you were really appalled
at murder having been committed, you could have told
the truth to the police when they first questioned you.

ROMAINE. I was afraid of Leonard.

SIR WILFRID. (*Gesturing towards the woeful figure of* LEON-
ARD) You were afraid of Leonard Vole—afraid of the
man whose heart and spirit you've just broken. I think
the Jury will know which of you to believe. (*He sits.*)

MYERS. (*Rising*) Romaine Heilger. I ask you once more, is
the evidence you have given the truth, the whole truth
and nothing but the truth?

ROMAINE. It is.

MYERS. My lord, that is the case for the prosecution. (*He
sits.*)

(ROMAINE *stands down and crosses to the door up* L. *The*
POLICEMAN *opens the door.*)

LEONARD. (*As* ROMAINE *passes him.*) Romaine!
USHER. (*Rising*) Silence!

(ROMAINE *exits up* L. *The* POLICEMAN *closes the door. The*
USHER *resumes his seat.*)

JUDGE. Sir Wilfrid.

SIR WILFRID. (*Rising*) My lord, members of the Jury, I will
not submit to you, as I might, that there is no case for
the prisoner to answer. There *is* a case. A case of very
strong circumstantial evidence. You have heard the
police and other expert witnesses. They have given fair,
impartial evidence as is their duty. Against them I have
nothing to say. On the other hand, you have heard
Janet MacKenzie and the woman who calls herself
Romaine Vole. Can you believe that their testimony is
not warped? Janet MacKenzie—cut out of her rich mistress's will because her position was usurped, quite un-
wittingly, by this unfortunate boy. (*He pauses.*) Romaine Vole—Heilger—whatever she calls herself, who
trapped him into marriage, whilst concealing from him
the fact that she was married already. That woman
owes him more than she can ever repay. She used him
to save her from political persecution. But she admits no

love for him. He has served his purpose. I will ask you to be very careful how you believe her testimony, the testimony of a woman who, for all we know, has been brought up to believe the pernicious doctrine that lying is a weapon to be used to serve one's own ends. Members of the Jury, I call the prisoner. Leonard Vole.

(*The* USHER *rises and crosses to the witness box.* LEONARD *rises, crosses and goes into the witness box. The* WARDER *follows* LEONARD *and stands behind him. The* USHER *picks up the Bible, hands it to* LEONARD *and holds up the oath card.*)

LEONARD. I swear by Almighty God that the evidence that I shall give shall be the truth, the whole truth and nothing but the truth. (*He puts the Bible on the ledge of the witness box.*)

(*The* USHER *replaces the oath card on the ledge of the witness box and sits* R. *of the table.*)

SIR WILFRID. Now, Mr. Vole, we have heard of your friendship with Miss Emily French. Now I want you to tell us how often you visited her.

LEONARD. Frequently.

SIR WILFRID. Why was that?

LEONARD. Well, she was awfully nice to me and I got fond of her. She was like my Aunt Betsy.

SIR WILFRID. That was an aunt who brought you up?

LEONARD. Yes. She was a dear. Miss French reminded me of her.

SIR WILFRID. You've heard Janet MacKenzie say Miss French thought you were a single man, and that there was some question of marrying you. Is there any truth in this?

LEONARD. Of course not. It's an absurd idea.

SIR WILFRID. Miss French knew that you were married?

LEONARD. Yes.

SIR WILFRID. So there was no question of marriage between you?

LEONARD. Of course not. I've told you, she treated me as though she was an indulgent aunt. Almost like a mother.

SIR WILFRID. And in return you did everything for her that you could.

LEONARD. (*Simply.*) I was very fond of her.

SIR WILFRID. Will you tell the Jury in your own words exactly what happened on the night of October the fourteenth?

LEONARD. Well, I'd come across a kind of a cat brush—a new thing in that line—and I thought it would please her. So I took it along that evening. I'd nothing else to do.

SIR WILFRID. What time was that?

LEONARD. Just before eight I got there. I gave her the cat brush. She was pleased. We tried it out on one of the cats and it was a success. Then we played a game of Double Demon—Miss French was very fond of Double Demon—and after that I left.

SIR WILFRID. Yes, but did you not . . .

JUDGE. Sir Wilfrid, I don't understand this piece of evidence at all. What is a cat brush?

LEONARD. It's a brush for brushing cats.

JUDGE. Oh!

LEONARD. A sort of brush and comb combined. Miss French kept cats—eight of them she had, and the house smelt a bit . . .

SIR WILFRID. Yes, yes.

LEONARD. I thought the brush might be useful.

SIR WILFRID. Did you see Janet MacKenzie?

LEONARD. No. Miss French let me in herself.

SIR WILFRID. Did you know Janet MacKenzie was out?

LEONARD. Well, I didn't think about it.

SIR WILFRID. At what time did you leave?

LEONARD. Just before nine. I walked home.

SIR WILFRID. How long did that take you?

LEONARD. Oh, I should say about twenty minutes to half an hour.

SIR WILFRID. So that you reached home . . . ?

LEONARD. I reached home at twenty-five minutes past nine.

SIR WILFRID. And your wife—I will call her your wife—was at home then?

LEONARD. Yes, of course she was. I—I think she must have gone mad. I . . .

SIR WILFRID. Never mind that now. Just go on with your story. Did you wash your coat when you got in?

LEONARD. No, of course I didn't.

SIR WILFRID. Who did wash your coat?

LEONARD. Romaine did, the next morning. She said it had got blood on it from a cut on my wrist.

SIR WILFRID. A cut on your wrist?

LEONARD. Yes. Here. (*He holds out his arm and shows his wrist.*) You can still see the mark.

SIR WILFRID. When was the first you heard of the murder?

LEONARD. I read about it in the evening paper the next day.

SIR WILFRID. And what did you feel?

LEONARD. I was stunned. I could hardly believe it. I was very upset too. The papers said it was a burglary. I never dreamed of anything else.

SIR WILFRID. And what happened next?

LEONARD. I read that the police were anxious to interview me, so of course I went along to the police station.

SIR WILFRID. You went along to the police station and made a statement?

LEONARD. Yes.

SIR WILFRID. You were not nervous? Reluctant to do so?

LEONARD. No, of course not. I wanted to help in any way possible.

SIR WILFRID. Did you ever receive any money from Miss French?

LEONARD. No.

SIR WILFRID. Were you aware that she had made a will in your favour?

LEONARD. She said she was ringing up her lawyers and going to make a new will. I asked her if she often made new wills and she said, "From time to time."

SIR WILFRID. Did you know what the terms of this new will were to be?

LEONARD. I swear I didn't.

SIR WILFRID. Had she ever suggested to you that she might leave you anything at all in her will?

LEONARD. No.

SIR WILFRID. You have heard the evidence that your wife— or the woman whom you considered as your wife—has given in Court.

LEONARD. Yes—I heard. I can't understand—I . . .

SIR WILFRID. (Checking him) I realize, Mr. Vole, that you are very upset, but I want to ask you to put aside all emotion and to answer the question plainly and simply. Was what that witness said true or untrue?

LEONARD. No, of course it wasn't true.

SIR WILFRID. You arrived home at nine-twenty-five that night, and had supper with your wife?

LEONARD. Yes.

SIR WILFRID. Did you go out again?

LEONARD. No.

SIR WILFRID. Are you right or left handed?

LEONARD. Right handed.

SIR WILFRID. I'm going to ask you just one more question, Mr. Vole. *Did you kill* Emily French?

LEONARD. No, I did not.

(SIR WILFRID *sits.*)

MYERS. (*Rising*) Have you ever tried to get money out of anybody?

LEONARD. No.

MYERS. How soon in your acquaintance with Miss French did you learn that she was a very wealthy woman?

LEONARD. Well, I didn't know she *was* rich when I first went to see her.

MYERS. But, having gained that knowledge, you decided to cultivate her acquaintance further?

LEONARD. I suppose that's what it looks like. But I really liked her, you know. Money had nothing to do with it.

MYERS. You would have continued to visit her, no matter how poor she'd been?

LEONARD. Yes, I would.

MYERS. You yourself are in poor circumstances?

LEONARD. You know I am.

MYERS. Kindly answer the question, yes or no.

JUDGE. You must answer the question, yes or no.

LEONARD. Yes.

MYERS. What salary do you earn?

LEONARD. Well, as a matter of fact I haven't got a job at the moment. Haven't had one for some time.

MYERS. You were recently discharged from your position?

LEONARD. No, I wasn't—I quit.

MYERS. At the time of your arrest how much money had you in the bank?

LEONARD. Well, actually only a few pounds. I was expecting some money in, in a week or two.

MYERS. How much ?

LEONARD. Not very much.

MYERS. I put it to you, you were pretty desperate for money?

LEONARD. Not desperate. I—well, I felt a bit worried.

MYERS. You were worried about money, you met a wealthy woman and you courted her acquaintance assiduously.

LEONARD. You make it sound all twisted. I tell you I liked her.

MYERS. We have heard that Miss French used to consult you on her income tax returns.

LEONARD. Yes, she did. You know what those forms are. You can't make head or tail of them—or she couldn't.

MYERS. Janet MacKenzie has told us that Miss French was a very good business woman, well able to deal with her own affairs.

LEONARD. Well, that's not what she said to me. She said those forms worried her terribly.

MYERS. In filling up her income tax forms for her you no doubt learned the exact amount of her income?

LEONARD. No.

MYERS. No?

LEONARD. Well—I mean naturally, yes.

MYERS. Yes, very convenient. How was it, Mr. Vole, that you never took your wife to see Miss French?

LEONARD. I don't know. It just didn't seem to crop up.

MYERS. You say Miss French knew you were married?

LEONARD. Yes.

MYERS. Yet she never asked you to bring your wife with you to the house?

LEONARD. No.

MYERS. Why not?

LEONARD. Oh, I don't know. She didn't like women, I don't think.

MYERS. She preferred, shall we say, personable young men? And you didn't insist on bringing your wife?

LEONARD. No, of course I didn't. You see, she knew my wife was a foreigner and she—oh, I don't know, she seemed to think we didn't get on.

MYERS. That was the impression you gave her?

LEONARD. No, I didn't. She—well, I think it was wishful thinking on her part.

MYERS. You mean she was infatuated with you?

LEONARD. No, she wasn't infatuated, but she, oh, it's like mothers are sometimes with a son.

MYERS. How?

LEONARD. They don't want him to like a girl or get engaged or anything of that kind.

MYERS. You hoped, didn't you, for some monetary advantage from your friendship with Miss French?

LEONARD. Not in the way you mean.

MYERS. Not in the way I mean? You seem to know what I mean better than I know myself. In what way then did you hope for monetary advantage? (He pauses.) I repeat, in what way did you hope for monetary advantage?

LEONARD. You see, there's a thing I've invented. A kind of windscreen wiper that works in snow. I was looking for someone to finance that and I thought perhaps Miss French would. But that wasn't the only reason I went to see her. I tell you I liked her.

MYERS. Yes, yes, we've heard that very often, haven't we—how much you liked her.

LEONARD. (*Sulkily.*) Well, it's true.

MYERS. I believe, Mr. Vole, that about a week before Miss French's death, you were making enquiries of a travel agency for particulars of foreign cruises.

LEONARD. Supposing I did—it isn't a crime, is it?

MYERS. Not at all. Many people go for cruises *when they can pay for it*. But you couldn't pay for it, could you, Mr. Vole?

LEONARD. I was hard up. I told you so.

MYERS. And yet you came into this particular travel agency—with a blonde—a strawberry blonde—I understand—and . . .

JUDGE. A strawberry blonde, Mr. Myers?

MYERS. A term for a lady with reddish fair hair, my lord.

JUDGE. I thought I knew all about blondes, but a strawberry blonde . . . Go on, Mr. Myers.

MYERS. (*To* LEONARD) Well?

LEONARD. My wife isn't a blonde and it was only a bit of fun, anyway.

MYERS. You admit that you asked for particulars, not of cheap trips, but of the most expensive and luxurious cruises. How did you expect to pay for such a thing?

LEONARD. I didn't.

MYERS. I suggest that you knew that in a week's time you would have inherited a large sum of money from a trusting elderly lady.

LEONARD. I didn't know anything of the kind. I just was feeling fed up—and there were the posters in the window—palm trees and coconuts and blue seas, and I went in and asked. The clerk gave me a sort of supercilious look—I *was* a bit shabby—but it riled me. And so I put on a bit of an act—(*He suddenly grins as though enjoying remembrance of the scene.*) and began asking for the swankiest tours there were—all *de luxe* and a cabin on the boat deck.

MYERS. You really expect the Jury to believe that?

LEONARD. I don't expect anyone to believe anything. But

that's the way it was. It was make-believe and childish
if you like—but it was fun and I enjoyed it. (*He looks
suddenly pathetic.*) I wasn't thinking of killing anybody
or of inheriting money.

MYERS. So it was a remarkable coincidence that Miss French
should be killed, leaving you her heir, only a few days
later.

LEONARD. I've told you—I didn't kill her.

MYERS. Your story is that on the night of the fourteenth, you
left Miss French's house at four minutes to nine, that
you walked home and you arrived there at twenty-five
minutes past nine, and stayed there the rest of the evening.

LEONARD. Yes.

MYERS. You have heard the woman Romaine Heilger rebut
that story in Court. You have heard her say that you
came in not at *twenty-five minutes* past nine but at *ten
minutes past ten.*

LEONARD. It's not true!

MYERS. That your clothes were bloodstained, that you
definitely admitted to her that you had killed Miss
French.

LEONARD. It's not true, I tell you. Not one word of it is true.

MYERS. Can you suggest any reason why this young woman,
who has been passing as your wife, should deliberately
give evidence she has given if it were not true?

LEONARD. No, I can't. That's the awful thing. There's no
reason at all. I think she must have gone mad.

MYERS. You think she must have gone mad? She seemed
extremely sane, and self-possessed. But insanity is the
only reason you can suggest.

LEONARD. I don't understand it. Ah, God, what's happened—
what's changed her?

MYERS. Very effective, I'm sure. But in this Court we deal
with facts. And the fact is, Mr. Vole, that we have only
your word for it that you left Emily French's house at
the time you say you did, and that you arrived home at
five and twenty minutes past nine, and that you did not
go out again.

LEONARD. (*Wildly*) Someone must have seen me—in the
street—or going into the house.

MYERS. One would certainly think so—but the only person
who did see you come home that night says it was at ten

minutes past ten. And that person says that you had blood on your clothes.

LEONARD. I cut my wrist.

MYERS. A very easy thing to do in case any questions should arise.

LEONARD. (*Breaking down*) You twist everything. You twist everything I say. You make me sound like a different kind of person from what I am.

MYERS. You cut your wrist deliberately.

LEONARD. No, I didn't. I didn't do anything, but you make it all sound as though I did. I can hear it myself.

MYERS. You came home at ten past ten.

LEONARD. No, I didn't. You've *got* to believe me. You've got to *believe* me.

MYERS. You killed Emily French.

LEONARD. I didn't do it.

(*The* LIGHTS *fade quickly, leaving two spots on* LEONARD *and* MYERS. *These fade too as he finishes speaking and the Curtain falls.*)

I didn't kill her. I've never killed anybody. Oh God! It's a nightmare. It's some awful, evil dream.

CURTAIN

Act Three

Scene I

SCENE: *The Chambers of Sir Wilfrid Robarts, Q.C. The same evening.*

When the Curtain rises, the stage is empty and in darkness. The window curtains are open. GRETA *enters immediately and holds the door open.* MAYHEW *and* SIR WILFRID *enter.* MAYHEW *carries his brief-case.*

GRETA. Good evening, Sir Wilfrid. It's a nasty night, sir. (GRETA *exits, closing the door behind her.*)

SIR WILFRID. Damned fog! (*He switches on the wall-brackets by the switch below the door and crosses to the window.*)

MAYHEW. It's a beast of an evening. (*He removes his hat and overcoat and hangs them on the pegs up* L.)

SIR WILFRID. (*Closing the window curtains*) Is there no justice? We come out of a stuffy Court Room gasping for fresh air, and what do we find? (*He switches on the desk lamp.*) Fog!

MAYHEW. It's not as thick as the fog we're in over Mrs. Heilger's antics. (*He crosses to the desk and puts his case on the up* L. *corner.*)

SIR WILFRID. That damned woman. From the very first moment I clapped eyes on her, I scented trouble. I knew she was up to something. A thoroughly vindictive piece of goods and much too deep for that simple young fool in the dock. But what's *her* game, John? What's she up to? Tell me that. (*He crosses below the desk to* L.)

MAYHEW. Presumably, it would seem, to get young Leonard Vole convicted of murder.

SIR WILFRID. (*Crossing down* R.) But why? Look what's he's done for her.

MAYHEW. He's probably done too much for her.

SIR WILFRID. (*Moving up* R. *of the desk*) And she despises him for it. That's likely enough. Ungrateful beasts, women. But why be vindictive? After all, if she was bored with him, all she had to do was walk out. (*He crosses above the desk to* L.) There doesn't seem to be any financial reason for her to remain with him.

GRETA. (*Enters and crosses to the desk. She carries a tray with two cups of tea.*) I've brought you your tea, Sir Wilfrid, and a cup for Mr. Mayhew, too. (*She puts one cup on each side of the desk.*)

SIR WILFRID. (*Sitting* L. *of the fireplace*) Tea? Strong drink is what we need.

GRETA. Oh, you know you like your tea really, sir. How did it go today?

SIR WILFRID. Badly.

(MAYHEW *sits* L. *of the desk.*)

GRETA. (*Crossing to* SIR WILFRID) Oh, no, sir. Oh, I do hope not. Because he didn't do it. I'm sure he didn't do it. (*She crosses to the door.*)

SIR WILFRID. You're still sure he didn't do it? (*He looks thoughtfully at her.*) Now why's that?

GRETA. (*Confidently*) Because he's not the sort. He's *nice*, if you know what I mean—ever so nice. He'd never go coshing an old lady on the head. But you'll get him off, won't you, sir?

SIR WILFRID. I'll—get—him—off.

(GRETA *exits.*)

(*He rises. Almost to himself.*) God knows how. Only one woman on the jury—pity—evidently the women like him—can't think why—he's not particularly— (*He crosses to* R. *of the desk.*) good looking. Perhaps he's got something that arouses the maternal instinct. Women want to mother him.

MAYHEW. Whereas Mrs. Heilger—is *not* the maternal type.

SIR WILFRID. (*Picking up his tea and crossing with it to* L.) No, she's the passionate sort. Hot blooded behind that cool self-control. The kind that would knife a man if he

double-crossed her. God, how I'd like to break her
down. Show up her lies. Show *her* up for what she is.

MAYHEW. (*Rising and taking his pipe from his pocket*)
Forgive me, Wilfrid, but aren't you letting this case
become a personal duel between you and her? (*He
moves to the fireplace, takes a pipe cleaner from the
jar on the mantelpiece and cleans his pipe.*)

SIR WILFRID. Am I? Perhaps I am. But she's an evil woman,
John. I'm convinced of that. And a young man's life
depends on the outcome of that duel.

MAYHEW. (*Thoughtfully*) I don't think the Jury liked her.

SIR WILFRID. No, you're right there, John. I don't think they
did. To begin with, she's a foreigner, and they distrust
foreigners. Then she's not married to the fellow—she's
more or less admitting to committing bigamy.

(MAYHEW *tosses the pipe cleaner into the fireplace, then
crosses to* L. *of the desk.*)

None of that goes down well. And at the end of it all,
she's not sticking to her man when he's down. We
don't like that in this country.

MAYHEW. That's all to the good.

SIR WILFRID. (*Crossing above the desk to* R. *of it*) Yes, but
it isn't enough. There's no corroboration of his statements whatsoever. (*He puts his tea on the desk.*)

(MAYHEW *crosses to* L.)

He admits being with Miss French that evening, his
fingerprints are all over the place, we haven't managed
to find anybody who saw him on the way home, and
there's the altogether damning matter of the will. (*He
stands above the desk.*) That travel-agency business
doesn't help. The woman makes a will in his favour
and immediately he goes enquiring about luxury cruises.
Couldn't be more unfortunate.

MAYHEW. (*Moving to the fireplace*) I agree. And his explanation was hardly convincing.

SIR WILFRID. (*With a sudden complete change of manner
and becoming very human*) And yet, you know, John,
my wife does it.

MAYHEW. Does what?

SIR WILFRID. (*Smiling indulgently.*) Gets travel agencies to
make out itineraries for extensive foreign tours. For

both of us. (*He takes the tobacco jar from the mantelpiece and puts it on the desk.*)

MAYHEW. Thank you, Wilfrid. (*He sits L. of the desk and fills his pipe.*)

SIR WILFRID. She'll work it all out to the last detail and bemoan the fact that the boat misses a connection at Bermuda. (*He moves to R. of the desk.*) She'll say to me that we could save time by flying but that we wouldn't see anything of the country, and (*He sits R. of the desk.*) what do I think? And I say: "It's all the same to me, my dear. Arrange it as you like." We both know that it's a kind of game, and we'll end up with the same old thing—staying at home.

MAYHEW. Ah, now with *my* wife, it's houses.

SIR WILFRID. Houses?

MAYHEW. Orders to view. Sometimes I think that there's hardly a house in England that's ever been up for sale that my wife hasn't been over. She plans how to apportion the rooms, and works out any structural alterations that will be necessary. She even plans the curtains and the covers and the general colour scheme. (*He rises, puts the tobacco jar on the mantelpiece and feels in his pocket for a match.*)

(SIR WILFRID *and* MAYHEW *look at each other and smile indulgently.*)

SIR WILFRED. H'm—well . . . (*He becomes the Q.C. again.*) The fantasies of our wives aren't evidence, worse luck. But it helps one to understand why young Vole went asking for cruise literature.

MAYHEW. Pipe dreams.

SIR WILFRID. (*Taking a matchbox from the desk drawer*) There you are, John. (*He puts the box on the desk.*)

MAYHEW. (*Crossing to L. of the desk and picking up the matchbox*) Thank you, Wilfrid.

SIR WILFRID. I think we've had a certain amount of luck with Janet MacKenzie.

MAYHEW. Bias, you mean?

SIR WILFRID. That's right. Overdoing her prejudice.

MAYHEW. (*Sitting L. of the desk*) That was a very telling point of yours about her deafness.

SIR WILFRID. Yes, yes, we got her there. But she got her own back over the wireless.

(MAYHEW *finds that the matchbox is empty, throws it in the waste-paper basket and puts his pipe in his pocket.*)

Not smoking, John?

MAYHEW. No, not just now.

SIR WILFRID. John, what really happened that night? Was it robbery with violence after all? The police have to admit that it might have been.

MAYHEW. But they don't really think so and they don't often make a mistake. That inspector is quite convinced that it *was* an inside job—that that window was tampered with from the inside.

SIR WILFRID. (*Rising and crossing below the desk to* L.) Well, he may be wrong.

MAYHEW. I wonder.

SIR WILFRID. But if so who was the man Janet MacKenzie heard talking to Miss French at nine-thirty? Seems to me there are two answers to that.

MAYHEW. The answers being . . . ?

SIR WILFRID. First that she made the whole thing up, when she saw that the police weren't satisfied about its being a burglary.

MAYHEW. (*Shocked*) Surely she wouldn't do a thing like that?

SIR WILFRID. (*Crossing to* c.) Well, what did she hear, then? Don't tell me it was a burglar chatting amicably with Miss French—(*He takes his handkerchief from his pocket.*) before he coshed her on the head, you old clown. (*He coshes* MAYHEW *with the handkerchief.*)

MAYHEW. That certainly seems unlikely.

SIR WILFRID. I don't think that that rather grim old woman would stick at making up a thing like that. I don't think she'd stick at anything, you know. No—(*Significantly.*) I don't think—she'd stick—at—*anything*.

MAYHEW. (*Horrified*) Good Lord! Do you mean . . . ?

CARTER. (*Enters and closes the door behind him.*) Excuse me, Sir Wilfrid. A young woman is asking to see you. She says it has to do with the case of Leonard Vole.

SIR WILFRID. (*Unimpressed.*) Mental?

CARTER. Oh, no, Sir Wilfrid. I can always recognize that type.

SIR WILFRID. (*Moving above the desk and picking up the tea-cups*) What sort of a young woman? (*He crosses to* c.)

CARTER. (*Taking the cups from* SIR WILFRID) Rather a common young woman, sir, with a free way of talking.

SIR WILFRID. And what does she want?

CARTER. (*Quoting somewhat distastefully*) She says she "knows something that might do the prisoner a bit of good."

SIR WILFRID. (*With a sigh*) Highly unlikely. Bring her in.

(CARTER *exits, taking the cups with him.*)

What do you think, John?

MAYHEW. Oh well, we can't afford to leave any stone unturned.

(CARTER *enters and ushers in a* WOMAN. *She appears to be aged almost thirty-five and is flamboyantly but cheaply dressed. Blonde hair falls over one side of her face. She is violently and crudely made up. She carries a shabby handbag.* MAYHEW *rises.*)

CARTER. The young lady. (CARTER *exits.*)

WOMAN. (*Looking sharply from* SIR WILFRID *to* MAYHEW) Here, what's this? Two o' yer? I'm not talking to two of yer. (*She turns to go.*)

SIR WILFRID. This is Mr. Mayhew. He is Leonard Vole's solicitor. I am Sir Wilfrid Robarts, Council for the Defence.

WOMAN. (*Peering at* SIR WILFRID) So you are, dear. Didn't recognize you without your wig. Lovely you all look in them wigs.

(MAYHEW *gives* SIR WILFRID *a nudge, then stands above the desk.*)

Havin' a bit of a confab, are you? Well, maybe I can help you if you make it worth my while.

SIR WILFRID. You know, Miss—er . . .

WOMAN. (*Crossing and sitting* L. *of the desk*) No need for names. If I did give you a name, it mightn't be the right one, might it?

SIR WILFRID. (*Standing* C.) As you please. You realize you are in duty bound to come forward to give any evidence that may be in your possession.

WOMAN. Aw, come off it! I didn't say I knew anything, did I? I've *got* something. That's more to the point.

MAYHEW. What is it you have got, madam?

WOMAN. Aye-aye! I was in court today. I watched the—that trollop give her evidence. So high and mighty about it too. She's a wicked one. A Jezebel, that's what she is.

SIR WILFRID. Quite so. But as to this special information you have . . .

WOMAN. (*Cunningly.*) Ah, but what's in it for me? It's valuable, what I've got. A hundred quid, that's what I want.

MAYHEW. I'm afraid we could not countenance anything of that character, but perhaps if you tell us a little more about what you have to offer . . .

WOMAN. You don't buy unless you get a butcher's, is that it?

SIR WILFRID. A butcher's?

WOMAN. A butcher's 'ook—look.

SIR WILFRID. Oh, yes—yes.

WOMAN. I've got the goods on her all right. (*She opens her handbag.*) It's letters, that's what it is. Letters.

SIR WILFRID. Letters written by Romaine Vole to the prisoner?

WOMAN. (*Laughing coarsely*) To the prisoner? Don't make me laugh. Poor ruddy prisoner, he's been took in by her all right. (*She winks.*) I've got something to *sell*, dear, and don't you forget it.

MAYHEW. (*Smoothly.*) If you will let us see these letters, we shall be able to advise you as to how pertinent they are.

WOMAN. Putting it in your own language, aren't you? Well, as I say, I don't expect you to buy without seeing. But fair's fair. If those letters will do the trick, if they'll get the boy off, and put that foreign bitch where she belongs, well, it's a hundred quid for me. Right?

MAYHEW. (*Taking his wallet from his pocket and extracting ten pounds*) If these letters contain information that is useful to the defence—to help your expenses in coming here—I am prepared to offer you ten pounds.

WOMAN. (*Almost screaming.*) Ten bloody quid for letters like these. Think again.

SIR WILFRID. (*Crossing to* MAYHEW *and taking the wallet from him*) If you have a letter there that will help to prove my client's innocence, twenty pounds would I think not be an unreasonable sum for your expenses. (*He crosses to* R. *of the desk, takes ten pounds from the wallet, returns the empty wallet to* MAYHEW, *and takes the first ten pounds from him.*)

WOMAN. Fifty quid and it's a bargain. That's if you're satisfied with the letters.

SIR WILFRID. Twenty pounds. (*He puts the notes on the desk.*)

(*The* WOMAN *watches him and wets her lips. It is too much for her.*)

WOMAN. All right, blast you. 'Ere, take 'em. Quite a packet of 'em. (*She takes the letters from her handbag.*) The top one's the one will do the trick. (*She puts the letters on the desk, then goes to pick up the money.*)

(SIR WILFRID *is too quick for the* WOMAN *and picks up the money. The* WOMAN *quickly retrieves the letters.*)

SIR WILFRID. Just a moment. I suppose this is her handwriting?

WOMAN. It's her handwriting all right. She wrote 'em. It's all fair and square.

SIR WILFRID. We have only your word for that.

MAYHEW. Just a moment. I have a letter from Mrs. Vole— not here, but at my office.

SIR WILFRID. Well, madam, it looks as though we'll have to trust you—(*He hands her the notes.*) for the moment. (*He takes the letter from her, smoothes them out and begins to read.*)

(*The* WOMAN *slowly counts the notes, carefully watching the* OTHERS *meanwhile.* MAYHEW *moves to* SIR WILFRID *and peers at the letters. The* WOMAN *rises and crosses towards the door.*)

(*To* MAYHEW.) It's incredible. Quite incredible.

MAYHEW. (*Reading over his shoulder*) The cold-blooded vindictiveness.

SIR WILFRID. (*Crossing to the* WOMAN) How did you get hold of these?

WOMAN. That'd be telling.

SIR WILFRID. What have you got against Romaine Vole?

(*The* WOMAN *crosses to the desk, suddenly and dramatically turns her head, swings the desk lamp so that it flows on to her face on the side that has been turned away from*

the audience, pushing her hair back as she does so, re-
vealing that her cheek is all slashed, scarred and dis-
figured. SIR WILFRID *starts back with an ejaculation.*)

WOMAN. See that?

SIR WILFRID. Did *she* do that to you?

WOMAN. (*Crossing to* c.) Not her. The chap I was going
    with. Going with him steady, I was too. He was a bit
    younger than me, but he was fond of me and I loved
    him. Then she came along. She took a fancy to him and
    she got him away from me. She started to see him on
    the sly and then one day he cleared out. I knew where
    he'd gone. I went after him and I found them together.
    (*She sits* L. *of the desk.*) I told 'er what I thought of
    'er and 'e set on me. In with one of the razor gangs, he
    was. He cut my face up proper. "There," he says, "no
    man'll ever look at you now."

SIR WILFRID. Did you go to the police about it?

WOMAN. Me? Not likely. 'Sides it wasn't 'is fault. Not really.
    It was hers, all hers. Getting him away from me, turning
    'im against me. But I waited my time. I followed 'er
    about and watched 'er. I know some of the things she's
    bin up to. I know where the bloke lives who she goes to
    see on the sly sometimes. That's how I got hold of them
    letters. So now you know the whole story, mister. (*She
    rises, thrusts her face forward and pushes her hair aside.*)
    Want to kiss me?

(SIR WILFRID *shrinks back.*)

I don't blame yer. (*She crosses to* L.)

SIR WILFRID. I'm deeply sorry, deeply sorry. Got a fiver, John?

(MAYHEW *shows his empty wallet.*)

(*He takes his wallet from his pocket and extracts a
fivepound note.*) Er—we'll make it another five pounds.

WOMAN. (*Grabbing the note*) 'Oldin' out on me, were yer?
    Willin' to go up another five quid. (*She advances on*
    SIR WILFRID.)

(SIR WILFRID *backs towards* MAYHEW.)

Ah, I knew I was being too soft with you. Those letters
are the goods, aren't they?

SIR WILFRID. They will, I think, be very useful. (*He turns to* MAYHEW *and holds out a letter.*) Here, John, have a butcher's at this one.

(*The* WOMAN *slips quickly out of the door.*)

MAYHEW. We'll have a handwriting expert on these for safety's sake, and he can give evidence if necessary.

SIR WILFRID. We shall require this man's surname and his address.

MAYHEW. (*Looking around*) Hullo, where has she gone? She mustn't leave without giving us further particulars. (*He crosses to* C.)

SIR WILFRID. (*Crosses and exits hurriedly. Off, calling*) Carter! Carter!

CARTER. (*Off.*) Yes, Sir Wilfrid?

SIR WILFRID. (*Off.*) Carter, where did that young woman go?

CARTER. (*Off.*) She went straight out, sir.

SIR WILFRID. (*Off.*) Well, you shouldn't have let her go. Send Greta after her.

CARTER. (*Off.*) Very good, Sir Wilfrid.

(SIR WILFRID *enters and crosses to* L. *of* MAYHEW.)

MAYHEW. She's gone?

SIR WILFRID. Yes, I've sent Greta after her, but there's not a hope in this fog. Damn! We must have this man's surname and address.

MAYHEW. We won't get it. She thought things out too carefully. Wouldn't give us her name, and slipped out like an eel as soon as she saw us busy with the letters. She daren't risk having to appear in the witness box. Look what the man did to her last time.

SIR WILFRID. (*Without conviction*) She'd have protection.

MAYHEW. Would she? For how long? He'd get her in the end, or his pals would. She's already risked something coming here. She doesn't want to bring the man into it. It's Romaine Heilger she's after.

SIR WILFRID. And what a beauty our Romaine is. But we've got something to go on at last. Now as to procedure . . .

CURTAIN

Scene II

SCENE: *The Old Bailey. The next morning.*

When the Curtain rises, the Court is awaiting the entry of the JUDGE. LEONARD *and the* WARDER *are seated in the dock. Two* BARRISTERS *are seated at the* L. *end of the back row of* BARRISTERS' *seats.* SIR WILFRID *and his* ASSISTANT *are in their places.* MAYHEW *is standing* L. *of the table talking to* SIR WILFRID. *The* CLERK OF THE COURT, *the* JUDGE'S CLERK *and the* STENOGRAPHER *are in their places. The three visible* MEMBERS OF THE JURY *are seated. The* POLICEMAN *is at the doors up* L. *The* USHER *is standing at the top of the steps up* R.C. MYERS, *his* ASSISTANT *and two* BARRISTERS *enter up* C. MYERS *crosses to* SIR WILFRID *and starts talking angrily. The* ASSISTANT *and the* BARRISTERS *take their seats. There are three KNOCKS on the* JUDGE'S *door. The* USHER *comes down the steps to* R.C.

USHER. Stand up.

(ALL *stand. The* JUDGE *and* ALDERMAN *enter by the* JUDGE'S *door and take their seats.*)

All persons who have anything further to do before my lady the Queen's justices of Oyer and Terminer and general gaol delivery for the jurisdiction of the Central Criminal Court draw near and give your attendance. God Save the Queen.

(*The* JUDGE *bows to the Court and* ALL *take their seats. The* USHER *sits on the stool down* R.)

SIR WILFRID. (*Rising*) My lord, since this was adjourned, certain evidence of a rather startling character has come into my hands. This evidence is such that I am taking it upon myself to ask your lordship's permission to have the last witness for the prosecution, Romaine Heilger, recalled.

(*The* CLERK *rises and whispers to the* JUDGE.)

JUDGE. When exactly, Sir Wilfrid, did this evidence come to your knowledge?

(*The* CLERK *sits.*)

SIR WILFRID. It was brought to me after the Court was adjourned last night.

MYERS. (*Rising*) My lord, I must object to my learned friend's request. The case for the prosecution is closed and . . .

(SIR WILFRID *sits.*)

JUDGE. Mr. Myers, I had not intended to rule on this question without first observing the customary formality of inviting your observations on the matter. Yes, Sir Wilfrid?

(MYERS *sits.*)

SIR WILFRID. (*Rising*) My lord, in a case where evidence vital to the prisoner comes into possession of his legal advisers at any time before the jury have returned their verdict, I contend that such evidence is not only admissible, but desirable. Happily there is clear authority to support my proposition, to be found in the case of the King against Stillman, reported in nineteen twenty-six *Appeal Cases* at page four-six-three. (*He opens a law volume in front of him.*)

JUDGE. You needn't trouble to cite the authority, Sir Wilfrid, I am quite familiar with it. I should like to hear the prosecution. Now, Mr. Myers.

(SIR WILFRID *sits.*)

MYERS. (*Rising*) In my respectful submission, my lord, the course my friend proposes is, save in exceptional circumstances, quite unprecedented. And what, may I ask, is this startling new evidence of which Sir Wilfrid speaks?

SIR WILFRID. (*Rising*) Letters, my lord. Letters from Romaine Heilger.

JUDGE. I should like to see these letters to which you refer, Sir Wilfrid.

(SIR WILFRID *and* MYERS *sit. The* USHER *rises, crosses to* SIR WILFRID, *collects the letters, passes them to the* CLERK, *who hands them to the* JUDGE. *The* JUDGE *studies the letters. The* USHER *resumes his seat.*)

MYERS. (*Rising*) My friend was good enough to tell me only as we came into Court that he intended to make this submission, so that I have had no opportunity to examine the authorities. But I seem to remember a case in, I think, nineteen thirty, the King against Porter, I believe . . .

JUDGE. No, Mr. Myers, the King against Potter, and it was reported in nineteen thirty one. I appeared for the prosecution.

MYERS. And if my memory serves me well, your lordship's similar objection was sustained.

JUDGE. Your memory for once serves you ill, Mr. Myers. My objection then was overruled by Mr. Justice Swindon —as yours is now, by me.

(MYERS *sits.*)

SIR WILFRID. (*Rising*) Call Romaine Heilger.

USHER. (*Rises and moves down* C.) Romaine Heilger.

POLICEMAN. (*Opens the door. Calling*) Romaine Heilger.

JUDGE. If these letters are authentic it raises very serious issues. (*He hands the letters to the* CLERK.)

(*The* CLERK *hands the letters to the* USHER, *who returns them to* SIR WILFRID. *During the slight wait that ensues,* LEONARD *is very agitated. He speaks to the* WARDER, *then puts his hands to his face. The* USHER *sits on the stool* R. *of the table.* MAYHEW *rises, speaks to* LEONARD *and calms him down.* LEONARD *shakes his head and looks upset and worried.* ROMAINE *enters up* L., *crosses and enters the witness box. The* POLICEMAN *closes the door.*)

SIR WILFRID. Mrs. Heilger, you appreciate that you are still on your oath?

ROMAINE. Yes.

JUDGE. Romaine Heilger, you are recalled to this box so that Sir Wilfrid may ask you further questions.

SIR WILFRID. Mrs. Heilger, do you know a certain man whose Christian name is Max?

ROMAINE. (*Starts violently at the mention of the name.*) I don't know what you mean.

SIR WILFRID. (*Pleasantly.*) And yet it's a very simple question. Do you or do you not know a man called Max?

ROMAINE. Certainly not.

SIR WILFRID. You're quite sure of that?

ROMAINE. I've never known anyone called Max. Never.

SIR WILFRID. And yet I believe it's a fairly common Christian name, or contraction of a name, in your country. You mean that you have never known anyone of that name?

ROMAINE. (*Doubtfully.*) Oh, in Germany—yes—perhaps, I do not remember. It is a long time ago.

SIR WILFRID. I shall not ask you to throw your mind back such a long way as that. A few weeks will suffice. Let us say—(*He picks up one of the letters and unfolds it, making rather a parade of it.*) the seventeenth of October last.

ROMAINE. (*Startled.*) What have you got there?

SIR WILFRID. A letter.

ROMAINE. I don't know what you're talking about.

SIR WILFRID. I'm talking about a letter. A letter written on the seventeenth of October. You remember that date, perhaps.

ROMAINE. Not particularly, why?

SIR WILFRID. I suggest that on that day, you wrote a certain letter—a letter addressed to a man called Max.

ROMAINE. I did nothing of the kind. These are lies that you are telling. I don't know what you mean.

SIR WILFRID. That letter was one of a series written to the same man over a considerable period of time.

ROMAINE. (*Agitated.*) Lies—all lies!

SIR WILFRID. You would seem to have been on—(*Significantly.*) intimate terms with this man.

LEONARD. (*Rising*) How dare you say a thing like that?

(*The* WARDER *rises and attempts to restrain* LEONARD.)

(*He waves the* WARDER *aside.*) It isn't true!

JUDGE. The prisoner in his own interest will remain silent.

(LEONARD *and the* WARDER *resume their seats.*)

SIR WILFRID. I am not concerned with the general trend of this correspondence. I am only interested in one particular letter. (*He reads.*) "My beloved Max. An extraordinary thing has happened. I believe all our difficulties may be ended . . ."

ROMAINE. (*Interrupting in a frenzy*) It's a lie—I never wrote it. How did you get hold of that letter? Who gave it to you?

SIR WILFRID. How the letter came into my possession is irrelevant.

ROMAINE. You stole it. You are a thief as well as a liar. Or did some woman give it to you? Yes, I am right, am I not?

JUDGE. Kindly confine yourself to answering Counsel's questions.

ROMAINE. But I will not listen.

JUDGE. Proceed, Sir Wilfrid.

SIR WILFRID. So far you have only heard the opening phrases of the letter. Am I to understand that you definitely deny writing it?

ROMAINE. Of course I never wrote it. It is a forgery. It is an outrage that I should be forced to listen to a pack of lies—lies made up by a jealous woman.

SIR WILFRID. I suggest it is *you* who have lied. You have lied flagrantly and persistently in this Court and upon oath. And the reason *why* you have lied is made clear by— (*He taps the letter.*) this letter—written down by you in black and white.

ROMAINE. You are crazy. Why should I write down a lot of nonsense?

SIR WILFRID. Because a way had opened before you to freedom—and in planning to take that way, the fact that an innocent man would be sent to his death meant nothing to you. You have even included that final deadly touch of how you yourself managed accidentally to wound Leonard Vole with a ham knife.

ROMAINE. (*Carried away with fury.*) I never wrote that. I wrote that he did it himself cutting the ham . . . (*Her voice dies away.*)

(*All eyes in court turn on her.*)

SIR WILFRID. (*Triumphantly.*) So you know what is in the letter—before I have read it.

ROMAINE. (*Casting aside all restraint*) Damn you! Damn you! Damn you!

LEONARD. (*Shouting*) Leave her alone. Don't bully her.

ROMAINE. (*Looking wildly around*) Let me get out of here— let me go. (*She comes out of the witness box.*)

(*The* USHER *rises and restrains* ROMAINE.)

JUDGE. Usher, give the witness a chair.

(ROMAINE *sinks on to the stool* R. *of the table, sobs hysterically and buries her face in her hands. The* USHER *crosses and sits on the stool down* R.)

Sir Wilfrid, will you now read the letter aloud so that the Jury can hear it.

SIR WILFRID. (*Reading*) "My beloved Max. An extraordinary thing has happened. I believe all our difficulties may be ended. I can come to you without any fear of endangering the valuable work you are doing in this country. The old lady I told you about has been murdered and I think Leonard is suspected. He was there earlier that night and his fingerprints will be all over the place. Nine-thirty seems to be the time. Leonard was home by then, but his alibi depends on me—on *me*. Supposing I say he came home much later and that he had blood on his clothes—he did have blood on his sleeve, because he cut his wrist at supper, so you see it would all fit in. I can even say he told me he killed her. Oh, Max, beloved! Tell me I can go ahead—it would be so wonderful to be free from playing the part of a loving, grateful wife. I know the Cause and the Party comes first, but if Leonard was convicted of murder, I could come to you safely and we could be together for always. Your adoring Romaine."

JUDGE. Romaine Heilger, will you go back into the witness box?

(ROMAINE *rises and enters the witness box.*)

You have heard that letter read. What have you to say?

ROMAINE. (*Frozen in defeat.*) Nothing.

LEONARD. Romaine, tell him you didn't write it. I know you didn't write it.

ROMAINE. (*Turning and fairly spitting out the words*) Of course I wrote it.

SIR WILFRID. That, my lord, concludes the case for the defence.

JUDGE. Sir Wilfrid, have you any evidence as to whom these letters were addressed?

SIR WILFRID. My lord, they came into my possession anonymously, and there has been as yet no time to ascertain any further facts. It would seem likely that he came to this country illegally and is engaged on some subversive operations here . . .

ROMAINE. You will never find out who he is—never. I don't care what you do to me. You shall never know.

JUDGE. Do you wish to re-examine, Mr. Myers?

(SIR WILFRID *sits.*)

MYERS. (*Rising rather unhappily*) Really, my lord, I find it somewhat difficult in view of these startling developments. (*To* ROMAINE.) Mrs. Heilger, you are, I think, of a highly nervous temperament. Being a foreigner you may not quite realize the responsibilities that lie upon you when you take the oath in an English court of law. If you have been intimidated into admitting something that is not true, if you wrote a letter under stress or in some spirit of make-believe, do not hesitate to say so now.

ROMAINE. Must you go on and on torturing me? I wrote the letter. Now let me go.

MYERS. My lord, I submit that this witness is in such a state of agitation that she hardly knows what she is saying or admitting.

JUDGE. You may remember, Mr. Myers, that Sir Wilfrid cautioned the witness at the time of her previous statement and impressed upon her the sacred nature of the oath she had taken.

(MYERS *sits.*)

Mrs. Heilger, I wish to warn you that this is not the end of the matter. In this country you cannot commit perjury without being brought to account for it, and I may tell you that I have no doubt proceedings for perjury will shortly be taken against you. The sentence for perjury can be severe. You may stand down.

(ROMAINE *stands down. The* POLICEMAN *opens the door.* ROMAINE *crosses and exits. The* POLICEMAN *closes the door.*)

Sir Wilfrid, will you now address the Jury on behalf of the defence?

SIR WILFRID. (*Rising*) Members of the Jury, when truth is clearly evident it speaks for itself. No words of mine I'm sure can add to the impression made upon you by the straightforward story which the prisoner has told, and by the very wicked attempt to incriminate him, evidence of which you have just witnessed . . .

(*As* SIR WILFRID *speaks the* LIGHTS *dim to black-out. After a few seconds the* LIGHTS *come up. The* JURY *are out but are just re-entering the box.*)

CLERK. (*Rising*) Vole, stand up.

(LEONARD *rises.*)

Members of the Jury, are you all agreed upon your verdict?

FOREMAN. (*Standing*) We are.

CLERK. Do you find the prisoner, Leonard Vole, guilty or not guilty?

FOREMAN. Not guilty, my lord.

(*A buzz of approbation goes round the court.*)

USHER. (*Rising and moving down* C.) Silence!

JUDGE. Leonard Vole, you have been found not guilty of the murder of Emily French on October fourteenth. You are hereby discharged and are free to leave the Court. (*He rises.*)

(ALL *rise. The* JUDGE *bows to the Court and exits up* R., *followed by the* ALDERMAN *and the* JUDGE'S CLERK.)

USHER. All persons who have anything further to do before my lady the Queen's justices of Oyer and Terminer and general gaol delivery for the jurisdiction of the Central Criminal Court may depart hence and give your attendance here again tomorrow morning at ten-thirty o'clock. God Save The Queen.

(*The* USHER, *the* JURY *and the* STENOGRAPHER *exit down* R. *The* BARRISTERS, ASSISTANTS *and the* CLERK OF THE COURT *exit up* C. *The* WARDER *and the* POLICEMAN *exit up* L. LEONARD *leaves the dock and crosses to* MAYHEW.)

MAYHEW. Congratulations, my boy!

LEONARD. I can't thank you enough.

MAYHEW. (*Tactfully indicating* SIR WILFRID) This is the man you've got to thank.

(LEONARD *crosses to* C. *to meet* SIR WILFRID, *but comes face to face with* MYERS, *who glares at him, and exits up* C. SIR WILFRID *crosses to* R. *of* LEONARD.)

LEONARD. (*Turning to* SIR WILFRED) Thank you, sir. (*His tone is less spontaneous than it was to* MAYHEW. *He dislikes* SIR WILFRID *it seems.*) You—you've got me out of a very nasty mess.

SIR WILFRID. Nasty mess! Do you hear that, John? Your troubles are over now, my boy.

MAYHEW. (*Moving to* L. *of* LEONARD) But it was a near thing, you know.

LEONARD. (*Unwillingly*) Yes, I suppose it was.

SIR WILFRID. If we hadn't been able to break that woman down . . .

LEONARD. Did you have to go for her the way you did? It was terrible the way she went to pieces. I can't believe . . .

SIR WILFRID. (*With all the force of his personality.*) Look here, Vole, you're not the first young man I've known who's been so crazy over a woman that he's been blinded to what she's really like. That woman did her level best to put a rope round your neck.

MAYHEW. And don't you forget it.

LEONARD. Yes, but why? I can't see why. She's always seemed so devoted. I could have sworn she loved me—and yet all the time she was going with this other fellow. (*He shakes his head.*) It's unbelievable—there's something there I don't understand.

WARDER. (*Enters up* L. *and moves to* L. *of the table.*) Just two or three minutes more, sir. We'll slip you out to a car by the side entrance.

LEONARD. Is there still a crowd?

(ROMAINE, *escorted by the* POLICEMAN, *enters up* L.)

POLICEMAN. (*In the doorway.*) Better wait in here, ma'am. The crowd's in a nasty mood. I'd let them disperse before you try to leave.

ROMAINE. (*Moving down* L. *of the table*) Thank you.

(*The* POLICEMAN *and the* WARDER *exit up* L. ROMAINE *crosses towards* LEONARD.)

SIR WILFRID. (*Intercepting* ROMAINE) No, you don't.

ROMAINE. (*Amused*) Are you protecting Leonard from me? Really, there's no need.

SIR WILFRID. You've done enough harm.

ROMAINE. Mayn't I even congratulate Leonard on being free?

SIR WILFRID. No thanks to you.

ROMAINE. And rich.

LEONARD. (*Uncertainly.*) Rich?

MAYHEW. Yes, I think, Mr. Vole, that you will certainly inherit a great deal of money.

LEONARD. (*Boyishly*) Money doesn't seem to mean so much after what I've been through. Romaine, I can't understand . . .

ROMAINE. (*Smoothly.*) Leonard, I can explain.

SIR WILFRID. No!

(SIR WILFRID *and* ROMAINE *look at each other like antagonists.*)

ROMAINE. Tell me, do those words the Judge said mean that I shall—go to prison?

SIR WILFRID. You will quite certainly be charged with perjury and tried for it. You will probably go to prison.

LEONARD. (*Awkwardly.*) I'm sure that—that everything will come right. Romaine, don't worry.

MAYHEW. Will you never see sense, Vole? Now we must consider practicalities—this matter of probate.

(MAYHEW *draws* LEONARD *down* R., *where they murmur together.* SIR WILFRID *and* ROMAINE *remain, measuring each other.*)

SIR WILFRID. It may interest you to know that I took your measure the first time we met. I made up my mind then to beat you at your little game, and by God I've done it. I've got him off—in spite of you.

ROMAINE. In *spite*—of me.

SIR WILFRID. You don't deny, do you, that you did your best to hang him?

ROMAINE. Would they have believed me if I had said that he was at home with me that night, and did not go out? Would they?

SIR WILFRID. (*Slightly uncomfortable*) Why not?

ROMAINE. Because they would have said to themselves: this woman loves this man—she would say or do anything

for him. They would have had sympathy with me, yes.
But they would not have *believed* me.

SIR WILFRID. If you'd been speaking the truth they would.

ROMAINE. I wonder. (*She pauses.*) I did not want their sympathy—I wanted them to dislike me, to mistrust me, to
be convinced that I was a liar. And then, when my lies
were broken down—then they believed . . . (*In the
Cockney accent of the* WOMAN *who visited* SIR WILFRID
at his office.) So now you know the whole story, mister
—like to kiss me?

SIR WILFRID. (*Thunderstruck.*) My God!

ROMAINE. (*As herself*) Yes, the woman with the letters. I
wrote those letters. I brought them to you. I was that
woman. It wasn't *you* who won freedom for Leonard. It
was *I*. And because of it I shall go to prison. (*Her eyes
close.*) But at the end of it Leonard and I will be together again. Happy—loving each other.

SIR WILFRID. (*Moved.*) My dear . . . But couldn't you trust
me? We believe, you know, that our British system of
justice upholds the truth. We'd have got him off.

ROMAINE. I couldn't risk it. (*Slowly.*) You see, you *thought*
he was innocent . . .

SIR WILFRID. (*With quick appreciation.*) And you *knew* he
was innocent . . .

ROMAINE. But you do not understand at all. *I* knew he was
guilty.

SIR WILFRID. (*Thunderstruck.*) But aren't you afraid?

ROMAINE. Afraid?

SIR WILFRID. Of linking your life with a murderer's.

ROMAINE. You don't understand—we love each other.

SIR WILFRID. The first time I met you I said you were a
very remarkable woman—I see no reason to change my
opinion. (*Crosses and exits up* C.)

WARDER. (*Off up* L.) It's no good going in there, miss. It's
all over.

(*There is a* COMMOTION *off up* L. *and then a* GIRL *comes
running on up* L. *She is a very young strawberry blonde
with a crude, obvious appeal. She rushes to* LEONARD
through the Q.C.'s *bench and meets him down* R.C.)

GIRL. Len, darling, you're free. (*She embraces him*) Isn't it
wonderful? They're trying to keep me out. Darling, it's
been awful. I've been nearly crazy.

ROMAINE. (*With sudden violent harshness.*) Leonard—who—is—this girl!

GIRL. (*To* ROMAINE, *defiantly.*) I'm Len's girl. I know all about *you.* You're not his wife. Never have been. (*She crosses to* R. *of* ROMAINE.) You're years older than him, and you just got hold of him—and you've done your best to hang him. But that's all over now. (*She turns to* LEONARD.) We'll go abroad like you said on one of your cruises—to all those grand places. We'll have a wonderful time.

ROMAINE. Is—this—true? Is she your girl, Leonard?

LEONARD. (*Hesitates, then decides that the situation must be accepted.*) Yes, she is.

(*The* GIRL *crosses above* LEONARD *to* R. *of him.*)

ROMAINE. After all I've done for you . . . What can *she* do for you that can compare with that?

LEONARD. (*Flinging off all disguise of manner, and showing coarse brutality.*) She's fifteen years younger than you are. (*He laughs.*)

(ROMAINE *flinches as though struck.*)

(*He crosses to* R. *of* ROMAINE. *Menacingly.*) I've got the money. I've been acquitted, and I can't be tried again, so don't go shooting off your mouth, or you'll just get *yourself* hanged as an accessory after the fact. (*He turns to the* GIRL *and embraces her.*)

ROMAINE. (*Picks up the knife from the table. Throwing her head back in sudden dignity.*) No, that will not happen. I shall not be tried as an accessory after the fact. I shall not be tried for perjury. I shall be tried for murder — (*She stabs* LEONARD *in the back.*) the murder of the only man I ever loved.

(LEONARD *drops. The* GIRL *screams.* MAYHEW *bends over* LEONARD, *feels his pulse and shakes his head.*)

(*She looks up at the* JUDGE's *seat.*) Guilty, my lord.

CURTAIN

TOWARDS ZERO

Presented by Peter Saunders at the St. James's Theatre, London, on the 4th September, 1956, with the following cast of characters:

(In the order of their appearance)

THOMAS ROYDE	Cyril Raymond
KAY STRANGE	Mary Law
MARY ALDIN	Gillian Lind
MATHEW TREVES	Frederick Leister
NEVILE STRANGE	George Baker
LADY TRESSILIAN	Janet Barrow
AUDREY STRANGE	Gwen Cherrell
TED LATIMER	Michael Scott
SUPERINTENDENT BATTLE, C.I.D., Scotland Yard	William Kendall
INSPECTOR LEACH, *local* C.I.D.	Max Brimmell
P. C. BENSON	Michael Nightingale

Directed by MURRAY MACDONALD

Décor by MICHAEL WEIGHT

SYNOPSIS OF SCENES

The action of the play passes in the drawing-room at Gull's Point, Lady Tressilian's house at Saltcreek, Cornwall.

ACT I
SCENE 1: A morning in September.
SCENE 2: After dinner, four days later.

ACT II
SCENE 1: Early the following morning.
SCENE 2: Two hours later.

ACT III
SCENE 1: The next morning.
SCENE 2: The same evening.

TIME: The present

Act One

Scene I

SCENE: *The drawing-room at Gull's Point, Lady Tressilian's house at Saltcreek, Cornwall. A morning in September. It is a large, very beautiful room, obviously belonging to somebody with exquisite taste. It has been furnished to combine elegance with comfort. There is a deep, arched alcove up* R. *with French windows opening on to a terrace overlooking the garden and tennis court. A large curved-bay window up* L., *with a built-in window-seat, shows a view across the river to Easterhead Bay, with a large hotel on the cliff opposite. This window is slightly raised above the rest of the stage on a platform or rostrum. A door down* L. *leads to the other parts of the house. There is a chaise-longue* R. C.; *easy chairs down* R. *and down* L. *and armchairs* L. C. *and* R. *In the alcove* R. *there is a bureau-bookcase with a carver chair, a small table and an upright chair. A waste-paper basket stands* L. *of the bureau. Down* R. *there is a small table, and on it a framed photograph of Audrey. A standing work-basket is* R. *of the armchair* L. C. *On the rostrum in the bay window is a low butler's tray with a variety of drinks and glasses. A large circular coffee table stands* C. *A low bookcase, with a table-lamp on it, is* L. *of the window and there is a corner table* R. *of the window. On the window-seat, at the* L. *end, is a portable record player with some loose records. At night the room is lit by electric-candle wall-brackets down* L. *and above and below the alcove* R. *The switches are below the door down* L.

When the curtain rises, the room is empty. An incongruous carpet sweeper stands negligently against the easy chair down L. Thomas Royde enters immediately by the French windows. He is a bronzed middle-aged man, good-looking in a rugged way. He carries a suitcase and a set of golf clubs. As he reaches the upstage end of the chaise, the door down L. is banged by someone as though rushing out of the room. Rodye shrugs, moves to the window bay, puts his case and clubs at the L. end of it, opens the C. sash of the window, then takes his pipe and pouch from his pocket and stands gazing out of the window and filling his pipe. Kay Strange rushes in R. She is dressed in tennis kit and carries a towel. Clearly upset about something, she does not see Royde, tosses the towel on the chaise, goes to the table down R. and takes a cigarette from the box on it. As she does so, she sees the photograph of Audrey, drops the cigarette, picks up the photograph, rips it from the frame, tears it in half and throws it angrily into the waste-paper basket. Royde turns sharply. Kay pauses a moment, then looks round and sees Royde. She looks at once like a guilty child and is for a moment too startled to say anything.

KAY. Oh! Who are you?

ROYDE. (*Moving to R. of the rostrum*) I've just walked up from the bus stop. I'm . . .

KAY. (*Interrupting.*) I know who you are. You're the man from Malaya.

ROYDE. (*Gravely.*) Yes, I'm the man from Malaya.

KAY. (*Moving to the coffee table* C.) I just—came in, to get a cigarette. (*She takes a cigarette from the box on the coffee table, crosses to the French windows and turns.*) Oh, hell, what's the good of explaining? What do I care what *you* think, anyway? (*Kay rushes out R. Royde stares thoughtfully after her. Mary Aldin enters L. She is a dark-haired woman of about thirty-six, pleasant and noncommittal in manner and entirely competent. Nevertheless there is something faintly intriguing about her reserve. Royde turns to Mary.*)

MARY. (*Moving L. C.*) Mr. Royde? (*Royde moves to R. of Mary and shakes hands with her.*) Lady Tressilian is not down yet. I am Mary Aldin—Lady Tressilian's dogsbody.

ROYDE. Dogsbody?

MARY. The official term is secretary—but as I don't know shorthand and such talents I have are purely domestic, "dogsbody" is a much better word.

ROYDE. I know all about you. Lady Tressilian told me in her Christmas letter what a wonderful difference you had made to her.

MARY. I've grown very fond of her. She has a lot of personality.

ROYDE. (*Moving to L. of the chaise*) That's quite an under-statement. (*He turns to Mary.*) How's her arthritis?

MARY. It makes her rather helpless, poor dear.

ROYDE. I'm sorry about that.

MARY. (*Moving on to the rostrum*) Can I offer you a drink?

ROYDE. No, thank you. (*He moves on to the R. end of the rostrum and looks out of the window.*) What's that great caravanserai over there?

MARY. That's the new *Easterhead Bay Hotel*. It was only finished last year—isn't it a horror? (*She closes the window.*) Lady Tressilian doesn't like this window opened, she's always afraid that someone might fall out. Yes, Easterhead Bay is a terrific resort, you know, nowadays. (*She crosses to the chaise, picks up Kay's towel and tidies the cushions.*) I suppose when you came here as a boy there was nothing the other side of the estuary except a few fishermen's cottages. (*She pauses.*) You did come here for your school holidays, didn't you? (*She puts the towel tidily on the end of the chaise.*)

ROYDE. Yes, old Sir Mortimer used to take me out sailing— he was mad keen on sailing.

MARY. Yes. He was drowned out there.

ROYDE. Lady Tressilian saw it happen, I wonder she can go on living here.

MARY. I think she preferred to remain with her memories. But she won't have any boat kept here—she even had the boathouse pulled down.

ROYDE. So if I want to sail or go for a row, I've got to go to the ferry.

MARY. (*Crossing to the butler's tray*) Or cross to the Easter-head side. That's where all the boats are nowadays.

ROYDE. (*Moving above the chaise.*) I hate changes. Always have. (*Rather self-consciously.*) May I ask who else is staying here?

MARY. Old Mr. Treves—you know him? (*Royde nods.*) And the Stranges.

ROYDE. (*Moving to* R *of her.*) The Stranges? You mean— Audrey Strange, Nevile's first wife?

MARY. Audrey, yes. But Nevile Strange and his—new wife are here, too.

ROYDE. Isn't that a bit odd?

MARY. Lady Tressilian thinks it very odd indeed.

ROYDE. Bit awkward—what? (*Mathew Treves enters by the French windows* R., *fanning himself with an old-fashioned panama hat. He is an elderly and distinguished lawyer of ripe experience and great shrewdness. He has retired from his London firm some years ago and is now a keen observer of human nature. His voice is dry and precise.*)

TREVES. (*As he enters.*) Rather too much glare on the terrace today . . . (*He sees Royde.*) Ah, Thomas. Nice to see you after all these years. (*He stands up* L. *of the chaise.*)

ROYDE. (*Moving to Treves.*) I'm very glad to be here. (*He shakes hands with Treves.*)

MARY. (*Moving to Royde's suitcase.*) Shall I take your things up to your room?

ROYDE. (*Crossing quickly to Mary.*) No, no, I can't let you do that. (*He picks up his suitcase and golf clubs. Mary leads the way to the door* L., *sees the sweeper and picks it up.*)

MARY. (*With a vexed exclamation.*) Really! Mrs. Barrett . . . These daily women are impossible. It makes Lady Tressilian very angry when things are left all over the place.

ROYDE. (*Following Mary to the door* L.) I think my sudden arrival on the terrace frightened the poor woman. (*He looks towards Treves. Treves smiles.*)

MARY. Oh, I see. (*Mary and Royde exit* L. *Treves turns to the bureau, sees the torn photograph in the waste-paper basket, stoops with a little difficulty and picks up the pieces. His eyebrows rise and he makes a little sound like "Tut, tut."*)

KAY. (*Off* L.; *calling.*) Where are you going to, Nevile?

NEVILE. (*Off* L.) Only into the house for a moment. (*Treves puts the pieces of the photograph into the waste-paper basket. Nevile Strange enters by the French windows* L. *He wears tennis kit and carries the remains of a glass of lemonade. He crosses to the coffee table and puts the glass on it.*) Isn't Audrey here?

TREVES. No.

NEVILE. Where is she? Do you know?

TREVES. I have no idea.

KAY. (*Off, calling.*) Nevile—Nevile. (*Treves moves down* R. *of the chaise.*)

NEVILE. (*Frowning.*) Oh, damn!

KAY. (*Off, nearer.*) Nevile.

NEVILE. (*Crossing to the French windows and calling.*) Coming—coming. (*Royde enters* L.)

ROYDE. (*Moving to* L. *of the coffee table.*) Nevile.

NEVILE. (*Moving to* R. *of the coffee table.*) Hullo, Thomas. (*They shake hands above the coffee table.*) What time did you get here?

ROYDE. Just now.

NEVILE. Must be quite a long time since I saw you last. When was it you were home, three years ago?

ROYDE. Seven.

NEVILE. Good Lord, is it, really? How time flies.

KAY. (*Off.*) Nevile!

NEVILE. (*Moving above the chaise.*) All right, Kay. (*Kay enters by the French windows* R.)

KAY. (*Moving to* R. *of Nevile.*) Why can't you come? Ted and I are waiting.

NEVILE. I just came to see if Audrey . . .

KAY. (*Turning away.*) Oh, bother Audrey—we can get on quite well . . . (*Kay and Nevile exit by the French windows* R. *Their voices die away.*)

ROYDE. And who is Kay?

TREVES. (*Moving below the chaise to* R. *of the coffee table.*) The present Mrs. Nevile Strange. (*Lady Tressilian enters* L. *Mary assists her on. Lady Tressilian uses a walking stick. She is a white-haired, aristocratic-looking woman, a little younger than Treves. Mary carries Lady Tressilian's sewing.*) Good morning, Camilla.

LADY TRESSILIAN. Good morning, Mathew. (*She greets Royde affectionately.*) Well, Thomas, so here you are. I'm very glad to see you.

ROYDE. (*Rather shyly.*) Very glad to be here. (*Mary puts the sewing in the work-box and arranges the cushion in the armchair* L. C.)

LADY TRESSILIAN. Tell me all about yourself.

ROYDE. (*Mumbling.*) Nothing to tell.

LADY TRESSILIAN. (*Studying him.*) You look exactly the same as you did at fourteen. That same boiled owl look. And no more conversation now than you had then. (*Treves moves up* c. *Mary moves to the butler's tray.*)

ROYDE. Never had the gift of the gab.

LADY TRESSILIAN. Then it's time you learnt. Have some sherry? Mathew? Thomas?

ROYDE. Thank you. (*Mary pours two glasses of sherry.*)

LADY TRESSILIAN. (*Indicating the sofa.*) Then go and sit down. Somebody's got to amuse me by bringing me all the gossip. (*She sits in the armchair* L. C.) Why can't you be more like Adrian? I wish you'd known his brother, Mary, a really brilliant young man, witty, amusing— (*Royde sits on the chaise.*) all the things that Thomas isn't. And don't go grinning at me, Thomas Royde, as though I were praising you. I'm scolding you.

ROYDE. Adrian was certainly the show man of our family.

MARY. (*Handing a glass of sherry to Treves.*) Did he—was he—killed in the war?

ROYDE. No, he was killed in a motor accident two years ago.

MARY. How dreadful! (*She hands a glass of sherry to Royde.*)

TREVES. The impossible way young people drive cars nowadays ... (*Lady Tressilian picks up her sewing.*)

ROYDE. In his case it was some fault in the steering. (*He takes his pipe from his pocket and looks at Lady Tressilian.*) I'm so sorry, may I? (*Mary pours another glass of sherry.*)

LADY TRESSILIAN. I wouldn't know you without your pipe. But don't think you can just sit back and puff contentedly while you're here. You've got to exert yourself and help.

ROYDE. (*Surprised.*) Help? (*Treves perches himself on the upstage end of the chaise.*)

LADY TRESSILIAN. We've got a difficult situation on our hands. Have you been told who's here? (*Mary takes the glass of sherry to Lady Tressilian. To Mary.*) No, no, much too early, pour it back into the decanter. (*Mary resignedly pours the glass of sherry into the decanter.*)

ROYDE. Yes, I've just heard.

LADY TRESSILIAN. Well, don't you think it's disgraceful?

ROYDE. Well ...

TREVES. You'll have to be a little more explicit, Camilla.

LADY TRESSILIAN. I intend to be. When I was a girl such things did not happen. Men had their affairs, naturally,

but they did *not* allow them to break up their married
life.

TREVES. Regrettable though the modern point of view may
be, one has to accept it, Camilla. (*Mary moves to the
easy chair down* L. *and sits on the upstage arm of it.*)

LADY TRESSILIAN. That's not the point. We were all delighted
when Nevile married Audrey. Such a sweet gentle girl.
(*To Royde.*) You were all in love with her—you, Adrian
and Nevile. Nevile won.

ROYDE. Naturally. He always wins.

LADY TRESSILIAN. Of all the defeatist . . .

ROYDE. I don't blame her, Nevile had everything—good looks,
first-class athlete—even had a shot at swimming the
channel.

TREVES. And all the kudos of that early Everest attempt—
never stuck up about it.

ROYDE. *Mens sana in corpore sana.*

LADY TRESSILIAN. Sometimes I think that's the only bit of
Latin you men ever learn in your expensive education.

TREVES. My dear Camilla, you must allow for its being invariably quoted by one's housemaster whenever he is
slightly embarrassed.

LADY TRESSILIAN. Mary, I wish you wouldn't sit on the arms
of chairs—you know how much I dislike it.

MARY. (*Rising.*) Sorry, Camilla. (*She sits in the easy chair
down* L. *Treves rises guiltily and quickly, then sits above
Royde on the chaise.*)

LADY TRESSILIAN. Now where was I?

MARY. You were saying that Audrey married Nevile.

LADY TRESSILIAN. Oh, yes. Well, Audrey married Nevile and
we were all delighted. Mortimer was particularly pleased,
wasn't he, Mathew?

TREVES. Yes, yes.

LADY TRESSILIAN. And they were very happy together until
this creature Kay came along; how Nevile could leave
Audrey for a girl like Kay I simply cannot imagine.

TREVES. I can—I've seen it happen so often.

LADY TRESSILIAN. Kay is quite the wrong wife for Nevile, no
background.

TREVES. But a singularly attractive young woman.

LADY TRESSILIAN. Bad stock, her mother was notorious all over
the Riviera.

ROYDE. What for?

LADY TRESSILIAN. Never you mind. What an upbringing for a girl. Kay made a dead set at Nevile from the moment they met, and never rested until she got him to leave Audrey and go off with her. I blame Kay entirely for the whole thing.

TREVES. (*Rising and moving above the coffee table, fairly amused.*) I'm sure you do. You're very fond of Nevile.

LADY TRESSILIAN. Nevile's a fool. Breaking up his marriage for a silly infatuation. It nearly broke poor Audrey's heart. (*To Royde.*) She went to your mother at the Vicarage and practically had a nervous breakdown.

ROYDE. Er—yes—I know.

TREVES. When the divorce went through, Nevile married Kay.

LADY TRESSILIAN. If I had been true to my principles I should have refused to receive them here.

TREVES. If one sticks too rigidly to one's principles one would hardly see anybody.

LADY TRESSILIAN. You're very cynical, Mathew—but it's quite true. I've accepted Kay as Nevile's wife—though I shall never really like her. But I must say I was dumbfounded and very much upset, wasn't I, Mary?

MARY. Yes, you were, Camilla.

LADY TRESSILIAN. When Nevile wrote asking if he could come home with Kay, under the pretext, if you please, that it would be nice if Audrey and Kay could be friends— (*Scornfully.*) friends—I said I couldn't entertain such a suggestion for a moment and that it would be very painful for Audrey.

TREVES. (*Putting his glass on the coffee table.*) And what did he say to that?

LADY TRESSILIAN. He replied that he had already consulted Audrey and she thought it a good idea.

TREVES. And did Audrey think it a good idea?

LADY TRESSILIAN. Apparently, yes. (*She tosses a knot of silk to Mary.*) Unravel that.

MARY. Well, she said she did, quite firmly.

LADY TRESSILIAN. But Audrey is obviously embarrassed and unhappy. If you ask me, it's just Nevile being like Henry the Eighth.

ROYDE. (*Puzzled.*) Henry the Eighth?

LADY TRESSILIAN. Conscience. Nevile feels guilty about Audrey and is trying to justify himself. (*Mary rises, moves above the armchair* L. C. *and puts the silks in the work-basket.*) Oh! I don't understand *any* of this modern nonsense. (*To Mary.*) Do you? (*Royde puts his glass on the coffee table.*)

MARY. In a way.

LADY TRESSILIAN. And you, Thomas?

ROYDE. Understand Audrey—but I don't understand Nevile. It's not like Nevile.

TREVES. I agree. Not like Nevile at all, to go looking for trouble. (*Mary transfers Royde's and Treves' glasses to the butler's tray.*)

MARY. Perhaps it was Audrey's suggestion.

LADY TRESSILIAN. Oh, no. Nevile says it was entirely his idea.

MARY. Perhaps he thinks it was. (*Treves looks sharply at Mary.*)

LADY TRESSILIAN. What a fool the boy is, bringing two women together who are both in love with him. (*Royde looks sharply at Lady Tressilian.*) Audrey has behaved perfectly, but Nevile himself has paid far too much attention to her, and as a result Kay has become jealous, and as she has no kind of self-control, it is all most embarrassing—(*To Treves.*) isn't it? (*Treves, gazing towards the French windows, does not hear.*) Mathew?

TREVES. There is undeniably a certain tension . . .

LADY TRESSILIAN. I'm glad you admit it. (*There is a knock on the door* L.) Who's that?

MARY. (*Moving to the door* L.) Mrs. Barrett, I expect, wanting to know something.

LADY TRESSILIAN. (*Irritably.*) I wish you could teach these women that they only knock on *bedroom* doors. (*Mary exits* L.) The last so-called butler we had, actually whistled, *Come into the garden, Maud,* as he served at table. (*Mary enters* L.)

MARY. It's only about the lunch, Camilla. I'll see to it. (*Mary exits* L.)

LADY TRESSILIAN. I don't know what I should do without Mary. She's so self-effacing that I sometimes wonder whether she *has* a self of her own.

TREVES. I know. She's been with you nearly two years now, but what's her background?

LADY TRESSILIAN. Her father was a professor of some kind, I believe. He was an invalid and she nursed him for years.

Poor Mary, she's never had any life of her own. And now, perhaps, it's too late. (*She rises and puts her sewing in the work-box.*)

TREVES. I wonder. (*He strolls to the French windows.*) They're still playing tennis. (*Royde rises, moves and stands behind Treves, gazing off* R.)

LADY TRESSILIAN. Nevile and Kay?

TREVES. No, Kay and that friend of hers from the *Easterhead Bay Hotel*—young Latimer.

LADY TRESSILIAN. That theatrical-looking young man. (*She moves to* L. *of the coffee table.*) Just the sort of friend she would have.

TREVES. One wonders what he does for a living.

LADY TRESSILIAN. Lives by his wits, I imagine.

TREVES. (*Moving slowly down* R.) Or by his looks. A decorative young man. (*Dreamily.*) Interesting shaped head. The last man I saw with a head shaped like that was at the Central Criminal Court—a case of brutal assault on an elderly jeweller.

LADY TRESSILIAN. Mathew! Do you mean to tell me . . . ?

TREVES. (*Perturbed.*) No, no, no, you misunderstand me. I am making no suggestion of any kind. I was only commenting on a matter of anatomical structure.

LADY TRESSILIAN. Oh, I thought . . .

TREVES. What reminded me of that was that I met a very old friend of mine this morning, Superintendent Battle of Scotland Yard. He's staying down here on holiday with his nephew who's in the local police.

LADY TRESSILIAN. You and your interest in criminology. The truth is I am thoroughly jumpy—I feel the whole time as though something was going to happen. (*She moves on to the rostrum.*)

TREVES. (*Crossing and standing down* R. *of Lady Tressilian.*) Yes, there is a suggestion of gunpowder in the air. One little spark might set off an explosion.

LADY TRESSILIAN. Must you talk as though you were Guy Fawkes? Say something cheerful.

TREVES. (*Turning and smiling at her.*) What can I say? "Men have died from time to time, and worms have eaten them—but not for love."

LADY TRESSILIAN. And he calls that cheerful. I shall go out on the terrace for a little. (*Treves crosses to the French windows and looks off. She moves up* L. *of the chaise.*

To Royde, confidentially.) Don't make a fool of yourself a second time.

ROYDE. What do you mean?

LADY TRESSILIAN. You know quite well what I mean. Last time, you let Nevile walk off with Audrey under your nose.

ROYDE. (*Moving below the chaise.*) Is it likely she'd have preferred me to Nevile?

LADY TRESSILIAN. (*Moving above the chaise.*) She might have —if you'd asked her. (*Royde moves to L. of Lady Tressilian.*) Are you going to ask her this time?

ROYDE. (*With sudden force.*) You bet your life I am. (*Audrey enters by the French windows. She is very fair and has an Undine-like look. There is something strange about her air of repressed emotion. With Royde she is natural and happy.*)

LADY TRESSILIAN. (*As Audrey enters.*) Thank God for that. (*Audrey, with hands outstretched, crosses below Treves and Lady Tressilian to R. of Royde.*)

AUDREY. Thomas—dear Thomas. (*Royde takes Audrey's hands. Lady Tressilian looks for a moment at Royde and Audrey.*)

LADY TRESSILIAN. Mathew, your arm. (*Treves assists Lady Tressilian, and exits with her by the French windows.*)

AUDREY. (*After a pause.*) It's lovely to see you.

ROYDE. (*Shyly.*) Good to see you.

AUDREY. (*Crossing below Royde to L.*) It's years since you've been home. Don't they give you any leave on rubber plantations?

ROYDE. I *was* coming home two years ago . . . (*He breaks off awkwardly.*)

AUDREY. Two years ago! And then you didn't.

ROYDE. My dear, you know—there were reasons.

AUDREY. (*Sitting in the armchair L. C; with affection*) Oh, Thomas—you look just the same as when we last met— pipe and all.

ROYDE. (*Moving to L. of the coffee table, after a pause*) Do I?

AUDREY. Oh, Thomas—I am so glad you've come back. Now, at last I can talk to someone. Thomas—there's something wrong.

ROYDE. Wrong?

AUDREY. Something's changed about this place. Ever since I arrived I've felt there was something not quite right.

Don't you feel there's something different? No—how can you, you've only just come. The only person who doesn't seem to feel it is Nevile.

ROYDE. Damn Nevile!

AUDREY. You don't like him?

ROYDE. (*With intensity.*) I hate his guts—always have. (*He quickly recovers himself.*) Sorry.

AUDREY. I—didn't know . . .

ROYDE. Lots of things one—doesn't know—about people.

AUDREY. (*Thoughtfully.*) Yes—lots of things.

ROYDE. Gather there's a spot of bother. What made you come here at the same time as Nevile and his new wife? Did you have to agree?

AUDREY. (*Rising and standing L. of the armchair L. c.*) Yes. Oh, I know you can't understand . . .

ROYDE. (*Moving to R. of the armchair L. c.*) But I do understand. I know all about it. (*Audrey looks doubtfully at Royde.*) I know exactly what you've been through—(*With meaning.*) But it's all *past*, Audrey, it's *over*. You must forget the past and think of the future. (*Nevile enters by the French windows and moves up R. of the chaise.*)

NEVILE. Hullo, Audrey, where have you been all the morning? (*Audrey moves to R. of the easy chair down L. Royde moves above the coffee table.*)

AUDREY. I haven't been anywhere particular.

NEVILE. I couldn't find you anywhere. What about coming down to the beach for a swim before lunch?

AUDREY. (*Crossing to the coffee table.*) No, I don't think so. (*She looks among the magazines on the table. Royde moves on to the rostrum.*) Have you seen this week's *London Illustrated News*?

NEVILE. (*Moving to R. of Audrey.*) No. Come on—the water will be really warm today.

AUDREY. Actually, I told Mary I'd go into Saltington with her to shop.

NEVILE. Mary won't mind. (*Audrey picks up a magazine. He takes her hand.*) Come on, Audrey.

AUDREY. No, really . . . (*Kay enters by the French windows.*)

NEVILE. (*As he sees Kay.*) I'm trying to persuade Audrey to come bathing.

KAY. (*Moving to R. of the chaise.*) Oh? And what does Audrey say?

AUDREY. Audrey says "no." (*Audrey withdraws her hand from Nevile's and exits* L.)

ROYDE. If you'll excuse me, I'll go and unpack. (*Royde pauses a moment by the bookshelves up* L., *selects a book, then exits* L.)

KAY. So that's that. Coming, Nevile?

NEVILE. Well, I'm not sure. (*He takes a magazine from the coffee table, sits on the chaise, leans back and puts his feet up.*)

KAY. (*Impatiently.*) Well, make up your mind.

NEVILE. I'm not sure I won't just have a shower and laze in the garden.

KAY. It's a perfect day for bathing. Come on.

NEVILE. What have you done with the boy friend?

KAY. Ted? I left him on the beach and came up to find you. You can laze on the beach. (*She touches his hair.*)

NEVILE. (*Moving her hand from his hair.*) With Latimer, I suppose? (*He shakes his head.*) Doesn't appeal to me a lot.

KAY. You don't like Ted, do you?

NEVILE. Not madly. But if it amuses you to pull him around on a string . . .

KAY. (*Tweaking his ear.*) I believe you're jealous.

NEVILE. (*Pushing her hand from his ear.*) Of Latimer? Nonsense, Kay.

KAY. Ted's very attractive.

NEVILE. I'm sure he is. He has that lithe South American charm.

KAY. You needn't sneer. He's very popular with women.

NEVILE. Especially with the ones over fifty.

KAY. (*Pleased.*) You are jealous.

NEVILE. My dear—I couldn't care less—he just doesn't count.

KAY. I think you're very rude about my friends. I have to put up with yours.

NEVILE. What do you mean by that?

KAY. (*Moving above the chaise to* R. *of the coffee table.*) Dreary old Lady Tressilian and stuffy old Mr. Treves and all the rest of them. (*She sits on the coffee table, facing Nevile.*) Do you think I find them amusing? (*Suddenly.*) Nevile, do we *have* to stay on here? Can't we go away—tomorrow? It's so boring . . .

NEVILE. We've only just come.

KAY. We've been here four days—four whole long days. Do
let's go, Nevile, please.

NEVILE. Why?

KAY. I want to go. We could easily find some excuse. Please,
darling.

NEVILE. Darling, it's out of the question. We came for a
fortnight and we're going to stay a fortnight. You don't
seem to understand. Sir Mortimer Tressilian was my
guardian. I came here for holidays as a boy. Gull's Point
was practically my home. Camilla would be terribly hurt.
(*He smiles.*)

KAY. (*Rising and moving to the window up* L.; *impatiently.*)
Oh, all right, all right. I suppose we have to suck up to
old Camilla, because of getting all that money when
she dies.

NEVILE. (*Rising and moving on to the rostrum, angrily.*) It's
not a question of sucking up. I wish you wouldn't look
at it like that. She's no control over the money. Old
Mortimer left it in trust to come to me and my wife at
her death. Don't you realize it's a question of *affection?*

KAY. Not with me, it isn't. She hates me.

NEVILE. Don't be stupid.

KAY. (*Moving to* L. *of the armchair* L. C.) Yes, she does. She
looks down that bony nose of hers at me, and Mary Aldin
talks to me as though I were someone she'd just met
on a train. They only have me here on sufferance. You
don't seem to know what goes on.

NEVILE. They always seem to me to be very nice to you.
(*He moves to the coffee table and throws the magazine
on it.*) You imagine things.

KAY. Of course they're polite. But they know how to get
under my skin all right. I'm an interloper. That's what
they feel.

NEVILE. Well—I suppose that's only natural . . .

KAY. Oh, yes, I daresay it's quite natural. They're devoted
to Audrey, aren't they? (*She turns and looks towards
the door* L.) Dear, well bred, cool, colorless Audrey.
Camilla has never forgiven me for taking Audrey's place.
(*She turns, moves above the armchair* L. C. *and leans on
the back of it.*) I'll tell you something—Audrey gives
me the creeps. You never know what she's thinking.

NEVILE. (*Sitting on the chaise.*) Oh, nonsense, Kay, don't
be absurd.

KAY. Audrey's never forgiven you for marrying me. Once or twice I've seen her looking at you—and the way she looked at you frightened me.

NEVILE. You're prejudiced, Kay. Audrey's been charming. No one could have been nicer.

KAY. It seems like that, but it isn't true. There's something behind it all. (*She runs above the chaise to* R. *of Nevile and kneels beside him.*) Let's go away—at once—before it's too late.

NEVILE. Don't be melodramatic. I'm not going to upset old Camilla just because you work yourself up into a state about nothing at all.

KAY. It isn't nothing at all. I don't think you know the first thing about your precious Audrey. (*Lady Tressilian and Treves enter by the French windows.*)

NEVILE. (*Furiously.*) She isn't my—precious Audrey. (*Lady Tressilian moves above the chaise.*)

KAY. Isn't she? Anyone would think so, the way you follow her about. (*She sees Lady Tressilian.*)

LADY TRESSILIAN. Are you going down to bathe, Kay?

KAY. (*Rising, nervously.*) Yes—yes, I was.

LADY TRESSILIAN. Almost high tide. It ought to be very pleasant. (*She knocks her stick against the leg of the chaise.*) What about you, Nevile?

NEVILE. (*Sulkily.*) I don't want to bathe.

LADY TRESSILIAN. (*To Kay.*) Your friend, I think, is down there waiting for you. (*Kay hesitates a moment, then crosses and exits by the French window. Treves moves down* R.) Nevile, you're behaving very badly. You really must stand up when I come into the room. What's the matter with you—forgetting your manners?

NEVILE. (*Rising quickly.*) I'm sorry.

LADY TRESSILIAN. (*Crossing to the armchair* L. C.) You're making us all very uncomfortable. I don't wonder your wife is annoyed.

NEVILE. My wife? Audrey?

LADY TRESSILIAN. Kay is your wife now.

NEVILE. With your High Church principles I wonder you admit the fact.

LADY TRESSILIAN. (*Sitting in the armchair* L. C.) Nevile, you are exceedingly rude. (*Nevile crosses to* R. *of Lady Tressilian, takes her hand and kisses her on the cheek.*)

NEVILE. (*With sudden disarming charm.*) I'm very sorry,

Camilla. Please forgive me. I'm so worried I don't know what I'm saying. (*Treves sits in the easy chair down* R.)

LADY TRESSILIAN. (*With affection.*) My dear boy, what else could you expect with this stupid idea of being all friends together?

NEVILE. (*Wistfully.*) It still seems to me the sensible way to look at things.

LADY TRESSILIAN. Not with two women like Audrey and Kay.

NEVILE. Audrey doesn't seem to care.

TREVES. How did the matter first come up, Nevile? (*Nevile withdraws his hand from Lady Tressilian's and moves down* L. *of the chaise.*)

NEVILE. (*Eagerly.*) Well, I happened to run across Audrey in London, quite by chance, and she was awfully nice about things—didn't seem to bear any malice or anything like that. While I was talking to her the idea came to me how sensible it would be if—if she and Kay could be friends—if we could all get together. And it seemed to me that this was the place where it could happen quite naturally.

TREVES. You thought of that—all by yourself?

NEVILE. Oh, yes, it was all my idea. And Audrey seemed quite pleased and ready to try.

TREVES. Was Kay equally pleased?

NEVILE. Well—no—I had a spot of bother with Kay. I can't think why. I mean if anyone was going to object, you'd think it would be Audrey.

LADY TRESSILIAN. (*Rising.*) Well, I'm an old woman. (*Treves rises.*) Nothing people do nowadays seems to make any sense. (*She moves to the door* L.)

TREVES. (*Crossing to the door* L.) One has to go with the times, Camilla. (*He opens the door.*)

LADY TRESSILIAN. I feel very tired. I shall rest before lunch. (*She turns to Nevile.*) But you must behave yourself, Nevile. With or without reason, Kay is jealous. (*She emphasizes her following words by banging her stick on the carpet.*) I will not have these discordant scenes in my house. (*She peaks off* L.) Ah, Mary—I shall lie down on the library sofa. (*Lady Tressilian exits* L. *Treves closes the door.*)

NEVILE. (*Sitting on the chaise.*) She speaks to me as though I were six.

TREVES. (*Moving up* R. C. *and standing with his back to the audience.*) At her age, she doubtless feels you *are* six.

NEVILE. (*Recovering his temper with an effort.*) Yes, I suppose so. It must be ghastly to be old.

TREVES. (*After a slight pause, turning.*) It has its compensations, I assure you. (*Dryly.*) There is no longer any question of emotional involvements.

NEVILE. (*Grinning.*) That's certainly something. (*He rises and moves above the chaise to the French windows.*) I suppose I'd better go and make my peace with Kay. I really can't see, though, why she has to fly off the handle like this. Audrey might very well be jealous of *her*, but I can't see why she should be jealous of Audrey. Can you? (*Nevile grins and exits by the French windows. Treves thoughtfully strokes his chin for a moment or two, then goes to the waste-paper basket, takes out the pieces of the torn photograph and turns to the bureau to put the pieces into a pigeon-hole. Audrey enters* L., *looking round rather cautiously for Nevile. She carries a magazine.*)

AUDREY. (*Crossing to the coffee table, surprised.*) What are you doing with my photograph? (*She puts the magazine on the table.*)

TREVES. (*Turning and holding out the pieces of the photograph.*) It seems to have been torn.

AUDREY. Who tore it?

TREVES. Mrs. Barrett, I suppose—that *is* the name of the woman in the cloth cap who cleans this room? I thought I would put it in here until it can be mended. (*Treves' eyes meet Audrey's for a moment, then he puts the pieces of the photograph in the bureau.*)

AUDREY. It wasn't Mrs. Barrett, was it?

TREVES. I have no information—but I should think probably not.

AUDREY. Was it Kay?

TREVES. I told you—I have no information. (*There is a pause, during which Audrey crosses to* R. *of the armchair* R.)

AUDREY. Oh, dear, this is all very uncomfortable.

TREVES. Why did you come here, my dear?

AUDREY. I suppose because I always come here at this time. (*She crosses and stands below the armchair* L. C.)

TREVES. But with Nevile coming here, wouldn't it have been better to have postponed your visit?

AUDREY. I couldn't do that. I have a job, you know. I have to earn my living. I have two weeks' holiday and once that is arranged I can't alter it.

TREVES. An interesting job?

AUDREY. Not particularly, but it pays quite well.

TREVES. (*Moving to* R. *of the coffee table.*) But, my dear Audrey, Nevile is a very well-to-do man. Under the terms of your divorce he has to make suitable provision for you.

AUDREY. I have never taken a penny from Nevile. I never shall.

TREVES. Quite so. Quite so. Several of my clients have taken that point of view. It has been my duty to dissuade them. In the end, you know, one must be guided by common sense. You have hardly any money of your own, I know. It is only just and right that you should be provided for suitably by Nevile, who can well afford it. Who were your solicitors, because I could . . .

AUDREY. (*Sitting in the armchair* L. C.) It's nothing to do with solicitors. I won't take anything from Nevile—anything at all.

TREVES. (*Eyeing her thoughtfully.*) I see—you feel strongly —very strongly.

AUDREY. If you like to put it that way, yes.

TREVES. Was it really Nevile's idea to come here all together?

AUDREY. (*Sharply.*) Of course it was.

TREVES. But you agreed?

AUDREY. I agreed. Why not?

TREVES. It hasn't turned out very well, has it?

AUDREY. That's not my fault.

TREVES. No, it isn't your fault—ostensibly.

AUDREY. (*Rising.*) What do you mean?

TREVES. I was wondering . . .

AUDREY. You know, Mr. Treves, sometimes I think I'm just a little frightened of you.

TREVES. Why should you be?

AUDREY. I don't know. You're a very shrewd observer. I sometimes . . . (*Mary enters* L.)

MARY. Audrey, will you go to Lady Tressilian? She's in the library.

AUDREY. Yes. (*Audrey crosses and exits* L. *Treves sits on the chaise. Mary goes to the butler's tray and collects the dirty sherry glasses.*)

TREVES. Miss Aldin, who do you think is behind this plan of meeting here?

MARY. (*Moving to* R. *of the butler's tray.*) Audrey.

TREVES. But why?

MARY. (*Moving to* L. *of Treves.*) I suppose—she still cares for him.

TREVES. You think it's that?

MARY. What else can it be? He's not really in love with Kay, you know.

TREVES. (*Primly.*) These sudden passionate infatuations are very often not of long duration.

MARY. You'd think Audrey would have more pride.

TREVES. In my experience, pride is a word often on women's lips—but they display little sign of it where love affairs are concerned.

MARY. (*With bitterness.*) Perhaps. I wouldn't know. (*She looks towards the French windows.*) Excuse me. (*Mary exits* L. *Royde enters by the French windows. He carries a book.*)

TREVES. Ah, Thomas, have you been down to the ferry?

ROYDE. (*Crossing to* C.) No, I've been reading a detective story. Not very good. (*He looks down at the book.*) Always seems to me these yarns begin in the wrong place. Begin with the murder. But the murder's not really the beginning.

TREVES. Indeed? Where would you begin?

ROYDE. As I see it, the murder is the end of the story. (*He sits in the armchair* L. C.) I mean, the real story begins long before—years before, sometimes. Must do. All the causes and events that bring the people concerned to a certain place on a certain day at a certain time. And then, over the top—zero hour.

TREVES. (*Rising.*) That is an interesting point of view.

ROYDE. (*Apologetically.*) Not very good at explaining myself, I'm afraid.

TREVES. (*Moving above the coffee table.*) I think you've put it very clearly, Thomas. (*He uses the coffee table as a globe.*) All sorts of people converging towards a given spot and hour—all going towards zero. (*He pauses briefly.*) Towards Zero. (*Treves looks at Royde, and the lights fade to Black-Out, as—the Curtain falls.*)

CURTAIN

Scene II

SCENE: *The same. After dinner, four days later. When the Curtain rises, the lights are on. The curtains of the bay window are half closed. The French windows are open, the curtains undrawn. The night is very warm, sultry and cloudy. Kay is seated on the chaise, smoking a cigarette. She is in evening dress and looks rather sulky and bored. Ted Latimer is standing on the rostrum, gazing out of the window. He is a very dark, good-looking man of about twenty-six. His dinner suit fits him a shade too well.*

KAY. (*After a pause.*) This is what I call a wildly hilarious evening, Ted.

LATIMER. (*Turning.*) You should have come over to the hotel as I suggested. (*He moves to the downstage edge of the rostrum.*) They've got a dance on. The band's not so hot, but it's fun.

KAY. I wanted to, but Nevile wasn't keen.

LATIMER. So you behaved like a dutiful wife.

KAY. Yes—and I've been rewarded by being bored to death.

LATIMER. The fate of most dutiful wives. (*He moves to the record player on the window-seat.*) Aren't there any dance records? We could at least dance.

KAY. There's nothing like that *here*. Only Mozart and Bach—all classical stuff.

LATIMER. (*Moving to the coffee table.*) Oh, well—at least we've been spared the old battleaxe tonight. (*He takes a cigarette from the box.*) Doesn't she ever appear at dinner, or did she just shirk it because I was there? (*He lights his cigarette.*)

KAY. Camilla always goes to bed at seven. She's got a groggy heart or something. She has her dinner sent up on a tray.

LATIMER. Not what you'd call a gay life.

KAY. (*Rising abruptly.*) I hate this place. (*She moves below the chaise then up R. of it.*) I wish to God we'd never come here.

LATIMER. (*Moving to* L. *of her.*) Steady, honey. What's the matter?

KAY. I don't know. (*She crosses and stands below the armchair* L. C.) It's just—sometimes I get—*scared*.

LATIMER. (*Moving to* R. *of the coffee table.*) That doesn't sound like you, Kay.

KAY. (*Recovering.*) It doesn't, does it? But there's something queer going on. I don't know what, but I'll swear that Audrey's behind it all.

LATIMER. It was a damn silly idea of Nevile's—coming here with you at the same time as his ex-wife.

KAY. (*Sitting in the armchair* L. C.) I don't think it *was* his idea. I'm convinced *she* put him up to it.

LATIMER. Why?

KAY. I don't know—to cause trouble probably.

LATIMER. (*Moving to Kay and touching her arm.*) What *you* want is a drink, my girl.

KAY. (*Moving his hand from her arm, irritably.*) I don't want a drink and I'm not your girl.

LATIMER. You would have been if Nevile hadn't come along. (*He moves to the butler's tray and pours two glasses of whisky and soda.*) Where *is* Nevile, by the way?

KAY. I've no idea.

LATIMER. They're not a very sociable crowd, are they? Audrey's out on the terrace talking to old Treves, and that fellow Royde's strolling about the garden all by himself, puffing at that eternal pipe of his. Nice, cheery lot.

KAY. (*Crossly.*) I wouldn't care a damn if they were all at the bottom of the sea—except Nevile.

LATIMER. I should have felt much happier, darling, if you'd included Nevile. (*He picks up the drinks and takes one to Kay.*) You drink that, my sweet. You'll feel much better. (*Kay takes her drink and sips it.*)

KAY. God, it's strong.

LATIMER. More soda?

KAY. No, thanks. I wish you wouldn't make it so clear you don't like Nevile.

LATIMER. Why should I like him? He's not my sort. (*Bitterly.*) The ideal Englishman—good at sport, modest, good-looking, always the little pukka sahbit. Getting everything he wants all along the line—even pinched my girl.

KAY. I wasn't your girl.

LATIMER. (*Moving above the coffee table.*) Yes, you were. If I'd been as well off as Nevile . . .

KAY. I didn't marry Nevile for his money.

LATIMER. Oh, I know, and I understand—Mediterranean nights and dewy-eyed romance . . .

KAY. I married Nevile because I fell in love with him.

LATIMER. I'm not saying you didn't, my sweet, but his money helped you to fall.

KAY. Do you *really* think that?

LATIMER. (*Moving up* C.) I try to—it helps soothe my injured vanity.

KAY. (*Rising and moving to* L. *of him.*) You're rather a dear, Ted—I don't know what I should do without you, sometimes.

LATIMER. Why try? I'm always around. You should know that by this time. The faithful swain—or should it be swine? Probably depends which you happen to be—the wife or the husband. (*He kisses Kay's shoulder. Mary enters* L. *She wears a plain dinner frock. Kay moves hastily on to the rostrum up* L.)

MARY. (*Pointedly.*) Have either of you seen Mr. Treves? Lady Tressilian wants him.

LATIMER. He's out on the terrace, Miss Aldin.

MARY. Thank you, Mr. Latimer. (*She closes the door.*) Isn't it stifling? I'm sure there's going to be a storm. (*She crosses to the French windows.*)

LATIMER. I hope it holds off until I get back to the hotel. (*He moves to* L. *of Mary and glances off.*) I didn't bring a coat. I'll get soaked to the skin going over in the ferry if it rains.

MARY. I daresay we could find you an umbrella if necessary, or Nevile could lend you his raincoat. (*Mary exits by the French windows.*)

LATIMER. (*Moving up* C.) Interesting woman, that—bit of a dark horse.

KAY. I feel rather sorry for her. (*She moves to the armchair* L. C., *sits and sips her drink.*) Slaving for that unpleasant old woman—and she won't get anything for it, either. All the money comes to me and Nevile.

LATIMER. (*Moving to* R. *of Kay.*) Perhaps she doesn't know that.

KAY. That would be rather funny. (*They laugh. Audrey and Treves enter by the French windows. Treves is wearing an old-fashioned dinner suit. Audrey is in evening dress. She notices Latimer and Kay together, then moves below the chaise. Treves stops in the doorway and speaks over his shoulder.*)

TREVES. I shall *enjoy* a little gossip with Lady Tressilian, Miss Aldin. With, perhaps, the remembering of a few old scandals. A touch of malice, you know, adds a certain savour to conversation. (*He crosses to the door* L.) Doesn't it, Audrey?

AUDREY. She chooses the person she wants and summons them by a kind of Royal Command.

TREVES. Very aptly put, Audrey. I am always sensible of the royal touch in Lady Tressilian's manner. (*Treves exits* L.)

AUDREY. (*Listlessly.*) It's terribly hot, isn't it? (*She sits on the chaise.*)

LATIMER. (*With a step towards the butler's tray.*) Would you—like a drink?

AUDREY. (*Shaking her head.*) No, thank you. I think I shall go to bed very soon. (*There is a short silence. Nevile enters* L. *He is wearing a dinner suit and is carrying a magazine.*)

KAY. What *have* you been doing all this time, Nevile?

NEVILE. I had a couple of letters to write—thought I might as well get 'em off my chest.

KAY. (*Rising.*) You might have chosen some other time. (*She moves to the butler's tray and puts her glass on it.*)

NEVILE. (*Crossing and standing above the coffee table.*) Better the hour, better the deed. By the way, here's the *Illustrated News.* Somebody wanted it.

KAY. (*Holding out her hand.*) Thank you, Nevile.

AUDREY. (*At almost the same moment.*) Oh! Thank you, Nevile. (*She holds out her hand. Nevile hesitates between them, smiling.*)

KAY. (*With a slight note of hysteria.*) I want it. Give it to me.

AUDREY. (*Withdrawing her hand, slightly confused.*) Oh, sorry. I thought you were speaking to me, Nevile. (*Nevile hesitates for a moment, then holds out the magazine to Audrey.*)

NEVILE. (*Quietly.*) Here you are, Audrey.

AUDREY. Oh, but I . . .

KAY. (*In suppressed fury, and almost crying.*) It is stifling in here. (*She moves quickly to the coffee table, picks up her evening bag and rushes below the chaise to the French windows.*) Let's go out in the air, Ted. I can't stand being cooped up in this lousy hole any longer. (*Kay almost stumbles as she exits by the French windows. Latimer, with an angry look at Nevile, follows Kay off. Nevile tosses the magazine on to the coffee table.*)

AUDREY. (*Rising, reproachfully.*) You shouldn't have done that, Nevile.

NEVILE. Why not?

AUDREY. (*Crossing below the coffee table and standing down L.*) It was stupid. You'd better go after Kay and apologize.

NEVILE. I don't see why I should apologize.

AUDREY. I think you'd better. You were very rude to your wife. (*Mary enters by the French windows and stands above the chaise.*)

NEVILE. (*In a low voice.*) You're my wife, Audrey. You always will be. (*He sees Mary.*) Ah—Miss Aldin—are you going up to Lady Tressilian? (*Audrey moves on to the L. end of the rostrum.*)

MARY. (*Crossing to L. C.*) Yes—when Mr. Treves comes down. (*Royde enters by the French windows and stands R. of the chaise. Nevile stares for a moment at Royde, then exits by the French windows. Wearily.*) Oh, dear! I don't think I've ever felt so tired in my life. If Lady Tressilian's bell rings tonight, I'm quite certain I shall never hear it. (*She sits in the armchair L. C.*)

AUDREY. (*Turning and moving to the downstage edge of the rostrum.*) What bell?

MARY. It rings in my room—in case Lady Tressilian should want anything in the night. It's one of those old-fashioned bells—on a spring and worked with a wire. It makes a ghastly jangle, but Lady Tressilian insists that it's more reliable than electricity. (*She yawns.*) Excuse me—it's this dreadful sultry weather, I think.

AUDREY. You ought to go to bed, Mary. You look worn out.

MARY. I shall—as soon as Mr. Treves has finished talking to Lady Tressilian. Then I shall tuck her up for the night and go to bed myself. Oh, dear. It's been a very trying day. (*Latimer enters by the French windows and moves down* R.)

ROYDE. It certainly has.

AUDREY. (*After a look at Latimer.*) Thomas! Let's go on to the terrace. (*She crosses to the French windows.*)

ROYDE. (*Moving to Audrey.*) Yes—I want to tell you about a detective story I've been reading . . . (*Audrey and Royde exit by the French windows. There is a pause, as Latimer looks after Royde and Audrey for a moment.*)

LATIMER. You and I, Miss Aldin, seem to be the odd men out. We must console each other. (*He moves to the butler's tray.*) Can I get you a drink?

MARY. No, thank you.

LATIMER. (*Pouring a drink for himself.*) One conjugal reconciliation in the rose garden, one faithful swain nerving himself to pop the question. Where do we come in? Nowhere. We're the outsiders. (*He moves to the downstage edge of the rostrum and raises his glass.*) Here's to the outsiders—and to hell with all those inside the ringed fence. (*He drinks.*)

MARY. How bitter you are.

LATIMER. So are you.

MARY. (*After a pause.*) Not really.

LATIMER. (*Moving below the coffee table to* R. *of it.*) What's it like, fetching and carrying, running up and down stairs, endlessly waiting on an old woman?

MARY. There are worse things.

LATIMER. I wonder. (*He turns and looks towards the terrace.*)

MARY. (*After a pause.*) You're very unhappy.

LATIMER. Who isn't?

MARY. Have—(*She pauses.*) you always been in love with Kay?

LATIMER. More or less.

MARY. And she?

LATIMER. (*Moving up* R. C.) I thought so—until Nevile came along. Nevile with his money and his sporting record. (*He moves to* L. *of the chaise.*) I could go climbing in the Himalayas if I'd ever had the cash.

MARY. You wouldn't want to.

LATIMER. Perhaps not. (*Sharply.*) What do you want out of life?

MARY. (*Rising, after a pause.*) It's almost too late.

LATIMER. But not quite.

MARY. No—not quite. (*She moves on to the rostrum.*) All I want is a little money—not very much—just enough.

LATIMER. Enough for what?

MARY. Enough to have some sort of life of my own before it's too late. I've never had anything.

LATIMER. (*Moving to* R. *of Mary.*) Do you hate them, too, those inside the fence?

MARY. (*Violently.*) Hate them—I . . . (*She yawns.*) No—no—I'm too tired to hate anybody. (*Treves enters* L.)

TREVES. Ah, Miss Aldin, Lady Tressilian would like you to go to her now if you will be so kind. I think she's feeling sleepy.

MARY. That's a blessing. Thank you, Mr. Treves. I'll go up at once. (*She crosses to the door* L.) I shan't come down again so I'll say good night now. Good night, Mr. Latimer. Good night, Mr. Treves.

LATIMER. Good night. (*Mary exits* L. *Treves moves on to the* L. *end of the rostrum.*) I must be running along myself. With luck I shall get across the ferry and back to the hotel before the storm breaks. (*He moves above the chaise. Royde enters by the French windows.*)

ROYDE. Are you going, Latimer? Would you like a raincoat?

LATIMER. No, thanks, I'll chance it.

ROYDE. (*Moving on to the rostrum.*) Hell of a storm coming.

TREVES. Is Audrey on the terrace?

ROYDE. I haven't the faintest idea. (*He crosses to the door* L.) I'm for bed. Good night. (*Royde exits* L. *There is a flash of lightning and a low rumble of thunder is heard off.*)

LATIMER. (*With malice.*) It would seem that the course of true love has not run smoothly. Was that thunder? Some way away still—(*He moves to the French windows.*) but I think I'll make it.

TREVES. I'll come with you and bolt the garden gate. (*He crosses to the French windows. Latimer and Treves exit by the French windows.*)

AUDREY. (*Off, to Latimer.*) Good night. (*Audrey enters rather quickly by the French windows. There is a flash of lightning and a rumble of thunder. Audrey stands for a moment looking around the room, then moves slowly on to the rostrum, sits on the window-seat and looks out at the night. Nevile enters by the French windows and moves above the chaise.*)

NEVILE. Audrey.

AUDREY. (*Rising quickly and moving to the* L. *end of the rostrum.*) I'm going to bed, Nevile. Good night.

NEVILE. (*Moving on to the rostrum.*) Don't go yet. I want to talk to you.

AUDREY. (*Nervously.*) I think you'd better not.

NEVILE. (*Moving to* R. *of her.*) I must. I've got to. Please listen to me, Audrey.

AUDREY. (*Backing to the* L. *wall of the window bay.*) I'd rather you didn't.

NEVILE. That means you know what I'm going to say. (*Audrey does not reply.*) Audrey, can't we go back to where we were? Forget everything that has happened?

AUDREY. (*Turning a little.*) Including—Kay?

NEVILE. Kay will be sensible.

AUDREY. What do you mean by—sensible?

NEVILE. (*Eagerly.*) I shall tell her the truth—that you are the only woman I've ever loved. That *is* the truth, Audrey. You've got to believe that.

AUDREY. (*Desperately.*) You loved Kay when you married her.

NEVILE. My marriage to Kay was the biggest mistake I ever made. I realize now what a damned fool I've been. I . . . (*Kay enters by the French windows.*)

KAY. (*Moving to* R. C.) Sorry to interrupt this touching scene, but I think it's about time I did.

NEVILE. (*Moving to* C. *of the rostrum.*) Kay, listen . . .

KAY. (*Furiously.*) Listen! I've heard all I want to hear—too much.

AUDREY. (*With relief.*) I'm going to bed. (*She moves to the door* L.) Good night.

KAY. (*Crossing to* R. *of Audrey.*) That's right. Go to bed! You've done all the mischief you wanted to do, haven't you? But you're not going to get out of it as easily as all that. I'll deal with you after I've had it out with Nevile.

AUDREY. (*Coldly.*) It's no concern of mine. Good night. (*Audrey exits* L. *There is a flash of lightning and a peal of thunder off.*)

KAY. (*Looking after Audrey.*) Of all the damned, cool . . .

NEVILE. (*Moving to* R. *of the coffee table.*) Look here, Kay, Audrey had absolutely nothing to do with this. It's not her fault. Blame me if you like . . .

KAY. (*Working herself up.*) And I do like. What sort of man do you think you are? (*She turns to Nevile. Her voice rises.*) You leave your wife, come bald-headed after me, get your wife to divorce you. Crazy about me one minute, tired of me the next. Now I suppose you want to go back to that—(*She looks towards the door* L.) whey-faced, mewling, double-crossing little cat . . .

NEVILE. (*Angrily.*) Stop that, Kay.

KAY. (*Moving on to the rostrum.*) That's what she is. A crafty, cunning, scheming, little . . .

NEVILE. (*Moving to Kay and gripping her arms.*) Stop it!

KAY. (*Releasing herself.*) Leave me alone! (*She moves slowly to* L. *of the chaise.*) What the hell do you want?

NEVILE. (*Turning and facing up stage.*) I can't go on. I'm every kind of worm you like to call me. But it's no good, Kay. I can't go on. (*Kay sits on the chaise. He turns.*) I think—really—I must have loved Audrey all the time. I've only just realized it. My love for you was—was a kind of madness. But it's no good—you and I don't belong. It's better to cut our losses. (*He moves above the chaise to* R. *of it.*)

KAY. (*In a deceptively quiet voice.*) What exactly are you suggesting, Nevile?

NEVILE. We can get a divorce. You can divorce me for desertion.

KAY. You'd have to wait three years for it.

NEVILE. I'll wait.

KAY. And then, I suppose, you'll ask dear, sweet, darling Audrey to marry you all over again? Is *that* the idea?

NEVILE. If she'll have me.

KAY. She'll have you all right. And where do I come in?

NEVILE. Naturally, I'll see you're well provided for.

KAY. (*Losing control of herself.*) Cut out the bribes. (*She rises and moves to Nevile.*) Listen to me, Nevile. I'll *not* divorce you. (*She beats her hands against his chest.*) You fell in love with me and you married me and I'm not going to let you go back to the sly little bitch who's got her hooks into you again.

NEVILE. (*Throwing Kay on to the chaise.*) Shut up, Kay. For God's sake. You can't make this kind of scene here.

KAY. She meant this to happen. It's what she's been playing for. She's probably gloating over her success now. But she's not going to bring it off. You'll see what I can do. (*She flings herself on the chaise in a paroxysm of hys-*

*terical sobbing. Nevile gives a despairing gesture. Treves
enters by the French windows and stands watching. At
the same moment there is a brilliant flash of lightning,
a rolling peal of thunder and the storm bursts as—the
curtain falls.)*

CURTAIN

Act Two

Scene I

SCENE: *The same. Early the following morning.*
*When the curtain rises, it is a fine morning with the sun
streaming in through the bay window. The French windows are open. The butler's tray has been removed. The
room is empty. Royde enters by the French windows.
He is sucking at his pipe which appears to have become
stopped up. He looks around for an ashtray, sees one on
the coffee table, moves to it and knocks out the ashes
from his pipe. Finding it is still stopped up, he takes a
penknife from his pocket and gently probes the bowl.
Treves enters down L.*

TREVES. Good morning, Thomas.

ROYDE. (*Moving above the coffee table.*) 'Morning. Going
to be another lovely day by the look of it.

TREVES. Yes. (*He goes on to the* L. *end of the rostrum and
looks out of the window.*) I thought possibly the storm
might have broken up the spell of fine weather, but it
has only removed that oppressive heat—which is all to
the good. (*He moves to the* R. *end of the rostrum.*)
You've been up for hours as usual, I presume?

ROYDE. Since just after six. Been for a walk along the cliffs.
Only just got back, as a matter of fact.

TREVES. Nobody else appears to be about yet. Not even Miss
Aldin.

ROYDE. Um.

TREVES. Possibly she is fully occupied attending to Lady Tressilian. I should imagine she may be rather upset after
that unfortunate incident last night. (*He moves to* L.
of the chaise.)

ROYDE. (*Blowing down his pipe.*) Bit of a rumpus, wasn't there?

TREVES. (*Moving down* R.) You have a positive genius for understatement, Thomas. That unpleasant scene between Nevile and Kay . . .

ROYDE. (*Surprised.*) Nevile and *Kay*? The row *I* heard was between Nevile and Lady Tressilian.

TREVES. (*Moving* R. *of the chaise.*) When was this?

ROYDE. Must have been about twenty past ten. They were going at it hammer and tongs. Couldn't help hearing. My room's practically opposite hers, you know.

TREVES. (*Moving above the chaise, troubled.*) Dear, dear, this is news to me.

ROYDE. Thought that was what you meant.

TREVES. (*Moving to* R. *of Royde.*) No, no, I was referring to a most distressing scene that took place in here earlier, to part of which I was a reluctant witness. That unfortunate young woman—er—Kay, had a fit of violent hysterics.

ROYDE. What was the row about?

TREVES. I'm afraid it was Nevile's fault.

ROYDE. That doesn't surprise me. He's been behaving like a damn fool. (*He moves on to the rostrum.*)

TREVES. I entirely agree. His conduct has been most reprehensible. (*He sighs and sits on the chaise.*)

ROYDE. Was—Audrey mixed up in the row?

TREVES. She was the cause of it. (*Kay enters quickly* L. *She looks subdued and tired. She carries her handbag.*)

KAY. Oh! Good—good morning.

TREVES. (*Rising.*) Good morning, Kay.

ROYDE. Good morning.

KAY. (*Moving* L. C.; *nervous and ill at ease.*) We're—we're the only ones up, aren't we?

TREVES. I think so. I haven't seen anyone else. I breakfasted in—er—solitary state.

ROYDE. Haven't had mine yet. Think I'll go and hunt some up. (*To Kay.*) Have you had breakfast?

KAY. No. I've only just come down. I—I don't want any breakfast. I feel like hell.

ROYDE. Um—could eat a house, myself. (*He crosses below Kay to the door* L.) See you later. (*Royde exits* L.)

KAY. (*With a step or two towards Treves, after a slight pause.*) Mr. Treves—I—I'm afraid I behaved—rather badly last night.

TREVES. It was very natural that you should be upset.

KAY. I lost my temper and I said a lot of—of foolish things.

TREVES. We are all apt to do that at times. You had every provocation. Nevile was, in my opinion, very much to blame.

KAY. He was led into it. Audrey's been determined to cause trouble between Nevile and me ever since we came here.

TREVES. (*Moving above the coffee table.*) I don't think you're being quite fair to her.

KAY. She planned this, I tell you. She knows that Nevile's always—always felt guilty at the way he treated her.

TREVES. (*Moving to* R. *of Kay.*) No, no, I'm sure you're wrong.

KAY. No, no, I'm not wrong. You see, Mr. Treves, I went over it all in the night, and Audrey thought that if she could get us all here together and—(*She crosses to* R. *of the coffee table.*) and pretend to be friendly and forgiving that she could get him back. She's worked on his conscience. Pale and aloof—creeping about like a—like a grey ghost. She knew what effect *that* would have on Nevile. He's always reproached himself because he thought he'd treated her badly. (*She sits on the chaise.*) Right from the beginning—or nearly the beginning— Audrey's shadow has been between us. Nevile couldn't quite forget about her—she was always there at the back of his mind.

TREVES. You can hardly blame her for that.

KAY. Oh, don't you *see*? She *knew* how Nevile felt. She *knew* what the result would be if they were thrown together again.

TREVES. I think you are giving her credit for more cunning than she possesses.

KAY. You're all on her side—all of you.

TREVES. My dear Kay!

KAY. (*Rising.*) You'd *like* to see Nevile go back to Audrey. I'm the interloper—I don't *belong*—Nevile said so last night and he was right. Camilla's always disliked me— she's put up with me for Nevile's sake. I'm supposed to see everyone's point of view but my own. What I feel or think doesn't matter. If *my* life is all smashed up it's just too bad, but it doesn't matter. It's only *Audrey* who matters.

TREVES. No, no, no.

KAY. (*Her voice rising.*) Well, she's not going to smash up my life. I don't care what I do to stop it, but I will. I'll make it impossible for Nevile to go back to her. (*Nevile enters* L.)

NEVILE. (*Taking in the situation.*) What's the matter *now*? More trouble?

KAY. What do you expect after the way you behaved last night? (*She sits on the chaise and takes a handkerchief from her bag. Treves moves on to the* R. *end of the rostrum.*)

NEVILE. (*Crossing slowly and standing up* L. *of Kay.*) It was you who made all the fuss, Kay. I was prepared to talk the matter over calmly.

KAY. Calmly! Did you imagine that I was going to accept your suggestion that I should divorce you, and leave the way clear for Audrey, as if—as if you were inviting me to—to go to a dance? (*Treves crosses to the* L. *of the rostrum.*)

NEVILE. No, but at least you needn't behave in this hysterical fashion when you're staying in other people's houses. For goodness' sake control yourself and try to behave properly.

KAY. Like *she* does, I suppose?

NEVILE. At any rate, Audrey doesn't make an exhibition of herself.

KAY. She's turning you against me—just as she intended.

NEVILE. Look here, Kay, this isn't Audrey's fault. I told you that last night. I explained the situation. I was quite open and honest about it.

KAY. (*Scornfully.*) Open and honest!

NEVILE. Yes. I can't help feeling the way I do.

KAY. How do you suppose I feel? You don't care about that, do you?

TREVES. (*Moving down* C. *and interposing.*) I really think, Nevile, that you should very seriously consider your attitude in this—er—matter. Kay is your wife. She has certain rights of which you cannot deprive her in this—this cavalier manner.

NEVILE. I admit that, but—I'm willing to do the—the right thing.

KAY. The *right* thing!

TREVES. Furthermore it is hardly the—er—proper procedure to discuss this under Lady Tressilian's roof. It is bound

to upset her very seriously. (*He crosses below Nevile to*
L. *of Kay*.) My sympathies are entirely with Kay, but I
think you *both* have a duty to your hostess and to your
fellow guests. I suggest that you postpone any further
discussion of the matter until your visit here has termi-
nated.

NEVILE. (*A little shamefacedly*.) I suppose you're right, Mr.
Treves—yes, of course, you're right. I'm willing. What
do you say, Kay?

KAY. As long as Audrey doesn't try and . . .

NEVILE. (*Sharply*.) Audrey hasn't tried anything.

TREVES. (*To Kay*.) Ssh! I think, my dear, you would be well
advised to agree to my suggestion. It is only a question
of a few more days.

KAY. (*Rising, ungraciously*.) Oh, very well then. (*She moves
to the French windows*.)

NEVILE. (*Relieved*.) Well, that's that. I'm going to get some
breakfast. (*He moves to the door* L.) We might all go
sailing later on. (*He goes on to the* L. *end of the rostrum
and glances out of the window*.) There's quite a good
breeze. (*He looks at Treves*.) Would you like to come?

TREVES. I'm afraid I'm a little too old for that sort of thing.
(*He crosses towards the door* L.)

NEVILE. What about you, Kay?

KAY. (*Moving* R. C.) What about Ted? We promised him
we'd go over this morning.

NEVILE. There's no reason why he shouldn't come, too. I'll
get hold of Royde and Audrey and see what they think
of the idea. It should be lovely out in the bay. (*Audrey
enters* L. *She looks worried*.)

AUDREY. (*Anxiously*.) Mr. Treves—what do you think we
ought to do? We can't wake Mary. (*Kay moves down* R.
of the chaise.)

NEVILE. Can't *wake* her? (*He moves off the rostrum to* C.)
What do you mean?

AUDREY. Just that. When Mrs. Barrett came, she took up
Mary's morning tea as usual. (*She moves slowly* L. C.)
Mary was fast asleep. Mrs. Barrett drew the curtains
and called to her, but Mary didn't wake up, so she left
the tea on the bedside table. She didn't bother much
when Mary didn't come down, but when Mary didn't
come down to fetch Camilla's tea, Mrs. Barrett went up
again. Mary's tea was stone cold and she was still asleep.

TREVES. (*Moving down* L. *of the armchair* L. C.) She was very tired last night, Audrey.

AUDREY. But this isn't a *natural* sleep, Mr. Treves. It *can't* be. Mrs. Barrett shook her—hard—and she didn't wake. I went in to Mary and I tried to wake her, too. There's definitely something wrong with her.

NEVILE. Do you mean she's unconscious?

AUDREY. I don't know. She looks very pale and she just lies there—like a log.

KAY. Perhaps she took some sleeping pills.

AUDREY. (*Moving* C.) That's what I thought, but it's so unlike Mary. (*She turns to Treves.*) What shall we do?

TREVES. I think you should get a doctor. She may be ill.

NEVILE. (*Crossing to the door* L.) I'll go and phone Lazenby and get him to come at once. (*Nevile exits quickly* L.)

TREVES. (*Moving* L. C.) Have you told Lady Tressilian, Audrey?

AUDREY. (*Moving* R. C.; *shaking her head.*) No, not yet. I didn't want to disturb her. They're making her some fresh tea in the kitchen. I'm going to take it up. I'll tell her then.

TREVES. I sincerely hope it's nothing serious.

KAY. She's probably taken an overdose of sleeping stuff. (*She sits in the easy chair down* R.)

TREVES. That *could* be extremely serious.

AUDREY. I can't imagine Mary doing such a thing. (*Royde enters* L.)

ROYDE. (*Moving between Treves and Audrey.*) I heard Strange telephoning Dr. Lazenby. What's the matter?

AUDREY. It's Mary. She's still asleep and we can't get her to wake up. Kay thinks she may have taken an overdose of some drug.

KAY. Something like that must have happened or you'd be able to wake her.

ROYDE. Sleeping stuff, do you mean? Shouldn't think she'd have needed anything like that last night. She was dog tired.

TREVES. I'm sure she wouldn't take any sort of drug, you know—in case the bell rang.

KAY. Bell?

ROYDE. There's a bell in her room. Lady Tressilian always rings it if she wants anything in the night. (*To Audrey.*) Remember she was telling us about it last night.

AUDREY. Mary wouldn't take anything that would stop her hearing the bell, in case it was urgent. (*Nevile enters quickly* L.)

NEVILE. Lazenby's coming round right away.

AUDREY. (*Crossing to the door* L.) Oh, good. Before he gets here I'd better go and see about Camilla's tea. She'll be wondering what's happened.

NEVILE. Can I help?

AUDREY. No, thank you. I can manage. (*Audrey exits* L. *Kay rises and moves up* R. *of the chaise.*)

ROYDE. (*Moving to the chaise.*) I wonder if it could be some kind of heart attack. (*He sits on the chaise. Treves sits in the armchair* L. C.)

NEVILE. (*Crossing and standing on the right end of the rostrum.*) It's not much use conjecturing, is it? Lazenby'll be able to tell us. Poor old Mary. I don't know what will happen if she's really ill.

TREVES. It would be disastrous. Lady Tressilian relies on Mary for everything.

KAY. (*Moving to* R. *of Nevile, hopefully.*) I suppose we should all have to pack up and go?

NEVILE. (*Smiling at Kay*). Perhaps it isn't anything serious after all. (*Kay moves down* R.)

ROYDE. Must be something pretty bad if she can't be wakened.

TREVES. It can't take Dr. Lazenby very long to get here, and then we shall know. He lives a very short distance away.

NEVILE. He ought to be here in about ten minutes, I should think.

TREVES. Possibly he will be able to relieve all our minds. I trust so.

NEVILE. (*With a determinedly cheerful air.*) No good looking on the black side of things, anyway.

KAY. (*Moving to* R. *of the chaise.*) Always the perfect optimist, aren't you, Nevile?

NEVILE. Well, things usually work out all right.

ROYDE. They certainly do for you.

NEVILE. (*Moving to* L. *of Royde.*) I don't quite know what you mean by that, Thomas.

ROYDE. (*Rising.*) I should have thought it was obvious.

NEVILE. What are you insinuating?

ROYDE. I'm not insinuating anything. I'm stating facts.

TREVES. (*Rising.*) Ssh! (*He moves* C. *and hastily changes the subject.*) Do you think—er—we ought to see if there is anything we could do to—er—help. Lady Tressilian might wish . . . (*Royde crosses above the others and stands on the left end of the rostrum.*)

NEVILE. If Camilla wants us to do anything she'll soon say so. I wouldn't interfere unless she does, if I were you. (*Audrey is heard to scream off* L. *Royde exits hurriedly. There is a short pause. Audrey, supported by Royde, enters* L. *She looks almost dazed.*)

AUDREY. Camilla—Camilla . . .

TREVES. (*Concerned.*) My dear! What's the matter?

AUDREY. (*In a husky whisper.*) It's—Camilla.

NEVILE. (*Surprised.*) Camilla? What's wrong with her?

AUDREY. She's—she's dead.

KAY. (*Sitting on the chaise.*) Oh, no, no.

NEVILE. It must have been her heart.

AUDREY. No—it—it wasn't her heart. (*She presses her hands to her eyes. They all stare at her. She shouts.*) There's blood—all over her head. (*She suddenly screams out hysterically.*) She's been murdered. Don't you understand? She's been murdered. (*Audrey sinks into the easy chair down* L. *and the lights fade to Black-Out, as—the Curtain falls.*)

CURTAIN

Scene II

SCENE: *The same. Two hours later. The furniture has been moved to make the room more suitable for the police interrogations. The coffee table has been moved into the alcove* R., *and the chaise on to the rostrum. A card table has been placed* R. C. *with the upright chair from the alcove* L. *of it. The armchair* L. C. *is now above the card table and the easy chair down* L. *is now* L. C. *On the card table is a small tray with a jug of water and two glasses. Also on the card table are a box of cigarettes, an ashtray and a box of matches. A copy of "The Times" lies half open on the window-seat.*

When the curtain rises, Treves is standing L. *of the card table, looking around the room. After a moment he moves up* C. *on the rostrum. Superintendent Battle enters* L. *He is a big man, aged about fifty, and is quietly dressed. His face is heavy but intelligent.*

TREVES. Ah. Battle.

BATTLE. That's fixed up, sir.

TREVES. It was all right, was it, Battle?

BATTLE. (*Crossing to* C.) Yes, sir. The Chief Constable got through to the Yard. As I happened to be on the spot they've agreed to let me handle the case. (*He moves down* R., *turns and looks around the room.*)

TREVES. (*Moving down* C.) I'm very glad. It's going to make it easier having you instead of a stranger. Pity to have spoilt your holiday, though.

BATTLE. Oh, I don't mind that, sir. I'll be able to give my nephew a hand. It'll be his first murder case, you see.

TREVES. (*Moving to the bureau chair.*) Yes, yes—I've no doubt he will find your experience of great help. (*He moves the chair to* R. *of the card table.*)

BATTLE. (*Crossing to* R. C.) It's a nasty business.

TREVES. Shocking, shocking. (*He crosses and stands below the easy chair* L. C.)

BATTLE. I've seen the doctor. Two blows were struck. The first was sufficient to cause death. The murderer must have struck again to make sure, or in a blind rage.

TREVES. Horrible. (*He sits in the easy chair* L. C.) I can't believe it could have been anyone in the house.

BATTLE. Afraid it was, sir. We've been into all that. No entry was forced. (*He moves in the direction of the French windows.*) All the doors and windows were fastened this morning as usual. And then there's the drugging of Miss Aldin—that must have been an inside job.

TREVES. How is she?

BATTLE. Still sleeping it off, but she was given a pretty heavy dose. It looks like careful planning on somebody's part. (*He crosses to* C.) Lady Tressilian might have pulled that bell which rings in Miss Aldin's room, if she'd been alarmed. That had to be taken care of—so Miss Aldin was doped.

TREVES. (*Troubled.*) It still seems to me quite incredible.

BATTLE. We'll get to the bottom of it, sir, in the end. (*He moves to* L. *of the card table.*) Death occurred, according to the doctor, between ten-thirty and midnight. Not earlier than ten-thirty, not later than midnight. That should be a help. (*He sits on the chair* L. *of the card table.*)

TREVES. Yes, yes. And the weapon used was a niblick?

BATTLE. Yes, sir. Thrown down by the bed, blood-stained and with white hairs sticking to it. (*Treves makes a gesture of repulsion.*) I shouldn't have deduced a niblick from the appearance of the wound, but apparently the sharp edge of the club didn't touch the head. The doctor says it was the rounded part of the club hit her.

TREVES. The—er—murderer was incredibly stupid, don't you think, to leave the weapon behind?

BATTLE. Probably lost his head. It happens.

TREVES. Possibly—yes, possibly. I suppose there are no finger-prints?

BATTLE. (*Rising and moving up* R. C.) Sergeant Pengelly is attending to that now, sir. I doubt if it's going to be as easy as that. (*Inspector Leach enters* L. *He is a youngish man, about thirty-eight to forty, thin and dark. He speaks with a slight Cornish accent. He carries a niblick golf club.*)

LEACH. (*Crossing above the easy chair* L. C. *to* L. *of Battle.*) See here, Uncle. Pengelly has brought up a beautiful set of dabs on this—clear as day.

BATTLE. (*Warningly.*) Be careful how you go handling that, my boy.

LEACH. It's all right, we've got photographs. Got specimens of the blood and hair, too. (*He shows the club to Battle.*) What do you think of these dabs? Clear as clear, aren't they? (*Battle inspects the fingerprints on the shaft of the club, then crosses to* R. *of Treves.*)

BATTLE. They're clear enough. What a fool! (*He shows the club to Treves.*)

LEACH. That's so to be sure.

BATTLE. All we've got to do now, my lad, is ask everyone nicely and politely if we may take their fingerprints—no compulsion, of course. Everyone will say "yes"—and one of two things will happen. Either none of the prints will agree, or else . . .

LEACH. It'll be in the bag, eh? (*He crosses to the door* L. *Battle nods.*)

TREVES. Doesn't it strike you as extremely odd, Battle, that the—er—murderer should have been so foolish as to leave such a damning piece of evidence behind—actually on the scene of the crime?

BATTLE. I've known 'em do things equally foolish, sir. (*He puts the club on the chaise.*) Well, let's get on with it. Where's everybody?

LEACH. (*Moving up* L.) In the library. Pollock is going through all their rooms. Except Miss Aldin's, of course. She's still sleeping off the effects of that dope.

BATTLE. We'll have 'em in here one at a time. (*To Treves.*) Which Mrs. Strange was it who discovered the murder?

TREVES. Mrs. Audrey Strange.

BATTLE. Oh, yes. Difficult when there are two Mrs. Stranges. Mrs. Audrey Strange is the divorced wife, isn't she?

TREVES. Yes. I explained to you the—er—situation.

BATTLE. Yes, sir. Funny idea of Mr. Strange's. I should have thought that most men . . . (*Kay enters quickly* L. *She is very upset and slightly hysterical.*)

KAY. (*Crossing towards the French windows, to Battle.*) I'm not going to stay cooped up in that damned library any longer. I want some air and I'm going out. You can do what the hell you like about it. (*Leach moves down* L.)

BATTLE. Just a minute, Mrs. Strange. (*Kay stops and turns by the French windows.*) There's no reason why you shouldn't go out if you wish, but it'll have to be later.

KAY. I want to go *now*.

BATTLE. I'm afraid that's impossible.

KAY. (*Moving slowly down* R.) You've no right to keep me here. I haven't done anything.

BATTLE. (*Soothingly.*) No, no, of course you haven't. But you see, there'll be one or two questions we'll have to ask you.

KAY. What sort of questions? I can't help you. I don't know anything about it.

BATTLE. (*Moving down* C.; *to Leach.*) Get Benson, will you, Jim? (*Leach nods and exits* L.) Now you just sit down here, Mrs. Strange—(*He indicates the chair* L. *of the card table*) and relax.

KAY. (*Moving and sitting* L. *of the card table.*) I've told you I don't know anything. Why do I have to answer a lot of questions when I don't know anything?

BATTLE. (*Moving above the card table and standing down* R. *of it, apologetically.*) We've got to interview everybody, you see. It's just part of the routine. Not very pleasant for you, or for us, but there you are.

KAY. Oh, well—all right. (*Police-Constable Benson enters* L. *Leach follows him on. Benson is a youngish man, fairish and very quiet. He moves to* L. *of the chaise and takes out a notebook and pencil.*)

BATTLE. (*Sitting* R. *of the card table.*) Now, just tell us about last night, Mrs. Strange.

KAY. What about last night?

BATTLE. What did you do—say from after dinner, onwards?

KAY. I had a headache. I—I went to bed quite early.

BATTLE. How early?

KAY. I don't know exactly. It was about a quarter to ten, I think.

TREVES. (*Interposing gently.*) Ten minutes to ten.

KAY. Was it? I wouldn't know to the minute.

BATTLE. We'll take it was ten minutes to ten. (*He makes a sign to Benson. Benson makes a note in his book.*) Did your husband accompany you?

KAY. No.

BATTLE. (*After a pause.*) What time did *he* come to bed?

KAY. I've no idea. You'd better ask *him* that.

LEACH. (*Crossing to* L. *of Kay.*) The door between your room and your husband's is locked. Was it locked when you went to bed?

KAY. Yes.

LEACH. Who locked it?

KAY. I did.

BATTLE. Was it usual for you to lock it?

KAY. No.

BATTLE. (*Rising.*) Why did you do so last night, Mrs. Strange? (*Kay does not reply. Leach moves up* R. C.)

TREVES. (*After a pause.*) I should tell them, Kay.

KAY. I suppose if I don't, you will. Oh, well, then. You can have it. Nevile and I had a row—a flaming row. (*Leach looks at Benson, who makes a note.*) I was furious with him. I went to bed and locked the door because I was still in a flaming rage with him.

BATTLE. I see—what was the trouble about?

KAY. Does it matter? I don't see how it concerns . . .

BATTLE. You're not compelled to answer, if you'd rather not.

KAY. Oh, I don't mind. My husband has been behaving like a perfect fool. It's all that woman's fault, though.

BATTLE. What woman?

KAY. Audrey—his first wife. It was she who got him to come here in the first place.

BATTLE. I understood that it was *Mr.* Strange's idea.

KAY. Well, it wasn't. It was hers.

BATTLE. But why should Mrs. Audrey Strange have suggested

it? (*During the following speech, Leach crosses slowly to the door* L.)

KAY. To cause trouble, I suppose. Nevile thinks it was his own idea—poor innocent. But he never thought of such a thing until he met Audrey in the Park one day in London, and she put the idea into his head and made him believe he'd thought of it himself. I've seen her scheming mind behind it from the first. She's never taken *me* in.

BATTLE. Why should she be so anxious for you all to come here together?

KAY. (*Quickly and breathlessly.*) Because she wanted to get hold of Nevile again. That's why. She's never forgiven him for going off with me. This is her revenge. She got him to fix it so that we'd be here together and then she got to work on him. She's been doing it ever since we arrived. (*Battle crosses above the card table to* C.) She's clever, damned clever. She knows just how to look pathetic and elusive. Poor sweet, injured little kitten—with all her blasted claws out.

TREVES. Kay—Kay . . .

BATTLE. I see. Surely, if you felt so strongly, you could have objected to this arrangement of coming here?

KAY. Do you think I didn't try? Nevile was set on it. He insisted.

BATTLE. But you're quite sure it wasn't his idea?

KAY. I'm positive. That white-faced little cat planned it all.

TREVES. You have no actual evidence on which to base such an assertion, Kay.

KAY. (*Rising and crossing to* R. *of Treves.*) I know, I tell you, and you know it, too, though you won't admit it. Audrey's been . . .

BATTLE. Come and sit down, Mrs. Strange. (*Kay crosses reluctantly to* L. *of the card table and sits.*) Did Lady Tressilian approve of the arrangement?

KAY. She didn't approve of anything in connection with me. Audrey was her pet. She disliked me for taking Audrey's place with Nevile.

BATTLE. Did you—quarrel with Lady Tressilian?

KAY. No.

BATTLE. After you'd gone to bed, Mrs. Strange, did you hear anything? Any unusual sounds in the house?

KAY. I didn't hear anything. I was so upset I took some sleeping stuff. I fell asleep almost at once.

BATTLE. (*Crossing to* R. *of the card table.*) What kind of sleeping stuff?

KAY. They're little blue capsules. I don't know what's in them. (*Battle looks at Benson, who makes a note.*)

BATTLE. (*Moving to the chaise.*) You didn't see your husband after you went up to bed?

KAY. No, no, no. I've already told you that I locked the door.

BATTLE. (*Picking up the niblick and bringing it to* L. *of Kay.*) Have you ever seen this before, Mrs. Strange?

KAY. (*Shrinking away.*) How—how horrible. Is that what—what it was done with?

BATTLE. We believe so. Have you any idea to whom it belongs?

KAY. (*Shaking her head.*) There are packets of golf clubs in the house. Mrs. Royde's—Nevile's—mine . . .

BATTLE. This is a man's club. It wouldn't be one of yours.

KAY. Then it must be . . . I don't know.

BATTLE. I see. (*He moves to the chaise and replaces the niblick on it.*) Thank you, Mrs. Strange, that's all for the present. (*Kay rises and moves down* R.)

LEACH. There's just one other thing. (*Kay turns. He crosses to* L. *of Kay.*) Would you object to letting Detective Sergeant Pengelly take your fingerprints?

KAY. My—fingerprints?

BATTLE. (*Smoothly.*) It's just a matter of routine, Mrs. Strange. We're asking everybody.

KAY. I don't mind anything—so long as I don't have to go back to that menagerie in the library.

LEACH. I'll arrange for Sergeant Pengelly to take your fingerprints in the breakfast room. (*Kay crosses below Leach to* L. C., *looks closely at Treves for a moment, then exits* L. *Leach crosses and exits* L. *Benson closes his notebook and waits stolidly.*)

BATTLE. Benson. Go and ask Pollock if he saw some small blue capsules in Mrs. Strange's room—Mrs. *Kay* Strange. I want a specimen of them.

BENSON. Yes, sir. (*He moves to the door* L.)

BATTLE. (*Moving* C.) Come back here when you've done that.

BENSON. Yes, sir. (*Benson exits* L.)

TREVES. (*Rising.*) Do you think the same drug was used to— er—dope Miss Aldin?

BATTLE. (*Moving on to the* R. *end of the rostrum.*) It's worth checking up on. Would you mind telling me, sir, who stands to gain by Lady Tressilian's death?

TREVES. Lady Tressilian had very little money of her own. The late Sir Mortimer Tressilian's estate was left in trust for her during her lifetime. On her death it is to be equally divided between Nevile and his wife.

BATTLE. Which wife?

TREVES. His first wife.

BATTLE. *Audrey* Strange?

TREVES. Yes. The bequest is quite clearly worded, "Nevile Henry Strange, and his wife, Audrey Elizabeth Strange, née Standish." The subsequent divorce makes no difference whatever to that bequest.

BATTLE. (*Moving down* R.) Mrs. Audrey Strange is of course fully aware of that?

TREVES. Certainly.

BATTLE. And the present Mrs. Strange—does she know that she gets nothing?

TREVES. Really I cannot say. (*His voice is doubtful.*) Presumably her husband has made it clear to her. (*He moves to* L. *of the card table.*)

BATTLE. If he hadn't she might be under the impression that she was the one who benefited?

TREVES. It's possible—yes. (*He sits* L. *of the card table.*)

BATTLE. Is the amount involved a large one, sir?

TREVES. Quite considerable. Approaching one hundred thousand pounds.

BATTLE. Whew! That's quite something, even in these days. (*Leach enters* L. *He is carrying a crumpled dinner jacket.*)

LEACH. (*Moving* L. C.) I say, take a look at this. Pollock has just found it bundled down in the bottom of Nevile Strange's wardrobe. (*Battle crosses to* R. *of Leach. He points to the sleeve.*) Look at these stains. That's blood, or I'm Marilyn Monroe.

BATTLE. (*Taking the jacket from Leach.*) You're certainly not Marilyn Monroe, Jim. It's spattered all up the sleeve as well. Any other suits in the room?

LEACH. Dark grey pinstripe hanging over a chair. And there's a lot of water round the wash basin on the floor—quite a pool of it. Looks as if it had slopped over.

BATTLE. Such as might have been made if he'd washed the blood off his hands in the devil of a hurry, eh?

LEACH. Yes. (*He takes some small tweezers from his pocket and picks some hairs off the inside of the collar.*)

BATTLE. Hairs! A woman's fair hairs on the inside of the collar.

LEACH. Some on the sleeve, too.

BATTLE. Red ones, these. Mr. Strange seems to have had his arm around one wife and the other one's head on his shoulder.

LEACH. Quite a Mormon. Looks bad for him, don't it?

BATTLE. We'll have to have the blood on this tested later to see if it's the same group as Lady Tressilian's.

LEACH. I'll try and arrange it, Uncle.

TREVES. (*Rising and moving down* R.; *very perturbed.*) I can't *believe*, I really can't believe that Nevile, whom I've known all his life, is capable of such a terrible act. There *must* be a mistake.

BATTLE. (*Moving and putting the jacket on the chaise.*) I hope so, I'm sure, sir. (*To Leach.*) We'll have Mr. Royde in next. (*Leach nods and exits* L.)

TREVES. I'm quite sure there must be some innocent explanation, Battle, for that stained dinner jacket. Quite apart from lack of motive, Nevile is . . .

BATTLE. Fifty thousand pounds is a pretty good motive, sir, to my mind.

TREVES. But Nevile is well off. He's not in need of money.

BATTLE. There may be something we know nothing about, sir. (*Benson enters* L. *and crosses to* L. *of Battle. He carries a small round box.*)

BENSON. Pollock found the pills, sir. (*He hands the box to Battle.*) Here you are.

BATTLE. (*Looking into the box.*) These are the things. I'll get the doctor to tell us whether they contain the same stuff that was given to Miss Aldin. (*He moves up* R. *Royde enters* L.)

ROYDE. (*Moving* L. C.) You want to see me?

BATTLE. (*Moving down* R. C.) Yes, Mr. Royde. (*He indicates the chair* L. *of the card table.*) Will you sit down, sir?

ROYDE. Rather stand.

BATTLE. Just as you like. (*Benson takes out his notebook and pencil. Treves sits in the easy chair down* R.) I'd like you to answer one or two questions, if you've no objection.

ROYDE. No objection at all. Nothing to hide.

BATTLE. (*Moving below the card table.*) I understand that you have only just returned from Malaya, Mr. Royde.

ROYDE. That's right. First time I've been home for seven years.

BATTLE. You've known Lady Tressilian for a long time?

ROYDE. Ever since I was a boy.

BATTLE. Can you suggest a reason why anyone should want to kill her?

ROYDE. No.

BATTLE. (*Moving up R. of the card table.*) How long have you known Mr. Nevile Strange?

ROYDE. Practically all my life.

BATTLE. (*Moving up R. C.*) Do you know him sufficiently well to be aware if he was worried over money?

ROYDE. No, but I shouldn't think so. Always seems to have plenty.

BATTLE. If there was any trouble like that, he wouldn't be likely to confide in you?

ROYDE. Very unlikely.

BATTLE. (*Moving down L. of the card table.*) What time did you go to bed last night, Mr. Royde?

ROYDE. Round about half past nine, I should think.

BATTLE. That seems to be very early.

ROYDE. Always go to bed early. Like to get up early.

BATTLE. I see. Your room is practically opposite Lady Tressilian's, isn't it?

ROYDE. Practically.

BATTLE. Did you go to sleep immediately you went to bed?

ROYDE. No. Finished a detective story I was reading. Not very good—it seems to me they always . . .

BATTLE. Yes, yes. Were you still awake at half past ten?

ROYDE. Yes.

BATTLE. (*Sitting L. of the card table.*) Did you—this is very important, Mr. Royde—did you hear any unusual sounds round about that time? (*Royde does not reply.*) I'll repeat that question. Did you . . . ?

ROYDE. There's no need. I heard you.

BATTLE. (*After a pause.*) Well, Mr. Royde?

ROYDE. Heard a noise in the attic over my head, rats, I expect. Anyway, that was later.

BATTLE. I don't mean that.

ROYDE. (*Looking at Treves, reluctantly.*) There was a bit of a rumpus.

BATTLE. What sort of rumpus?

ROYDE. Well—an argument.

BATTLE. An argument? Who was the argument between?

ROYDE. Lady Tressilian and Strange.

BATTLE. Lady Tressilian and Mr. Strange were quarreling?

ROYDE. Well, yes. I suppose you'd call it that.

BATTLE. (*Rising and moving to* R. *of Royde.*) It's not what
    I would call it, Mr. Royde. Do you call it that?

ROYDE. Yes.

BATTLE. Thank you. What was this quarrel about?

ROYDE. Didn't listen. Not my business.

BATTLE. But you are quite sure they *were* quarreling?

ROYDE. Sounded like it. Their voices were raised pretty high.

BATTLE. Can you place the time exactly?

ROYDE. About twenty past ten I should think.

BATTLE. Twenty past ten. You didn't hear anything else?

ROYDE. Strange slammed the door when he left.

BATTLE. You heard nothing more after that?

ROYDE. (*Crossing below Battle to the card table.*) Only rats.
    (*He knocks out his pipe in the ashtray.*)

BATTLE. (*Moving to the chaise.*) Never mind the rats. (*He
    picks up the niblick. Royde fills and lights his pipe. He
    moves to* L. *of Royde.*) Does this belong to you, Mr.
    Royde? (*Royde, engrossed with his pipe, does not reply.*)
    Mr. Royde!

ROYDE. (*Looking at the niblick.*) No. All my clubs have got
    T.R. scratched on the shaft.

BATTLE. Do you know to whom it does belong?

ROYDE. No idea. (*He moves up* R.)

BATTLE. (*Replacing the niblick on the chaise.*) We shall
    want to take your fingerprints, Mr. Royde. Have you any
    objection to that?

ROYDE. Not much use objecting, is it? Your man's already
    done it. (*Benson laughs quietly.*)

BATTLE. Thank you, then, Mr. Royde. That's all for the
    present.

ROYDE. Do you mind if I go out for a bit? Feel like some
    fresh air. Only out on the terrace, if you want me.

BATTLE. That'll be quite all right, sir.

ROYDE. Thanks. (*Royde exits by the French windows. Benson
    sits on the window-seat.*)

BATTLE. (*Moving* C.) The evidence seems to be piling up
    against Mr. Strange, sir.

TREVES. (*Rising and moving to R. of the card table.*) It's incredible—incredible. (*Leach enters L. and crosses to L. C.*)

LEACH. (*Jubilantly.*) The fingerprints are Nevile Strange's all right.

BATTLE. That would seem to clinch it, Jim. He leaves his weapon—he leaves his fingerprints; I wonder he didn't leave his visiting card.

LEACH. Been easy, hasn't it?

TREVES. It *can't* have been Nevile. There must be a mistake. (*He pours himself a glass of water.*)

BATTLE. It all adds up. We'll see what Mr. Strange has to say, anyhow. Bring him in, Jim. (*Leach exits L.*)

TREVES. I don't understand it. I'm sure there's something wrong. (*Battle moves down L. C.*) Nevile's not a complete and utter fool. Even if he were capable of committing such a brutal act—which I refuse to believe— would he have left all this damning evidence strewn about so carelessly? (*He moves up R.*)

BATTLE. Well, sir, apparently he did. (*He moves to R. of the easy chair L. C.*) You can't get away from facts. (*Nevile and Leach enter L. Nevile looks worried and a little nervous. He stands a moment in the doorway. He indicates the chair L. of the card table.*) Come and sit down, Mr. Strange.

NEVILE. (*Crossing to the chair L. of the card table.*) Thank you. (*He sits. Treves crosses slowly above the others and stands down L.*)

BATTLE. We should like you to answer certain questions, but it's my duty to caution you that you are not bound to answer these questions unless you wish.

NEVILE. Go ahead. Ask me anything you wish.

BATTLE. (*Moving C.*) You realize that anything you say will be taken down in writing and may subsequently be used in evidence in a court of law?

NEVILE. Are you threatening me?

BATTLE. No, no, Mr. Strange. Warning you.

TREVES. (*Moving below the easy chair L. C.*) Superintendent Battle is obliged to conform to the regulations, Nevile. You need say nothing unless you wish to?

NEVILE. Why shouldn't I wish to?

TREVES. It might be wiser not to.

NEVILE. Nonsense! Go ahead, Superintendent. Ask me any-

thing you like. (*Treves makes a despairing gesture and
sits in the easy chair* L. C. *Benson rises.*)

BATTLE. (*Crossing below Nevile and standing down* R.) Are
you prepared to make a statement?

NEVILE. If that's what you call it. I'm afraid, though, I can't
help you very much.

BATTLE. Will you begin by telling us exactly what you did
last night? From dinner onwards? (*He sits* R. *of the
card table.*)

NEVILE. Let me see. Immediately after dinner I went up to
my room and wrote a couple of letters—I'd been putting
them off for a long time and I thought I might as well
get them done. When I'd finished I came down here.

BATTLE. What time would that be?

NEVILE. I suppose it was about a quarter past nine. That's as
near as dammit, anyhow. (*Battle helps himself to a
cigarette.*)

BATTLE. (*Offering the cigarettes to Nevile.*) I'm so sorry.

NEVILE. No, thank you.

BATTLE. What did you do after that? (*He lights his cigarette.*)

NEVILE. I talked to—to Kay, my wife, and Ted Latimer.

BATTLE. Latimer—who's he?

NEVILE. A friend of ours who's staying at the *Easterhead Bay
Hotel.* He'd come over for dinner. He left soon after
and everybody else went off to bed.

BATTLE. Including your wife?

NEVILE. Yes, she was feeling a bit off color.

BATTLE. (*Rising.*) I understand there was some sort of—
unpleasantness?

NEVILE. Oh—(*He looks at Treves.*) you've heard about that,
have you? It was purely a domestic quarrel. Can't have
anything to do with this horrible business.

BATTLE. I see. (*He crosses below the table and moves up* C.
After a pause.) After everybody else had gone to bed,
what did you do then?

NEVILE. I was a bit bored. It was still fairly early and I decided to go across to the *Easterhead Bay Hotel.*

BATTLE. In the storm? It had broken by this time, surely?

NEVILE. Yes, it had. But it didn't worry me. I went upstairs
to change . . .

BATTLE. (*Moving quickly to Nevile, breaking in quickly.*)
Change into what, Mr. Strange?

NEVILE. I was wearing a dinner jacket. As I proposed to take the ferry across the river and it was raining pretty heavily, I changed. Into a grey pinstripe—(*He pauses.*) if it interests you.

BATTLE. (*After a pause.*) Go on, Mr. Strange.

NEVILE. (*Showing signs of increasing nervousness.*) I went up to change, as I said. I was passing Lady Tressilian's door, which was ajar, when she called, "Is that you, Nevile?" and asked me to come in. I went in and—and we chatted for a bit.

BATTLE. How long were you with her?

NEVILE. About twenty minutes, I suppose. When I left her I went to my room, changed, and hurried off. I took the latchkey with me because I expected to be late.

BATTLE. What time was it then?

NEVILE. (*Reflectively.*) About half past ten, I should think, I just caught the ten-thirty-five ferry and went across to the Easterhead side of the river. I had a drink or two with Latimer at the hotel and watched the dancing. Then we had a game of billiards. In the end I found I'd missed the last ferry back. It goes at one-thirty. Latimer very decently got out his car and drove me home. It's fifteen miles round by road, you know. (*He pauses.*) We left the hotel at two o'clock and reached here at half past. Latimer wouldn't come in for a drink, so I let myself in and went straight up to bed. (*Battle and Treves exchange looks.*)

BATTLE. (*Crossing below Nevile to R. of the card table.*) During your conversation with Lady Tressilian—was she quite normal in her manner? (*He stubs out his cigarette in the ashtray on the card table.*)

NEVILE. Oh, yes, quite.

BATTLE. (*Moving above the card table.*) What did you talk about?

NEVILE. This and that.

BATTLE. (*Moving behind Nevile.*) Amiably?

NEVILE. Of course.

BATTLE. (*Moving down L. C.; smoothly.*) You didn't have a violent quarrel?

NEVILE. (*Rising, angrily.*) What the devil do you mean?

BATTLE. You'd better tell the truth, Mr. Strange. I'll warn you—you were overheard.

NEVILE. (*Crossing slowly below the card table to* R. *of it*) Well, we *did* have a difference of opinion. She—she disapproved of my behaviour over—over Kay and—and my first wife. I may have got a bit heated, but we parted on perfectly friendly terms. (*He bangs his fist on the table. With a sudden burst of temper.*) I didn't bash her over the head because I lost my temper—if that's what you think. (*Battle moves to the chaise, picks up the niblick, then moves to* L. *of the card table.*)

BATTLE. Is this your property, Mr. Strange?

NEVILE. (*Looking at the niblick.*) Yes. It's one of Walter Hudson's niblicks from *St. Egbert's.*

BATTLE. This is the weapon we think was used to kill Lady Tressilian. Have you any explanation for your finger-prints being on the grip?

NEVILE. But—of course they would be—it's my club. I've often handled it.

BATTLE. Any explanation, I mean, for the fact that your fingerprints show that you were the *last* person to have handled it?

NEVILE. That's not true. It *can't* be. Somebody could have handled it after me—someone wearing gloves.

BATTLE. Nobody could have handled it in the sense you mean —by raising it to strike—without blurring your own marks.

NEVILE. (*Staring at the niblick in sudden realization.*) It can't be! (*He sits* R. *of the card table and covers his face with his hands.*) Oh, God! (*After a pause he takes his hands away and looks up.*) It isn't that! It simply isn't true. You think I killed her, but I didn't. I swear I didn't. There's some horrible mistake. (*Battle replaces the niblick on the chaise.*)

TREVES. (*Rising and crossing to* L. *of the card table.*) Can't you think of any explanation to account for those fingerprints, Nevile? (*Battle picks up the dinner jacket.*)

NEVILE. No—no—I can't think—of anything. (*Treves moves above the card table.*)

BATTLE. (*Moving to* L. *of the card table.*) Can you explain why the cuffs, and sleeve of this dinner jacket—*your* dinner jacket—are stained with blood?

NEVILE. (*In a horror-stricken whisper.*) Blood? It couldn't be.

TREVES. You didn't, for instance, cut yourself?

NEVILE. (*Rising and pushing his chair violently backwards.*)

No—no, of course I didn't. It's fantastic—simply fantastic. It's none of it *true*.

BATTLE. The facts are true enough, Mr. Strange.

NEVILE. But why should I do such a dreadful thing? It's unthinkable—unbelievable. I've known Lady Tressilian all my life. (*He moves to* R. *of Treves.*) Mr. Treves—you don't believe it, do you? You don't believe that I would do a thing like this? (*Battle replaces the jacket on the chaise.*)

TREVES. No, Nevile, I can't believe it.

NEVILE. I didn't. I swear I didn't. What reason could I have . . . ?

BATTLE. (*Turning and standing on the rostrum.*) I believe that you inherit a great deal of money on Lady Tressilian's death, Mr. Strange.

NEVILE. (*Moving down* R.) You mean—You think that . . . ? It's ridiculous! I don't need money. I'm quite well off. You've only to enquire at my bank . . . (*Treves sits* R. *of the card table.*)

BATTLE. We shall check up on that. But there may be some reason why you suddenly require a large sum of money—some reason unknown to anyone except yourself.

NEVILE. There's nothing of the sort.

BATTLE. As to that—we shall see.

NEVILE. (*Crossing slowly below the card table to* R. *of Battle.*) Are you going to arrest me?

BATTLE. Not yet—we propose to give you the benefit of the doubt.

NEVILE. (*Bitterly.*) You mean that you've made up your mind I did it, but you want to be sure of my motive so as to clinch the case against me. (*He moves above the armchair* R. C.) That's it, isn't it? (*He grips the back of the armchair.*) My God! It's like some awful dream. Like being caught in a trap and you can't get out. (*He pauses.*) Do you want me any more now? I'd like to—to get out—by myself—and think over all this. It's been rather a shock.

BATTLE. We've finished with you for the present, sir.

NEVILE. Thank you.

BATTLE. (*Moving down* L. C.) Don't go *too* far away, though, will you, sir?

NEVILE. (*Moving to the French windows.*) You needn't

worry. I shan't try and run away—if *that's* what you mean. (*He glances off* R.) I see you've taken your precautions, anyway. (*Nevile exits by the French windows. Benson sits on the window-seat.*)

LEACH. (*Moving to* L. *of Battle.*) He did it all right.

BATTLE. (*Moving* C.) I don't know, Jim. If you want the truth, I don't like it. I don't like *any* of it. There's *too much* evidence against him. Besides, it doesn't quite fit. Lady Tressilian calls him into the room, and he goes happening to have a niblick in his hand. Why?

LEACH. So as to bash her over the head.

BATTLE. Meaning it's premeditated? All right, he's drugged Miss Aldin. But he can't count on her being asleep so soon. He couldn't count on *anybody* being asleep so soon.

LEACH. Well then, say he's cleaning his clubs. Lady T calls him. They have a row—he loses his temper and bashes her with the club he just *happens* to be holding.

BATTLE. That doesn't account for the drugging of Mary Aldin. And she *was* drugged—the doctor says so. Of course—(*Meditatively.*) she could have drugged herself.

LEACH. Why?

BATTLE. (*Moving to* L. *of the card table, to Treves.*) Is there any possible motive in Miss Aldin's case?

TREVES. Lady Tressilian left her a legacy—not a very large one—a few hundreds a year. As I told you, Lady Tressilian had very little personal fortune.

BATTLE. A few hundreds a year. (*He sits* L. *of the card table.*)

TREVES. (*Rising and moving down* R.) I agree. An inadequate motive.

BATTLE. (*Sighing.*) Well, let's see the first wife. Jim, get Mrs. Audrey Strange. (*Leach exits* L.) There's something peculiar about this business, sir. A mixture of cold premeditation and unpremeditated violence, and the two don't mix.

TREVES. Exactly, Battle. The drugging of Miss Aldin suggests premeditation . . .

BATTLE. And the way the murder was carried out looks as though it was done in a fit of blind rage. Yes, sir. It's all *wrong*.

TREVES. Did you notice what he said—about a trap?

BATTLE. (*Thoughtfully.*) "A trap." (*Leach enters* L. *and holds the door open. Audrey enters* L. *She is very pale but completely composed. Benson rises. Treves moves up* R. *Leach exits* L. *and closes the door.*)

AUDREY. (*Crossing to* C.) You wish to see me?

BATTLE. (*Rising.*) Yes. (*He indicates the chair* L. *of the card table.*) Please sit down, Mrs. Strange. (*Audrey crosses quickly to the chair* L. *of the card table and sits.*) You've already told me how you came to make the discovery, so we needn't go into that again.

AUDREY. Thank you.

BATTLE. (*Moving down* R.) I'm afraid, however, that I shall have to ask you several questions that you may find embarrassing. You are not compelled to answer them unless you like.

AUDREY. I don't mind. I only wish to help. (*Treves moves slowly down* L.)

BATTLE. First of all, then, will you tell us what you did after dinner last night?

AUDREY. I was on the terrace for some time talking to Mr. Treves. Then Miss Aldin came out to say that Lady Tressilian would like to see him in her room, and I came in here. I talked to Kay and Mr. Latimer and, later, to Mr. Royde and Nevile. Then I went up to bed.

BATTLE. What time did you go to bed?

AUDREY. I think it was about half past nine. I'm not sure of the time exactly. It may have been a little later.

BATTLE. There was some sort of trouble between Mr. Strange and his wife, I believe. Were you mixed up in that?

AUDREY. Nevile behaved very stupidly. I think he was rather excited and overwrought. I left them together and went to bed. I don't know what happened after that, naturally. (*Treves sits in the easy chair* L. C.)

BATTLE. Did you go to sleep at once?

AUDREY. No. I was reading for some little while.

BATTLE. (*Moving on to the rostrum.*) And you heard nothing unusual during the night?

AUDREY. No, nothing. My room is on the floor above Cam— Lady Tressilian's. I wouldn't have heard anything.

BATTLE. (*Picking up the niblick.*) I'm sorry, Mrs. Strange— (*He moves to* L. *of Audrey and shows her the niblick.*) we believe this was used to kill Lady Tressilian. It has been identified by Mr. Strange as his property. It also bears his fingerprints.

AUDREY. (*Drawing in her breath sharply.*) Oh, you—you're not suggesting that it was—*Nevile* ...

BATTLE. Would it surprise you?

AUDREY. Very much. I'm sure you're quite wrong, if you think so. Nevile would never do a thing like that. Besides, he had no reason.

BATTLE. Not if he wanted money very urgently?

AUDREY. He wouldn't. He's not an extravagant person—he never has been. You're quite, quite wrong if you think it was Nevile.

BATTLE. You don't think he would be capable of violence in a fit of temper?

AUDREY. Nevile? Oh, no!

BATTLE. (*Moving and replacing the niblick on the chaise.*) I don't want to pry into your private affairs, Mrs. Strange, but will you explain why you are here? (*He moves to L. of Audrey.*)

AUDREY. (*Surprised.*) Why? I always come here at this time.

BATTLE. But not at the same time as as your ex-husband.

AUDREY. He did ask me if I'd mind.

BATTLE. It was his suggestion?

AUDREY. Oh, yes.

BATTLE. Not yours?

AUDREY. No.

BATTLE. But you agreed?

AUDREY. Yes, I agreed—I didn't feel that I could very well refuse.

BATTLE. Why not? You must have realized that it might be embarrassing?

AUDREY. Yes—I did realize that.

BATTLE. You were the injured party?

AUDREY. I beg your pardon?

BATTLE. It was you who divorced your husband?

AUDREY. Oh, I see—yes.

BATTLE. Do you feel any animosity towards him, Mrs. Strange?

AUDREY. No—none at all.

BATTLE. You have a very forgiving nature. (*Audrey does not reply. He crosses and stands down R.*) Are you on friendly terms with the present Mrs. Strange?

AUDREY. I don't think she likes me very much.

BATTLE. Do *you* like her?

AUDREY. I really don't know her.

BATTLE. (*Moving to* R. *of the card table.*) You are quite
    sure it was not your idea—this meeting?

AUDREY. Quite sure.

BATTLE. I think that's all, Mrs. Strange, thank you.

AUDREY. (*Rising, quietly.*) Thank you. (*She crosses to the
    door* L. *then hesitates, turns and moves* L. C. *Treves rises.
    Nervously and quickly.*) I would just like to say—you
    think Nevile did this—that he killed her because of the
    money? I'm quite sure that isn't so. Nevile never cared
    much about money. I do know that. I was married to
    him for several years, you see. It—it—isn't *Nevile.* I
    know my saying this isn't of any value as evidence—but
    I do wish you would believe it. (*Audrey turns quickly
    and exits* L. *Benson sits on the window-seat.*)

BATTLE. (*Moving* R. C.) It's difficult to know what to make
    of *her,* sir. I've never seen anyone so devoid of emotion.

TREVES. (*Moving* L. C.) H'm. She didn't show any, Battle,
    but it's there—some very strong emotion. I thought—
    but I may have been wrong . . . (*Mary, assisted by
    Leach, enters* L. *Mary is wearing a dressing-gown. She
    sways a little. He moves to Mary.*) Mary! (*He leads her
    to the easy chair* L. C. *Mary sits in the easy chair* L. C.)

BATTLE. Miss Aldin! You shouldn't . . .

LEACH. She insisted on seeing you, Uncle. (*He stands above
    the door* L.)

MARY. (*Faintly.*) I'm all right. I just feel—a little dizzy still.
    (*Treves crosses to the card table and pours a glass of
    water.*) I had to come. They told me something about
    your suspecting Nevile. Is that true? Do you suspect
    Nevile? (*Treves crosses with the glass of water to* R. *of
    Mary.*)

BATTLE. (*moving down* R. C.) Who told you so?

MARY. The cook. She brought me up some tea. She heard
    them talking in his room. And then—I came down—
    and I saw Audrey—and she said it *was* so. (*She looks
    from one to the other.*)

BATTLE. (*Moving down* R.; *evasively.*) We are not con-
    templating an arrest—at this moment.

MARY. But it *can't* have been Nevile. I had to come and tell
    you. Whoever did it, it wasn't Nevile. That I *know.*

BATTLE. (*Crossing to* C.) How do you know?

MARY. Because I saw her—Lady Tressilian—alive after Nevile
    had left the house.

BATTLE. What?

MARY. My bell rang, you see. I was terribly sleepy. I could only just get up. It was a minute or two before half past ten. As I came out of my room Nevile was in the hall below. I looked over the banisters and saw him. He went out of the front door and slammed it behind him. Then I went in to Lady Tressilian.

BATTLE. And she was alive and well?

MARY. Yes, of course. She seemed a little upset and said Nevile had shouted at her.

BATTLE. (*To Leach.*) Get Mr. Strange. (*Leach crosses and exits by the French windows. Mary takes the glass from Treves and sips the water. He sits on the chair L. of the card table.*) What did Lady Tressilian say exactly?

MARY. She said——(*She thinks.*) Oh, dear, what did she say? She said, "Did I ring for you? I can't remember doing so. Nevile has behaved very badly—losing his temper—shouting at me. I feel most upset." I gave her some aspirin and some hot milk from the thermos and she settled down. Then I went back to bed. I was desperately sleepy. Dr. Lazenby asked me if I'd taken any sleeping pills . . .

BATTLE. Yes, we know . . . (*Nevile and Leach enter by the French windows. Kay follows them on and stands down R. of the card table. Leach stands up R. He rises and moves L. C.*) You are a very lucky man, Mr. Strange.

NEVILE. (*Moving above the card table.*) Lucky? Why?

BATTLE. Miss Aldin saw Lady Tressilian alive *after* you left the house, and we've already established you were on the ten-thirty-five ferry.

NEVILE. (*Bewildered.*) Then—that lets me out? But the blood-stained jacket—(*He moves to R. of the chaise.*) The niblick with my fingerprints on it . . . ? (*Kay sits in the easy chair down R.*)

BATTLE. (*Moving to L. of the chaise.*) Planted. Very ingeniously planted. Blood and hair smeared on the niblick head. *Someone* put on your jacket to commit the crime and then stuffed it away in your wardrobe to incriminate you.

NEVILE. (*Moving behind the chair L. of the card table.*) But why? I can't believe it.

BATTLE. (*Impressively.*) Who hates you, Mr. Strange? Hates

you so much that they wanted you to be hanged for a
murder you didn't commit?

NEVILE. (*After a pause; shaken.*) Nobody—nobody . . .
(*Royde enters by the French windows and moves slowly
towards the card table as—*)

THE CURTAIN FALLS

Act Three

Scene I

SCENE: *The same. The next morning.*
*Most of the furniture has been replaced in its original
position, but the coffee table is now on the rostrum
up* C. *and the work-basket has been removed.*

*When the curtain rises it is about eleven o'clock. The
sun is shining brightly and the bay and French windows
are open. Royde is standing on the rostrum, gazing out
of the window. Mary enters by the French windows. She
looks a little pale and worried. She moves above the
chaise and sees Royde.*

MARY. Oh, dear!

ROYDE. (*Closing the window and turning.*) Anything the
matter?

MARY. (*Laughing with a slight note of hysteria.*) Nobody but
you could say a thing like that, Thomas. A murder in the
house and you just say "Is anything the matter?" (*She
sits on the chaise, at the upstage end.*)

ROYDE. I meant anything fresh.

MARY. Oh, I know what you meant. It's really a wonderful
relief to find anyone so gloriously just-the-same-as-usual
as you are.

ROYDE. Not much good, is it, getting all het up over things?

MARY. No, you're very sensible, of course. It's how you manage to do it, beats me.

ROYDE. (*Moving down* L. C.) I'm not so—close to things as
you are.

MARY. That's true. I don't know what we should have done
without you. You've been a tower of strength.

ROYDE. The human buffer, eh?

MARY. The house is still full of policemen.

ROYDE. Yes, I know. Found one in the bathroom this morning. I had to turf him out before I could shave. (*He sits in the armchair* L. C.)

MARY. I know—you come across them in the most unexpected places. (*She rises.*) They're looking for something. (*She shivers and moves up* R.) It was a very near thing for poor Nevile, wasn't it?

ROYDE. Yes, very near. (*Grimly.*) I can't help feeling pleased he's had a bit of a kick in the pants. He's always so damned complacent.

MARY. It's just his manner.

ROYDE. He's had the devil's own luck. If it had been some other poor chap with all that evidence piled against him, he wouldn't have had a hope.

MARY. It *must* have been someone from outside.

ROYDE. It wasn't. They've proved *that*. Everything was fastened up and bolted in the morning. (*Mary moves to the* C. *bay window and examines the catch.*) Besides, what about your dope? That must have been someone in the house.

MARY. (*Shaking her head.*) I just can't believe it could have been one of—us. (*She moves to the* R. *end of the rostrum. Latimer enters by the French windows. He carries his jacket.*)

LATIMER. (*Moving to* R. *of the chaise.*) Hullo, Royde. Good morning, Miss Aldin. I'm looking for Kay. Do you know where she is?

MARY. I think she's up in her room, Mr. Latimer.

LATIMER. (*Putting his jacket over the upstage end of the chaise.*) I thought she might like to come and have lunch at the hotel. Not very cheerful for her here, in the circumstances.

MARY. You can hardly expect us to be very cheerful after what's happened, can you?

LATIMER. (*Moving down* R.) That's what I meant. It's different for Kay, though, you know. The old girl didn't mean so much to her.

MARY. Naturally. She hasn't known Lady Tressilian as long as we have.

LATIMER. Nasty business. I've had the police over at the hotel this morning.

MARY. What did they want?

LATIMER. Checking up on Strange, I suppose. They asked

me all sorts of questions. I told them he was with me
from after eleven until half past two, and they seemed
satisfied. Lucky thing for him that he decided to follow me over to the hotel that night, wasn't it?

ROYDE. (*Rising.*) Very lucky. (*He moves to the door* L.) I'm
going upstairs, Latimer. I'll tell Kay you're here, if I
can find her.

LATIMER. Thanks. (*Royde exits* L. *He looks toward the door*
L. *for a moment, then goes to his jacket and takes his
cigarettes from the pocket.*) A queer chap. Always seems
to be keeping himself bottled up and afraid the cork
might come out. Is Audrey going to reward at long last
the dog-like devotion of a lifetime? (*He lights a cigarette for himself.*)

MARY. (*Crossing to the door* L.; *annoyed.*) I don't know,
and it's no business of ours. (*She hesitates and turns.*)
When you saw the police did they say anything—I
mean—did you get any idea as to who they suspect
now? (*She moves to* L. *of the armchair* L. C.)

LATIMER. They weren't making any confidences.

MARY. I didn't suppose they were, but I thought, perhaps
from the questions they asked . . . (*Kay enters* L.)

KAY. (*Crossing to Latimer.*) Hullo, Ted. It was sweet of you
to come over.

LATIMER. I thought you could probably do with a bit of
cheering up, Kay.

KAY. My God, how right you were. It was bad enough before
in this house, but *now* . . .

LATIMER. What about a run in the car and lunch at the
hotel—or anywhere else you like? (*Mary moves down
L.*)

KAY. I don't know what Nevile's doing . . .

LATIMER. I'm not asking Nevile—I'm asking *you*.

KAY. I couldn't come without Nevile, Ted. I'm sure it would
do him good to get away from here for a bit.

LATIMER. (*Shrugging his shoulders.*) All right—bring him
along if you want to, Kay. I'm easy.

KAY. Where *is* Nevile, Mary?

MARY. I don't know. I think he's in the garden somewhere.

KAY. (*Crossing to the French windows.*) I'll see if I can find
him. I won't be long, Ted. (*Kay exits by the French
windows.*)

LATIMER. (*Moving up* R.; *angrily.*) What she sees in him I
can't think. He's treated her like dirt.

MARY. (*Moving up* L. *of the armchair* L. C.) I think she'll forgive him.

LATIMER. She shouldn't—now she's got her share of the old girl's money—she can go where she pleases, do what she likes. She's got a chance now of having a life of her own.

MARY. (*Sitting in the armchair* L. C.; *with obscure feeling.*) Can one ever really have a life of one's own? Isn't that just the illusion that lures us on—thinking—planning—for a future that will never really exist?

LATIMER. That wasn't what you were saying the other night.

MARY. I know. But that seems a long time ago. So much has happened since then.

LATIMER. Specifically, one murder.

MARY. You wouldn't talk so flippantly about murder if . . .

LATIMER. If what, Miss Aldin? (*He moves to* R. *of Mary.*)

MARY. If you had been as close to murder as I have.

LATIMER. This time it is better to be an outsider. (*Kay and Nevile enter by the French windows. Kay looks a little annoyed.*)

KAY. (*As she enters.*) It's no good, Ted. (*She goes on to the* R. *end of the rostrum.*) Nevile won't come so we can't go.

NEVILE. (*Moving down* R.) I don't see very well how we can. It's awfully nice of you, Latimer, but it would hardly be the thing, would it, after what's happened?

LATIMER. (*Moving above the chaise.*) I don't see what harm it would do to go out to lunch—you've got to eat.

NEVILE. We can eat here. (*He crosses to* R. *of Kay.*) Hang it all, Kay, we can't go joy-riding about the country. The inquest hasn't been held yet.

LATIMER. If you feel like that about it, Strange, I suppose we'd better call it off. (*He picks up his jacket and moves to the French windows.*)

MARY. (*Rising.*) Perhaps you would care to stay and lunch with *us*, Mr. Latimer?

LATIMER. Well, that's very nice of you, Miss Aldin . . .

NEVILE. (*Moving above the chaise.*) Yes, do, Latimer.

KAY. (*Moving to* L. *of the rostrum.*) Will you, Ted?

LATIMER. (*Moving to* R. *of the chaise.*) Thanks, I'd like to.

MARY. You'll have to take pot luck. I'm afraid the domestic arrangements are just a little disorganized with the police popping in and out of the kitchen every two minutes.

LATIMER. If it's going to be any trouble . . .

MARY. (*Moving to the door* L.) Oh, no—it'll be no trouble at all. (*Audrey enters* L. *Kay looks at the magazines on the coffee table.*)

AUDREY. Has anyone seen Mr. Treves this morning?

NEVILE. I haven't seen him since breakfast. (*Latimer moves down* R.)

MARY. He was talking to the Inspector in the garden about half an hour ago. Do you want him particularly?

AUDREY. (*Crossing to* L. C.) Oh, no—I just wondered where he was.

NEVILE. (*Looking off* R.) They're coming now. Not Mr. Treves. Superintendent Battle and Inspector Leach.

MARY. (*Nervously.*) What do you think they want now? (*They all wait nervously. Battle and Leach enter by the French windows. Leach carries a long brown-paper parcel. He stands* R. *of the chaise.*)

BATTLE. (*Crossing to* R. C.) Hope we're not disturbing you all. There are one or two things we'd like to know about.

NEVILE. I should have thought you'd exhausted everything by now, Superintendent.

BATTLE. Not quite, Mr. Strange. (*He takes a small chamois leather glove from his pocket.*) There's this glove, for instance—who does it belong to? (*They all stare at the glove without answering. To Audrey.*) Is it yours, Mrs. Strange?

AUDREY. (*Shaking her head.*) No, no, it isn't mine. (*She sits in the armchair* L. C.)

BATTLE. (*Holding the glove out towards Mary.*) Miss Aldin?

MARY. I don't think so. I have none of that color. (*She sits in the easy chair down* L.)

BATTLE. (*To Kay.*) What about you?

KAY. No. I'm sure it doesn't belong to *me*.

BATTLE. (*Moving to Kay.*) Perhaps you'd just slip it on? It's the left hand glove. (*Kay tries on the glove but it is too small. He crosses to Mary.*) Will you try, Miss Aldin? (*Mary tries on the glove but it is too small. He moves to* L. *of Audrey.*) I think you'll find it fits *you* all right. Your hand is smaller than the other two ladies'. (*Audrey reluctantly takes the glove.*)

NEVILE. (*Moving* R. C. *sharply.*) She's already told you that it isn't her glove.

BATTLE. (*Blandly.*) Perhaps she made a mistake—or forgot.

AUDREY. It may be mine—gloves are so alike, aren't they?

BATTLE. Try it on, Mrs. Strange. (*Audrey slips the glove on her left hand.*) It seems as if it is yours —at any rate it was found outside your window, pushed down into the ivy—with the other one that goes with it.

AUDREY. (*With difficulty.*) I—I don't know—anything about it. (*She hastily removes the glove and gives it to Battle.*)

NEVILE. Look here, Superintendent, what are you driving at?

BATTLE. (*Crossing to* L. *of Nevile.*) Perhaps I might have a word with you *privately*, Mr. Strange?

LATIMER. (*Moving to the French windows.*) Come on, Kay, let's go out in the garden. (*Kay and Latimer exit by the French windows.*)

BATTLE. There's no need to disturb everybody. (*To Nevile.*) Isn't there somewhere else we could . . . ?

MARY. (*Rising quickly.*) I was just going, in any case. (*To Audrey.*) You coming with me, Audrey?

AUDREY. (*Almost in a dream.*) Yes—yes. (*She nods in a dazed, frightened manner, and rises slowly. Mary puts her arm around Audrey, and they exit* L.)

NEVILE. (*Sitting on the chaise.*) Now, Superintendent? What's this absurd story about gloves outside Audrey's window?

BATTLE. It's not absurd, sir. We've found some very curious things in this house.

NEVILE. Curious? What do you mean by *curious*?

BATTLE. Give us the exhibit, Jim. (*Leach moves to* R. *of Battle, extracts a heavy, steel-headed poker from his parcel, hands it to Battle, then moves down* L. C. *He shows the poker to Nevile.*) Old-fashioned Victorian fire-iron.

NEVILE. You think that this——

BATTLE. ——was what was really used? Yes, Mr. Strange, I do.

NEVILE. But why? There's no sign . . .

BATTLE. Oh, it's been cleaned, and put back in the grate of the room where it belonged. But you can't remove bloodstains as easily as all that. We found traces all right. (*He moves up* C. *and puts the poker on the window-seat.*)

NEVILE. (*Hoarsely.*) Whose room was it in?

BATTLE. (*With a quick glance at Nevile.*) We'll come to that presently. I've got another question to ask you. That dinner jacket you wore last night, it's got fair hairs on the inside of the collar and on the shoulders. Do you know how they got there? (*He moves to the* L. *end of the rostrum.*)

NEVILE. No.

BATTLE. (*Crossing and standing up* R.) They're a lady's hairs, sir. Fair hairs. There were several red hairs, as well, on the sleeves.

NEVILE. These would be my wife's—Kay's. You are suggesting that the others are Audrey's?

BATTLE. Oh, they are, sir. Unquestionably. We've had them compared with hairs from her brush.

NEVILE. Very likely they are. What about it? I remember I caught my cuff button in her hair the other night on the terrace.

LEACH. In that case the hairs would be on the cuff, sir. Not on the inside of the collar.

NEVILE. (*Rising.*) What are you insinuating?

BATTLE. There are traces of powder, too, inside the jacket collar. Primavera Naturelle, a very pleasant-scented powder and expensive. It's no good telling me that *you* use it, Mr. Strange, because I shan't believe you. And Mrs. Kay Strange uses Orchid Sun Kiss. Mrs. Audrey Strange uses Primavera Naturelle.

NEVILE. Supposing she does?

BATTLE. It seems obvious that on some occasion Mrs. Audrey Strange actually *wore* your dinner jacket. It's the only reasonable way the hairs and the powder could have got *inside* the collar. You've seen the glove that was found in the ivy outside her window. It's hers all right. It was the left hand glove. Here's the right hand one. (*He takes the glove from his pocket and holds it up. It is crumpled and stained with dried blood.*)

NEVILE. (*Huskily.*) What—what's that on it?

BATTLE. Blood, Mr. Strange. (*He holds the glove out to Leach. Leach moves on to the rostrum and takes the glove from Battle.*) Blood of the same group as Lady Tressilian's. An unusual blood group.

NEVILE. (*Moving slowly down* R.) Good God! Are you suggesting that Audrey—*Audrey*—would make all these elaborate preparations to kill an old lady she had known for years so that she could get hold of that money? (*His voice rises.*) Audrey? (*Royde enters quickly* L.)

ROYDE. (*Crossing to* L. *of the chaise.*) Sorry to interrupt, but I'd like to be in on this.

NEVILE. (*Annoyed.*) Do you mind, Thomas? This is all rather private.

ROYDE. I'm afraid I don't care about that. You see, I heard Audrey's name mentioned . . .

NEVILE. (*Moving to* R. *of the chaise, angrily.*) What the hell has Audrey's name got to do with you?

ROYDE. What has it to do with you, if it comes to that? I came here meaning to ask her to marry me, and I think she knows it. What's more, I mean to marry her.

NEVILE. I think you've got a damn nerve . . .

ROYDE. You can think what you like. I'm stopping here. (*Battle coughs.*)

NEVILE. Oh, all right! Sorry, Superintendent, for the interruption. (*To Royde.*) The Superintendent is suggesting that Audrey—*Audrey* committed a brutal assault on Camilla and killed her. Motive—money.

BATTLE. (*Moving down* L. C.) I didn't say the motive was money. I don't think it was, though fifty thousand pounds is a very sizeable motive. No, I think that this crime was directed against *you*, Mr. Strange.

NEVILE. (*Startled.*) Me?

BATTLE. I asked you—yesterday—who hated you. The answer, I think, is Audrey Strange.

NEVILE. Impossible. Why should she? I don't understand.

BATTLE. Ever since you left her for another woman, Audrey Strange has been brooding over her hatred of you. In my opinion—and strictly off the record—I think she's become mentally unbalanced. I daresay we'll have these high-class doctors saying so with a lot of long words. Killing you wasn't enough to satisfy her hate. She decided to get you hanged for murder. (*Royde moves up to* R.)

NEVILE. (*Shaken.*) I'll never believe that. (*He perches on the back of the chaise.*)

BATTLE. She wore your dinner jacket, she planted your niblick, smearing it with Lady Tressilian's blood and hair. The only thing that saved you was something she couldn't foresee. Lady Tressilian rang her bell for Miss Aldin after you'd left . . .

NEVILE. It isn't true—it can't be true. You've got the whole thing wrong. Audrey's never borne a grudge against me. She's always been gentle—forgiving.

BATTLE. It's not my business to argue with you, Mr. Strange.

I asked for a word in private because I wanted to prepare you for what's about to happen. I'm afraid I shall have to caution Mrs. Audrey Strange and ask her to accompany me ...

NEVILE. (*Rising.*) You mean—you're going to *arrest* her?

BATTLE. Yes, sir.

NEVILE. (*Crossing below the chaise to* R. *of Battle.*) You can't—you can't—it's preposterous. (*Royde moves to* L. *of Nevile.*)

ROYDE. (*Pushing Nevile down on to the chaise.*) Pull yourself together, Strange. Don't you see that the only thing that can help Audrey now is for you to forget all your ideas of chivalry and come out with the truth?

NEVILE. The truth? You mean ...?

ROYDE. I mean the truth about Audrey and Adrian. (*He turns to Battle.*) I'm sorry, Superintendent, but you've got your *facts* wrong. Strange didn't leave Audrey for another woman. *She* left him. She ran away with my brother Adrian. Then Adrian was killed in a car accident on his way to meet her. Strange behaved very decently to Audrey. He arranged for her to divorce *him* and agreed to take the blame.

NEVILE. I didn't want her name dragged through the mud. I didn't know anyone knew.

ROYDE. Adrian wrote to me and told me all about it just before he was killed. (*To Battle.*) You see, that knocks your motive out, doesn't it? (*He moves up to* R. C.) Audrey has no *cause* to hate Strange. On the contrary, she has every reason to be grateful to him.

NEVILE. (*Rising; eagerly.*) Royde's right. He's right. That cuts out the motive. Audrey can't have done it. (*Kay enters quickly by the French windows. Latimer slowly follows Kay on and stands down* R.)

KAY. She did. She did. Of course she did.

NEVILE. (*Angrily.*) Have you been listening?

KAY. Of course I have. And Audrey did it, I tell you. I've known she did it all the time. (*To Nevile.*) Don't you understand? She tried to get you hanged.

NEVILE. (*Crossing to* R. *of Battle.*) You won't go through with it—not now?

BATTLE. (*Slowly.*) I seem to have been wrong—about the motive. But there's still the money.

KAY. (*Moving below the chaise.*) What money?

BATTLE. (*Crossing below Nevile to* L. *of Kay.*) Fifty thousand pounds comes to Mrs. Audrey Strange at Lady Tressilian's death.

KAY. (*Dumbfounded.*) To *Audrey?* To *me.* The money comes to Nevile and his wife. I'm his wife. Half the money comes to me. (*Nevile moves slowly down* L.)

BATTLE. I am informed—definitely—that the money was left in trust for Nevile Strange and "his wife Audrey Strange." She gets it, not you. (*He makes a sign to Leach. Leach exits quickly* L. *Royde crosses slowly and stands up* L.)

KAY. (*With a step towards Nevile.*) But you told me—you let me think . . .

NEVILE. (*Mechanically.*) I thought you knew. We—I get fifty thousand. Isn't that enough? (*He moves to* L. *of the chaise.*)

BATTLE. Apart from all questions of motive, facts are facts. The facts point to her being guilty. (*Kay sits on the chaise.*)

NEVILE. All the facts showed that *I* was guilty yesterday.

BATTLE. (*Slightly taken aback.*) That's true. (*He moves a little up* C.) But are you seriously asking me to believe that there's someone who hates *both* of you? Someone who, if the plan failed against you, laid a second trail to Audrey Strange? Can you think of anyone who hates both you *and* your former wife sufficiently for that?

NEVILE. (*Crushed.*) No—no.

KAY. Of course Audrey did it. She planned it . . . (*Audrey enters* L. *She moves like a sleepwalker. Leach follows her on.*)

AUDREY. (*Moving up* L. C.) You wanted me, Superintendent? (*Royde moves quietly behind Audrey. Nevile faces Audrey, his back to the audience.*)

BATTLE. (*Becoming very official.*) Audrey Strange, I arrest you on the charge of murdering Camilla Tressilian on Thursday last, September the twenty-first. I must caution you that anything you say will be written down and may be used in evidence at your trial. (*Kay rises and moves to Latimer. Leach takes a notebook and pencil from his pocket, and stands waiting. Audrey stares straight at Nevile as though hypnotized.*)

AUDREY. So—it's come at last—it's come.

NEVILE. (*Turning away.*) Where's Treves? Don't say anything. I'm going to find Treves. (*Nevile exits by the*

French windows. Off. Calling.) Mr. Treves. (*Audrey sways and Royde holds her.*)

AUDREY. Oh—there's no escape—no escape. (*To Royde.*) Dear Thomas, I'm so glad—it's all over—all over. (*She looks at Battle.*) I'm quite ready. (*Leach writes down Audrey's words. Battle is impassive. The others stare at Audrey, stupefied. Battle makes a sign to Leach, who opens the door L. Audrey turns and exits slowly L., followed by Battle and the others. The lights fade to Black-Out as—*)

THE CURTAIN FALLS

Scene II

SCENE: *The same. The same evening.*

When the curtain rises the windows and curtains are closed and the room is in darkness. Nevile is standing down L. He crosses to the French windows, draws the curtains, opens the windows to get some air, then moves above the chaise. The door L. opens and a shaft of light illuminates Nevile. Treves enters down L.

TREVES. Ah, Nevile. (*He switches on the lights, closes the door and moves L. C.*)

NEVILE. (*Quickly and eagerly.*) Did you see Audrey?

TREVES. Yes, I've just left her.

NEVILE. How is she? Has she got everything she wants? I tried to see her this afternoon, but they wouldn't let me.

TREVES. (*Sitting in the armchair L. C.*) She doesn't wish to see anybody at present.

NEVILE. Poor darling. She must be feeling awful. We've got to get her out of it.

TREVES. I am doing everything that's possible, Nevile.

NEVILE. (*Moving down R.*) The whole thing's an appalling mistake. Nobody in their right senses would ever believe that *Audrey* would be capable—(*He moves R. of the chaise, then stands up R. C.*) of killing anyone—like that.

TREVES. (*Warningly.*) The evidence is very strong against her.

NEVILE. I don't care a damn for the evidence.

TREVES. I'm afraid the police are more practical.

NEVILE. *You* don't believe it, do you? You don't believe . . .

TREVES. I don't know *what* to believe. Audrey has always been—an enigma.

NEVILE. (*Sitting on the chaise.*) Oh, nonsense! She's always been sweet and *gentle*.

TREVES. She has always appeared so, certainly.

NEVILE. Appeared so? She *is*. Audrey and—and violence of any sort just don't go together. Only a muddle-headed fool like Battle would believe otherwise.

TREVES. Battle is far from being a muddle-headed fool, Nevile. I have always found him particularly shrewd.

NEVILE. Well, he hasn't proved himself very shrewd over this. (*He rises and moves up* R.) Good God, you don't *agree* with him, do you? You can't believe this utterly stupid and fantastic story—that Audrey planned all this to—to get back on me for marrying Kay. It's too absurd.

TREVES. Is it? Love turns to hate very easily, you know, Nevile.

NEVILE. But she had no *reason* to hate me. (*He moves* R. C.) That motive was exploded when I told them about—about Adrian.

TREVES. I must confess that *that* was a surprise to me. I was always under the impression that *you* left Audrey.

NEVILE. I let everyone think so, of course. What else could I do? It's always so much worse for the woman—she'd have had to face the whole wretched business alone—with all the gossip and—and mud-slinging. I couldn't let her do that.

TREVES. It was very—generous of you, Nevile.

NEVILE. (*Sitting on the chaise.*) Anybody would have done the same. Besides, in a way, it was my fault.

TREVES. Why?

NEVILE. Well—I'd met Kay, you see—while we were at Cannes—and I—I admit I was attracted. I flirted with her—in a harmless sort of way, and Audrey got annoyed.

TREVES. You mean she was jealous?

NEVILE. Well—yes, I think so.

TREVES. (*Rising.*) If that was the case she couldn't have been —really—in love with Adrian.

NEVILE. I don't think she was.

TREVES. Then she left you for Adrian in a fit of pique—because she resented your—er—attentions to Kay?

NEVILE. Something like that.

TREVES. (*Moving to* L. *of Nevile.*) If that was the case, the original motive *still* holds good.

NEVILE. What do you mean?

TREVES. If Audrey was in love with you—if she only ran away with Adrian in a fit of pique—then she might still have *hated* you for marrying Kay.

NEVILE. (*Sharply.*) No! She never hated me. She was very understanding about the whole thing.

TREVES. Outwardly—perhaps. What was she like *underneath*?

NEVILE. (*Rising, almost in a whisper.*) You believe she did it, don't you? You believe she killed Camilla—in that horrible way? (*He pauses and crosses to the armchair* L. C.) It wasn't Audrey. I'll swear it wasn't Audrey. I know her, I tell you. I lived with her for four years—you can't do that and be mistaken in a person. But if *you* think she's guilty, what hope is there?

TREVES. I'll give you my candid opinion, Nevile. I don't think there is *any* hope. I shall brief the best possible counsel, of course, but there's very little case for the defence. Except insanity. I doubt if we'll get very far with that. (*Nevile drops into the armchair* L. C. *and covers his face with his hands.*)

NEVILE. (*Almost inaudibly.*) Oh, God! (*Mary enters* L. *She is very quiet and clearly under strain.*)

MARY. (*Not realizing that Nevile is there.*) Mr. Treves! (*She sees Nevile.*) Er—there are sandwiches in the dining-room when anyone wants them. (*She moves to* L. *of Nevile.*)

NEVILE. (*Turning away.*) Sandwiches!

TREVES. (*Moving up* R. C.; *mildly.*) Life has to go on, Nevile.

NEVILE. (*To Mary.*) Do *you* think she did it, Mary?

MARY. (*After a definite pause.*) No. (*She takes Nevile's hand.*)

NEVILE. Thank God somebody besides me believes in her. (*Kay enters by the French windows.*)

KAY. (*Moving to* R. *of the chaise.*) Ted's just coming. He's running the car round into the drive. I came up through the garden.

NEVILE. (*Rising and moving above the chaise.*) What's Latimer coming here for? Can't he keep away for five minutes?

TREVES. I sent for him, Nevile. Kay very kindly took the message. I also asked Battle to come. I would prefer not to explain in detail. Let us say, Nevile, that I am trying out a last forlorn hope.

NEVILE. To save Audrey?

TREVES. Yes.

KAY. (*To Nevile.*) Can't you think of anything else but Audrey?

NEVILE. No, I can't. (*Kay moves to the easy chair down* R. *Latimer enters by the French windows and crosses to* R. *of Treves.*)

LATIMER. I came as quickly as I could, Mr. Treves. Kay didn't say what you wanted me for, only that it was urgent.

KAY. (*Sitting in the easy chair down* R.) I said what I was told to say. I haven't the faintest idea what it's all about.

MARY. (*Crossing to the chaise and sitting.*) We're all in the dark, Kay. As you heard, Mr. Treves is trying to help Audrey.

KAY. Audrey, Audrey, Audrey. It's *always* Audrey. I suppose she'll haunt us for the rest of our lives.

NEVILE. (*Moving down* R. *of the chaise.*) That's a beastly thing to say, Kay.

LATIMER. (*Angrily.*) Can't you see that her nerves are all in shreds?

NEVILE. So are everybody's. (*Latimer moves and stands above Kay. Royde enters* L.)

ROYDE. Superintendent Battle is here. (*To Treves.*) He says he's expected.

TREVES. Bring him in. (*Royde turns and beckons off. Battle enters* L.)

BATTLE. Good evening. (*He looks enquiringly at Treves.*)

TREVES. (*Moving down* C.) Thank you for coming, Superintendent. It is good of you to spare the time.

NEVILE. (*Bitterly.*) Especially when you've got your victim.

TREVES. I don't think that kind of remark is going to get us anywhere, Nevile. Battle has only done his duty as a police officer.

NEVILE. (*Moving up* R.) I'm—I'm sorry, Battle.

BATTLE. That's all right, sir.

TREVES. (*Indicating the easy chair* L. C.) Sit down, Battle.

BATTLE. (*Sitting in the easy chair* L. C.) Thank you, sir.

TREVES. Mr. Royde said something to me the other day, Battle, that I've thought about a great deal since.

ROYDE. (*Surprised.*) I did?

TREVES. Yes, Thomas. You were talking about a detective story you were reading. You said they all begin in the *wrong* place. The murder should not be the *beginning* of the story but the end. And, of course, you were right. A murder *is* the culmination of a lot of different circumstances, all converging at a given moment at a given point. Rather fancifully you called it *Zero Hour*.

ROYDE. I remember.

NEVILE. (*Impatiently.*) What's this got to do with Audrey?

TREVES. A great deal—*it's Zero Hour now.* (*There is a rather uncomfortable pause.*)

MARY. But Lady Tressilian was murdered three days ago.

TREVES. It is not exactly Lady Tressilian's murder that I am talking about now. There are different kinds of murder. Superintendent Battle, when I put it to you, will you allow that all the evidence against Audrey Strange *could* have been faked? The weapon taken from her fender. *Her* gloves, stained with blood, and hidden in the ivy outside her window. *Her* face powder, dusted on the inside of Nevile's dinner jacket. Hairs from *her* brush placed there as well?

BATTLE. (*Stirring uncomfortably.*) I suppose it *could* have been done, but . . .

KAY. But she admitted she was guilty—herself—when you arrested her.

ROYDE. (*Moving down* L.) No, she didn't.

KAY. She said that she couldn't escape.

MARY. She said that she was glad it was all over.

KAY. What more do you want? (*Treves holds up a hand. They subside. Nevile crosses slowly and stands on the* L. *end of the rostrum.*)

TREVES. (*Moving to* C. *of the rostrum.*) Do you remember, Thomas, that when the Superintendent here was questioning you as to what you had heard on the night of the murder, you mentioned rats? Rats in the attic—over your head?

ROYDE. (*Sitting in the easy chair down* L.) Yes.

TREVES. That remark of yours interested me. I went up to the attic floor—I will admit, with no very clear idea in my head. The attic directly over your bedroom, Thomas, is used as a lumber room. It is full of what may be termed junk. Unwanted junk. There was heavy dust over everything except one thing. (*He crosses to the bureau.*) But there was one thing that was *not* covered with dust.

(*He takes out a long coil of thin rope which has been concealed in the corner* R. *of the bureau.*) This. (*He crosses to* R. *of Battle. Battle takes the rope. His eyebrows rise in surprise.*)

BATTLE. It's damp.

TREVES. Yes, it's still damp. No dust on it—and damp. Thrown into the lumber room where someone thought it would never be noticed.

BATTLE. Are you going to tell us, sir, what it means? (*He returns the rope to Treves.*)

TREVES. (*Moving on to the rostrum.*) It means that during the storm on the night of the murder, that rope was hanging from one of the windows of this house. Hanging from a window down to the water below. (*He tosses the rope on to the coffee table.*) You said, Superintendent, that no one could have entered this house to commit murder from outside that night. That isn't quite true. Someone could have entered from outside—(*Latimer moves very slowly above the chaise.*) if this rope was hanging ready for them to climb up from the estuary.

BATTLE. You mean someone came from the other side? The Easterhead side?

TREVES. Yes. (*He turns to Nevile.*) You went over on the ten-thirty-five ferry. You must have got to the *Easterhead Bay Hotel* at about a quarter to eleven—but you weren't able to find Mr. Latimer for some time, were you? (*Latimer makes a move as though to speak, then stops himself.*)

NEVILE. No, that's true. I looked all around, too. He wasn't in his room—they telephoned up.

LATIMER. Actually, I was sitting out on the glass-enclosed terrace with a fat, talkative body from Lancashire. (*Easily.*) She wanted to dance—but I stalled her off. Too painful on the feet.

TREVES. (*Moving* C.) Strange wasn't able to find you until half past eleven. Three-quarters of an hour. Plenty of time . . . .

LATIMER. Look here, what do you mean?

NEVILE. Do you mean that *he* . . . ? (*Kay shows every sign of violent agitation, rises and moves to Latimer.*)

TREVES. Plenty of time to strip, swim across the estuary—it's narrow just here—swarm up the rope—do what you had to do—swim back, get into your clothes and meet Nevile in the lounge of the hotel.

LATIMER. Leaving the rope hanging from the window? You're crazy—the whole thing's crazy.

TREVES. (*With a slight glance towards Kay.*) The same person who arranged the rope for you could have drawn it up again and put it in the attic.

LATIMER. (*Frenzied.*) You can't do this to me. You can't frame me—and don't you try. I couldn't climb up a rope all that way—and anyway, I can't swim. I tell you, I can't swim.

KAY. No, Ted can't swim. It's true, I tell you, he can't swim.

TREVES. (*Gently.*) No, you can't swim. I have ascertained that fact. (*He moves on to the rostrum. Kay moves down. To Nevile.*) But you're a very fine swimmer, aren't you, Nevile? And you're an expert climber. It would be child's play to you to swim across, climb up the rope you'd left ready—(*Latimer moves R. of the chaise.*) go along to Lady Tressilian's room, kill her, and go back the way you came. Plenty of time to dispose of the rope when you got back at two-thirty. You didn't see Latimer at the hotel between ten-forty-five and eleven-thirty—but he didn't see you either. It cuts both ways. (*Battle rises and stands in front of the door L.*)

NEVILE. I never heard such rubbish! Swim across—kill Camilla. Why ever should I do such a fantastic thing?

TREVES. Because you wanted to hang the woman who had left you for another man. (*Kay collapses in the easy chair down R. Mary rises, moves to Kay and comforts her. Royde rises and moves to L. of the armchair L. C.*) She had to be punished—your ego has been swelling for a long time—nobody must dare to oppose you.

NEVILE. Is it likely I'd fake all those clues against *myself?*

TREVES. (*Crossing to L. of Nevile.*) It's exactly what you did do—and took the precaution of ringing Lady Tressilian's bell by pulling the old-fashioned bell wire outside her room, to make sure that Mary would see you leaving the house. Lady Tressilian didn't remember ringing that bell. *You* rang it.

NEVILE. (*Moving to the French windows.*) What an absurd pack of lies. (*Leach appears at the French windows.*)

TREVES. *You* murdered Lady Tressilian—but the real murder, the murder that you gloated over secretly, was the murder of Audrey Strange. You wanted her not only to die—but to suffer. You wanted her to be afraid—she was afraid—of you. You enjoyed the idea of her suffering, didn't you?

NEVILE. (*Sitting on the chaise, thickly.*) All—a tissue of lies.

BATTLE. (*Crossing to* L. *of Nevile.*) Is it? I've met people like you before—people with a mental kink. Your vanity was hurt when Audrey Strange left you, wasn't it? You loved her and she had the colossal impertinence to prefer another man. (*Nevile's face shows momentary agreement. He watches Nevile narrowly.*) You wanted to think of something special—something clever, something quite out of the way. The fact that it entailed the killing of a woman who had been almost a mother to you didn't worry you.

NEVILE. (*With resentment.*) She shouldn't have ticked me off like a child. But it's lies—all lies. And I haven't got a mental kink.

BATTLE. (*Watching Nevile.*) Oh, yes, you have. Your wife flicked you on the raw, didn't she, when she left you? You—the wonderful Nevile Strange. You saved your pride by pretending that *you'd* left *her*—and you married another girl just to bolster up that story.

KAY. Oh. (*She turns to Mary. Mary puts her arm around Kay.*)

BATTLE. But all the time you were planning what you'd do to Audrey. Pity you didn't have the brains to carry it out better.

NEVILE. (*Almost whimpering.*) It's not true.

BATTLE. (*Inexorably breaking him down.*) Audrey's been laughing at you—while you've been preening yourself and thinking how clever you were. (*He raises his voice and calls.*) Come in, Mrs. Strange. (*Audrey enters* L. *Nevile gives a strangled cry and rises. Royde moves to Audrey and puts an arm around her.*) She's never been really under arrest, you know. We just wanted to keep her out of your crazy reach. There was no knowing what you might do if you thought your silly childish plan was going wrong. (*Benson appears at the French windows. Leach moves above the chaise.*)

NEVILE. (*Breaking down and screaming with rage.*) It wasn't silly. It was clever—it *was* clever. I thought out every detail. How was *I* to know that Royde knew the truth about Audrey and Adrian? Audrey and Adrian . . . (*He suddenly loses control and screams at Audrey.*) How dare you prefer Adrian to me? God damn and blast

your soul, you *shall* hang. They've *got* to hang you.
They've got to. (*He makes a dash towards Audrey.
Battle makes a sign to Leach and Benson, who move
one each side of Nevile. Audrey clings to Royde. Half sobbing.*) Leave me alone. I want her to die *afraid*—to die
afraid. I hate her. (*Audrey and Royde turn away from
Nevile and move up* L.)

MARY. (*Moving to the chaise and sitting, almost inaudibly.*)
Oh, God!

BATTLE. Take him away, Jim. (*Leach and Benson close in on
Nevile.*)

NEVILE. (*Suddenly quite calm.*) You're making a great mistake, you know. I can . . . (*Leach and Benson lead
Nevile to the door* L. *Nevile suddenly kicks Benson on
the shin, pushes him into Leach, and dashes off* L.
Leach and Benson dash off after Nevile.)

BATTLE. (*In alarm.*) Look out! Stop him. (*Battle dashes off*
L. *Off. Shouting.*) After him—don't let him get away.
(*Treves and Royde run out* L. *Audrey moves slowly to* C.
of rostrum.)

ROYDE. (*Off; shouting.*) He's locked himself in the dining-
room.

BATTLE. (*Off; shouting.*) Break the door open. (*The sound
of heavy blows on wood is heard off. Kay rises.*)

KAY. (*Burying her face in Latimer's shoulder.*) Ted—oh,
Ted . . . (*She sobs. There is a crash of breaking glass off,
followed by the sound of the door breaking open.*)

BATTLE. (*Off; shouting.*) Jim—you go down by the road.
I'll take the cliff path. (*Battle enters quickly* L., *and
crosses quickly to the French windows. He looks worried.
Breathlessly.*) He flung himself through the dining-room
window. It's a sheer drop to the rocks below. I shouldn't
think there was a chance. (*Battle exits by the French
windows. Benson enters* L., *crosses, exits by the French
windows, and is heard to give three shrill blasts on his
whistle.*)

KAY. (*Hysterically.*) I want to get away. I can't . . .

MARY. (*Rising and moving* C.) Why don't you take her back
to the hotel with you, Mr. Latimer?

KAY. (*Eagerly.*) Yes, Ted, please—anything to get away from
here.

MARY. Take her. I'll have her things packed and sent over.

LATIMER. (*Gently.*) Come along. (*Kay exits with Latimer
by the French windows. Mary nods and exits* L. *Audrey*

*moves to the chaise, sits on it, with her back to the bay
window, and sobs. There is a slight pause, then the
curtains of the bay window are parted a little. Nevile
enters quietly over the sill of the bay window. His hair
is dishevelled and there are streaks of dirt on his face
and hands. There is a cruel and devilish smile on his
face as he looks at Audrey. He moves silently towards
her.)*

NEVILE. Audrey! *(Audrey turns quickly and sees Nevile. In
a low, tense voice.)* You didn't think I'd come back, did
you? I was too clever for them, Audrey. While they
were breaking open the door I flung a stool through the
window and climbed out on to the stone ledge. Only a
man who is used to mountain climbing could have done
it—a man with strong fingers—like mine. *(He moves
slowly nearer and nearer to Audrey.)* Strong fingers,
Audrey—and a soft throat. They wouldn't hang you as
I wanted them to, would they? But you're going to die
just the same. *(His fingers close on her throat.)* You'll
never belong to anyone but me. *(Leach dashes in L.
Benson dashes in by the French windows. Leach and
Benson drag Nevile from Audrey and exit with him by
the French windows. Audrey is left gasping for breath
on the chaise. Royde enters L. He stares in a puzzled
way towards the French windows and crosses towards
them. He has almost passed the upstage end of the
chaise when he realizes Audrey is there.)*

ROYDE. *(Stopping and turning to Audrey.)* I say, are you all
right?

AUDREY. Am I all right? Oh, Thomas! *(She laughs. Royde,
with his arms outstretched, moves towards Audrey as—)*

THE CURTAIN FALLS

VERDICT

CAST

(In order of their appearance)

LESTER COLE
MRS. ROPER
LISA KOLETZKY
PROFESSOR KARL HENDRYK
DR. STONER
ANYA HENDRYK
HELEN ROLLANDER
SIR WILLIAM ROLLANDER
DETECTIVE INSPECTOR OGDEN
POLICE SERGEANT PEARCE

SYNOPSIS OF SCENES

ACT I

SCENE 1 An afternoon in early spring.
SCENE 2 A fortnight later. Afternoon.

ACT II

SCENE 1 Four days later. About midday.
SCENE 2 Six hours later. Evening.
SCENE 3 Two months later. Late afternoon.

TIME: The Present.

Act One

Scene I

SCENE: *The living room of* PROFESSOR HENDRYK's *flat in Bloomsbury. An afternoon in early spring.*

The flat is the upper floor of one of the old houses in Bloomsbury. It is a well-proportioned room with comfortable, old-fashioned furniture. The main feature that strikes the eye is books; books everywhere, in shelves against the wall, lying on tables, on chairs, on the sofa and piled up in heaps on the floor. Double doors up C *lead to an entrance hall with the door to* LISA's *bedroom, facing. In the hall, the front door is* R *and a passage leads off* L *to the kitchen. In the room the door to* ANYA's *bedroom is down* R *and there is a sash window* L *leading on to a small balcony with ivy-covered railings, overlooking the street below and a row of houses opposite.* KARL's *desk is in front of the window with a chair in front of it. The desk is filled with books as well as the telephone, blotter, calendar, etc. Below the desk is a record cabinet, filled with records, more books and odd lecture papers. There is a record player on top. Built into the walls either side of the double doors are bookcases. Below the left one is* ANYA's *small work-table. Between the doors and the bookcase* L *of it there is a three-tiered, round table with books in each tier and a plant on the top one. Against the wall below the door* R *is a small console table with a plant on top and books piled below. Hanging on the wall above the door down* R *is a small set of shelves with more books and* ANYA's *medicine in one corner. Under the shelves is a small cupboard with further books. The cupboards are underneath. In front of these shelves, there is a library ladder. A sofa is* RC *with a circular table*

*behind it. Chairs stand above and L of the table. All
three pieces of furniture have books on them. A large red
armchair is LC, with still more books on it. At night the
room is lit by wall-brackets each side of the window and
table-lamps on the desk, on the table RC and on the
cupboard R. There are switches L of the double doors.
In the hall there is a chair R of the bedroom door.*

When the CURTAIN *rises, the double doors are open.
The stage is in darkness. When the lights come up*
LESTER COLE *is precariously balanced on the library
ladder. He is a clumsy but likeable young man of about
twenty-four, with a tousled head of hair. He is shabbily
dressed. There is a pile of books on the top of the
ladder.* LESTER *reaches up to the top shelf, selects a
book now and again, pauses to read a passage and
either adds it to the pile on the ladder or replaces it
on the shelf.*

MRS. ROPER. (*off* L *in the Hall*) All right, Miss Koletzky, I'll
see to it before I go home.

(MRS. ROPER *enters the hall from* L. *She is a rather shifty
and unpleasant cleaning woman. She is carrying her
outdoor clothes and a shopping bag. She crosses to* R *of
the hall, then returns with great stealth, entering the
room with her back against the right-hand door. She
obviously does not see* LESTER *who is engrossed in a
book. She creeps towards the downstage end of the
desk where there is a packet of cigarettes. She is just
about to pocket them when* LESTER *shuts his book with
a bang.* MRS. ROPER, *startled out of her wits, spins
round.*)

Oh, Mr. Cole—I didn't know you were still here.

(LESTER *goes to return the book to the top shelf and nearly
overbalances.*)

Do be careful. (*She crosses above the armchair* LC *to* R
of it and puts her bag on the floor) That thing's not
safe, really it isn't. (*She puts on her hat*) Come to
pieces any minute, it might, and where would you be
then, I'd like to know? (*She puts on her coat*)
LESTER. Where indeed?

(The lights begin to fade slowly for sunset.)

MRS. ROPER. Only yesterday I read in the papers of a gentle-man as fell off a pair of steps in his library. Thought nothing of it at the time—but later he was took bad and they rushed him to hospital. *(She puts her scarf around her neck)* Broken rib what had penetrated the lung. *(With satisfaction)* And the next day he was— *(She gives her scarf a final pull round her throat)* dead.

LESTER. What jolly papers you read, Mrs. Roper. *(He becomes engrossed in a book and ignores MRS. ROPER)*

MRS. ROPER. And the same will happen to you if you go stretching over like that. *(She glances at the desk where the cigarettes are, then back at LESTER again. Seeing that he is taking no notice of her she starts to sidle over to the desk, humming quietly to herself and keeping an eye on LESTER. She empties the cigarettes from the packet into her pocket, then moves to C holding the empty packet)* Oh, look! The professor's run out of cigarettes again.

(A clock strikes five somewhere outside the window.)

I'd better slip out and get him another twenty before they shut. Tell Miss Koletzky I won't be long fetching back that washing. *(She picks up her bag, goes into the hall and calls)* Bye!

(MRS. ROPER exits in the hall to R. The front door is heard opening and closing.)

LESTER. *(without taking his nose out of the book)* I'll tell her.

(A door is heard to slam off L in the hall. LESTER jumps, knocking the pile of books off the top of the steps. LISA KOLETZKY enters up C from L. She is a tall, handsome, dark woman of thirty-five, with a strong and rather enigmatic personality. She is carrying a hot-water bottle.)

Sorry, Miss Koletzky, I'll pick 'em up. *(He comes down the ladder and picks up the books)*

LISA. *(moving C)* It does not matter. A few more books here and there are of no consequence.

LESTER. (*placing the books on the table* RC) You startled me, you see. How is Mrs. Hendryk?

LISA. (*tightening the stopper on the bottle*) The same as usual. She feels the cold. I have a fresh bottle here for her.

LESTER. (*moving to* R *of the sofa*) Has she been ill for a very long time?

LISA. (*sitting on the left arm of the sofa*) Five years.

LESTER. Will she ever get any better?

LISA. She has her bad and her good days.

LESTER. Oh, yes, but I mean really better.

(LISA *shakes her head.*)

I say, that's tough going, isn't it?

LISA (*rather foreign*) As you say, it is "tough going."

LESTER. (*climbing up the ladder and falling up before reaching the top*) Can't the doctors do anything?

LISA. No. She has one of these diseases for which at present there is no known cure. Some day perhaps they will discover one. In the meantime—(*She shrugs her shoulders*) she can never get any better. Every month, every year, she gets a little weaker. She may go on like that for many, many years.

LESTER. Yes, that is tough. It's tough on him. (*He comes down the ladder*)

LISA. As you say, it is tough on him.

LESTER. (*moving to* R *of the sofa*) He's awfully good to her, isn't he?

LISA. He cares for her very much.

LESTER. (*sitting on the right arm of the sofa*) What was she like when she was young?

LISA. She was very pretty. Yes, a very pretty girl, fair-haired and blue-eyed and always laughing.

LESTER. (*bewildered by life*) You know, it gets me. I mean, time—what it does to you. How people change. I mean, it's hard to know what's real and what isn't—or if anything is real.

LISA. (*rising and crossing to the door down* R) This bottle seems to be real.

(LISA *exits down* R *leaving the door open.* LESTER *rises, collects his satchel from the table* RC, *crosses to the arm-*

chair LC *and puts some books from the chair into the*
satchel. LISA *can be heard talking to* ANYA, *but the*
words are indistinguishable. LISA *re-enters down* R.)

LESTER. (*guiltily*) The professor said it would be all right to
take anything I wanted.

LISA. (*moving to* R *of the table* RC *and glancing at the books*)
Of course, if he said so.

LESTER. He's rather wonderful, isn't he?

LISA. (*absorbed in a book*) Hmm?

LESTER. The Prof., he's wonderful. We all think so, you
know. Everybody's terrifically keen. The way he puts
things. All the past seems to come alive. (*He pauses*)
I mean, when he talks about it you see what everything
means. He's pretty unusual, isn't he?

LISA. He has a very fine brain.

LESTER. (*sitting on the right arm of the armchair*) Bit of
luck for us that he had to leave his own country and
came here. But it isn't only his brain, you know, it's
something else.

(LISA *selects a "Walter Savage Landor," moves and sits on*
the sofa at the left end.)

LISA. I know what you mean. (*She reads*)

LESTER. You just feel that he knows all about you. I mean,
that he knows just how difficult everything is. Because
you can't get away from it—life is difficult, isn't it?

LISA. (*still reading*) I do not see why it should be so.

LESTER. (*startled*) I beg your pardon?

LISA. I don't see why you say—and so many people say—that
life is difficult. I think life is very simple.

LESTER. Oh, come now—hardly simple.

LISA. But, yes. It has a pattern, the sharp edges, very easy to
see.

LESTER. Well, I think it's just one unholy mess. (*Doubtfully,*
but hoping he is right) Perhaps you're a kind of
Christian Scientist?

LISA. (*laughing*) No, I'm not a Christian Scientist.

LESTER. But you really think life's easy and happy?

LISA. I did not say it was easy or happy. I said it was simple.

LESTER. (*rising and crossing to* L *of the sofa*) I know you're
awfully good—(*Embarrassed*) I mean, the way you look
after Mrs. Hendryk and everything.

LISA. I look after her because I want to do so, not because it is good.

LESTER. I mean, you could get a well-paid job if you tried.

LISA. Oh, yes, I could get a job quite easily. I am a trained physicist.

LESTER. (*impressed*) I'd no idea of that. But then, surely you ought to get a job, oughtn't you?

LISA. How do you mean—ought?

LESTER. Well, I mean it's rather a waste, isn't it, if you don't? Of your ability, I mean.

LISA. A waste of my training, perhaps, yes. But ability—I think what I am doing now I do well, and I like doing it.

LESTER. Yes, but . . .

(*The front door is heard opening and closing.* KARL HENDRYK *enters up* C *from* R. *He is a virile and good-looking man of forty-five. He is carrying a brief-case and a small bunch of spring flowers. He switches on the wall-brackets, the table-lamp* R *and the table-lamp* RC *by the switches* L. *of the door. He smiles at* LISA *who rises as he moves* C, *and his face lights up with pleasure to see* LESTER.)

KARL. Hello, Lisa.

LISA. Hello, Karl.

KARL. Look—spring. (*He hands her the flowers*)

LISA. How lovely. (*She moves round below the sofa, puts the flowers on the table* RC, *then continues round the table and takes* KARL's *coat and hat.*)

(LISA *exits off* C *to* L *with the hat and coat.*)

KARL. So you have come for more books? Good. Let me see what you are taking.

(*They look over the books together.*)

Yes, Loshen is good—very sound. And the Verthmer. Salzen—I warn you—he is very unsound.

LESTER. Then, perhaps, sir, I'd better not . . .

KARL. No. No, take it. Read it. I warn you out of my own experience, but you must make your own judgements.

LESTER. Thank you, sir. I'll remember what you say. (*He crosses above* KARL *to the table* RC *and picks up a book*) I brought the Loftus back. It is just as you said—he really makes one think. (*He replaces the book on the table*)

(KARL *crosses above the armchair to the desk, takes some books from his brief-case and puts them on the desk.*)

KARL. Why not stay and have some supper with us? (*He switches on the desk lamp*)

LESTER. (*putting books in his satchel*) Thank you so much, sir, but I've got a date.

KARL. I see. Well, good-bye till Monday, then. Take care of the books.

(LISA *enters up* C *from* L *and crosses to* R *of the table* RC)

LESTER. (*flushing guiltily*) Oh, I will, sir. I'm awfully sorry—more sorry than I can tell you—about losing that other one.

KARL. (*sitting at the desk*) Think no more about it. I have lost books myself in my time. It happens to all of us.

LESTER. (*moving to the doors up* C) You've been awfully good about it. Awfully good. Some people wouldn't have lent me any more books.

KARL. Tcha! That would have been foolish. Go on, my boy.

(LESTER *exits rather unwillingly by the hall to* R.)

(*To* LISA) How is Anya?

LISA. She has been very depressed and fretful this afternoon, but she settled down for a little sleep. I hope she is asleep, now.

KARL. I won't wake her if she is asleep. My poor darling, she needs all the sleep she can get.

LISA. I'll get some water for the flowers.

(LISA *takes a vase from the shelf* R *and comes back into the room. He glances quickly round, makes sure he is alone with Karl and moves to* R *of the armchair.*)

LESTER. (*with a rush*) I've got to tell you, sir, I must. I—I didn't lose that book.

(LISA *enters from up* C *and* L *with the flowers in the vase, crosses very quietly to* L *of the table and* RC *and puts the vase on it.*)

      I—I sold it.

KARL. (*not turning and not really surprised but kindly nodding his head*) I see. You sold it.

LESTER. I never meant to tell you. I don't know why I have. But I just felt you'd got to know. I don't know what you'll think of me.

KARL. (*turning round; thoughtfully*) You sold it. For how much?

LESTER. (*slightly pleased with himself*) I got two pounds for it. Two pounds.

KARL. You wanted the money?

LESTER. Yes, I did. I wanted it badly.

KARL. (*rising*) What did you want the money for?

LESTER. (*giving* KARL *a rather shifty glance*) Well, you see, my mother's been ill lately and . . . (*He breaks off and moves away from* KARL *down* C) No, I won't tell you any more lies. I wanted it—you see, there was a girl. I wanted to take her out, and . . .

(KARL *suddenly smiles at* LESTER *and crosses below the arm-chair to* L *of him.*)

KARL. Ah! You wanted it to spend on a girl. I see. Good. Very good—very good, indeed.

LESTER. Good? But . . .

KARL. So natural. Oh, yes, it was very wrong of you to steal my book and to sell it and to lie to me about it. But if you have to do bad things I am glad that you do them for a good motive. And at your age there is no better motive than that—to go out with a girl and enjoy yourself. (*He pats* LESTER *on the shoulder*) She is pretty, your girl?

LESTER. (*self-consciously*) Well, naturally, I think so. (*He gains confidence*) Actually, she's pretty marvellous.

KARL. (*with a knowing chuckle*) And you had a good time on the two pounds?

LESTER. In a way. Well, I mean, I began by enjoying it awfully. But—but I did feel rather uncomfortable.

KARL. (*sitting on the right arm of the armchair*) You felt uncomfortable—yes, that's interesting.

LESTER. Do believe me, sir, I am terribly sorry and ashamed, and it won't happen again. And I'll tell you this, too. I'm going to save up and buy that book back and bring it back to you.

KARL. (*gravely*) Then you shall do so if you can. Now, cheer up—that's all over and forgotten.

(LESTER *throws* KARL *a grateful glance and exits by the hall to* R. LISA *comes slowly forward towards* KARL)

(*He nods his head*) I'm glad he came and told me about it himself. I hoped he would, but of course I wasn't at all sure.

LISA. (*moving* RC) You knew, then, that he'd stolen it?

KARL. Of course I knew.

LISA. (*puzzled*) But you didn't let him know that you knew.

KARL. No.

LISA. Why?

KARL. Because, as I say, I hoped he would tell me about it himself.

LISA. (*after a pause*) Was it a valuable book?

KARL. (*rising and moving to the desk*) Actually, it's quite irreplaceable.

LISA. (*turning away*) Oh, Karl.

KARL. Pood devil—so pleased to have got two pounds for it. The dealer who bought it off him will probably have sold it for forty or fifty pounds by now.

LISA. So he won't be able to buy it back?

KARL. (*sitting at the desk*) No.

LISA. (*crossing to* R *of the armchair*) I don't understand you, Karl. (*She begins to lose her temper*) It seems to me sometimes you go out of your way to let yourself be played upon—you allow yourself to have things stolen from you, to be deceived . . .

KARL. (*gently but amused*) But, Lisa, I wasn't deceived.

LISA. Well, that makes it worse. Stealing is stealing. The way you go on positively encourages people to steal.

KARL. (*becoming thoughtful*) Does it? I wonder. I wonder.

(LISA *is very angry now and starts pacing below the sofa and back up* C.)

LISA. How angry you make me.

KARL. I know. I always make you angry.

LISA. (*moving up* R) That miserable boy . . .

KARL. (*rising and standing up* LC) That miserable boy has the makings of a very fine scholar—a really fine scholar. That's rare, you know, Lisa. That's very rare. There are so many of these boys and girls, earnest, wanting to learn, but not the real thing.

(LISA *sits on left arm of the sofa.*)

(*He moves to* L *of* LISA) But Lester Cole is the real stuff of which scholars are made.

(LISA *has calmed down by now and she puts her arm affectionately on* KARL's *arm.*)

(*He smiles ruefully. After a pause*) You've no idea of the difference one Lester Cole makes to a weary professor's life.

LISA. I can understand that. There is so much mediocrity.

KARL. Mediocrity and worse. (*He gives* LISA *a cigarette, lights it, then sits* C *of the sofa*) I'm willing to spend time on the conscientious plodder, even if he isn't very bright, but the people who want to acquire learning as a form of intellectual snobbery, to try it on as you try on a piece of jewellery, who want just a smattering and only a smattering, and who ask for their food to be pre-digested, that I won't stand for. I turned one of them down today.

LISA. Who was that?

KARL. A very spoiled young girl. Naturally she's at liberty to attend classes and waste her time, but she wants private tuition—special lessons.

LISA. Is she prepared to pay for them?

KARL. That is her idea. Her father, I gather, has immense wealth and has always bought his daughter everything she wanted. Well, he won't buy her private tuition from me.

LISA. We could do with the money.

KARL. I know. I know, but it's not a question of money—it's the time, you see, Lisa. I really haven't got the time. There are two boys, Sydney Abrahamson—you know him—and another boy. A coal miner's son. They're both keen, desperately keen, and I think they've got the stuff in them. But they're handicapped by a bad superficial education. I've got to give them private time if they're to have a chance.

(LISA *rises, crosses above the armchair and flicks her cigarette ash into the ashtray on the desk.*)

And they're worth it, Lisa, they're worth it. Do you understand?

LISA. I understand that one cannot possibly change you, Karl. You stand by and smile when a student helps himself to a valuable book, you refuse a rich pupil in favour of a penniless one. (*She crosses to* C) I'm sure it is very noble, but nobility doesn't pay the baker and the butcher and the grocer.

KARL. But surely, Lisa, we are really not so hard up.

LISA. No, we are not really so hard up, but we could always do with some more money. Just think what we could do with this room.

(*The thumping of a stick is heard off* R.)

Ah! Anya is awake.

KARL. (*rising*) I'll go to her.

KARL *exits down* R. LISA *smiles, sighs, and shakes her head, then collects the books from the armchair and puts them on the table* RC. *The music of a barrel organ is heard off.* LISA *picks up the "Walter Savage Landor" from the table* RC, *sits on the left arm of the sofa and reads.* MRS. ROPER *enters the hall from* R. *She carries a large parcel of washing. She exits in the hall to* L, *deposits the parcel, then re-enters and comes into the room with her shopping bag.*

MRS. ROPER. I got the washing. (*She goes to the desk*) And I got a few more fags for the professor—he was right out again. (*She takes a packet of cigarettes from her shopping bag and puts them on the desk*) Oh! Don't they carry on when they run out of fags? You should have heard Mr. Freemantel at my last place. (*She puts her bag on the floor* R *of the armchair*) Screamed blue murder he did if he hadn't got a fag. Always sarcastic to his wife, he was. They were incompatible—you know, he had a secretary. Saucy cat! When the divorce came up, I could have told them a thing or two, from what I saw. I would have done, too, but for Mr. Roper. I thought it was only right, but he said, "No, Ivy, never spit against the wind."

(*The front door bell rings.*)

Shall I see who it is?

LISA. (*rising*) If you please, Mrs. Roper.

(MRS. ROPER *exits by the hall to* R.)

DOCTOR. (*off*) Good evening, Mrs. Roper.

(MRS. ROPER *re-enters.* DOCTOR STONER *follows her on. He is a typical family doctor of the old school, aged about sixty. He is affectionately at home.*)

MRS. ROPER. (*as she enters*) It's the doctor.

DOCTOR. Good evening, Lisa, my dear. (*He stands up* R *and looks around the room at the masses of books everywhere*)

LISA. (*moving to* R *of the table* RC) Hello, Doctor Stoner.

MRS. ROPER. (*picking up her bag*) Well, I must be off. Oh, Miss Koletzky, I'll bring in another quarter of tea in the morning, we're right out again. 'Bye!

(MRS. ROPER *exits up* C, *closing the doors behind her. The* DOCTOR *crosses below the sofa to* R *of it.*)

DOCTOR. Well, Lisa, and how goes it?

(LISA *moves about the table* RC *and marks her place in the book, with a piece of flower wrapping paper.*)

Has Karl been buying books again, or is it only my fancy that there are more than usual? (*He busies himself clearing the books from the sofa and putting them on the table* RC)

(LISA *picks up the remainder of the wrapping paper, crosses to the waste-paper basket above the desk and drops the paper in it.*)

LISA. (*moving to* L *of the sofa*) I have forbidden him to buy more, Doctor. Already there is practically nowhere to sit down.

DOCTOR. You are quite right to read him the riot act, Lisa, but you won't succeed. Karl would rather have a book for dinner than a piece of roast beef. How is Anya?

LISA. She has been very depressed and in bad spirits today. Yesterday she seemed a little better and more cheerful.

DOCTOR. (*sitting on the sofa at the right end*) Yes, yes, that's the way it goes. (*He sighs*) Is Karl with her now?

LISA. Yes.
DOCTOR. He never fails her.

(*The barrel organ music ceases.*)

You realize, my dear, don't you, that Karl is a very remarkable man? People feel it, you know, they're influenced by him.
LISA. He makes his effect, yes.
DOCTOR. (*sharply*) Now, what do you mean by that, young woman?
LISA. (*taking the book from under her arm*) "There are no fields of amaranth this side of the grave."

(*The* DOCTOR *takes the book from* LISA *and looks at the title.*)

DOCTOR. H'm. Walter Savage Landor. What's your exact meaning, Lisa, in quoting him?
LISA. Just that you know and I know that there are no fields of amaranth this side of the grave. But Karl doesn't know. For him the fields of amaranth are here and now, and that can be dangerous.
DOCTOR. Dangerous—to him?
LISA. Not only to him. Dangerous to others, to those who care for him, who depend on him. Men like Karl . . . (*She breaks off*)
DOCTOR. (*after a pause*) Yes?

(*Voices are heard off down* R, *and as* LISA *hears them she moves to the work-table up* L *and sets it* R *of the armchair.* KARL *enters down* R *pushing* ANYA HENDRYK *in a wheelchair.* ANYA *is a woman of about thirty-eight, fretful and faded with a trace of former prettiness. On occasions her manner shows she has at one time been a coquettish and pretty young girl. Mostly she is a querulous and whining invalid.*)

KARL. (*as he enters*) I thought I heard your voice, Doctor.
DOCTOR. (*rising*) Good evening, Anya, you look very well this evening.

(KARL *pushes the wheelchair to* C *and sets it* R *of the worktable.*)

ANYA. I may look well, Doctor, but I don't feel it. How can
I feel well cooped up here all day?

DOCTOR. (*Cheerfully*) But you have that nice balcony outside
your bedroom window. (*He sits on the sofa*) You can
sit out there and get the air and the sunshine and see
what's going on all around you.

ANYA. As if there's anything worth looking at going on round
me. All these drab houses and all the drab people who
live in them. Ah, when I think of our lovely little house
and the garden and all our nice furniture—everything
gone. It's too much, Doctor, it's too much to lose everything you have.

KARL. Come, Anya, you still have a fine upstanding husband.

(LISA *brings the flowers from the table* RC *and puts them on
the work-table.*)

ANYA. Not such an upstanding husband as he was—(*To* LISA)
is he?

(LISA *laughs at* ANYA's *little joke and exits up* C.)

You stoop, Karl, and your hair is grey.

KARL. (*sitting on the left arm of the sofa*) That is a pity,
but you must put up with me as I am.

ANYA. (*miserably*) I feel worse every day, Doctor. My back
aches and I've got a twitching in this left arm. I don't
think that last medicine suits me.

DOCTOR. Then we must try something else.

ANYA. The drops are all right, the ones for my heart, but Lisa
only gives me four at a time. She says that you said I
mustn't take more. But I think I've got used to them
and it would be better if I took six or eight.

DOCTOR. Lisa is carrying out my orders. That is why I have
told her not to leave them near you in case you should
take too many. They are dangerous, you know.

ANYA. It's just as well you don't leave them near me. I'm
sure if you did, one day I should take the whole bottle
and finish it all.

DOCTOR. No, no, my dear. You wouldn't do that.

ANYA. What good am I to anyone, just lying there, ill and a
nuisance to everyone? Oh, I know they're kind enough,
but they must feel me a terrible burden.

KARL. (*rising and affectionately patting* ANYA's *shoulder*) You are not a burden to me, Anya.

ANYA. That's what you say, but I must be.

KARL. No, you're not.

ANYA. I know I am. It's not as though I am gay and amusing like I used to be. I'm just an invalid now, fretful and cross with nothing amusing to say or do.

KARL. No, no, my dear.

ANYA. If I were only dead and out of the way, Karl could marry—a young handsome wife who would help him in his career.

KARL. You would be surprised if you knew how many men's careers have been ruined by marrying young handsome wives when they themselves are middle-aged.

ANYA. You know what I mean. I'm just a burden on you.

(KARL *shakes his head at* ANYA, *gently smiling*.)

DOCTOR. (*writing a prescription on his pad*) We'll try a tonic. A new tonic.

(LISA *enters up* C. *She carries a tray of coffee for four which she puts on the table* RC.)

LISA. Have you seen your flowers, Anya? Karl brought them for you. (*She pours the coffee*)

(KARL *moves above the work-table and picks up the vase for* ANYA *to see*.)

ANYA. I don't want to be reminded of spring. Spring in this horrible city. You remember the woods and how we went and picked the little wild daffodils? Ah, life was so happy, then, so easy. We didn't know what was coming. Now, the world is hateful, horrible, all drab grey, and our friends are scattered, and most of them are dead, and we have to live in a foreign country.

(LISA *hands a cup of coffee to the doctor*.)

DOCTOR. Thank you, Lisa.

KARL. There are worse things.

ANYA. I know you think I complain all the time, but—if I were well I should be brave and bear it all.

(ANYA *puts her hand out and* KARL *kisses it.* LISA *hands a cup of coffee to* ANYA.)

KARL. I know, my dear, I know. You have a lot to bear.
ANYA. You don't know anything about it.

(*The front-door bell rings.* LISA *exits in the hall to* R.)

You're well and strong and so is Lisa. What have I ever done that this should happen to me?
KARL. (*taking her hand in his*) Dearest—dearest—I understand.
LISA. (*off*) Good afternoon.
HELEN. (*off*) Could I see Professor Hendryk, please?
LISA. (*off*) Would you come this way, please.

(LISA *enters up* C *from* R. HELEN ROLLANDER *follows her on.* HELEN *is a beautiful and self-assured girl of about twenty-three.* KARL *moves above the armchair.*)

(*She stands* L *of the doors*) Miss Rollander to see you, Karl.

(HELEN *goes straight toward* KARL. *Her manner is assured and charming.* LISA *watches her sharply. The* DOCTOR, *rising, is intrigued and interested.*)

HELEN. I do hope you don't mind my butting in like this. I got your private address from Lester Cole.

(LISA *crosses to the table* RC *and pours more coffee.*)

KARL. (*moving up* L *of* ANYA) Of course I do not mind. May I introduce you to my wife—Miss Rollander.

(HELEN *stands* R *of* ANYA. LISA *gives* KARL *a cup of coffee.*)

HELEN. (*with great charm*) How do you do, Mrs. Hendryk?
ANYA. How do you do? I am, you see, an invalid. I cannot get up.
HELEN. Of course not. I'm so sorry. I hope you don't mind my coming, but I'm a pupil of your husband's. I wanted to consult him about something.
KARL. (*indicating them in turn*) This is Miss Koletzky and Dr. Stoner.
HELEN. (*to* LISA) How do you do? (*She crosses to the* DOCTOR *and shakes hands*) How do you do? (*She moves up* C)

DOCTOR. How do you do?

HELEN. (*looking round the room*) So this is where you live. Books, books, and books. (*She moves down to the sofa, then sits on it*)

DOCTOR. Yes, Miss Rollander, you are very fortunate in being able to sit down. I cleared that sofa only five minutes ago.

HELEN. Oh, I'm always lucky.

KARL. Would you like some coffee?

HELEN. No, thank you. Professor Hendryk, I wonder if I could speak to you for a moment alone?

(LISA *looks up sharply from her coffee at* KARL.)

KARL. (*rather coldly*) I'm afraid our accommodation is rather limited. This is the only sitting-room.

HELEN. Oh, well, I expect you know what I'm going to say. You told me today that your time was so taken up that you couldn't accept any more private pupils. I've come to ask you to change your mind, to make an exception in my favour.

KARL *crosses above* ANYA *to* L *of* HELEN, *looks at* LISA *as he passes and hands her his cup and saucer.*

KARL. I'm very sorry, Miss Rollander, but my time is absolutely booked up.

(HELEN *speaks with great pace and assurance, almost gabbling.*)

HELEN. You can't put me off like that. I happen to know that after you refused me you agreed to take Sydney Abrahamson privately, so you see you had got time. You preferred him to me. Why?

KARL. If you want an honest answer . . .

HELEN. I do. I hate beating about the bush.

KARL. I think Sydney is more likely to profit than you are.

HELEN. Do you mean you think he's got a better brain than I have?

KARL. No, I would not say that, but he has, shall I say, a greater desire for learning.

HELEN. Oh, I see. You think I'm not serious?

(KARL *does not answer.*)

But I am serious. The truth is you're prejudiced. You
think that because I'm rich, because I've been a deb,
and done all the silly things that debs do—you think
I'm not in earnest.

ANYA. (*finding* HELEN's *chatter is too much; interrupting*)
Karl.

HELEN. But, believe me, I am.

ANYA. Oh, dear—I wonder—Karl!

KARL. (*moving to R of* ANYA) Yes, my darling?

ANYA. My head—I don't feel terribly well.

(HELEN *is put out by* ANYA's *interruption, and takes some
cigarettes and a lighter from her handbag.*)

I'm sorry—er—Miss Rollander, but if you'll excuse me
I think I'll go back to my own room.

HELEN. (*rather bored*) Of course, I quite understand.

(KARL *pushes the chair towards the door down* R. *The* DOCTOR
*moves to the door, opens it and takes charge of the
chair.* KARL *stands* R *of the sofa.*)

ANYA. My heart feels—very odd tonight. Doctor, don't you
think you could . . . ?

DOCTOR. Yes, yes, I think we can find something that will
help you. Karl, will you bring my bag?

(*The* DOCTOR *wheels* ANYA *off down* R. KARL *picks up the*
DOCTOR's *bag.*)

KARL. (*to* HELEN) Excuse me please.

(KARL *exits down* R.)

HELEN. Poor Mrs. Hendryk, has she been an invalid long? (*She
lights her cigarette*)

LISA. (*drinking her coffee and watching* HELEN) Five years.

HELEN. Five years! Poor man.

LISA. Poor man?

HELEN. I was thinking of him dancing attendance on her all
the time. She likes him to dance attendance, doesn't
she?

LISA. He's her husband.

HELEN. (*rising, crossing below the armchair and standing
down* L) He's a very kind man, isn't he? But one can

be too kind. Pity is weakening, don't you think? I'm afraid I'm not in the least kind. I never pity anybody. I can't help it, I'm made that way. (*She sits on the left arm of the armchair*)

(LISA *moves to the work-table and takes* ANYA's *cup and saucer to the tray.*)

Do you live here, too?

LISA. I look after Mrs. Hendryk and the flat.

HELEN. Oh, you poor dear, how awful for you.

LISA. Not at all. I like it.

HELEN. (*vaguely*) Don't they have household helps or something who go around and do that sort of thing for invalids? (*She rises and moves above the armchair*) I should have thought it would be much more fun for you to train for something and take a job.

LISA. There is no need for me to train. I am already a trained physicist.

HELEN. Oh, but then you could get a job quite easily. (*She stubs out her cigarette in the ashtray on the desk*)

LISA. I already have a job—here.

(KARL *enters down* R, *collects the bottle of medicine and glass from the shelves by the door, then moves to the bookshelves up* R. LISA *picks up the coffee and tray and exits with it up* C.)

HELEN. (*crossing below the armchair to* C) Well, Professor Hendryk, can I come?

KARL. I'm afraid the answer is no. (*He pours some water from the jug on the bookcase shelf into the medicine glass, then moves to the door down* R)

HELEN. (*crossing to* KARL) You don't understand. I want to come. I want to be taught. Oh, please, you can't refuse me. (*She comes close to him and puts a hand on his arm*)

KARL. (*drawing back a little*) But I can refuse you, you know. (*He smiles at her quite gently and kindly*)

HELEN. But why, why? Daddy'll pay you heaps if you let me come. Double the ordinary fee. I know he will.

KARL. I'm sure your father would do anything you ask him, but it's not a question of money.

(HELEN *turns to* C. LISA *enters up* C *and stands above the table* RC.)

(*He turns to* LISA) Lisa, give Miss Rollander a glass of sherry, will you. I must go back to Anya. (*He turns to go*)

HELEN. Professor Hendryk!

KARL. My wife is having one of her bad days. I know you'll excuse me if I go back to her now.

(KARL *smiles very charmingly at* HELEN *then exits down* R. HELEN *looks after him.* LISA *takes a bottle of sherry from the bookcase, cupboard* R. HELEN, *after a slight pause, makes a decision and collects her handbag and gloves from the sofa.*)

HELEN. No, thanks, I don't want any sherry. I'll be going now. (*She moves towards the double doors, then pauses and looks back*)

(*The* DOCTOR *enters down* R *and stands by the door.*)

I shall get my own way, you know. I always do.

(HELEN *sweeps out up* C.)

LISA. (*taking some glasses from the cupboard*) You will have a glass of sherry, Doctor?

DOCTOR. Thank you. (*He crosses to* LC *and puts his bag down*) That's a very determined young woman.

LISA. (*pouring two glasses of sherry*) Yes. She has fallen in love with Karl, of course.

DOCTOR. I suppose that happens fairly often?

LISA. Oh, yes. I remember being frightfully in love myself with my professor of mathematics. He never even noticed me. (*She crosses to the* DOCTOR, *hands him a glass of sherry, then sits on the left arm of the sofa*)

DOCTOR. But you were probably younger than that girl.

LISA. Yes, I was younger.

DOCTOR. (*sitting in the armchair*) You don't think that Karl may respond?

LISA. One never knows. I don't think so.

DOCTOR. He's used to it, you mean?

LISA. He's not used to it, to it from quite that type of girl. Most of the students are rather an unattractive lot, but this girl has beauty and glamour and money—and she wants him very badly.

DOCTOR. So you are afraid.

LISA. No, I'm not afraid, not for Karl. I know what Karl is. I know what Anya means to him and always will. If I am afraid . . . (*She hesitates*)

DOCTOR. Yes?

LISA. Oh, what does it matter? (*She takes refuge in her sherry*)

(KARL *enters down* R.)

KARL. (*crossing to* RC) So my importunate young lady has gone.

(LISA *rises and pours a glass of sherry for* KARL.)

DOCTOR. A very beautiful girl. Are many of your students like that, Karl?

KARL. Fortunately, no, or we should have more complications than we have already. (*He sits on the sofa at the left end*)

DOCTOR. (*rising*) You must be careful, my boy. (*He sets down his glass and picks up his bag, then moves up* C)

KARL. (*amused*) Oh, I am careful. I have to be.

(LISA *moves up* RC.)

DOCTOR. And if you do give her private lessons, have Lisa there as chaperone. Good night, Lisa.

LISA. Good night, Doctor.

(*The* DOCTOR *exits up* C, *closing the doors behind him.* LISA *moves to* L *of* KARL *and hands him the glass of sherry. There is a pause.*)

(*She moves to the door down* R) I'd better go to Anya.

KARL. No. She said she wanted to be left to rest a little. (*He pauses*) I'm afraid it upset her, that girl coming.

LISA. Yes, I know.

KARL. It's the contrast between her life and—the other. And she says she gets jealous, too. Anya's always convinced I'm going to fall in love with one of my students.

LISA. (*sitting beside* KARL *on the sofa*) Perhaps you will.

KARL. (*sharply and significantly*) Can you say that?

LISA. (*turning away and shrugging her shoulders*) It might happen.

KARL. Never. And you know it.

(*There is a rather constrained pause. They both stare into their glasses.*)

Why do you stay with us?

(LISA *does not answer.*)

(*After a pause*) Why do you stay with us?

LISA. You know perfectly why I stay.

KARL. I think it's wrong for you. I think perhaps you should go back.

LISA. Go back? Go back where?

KARL. There's nothing against you and never was. You could go back and take up your old post. They'd leap at the chance of having you.

LISA. Perhaps, but I don't want to go.

KARL. But perhaps you should go.

LISA. Should go? Should go? What do you mean?

KARL. This is no life for you.

LISA. It's the life I choose.

KARL. It's wrong for you. Go back. Go away. Have a life of your own.

LISA. I have a life of my own.

KARL. You know what I mean. Marry. Have children.

LISA. I do not think I shall marry.

KARL. Not if you stay here, but if you go away . . .

LISA. Do you want me to go? (*She pauses*) Answer me, do you want me to go?

KARL. (*with difficulty*) No, I don't want you to go.

LISA. Then don't let's talk about it. (*She rises, takes* KARL's *glass and puts it with her own on the bookcase shelf*)

KARL. Do you remember the concert in the Kursaal that day? It was August and very hot. An immensely fat soprano sang the Liebestod. She did not sing it well, either. We were not impressed, either of us. You had a green coat and skirt and a funny little velvet hat. Odd isn't it, how there are some things that one never forgets, that one never will forget? I don't know what happened the day before that, or what happened the day after it, but I remember that afternoon very well. The gold chairs and the platform, the orchestra wiping their foreheads and the fat soprano bowing and kissing her hand. And then they played the Rachmaninoff piano concerto. Do you remember, Lisa?

LISA. (*calmly*) Of course.

(KARL *hums the tune of the* "*Rachmaninoff piano con-*
   certo.")

KARL. I can hear it now. (*He hums*)

                 (*The front-door bell rings.*)

   Now, who's that?

          (LISA *turns abruptly and exits up* C *to* R.)

ROLLANDER. (*off*) Good evening. Is Professor Hendryk in?

      (KARL *picks up a book and glances through it.*)

LISA. (*off*) Yes. Will you come in, please?

(SIR WILLIAM ROLLANDER *enters up* C *from* R. *He is a tall,
   grey-haired man of forceful personality.* LISA *follows
   him on, closes the doors and stands behind the armchair.*)

ROLLANDER. (*moving down* C.) Professor Hendryk? My name
   is Rollander. (*He holds out his hand*)

(KARL *rises, puts his book on the table* RC *and shakes* ROL-
   LANDER'S *hand.*)

KARL. How do you do? This is Miss Koletzky.
ROLLANDER. How do you do?
LISA. How do you do?
ROLLANDER. I have a daughter who studies under you, Pro-
   fessor Hendryk.
KARL. Yes, that is so.
ROLLANDER. She feels that the attending of lectures in a class
   is not sufficient for her. She would like you to give her
   extra private tuition.
KARL. I'm afraid that is not possible. (*He moves away below
   the right end of the sofa*)
ROLLANDER. Yes, I know that she has already approached
   you on the matter and that you have refused. But I
   should like to reopen the subject if I may.

              (LISA *sits in the desk chair.*)

KARL. (*calmly*) Certainly, Sir William, but I do not think
   that you will alter my decision.
ROLLANDER. I should like to understand first your reasons for
   refusing. They are not quite clear to me.

KARL. They are quite simple. Please do sit down. (*He in-dicates the sofa*) Your daughter is charming and intelligent, but she is not in my opinion the stuff of which true scholars are made.

ROLLANDER. (*sitting on the sofa at the left end*) Isn't that rather an arbitrary decision?

KARL. (*smiling*) I think you have the popular belief that learning is a thing that can be stuffed into people as you put stuffing into a goose. (*He sits on the right arm of the sofa*) Perhaps it would be easier for you to understand if it was a question of music. If your daughter had a pretty and tuneful voice and you brought her to a singing teacher and wanted her trained for opera, a conscientious and honest teacher would tell you frankly that her voice was not suitable for opera. Would never be suitable with all the training in the world.

ROLLANDER. Well, you're the expert. I must, I suppose, bow to your ruling on that.

KARL. Do you, yourself, really believe that your daughter wants to take up an academic career?

ROLLANDER. No, quite frankly, I do not think so. But she thinks so, Professor Hendryk. Shall we put it as simply as this, that I want my daughter to have what she wants.

KARL. A common parental weakness.

ROLLANDER. As you say, a common parental weakness. My position, however, is more uncommon than that of some parents. I am, as you may or may not know, a rich man —to put it simply.

KARL. I am aware of that, Sir William. I read the newspapers. I think it was only a few days ago that I read the description of the exotically fitted luxury car which you were having specially built as a present for your daughter.

ROLLANDER. Oh, that! Probably seems to you foolish and ostentatious. The reasons behind it, let me tell you, are mainly business ones. Helen's not even particularly interested in the car. Her mind at the moment is set on serious subjects. That, I may say, is something for a change, for which I am thankful. She's run around for a couple of years now with a set of people whom I don't much care for. People without a thing in their heads except pleasure. Now she seems to want to go in for serious study and I am behind her one hundred per cent.

KARL. I can quite understand your point of view, but . . .

ROLLANDER. I'll tell you a little more, Professor Hendryk. Helen is all that I have. Her mother died when she was seven years old. I loved my wife and I've never married again. All that I have left of her is Helen. I've always given Helen every single mortal thing she wanted.

KARL. That was natural, I'm sure, but has it been wise?

ROLLANDER. Probably not, but it's become a habit of life, now. And Helen's a fine girl, Professor Hendryk. I dare say she's made her mistakes, she's been foolish, but the only way you can learn about life is by experience. The Spanish have a proverb, " 'Take what you want and pay for it,' says God." That's sound, Professor Hendryk, very sound.

KARL. (*rising and crossing to* R *of the work-table*) The payment may be high.

ROLLANDER. Helen wants private tuition from you. I want to give it to her. I'm prepared to pay your price.

KARL. (*coldly*) It's not a question of price, Sir William. I'm not in the market for the highest fees I can get. I have a responsibility to my profession. My time and energy are limited. I have two good scholars, poor men, but they rate with me in priority above your daughter. You will forgive me for speaking frankly.

ROLLANDER. I appreciate your point of view, but I am not so insensitive as you may think. I quite realize it isn't just a question of money. But in my belief, Professor Hendryk—and I'm a business man—every man has his price.

(KARL *shrugs his shoulders and sits in the armchair.*)

KARL. You are entitled to your opinion.

ROLLANDER. Your wife is, I believe, suffering from disseminated sclerosis.

KARL. (*surprised*) That is quite true. But how—did you . . . ?

ROLLANDER. (*interrupting*) When I approach a proposition I find out all about it beforehand. That disease, Professor Hendryk, is one about which very little is known. It responds to palliatives but there is no known cure, and although the subject of it may live for many years, complete recovery is unknown. That, I think, speaking in non-medical terms, is fairly correct?

KARL. Yes, that is correct.

ROLLANDER. But you may have heard or read of a sensational new treatment started in America, of which there are great hopes. I don't pretend to speak with any kind of medical knowledge or accuracy, but I believe that a new expensively produced antibiotic has been discovered which has an appreciable effect upon the course of the disease. It is at present unprocurable in England, but a small quantity of the drug—or whatever you call it— has been sent to this country and will be used on a few specially selected cases. I have influence in that direction, Professor Hendryk. The Franklin Institute, where this work is going on, will accept your wife as a patient if I exert my influence there.

(LISA *rises and moves to* L *of* KARL.)

KARL. (*quietly*) Bribery and corruption.
ROLLANDER. (*unoffended*) Oh, yes, just as you say. Bribery and corruption. Not personal bribery, it wouldn't work in your case. You would turn down any financial offer I made you. But can you afford to turn down a chance of your wife's recovering her health?

(*There is a pause, then* KARL *rises and goes to the double doors up* C. *He stands there for quite a while, then turns and comes down* C.)

KARL. You are quite right, Sir William. I will accept your daughter as a pupil. I will give her private tuition and as much care and attention as I would my best pupil. Does that satisfy you?
ROLLANDER. It will satisfy her. She is the kind of girl who doesn't take no for an answer. (*He rises and faces* KARL C) Well, you have my word for it that when they are ready at the Franklin Institute, your wife will be accepted as a patient. (*He shakes hands with* KARL) That will probably be in about two months' time.

(LISA *moves to the doors* C, *opens them, then stands to one side.*)

It only remains for me to hope the treatment will be as successful as these cases in the United States seem to have been, and that I may congratulate you in a year's

time on your wife's being restored to health and strength.
Good night, Professor Hendryk. (*He starts to go, then
stops and turns*) By the way my daughter is waiting in
the car downstairs to hear the result of my embassy. Do
you mind if she comes up for a moment or two? I
know she'd like to thank you.

KARL. Certainly, Sir William.

(ROLLANDER *exits up* C *to* R. LISA *follows him off.* KARL
moves to the desk chair and leans on the back of it.)

ROLLANDER. (*off*) Good night.
LISA. (*off*) Good night, Sir William.

(LISA *re-enters, leaving the doors open. She stands up* LC.)

So the girl wins.
KARL. Do you think I should have refused?
LISA. No.
KARL. I have made Anya suffer so much already. For sticking
to my principles I was turned out of the university at
home. Anya has never really understood why. She never
saw my point of view. It seemed to her that I behaved
foolishly and quixotically. She suffered through it far
more than I did. (*He pauses*) So now there is a chance
of recovery and she must have it. (*He sits at the desk*)
LISA. What about those two students? Won't one of them
have to go to the wall?
KARL. Of course not. I shall make the time. I can sit up late
at night to do my own work.
LISA. You're not so young as you were, Karl. You're already
overworking yourself.
KARL. Those two boys mustn't suffer.
LISA. If you have a breakdown, everybody will suffer.
KARL. Then I mustn't have a breakdown. It's fortunate that
no principle is involved here.
LISA. Very fortunate—(*She looks towards the door down* R)
for Anya.
KARL. What do you mean by that, Lisa?
LISA. Nothing, really.
KARL. I don't understand. I'm a very simple man.
LISA. Yes. That's what's so frightening about you.

(*The thump of* ANYA'*s stick is heard off* R.)

KARL. (*rising*) Anya is awake. (*He moves towards the door down* R)

LISA. (*moving down* C) No, I'll go. Your new pupil will want to see you. (*She goes towards the door down* R)

KARL. (*as she passes him*) You do believe that I have done right? (*He moves and stands below the armchair*)

(HELEN *enters up* C *from* R.)

LISA. (*pausing at the doorway and turning to* KARL) What is right? How do we ever know till we see the results?

(LISA *exits down* R.)

HELEN. (*in the doorway*) The door was open so I came straight in. Is that all right?

KARL. (*rather far away and staring after* LISA) Of course.

HELEN. (*moving to* R *of the armchair*) I do hope you're not angry. I dare say you feel I'm not much good as a scholar. But you see, I've never had any proper training. Only a silly sort of fashionable education. But I will work hard, I will, really.

KARL. (*coming back to earth*) Good. (*He goes to the desk and makes some notes on a sheet of paper*) We will commence a serious life of study. I can lend you some books. You shall take them away and read them, then you will come at an hour that we fix and I shall ask you certain questions as to the conclusions you draw from them. (*He turns to* HELEN) You understand?

HELEN. (*moving up* C) Yes. May I take the books now? Daddy's waiting for me in the car.

KARL. Yes. That is a good idea. You'll need to buy these. (*He gives her the list he has written*) Now, let me see. (*He goes to the bookcase* R *of the double doors and picks out two large volumes, murmuring under his breath as he does so.*)

(HELEN *watches* KARL.)

KARL. (*Almost to himself as he picks the volumes*) You must have Lecomte, yes, and possibly Wertfor. (*To* HELEN) Do you read German? (*He moves to* L *of the table* RC)

HELEN. (*moving to* L *of* KARL) I know a little hotel German.

KARL. (*sternly*) You must study German. It is impossible to get anywhere without knowing French and German thoroughly. You should study German grammar and composition three days a week.

(HELEN *makes a slight grimace.*)

(*He looks sharply at* HELEN *and hands her the two books*) The books are rather heavy, I'm afraid.

HELEN. (*taking the books and nearly dropping them*) Ooh— I should say they are. (*She sits on the left arm of the sofa and glances through the books*) It looks rather difficult. (*She leans on* KARL's *shoulder slightly as she looks at the books*) You want me to read all of it?

KARL. I should like you to read it through with especial attention to chapter four and chapter eight.

HELEN. (*leaning almost against him*) I see.

KARL. (*crossing to the desk*) Shall we say next Wednesday afternoon at four o'clock?

HELEN. (*rising*) Here? (*She puts the books on the sofa*)

KARL. No. At my room in the university.

HELEN (*rather pleased*) Oh, thank you, Professor Hendryk. (*She crosses above the armchair to* R *of* KARL) I really am grateful. I am indeed, and I shall try very hard. Please don't be against me.

KARL. I'm not against you.

HELEN. Yes, you are. You feel you've been bullied into this by me and my father. But I'll do you credit. I will, really.

KARL. (*smiling*) Then that is understood. There is no more to be said.

HELEN. It's sweet of you. Very sweet of you. I am grateful. (*She gives* KARL *a sudden quick kiss on the cheek, then turns away, gathers up the books, moves up* C *and stands in the doorway, smiling at* KARL. *Coyly*) Wednesday. At four?

(HELEN *exits up* C *to* R, *leaving the doors open.* KARL *looks after her with some surprise. His hand goes to his cheek and he finds lipstick on it. He wipes his cheek with his handkerchief, smiles, then shakes his head a little doubtfully. He goes to the record player, puts on the record of the "Rachmaninoff Piano Concerto," switches on, then goes to the desk and sits. He starts to do a little work, but pauses to listen to the music.* LISA *enters down* R. *She stands there a moment, listening and watching*

KARL, *but he is not aware that she is there. Her hands go up slowly to her face as she tries to retain composure, then suddenly she breaks down, rushes to the sofa and slumps on to the right end of it.*)

LISA. Don't. Don't. Take it off.

(KARL, *startled, swings round.*)

KARL. (*puzzled*) It's the Rachmaninoff, Lisa. You and I have always loved it.

LISA. I know. That's why I can't bear it just now. Take it off.

(KARL *rises and stops the music.*)

KARL. (*crossing to* L *of the sofa*) You know, Lisa. You've always known.

LISA. Don't. We've never said anything.

KARL. But we've known, haven't we?

LISA. (*in a different, matter-of-fact voice*) Anya is asking for you.

KARL. (*coming out of a kind of dream*) Yes. Yes, of course. I'll go to her.

(KARL *crosses and exits down* R. LISA *stares after him in an attitude of despair.*)

LISA. Karl. (*She beats her hands on the sofa*) Karl. Oh, Karl.

LISA *collapses miserably, her head in her hands, over the right arm of the sofa as the lights BLACK-OUT and*

the CURTAIN *falls.*

Scene II

SCENE: *The same. A fortnight later. Afternoon.*

When the CURTAIN *rises, the lights come up. The right half of the double doors is open.* ANYA *is in her wheel-chair* C, *with her work-table* L *of her. She is knitting.* KARL *is seated at the desk, making notes from various books.* MRS. ROPER *is dusting the shelves of the bookcase* R. *Her vacuum cleaner is below the sofa.* LISA *enters from her bedroom, comes into the room and picks up her handbag from the armchair. She is dressed ready for going out.*

ANYA. *(vexedly; half crying)* I've dropped another stitch. Two stitches. Oh, dear!

(LISA *replaces her handbag on the armchair, leans over the work-table and takes the knitting.*)

LISA. I'll pick them up for you.

ANYA. It's no good my trying to knit. Look at my hands. They won't keep still. It's all hopeless.

(MRS. ROPER *moves to* R *of the table* RC *and dusts the books on it.*)

MRS. ROPER. Our life's a vale of tears, they do say. Did you see that piece in the paper this morning? Two little girls drowned in a canal. Lovely children, they were. *(She leaves the duster on the table* RC, *moves below the sofa, picks up the vacuum cleaner and moves towards the door down* R) By the way, Miss Koletzky, we're out of tea again.

(MRS. ROPER *exits down* R. LISA *has sorted out the knitting and returns it to* ANYA.)

LISA. There. That's all right now.

ANYA. Shall I ever get well again?

(MRS. ROPER *re-enters down* R, *collects her duster on the table* RC.)

(Wistfully and rather sweetly) I want so much to get well.

MRS. ROPER. 'Course you will, dearie, of course you will. Never say die. *(She dusts the chair* L *of the table* RC) My Joyce's eldest he has fits something shocking. Doctor says he'll grow out of it, but I don't know myself. *(She crosses above the table* RC *to the door down* R, *giving an odd flick with the duster here and there)* I'll do the bedroom now, shall I? So that it'll be ready for you when the doctor comes.

LISA. If you please, Mrs. Roper.

(MRS. ROPER *exits down* R, *leaving the door open.*)

ANYA. You'd better go, Lisa, you'll be late.

LISA. (*hesitating*) If you would like me to stay . . .

ANYA. No, of course I don't want you to stay. Your friends
are only here for one day. Of course you must see them.
It's bad enough to be a helpless invalid without feeling
that you're spoiling everybody else's pleasure.

(MRS. ROPER, *off, interrupts the calm with the sound of the
vacuum cleaner and by singing an old music hall song
in a raucous voice.*)

KARL. Oh, Please!

LISA. (*crossing to the door down* R *and calling*) Mrs. Roper.
Mrs. Roper.

(*The vacuum and the singing stop.*)

Do you mind? The Professor is trying to work.

MRS. ROPER. (*off*) Sorry, miss.

(LISA *crosses above* ANYA *to the armchair and picks up her
handbag. She is rather amused at the incident, and* KARL
and ANYA *join in.* KARL *fills his brief-case with papers
and books.*)

ANYA. Do you remember our little Mitzi?

LISA. Ah, yes, Mitzi.

ANYA. Such a nice, willing little maid. Always laughing and
such pretty manners. She made good pastry, too.

LISA. She did.

KARL. (*rising and picking up his brief-case*) There now, I am
all ready for my lecture.

LISA. (*moving to the doors up* C) I'll be back as soon as I
can, Anya. Good-bye, Anya.

ANYA. Enjoy yourself.

LISA. Good-bye, Karl.

KARL. Good-bye, Lisa.

(LISA *exits up* C *to* R.)

(*He moves below the armchair*) Someday, sweetheart,
you will be well and strong. (*He sits in the armchair and
fastens his brief-case*)

ANYA. No, I shan't. You talk to me as though I were a child or an imbecile. I'm ill. I'm very ill and I get worse and worse. You all pretend to be so bright and cheerful about it. You don't know how irritating it is.

KARL. (*gently*) I am sorry. Yes, I can see it must be very irritating sometimes.

ANYA. And I irritate and weary you.

KARL. Of course you don't.

ANYA. Oh, yes, I do. You're so patient and so good, but really you must long for me to die and set you free.

KARL. Anya, Anya, don't say these things. You know they are not true.

ANYA. Nobody ever thinks of me. Nobody ever considers me. It was the same when you lost your Chair at the university. Why did you have to take the Schultzes in?

KARL. They were our friends, Anya.

ANYA. You never really liked Schultz or agreed with his views. When he got into trouble with the police we should have avoided them altogether. It was the only safe thing to do.

KARL. It was no fault of his wife and children, and they were left destitute. Somebody had to help them.

ANYA. It need not have been us.

KARL. But they were our friends, Anya. You can't desert your friends when they are in trouble.

ANYA. You can't, I know that. But you didn't think of me. The result of it was you were told to resign and we had to leave our home and our friends and come away to this cold, grey, horrible country.

KARL. (*rising, crossing and putting his brief-case on the left arm of the sofa*) Come now, Anya, it's not so bad.

ANYA. Not for you, I dare say. They've given you a post at the university in London and it's all the same to you, as long as you have books and your studies. But I'm ill.

KARL. (*crossing to* R *of* ANYA) I know, dearest.

ANYA. And I have no friends here. I lie alone day after day with no-one to speak to, nothing interesting to hear, no gossip. I knit and I drop the stitches.

KARL. There now . . .

ANYA. You don't understand. You don't understand anything. You can't really care for me, or you would understand.

KARL. Anya, Anya. (*He kneels beside her*)

ANYA. You're selfish, really, selfish and hard. You don't care for anyone but yourself.

KARL. My poor Anya.

ANYA. It's all very well to say "poor Anya." Nobody really cares about me or thinks about me.

KARL. (*gently*) I think about you. I remember when I saw you first. In your little jacket all gaily embroidered in wool. We went for a picnic up the mountains. Narcissus were out. You took off your shoes and walked through the long grass. Do you remember? Such pretty little shoes and such pretty little feet.

ANYA. (*with a sudden pleased smile*) I always had small feet.

KARL. The prettiest feet in the world. The prettiest girl. (*He gently strokes her hair*)

ANYA. Now I'm faded and old and sick. No use to anybody.

KARL. To me you are the same Anya. Always the same.

(*The front door bell rings.*)

(*He rises*) That's Dr. Stoner, I expect. (*He goes behind the wheel-chair and straightens the cushions.*)

(MRS. ROPER *enters down* R.)

MRS. ROPER. Shall I see who it is?

(MRS. ROPER *exits up* C *to* R. KARL *goes to the desk, picks up a couple of pencils and puts them in his pocket. There is a sound of the front door opening and closing and voices off.* MRS. ROPER *enters up* C *from* R. HELEN *follows her on. She is carrying the two books which she borrowed.*)

It's a young lady to see you, sir. (*She moves slowly down* R)

(KARL *moves up* LC.)

HELEN. (*moving to* R *of* KARL) I've brought some of your books back. I thought you might be wanting them. (*She stops on seeing* ANYA *and her face drops*)

(MRS. ROPER *exits down* R.)

KARL. (*taking the books from* HELEN *and moving to* L *of* ANYA) Dearest, you remember Miss Rollander?

HELEN. (*moving up* R *of* ANYA) How are you, Mrs. Hendryk?
I do hope you are feeling better.

ANYA. I never feel better.

HELEN. (*devoid of feeling*) I am sorry. (*She goes above the
table* RC)

(*The front door bell rings.* KARL *goes to the desk, puts the
books down, then moves up* C.)

KARL. That'll be Dr. Stoner now.

(KARL *exits up* C *to* R. MRS. ROPER *enters down* R, *carrying a
waste-paper basket. She goes to the shelf below the
bookcase* R *and empties an ashtray into the basket.*
HELEN *glances idly through a book on the table* RC.)

MRS. ROPER. I'll finish the bedroom later. I'd better slip out
for the tea before he shuts.

KARL. (*off*) Hello, Doctor. Come in.

DOCTOR. (*off*) Well, Karl, it's a lovely day.

(KARL *enters up* C *from* R *and stands* L *of the doorway. The
DOCTOR follows him on.*)

KARL. I'd like a word with you alone, Doctor.

(MRS. ROPER *exits up* C *to* L, *leaving the door open.*)

DOCTOR. Yes, of course. (*He moves to* L *of* ANYA) Well,
Anya, it's a lovely spring day.

ANYA. Is it?

KARL. (*moving down* C) Will you excuse us a moment?
(*He crosses below the sofa to the door down* R)

HELEN. (*moving to* R *of the table* RC) Yes, of course.

DOCTOR. Good afternoon, Miss Rollander.

HELEN. Good afternoon, Doctor.

(*The* DOCTOR *crosses below* KARL *and exits down* R. KARL
follows him off, closing the door behind him. MRS.
ROPER *comes into the hall from* L. *She carries her coat
and shopping bag. She leaves the bag in the hall, comes
into the room and puts on her coat.*)

MRS. ROPER. It's too hot for the time of the year—

(HELEN *moves around* R *of the sofa and sits on it at the
right end, takes a cigarette case from her handbag and
lights a cigarette.*)

—gets me in the joints it does when it's like that. So stiff I was this morning I could hardly get out of bed. I'll be right back with the tea, Mrs. Hendryk. Oh, and about the tea, I'll get half a pound shall I?

ANYA. If you like, if you like.

MRS. ROPER. Ta-ta, so long.

(MRS. ROPER *goes into the hall, collects her shopping bag and exits to* R.)

ANYA. It is she who drinks the tea. She always says we need more tea, but we use hardly any. We drink coffee.

HELEN. I suppose these women always pinch things, don't they?

ANYA. And they think we are foreigners and we shall not know.

(*There is a pause.* ANYA *knits.*)

I'm afraid it is very dull for you, Miss Rollander, with only me to talk to. Invalids are not very amusing company.

(HELEN *rises, moves up* R *and looks at the books in the bookcase.*)

HELEN. I really only came to bring back those books.

ANYA. Karl has too many books. Look at this room—look at the books everywhere. Students come and borrow the books and read them and leave them about, and then take them away and lose them. It is maddening—quite maddening.

HELEN. Can't be much fun for you.

ANYA. I wish I were dead.

HELEN. (*turning sharply to look at* ANYA) Oh, you mustn't say that.

ANYA. But it's true. I'm a nuisance and a bore to everybody. To my cousin, Lisa, and to my husband. Do you think it is nice to know one is a burden on people?

HELEN. Do you? (*She turns away to the bookcase*)

ANYA. I'd be better dead, much better dead. Sometimes I think I will end it all. It will be quite easy. Just a little overdose of my heart medicine and then everybody will be happy and free and I'd be at peace. Why should I go on suffering?

(HELEN *crosses above the armchair to the desk and looks out of the window.*)

HELEN. (*bored and unsympathetic; with a sigh*) Must be awful for you.

ANYA. You don't know, you can't possibly understand. You're young and good-looking and rich and have everything you want. And here am I, miserable, helpless, always suffering, and nobody cares. Nobody really cares.

(*The* DOCTOR *enters down* R *and crosses to* R *of* ANYA. KARL *follows him on and stands below the sofa.* HELEN *turns.*)

DOCTOR. Well, Anya, Karl tells me you're going into the clinic in about two weeks' time.

ANYA. It won't do any good. I'm sure of it.

DOCTOR. Come, come, you mustn't say that. I was reading a most interesting article in The Lancet the other day, which dealt with the matter. Only an outline, but it was interesting. Of course we're very cautious in this country about the prospect of this new treatment. Afraid to commit ourselves. Our American cousins rush ahead, but there certainly seems to be a good chance of success with it.

ANYA. I don't really believe in it, it won't do any good.

DOCTOR. Now, Anya, don't be a little misery. (*He pushes the wheel-chair towards the door down* R)

(KARL *moves to the door down* R *and holds it open.*)

We'll have your weekly overhaul now and I'll see whether you're doing me credit as a patient or not.

ANYA. I can't knit any more, my hands shake so, I drop the stitches.

(KARL *takes the chair from the* DOCTOR *and pushes* ANYA *off down* R.)

KARL. There's nothing in that, is there, Doctor?

DOCTOR. No, no, nothing at all.

(KARL *exits with* ANYA *down* R. *The* DOCTOR *follows them off.* KARL *re-enters and closes the door. He rather ignores* HELEN *who stubs out her cigarette in the ashtray on the desk and crosses to* LC.)

KARL. (*collecting his brief-case*) I'm afraid I have to go out, I have a lecture at half past four.

HELEN. Are you angry with me for coming?

KARL. (*formally*) Of course not. It is very kind of you to return the books.

HELEN. (*moving to L of KARL*) You are angry with me. You've been so brusque—so abrupt, lately. What have I done to make you angry? You were really cross yesterday.

KARL. (*crossing above HELEN to the desk*) Of course I was cross. (*He takes a book from the desk and crosses below HELEN to L of the sofa*) You say that you want to learn, that you want to study and take your diploma, and then you do not work.

HELEN. Well, I've been rather busy lately—there's been a lot on . . .

KARL. You're not stupid, you've got plenty of intelligence and brains, but you don't take any trouble. How are you getting on with your German lessons?

HELEN. (*very off-handedly*) I haven't arranged about them yet.

KARL. But you must, you must. It's essential that you should be able to read German. (*He crosses above the table RC to the bookcase R and takes a book*) The books I give you to read, you do not read properly. I ask you questions and your answers are superficial. (*He puts the books in his brief-case*)

(*HELEN moves below the sofa.*)

HELEN. (*kneeling on the sofa in rather a languid pose*) It's such a bore, working.

KARL. But you were eager to study, to take your diploma.

HELEN. The diploma can go to hell for all I care.

KARL. (*dumping his brief-case on the left arm of the sofa in amazement*) Then I don't understand. You force me to teach you, you made your father come to me.

HELEN. I wanted to see you, to be near you. Are you quite blind, Karl? I'm in love with you.

KARL. (*turning and taking a pace to C; amazed*) What? But, my dear child . . .

HELEN. Don't you like me even a little bit?

KARL. (*crossing and standing down R*) You're a very desirable young woman but you must forget this nonsense.

HELEN. (*rising and standing behind* KARL) It's not nonsense, I tell you I love you. Why can't we be simple and natural about it all? I want you and you want me. You know you do—you're the kind of man I want to marry. Well, why not? Your wife's no good to you.

KARL. How little you understand. You talk like a child. I love my wife. (*He crosses to* C)

HELEN. (*sitting on the sofa*) Oh, I know. You're a terribly kind person. You look after her and bring her cups of Bengers and all that, no doubt. But that isn't love.

KARL. (*crossing below the sofa to* R; *rather at a loss what to say*) Isn't it? I think it is. (*He sits on the right arm of the sofa*)

HELEN. Of course you must see that she's properly looked after, but it needn't interfere with your life as a man. If we have an affair together your wife needn't know about it.

KARL. (*firmly*) My dear child, we're not going to have an affair.

HELEN. I had no idea you were so straight-laced. (*She is struck by an idea*) I'm not a virgin, you know, if that's what's worrying you. I've had lots of experience.

KARL. Helen, don't delude yourself. I am not in love with you.

HELEN. You may go on saying that till you're blue in the face, but I don't believe you.

KARL. Because you don't want to believe me. But it is true. (*He rises and moves down* R) I love my wife. She is dearer to me than anyone in the world.

HELEN. (*like a bewildered child*) Why? Why? I mean, what can she possibly give you? I could give you everything. Money for research or for whatever you wanted.

KARL. But you would still not be Anya. (*He sits on the right arm of the sofa*) Listen . . .

HELEN. I dare say she was pretty and attractive once, but she's not like that now.

KARL. She is. We don't change. There is the same Anya there still. Life does things to us. Ill health, disappointment, exile, all these things form a crust covering over the real self. But the real self is still there.

HELEN. (*rising, impatiently, moving down* LC *and turning to face* KARL) I think you're talking nonsense. If it were a real marriage—but it isn't. It can't be, in the circumstances.

KARL. It is a real marriage.

HELEN. Oh, you're impossible! (*She moves down* L)

KARL. (*rising*) You see, you are only a child, you don't understand.

(HELEN *crosses above the armchair to* L *of* KARL. *She is losing her temper.*)

HELEN. You are the child, wrapped up in a cloud of sentimentality, and pretence. You even humbug yourself. If you had courage—now, I've got courage and I'm a realist. I'm not afraid to look at things and see them as they are.

KARL. You are a child that hasn't grown up.

HELEN. (*exasperated*) Oh! (*She crosses above the armchair to the desk and stares rather furiously out of the window*)

(*The* DOCTOR *pushes* ANYA *in down* R.)

DOCTOR. (*as they enter; cheerfully*) All very satisfactory.

(KARL *takes over from the* DOCTOR *and pushes* ANYA *to her usual place* C.)

(*The* DOCTOR *goes up* C.)

ANYA. (*as she is going across*) That's what he says. All doctors are liars.

(KARL *collects his brief-case.*)

DOCTOR. Well, I must be off. I have a consultation at half-past four. Good-bye, Anya. Good afternoon, Miss Rollander. I'm going up Gower Street, Karl, I can give you a lift if you like.

KARL. Thank you, Doctor.

DOCTOR. I'll wait downstairs in the car.

(*The* DOCTOR *exits up* C, *closing the door behind him.* KARL *closes his brief-case and moves to* R *of* ANYA)

ANYA. Karl, forgive me, Karl.

KARL. Forgive you, sweetheart? What is there to forgive?

ANYA. Everything. My moods, my bad temper. But it isn't really me, Karl. It's just the illness. You do understand?

KARL. (*with his arm affectionately round her shoulders*) I understand.

(HELEN *half turns her head to look at them, frowns, and turns back to the window.*)

Nothing you say will ever hurt me because I know your heart.

(KARL *claps* ANYA's *hand, they look at each other, and then she kisses his hand.*)

ANYA. Karl, you will be late for your lecture. You must go.

KARL. I wish I didn't have to leave you.

ANYA. Mrs. Roper will be back any minute and she will stay with me till Lisa gets back.

HELEN. I'm not going anywhere in particular, I can stay with Mrs. Hendryk till Miss Koletzky gets back.

KARL. Would you, Helen?

HELEN. Of course.

KARL. That's very kind of you. (*To* ANYA) Good-bye, darling.

ANYA. Good-bye.

KARL. Thank you, Helen.

(KARL *exits up* C, *closing the door behind him. The daylight starts to fade.*)

HELEN. (*crossing above the wheel-chair to the sofa*) Is Miss Koletzky a relation? (*She sits on the sofa*)

ANYA. Yes, she's my first cousin. She came to England with us and has stayed with us ever since. This afternoon she has gone to see some friends who are passing through London. They are at the Hotel Russell, not very far away. It is so seldom we see friends from our own country.

HELEN. Would you like to go back?

ANYA. We cannot go back. A friend of my husband's, another professor, fell into disgrace because of his political view—he was arrested.

HELEN. How did that affect Professor Hendryk?

ANYA. His wife and children, you see, were left quite destitute. Professor Hendryk insisted that we should take them into our house. But when the authorities got to hear about it, they forced him to resign his position.

HELEN. Really, it didn't seem worth it, did it?

ANYA. That's what I felt, and I never liked Maria Schultz in
in the least. She was a most tiresome woman, always
carping and criticizing and moaning about something or
other. And the children were very badly behaved and
very destructive. It seems too bad that because of them
we had to leave our nice home and come over here
practically as refugees. This will never be home.

HELEN. It does seem rather rough luck on you.

ANYA. Men don't think of that. They only think of their
ideas of what is right, or just, or one's duty.

HELEN. I know. Such an awful bore. But men aren't realists
like we are.

(*There is a pause as* HELEN *lights a cigarette she has taken
from a case in her handbag. A clock outside strikes
four.*)

ANYA. (*looking at her watch*) Lisa never gave me my medicine
before she went out. She is very tiresome sometimes the
way she forgets things.

HELEN. (*rising*) Can I do anything?

ANYA. (*pointing to the shelves on the wall down* R) It's on
the little shelf over there.

(HELEN *moves to the shelves down* R.)

The little brown bottle. Four drops in water.

(HELEN *stubs out her cigarette in the ashtray on the cupboard* R, *and takes the bottle of medicine and a glass
from the shelves.*)

It's for my heart, you know. There's a glass over there
and a dropper.

(HELEN *moves to the bookshelves* R.)

Be careful, it's very strong. That's why they keep it out
of reach. Sometimes I feel so terribly depressed and I
threaten to kill myself, and they think perhaps if I
had it near me I'd yield to temptation and take an
overdose.

HELEN. (*taking the dropper-stopper from the bottle*) You
often want to, I suppose?

ANYA. (*complacently*) Oh, yes, one feels so often that one
would be better dead.

HELEN. Yes, I can understand that.

ANYA. But, of course, one must be brave and go on.

(HELEN's *back is towards* ANYA. *She throws a quick glance over her shoulder.* ANYA *is not looking her way but is engrossed in her knitting.* HELEN *tilts the bottle and empties all the contents into the glass, adds some water then takes the glass to* ANYA.)

HELEN. (R of ANYA) Here you are.

ANYA. Thank you, my dear. (*She takes the glass in her left hand and sips*)

(HELEN *stands up* R of ANYA.)

It tastes rather strong.

HELEN. Four drops, you said?

ANYA. Yes, that's right. (*She drinks it down quickly, then leans back and puts the glass on her work-table*)

(HELEN, *tensely strung up, stands watching* ANYA.)

The Professor works much too hard, you know. He takes more pupils than he ought to do. I wish—I wish he could have an easier life.

HELEN. Perhaps some day he will.

ANYA. I doubt it. (*With a little tender smile*) He's so good to everyone. So full of kindness. He is so good to me, so patient. (*She catches her breath*) Ah!

HELEN. What is it?

ANYA. Just—I don't seem to be able to get my breath. You're sure you didn't give me too much?

HELEN. I gave you the right dose.

ANYA. I'm sure—I'm sure you did. I didn't mean—I didn't think . . . (*Her words get slower as she settles back almost as if she is about to go to sleep. Her hand comes up very slowly toward her heart*) How strange—how very—strange. (*Her head droops sideways on the pillow*)

(HELEN *moves* R of ANYA *and watches her. She is now looking frightened. Her hand goes to her face and then down again.*)

HELEN. (*in a low voice*) Mrs. Hendryk.

(*There is silence.*)

(*A little louder*) Mrs. Hendryk.

(HELEN MOVES TO R of ANYA, *takes her wrist and feels the pulse. When she finds that it has stopped she gasps and flings the hand down in horror, then backs slightly down* R. *She moves below the armchair, round it and stands above the work-table, without taking her eyes off* ANYA. *She stands staring for some moments at* ANYA, *then shakes herself back to reality, sees the glass on the work-table, picks it up and wipes it on her handkerchief, then leans over and puts it carefully into* ANYA's *left hand. She then goes and leans exhausted over the left arm of the sofa. Again she pulls herself together, moves to the bookcase* R *and picks up the medicine bottle and dropper. She wipes her fingerprints off the bottle and crosses to* R *of* ANYA. *She gently presses* ANYA's *right hand round the bottle, then moves above the work-table, puts the bottle down, takes the dropper out and leaves it beside the bottle. She moves slightly up* C, *looks around, then goes quickly to the sofa for her bag and gloves and moves quickly to the doors up* C. *She stops suddenly and dashes to the shelf for the water jug, wiping it with her handkerchief as she crosses to the work-table, where she puts down the jug. She again goes to the doors up* C. *The sound of a barrel organ is heard off.* HELEN *flings open the right door and exits in the hall to* R. *The front door is heard to slam. There is quite a pause, then the front door is heard opening and closing.* MRS. ROPER *pops her head in the doorway up* C.)

MRS. ROPER. I got the tea.

(MRS. ROPER *withdraws her head and disappears to* L. *She reappears in the doorway, taking off her hat and coat. These she hangs on a hook off* R *of the double doors.*)

And I got the bacon and a dozen boxes of matches. Isn't everything a price these days? I tried to get some kidneys for young Muriel's supper, tenpence each they were, and they looked like little shrunken heads. (*She crosses above the table* RC *towards the door down* R) She'll have to have what the others have and like it. I keep telling her money doesn't grow on trees.

(MRS. ROPER *exits down* R. *There is a considerable pause, then the front door opens and closes.* LISA *enters up* C *from* R, *putting her doorkey into her bag.*)

LISA. (*as she enters*) Have I been long? (*She crosses to the desk, glances at* ANYA *and thinking she is asleep, smiles, turns to the window and removes her hat. After putting her hat on the desk she turns towards* ANYA *and begins to realize that possibly* ANYA *is more than asleep*) Anya? (*She rushes to* R *of* ANYA *and lifts her head. She takes her hand away and* ANYA'S *head falls again. She sees the bottle on the work-table, moves above the wheel-chair, picks up the glass and then the bottle.*)

(MRS. ROPER *enters down* R *as* LISA *is holding the bottle.*)

MRS. ROPER. (*startled*) Oh, I didn't hear you come in, miss. (*She moves up* R)

LISA. (*putting the bottle down with a bang; startled by* MRS. ROPER'S *sudden appearance*) I didn't know you were here, Mrs. Roper.

MRS. ROPER. Is anything wrong?

LISA. Mrs. Hendryk—I think Mrs. Hendryk is dead. (*She moves to the telephone, lifts the receiver and dials*)

MRS. ROPER *moves slowly up* L *of* ANYA, *sees the bottle, then turns slowly round to stare at* LISA, *who is waiting impatiently for someone to answer her call. She has her back to* MRS. ROPER *and does not see the look. The lights* BLACK-OUT *as—*

the CURTAIN *falls.*

Act Two

Scene I

SCENE: *The same. Four days later. About midday.*

When the CURTAIN *rises, the lights come up. The room is empty. It is much the same as before except that* ANYA'S *wheelchair has gone. The doors are all closed. After a moment,* KARL *enters up* C, *moves down* C, *pauses for a moment and looks where the wheelchair used to be, then sits in the armchair.* LISA *enters up* C *and goes to the desk. She wears outdoor clothes. The* DOCTOR *enters up* C, *looks at the others, then moves below the sofa.* LESTER *enters up* C *and stands rather awkwardly up* C. *They all enter very slowly and are very depressed.*

DOCTOR. (*rather uncomfortably*) Well, that's over.

LISA. (*removing her gloves and hat*) I have never been to an inquest in this country before. Are they always like that?

DOCTOR. (*still a little ill at ease*) Well, they vary, you know, they vary. (*He sits on the sofa at the right end*)

LISA. (*after a pause*) It seems so business-like, so unemotional.

DOCTOR. Well, of course, we don't go in for emotion much. It's just a routine business enquiry, that's all.

LESTER. (*moving up* L *of the sofa; to the* DOCTOR) Wasn't it rather an odd sort of verdict? They said she died from an overdose of stropanthin but they didn't say how it was administered. I should have thought they'd have said suicide while the balance of the mind was disturbed and have done with it.

(LISA *sits at the desk.*)

KARL. (*rousing himself*) I cannot believe that Anya committed suicide.

LISA. (*thoughtfully*) I should not have said so, either.

LESTER. (*moving* LC) All the same, the evidence was pretty clear. Her fingerprints on the bottle and on the glass.

KARL. It must have been some kind of accident. Her hand shook a great deal, you know. She must have poured in far more than she realized. The curious thing is that I can't remember putting the bottle and glass beside her, yet I suppose I must have done.

(LISA *rises and moves to* L *of* KARL. LESTER *sits on the left arm of the sofa.*)

LISA. It was my fault. I should have given her the drops before I went out.

DOCTOR. It was nobody's fault. Nothing is more unprofitable than accusing oneself of having left undone something one should have done or the opposite. These things happen and they're very sad. Let's leave it at that— (*Under his breath and not to the others*) if we can.

KARL. You don't think Anya took an overdose, deliberately, Doctor?

DOCTOR. (*slowly*) I shouldn't have said so.

LESTER. (*rising and moving* LC) She did talk about it, you know. I mean, when she got depressed.

(LISA *moves to the desk.*)

DOCTOR. Yes, yes, nearly all chronic invalids talk about suicide. They seldom commit it.

LESTER. (*after a pause; embarrassed*) I say, I do hope I'm not butting in, coming here. (*He moves* C) I expect you want to be alone. I shouldn't . . .

KARL. No, no, my dear boy, it was kind of you.

LESTER. I just thought perhaps there was something I could do. (*He turns up stage in embarrassment and falls over the chair* L *of the table, then moves to* R *of* KARL) I'd do anything—(*He looks devoutly at* KARL) if only I could do something to help.

KARL. Your sympathy helps. Anya was very fond of you, Lester.

(MRS. ROPER *enters up* C. *She wears a rusty black costume and hat. She carries a tray of coffee for four and a plate of sandwiches.* LESTER *goes to the desk.*)

MRS. ROPER. (*in a suitably muted voice*) I've made some coffee and some little sandwiches. (*She puts the tray on the table* RC. *To* KARL) I thought, sir, as you'd need something to keep your strength up.

(LISA *crosses to the tray and pours the coffee.*)

KARL. Thank you, Mrs. Roper.

MRS. ROPER. (*with conscious virtue*) I hurried back from the inquest as fast as I could, sir—(*She moves* C) so as to have things ready when you come.

KARL. (*realizing* MRS. ROPER's *rather unusual costume of rusty black with a hat*) Did you go to the inquest, then?

MRS. ROPER. 'Course I did. I felt I had an interest, like. Poor, dear lady. (*She leans across the sofa to the* DOCTOR) Low in her spirits, wasn't she? I thought I'd go as a sign of respect, if nothing more. I can't say as it's been very nice, though, having the police here asking questions.

(*During this scene with* MRS. ROPER, *the others all avoid looking at her directly in the hope that she will stop talking and leave, but she persists in trying to start a conversation first with one and then the other.*)

DOCTOR. (*rising*) These routine enquiries have to be made, Mrs. Roper. (*He takes a cup of coffee to* KARL, *then goes above* MRS. ROPER *to the tray.*)

MRS. ROPER. Of course, sir.

DOCTOR. Whenever a certificate cannot be given, there has to be a coroner's enquiry.

MRS. ROPER. Oh, yes, sir, I'm sure it's very right and proper, but it's not very nice. That's what I say.

(*The* DOCTOR *takes a cup of coffee for himself, then sits on the sofa.*)

MRS. ROPER. It's not what I've been accustomed to. My husband, he wouldn't like it at all if I were to be mixed up in anything of that sort.

LISA. I don't see that you are mixed up in it in any way, Mrs. Roper.

MRS. ROPER. (*moving eagerly towards* LISA) Well, they asked
me questions, didn't they, as to whether she was low in
her spirits and whether she'd ever talked about anything of the kind. (*She moves to* R *of* KARL. *Rather
significantly*) Oh, quite a lot of questions they asked me.

KARL. Well, that is all over now, Mrs. Roper. I don't think
you need worry any further.

MRS. ROPER. (*rather squashed*) No, sir, thank you, sir.

(MRS. ROPER *exits up* C, *closing the doors behind her.*)

DOCTOR. All ghouls, you know, these women. Nothing they
like better than illnesses, deaths, and funerals. An inquest, I expect, is an added joy.

LISA. Lester—coffee?

LESTER. Thanks so much. (*He crosses to the chair* R *of the
table* RC, *sits, helps himself to coffee, then becomes engrossed in a book*)

(LISA *crosses to the desk.*)

KARL. It must have been some kind of accident, it must.

DOCTOR. I don't know. (*He sips his coffee*) Not quite the
same as your coffee, Lisa, my dear.

LISA. (*crossing below the armchair and sofa and standing
down* R) I expect it's been boiling hard for half an hour.

KARL. It was kindly meant.

LISA. (*turning to the door down* R; *over her shoulder*) I
wonder.

(LISA *exits down* R, *leaving the door open. The* DOCTOR *rises,
takes the plate of sandwiches from the tray and crosses
to* KARL.)

DOCTOR. Have a sandwich?

KARL. No, thank you.

DOCTOR. (*moving to the table* RC *and putting the sandwiches
in front of* LESTER) Finish them up, my boy. Always
hungry at your age.

(LESTER, *by now deep in the book, does not look up but
automatically helps himself to a sandwich.*)

LESTER. Well, thanks. I don't mind if I do.

LISA. (*off; calling*) Karl.

KARL. (*rising and putting his cup on the work-table*) Excuse me a moment. (*He calls and crosses to the door down* R) Yes, I am coming.

(KARL *exits down* R, *closing the door behind him.*)

LESTER. He's terribly cut-up, isn't he, Doctor?

DOCTOR. (*taking out his pipe*) Yes.

LESTER. It seems odd in a way, at least I don't mean odd, because, I suppose—what I mean is, it's so difficult to understand what other people feel like.

DOCTOR. (*moving down* C *and lighting his pipe*) Just what are you trying to say, my boy?

LESTER. Well, what I mean is, poor Mrs. Hendryk being an invalid and all that, you'd think, wouldn't you, that he'd get a bit impatient with her or feel himself tied.

(*The* DOCTOR *puts the matchstick in the ashtray on the table* RC, *then sits on the sofa at the left end.*)

And you'd think that really, underneath, he'd be glad to be free. Not a bit. He loved her. He really loved her.

DOCTOR. Love isn't just glamour, desire, sex appeal—all the things you young people are so sure it is. That's nature's start of the whole business. It's the showy flower, if you like. But love's the root. Underground, out of sight, nothing much to look at, but it's where the life is.

LESTER. I suppose so, yes. But passion doesn't last, sir, does it?

DOCTOR. (*despairingly*) God give me strength. You young people know nothing about these things. You read in the papers of divorces, of love tangles with a sex angle to everything. Study the columns of deaths sometimes for a change. Plenty of records there of Emily this and John that dying in their seventy-fourth year, beloved wife of So-and-so, beloved husband of someone else. Unassuming records of lives spent together, sustained by the root I've just talked about which still puts out its leaves and its flowers. Not showy flowers, but still flowers.

LESTER. I suppose you're right. I've never thought about it. (*He rises, moves and sits* R *of the* DOCTOR *on the sofa*) I've always thought that getting married is taking a bit of a chance, unless, of course, you meet a girl who . . .

DOCTOR. Yes, yes, that's the recognized pattern. You meet a girl—or you've already met a girl—who's different.

LESTER. (*earnestly*) But really, sir, she is different.

DOCTOR. (*good-humouredly*) I see. Well, good luck to you, young fellow.

(KARL *enters down* R. *He carries a small pendant. The* DOCTOR *rises.* KARL *crosses to* C, *looking at the pendant.*)

KARL. Will you give this to your daughter, Doctor? It was Anya's and I know she would like Margaret to have it. (*He turns and hands the pendant to the* DOCTOR)

DOCTOR. (*moved*) Thank you, Karl. I know Margaret will appreciate the gift. (*He puts the pendant in his wallet then moves towards the doors up* C) Well, I must be off. Can't keep my surgery patients waiting.

LESTER. (*rising and moving up* RC; *to* KARL) I'll go, too, if you're sure there's nothing I can do for you, sir.

KARL. As a matter of fact there is.

(LESTER *looks delighted.*)

Lisa has been making up some parcels of clothes and things like that—she is sending them to the East London Mission. If you would help her to carry them to the post office . . .

LESTER. Of course I will.

(LESTER *exits down* R.)

DOCTOR. Good-bye, Karl.

(*The* DOCTOR *exits up* C. LESTER *enters down* R. *He carries a large box wrapped in brown paper, which he takes to the desk and fastens with sellotape.* LISA *enters down* R. *She carries a brown paper parcel and a small drawer containing papers, letters, etc., and a small trinket box.*)

LISA. (*moving below the sofa*) If you would look through these, Karl. (*She puts the drawer on the sofa*) Sit down here and go through these, quietly and alone. It has to be done and the sooner the better.

KARL. How wise you are, Lisa. One puts these things off and dreads them—dreads the hurt. As you say, it's better to do it and finish.

LISA. I shan't be long. Come along, Lester.

(LISA *and* LESTER *exit up* C, *closing the doors behind them.*
    KARL *collects the waste-paper basket from the desk, sits
    on the sofa, puts the drawer on his knee and starts to
    go through the letters.*)

KARL. (*reading a letter*) So long ago, so long ago.

(*The front door bell rings.*)

Oh, go away whoever you are.

MRS. ROPER. (*off*) Would you come inside, please.

(MRS. ROPER *enters up* C *from* R *and stands to one side.*)

It's Miss Rollander, sir.

(HELEN *enters up* C *from* R *and moves down* C. KARL *rises
    and puts the drawer on the table* RC. MRS. ROPER *exits
    up* C *to* L, *leaving the door open.*)

HELEN. I do hope I'm not being a nuisance. I went to the
    inquest, you see, and afterwards I thought I must come
    on here and speak to you. But if you'd rather I went
    away . . .

KARL. No, no, it was kind of you.

(MRS. ROPER *enters up* C *from* L, *putting on her coat.*)

MRS. ROPER. I'll just pop out and get another quarter of tea
    before he closes. We're right out again.

KARL. (*fingering the letters in the drawer; far away*) Yes, of
    course, Mrs. Roper.

MRS. ROPER. Oh, I see what you're doing, sir. And a sad
    business it always is. My sister now, she's a widder. Kep'
    all her husband's letters, she did, what he wrote her
    from the Middle East. And she'll take them out and
    cry over them, like as not.

(HELEN, *rather impatient about* MRS. ROPER's *chatter, moves
    above the armchair.*)

The heart doesn't forget, sir, that's what I say. The
    heart doesn't forget.

KARL. (*crossing below the sofa to* R *of it*) As you say, Mrs.
    Roper.

MRS. ROPER. Must have been a terrible shock to you, sir,
    wasn't it? Or did you expect it?

KARL. No, I did not expect it.

MRS. ROPER. Can't imagine how she came to do such a thing. (*She stares, fascinated, at the place where* ANYA'S *chair used to be*) It don't seem right, sir, not right at all.

KARL. (*sadly exasperated*) Did you say you were going to get some tea, Mrs. Roper?

MRS. ROPER. (*still staring at the wheel-chair's place*) That's right, sir, and I must hurry, sir—(*She backs slowly up* C) because that grocer there, he shuts at half past twelve.

(MRS. ROPER *exits up* C, *closing the door behind her.*)

HELEN. (*moving* C) I was so sorry to hear . . .

KARL. (*moving down* R) Thank you.

HELEN. Of course she'd been ill a long time, hadn't she? She must have got terribly depressed.

KARL. Did she say anything to you before you left her that day?

HELEN. (*nervously moving above the armchair and round to* L *of it*) No, I—I don't think so. Nothing particular.

KARL. (*moving below the sofa*) But she was depressed—in low spirits?

HELEN. (*rather grasping at a straw*) Yes. (*She moves below the armchair*) Yes, she was.

KARL. (*a shade accusingly*) You went away and left her—alone—before Lisa returned.

HELEN. (*sitting in the armchair; quickly*) I'm sorry about that. I'm afraid it didn't occur to me.

(KARL *moves up* C.)

I mean she said she was perfectly all right and she urged me not to stay, and—well as a matter of fact, I—I thought she really wanted me to go—and so I did. Of course, now . . .

KARL. (*moving down* R) No, no. I understand. I can see that if my poor Anya had this in her mind she might have urged you to go.

HELEN. And in a way, really, it's the best thing that could have happened, isn't it?

KARL. (*moving towards her; angrily*) What do you mean—the best thing that could have happened? (*He moves up* C)

HELEN. (*rising*) For you, I mean. And for her, too. She wanted to get out of it all, well, now she has. So everything is all right, isn't it? (*She moves up* LC, *between the armchair and the desk*)

KARL. (*moving up* RC) It's difficult for me to believe that she did want to get out of it all.

HELEN. She said so—after all, she couldn't have been happy, could she?

KARL. (*thoughtfully*) Sometimes she was very happy.

HELEN. (*circling the armchair*) She couldn't have been, knowing she was a burden on you.

KARL. (*moving below the sofa; beginning to lose his temper*) She was never a burden to me.

HELEN. Oh, why must you be so hypocritical about it all? I know you were kind to her and good to her, but let's face facts, to be tied to a querulous invalid is a drag on any man. Now, you're free. You can go ahead. You can do anything—anything. Aren't you ambitious?

KARL. I don't think so.

HELEN. But you are, of course you are. I've heard people talk about you, I've heard people say that that book of yours was the most brilliant of the century.

KARL. (*sitting on the sofa at the left end*) Fine words, indeed.

HELEN. And they were people who knew. You've had offers, too, to go to the United States, to all sorts of places. Haven't you? You turned them down because of your wife whom you couldn't leave and who couldn't travel. (*She kneels at the left end of the sofa*) You've been tied so long, you hardly know what it is to feel free. Wake up, Karl, wake up. Be yourself. You did the best you could for Anya. Well, now it's over. You can start to enjoy yourself, to live life as it really ought to be lived.

KARL. Is this a sermon you're preaching me, Helen?

HELEN. It's only the present and the future that matter.

KARL. The present and the future are made up of the past.

HELEN. (*rising and moving* LC) You're free. Why should we go on pretending we don't love each other?

KARL. (*rising and crossing to the armchair; firmly and almost harshly*) I don't love you, Helen, you must get that into your head. I don't love you. You're living in a fantasy of your own making.

HELEN. I'm not.

KARL. You are. I hate to be brutal, but I've got to tell you now I've no feelings for you of the kind you imagine. (*He sits in the armchair*)

HELEN. You must have. You must have. (*She moves down RC*) After what I've done for you. Some people wouldn't have had the courage, but I had. I loved you so much that I couldn't bear to see you tied to a useless querulous woman. You don't know what I'm talking about, do you? I killed her. Now, do you understand? I killed her.

KARL. (*utterly stupefied*) You killed . . . I don't know what you're saying.

HELEN. (*moving down R of KARL*) I killed your wife. I'm not ashamed of it. People who are sick and worn out and useless should be removed so as to leave room for the ones who matter.

KARL. (*rising and backing away down L*) You killed Anya?

HELEN. She asked for her medicine. I gave it to her. I gave her the whole bottleful.

KARL. (*backing further away from her up L; aghast*) You—you . . .

HELEN. (*moving C*) Don't worry. Nobody will ever know. I thought of everything. (*She speaks rather like a confident, pleased child*) I wiped off all the fingerprints—(*She moves level with KARL*) and put her own fingers first round the glass and then round the bottle. So that's all right, you see. (*She moves to R of him*) I never really meant to tell you, but I just suddenly felt that I couldn't bear there to be any secrets between us. (*She puts her hands on KARL*)

KARL. (*pushing her away*) You killed Anya.

HELEN. If you once got used to the idea . . .

KARL. You—killed—Anya. (*Every time he repeats the words, his consciousness of her act grows greater and his tone more menacing. He seizes her suddenly by the shoulders and shakes her like a rat, then forces her above the left end of the sofa*) You miserable immature child—what have you done? Prating so glibly of your courage and your resource. You killed my wife—my Anya. Do you realize what you've done? Talking about things you don't understand, without conscience, without pity. I could take you by the neck and strangle you here and now. (*He seizes her by the throat and starts to strangle her*)

(HELEN *is forced backwards over the back of the sofa.* KARL *eventually flings her away and she falls face downwards over the left arm of the sofa, gasping for breath.*)

Get out of here. Get out before I do to you what you did to Anya.

(HELEN *is still gasping for breath and sobbing.* KARL *staggers to the desk chair and leans on the back, near collapse.*)

HELEN. (*broken and desperate*) Karl.
KARL. Get out. (*He shouts*) Get out, I say.

(HELEN, *still sobbing, rises, staggers to the armchair, collects her handbag and gloves, and as in a trance, exits up* C. *to* R. KARL *sinks on to the desk chair and buries his head in his hands. There is a pause, then the front door is heard closing.* LISA *enters the hall from* R.)

LISA. (*calling*) I'm back, Karl.

(LISA *exits to her bedroom.* KARL *rises, crosses slowly to the sofa and almost collapses on to it.*)

KARL. My poor Anya.

(*There is a pause.* LISA *enters from her bedroom and comes into the room. She is tying an apron on as she enters, and goes to look out the window.*)

LISA. (*casually*) I met Helen on the stairs. She looked very strange. Went past me as though she didn't see me. (*She finishes her apron, turns and sees* KARL) Karl, what has happened? (*She crosses to him*)
KARL. (*quite simply*) She killed Anya.
LISA (*startled*) What!
KARL. She killed Anya. Anya asked for her medicine and that miserable child gave her an overdose deliberately.
LISA. But Anya's fingerprints were on the glass.
KARL. Helen put them there after she was dead.
LISA. (*a calm, matter-of-fact mind dealing with the situation*) I see—she thought of everything.
KARL. I knew. I always knew that Anya wouldn't have killed herself.
LISA. She's in love with you, of course.
KARL. Yes, yes. But I never gave her any reason to believe that I cared for her. I didn't, Lisa, I swear I didn't.

LISA. I don't suppose you did. She's the type of girl who would assume that whatever she wanted must be so. (*She moves to the armchair and sits*)

KARL. My poor, brave Anya.

(*There is a long pause.*)

LISA. What are you going to do about it?

KARL. (*surprised*) Do?

LISA. Aren't you going to report it to the police?

KARL. (*startled*) Tell the police?

LISA. (*still calm*) It's murder, you know.

KARL. Yes, it was murder.

LISA. Well, you must report what she said to the police.

KARL. I can't do that.

LISA. Why not? Do you condone murder?

(KARL *rises, paces up* C, *turns slowly to* L, *then crosses above the armchair to* L *of it.*)

KARL. But I can't let that girl . . .

LISA. (*restraining herself; calmly*) We've come of our own accord, as refugees, to a country where we live under the protection of its laws. I think we should respect its law, no matter what our own feelings on the subject may be.

KARL. You seriously think I should go to the police?

LISA. Yes.

KARL. Why?

LISA. It seems to me pure common sense.

KARL. (*sitting at the desk*) Common sense! Common sense! Can one rule one's life by common sense?

LISA. You don't, I know. You never have. You're softhearted, Karl. I'm not.

KARL. Is it wrong to feel pity? Can mercy ever be wrong?

LISA. It can lead to a lot of unhappiness.

KARL. One must be prepared to suffer for one's principles.

LISA. Perhaps. That is your business. (*She rises and crosses to* L *of the table* RC) But other people suffer for them as well. Anya suffered for them.

KARL. I know, I know. But you don't understand.

LISA. (*turning to face* KARL) I understand very well.

KARL. What do you want me to do?

LISA. I have told you. Go to the police. Anya has been murdered. This girl has admitted to murdering her. The police must be told.

KARL. (*rising and crossing above the armchair to* C) You haven't thought, Lisa. The girl is so young. She is only twenty-three.

LISA. Whereas Anya was thirty-eight.

KARL. If she is tried and condemned—what good will it do? Can it bring Anya back? Don't you see, Lisa, revenge can't bring Anya back to life again.

LISA. No. Anya is dead.

KARL. (*crossing to the sofa and sitting*) I wish you could see it my way.

LISA. (*moving to* L *of the sofa*) I can't see it your way. I loved Anya. We were cousins and friends. We went about as girls together. I looked after her when she was ill. I know how she tried to be brave, how she tried not to complain. I know how difficult life was for her.

KARL. Going to the police won't bring Anya back.

(LISA *does not answer but turns and moves up* RC.)

And don't you see, Lisa, I'm bound to feel responsible myself. I must in some way have encouraged the girl.

LISA. You didn't encourage her. (*She moves to* L *of the sofa and kneels, facing* KARL) Let's speak plainly. She did her utmost to seduce you, and failed.

KARL. No matter how you put it, I feel responsible. Love for me was her motive.

LISA. Her motive was to get what she wanted, as she always has got everything she wanted all her life.

KARL. That's just what has been her tragedy. She has never had a chance.

LISA. And she's young and beautiful.

KARL. (*sharply*) What do you mean?

LISA. I wonder if you'd be so tender if she were one of your plain girl students.

KARL. (*rising*) You can't think . . .

LISA. (*rising*) What can't I think?

KARL. That I want that girl . . .

LISA. (*moving slowly down* L) Why not? Aren't you attracted to her? Be honest with yourself. Are you sure you're not really a little in love with the girl?

KARL. (*crossing to* R *of* LISA) You can say that? You? When you know—when you've always known . . . ? It's you I love. You! I lie awake at nights thinking about you, longing for you. Lisa, Lisa . . .

KARL *takes* LISA *in his arms. They embrace passionately. There is a shadowy figure in the doorway up* C. *After a pause, the door closes with a bang. This makes* KARL *and* LISA *move apart and look at the door. They do not see who it was and the audience are left unaware of the identity of the eavesdropper. The lights* BLACK-OUT *as—*

The CURTAIN *falls.*

Scene II

SCENE: *The same. Six hours later. Evening.*

When the CURTAIN *rises, the lights come up a very little, leaving most of the room in darkness.* LISA *is seated on the sofa, at the right end, smoking. She is almost invisible. The front door is heard opening and closing and there is the sound of voices in the hall.* KARL *enters up* C. *He has a newspaper in his overcoat pocket. The* DOCTOR *follows him on.*

KARL. Nobody's at home. I wonder . . .

(*The* DOCTOR *switches on the lights by the switch* L *of the double doors, and he and* KARL *see* LISA.)

DOCTOR. Lisa! Why are you sitting here in the dark?

(KARL *goes to the desk chair and puts his coat over the back of it.*)

LISA. I was just thinking.

(KARL *sits in the armchair.*)

DOCTOR. I met Karl at the end of the street and we came along together. (*He puts his coat on the chair above the table* RC) D'you know what I prescribe for you, Karl? A little alcohol. A stiff brandy, eh, Lisa?

(LISA *makes a slight move.*)

No—I know my way about. (*He goes to the cupboard under the bookcase* R, *takes out a bottle of brandy and a glass, and pours a stiff drink*) He's had a shock, you know. A bad shock.

KARL. I have told him about Helen.

DOCTOR. Yes, he told me.

LISA. It's not been such a shock, I gather?

DOCTOR. I've been worried, you know. I didn't think Anya was a suicidal type and I couldn't see any possibility of an accident. (*He crosses to* R *of* KARL *and gives him the brandy*) And then the inquest aroused my suspicions. Clearly the police were behind the verdict. (*He sits* L *of* LISA *on the sofa*) Yes, it looked fishy. The police questioned me fairly closely and I couldn't help seeing what they were driving at. Of course, they didn't actually say anything.

LISA. So you were not surprised?

DOCTOR. No, not really. That young woman thought she could get away with anything. Even murder. Well, she was wrong.

KARL. (*in a low voice*) I feel responsible.

DOCTOR. Karl, take it from me, you weren't responsible in any way. Compared to that young woman you're an innocent in arms. (*He rises and moves up* C) Anyway, the whole thing's out of your hands now.

LISA. You think he should go to the police?

DOCTOR. Yes.

KARL. No.

DOCTOR. Because you insist on feeling partly responsible? You're too sensitive.

KARL. Poor wretched child.

DOCTOR. (*crossing above the armchair and standing down* L) Callous, murdering little bitch! That's nearer the mark. And I shouldn't worry before you need. Ten to one it'll never come to an arrest. (*He crosses below* KARL *to* RC) Presumably she'll deny everything—and there's got to be evidence, you know. The police may be quite sure who's done a thing, but be unable to make out a case. The girl's father is a very important person. One of the richest men in England. That counts.

KARL. There I think you are wrong.

DOCTOR. Oh, I'm not saying anything against the police. (*He moves up* C) If they've got a case they'll go ahead,

without fear or favour. All I mean is that they'll have to
scrutinize their evidence with extra care. And on the
face of it there can't really be much evidence, you
know. Unless, of course, she breaks down and confesses
the whole thing. And I should imagine she's much too
hard-boiled for that.

KARL. She confessed to me.

DOCTOR. That's different. Though as a matter of fact I can't
see why she did. (*He moves and sits on the left arm of
the sofa*) Seems to me a damn silly thing to do.

LISA. Because she was proud of it.

DOCTOR. (*looking curiously at her*) You think so?

KARL. It is true—that's what is so terrible.

(*The front door bell rings.*)

Who can that be?

DOCTOR. One of your boys or girls, I expect. (*He rises*) I'll
get rid of them.

(*The* DOCTOR *exits up* C *to* R. KARL *rises and puts his glass
on the desk.*)

OGDEN. (*off*) Could I see Professor Hendryk, please?

DOCTOR. (*off*) Would you come this way, please.

(*The* DOCTOR *enters up* C *from* R *and stands to one side.*)

It's Inspector Ogden.

(DETECTIVE INSPECTOR OGDEN *and* POLICE SERGEANT PEARCE
enter up C *from* R. OGDEN *has a pleasant manner and a
poker face. The* SERGEANT *closes the doors, then stands
above the table* RC.)

OGDEN. (*very pleasantly*) I hope we're not disturbing you,
Professor Hendryk.

KARL. (*moving down* L) Not at all.

OGDEN. Good evening, Miss Koletzky. I expect you didn't
think you would see me again——but we have a few more
questions to ask. It was an open verdict, you understand.
Insufficient evidence as to how the deceased lady came
to take the fatal dose.

KARL. I know.

OGDEN. Have your own ideas changed as to that, sir, since we
first talked about it?

(KARL *looks quickly at* LISA. OGDEN *and the* SERGEANT *note the look and exchange quick glances. There is a pause.*)

KARL. (*deliberately*) They have not changed. I still think it must have been some sort of—accident.

(LISA *turns away. The* DOCTOR *almost snorts and turns aside.*)

OGDEN. But definitely not suicide.

KARL.. Definitely not suicide.

OGDEN. Well, you're quite right as to that, sir. (*With emphasis*) It was not suicide.

(KARL *and* LISA *turn to* OGDEN.)

LISA. (*quietly*) How do you know?

OGDEN. By evidence that was not given at the inquest. Evidence as to the fingerprints found on the bottle containing the fatal drug—and on the glass, also.

KARL. You mean . . . But they were my wife's fingerprints, weren't they?

OGDEN. Oh, yes, sir. They were your wife's fingerprints. (*Softly*) But she didn't make them. (*He moves the chair* L *of the table* RC *and sets it* L *of the sofa*)

(*The* DOCTOR *and* KARL *exchange looks.*)

KARL. What do you mean?

OGDEN. It's the sort of thing that an amateur criminal thinks is so easy. To pick up a person's hand and close it round a gun or a bottle or whatever it may be. (*He sits on the chair he has placed* C) But actually it's not so easy to do.

(KARL *sits in the armchair.*)

The position of those fingerprints is such that they couldn't have been made by a living woman grasping a bottle. That means that somebody else took your wife's hand and folded the fingers round the bottle and the glass so as to give the impression that your wife committed suicide. A rather childish piece of reasoning and done by someone rather cocksure of their own ability. Also, there ought to have been plenty of other prints on the bottle, but there weren't—it had been wiped

clean before your wife's were applied. You see what
that means?

KARL. I see what it means.

OGDEN. There would be no reason to do such a thing if it
was an accident. That only leaves one possibility.

KARL. Yes.

OGDEN. I wonder if you do see, sir. It means—an ugly word
—murder.

KARL. Murder.

OGDEN. Doesn't that seem very incredible to you, sir?

KARL. (*more to himself than* OGDEN) You cannot know how
incredible. My wife was a very sweet and gentle woman.
It will always seem to me both terrible and unbelievable
that anyone should have—killed her.

OGDEN. You, yourself . . .

KARL. (*sharply*) Are you accusing me?

OGDEN. (*rising*) Of course not, sir. If I'd any suspicions con-
cerning you, I should give you the proper warning. No,
Professor Hendryk, we've checked your story and your
time is fully accounted for. (*He resumes his seat*) You
left here in the company of Dr. Stoner and he states that
there was no medicine bottle or glass on your wife's table
at that time. Between the time you left and the time
Miss Koletzky says she arrived here and found your wife
dead, every moment of your time is accounted for. You
were lecturing to a group of students at the university.
No, there is no suggestion of your having been the
person to put the fingerprints on the glass.

(*The* DOCTOR *moves down* L.)

What I am asking you, sir, is whether you have any
idea yourself as to who could have done so?

(*There is quite a long pause.* KARL *stares fixedly ahead of
him.*)

KARL. (*presently*) I—(*He pauses*) cannot help you.

(OGDEN *rises and as he replaces the chair beside the table,
he exchanges glances with the* SERGEANT, *who moves to
the door down* R.)

OGDEN. (*moving* C) You will appreciate, of course, that this
alters things. I wonder if I might have a look round the

flat. Round Mrs. Hendryk's bedroom in particular. I can get a search warrant if necessary, but ...

KARL. Of course. Look anywhere you please. (*He rises*)

(LISA *rises.*)

My wife's bedroom—(*He indicates the door down* R) is through there.

OGDEN. Thank you.

KARL. Miss Koletzky has been sorting through her things.

(LISA *crosses to the door* R *and opens it.* OGDEN *and the* SERGEANT *exit down* R. LISA *turns and looks at* KARL, *then exits down* R, *closing the door behind her.*)

DOCTOR. (*moving up* L *of the armchair*) I've known you long enough, Karl, to tell you plainly that you're being a fool.

KARL. (*moving up* R *of the armchair*) I can't be the one to put them on her track. They'll get her soon enough without my help.

DOCTOR. I'm not so sure of that. And it's all high-faultin' nonsense. (*He sits in the armchair*)

KARL. She didn't know what she was doing.

DOCTOR. She knew perfectly.

KARL. She didn't know what she was doing because life has not yet taught her understanding and compassion. (*He moves above the armchair*)

(LISA *enters down* R, *closing the door behind her.*)

LISA. (*moving* RC; *to the* DOCTOR) Have you made him see sense?

DOCTOR. Not yet.

(LISA *shivers.*)

You're cold.

LISA. No—I'm not cold. I'm afraid. (*She moves towards the doors up* C) I shall make some coffee.

(LISA *exits up* C. *The* DOCTOR *rises and moves below the sofa.*)

KARL. (*moving down* L *of the armchair*) I wish I could get you and Lisa to see that revenge will not bring Anya back to life again.

DOCTOR. (*moving up* LC) And suppose our little beauty goes
  on disposing of wives that happen to stand in her way?
KARL. I will not believe that.

(*The* SERGEANT *and* OGDEN *enter down* R. *The sergeant
  stands above the table* RC *and* OGDEN *stands down* R.)

OGDEN. I gather some of your wife's clothing and effects have
  already been disposed of?
KARL. Yes. They were sent off to the East London Mission,
  I think.

(*The* SERGEANT *makes a note.*)

OGDEN. (*moving to* R *of the sofa*) What about papers, letters?
KARL. (*crossing to the table* RC) I was going through them
  this morning. (*He indicates the little drawer*) Though
  what you expect to find . . .
OGDEN. (*evading the issue; vaguely*) One never knows. Some
  note, a memorandum set down . . .
KARL. I doubt it. Still, look through them, of course, if you
  must. I don't expect you'll find . . . (*He picks up a
  bundle of letters tied with ribbon*) Will you need these?
  They are the letters I wrote to my wife many years ago.
OGDEN. (*gently*) I'm afraid I must just look through them.
  (*He takes the letters from* KARL.)

(*There is quite a pause, then* KARL *turns impatiently towards
  the doors up* C.)

KARL. I shall be in the kitchen if you want me, Inspector
  Ogden.

(*The* DOCTOR *opens the right half of the doors up* C. KARL
  exits up C. *The* DOCTOR *follows him off, closing the
  door behind him.* OGDEN *moves to* R *of the table* RC.)

SERGEANT. Do you think he was in on it?
OGDEN. No, I don't. (*He starts to go through the papers in
  the drawer*) Not beforehand. Hadn't the faintest idea, I
  should say. (*Grimly*) But he knows now—and it's been
  a shock to him.
SERGEANT. (*also going through the papers, etc., in the drawer*)
  He's not saying anything.
OGDEN. No. That would be too much to expect. Doesn't

seem to be much here. Not likely to be, under the circumstances.

SERGEANT. If there had been, our Mrs. Mop would have known about it. I'd say she was a pretty good snooper. That kind always knows the dirt. And did she enjoy spilling it!

OGDEN. (*with distaste*) An unpleasant woman.

SERGEANT. She'll do all right in the witness-box.

OGDEN. Unless she overdoes it. Well, nothing additional here. We'd better get on with the job. (*He moves to the doors up* C, *opens one and calls*) Will you come in here, please. (*He moves below the armchair*)

(LISA *enters up* C *and moves down* C. *The* DOCTOR *enters up* C *and moves down* R *of the sofa.* KARL *enters up* C *and stands up* L *of the sofa. The* SERGEANT *moves to the doors up* C, *closes them and stands in front of them.*)

Miss Koletzky, there are some additional questions I would like to ask you. You understand that you are not forced to answer anything unless you please.

LISA. I do not want to answer any questions.

OGDEN. Perhaps you're wise. Lisa Koletzky, I arrest you on the charge of administering poison to Anya Hendryk on March the fifth last—

(KARL *moves to* R *of* LISA.)

—and it is my duty to warn you that anything you say will be taken down and may be used in evidence.

KARL. (*horror struck*) What's this? What are you doing? What are you saying?

OGDEN. Please, Professor Hendryk, don't let's have a scene.

KARL. (*moving behind* LISA *and holding her in his arms*) But you can't arrest Lisa, you can't, you can't. She's done nothing.

LISA. (*gently pushing* KARL *away; in a loud, clear, calm voice*) I did not murder my cousin.

OGDEN. You'll have plenty of opportunity to say everything you want, later.

(KARL, *losing restraint, advances on* OGDEN *but the* DOCTOR *holds his arm.*)

KARL. (*pushing the* DOCTOR *away; almost shouting*) You can't do this. You can't.

OGDEN. (*to* LISA) If you need a coat or a hat . . .

LISA. I need nothing.

(LISA *turns and looks at* KARL *for a moment, then turns and goes up* C. *The* SERGEANT *opens the door.* LISA *exits up* C. OGDEN *and the* SERGEANT *follow her off.* KARL *suddenly makes a decision and runs after them.*)

KARL. Inspector Ogden! Come back. I must speak to you.

(*He moves* RC)

OGDEN. (*off*) Wait in the hall, Sergeant.

SERGEANT. (*off*) Yes, sir.

(OGDEN *enters up* C. *The* DOCTOR *crosses to* LC.)

OGDEN. Yes, Professor Hendryk?

KARL. (*moving to* L *of the sofa*) I have something to tell you. I know who killed my wife. It was not Miss Koletzky.

OGDEN. (*politely*) Who was it, then?

KARL. It was a girl called Helen Rollander. She is one of my pupils. (*He crosses and sits in the armchair*) She—she formed an unfortunate attachment to me.

(*The* DOCTOR *moves to* L *of the armchair.*)

She was alone with my wife on the day in question, and she gave her an overdose of the heart medicine.

OGDEN. (*moving down* C) How do you know this, Professor Hendryk?

KARL. She told me herself, this morning.

OGDEN. Indeed? Were there any witnesses?

KARL. No, but I am telling you the truth.

OGDEN. (*thoughtfully*) Helen—Rollander. You mean the daughter of Sir William Rollander?

KARL. Yes. Her father is William Rollander. He is an important man. Does that make any difference?

OGDEN. (*moving below the left end of the sofa*) No, it wouldn't make any difference—if your story were true.

KARL. (*rising*) I swear to you that it's true.

OGDEN. You are very devoted to Miss Koletzky, aren't you?

KARL. Do you think I would make up a story just to protect her?

OGDEN. (*moving* C) I think it is quite possible—you are on terms of intimacy with Miss Koletzky, aren't you?

KARL. (*dumbfounded*) What do you mean?

OGDEN. Let me tell you, Professor Hendryk, that your daily woman, Mrs. Roper, came along to the police station this afternoon and made a statement.

KARL. Then it was Mrs. Roper who . . .

OGDEN. It is partly because of that statement that Miss Koletzky has been arrested.

KARL. (*turning to the* DOCTOR *for support*) You believe that Lisa and I . . .

OGDEN. Your wife was an invalid. Miss Koletzky is an attractive young woman. You were thrown together.

KARL. You think we planned together to kill Anya.

OGDEN. No, I don't think you planned it. I may be wrong there, of course.

(KARL *circles the armchair to* C.)

I think all the planning was done by Miss Koletzky. There was a prospect of your wife's regaining her health owing to a new treatment. I think Miss Koletzky was taking no chance of that happening.

KARL. But I tell you that it was Helen Rollander.

OGDEN. You tell me, yes. It seems to me a most unlikely story. (*He moves up* C)

(KARL *crosses and stands down* R.)

Is it plausible that a girl like Miss Rollander who's got the world at her feet and who hardly knows you, would do a thing like that? Making up an accusation of that kind reflects little credit on you, Professor Hendryk— trumping it up on the spur of the moment because you think it cannot be contradicted.

KARL. (*moving to* R *of* OGDEN) Listen. Go to Miss Rollander. Tell her that another woman has been arrested for the murder. Tell her, from me, that I know—know—that with all her faults, she is decent and honest. I swear that she will confirm what I have told you.

OGDEN. You've thought it up very cleverly, haven't you?

KARL. What do you mean?

OGDEN. What I say. But there's no-one who can confirm your story.

KARL. Only Helen herself.

OGDEN. Exactly.

KARL. And Dr. Stoner knows. I told him.

OGDEN. He knows because you told him.

DOCTOR. I believe it to be the truth, Inspector Ogden. If you remember, I mentioned to you that when we left Mrs. Hendryk that day, Miss Rollander remained behind to keep her company.

OGDEN. A kind offer on her part. (*He crosses to* R *of the* DOCTOR) We interviewed Miss Rollander at the time and I see no reason to doubt her story. She stayed for a short time and then Mrs. Hendryk asked her to leave since she felt tired. (*He moves above the armchair*)

KARL. Go to Helen now. Tell her what has happened. Tell her what I have asked you to tell her.

OGDEN. (*to the* DOCTOR) Just when did Professor Hendryk tell you that Miss Rollander had killed his wife? Within the last hour, I should imagine.

DOCTOR. That is so.

KARL. We met in the street. (*He moves below the sofa*)

OGDEN. Didn't it strike you that if this was true, he would have come to us as soon as she admitted to him what she had done?

DOCTOR. He's not that kind of man.

OGDEN. (*ruthlessly*) I don't think you're really aware what kind of man he is. (*He moves to* KARL's *coat on the desk chair*) He's a quick and clever thinker, and he's not over scrupulous.

(KARL *starts toward the* INSPECTOR, *but the* DOCTOR *crosses quickly to* L *of* KARL *and restrains him.*)

This is your coat and an evening paper, I see. (*He draws the evening paper from the pocket*)

(KARL *moves down* R *of the sofa. The* DOCTOR *moves up* L *of the sofa.*)

KARL. Yes, I bought it on the corner, just before I came in. I haven't had time to read it, yet.

OGDEN. (*moving* C) Are you sure?

KARL. Yes—(*He moves* RC) I am quite sure.

OGDEN. I think you did. (*He reads from the paper*) "Sir William Rollander's only daughter, Helen Rollander, was the victim of a regrettable accident this morning. In crossing the road she was knocked down by a lorry. The lorry driver claims that Miss Rollander gave him no time to brake. She walked straight into the road without looking right or left, and was killed instantly."

(KARL *slumps on to the sofa.*)

I think that when you saw that paragraph, Professor Hendryk, you saw a way out to save your mistress by accusing a girl who could never refute what you said—because she was dead.

The lights BLACK-OUT *as—*

The CURTAIN *falls.*

Scene III

SCENE: *The same. Two months later. Late afternoon.*

When the CURTAIN *rises, the lights come up.* KARL *is seated on the sofa. The* DOCTOR *is leaning against the table* RC, *reading the "Walter Savage Landor."* LESTER *is pacing up and down* LC. *The telephone rings. They all start.* LESTER, *who is nearest to the telephone, lifts the receiver.*

LESTER. (*into the telephone*) Hello? . . . No. (*He replaces the receiver*) These reporters never stop. (*He moves down* L)

(*The* DOCTOR *crosses and sits in the armchair.* KARL *rises and circles the sofa to* C.)

KARL. I wish I had stayed in court. Why didn't you let me stay?

DOCTOR. Lisa specially asked that you shouldn't remain in court to hear the verdict. We've got to respect her wish.

KARL. You could have stayed.

DOCTOR. She wanted me to be with you. The lawyers will let us know at once . . .

KARL. They can't find her guilty. They can't. (*He moves up R*)

LESTER. (*moving down C*) If you'd like me to go back there . . .

DOCTOR. You stay here, Lester.

LESTER. If I'm any use. If there's anything I could do . . .

DOCTOR. You can answer that damn telephone that keeps ringing.

KARL. (*moving below the sofa*) Yes, my dear boy. Stay. Your presence here helps me.

LESTER. Does it? Does it, really?

KARL. She must be, she will be acquitted. I can't believe that innocence can go unrecognized. (*He sits on the sofa*)

(LESTER *moves up* C.)

DOCTOR. Can't you? I can. One's seen it often enough. And you've seen it, Karl, time and time again. Mind you, I think she made a good impression on the jury.

LESTER. But the evidence was pretty damning. It's that frightful Roper woman. The things she said. (*He sits L of the table RC*)

DOCTOR. She believed what she was saying, of course. That's what made her so unshakeable under cross-examination. It's particularly unfortunate that she should have seen you and Lisa embracing each other on the day of the inquest. She did see it, I suppose.

KARL. Yes, she must have seen it. It was true. It's the first time I have ever kissed Lisa.

DOCTOR. And a thoroughly bad time to choose. It's really a thousand pities that snooping woman never saw or heard anything that passed between you and Helen. "A very nice young lady"—that's all she had to say.

KARL. It is so odd to tell the truth and not be believed.

DOCTOR. All you've done is to bring down a lot of odium on yourself, for cooking up a scurrilous story about a girl who is dead.

KARL. (*rising and moving up* C) If I'd only gone to the police right away, the moment she'd told me . . .

DOCTOR. If only you had. It's particularly unfortunate that you only came out with the story after you'd bought a paper containing the news that she's dead. And your reasons for not going to the police didn't sound credible in the least.

(KARL *moves down* L.)

Though they are to me, of course, because I know the incredible fool you are. The whole set of circumstances is thoroughly damnable. The Roper woman coming in to find Lisa standing by the body and holding the bottle in gloved fingers. The whole thing has built itself up in the most incredible fashion.

(KARL *crosses and stands down* R. *The telephone rings.*)

KARL. Is that . . . ? Can it . . . ?

(*There is a moment's agonizing pause, then the* DOCTOR *motions to* LESTER *who rises, goes to the telephone and lifts the receiver.*)

LESTER. (*into the telephone*) Yes? . . . Hello? . . . Go to hell! (*He slams the receiver down and stands* R *of the desk*)

DOCTOR. Ghouls, that's what they are, ghouls.

KARL. (*moving up* R) If they find her guilty, if they . . .

DOCTOR. Well, we can appeal, you know.

KARL. (*moving down* C *and then below the sofa*) Why should she have to go through all this? Why should she be the one to suffer? I wish I were in her place.

DOCTOR. Yes, it's always easier when it's oneself.

KARL. After all, I'm partly responsible for what happened . . .

DOCTOR. (*interrupting*) I've told you that's nonsense.

KARL. But Lisa has done nothing. Nothing. (*He moves down* C, *then goes up* R)

DOCTOR. (*after a long pause; to* LESTER) Go and make us some coffee, boy, if you know how.

LESTER. (*indignantly*) Of course I know how. (*He moves up* C)

(*The telephone rings.* LESTER *makes a move to answer it.*)

KARL. (*stopping* LESTER) Don't answer it.

(*The telephone goes on ringing.* LESTER *hesitates then exits up* C *to* L. *The telephone goes on ringing solidly.* KARL *eventually rushes to it and picks up the receiver.*)

(*Into the telephone*) Leave me alone, can't you. Leave
me alone. (*He slams down the receiver and sinks into
the desk chair*) I can't bear it. I can't bear it.

DOCTOR. (*rising and moving to* KARL) Patience, Karl. Courage.

KARL. What good is it saying that to me?

DOCTOR. Not much, but there's nothing else to say, is there?
There's nothing that can help you now except courage.

KARL. I keep thinking of Lisa. Of what she must be suffering.

DOCTOR. I know. I know.

KARL. She's so brave. So wonderfully brave.

DOCTOR. (*moving* C) Lisa is a very wonderful person. I have
always known that.

KARL. I love her. Did you know I loved her?

DOCTOR. Yes, of course I knew. You've loved her for a long
time.

KARL. Yes. Neither of us ever acknowledged it, but we knew.
It didn't mean that I didn't love Anya. I did love Anya.
I shall always love her. I didn't want her to die.

DOCTOR. I know, I know. I've never doubted that.

KARL. It's strange, perhaps, but one can love two women at
the same time.

DOCTOR. Not at all strange. It often happens. (*He moves behind* KARL) And you know what Anya used to say to
me? "When I'm gone, Karl must marry Lisa." That's
what she used to say. "You must make him do it,
Doctor," she used to say. "Lisa will look after him and
be good to him. If he doesn't think of it you must put
it into his head." That's what she used to say to me.
I promised her that I would.

KARL. (*rising*) Tell me, really, Doctor. Do you think they'll
acquit her? Do you?

DOCTOR. (*gently*) I think—you ought to prepare yourself . . .

KARL. (*moving below the armchair*) Even her counsel didn't
believe me, did he? He pretended to, of course, but he
didn't believe me. (*He sits in the armchair*)

DOCTOR. No, I don't think he did, but there are one or two
sensible people on the jury—I think. (*He moves down
L*) That fat woman in the funny hat listened to every
word you were saying about Helen, and I noticed her
nodding her head in complete agreement. She probably
has a husband who went off the rails with a young girl.
You never know what queer things influence people.

(The telephone rings.)

KARL. *(rising)* This time it must be.

(The DOCTOR *moves to the telephone and lifts the receiver.)*

DOCTOR. *(into the telephone)* Hello? . . .

*(*LESTER *enters up* C *from* L, *carrying a tray with three cups of coffee on it. The coffee has slopped into the saucers.)*

KARL. Well?

LESTER. Is that . . . ? *(He puts the tray on the table* RC *and pours the coffee into the cup from one of the saucers)*

DOCTOR. *(into the telephone)* No . . . No, I'm afraid he can't. *(He slams down the receiver)* Another of the ghouls. *(He crosses to the sofa and sits)*

KARL. What can they hope to get out of it?

DOCTOR. Increased circulation, I suppose.

LESTER. *(handing a cup of coffee to* KARL) I hope it's all right. It took me some time to find everything.

KARL. Thank you. *(He crosses to the desk chair and sits)*

*(*LESTER *hands a cup of coffee to the* DOCTOR, *then takes his own and stands* RC. *They sip their coffee. There is quite a pause.)*

DOCTOR. Have you ever seen herons flying low over a river bank?

LESTER. No, I don't think I have. Why?

DOCTOR. No reason.

LESTER. What put it into your head?

DOCTOR. I've no idea. Just wishing, I suppose, that all this wasn't true and that I was somewhere else.

LESTER. Yes, I can see that. *(He moves up* C) It's so awful, not being able to do anything.

DOCTOR. Nothing's so bad as waiting.

LESTER. *(after a pause)* I don't believe, you know, that I've ever seen a heron.

DOCTOR. Very graceful birds.

KARL. Doctor, I want you to do something for me.

DOCTOR. *(rising)* Yes? What is it?

KARL. I want you to go back to the court.

DOCTOR. *(crossing to* KARL *and putting his cup on the work-table as he passes)* No, Karl.

KARL. Yes, I know that you promised. But I want you to go back.

DOCTOR. Karl—Lisa . . .

KARL. If the worst happens, I would like Lisa to be able to see you there. And if it isn't the worst—well, then she'll need someone to look after her, to get her away, to bring her here.

(*The* DOCTOR *stares at* KARL *for a moment or two.*)

I know I'm right.

DOCTOR. (*deciding*) Very well.

LESTER. (*to the* DOCTOR) I can stay and . . .

(KARL *looks at the* DOCTOR *and shakes his head very slightly. The* DOCTOR *is quick to take the hint.*)

DOCTOR. No, you come with me, Lester. (*He moves up* C) There are times when a man has got to be alone. That's right, isn't it, Karl?

KARL. Don't worry about me. I want to stay here quietly with Anya.

DOCTOR. (*pulling round sharply as he is on his way to the door*) What did you say? With Anya?

KARL. Did I say that? That's what it seems like. Leave me here. I shan't answer the telephone if it rings. I shall wait now until you come.

(LESTER *exits up* C. *The* DOCTOR *follows him off and closes the door.* KARL *leans back in his chair. The clock chimes six.*)

"While the light lasts I shall remember,
And in the darkness I shall not forget."

(*There is a pause then the telephone rings.* KARL *rises, ignores the telephone, takes his coffee cup to the tray, at the same time collecting the* DOCTOR's *cup as he passes the work-table. He then exits with the tray up* C *to* L. *While he is off, the telephone stops ringing.* KARL *re-enters and moves down* L, *leaving the door open. He pauses for a moment, staring at the work-table, then goes to the record cabinet and takes the Rachmaninoff record from it. He goes to the desk and sits, putting the record on the desk in front of him.* LISA *suddenly enters up* C *from* R,

shuts the door behind her and leans against it. KARL
rises and turns.)

KARL. Lisa! Lisa! (*He goes towards her as though he can
hardly believe his eyes*) Is it true? Is it?

LISA. They found me not guilty.

KARL. (*attempting to take her in his arms*) Oh, my darling,
I'm so thankful. No-one shall ever hurt you again, Lisa.

LISA. (*pushing him away*) No.

KARL. (*realizing her coldness and aloofness*) What do you
mean?

LISA. I've come here to get my things.

KARL. (*backing above the armchair*) What do you mean—
your things?

LISA. Just a few things that I need. Then I am going away.

KARL. What do you mean—going away?

LISA. I'm leaving here.

KARL. But surely—that's ridiculous! D'you mean because of
what people would say? Does that matter now?

LISA. You don't understand. I am going away for good.

KARL. Going away—where?

LISA. (*moving slowly down* C) What does it matter? Somewhere. I can get a job. There'll be no difficulty about
that. I may go abroad. I may stay in England. Wherever
I go I'm starting a new life.

KARL. A new life? You mean—without me?

LISA. Yes. Yes, Karl. That's just what I do mean. Without
you.

KARL. (*backing down* L) But why? Why?

LISA. (*up* R *of the armchair*) Because I've had enough.

KARL. I don't understand you.

LISA. (*moving to the sofa*) We're not made to understand
each other. We don't see things the same way, and I'm
afraid of you.

KARL. How can you be afraid of me?

LISA. Because you're the kind of man who always brings
suffering.

KARL. No.

LISA. It's true.

KARL. No.

LISA. I see people as they are. Without malice and without
entering into judgement, but without illusions, either. I
don't expect people to be wonderful or life to be wonder-

ful, and I don't particularly want to be wonderful myself.
If there are fields of amaranth—they can be on the
other side of the grave as far as I am concerned.

KARL. Fields of amaranth? What are you talking about?

LISA. I'm talking about you, Karl. You put ideas first, not
people. Ideas of loyalty and friendship and pity. And
because of that the people who are near, suffer. (*She
moves to* R *of the armchair*) You knew you'd lose your
job if you befriended the Schultzes. And you knew, you
must have known, what an unhappy life that would
mean for Anya. But you didn't care about Anya. You
only cared about your ideas of what was right. But
people matter, Karl. They matter as much as ideas.
Anya mattered, I matter. Because of your ideas, because
of your mercy and compassion for the girl who killed
your wife, you sacrificed me. I was the one who paid
for your compassion. But I'm not ready to do that any
more. I love you, but love isn't enough. You've more in
common with the girl Helen than you have with me.
She was like you—ruthless. She went all out for the
things she believed in. She didn't care what happened
to people as long as she got her own way.

KARL. (*moving towards the armchair*) Lisa, you can't mean
what you are saying. You can't.

LISA. I do mean it. I've been thinking it really for a long
time. (*She moves below the left end of the sofa*) I've
thought of it all these days in court. I didn't really think
they'd acquit me. I don't know why they did. The judge
didn't seem to think there was much reasonable doubt.
But I suppose some of the jury believed me. There was
one little man who kept on looking at me as though he
was sizing me up. Just a commonplace ordinary little man
—but he looked at me and thought I hadn't done it—or
perhaps he thought I was the kind of woman that he'd
like to go to bed with and he didn't want me to suffer.
I don't know what he thought—but—he was a person
looking at another person and he was on my side and
perhaps he persuaded the others. And so I'm free. I've
been given a second chance to start life again. I'm
starting again—alone.

(LISA *exits down* R. KARL *crosses and sits on the sofa.*)

KARL. (*pleadingly*) Lisa. You can't mean it. You can't be so cruel. You must listen. Lisa. I implore you.

(LISA *re-enters down* R. *She carries a small silver photo frame. She remains down* R, *facing* KARL.)

LISA. No, Karl. What happens to the women who love you? Anya loved you and she died. Helen loved you and she's dead. I—have been very near death. I've had enough. I want to be free of you—for ever.

KARL. But where will you go?

(*There is a pause as* LISA *crosses below* KARL *to* C.)

LISA. You told me to go away and marry and have children. Perhaps that's what I'll do. If so, I'll find someone like that little man on the jury, someone who'll be human and a person, like me. (*She suddenly cries out*) I've had enough. I've loved you for years and it's broken me. I'm going away and I shall never see you again. Never!

KARL. Lisa!

LISA. (*moving down* L) Never!

(*The* DOCTOR *is suddenly heard calling from the hall.*)

DOCTOR. (*off; calling*) Karl! Karl!

(*The* DOCTOR *enters up* C *from* R *and moves towards* KARL, *without noticing* LISA.)

It's all right, my boy. She's acquitted. (*During this he is quite out of breath*) Do you understand? She's acquitted. (*He suddenly sees* LISA *and crosses to her with outstretched arms*) Lisa—my dear Lisa. Thank God we've got you safe. It's wonderful. Wonderful!

LISA. (*trying to respond to him*) Yes, it's wonderful.

DOCTOR. (*holding her away from him and looking her up and down*) How are you? A little fine drawn—thinner —only natural with all you've been through. But we'll make it up to you. (*He crosses above the armchair to* KARL) We'll look after you. As for Karl here, you can imagine the state he's been in. Ah, well, thank God that's all over now. (*He turns to* KARL) What do you say—shall we go out—celebrate? A bottle of champagne —eh? (*He beams expectantly*)

LISA. (*forcing a smile*) No, Doctor—not tonight.

DOCTOR. Ah, what an old fool I am. Of course not. You need rest.

LISA. I am all right. (*She moves towards the doors up* C) I must just get my things together.

DOCTOR. (*moving to* LISA) Things?

LISA. I am not—staying here.

DOCTOR. But . . . (*Enlightened*) Oh, I see—well, perhaps that is wise—with people like your Mrs. Roper about, with their evil minds and tongues. But where will you go? To an hotel? Better come to us. Margaret will be delighted. It's a very tiny room that we have, but we'll look after you well.

LISA. How kind you are. But I have all my plans made. Tell, —tell Margaret that I will come to see her very soon.

(LISA *goes into the hall and exits to her bedroom. The* DOCTOR *turns back to* KARL *and begins to realize that all is not well.*)

DOCTOR. (*moving* C) Karl—is anything wrong?

KARL. What should be wrong?

DOCTOR. (*semi-relieved*) She has been through a terrible ordeal. It takes a little time to—to come back to normal. (*He looks around*) When I think we sat here—waiting —with that damn telephone ringing all the time— hoping—fearing—and now—all over.

KARL. (*tonelessly*) Yes—all over.

DOCTOR. (*robustly*) No decent jury would ever have convicted her. (*He moves and sits* L *of* KARL *on the sofa*) I told you so. You look half dazed still, Karl. Can't you believe it yet? (*He takes* KARL *affectionately by the shoulder*) Karl, snap out of it. We've got our Lisa back again.

(KARL *turns sharply away.*)

Oh, I know—I'm clumsy—it takes a little time to get used to the joy.

(LISA *enters from her bedroom and comes into the room. She carries a hold-all which she puts on the floor up* C. *She avoids looking at* KARL *and stands up* LC.)

LISA. I'm going now.

DOCTOR. (*rising*) I'll get a taxi for you.

LISA. (*sharply*) No—please—I'd rather be alone. (*She turns away* L)

(*The* DOCTOR *is slightly taken aback. She relents, moves to the* DOCTOR *and puts her hands on his shoulders.*)

Thank you—for all your kindness—for all you did for Anya—you have been a good friend—I shall never forget.

(LISA *kisses the* DOCTOR, *picks up her hold-all and without once looking at* KARL *exits up* C *to* R.)

DOCTOR. (*moving to* KARL) Karl—what does this mean? There is something wrong.

KARL. Lisa is going away.

DOCTOR. Yes, yes—temporarily. But—she is coming back.

KARL. (*turning to face the* DOCTOR) No, she is not coming back.

DOCTOR. (*appalled*) What do you mean?

KARL. (*with complete conviction and force*) She—is—not—coming—back.

DOCTOR. (*incredulously*) Do you mean—you have parted?

KARL. You saw her go—that was our parting.

DOCTOR. But—why?

KARL. She had had enough.

DOCTOR. Talk sense, man.

KARL. It's very simple. She has suffered. She doesn't want to suffer any more.

DOCTOR. Why should she suffer?

KARL. It seems—I am a man—who brings suffering to those who love him.

DOCTOR. Nonsense!

KARL. Is it? Anya loved me and she is dead. Helen loved me and she died.

DOCTOR. Did Lisa say that to you?

KARL. Yes. Am I such a man? Do I bring suffering to those who love me? What did she mean when she talked of fields of amaranth?

DOCTOR. Fields of amaranth. (*He thinks for a moment, then recollects, moves to the table* RC, *picks up the "Walter Savage Landor" and gives it to* KARL) Yes, I was reading there. (*He points to the quotation*)

KARL. Please leave me.

DOCTOR. I'd like to stay.

KARL. I must get used to being alone.

DOCTOR. (*moving up* C, *then hesitating and returning to* KARL) You don't think . . . ?

KARL. She will not come back.

(*The* DOCTOR *exits reluctantly up* C *to* R.)

(*He rises, crosses to the desk, switches on the desk light, draws the curtains, then sits at the desk and reads*) "There are no fields of Amaranth this side of the grave. There are no voices, oh Rhodope, that are not soon mute, however tuneful: there is no name, with whatever emphasis of passionate love repeated, of which the echo is not faint at last . . ." (*He puts the book gently on the desk, rises, picks up the record, goes to the record player, puts on the record, switches on, then goes slowly to the armchair and sinks into it*) Lisa—Lisa— how can I live without you? (*He drops his head into his hands*)

(*The door up* C *opens slowly.* LISA *enters up* C, *moves slowly to* R *of* KARL *and puts her hand gently on his shoulder.*)

(*He looks up at* LISA) Lisa? You've come back. Why?

LISA. (*kneeling at* KARL's *side*) Because I am a fool.

LISA *rests her head on* KARL's *lap, he rests his head on hers and the music builds up as—*

The CURTAIN *falls.*

GO BACK FOR MURDER

Presented by Peter Saunders at the Duchess Theatre, London, on the 23rd March, 1960, with the following cast of characters:

(in the order of their appearance)

JUSTIN FOGG	Robert Urquhart
TURNBALL	Peter Hutton
CARLA	Ann Firbank
JEFF ROGERS	Mark Eden
PHILIP BLAKE	Anthony Marlowe
MEREDITH BLAKE	Laurence Hardy
LADY MELKSHAM	Lisa Daniely
MISS WILLIAMS	Margot Boyd
ANGELA WARREN	Dorothy Bromiley
CAROLINE CRALE	Ann Firbank
AMYAS CRALE	Nigel Green

Directed by HUBERT GREGG

Décor by MICHAEL WEIGHT

SYNOPSIS OF SCENES

ACT I

London

SCENE 1 A lawyer's office
SCENE 2 A City office
SCENE 3 A room in an hotel suite
SCENE 4 A bed-sitting-room
SCENE 5 A table in a restaurant

ACT II

Alderbury, a house in the West of England

Time—the present. Autumn

AUTHOR'S NOTES

Carla and her mother, Caroline Crale, are played by the same actress.

As regards the characters in Act II, PHILIP is not greatly changed, but his hair is not grey at the temples, and he is more slender, his manner is less pompous. MEREDITH is less vague, and more alert, his face is less red, and there is no grey in his hair. There is very little change in MISS WILLIAMS, except that she is also not so grey. ANGELA can have plaits, or long hair. ELSA must present the greatest change from LADY MELKSHAM, young, and eager, with her hair on her neck. CAROLINE is distinguishable from CARLA by a different hair style, as well as by an older make-up. Her voice, too, must be different, deeper in tone, and her manner more impulsive and intense.

Each scene of Act I represents a small portion of a room. In the original production the scenes were on trucks, but the whole of this Act can be quite simply staged by lighting up different parts of the stage in turn, or by cut-outs.

Act One

Scene I

SCENE: *Justin Fogg's room in the offices of Fogg, Fogg, Bamfylde and Fogg, Solicitors. An early autumn afternoon in London.*

The room is rather old-fashioned and cramped for space. The walls are lined with books. An arch up LC *leads to the rest of the building and there is a sash window across the corner up* R. *A large desk and swivel chair stand in front of the window. There is a chair* C *for visitors, and a table covered with files is against the wall* L. *There is a telephone on the desk.*

When the CURTAIN *rises, the stage is in darkness, then the* LIGHTS *come up.* JUSTIN FOGG *is seated at the desk, speaking into the telephone. The window is half-open.* JUSTIN *is a young man in the early thirties, sober, staid, but likeable.*

JUSTIN. *(into the telephone)* I quite see your point, Mrs. Ross, but the Law can't be hurried, you know——

*(*TURNBALL, *an elderly clerk, appears in the archway. He is carrying a file)*—we have to wait for their solicitors to reply to our letter . . .

*(*TURNBALL *coughs)*

(To Turnball) Come in, Turnball. *(Into the telephone)* No, it would be *most* inadvisable for you to take *any* steps yourself . . . Yes, we will keep you informed. *(He replaces the receiver)* Women!

618

(TURNBALL *places the file on the desk in front of Justin*)

Miss Le Marchant?

TURNBALL. She's here now, sir.

JUSTIN. Show her in, Turnball. I don't want any interruptions *at all*. Put anything urgent through to Mr. Grimes.

TURNBALL. Very good, sir.

(TURNBALL *exits.* JUSTIN *rises, crosses to the table* L, *selects a file, returns to his desk, sits, and puts Turnball's file in the desk drawer.* TURNBALL *re-enters and stands to one side*)

(*He announces*) Miss Le Marchant.

(CARLA *enters. She is aged twenty-one, pretty, and determined. She wears a coat and carries bag and gloves. She speaks with a Canadian accent.* TURNBALL *exits*)

JUSTIN. (*rising, moving to Carla and offering his hand*) How do you do?

CARLA. How do you do, Mr. Fogg? (*She looks at him in dismay, ignoring his outstretched hand*) But you're *young!*

(JUSTIN *looks at Carla for a moment, amused, although still formal*)

JUSTIN. Thank you. But I can assure you I'm a fully qualified solicitor.

CARLA. I'm sorry—it's just—that I expected you to be—rather old.

JUSTIN. Oh, you expected my father? He died two years ago.

CARLA. I see. I'm sorry. It was stupid of me. (*She offers him her hand*)

(JUSTIN *shakes hands with Carla*)

JUSTIN. (*indicating the chair* C) Do sit down.

(CARLA *sits* C)

(*He returns to his desk and sits at it*) Now, tell me what I can do for you.

(*There is a pause whilst* CARLA *looks at Justin, a little uncertain how to begin*)

CARLA. Do you know who I am?

JUSTIN. Miss Carla Le Marchant of Montreal.

CARLA. (*looking away*) My name isn't really Le Marchant.

JUSTIN. Oh, yes, it is. Legally.

CARLA. (*leaning forward*) So—you *do* know all about me?

JUSTIN. We have acted for Mr. Robert Le Marchant over a number of years.

CARLA. All right, then, let's get down to it. My name may be legally Le Marchant by adoption—or deed poll—or habeas corpus—or whatever the legal jargon is. (*She removes her gloves*) But I was born—(*she pauses*) Caroline Crale. Caroline was my mother's name, too. My father was Amyas Crale. Sixteen years ago my mother stood her trial for poisoning my father. They found her—guilty. (*She takes a deep breath. Defiantly*) That's right, isn't it?

JUSTIN. Yes, those are the facts.

CARLA. I only learned them six months ago.

JUSTIN. When you came of age?

CARLA. Yes. I don't think they wanted me to know. Uncle Robert and Aunt Bess, I mean. They brought me up believing my parents were killed in an accident when I was five years old. But my mother left a letter for me —to be given me when I was twenty-one, so they had to tell me all about it.

JUSTIN. Unfortunate.

CARLA. Do you mean you think they ought not to have told me?

JUSTIN. No, no, I don't mean that at all. I meant it was unfortunate for *you*—it must have been a bad shock.

CARLA. Finding out that my father was murdered and that my mother did it?

JUSTIN. (*after a pause; kindly*) There were—extenuating circumstances, you know.

CARLA. (*firmly*) It's not extenuating circumstances I'm interested in. It's facts.

JUSTIN. Yes, facts. Well, you've got your facts. Now—you can put the whole thing behind you. (*He smiles encouragingly*) It's your future that matters now, you know, not the past. (*He rises and crosses above the desk of the table* L)

CARLA. I think, before I can go forward—I've got to—go back.

(JUSTIN, *arrested and puzzled, turns to Carla*)

JUSTIN. I beg your pardon?

CARLA. It's not as simple as you make it sound. (*She pauses*)
I'm engaged—or I was engaged—to be married.

(JUSTIN *picks up the cigarette box from the table* L *and offers
it to* CARLA *who takes a cigarette*)

JUSTIN. I see. And your fiancé found out about all this?

CARLA. Of course, I told him.

JUSTIN. And he—er—reacted unfavourably? (*He replaces the
box on the table*)

CARLA. (*without enthusiasm*) Not at all. He was perfectly
splendid. Said it didn't matter at all.

JUSTIN. (*puzzled*) Well, then?

CARLA. (*looking up at Justin*) It isn't what a person *says* . . .
(*She leaves it at that*)

JUSTIN. (*after a moment*) Yes, I see. (*He lights Carla's
cigarette with the lighter from the table* L) At least, I
think I do.

CARLA. Anyone can *say* things. It's what they *feel* that
matters.

JUSTIN. Don't you think that perhaps you're super-sensitive?

CARLA. (*firmly*) No.

JUSTIN. But, my dear girl . . .

CARLA. Would *you* like to marry the daughter of a murderess?
(*She looks at Justin*)

(JUSTIN *looks down*)

(*Quietly*) You see, you wouldn't.

JUSTIN. You didn't give me time to answer. I wouldn't particularly *want* to marry the daughter of a murderer, or
of a drunkard or of a dope-fiend or of anything else
unpleasant. (*He picks up the cigarette box, crosses above
Carla to the desk and puts the lighter and cigarette box
on it*) But what the hell, if I loved a girl, she could be
the daughter of Jack the Ripper for all I cared.

CARLA. (*looking around the room*) I don't believe you would
mind as much as Jeff does. (*She shivers*)

JUSTIN. Do you find it cold?

CARLA. I think your central heating's kind of low.

JUSTIN. It's kind of non-existent, I'm afraid. (*He smiles*) I mean, we haven't any. Shall I get them to light the fire for you?

CARLA. No, please.

(JUSTIN *looks at the window, sees it is open, quickly closes it, then leans over the desk to Carla*)

JUSTIN. This Mr.—er . . . Jeff . . . ?

CARLA. You'll see him. He's coming to call for me, if you don't mind. (*She looks at her wrist-watch*) Hell, I'm wasting time. I didn't come to consult you about my love life. (*Struck*) At least, I suppose I did. I've got to find out the truth, you see.

JUSTIN. I told you just now that there were extenuating circumstances. Your mother was found guilty, but the jury made a strong recommendation to mercy. Her sentence was commuted to imprisonment.

CARLA. And she died in prison three years later.

JUSTIN. (*sitting at the desk*) Yes.

CARLA. In her letter, my mother wrote that she wanted me to know definitely that she was innocent. (*She looks defiantly at Justin*)

JUSTIN. (*unimpressed*) Yes.

CARLA. You don't believe it?

JUSTIN. (*carefully finding his words*) I think—a devoted mother—might want to do the best she could for her daughter's peace of mind.

CARLA. No, no, *no!* She wasn't like that. She never told lies.

JUSTIN. How can you know? You were a child of five when you saw her last.

CARLA. (*passionately*) I do know. My mother didn't tell lies. When she took a thorn out of my finger once, she said it would hurt. And going to the dentist. All those things. She was never one to sugar the pill. What she said was always *true*. (*She rises quickly, and turns up* L) And if she says she was innocent then she *was* innocent. You don't believe me—but it's *so*. (*She takes a handkerchief from her bag and dabs her eyes*)

JUSTIN. (*rising*) It's better, always, to face the truth.

CARLA. (*turning to him*) That is the truth.

JUSTIN. (*shaking his head; quietly*) It isn't the truth.

CARLA. How can you be so sure? Does a jury never make a mistake?

JUSTIN. There are probably several guilty people walking around free, yes, because they've been given the benefit of the doubt. But in your mother's case—there wasn't any doubt.

CARLA. You weren't there. It was your father who attended the case . . .

JUSTIN. (*interrupting*) My father was the solicitor in charge of the defence, yes.

CARLA. Well—*he* thought her innocent, didn't he?

JUSTIN. Yes. (*Embarrassed*) Yes, of course. You don't quite understand these things . . .

CARLA. (*cynically*) You mean that it was *technical* only?

(JUSTIN *is slightly at a loss how to explain*)

(*She moves* C, *in front of her chair*) But he himself, personally—what did *he* think?

JUSTIN. (*stiffly*) Really, I've no idea.

CARLA. Yes, you have. He thought she was guilty. (*She turns and faces* L) And you think so, too. (*She pauses, then turns to Justin*) But how is it that you remember it all so well?

JUSTIN. (*looking steadily at her*) I was eighteen—just going up to Oxford—not in the firm, yet—but—interested. (*Remembering*) I was in court every day.

CARLA. What did you think? Tell me. (*She sits* C. *Eagerly*) I have to know.

JUSTIN. Your mother loved your father desperately—but he gave her a raw deal—he brought his mistress into the house—subjected your mother to humiliation and insult. Mrs. Crale endured more than any woman could be expected to endure. He drove her too far. The means were to hand—try and understand. Understand and forgive. (*He crosses above the desk and stands down* L)

CARLA. I don't need to forgive. She didn't do it.

JUSTIN. (*turning to her*) Then who the devil did?

(CARLA, *taken aback, looks up at Justin*)

(*He crosses below Carla to* R) Well, that's the point, isn't it? Nobody else had the slightest motive. If you were to read up the reports of the case . . .

CARLA. I have. I've gone to the files. I've read up every single detail of the trial.

(JUSTIN *crosses behind the desk and goes through the file he put on it*)

JUSTIN. Well, then, take the facts. Aside from your mother
    and father, there were five people in the house that day.
    There were the Blakes—Philip and Meredith, two
    brothers, two of your father's closest friends. There was
    a girl of fourteen, your mother's half-sister—Angela
    Warren, and her governess—Miss—something or other,
    and there was Elsa Greer, your father's mistress—and
    there wasn't the least suspicion against any of them—
    and besides, if you'd seen . . . (*He breaks off*)
CARLA. (*eagerly*) Yes—go on . . .
JUSTIN. (*turning to the window; with feeling*) If you'd
    seen her standing there in the witness-box. So brave, so
    polite—bearing it all so patiently, but never—for one
    moment—fighting. (*He looks at Carla*) You're like her,
    you know, to look at. It might *be* her sitting there.
    There's only one difference. You're a fighter. (*He looks
    in the file*)
CARLA. (*looking out front; puzzled*) She didn't fight—why?
JUSTIN. (*crossing down* L) Montagu Depleach led for the
    defence. I think now that may have been a mistake. He
    had an enormous reputation, but he was—theatrical.
    His client had to play up. But your mother didn't play
    up.
CARLA. Why?
JUSTIN. She answered his questions with all the right answers
    —but it was like a docile child repeating a lesson—it
    didn't give old Monty his chance. He built up to the
    last question—"I ask you, Mrs. Crale, *did* you kill
    your husband?" And she said: "No—er—no, really I
    d-didn't." She stammered. It was a complete anti-climax,
    utterly unconvincing.
CARLA. And then what happened?
JUSTIN. (*crossing above Carla to the desk*) Then it was
    Asprey's turn. He was Attorney-General, later. Quiet,
    but quite deadly. Logic—after old Monty's fireworks.
    He made mincemeat of her. Brought out every damning
    detail. I—I could hardly bear it . . .
CARLA. (*studying him*) You remember it all very well.
JUSTIN. Yes.
CARLA. Why?
JUSTIN. (*taken aback*) I suppose . . .
CARLA. Yes?
JUSTIN. I was young, impressionable.
CARLA. You fell in love with my mother.

(JUSTIN *forces a laugh and sits at the desk*)

JUSTIN. Something of the kind—she was so lovely—so helpless—she'd been through so much—I—I'd have died for her. (*He smiles*) Romantic age—eighteen.

CARLA. (*frowning*) You'd have died for her—but you thought her guilty.

JUSTIN. (*firmly*) Yes, I did.

(CARLA *is really shaken. She bends her head, fighting back her tears.* TURNBALL *enters and moves to* L *of the desk*)

TURNBALL. A Mr. Rogers is here, sir, asking for Miss Le Marchant. (*He looks at Carla*)

CARLA. Jeff. (*To Turnball*) Please—ask him to wait.

TURNBALL. Certainly, Miss Le Marchant.

(TURNBALL *looks closely at Carla for a moment, then exits*)

CARLA. (*looking after Turnball*) He looked at me . . . (*She breaks off*)

JUSTIN. Turnball was at your mother's trial. He's been with us for nearly forty years.

CARLA. Please, ask him back.

(JUSTIN *rises and moves to the arch*)

JUSTIN. (*calling*) Turnball. (*He returns to* R *of the desk*)

(TURNBALL *enters*)

TURNBALL. Yes, sir?

(JUSTIN *motions to Carla.* TURNBALL *moves down* L *of Carla*)

CARLA. Mr. Turnball—I'm Carla Crale. I believe you were at my mother's trial.

TURNBALL. Yes, Miss Crale, I was. Er—I knew at once who you were.

CARLA. Because I'm so like my mother?

TURNBALL. The dead spit of her, if I may put it so.

CARLA. What did you think—at the trial? Did you think she was guilty?

(TURNBALL *looks at Justin.* JUSTIN *nods for Turnball to answer*)

TURNBALL. (*kindly*) You don't want to put it that way. She was a sweet, gentle lady—but she'd been pushed too far. As I've always seen it, she didn't rightly know what she was doing.

CARLA. (*to herself; ironically*) Extenuating circumstances. (*She looks at Justin*)

(JUSTIN *sits at the desk. After a while,* CARLA *looks back at Turnball*)

TURNBALL. (*after a pause*) That's right. The other woman—that Elsa Greer—she was a hussy if ever there was one. Sexy, if you'll excuse the word. And your father was an artist—a really great painter; I understand some of his pictures are in the Tate Gallery—and you know what artists are. That Greer girl got her hooks into him good and proper—a kind of madness it must have been. Got him so he was going to leave his wife and child for her. Don't ever blame your mother, Miss Crale. Even the gentlest lady can be pushed too far.

JUSTIN. Thank you, Turnball.

(TURNBALL *looks from Carla to Justin, then exits*)

CARLA. He thinks as you do—guilty.

JUSTIN. A gentle creature—pushed too far.

CARLA. (*acquiescing*) I—suppose so—yes. (*With sudden energy*) No! I don't believe it. I won't believe it. You—you've got to help me.

JUSTIN. To do what?

CARLA. Go back into the past and find out the truth.

JUSTIN. You won't believe the truth when you hear it.

CARLA. Because it *isn't* the truth. The defence was suicide, wasn't it?

JUSTIN. Yes.

CARLA. It *could* have been suicide. My father *could* have felt that he'd messed up everything, and that he'd be better out of it all.

JUSTIN. It was the only defence possible—but it wasn't convincing. Your father was the last man in the world to take his own life.

CARLA. (*doubtfully*) Accident?

JUSTIN. Conine—a deadly poison, introduced into a glass of beer by accident?

CARLA. All right, then. There's only one answer. Someone else.

(JUSTIN *begins to thumb through the file on his desk, which contains separate sheafs of notes on each person connected with the case*)

JUSTIN. One of the five people there in the house. Hardly Elsa Greer. She'd got your father besotted about her, and he was going to get a divorce from his wife and marry her. Philip Blake? He was devoted to your father and always had been.

CARLA. (*weakly*) Perhaps *he* was in love with Elsa Greer, too.

JUSTIN. He certainly was not. Meredith Blake? He was your father's friend, too, one of the most amiable men that ever lived. Imagination boggles at the thought of his murdering anyone.

CARLA. All right. All right. Who else do we have?

JUSTIN. Angela Warren, a schoolgirl of fourteen? And the governess, Miss Whoever her name is.

CARLA. (*quickly*) Well, what about Miss Whoever her name was?

JUSTIN. (*after a slight pause*) I see the way your mind is working. Frustration, lonely spinster, repressed love for your father. Let me tell you that Miss—Williams—(*he looks in the file*) yes, that was her name—Williams— wasn't like that, at all. She was a tartar, a woman of strong character, and sound commonsense. (*He closes the file*) Go and see her for yourself if you don't believe me.

CARLA. That's what I'm going to do.

JUSTIN. (*looking up*) What?

CARLA. (*stubbing out her cigarette in the ashtray on the desk*) I'm going to see them *all*. (*She rises*) That's what I want you to do for me. Find out where they all are. Make appointments for me with them.

JUSTIN. With what reason?

CARLA. (*crossing to* L) So that I can ask them questions, make them remember.

JUSTIN. What can they remember that could be useful after sixteen years?

CARLA. (*putting on her gloves*) Something, perhaps, that they never thought of at the time. Something that wasn't evidence—not the sort of thing that would come out in court. It will be like patchwork—a little piece of this and a little piece of that. And in the end, who knows, it might add up to something.

JUSTIN. Wishful thinking. You'll only give yourself more pain in the end. (*He puts the file in the desk drawer*)

CARLA. (*defiantly*) My mother was innocent. I'm starting from there. And you're going to help me.

JUSTIN. (*stubbornly*) That's where you're wrong. (*He rises*) I'm not going to help you to chase a will-o'-the-wisp.

(CARLA *and* JUSTIN *stare at each other.*)

(JEFF ROGERS *suddenly strides in.* TURNBALL, *indignantly protesting, follows him on.* JEFF *is a big, slick, self-satisfied man of thirty-five, good-looking and insensitive to others. He wears an overcoat and carries a hat, which he throws on to the desk*)

JEFF. (*standing above the desk*) Sorry to bust in, but all this sitting around in waiting-rooms gives me claustrophobia. (*To Carla*) Time means nothing to you, honey. (*To Justin*) I take it you're Mr. Fogg? Pleased to meet you.

(JEFF *and* JUSTIN *shake hands*)

TURNBALL. (*in the archway; to Justin*) I'm extremely sorry, sir. I was—er—quite unable to restrain this—gentleman.

JEFF. (*cheerily*) Forget it, Pop. (*He slaps Turnball on the back*)

(TURNBALL *winces*)

JUSTIN. It's quite all right, Turnball.

(TURNBALL *exits*)

JEFF. (*calling*) No hard feelings, Turnball. (*To Carla*) Well, I suppose you haven't finished your business, Carla?

CARLA. But I have. I came to ask Mr. Fogg something— (*coldly*) and he's answered me.

JUSTIN. I'm sorry.

CARLA. All right, Jeff. Let's go. (*She moves to the arch*)

JEFF. Oh, Carla——

(CARLA *stops and turns*)

—I rather wanted to have a word with Mr. Fogg, myself —about some affairs of mine here. Would you mind? I'll only be a few minutes.

(CARLA *hesitates*)

CARLA. I'll go and soothe Mr. Turnball's feelings. He was absolutely horrified by your behaviour.

(CARLA *exits*)

JEFF. (*moving to the arch and calling*) That's right, darling. Tell him I'm an overseas hick who knows no better. (*He laughs loudly and turns*) That old boy's like something out of Dickens.

JUSTIN. (*dryly*) Come in, Mr.—er . . . (*He looks unsuccessfully for Jeff's name on the band inside his hat*)

JEFF. (*not listening*) I wanted to have a word with you, Mr. Fogg. (*He moves down* C) It's this business about Carla's mother. The whole thing's given her a bit of a jolt.

JUSTIN. (*very cold and legal*) Not unnaturally.

JEFF. It's a shock to learn suddenly that your mother was a cold-blooded poisoner. I don't mind telling you that it was a bit of a jolt to *me*, too.

JUSTIN. Indeed!

(JEFF *moves and sits on the upstage end of the desk*)

JEFF. There I was, all set to marry a nice girl, uncle and aunt some of the nicest people in Montreal, a well-bred girl, money of her own, everything a man could want. And then—out of the blue—*this*.

JUSTIN. It must have upset you.

JEFF. (*with feeling*) Oh, it did.

JUSTIN. (*quietly*) Sit down, Mr.—er . . .

JEFF. What?

JUSTIN. (*nodding towards the chair* C) On the chair.

(JEFF *looks at the chair* C, *then rises, moves to the chair and sits on it*)

JEFF. Oh, I'll admit that, just at first, I thought of backing out—you know, kids—things like that?

JUSTIN. You have strong views about heredity?

JEFF. You can't do any cattle breeding without realizing that certain strains repeat themselves. "Still," I said to myself, "it isn't the girl's fault. She's a fine girl. You can't let her down. You've just got to go through with it."

(JUSTIN *picks up the box of cigarettes and lighter and crosses above Jeff to* L *of him*)

JUSTIN. Cattle breeding.

JEFF. So I told her it made no difference at all. (*He takes a packet of American cigarettes and a lighter from his pocket*)

JUSTIN. But it does?

JEFF. (*taking a cigarette from his packet*) No, no, I've put it behind me. But Carla's got some morbid idea in her head of raking the whole thing up. That's got to be stopped. (*He offers Justin a cigarette*)

JUSTIN. Yes? No. (*He puts the cigarette box quickly on the table* L)

JEFF. She'll only upset herself. Let her down lightly—but let your answer be "No." See?

(JEFF *lights his cigarette. At the same moment,* JUSTIN *flicks the lighter he holds, sees Jeff has his own, so extinguishes it quickly, and puts it on the table* L)

JUSTIN. I see.

JEFF. Of course—I suppose making all these enquiries would be quite—er—good business for your firm. You know, fees, expenses, all that . . .

JUSTIN. (*crossing below Jeff to* R) We are a firm of solicitors, you know, not inquiry agents.

JEFF. Sorry, must have explained myself clumsily.

JUSTIN. Yes.

JEFF. What I want to say is—I'll stump up the necessary—but drop it.

JUSTIN. (*moving behind the desk*) You will excuse me, Mr.—er . . . but Miss Le Marchant is my client.

JEFF. (*rising*) Yep, well, if you're acting for Carla, you must agree that it's best for her not to go harrowing herself raking up the past. Make her give it up. Once we're married, she'll never think of it again.

JUSTIN. And will you never think of it again?

JEFF. That's a good question. Yes, I dare say I'll have one or two nasty moments.

JUSTIN. If the coffee should taste bitter . . . ?

JEFF. That sort of thing.

JUSTIN. Which won't be very pleasant for her.

JEFF. (*cheerily*) Well, what can a man do? You can't undo the past. Glad to have met you, Fogg. (*He offers his hand*)

(JUSTIN *looks at Jeff's hand, then picks up Jeff's hat from the desk and puts it in the outstretched hand.* JEFF *exits.* JUSTIN *turns to the window, opens it wide, then lifts the telephone receiver*)

JUSTIN. (*into the telephone*) Has Miss Le Marchant left yet? . . . Well, ask her to come back for a moment. I shan't keep her long. (*He replaces the receiver, crosses to the table* L, *takes a cigarette from the box, lights it, then returns to* R *of the desk*)

(CARLA *enters*)

CARLA. (*looking coldly at Justin*) Yes?
JUSTIN. I've changed my mind.
CARLA. (*startled*) What?
JUSTIN. That's all. I've changed my mind. I will fix up an appointment for you to see Mr. Philip Blake here. I will let you know when.

(CARLA *smiles*)

Go on. Don't keep Mr.—er . . . don't keep him waiting. He wouldn't be pleased. You'll be hearing from me. (*He ushers Carla to the arch*)

(CARLA *exits*)

(*He goes to the desk and lifts the receiver. Into the telephone*) Get me Kellway, Blake and Leverstein, will you? I want to speak to Mr. Philip Blake personally. (*He replaces the receiver*) Cattle breeding!

The lights dim to BLACK-OUT

Scene II

SCENE: *Justin Fogg's room.*

It is a very handsome room. A door up R *leads to the outer office. Up* L *is a cupboard for drinks, let into the wall. A large and ornate desk is* L *with a damask-covered swivel chair behind it. A chair, to match, for visitors is down* R. *There are shaded, electric wall-brackets* R *and* L. *On the desk there is an intercom in addition to the telephone.*

When the LIGHTS *come up,* PHILIP BLAKE *is sitting at the desk, smoking and reading the "Financial Times." He is a good-looking man of fifty odd, grey at the temples, with a slight paunch. He is self-important, with traces of nervous irritability. He is very sure of himself. The intercom buzzes.* PHILIP *presses the switch.*

PHILIP. *(into the intercom)* Yes?
VOICE. *(through the intercom)* Miss Le Marchant's here, Mr. Blake.
PHILIP. Ask her to come in.
VOICE. Yes, Mr. Blake.

(PHILIP *releases the switch, frowns, folds his newspaper and lays it on the desk, rises, moves down* L *of the desk, turns and faces the door. He shows slight traces of uneasiness while he waits.* CARLA *enters. She wears a different coat, and carries different gloves and handbag)*

PHILIP. Good Lord.

(PHILIP *and* CARLA *look at each other for a moment, then* CARLA *closes the door and moves down* C)

Well, so it's Carla. *(He recovers himself and shakes hands with her)* Little Carla! *(With rather forced geniality)* You were—what—five years old when I saw you last.
CARLA. Yes. I must have been just about. *(She screws up her eyes)* I don't think I remember you . . .
PHILIP. I was never much of a children's man. Never knew what to say to them. Sit down, Carla.

(CARLA *sits on the chair down* R *and places her handbag on the floor beside the chair)*

(He offers the box of cigarettes from the desk) Cigarette?

(CARLA *declines)*

(He replaces the box on the desk, moves behind the desk and looks at his watch) I haven't much time, but . . . *(He sits at the desk)*
CARLA. I know you're a terribly busy person. It's good of you to see me.

PHILIP. Not at all. You're the daughter of one of my oldest
and closest friends. You remember your father?

CARLA. Yes. Not very clearly.

PHILIP. You should. Amyas Crale oughtn't to be forgotten.
(*He pauses*) Now, what's this all about? This lawyer
chap—Fogg—son of old Andrew Fogg, I suppose——

(CARLA *nods*)

—wasn't very clear about why you wanted to see me.
(*There is a trace of sarcasm in his voice during the
following sentence*) But I gathered that it wasn't just a
case of looking up your father's old friends?

CARLA. No.

PHILIP. He told me that you'd only recently learnt the facts
about your father's death. Is that right?

CARLA. Yes.

PHILIP. Pity, really, you ever had to hear about it at all.

CARLA. (*after a pause; firmly*) Mr. Blake, when I came in
just now you were startled. You said "Good Lord!"
Why?

PHILIP. Well, I . . .

CARLA. Did you think, just for the moment, that it was my
mother standing there?

PHILIP. There is an amazing resemblance. It startled me.

CARLA. You—you didn't like her?

PHILIP. (*dryly*) Could you expect me to? She killed my best
friend.

CARLA. (*stung*) It *could* have been suicide.

PHILIP. Don't run away with that idea. Amyas would never
have killed himself. He enjoyed life far too much.

CARLA. He was an artist, he could have had temperamental
ups and downs.

PHILIP. He didn't have that kind of temperament. Nothing
morbid or neurotic about Amyas. He had his faults, yes
—he chased women, I'll admit—but most of his affairs
were quite short lived. He always went back to Caroline.

CARLA. What fun that must have been for her!

PHILIP. She'd known him since she was twelve years old. We
were all brought up together.

CARLA. I know so little. Tell me.

PHILIP. (*sitting back comfortably in his chair*) She used to
come and stay at Alderbury for the holidays with the
Crales. My family had the big house next door. We all

ran wild together. Meredith, my elder brother, and Amyas were much of an age. I was a year or two younger. Caroline had no money of her own, you know. I was a younger son, out of the running, but both Meredith and Amyas were quite good catches.

CARLA. How cold-blooded you make her sound.

PHILIP. She *was* cold-blooded. Oh, she appeared impulsive, but behind it there was a cold calculating devil. And she had a wicked temper. You know what she did to her baby half-sister?

CARLA. (*quickly*) No?

PHILIP. Her mother had married again, and all the attention went to the new baby—Angela. Caroline was jealous as hell. She tried to kill the baby.

CARLA. No!

PHILIP. Went for her with a pair of scissors, I believe. Ghastly business. The child was marked for life.

CARLA. (*outraged*) You make her sound a—a monster!

PHILIP. (*shrugging*) Jealously is the devil.

CARLA. (*studying him*) You hated her—didn't you?

PHILIP. (*startled*) That's putting it rather strongly.

CARLA. No, it's true.

PHILIP. (*stubbing out his cigarette*) I suppose I'm bitter. (*He rises, moves to* R *of the desk and sits on the downstage corner of it*) But it seems to me that you've come over here with the idea in your head that your mother was an injured innocent. That isn't so. There's Amyas's side of it, too. He was your father, girl, and he loved life . . .

CARLA. I know. I know all that.

PHILIP. You've got to see this thing as it was. Caroline was no good. (*He pauses*) She poisoned her husband. And what I can't forget, and never will forget, is that *I* could have saved him.

CARLA. How?

PHILIP. My brother Meredith had a strange hobby. He used to fiddle about with herbs and hemlock and stuff and Caroline had stolen one of his patent brews.

CARLA. How did you know that it was *she* who had taken it?

PHILIP. (*grimly*) I knew all right. And I was fool enough to hang about waiting to talk it over with Meredith. Why I hadn't the sense to realize that *Caroline* wouldn't wait, I can't think. She'd pinched the stuff to use—and by God, she used it at the first opportunity.

CARLA. You *can't* be sure it was she who took it.

PHILIP. My dear girl, she *admitted* taking it. Said she'd taken it to do away with herself.

CARLA. That's possible, isn't it?

PHILIP. Is it? (*Caustically*) Well, she *didn't* do away with herself.

(CARLA *shakes her head. There is a silence*)

(*He rises and makes an effort to resume a normal manner*) Have a glass of sherry? (*He moves below and* L *of the desk to the cupboard up* L, *takes out a decanter of sherry and a glass and puts them on the desk*) Now, I suppose I've upset you? (*He pours a glass of sherry*)

CARLA. I've got to find out about things.

PHILIP. (*crossing and handing the glass to Carla*) There was a lot of sympathy for her at the trial, of course. (*He moves behind the desk*) Amyas behaved badly, I'll admit, bringing the Greer girl down to Alderbury. (*He replaces the decanter in the cupboard*) And she *was* pretty insolent to Caroline.

CARLA. Did you like her?

PHILIP. (*guardedly*) Young Elsa? Not particularly. (*He turns to the cupboard, takes out a bottle of whisky and a glass and puts them on the desk*) She wasn't my type, damnably attractive, of course. Predatory. Grasping at everything she wanted. (*He pours whisky for himself*) All the same, I think she'd have suited Amyas better than Caroline did. (*He replaces the bottle in the cupboard*)

CARLA. Weren't my mother and father happy together?

PHILIP. (*with a laugh*) They never stopped having rows. His married life would have been one long *hell* if it hadn't been for the way of escape his painting gave him. (*He squirts soda into his drink and sits at the desk*)

CARLA. How did he meet Elsa?

PHILIP. (*vaguely*) Some Chelsea party or other. (*He smiles*) Came along to me—told me he'd met a marvellous girl —absolutely different from any girl he'd met before. Well, I'd heard *that* often enough. He'd fall for a girl like a ton of bricks, and a month later, when you mentioned her, he'd stare at you and wonder who the hell you were talking about. But it didn't turn out that way with Elsa. (*He raises his glass*) Good luck, m'dear. (*He drinks*)

(CARLA *sips her sherry*)

CARLA. She's married now, isn't she?

PHILIP. (dryly) She's run through three husbands. A test pilot who crashed himself, some explorer chap whom she got bored with. She's married now to old Lord Melksham, a dreamy peer who writes mystical poetry. I should say she's about had *him* by now. (*He drinks*)

CARLA. Would she have gotten tired of my father, I wonder?

PHILIP. Who knows?

CARLA. I must meet her.

PHILIP. Can't you let things go?

CARLA. (*rising and putting her glass on the desk*) No, I've got to understand.

PHILIP. (*rising*) Determined, aren't you?

CARLA. Yes, I'm a fighter. But my mother—wasn't.

(*The intercom buzzes.* CARLA *turns and picks up her bag*)

PHILIP. Where did you get that idea? Caroline was a terrific fighter. (*He presses the switch. Into the intercom*) Yes?

VOICE. (*through the intercom*) Mr. Foster's here, Mr. Blake.

PHILIP. Tell him I won't keep him a moment.

VOICE. Yes, sir.

(PHILIP *releases the switch*)

CARLA. (*struck*) Was she? Was she really? But—she didn't fight at her trial.

PHILIP. No.

CARLA. Why didn't she?

PHILIP. Well, since she knew she was guilty . . . (*He rises*)

CARLA. (*angrily*) She wasn't guilty!

PHILIP. (*angrily*) You're obstinate, aren't you? After all I've told you!

CARLA. You still hate her. Although she's been dead for years. Why?

PHILIP. I've told you . . .

CARLA. Not the real reason. There's something else.

PHILIP. I don't think so.

CARLA. You hate her—now why? I shall have to find out. Good-bye, Mr. Blake. Thank you.

PHILIP. Good-bye.

(CARLA *moves to the door and exits, leaving the door open*)

(*He stares after her for a moment, slightly perplexed, then he closes the door, sits at the desk and presses the*

intercom switch. Into the intercom) Ask Mr. Foster to
come in.
VOICE. (*through the intercom*) Yes, sir.

PHILIP *sits back in his chair and picks up his drink as*

the lights dim to BLACK-OUT

Scene III

SCENE: *The sitting-room of an hotel suite.*

There is an arch back C *leading to a small entrance
hall with a door* L. *There is a long window* R. *A french
settee stands* L *with an armchair to match* R. *In front
of the settee there is a long stool, and a small table
with a house telephone stands under the window. There
are electric wall-brackets* R *and* L *of the arch. In the hall
there is a console table and a row of coathooks on the
wall* R.

When the LIGHTS *come up,* JUSTIN *is by the armchair,
placing some files in his brief-case. His coat is on the
settee.* CARLA *enters the hall from* L, *puts her gloves and
handbag on the hall table, removes her coat and hangs
it on the hooks.*

CARLA. Oh, I'm so glad you're here.
JUSTIN. (*surprised and pleased*) Really? (*He put his brief-
case on the armchair and moves down* R) Meredith
Blake will be here at three o'clock.
CARLA. Good! What about Lady Melksham?
JUSTIN. She didn't answer my letter.
CARLA. Perhaps she's away?
JUSTIN. (*crossing to* L *of the arch*) No, she's not away. I
took steps to ascertain that she's at home.
CARLA. I suppose that means that she's going to ignore the
whole thing.
JUSTIN. Oh, I wouldn't say that. She'll come all right.
CARLA. (*moving* C) What makes you so sure?
JUSTIN. Well, women usually . . .

CARLA. (*with a touch of mischief*) I see—you're an authority on women.

JUSTIN. (*stiffly*) Only in the legal sense.

CARLA. And—strictly in the legal sense . . . ?

JUSTIN. Women usually want to satisfy their curiosity.

(CARLA *sees Justin's coat on the settee, crosses and picks it up*)

CARLA. I really do like you—you make me feel much better. (*She moves towards the hooks*)

(*The telephone rings*)

(*She thrusts the coat at Justin, crosses and lifts the telephone receiver. Into the telephone*) Hello? . . .

(JUSTIN *hangs his coat in the hall*)

Oh, ask him to come up, will you? (*She replaces the receiver and turns to Justin*) It's Meredith Blake. Is he like his hateful brother?

JUSTIN. (*moving* C) A very different temperament, I should say. Do you need to feel better?

CARLA. What?

JUSTIN. You said just now I made you feel better. Do you need to feel better?

CARLA. Sometimes I do. (*She gestures to him to sit on the settee*)

(JUSTIN *sits on the settee*)

I didn't realize what I was letting myself in for.

JUSTIN. I was afraid of that.

CARLA. I could still—give it all up—go back to Canada—forget. Shall I?

JUSTIN. (*quickly*) No! No—er—not now. You've got to go on.

CARLA. (*sitting in the armchair*) That's not what you advised in the first place.

JUSTIN. You hadn't started then.

CARLA. You still think—that my mother was guilty, don't you?

JUSTIN. I can't see any other solution.

CARLA. And yet you want me to go on?

JUSTIN. I want you to go on until *you* are satisfied.

(*There is a knock on the hall door.* CARLA *and* JUSTIN *rise.* CARLA *goes to the hall, opens the door and steps back.*

JUSTIN *crosses to* R *of the armchair and faces the hall.*
MEREDITH BLAKE *enters the hall from* L. *He is a pleasant,
rather vague man with a thatch of grey hair. He gives
the impression of being rather ineffectual and irresolute.
He wears country tweeds with hat, coat and muffler*)

MEREDITH. Carla. My dear Carla. (*He takes her hands*) How
time flies. May I? (*He kisses her*) It seems incredible
that the little girl I knew should have grown up into a
young lady. How like your mother you are, my dear. My
word!

CARLA. (*slightly embarrassed; gesturing to Justin*) Do you
know Mr. Fogg?

MEREDITH. My word, my word! (*He pulls himself together*)
What? (*To Justin*) Ah, yes, I knew your father, didn't
I? (*He steps into the room*)

(CARLA *closes the door then moves into the room and stands*
L *of the arch*)

JUSTIN. (*moving to* R *of Meredith*) Yes, sir. (*He shakes
hands*) May I take your coat?

MEREDITH. (*unbuttoning his coat; to Carla*) And now—tell
me all about yourself. You're over from the States—

(JUSTIN *takes Meredith's hat*)

—thank you—no, Canada. For how long?

CARLA. I'm not quite sure—yet.

(JUSTIN *eyes Carla*)

MEREDITH. But you are definitely making your home overseas?

CARLA. Well—I'm thinking of getting married.

MEREDITH. (*removing his coat*) Oh, to a Canadian?

CARLA. Yes.

(MEREDITH *hands his coat and muffler to* JUSTIN *who hangs
them with the hat, in the hall*)

MEREDITH. Well, I hope he's a nice fellow and good enough
for you, my dear.

CARLA. Naturally I think so. (*She gestures to Meredith to
sit in the armchair*)

(MEREDITH *goes to sit in the armchair, sees Justin's brief-case
and picks it up.* JUSTIN *moves above the armchair*)

MEREDITH. Good. If you're happy, then I'm very happy for you. And so would your mother have been.

CARLA. (*sitting on the settee at the upstage end*) Do you know that my mother left a letter for me in which she said she was innocent?

MEREDITH. (*turning and looking at Carla; sharply*) Your mother wrote *that*?

CARLA. Does it surprise you so much?

(JUSTIN *sees* MEREDITH *is uncertain what to do with the brief-case and offers to take it*)

MEREDITH. Well, I shouldn't have thought Caroline . . . (*He hands the brief-case to Justin*)

(JUSTIN *puts the brief-case on the table* R)

I don't know—I suppose she felt—(*he sits in the arm-chair*) it would distress you less . . .

CARLA. (*passionately*) It doesn't occur to you that what she wrote me might be true?

MEREDITH. Well, yes—of course. If she solemnly wrote that when she was dying—well, it stands to reason that it must be true—doesn't it? (*He looks up at Justin for support*)

(*There is a pause*)

CARLA. What a rotten liar you are. (*She rises*)

MEREDITH. (*shocked*) Carla!

(CARLA *goes into the hall and picks up her handbag*)

CARLA. Oh, I know it was meant to be kind. But kindness doesn't really help. I want you to tell me all about it. (*She steps into the room and searches in her bag*)

MEREDITH. You know the facts—(*to Justin*) doesn't she?

JUSTIN. (*crossing down* L) Yes, sir, she does.

MEREDITH. Going over them will be painful—and quite un-profitable. Better let the whole thing rest. You're young and pretty and engaged to be married and that's all that really matters.

(JUSTIN *sees* CARLA *searching in her bag, takes out his ciga-rette case and offers it to her.* MEREDITH *takes a snuff-box from his waistcoat pocket*)

JUSTIN. (*to Carla*) You looking for one of these?

MEREDITH. (*offering the snuff-box to Carla*) Have a pinch

of . . . No, I don't suppose you do, but I'll . . . (*He offers the box to Justin*) Oh, will you?

(JUSTIN *declines.* CARLA *takes a cigarette from* JUSTIN *who also takes one*)

CARLA. I've asked your brother Philip, you know. (*She puts her bag on the stool*)

(JUSTIN *lights the cigarettes with his lighter*)

MEREDITH. Oh—Philip! You wouldn't get much from him. Philip's a busy man. So busy making money, that he hasn't time for anything else. If he did remember anything, he'd remember it all wrong. (*He sniffs the snuff*)

CARLA. (*sitting on the settee at the upstage end*) Then *you* tell me.

(JUSTIN *sits on the settee at the downstage end*)

MEREDITH. (*guardedly*) Well—you'd have to understand a bit about your father—first.

CARLA. (*matter-of-fact*) He had affairs with other women and made my mother very unhappy.

MEREDITH. Well—er—yes—(*he sniffs*) but these affairs of his weren't really important until Elsa came along.

CARLA. He was painting her?

MEREDITH. Yes, my word—(*he sniffs*) I can see her now. Sitting on the terrace where she posed. Dark—er—shorts and a yellow shirt. "Portrait of a girl in a yellow shirt," that's what he was going to call it. It was one of the best things Amyas ever did. (*He puts his snuff-box in his pocket*)

CARLA. What happened to the picture?

MEREDITH. I've got it. I bought it with the furniture. I bought the house, too. Alderbury. It adjoins my property, you know. I didn't want it turned into a building estate. Everything was sold by the executors and the proceeds put in trust for you. But you know that, I expect.

CARLA. I didn't know you'd bought the house.

MEREDITH. Well, I did. It's let to a Youth Hostel. But I keep one wing just as it was, for myself. I sold off most of the furniture . . .

CARLA. But you kept the picture. Why?

MEREDITH. (*as though defending himself*) I tell you, it was the best thing Amyas ever did. My word, yes! It goes to the nation when I die. (*He pauses*)

(CARLA *stares at Meredith*)

Well, I'll try to tell you what you want to know. Amyas brought Elsa down there—ostensibly because he was painting her. She hated the pretence. She—she was so wildly in love with him and wanted to have it out with Caroline then and there. She felt in a false position. I—I understood her point of view.

CARLA. (*coldly*) You sound most sympathetic towards her.

MEREDITH. (*horrified*) Not at all. My sympathies were all with Caroline. I'd always been—well, in love with Caroline. I asked her to marry me—but she married Amyas instead. Oh, I can understand it—he was a brilliant person and very attractive to women, but he didn't look after her the way I'*d* have looked after her. I remained her friend.

CARLA. And yet you believed she committed murder?

MEREDITH. She didn't really know what she was doing. There was a terrific scene—she was overwrought . . .

CARLA. Yes?

MEREDITH. And that same afternoon she took the conine from my laboratory. But I swear there was no thought of murder in her mind when she took it—she had some idea of—of—doing away with herself.

CARLA. But as your brother Philip said, "She *didn't* do away with herself."

MEREDITH. Things always look better the next morning. And there was a lot of fuss going on, getting Angela's things ready for school—that was Angela Warren, Caroline's half-sister. She was a real little devil, always scrapping with someone, or playing tricks. She and Amyas were forever fighting, but he was very fond of her—and Caroline adored her.

CARLA. (*quickly*) After once trying to kill her?

MEREDITH. (*looking at Carla; quickly*) I've always been sure that that story was grossly exaggerated. Most children are jealous of the new baby.

CARLA. (*after puffing at her cigarette*) My father was found dead—after lunch, wasn't he?

MEREDITH. Yes. We left him on the terrace, painting. He often wouldn't go in to lunch. The glass of beer that Caroline had brought him was there by his side—empty. I suppose the stuff was already beginning to work. There's no pain—just a slow—paralysis. Yes.

When we came out after lunch—he was dead. The whole thing was a nightmare.

CARLA. (*rising; upset*) A nightmare . . .

MEREDITH. (*rising*) I'm sorry, my dear. I didn't want to talk about it to you. (*He looks at Justin*)

CARLA. If I could go down there—to where it happened. Could I?

MEREDITH. Of course, my dear. You're only to say the word.

CARLA. (*moving c and turning to face Justin*) If we could go over it there—all of us . . .

MEREDITH. What do you mean by all of us?

CARLA. (*turning to face Meredith*) Your brother Philip and you, and the governess, and Angela Warren, and—yes—even Elsa.

MEREDITH. I hardly think Elsa would come. She's married, you know.

CARLA. (*wryly*) Several times, I hear.

MEREDITH. She's changed very much. Philip saw her at a theatre one night.

CARLA. Nothing lasts. You loved my mother once—but *that* didn't last, did it? (*She stubs out her cigarette in the ashtray on the stool*)

MEREDITH. What?

CARLA. (*crossing down L*) Everything's different from what I thought it would be. I can't seem to find my way.

(JUSTIN *rises*)

If I could go down to Alderbury . . .

MEREDITH. You're welcome at any time, my dear. Now, I'm afraid I must . . .

(CARLA *gazes out front*)

JUSTIN. (*moving to the hall*) I'll get your coat, sir. (*He sees Carla is in a brown study*) Carla's most grateful to you, sir. (*He takes Meredith's coat, hat and muffler from the hooks*)

CARLA. (*recollecting herself*) Oh, yes. Yes, thank you for coming.

(MEREDITH *goes to the hall where* JUSTIN *helps him on with his coat*)

MEREDITH. Carla, the more I think of it all . . .

CARLA. Yes?

MEREDITH. (*moving c*) I believe, you know, that it's quite

possible Amyas did commit suicide. He may have felt
more remorseful than we know. (*He looks hopefully at
Carla*)

CARLA. (*unconvinced*) It's a nice thought.

MEREDITH. Yes, yes—well, good-bye, my dear.

CARLA. Good-bye.

MEREDITH. (*taking his hat from Justin*) Good-bye, Mr. Fogg.

JUSTIN. (*opening the door*) Good-bye, sir.

MEREDITH. (*mumbling*) Good-bye. Good-bye.

(MEREDITH *exits.* JUSTIN *closes the door and moves* c)

CARLA. Well!

JUSTIN. Well!

CARLA. What a fool!

JUSTIN. Quite a nice kindly fool.

(*The telephone rings*)

CARLA. (*crossing to the telephone*) He doesn't believe anything of the sort. (*She lifts the receiver*) Why does he
say so? (*Into the telephone*) Yes? . . . Yes. I see. (*She
replaces the receiver. Disappointed*) She's not coming.

JUSTIN. Lady Melksham?

CARLA. Yes. Unavoidably prevented.

(JUSTIN *goes into the hall and collects his coat*)

JUSTIN. Don't worry, we'll think of something.

CARLA. (*looking out of the window*) I've got to see her, she's
the hub of it all.

JUSTIN. (*moving* c *and putting on his coat*) You're going
to take tea with Miss Williams, aren't you?

CARLA. (*flatly*) Yes.

JUSTIN. (*rather eagerly*) Want me to come with you?

CARLA. (*without interest*) No, there's no need.

JUSTIN. Maybe there'll be a letter from Angela Warren in
tomorrow's post. I'll phone you if I may?

CARLA. (*still looking through the window*) Please.

JUSTIN. (*after a pause*) What a fool your father was.

(CARLA *turns*)

Not to recognize quality when he had it.

CARLA. What do you mean?

JUSTIN. Elsa Greer was pretty brash, you know, crude allure,
crude sex, crude hero worship.

CARLA. Hero worship?

JUSTIN. Yes. Would she have made a dead set at your father if he hadn't been a celebrated painter? Look at her subsequent husbands. Always attracted by a somebody— a big noise in the world—never the man himself. But Caroline, your mother, would have recognized quality in a—(*he pauses and self-consciously gives a boyish smile*) well—even in a solicitor.

(CARLA *picks up Justin's brief-case and looks at him with interest*)

CARLA. I believe you're still in love with my mother. (*She holds out the brief-case*)

JUSTIN. Oh, no. (*He takes the brief-case and smiles*) I move with the times, you know.

(CARLA *is taken aback, but is pleased and smiles*)

Good-bye.

(JUSTIN *exits.* CARLA *looks after him, taking in what he has said. The telephone rings.* CARLA *lifts the receiver. The light starts to dim as twilight falls*)

CARLA. (*into the telephone*) Hullo? . . . Yes . . . Oh, it's out, Jeff . . . (*She takes the whole instrument and sits in the armchair with it, tucking one leg under her*) It may be a silly waste of time, but it's my time and if I . . . (*She straightens the seam of her stocking*) What? . . . (*Crossly*) You're quite wrong about Justin. He's a good friend—which is more than you are . . . All right, so I'm quarrelling . . . No, I don't want to dine with you . . . I don't want to dine with you anywhere.

(ELSA MELKSHAM *enters the hall from* L, *quietly closes the door and stands in the hall, looking at Carla.* ELSA *is tall, beautiful, very made-up and extremely smart. She wears hat and gloves, and a red velvet coat over a black dress, and carries her handbag*)

At the moment your stock is pretty low with me. (*She bangs the receiver down, rises and puts the instrument on the table* R)

ELSA. Miss Le Marchant—or do I say "Miss Crale"?

(CARLA, *startled, turns quickly*)

CARLA. So you've come after all?

ELSA. I always meant to come. I just waited until your legal
   adviser had faded.

CARLA. You don't like lawyers?

ELSA. I prefer, occasionally, to talk woman to woman. Let's
   have some light. (*She switches on the wall-brackets by
   the switch* L *of the arch then moves down* C *and looks
   hard at Carla*) Well, you don't look very much like the
   child I remember.

CARLA. (*simply*) I'm like my mother.

ELSA. (*coldly*) Yes. That doesn't particularly prejudice me in
   your favour. Your mother was one of the most loath-
   some women I've ever known.

CARLA. (*hotly*) I've no doubt she felt the same about you.

ELSA. (*smiling*) Oh, yes, the feeling was mutual. (*She sits on
   the settee at the upstage end*) The trouble with Caroline
   was that she wasn't a very good loser.

CARLA. Did you expect her to be?

ELSA. (*removing her gloves; amused*) Really, you know, I
   believe I did. I must have been incredibly young, and
   naïve. Because I myself couldn't understand clinging on
   to a man who didn't want me, I was quite shocked that
   she didn't feel the same. But I never dreamt that she'd
   kill Amyas rather than let me have him.

CARLA. She didn't kill him.

ELSA. (*without interest*) She killed him all right. She
   poisoned him more or less in front of my eyes—in a
   glass of iced beer. And I never dreamed—never guessed
   . . . (*With a complete change of manner*) You think
   at the time that you will never forget—that the pain
   will always be there. And then—it's all gone—gone—like
   that. (*She snaps her fingers*)

CARLA. (*sitting in the armchair*) How old were you?

ELSA. Nineteen. But I was no injured innocent. Amyas Crale
   didn't seduce a trusting young girl. It wasn't like that
   at all. I met him at a party and I fell for him right away.
   I knew he was the only man in the world for me. (*She
   smiles*) I think he felt the same.

CARLA. Yes.

ELSA. I asked him to paint me. He said he didn't do portraits.
   I said what about the portrait he'd done of Marna
   Vadaz, the dancer. He said special circumstances had
   led to that. I knew they'd had an affair together. I said,
   "I *want* you to paint me." He said, "You know what'll

happen? I shall make love to you." I said, "Why not?" And he said, "I'm a married man, and I'm very fond of my wife." I said that now we'd got that settled, when should we start the sittings? He took me by the shoulders and turned me towards the light and looked me over in a considering sort of way. Then he said, "I've often thought of painting a flight of outrageously coloured Australian macaws alighting on St. Paul's Cathedral. If I painted you in your flamboyant youth against a background of nice traditional English scenery, I believe I'd get the same effect." (*She pauses. Quickly*) So it was settled.

CARLA. And you went down to Alderbury.

(ELSA *rises, removes her coat, puts it on the downstage end of the settee and moves* C)

ELSA. Yes. Caroline was charming. She could be, you know. Amyas was very circumspect. (*She smiles*) Never said a word to me his wife couldn't have overheard. I was polite and formal. Underneath, though, we both knew ... (*She breaks off*)

CARLA. Go on.

ELSA. (*putting her hands on her hips*) After ten days he told me I was to go back to London.

CARLA. Yes?

ELSA. I said, "The picture isn't finished." He said, "It's barely begun. The truth is I can't paint you, Elsa." I asked him why, and he said that I knew very well "why" and that's why I'd got to clear out.

CARLA. So—you went back to London?

ELSA. Yes, I went. (*She moves up* C *and turns*) I didn't write to him. I didn't answer his letters. He held out for a week. And then—he came. I told him that it was fate and it was no use struggling against it, and he said, "You haven't struggled much, have you, Elsa?" I said I hadn't struggled at all. It was wonderful and more frightening than mere happiness. (*She frowns*) If only we'd kept away—if only we hadn't gone back.

CARLA. Why did you?

ELSA. The unfinished picture. It haunted Amyas. (*She sits on the settee at the upstage end*) But things were different this time—Caroline had caught on. I wanted to have the whole thing on an honest basis. All Amyas would say was, "To hell with honesty. I'm painting a picture."

(CARLA *laughs*)

Why do you laugh?

CARLA. (*rising and turning to the window*) Because I know just how he felt.

ELSA. (*angrily*) How should *you* know?

CARLA. (*simply*) Because I'm his daughter, I suppose.

ELSA. (*distantly*) Amyas's daughter. (*She looks at Carla with a new appraisement*)

CARLA. (*turning and crossing above the armchair to* c) I've just begun to know that. I hadn't thought about it before. I came over because I wanted to find out just what happened sixteen years ago. I am finding out. I'm beginning to know the people—what they felt, what they are like. The whole thing's coming alive, bit by bit.

ELSA. Coming alive? (*Bitterly*) I wish it would.

CARLA. My father—you—Philip Blake—Meredith Blake. (*She crosses down* L) And there are two more. Angela Warren . . .

ELSA. Angela? Oh, yes. She's quite a celebrity in her way— one of those tough women who travel to inaccessible places and write books about it. She was only a tiresome teenager then.

CARLA. (*turning*) How did *she* feel about it all?

ELSA. (*uninterested*) I don't know. They hustled her away, I think. Some idea of Caroline's that contact with murder would damage her adolescent mind—though I don't know why Caroline should have bothered about damage to her mind when she had already damaged her face for her. When I heard that story I ought to have realized what Caroline was capable of, and when I actually *saw* her take the poison . . .

CARLA. (*quickly*) You *saw* her?

ELSA. Yes. Meredith was waiting to lock up his laboratory. Caroline was the last to come out. I was just before her. I looked over my shoulder and saw her standing in front of a shelf with a small bottle in her hand. Of course, she might only have been looking at it. How was I to know?

CARLA. (*crossing to* c) But you suspected?

ELSA. I thought she meant it for herself.

CARLA. Suicide? And you didn't *care*?

ELSA. (*calmly*) I thought it might be the best way out.

CARLA. (*crossing above the armchair to the window*) Oh, no . . .

ELSA. Her marriage to Amyas had been a failure from the start—if she'd really cared for him as much as she pretended, she'd have given him a divorce. There was plenty of money—and she'd probably have married someone else who would have suited her better.

CARLA. How easily you arrange other people's lives. (*She moves down* R) Meredith Blake says I may come down to Alderbury. I want to get everyone there. Will you come?

ELSA. (*arrested, but attracted by the idea*) Come down to Alderbury?

CARLA. (*eagerly*) I want to go over the whole thing on the spot. I want to see it as though it were happening all over again.

ELSA. Happening all over again . . .

CARLA. (*politely*) If it's too painful for you . . .

ELSA. There are worse things than pain. (*Harshly*) It's forgetting that's so horrible—it's as though you were dead yourself. (*Angrily*) You—stand there so damned young and innocent—what do you know about loving a man? I loved Amyas. (*With fire*) He was so alive, so full of life and vigour, such a man. And she put an end to all that—your mother. (*She rises*) She put an end to Amyas so that I shouldn't have him. And they didn't even hang her. (*She pauses. In an ordinary tone*) I'll come to Alderbury. I'll join your circus. (*She picks up her coat and holds it out to Carla*)

(CARLA *crosses to Elsa and helps her on with her coat*)

Philip, Meredith—Angela Warren—all four of us.

CARLA. Five.

ELSA. Five?

CARLA. There was a governess.

ELSA. (*collecting her bag and gloves from the settee*) Oh, yes, the governess. Very disapproving of me and Amyas. Devoted to Caroline.

CARLA. Devoted to my mother—*she'll* tell me. I'm going to see her next. (*She goes into the hall and opens the door*)

ELSA. (*moving to the hall*) Perhaps you'll get your legal *friend* to telephone me, will you?

(ELSA *exits.* CARLA *closes the door and moves* C)

CARLA. The governess!

The LIGHTS *dim to* BLACK-OUT

Scene IV

SCENE: *Miss Williams' bed-sitting-room.*

It is an attic room with a small window in the sloping roof L. *The door is presumed to be in the "fourth wall." There is a fireplace, fitted with a gas fire, back* C. *There is a divan with cover and cushions* R. *A gate-legged table stands under the window. A small table with a table-lamp on it is* R *of the fireplace. Upright chairs stand* L *of the fireplace and down* L *and there is an old-fashioned armchair with a footstool under it,* C. *An electric kettle is plugged into the skirting,* R *of the fireplace.*

When the LIGHTS *come up, the lamp is on, but the window curtains are not yet closed. A tray of tea for two is on the table* L. *The kettle is steaming and the teapot is beside it. The gas fire is lit.* MISS WILLIAMS *is seated in the armchair* C. *She is sixty odd, intelligent, with clear enunciation and a pedagogic manner. She wears a tweed skirt and blouse, with a cardigan and a scarf round her shoulders.* CARLA *is seated on the divan, looking through a photograph album. She wears a brown dress.*

CARLA. I *do* remember you. It's all coming back. I didn't think I did.

MISS WILLIAMS. You were only five years old.

CARLA. You looked after me?

MISS WILLIAMS. No, you were not my responsibility. I was in charge of Angela. Ah, the kettle's boiling. (*She rises, picks up the teapot and makes the tea*) Now, are you going to be happy there, dear?

CARLA. I'm fine, thanks.

MISS WILLIAMS. (*pointing to the album*) That's Angela—you were only a baby when that was taken.

CARLA. What was she like?

MISS WILLIAMS. (*putting down the kettle*) One of the most interesting pupils I ever had. Undisciplined, but a first-class brain. She took a first at Somerville and you may have read her book on the rock paintings of the Hazelpa?

CARLA. Um?

MISS WILLIAMS. It was very well reviewed. Yes, I'm very proud of Angela. (*She puts the teapot on the tray* L) Now, we'll just let that stand a minute, shall we?

CARLA. (*putting the album on the upstage end of the divan*) Miss Williams, you know why I've come?

MISS WILLIAMS. Roughly, yes. (*She moves to the fireplace*) You have just learnt the facts about the tragedy that ended your father's life, and you want fuller information about the whole matter. (*She switches off the kettle*)

CARLA. And, I suppose, like everybody else, you think I ought to forget the whole thing?

MISS WILLIAMS. Not at all. It appears to be perfectly natural that you should want to understand. Then, and only then, can you forget about it.

CARLA. Will you tell me everything?

MISS WILLIAMS. Any questions you like to put to me I will answer to the full extent of my knowledge. Now, where's my little footstool? I have a little footstool somewhere. (*She turns the armchair to face the divan and looks around for the footstool*)

CARLA. (*rising and drawing the footstool out from under the armchair*) Here we are.

MISS WILLIAMS. Thank you, dear. (*She seats herself comfortably in the armchair and puts her feet on the footstool*) I like to keep my feet off the ground.

CARLA. I think—first—that I'd like to know just what my father and mother were like—what *you* thought they were like, I mean. (*She sits on the divan*)

MISS WILLIAMS. Your father, as you know, has been acclaimed as a great painter. I, of course, am not competent to judge. I do not, myself, admire his paintings. The drawing seems to me faulty and the colouring exaggerated. However, that may be, I have never seen why the possession of what is called the artistic temperament should excuse a man from ordinary decent behaviour. Your mother had a great deal to put up with where he was concerned.

CARLA. And she minded?

MISS WILLIAMS. She minded very much. Mr. Crale was not a faithful husband. She put up with his infidelities and forgave him for them—but she did not take them meekly. She remonstrated—and with spirit.

CARLA. You mean they gave each other hell?

MISS WILLIAMS. (*quietly*) That would not be my description. (*She rises and crosses below the armchair to the table* L) There were quarrels, yes, but your mother had dignity, and your father was in the wrong. (*She pours the tea*)

CARLA. Always?

MISS WILLIAMS. (*firmly*) Always. I was—very fond of Mrs. Crale. And very sorry for her. She had a lot to bear. If I had been Mr. Crale's wife, I should have left him. No woman should submit to humiliation at her husband's hands.

CARLA. You didn't like my father?

MISS WILLIAMS. (*tight-lipped*) I disliked him—very much.

CARLA. But he was really fond of my mother?

(MISS WILLIAMS *picks up a cup of tea and the sugar bowl and crosses to Carla*)

MISS WILLIAMS. I believe honestly that he cared for her— but men . . . ! (*She sniffs, then hands the cup of tea to Carla*)

CARLA. (*slightly amused*) You don't think much of men?

MISS WILLIAMS. (*with slight fanaticism*) Men still have the best of this world. I hope it will not always be so. (*She thrusts the sugar bowl at Carla*) Sugar?

CARLA. I don't take it, thanks. And then Elsa Greer came along?

(MISS WILLIAMS *crosses to the table, puts down the sugar bowl and picks up her cup of tea*)

MISS WILLIAMS. (*with distaste*) Yes. Ostensibly to have her portrait painted; they made poor progress with the picture. (*She crosses to* C) Doubtless they had other things to talk about. It was obvious that Mr. Crale was infatuated with the girl and that she was doing nothing to discourage him. (*She sniffs, then sits in the armchair*)

CARLA. What did *you* think of her?

MISS WILLIAMS. I thought she was good-looking, but stupid. She had had, presumably, an adequate education, but she never opened a book, and was quite unable to converse on any intellectual subject. All she ever thought about was her own personal appearance—and men, of course.

CARLA. Go on.

MISS WILLIAMS. Miss Greer went back to London, and very pleased we were to see her go. (*She pauses and sips her tea*) Then Mr. Crale went away and I knew, and so did Mrs. Crale, that he had gone after the girl. They reappeared together. The *sittings* were to be continued, and we all knew what *that* meant. The girl's manner became increasingly insolent, and she finally came out into the open with some outrageous remarks about what *she* would do at Alderbury when she was mistress there.

CARLA. (*horrified*) Oh, no!

MISS WILLIAMS. Yes, yes, yes. (*She pauses and sips her tea*) Mr. Crale came in, and his wife asked him outright if it was true that he planned to marry Elsa. There he stood, a great giant of a man, looking like a naughty schoolboy. (*She rises, goes to the table L, puts down her cup, picks up a plate of biscuits and crosses to Carla*) My blood boiled. I really could have killed him. Do have one of these biscuits, they're Peek Frean's.

CARLA. (*taking a biscuit*) Thank you. What did my mother do?

MISS WILLIAMS. I think she just went out of the room. I know I—I tried to say something to her of what I felt, but she stopped me. "We must all behave as usual," she said. (*She crosses and puts the plate on the table L*) They were all going over to tea with Mr. Meredith Blake that afternoon. Just as she was going, I remember she came back and kissed me. She said, "You're such a comfort to me." (*Her voice breaks a little*)

CARLA. (*sweetly*) I'm sure you were.

MISS WILLIAMS. (*crossing to the fireplace, picking up the kettle and unplugging it*) Never blame her for what she did, Carla. It is for you, her daughter, to understand and forgive.

CARLA. (*slowly*) So even you think she did it.

MISS WILLIAMS. (*sadly*) I *know* she did it.

CARLA. Did she *tell* you she did it?

MISS WILLIAMS. (*taking the kettle to the table* L) Of course not. (*She refills the teapot*)

CARLA. What *did* she say?

MISS WILLIAMS. She took pains to impress upon me that it must be suicide.

CARLA. You didn't—believe her?

MISS WILLIAMS. I said, "Certainly, Mrs. Crale, it *must* have been suicide."

CARLA. But you didn't believe what you were saying.

MISS WILLIAMS. (*crossing to the fireplace and replacing the kettle*) You have got to understand, Carla, that I was entirely on your mother's side. My sympathies were with *her*—not with the police. (*She sits in the armchair*)

CARLA. But murder . . . (*She pauses*) When she was charged, you wanted her acquitted?

MISS WILLIAMS. Certainly.

CARLA. On any pretext?

MISS WILLIAMS. On any pretext.

CARLA. (*pleading*) She *might* have been innocent.

MISS WILLIAMS. No.

CARLA. (*defiantly*) She *was* innocent.

MISS WILLIAMS. No, my dear.

CARLA. She was—she *was*. She wrote it to me. In a letter she wrote when she was dying. She said I could be *sure* of that.

(*There is a stunned silence*)

MISS WILLIAMS. (*in a low voice*) That was wrong—very wrong of her. To write a lie—and at such a solemn moment. I should not have thought that Caroline Crale would have done a thing like that. She was a truthful woman.

CARLA. (*rising*) It could be the truth.

MISS WILLIAMS. (*definitely*) No.

CARLA. You can't be positive. You *can't!*

MISS WILLIAMS. I *can* be positive. Of all the people connected with the case, I *alone* can be *sure* that Caroline Crale was guilty. Because of something I saw. I withheld it from the police—I have never told anyone. (*She rises*) But you must take it from me, Carla, quite definitely,

that your mother *was* guilty. Now, can I get you some
more tea, dear? We'll both have some, shall we? It
sometimes gets rather chilly in this room. (*She takes
Carla's cup and crosses to the table* L)

CARLA *looks distracted and bewildered as—*

the LIGHTS *dim to* BLACK-OUT

Scene V

SCENE: *A table in a restaurant.*
  *The table is in an alcove decorated in delicate Oriental
style, equipped with three banquettes.*

When the LIGHTS *come up,* CARLA *is seated* R *of the
table and* ANGELA WARREN *is seated above and* C *of it.
They are just finishing lunch.* CARLA *is wearing a mink-
trimmed coat.* ANGELA *is a tall woman of thirty, of distinguished appearance, well-dressed in a plain suit with
a mannish hat. There is a not too noticeable scar on her
left cheek.*

ANGELA. (*putting down her brandy glass*) Well, now that
we've finished our meal, Carla, I'm prepared to talk. I
should have been sorry if you'd gone back to Canada
without our being able to meet. (*She offers Carla a cigarette from a leather case*)

(CARLA *declines and takes a cigarette from an American
pack on the table*)

  (*She takes one of her own cigarettes*) I wanted to fix
it before, but I've had a hundred and one things to do
before leaving tomorrow. (*She lights Carla's cigarette
and then her own with a lighter which matches her case*)
CARLA. I know how it is. You're going by sea?
ANGELA. Yes, much easier when you're carting out a lot of
equipment.
CARLA. I told you I saw Miss Williams?
ANGELA. (*smiling*) Dear Miss Williams. What a life I used to

lead her. Climbing trees and playing truant, and plagu-
ing the life out of everyone all round me. I was jealous,
of course.

CARLA. (*startled*) Jealous?

ANGELA. Yes—of Amyas. I'd always come first with Caroline
and I couldn't bear her to be absorbed in him. I played all
sorts of tricks on him—put—what was it, now—some
filthy stuff—valerian, I think, in his beer, and once I
put a hedgehog in his bed. (*She laughs*) I must have
been an absolute menace. How right they were to pack
me off to school. Though, of course, I was furious at
the time.

CARLA. How much do you remember of it all?

ANGELA. Of the actual happening? Curiously little. We'd had
lunch—and then Caroline and Miss Williams went into
the garden room, and then we all came in and Amyas
was dead and there was telephoning, and I heard Elsa
screaming somewhere—on the terrace, I think with
Caroline. I just wandered about, getting in everyone's
way.

CARLA. I can't think why *I* don't remember anything. After
all, I was five. Old enough to remember *something*.

ANGELA. Oh, you weren't there. You'd gone away to stay with
your godmother, old Lady Thorpe, about a week before.

CARLA. Ah!

ANGELA. Miss Williams took me into Caroline's room. She
was lying down, looking very white and ill. I was
frightened. She said I wasn't to think about it—I was to
go to Miss Williams' sister in London, and then on
to school in Zurich as planned. I said I didn't want to
leave her—and then Miss Williams chipped in and said
in that authoritative way of hers—(*she mimics Miss
Williams*) "The best way you can help your sister,
Angela, is to do what she wants you to do without making any fuss." (*She sips her brandy*)

CARLA. (*amused*) I know just what you mean. There's something about Miss Williams which makes you feel you've
just got to go along with her.

ANGELA. The police asked me a few questions, but I didn't
know why. I just thought there had been some kind of
accident, and that Amyas had taken poison by mistake.
I was abroad when they arrested Caroline, and they kept
it from me as long as they could. Caroline wouldn't let

me go and see her in prison. She did everything she could to keep me out of it all. That was just like Caroline. She always tried to stand between me and the world.

CARLA. She must have been very fond of you.

ANGELA. It wasn't that. (*She touches her scar*) It was because of this.

CARLA. That happened when you were a baby.

ANGELA. Yes. You've heard about it. It's the sort of thing that happens—an older child gets mad with jealousy and chucks something. To a sensitive person, like Caroline, the horror of what she had done never quite left her. Her whole life was one long effort to make up to me for the way she had injured me. Very bad for *me*, of course.

CARLA. Did you ever feel vindictive about it?

ANGELA. Towards Caroline? Because she had spoiled my beauty? (*She laughs*) I never had much to spoil. No, I never gave it a second thought.

(CARLA *picks up her bag from the seat beside her, takes out a letter and hands it to Angela*)

CARLA. She left a letter for me—I'd like you to read it.

(*There is a pause as* ANGELA *reads the letter.* CARLA *stubs out her cigarette*)

I'm so confused about her. Everyone seems to have seen her differently.

ANGELA. She had a lot of contradictions in her nature. (*She turns a page and reads*) ". . . want you to know that I did not kill your father." Sensible of her. You might have wondered. (*She folds the letter and puts it on the table*)

CARLA. You mean—you believe she *wasn't* guilty?

ANGELA. Of course she wasn't guilty. Nobody who knew Caroline could have thought for one moment that she was guilty.

CARLA. (*slightly hysterical*) But they do—they all do—except you.

ANGELA. More fool they. Oh, the evidence was damning enough, I grant you, but anybody who knew Caroline well should know that she couldn't commit murder. She hadn't got it in her.

CARLA. What about . . . ?

ANGELA. (*pointing to her scar*) This? How can I explain? (*She stubs out her cigarette*) Because of what she did to me, Caroline was always watching herself for violence. I think she decided that if she was violent in speech she would have no temptation to violence in action. She'd say things like, "I'd like to cut So-and-so in pieces and boil him in oil." Or she'd say to Amyas, "If you go on like this, I shall *murder* you." Amyas and she had the most fantastic quarrels, they said the most outrageous things to each other. They both loved it.

CARLA. They *liked* quarrelling?

ANGELA. Yes. They were that kind of couple. Living that way, with continual rows and makings up, was their idea of fun.

CARLA. (*sitting back*) You make everything sound different. (*She picks up the letter and puts it in her bag*)

ANGELA. If only *I* could have given evidence. But I suppose the sort of thing I could have said wouldn't count as evidence. But you needn't worry, Carla. You can go back to Canada and be quite sure that Caroline *didn't* murder Amyas.

CARLA. (*sadly*) But then—who did?

ANGELA. Does it matter?

CARLA. Of course it matters.

ANGELA. (*in a hard voice*) It must have been some kind of accident. Can't you leave it at that?

CARLA. No, I can't.

ANGELA. Why not?

(CARLA *does not answer*)

Is it a man? (*She sips her brandy*)

CARLA. Well—there is a man, yes.

ANGELA. Are you engaged?

(CARLA, *slightly embarrassed, takes a cigarette from her packet*)

CARLA. I don't know.

ANGELA. He minds about this?

CARLA. (*frowning*) He's very magnanimous.

ANGELA. (*appreciatively*) How bloody! I shouldn't marry him.

CARLA. I'm not sure that I want to.

ANGELA. Another man? (*She lights Carla's cigarette*)

CARLA. (*irritably*) Must everything be a man?

ANGELA. Usually seems to be. I prefer rock paintings.

CARLA. (*suddenly*) I'm going down to Alderbury tomorrow. I want all the people concerned to be there. I wanted you as well.

ANGELA. Not me. I'm sailing tomorrow.

CARLA. I want to re-live it—as though I were my mother and not myself. (*Strongly*) Why didn't she fight for her life? Why was she so defeatist at her trial?

ANGELA. I don't know.

CARLA. It wasn't like her, was it?

ANGELA. (*slowly*) No, it wasn't like her.

CARLA. It *must* have been one of those four other people.

ANGELA. How persistent you are, Carla.

CARLA. I'll find out the truth in the end.

ANGELA. (*struck by Carla's sincerity*) I almost believe you will. (*She pauses*) I'll come to Alderbury with you. (*She picks up her brandy glass*)

CARLA. (*delighted*) You will? But your boat sails tomorrow.

ANGELA. I'll take a plane instead. Now, are you sure you won't have some brandy? I'm going to have some more if I can catch his eye. (*She calls*) Waiter!

CARLA. I'm *so* glad you're coming.

ANGELA. (*sombrely*) Are you? Don't hope for too much. Sixteen years. It's a long time ago.

ANGELA *drains her glass as the* LIGHTS *dim to* BLACK-OUT *and—*

the CURTAIN *falls*

Act Two

SCENE: *Alderbury, a house in the West of England.*

The scene shows a section of the house, with the Garden Room R and the terrace L with communicating french windows between them. The room is at an angle, so that the terrace extends and tapers off below it to R. Doors back C, in the room, and at the upstage end of the terrace, lead to the house. An exit, at the upstage end of a vine-covered pergola L, leads to the garden. There is another door down R in the room. Above this door is a small alcove with shelves for decorative plates and ornaments. A console table stands under the shelves. There is a table L of the door C, on which there is a telephone and a carved wooden head. On the wall above the table is the portrait of Elsa, painted by Amyas. There is a sofa R of the door C, with a long stool in front of it. Armchairs stand R and L, and there is an occasional table L of the armchair R. There is a stone bench C of the terrace.

When the CURTAIN *rises, the stage is in darkness, then the* LIGHTS *come up to show the house shrouded in darkness and the terrace bathed in moonlight. The long stool is on the sofa and both are covered with a dust sheet. The armchairs are also covered with dust sheets. The window curtains are closed. After a few moments, voices are heard off up* C.

CARLA. (*off*) Which way do we go?

MEREDITH. (*off*) This way, mind that little step. (*He is heard to stumble*) I always used to fall over it.

JUSTIN. (*off; stumbling*) Good heavens! Shall I leave the door?

MEREDITH. (*off*) Few things as depressing as an unlived-in house. I do apologize.

(MEREDITH *enters up* C *and the* LIGHTS *on the room snap up.*
He wears an overcoat, and has an old fishing hat, pulled
down. He moves down R. CARLA *follows Meredith on.*
She wears a loose coat and a head scarf. She moves L.
JUSTIN *enters last. He carries his bowler hat. He moves*
down C, *turns and looks around the room*)

This is what we call the garden room. Cold as a
morgue. Looks like a morgue, too, doesn't it? (*He*
laughs and rubs his hands) Not that I've ever seen the
inside of a—hum . . . I'll just remove these. (*He goes*
to the sofa and removes the dust sheet)

JUSTIN. Let me help you. (*He moves to* L *of the sofa and*
takes the dust sheet from Meredith)

(CARLA *moves to the armchair* L *and removes the dust sheet*
which she gives to Justin)

MEREDITH. This bit of the house has been shut up, you see,
ever since . . . (*He indicates the long stool on the sofa*)
Ah, that's an old friend. (*He takes the stool from the*
sofa) Let me see, I think it went somewhere there. (*He*
places the stool RC) It's sad, somehow. It was so alive,
once, and now it's dead.

(CARLA *sits on the left end of the stool and looks at the*
portrait)

CARLA. Is that the picture?
MEREDITH. What? Yes. Girl in a yellow shirt.
CARLA. You left it here?
MEREDITH. Yes. I—somehow couldn't bear to look at it. It
reminded me too much . . . (*He recollects himself,*
crosses to the french windows and opens the curtains)
CARLA. How she's changed.
MEREDITH. (*turning*) You've seen her?
CARLA. Yes.
MEREDITH. (*crossing to the armchair* R *and removing the dust*
sheet) I haven't seen her for years.
CARLA. She's beautiful still. But not like that. So alive and
triumphant—and young. (*She draws a breath and faces*
front) It's a wonderful portrait.
MEREDITH. Yes—(*he points* L) and that is where he painted
her—out there on the terrace. Well, I'll just dispose of
these—(*he takes the dust sheets from Justin*) in the
next room, I think.

(MEREDITH *exits* R. CARLA *rises, goes to the french windows, unlocks them and moves onto the terrace.* JUSTIN *looks at her, then follows and stands on the step just outside the windows*)

CARLA. Justin—do you think this scheme of mine is quite crazy? Jeff thinks I'm mad.

JUSTIN. (*crossing to the exit above the pergola and looking off*) I shouldn't let that worry you.

(MEREDITH *enters down* R *and crosses to the french windows*)

CARLA. (*sitting on the bench*) I don't.

MEREDITH. I'll just go and meet the others.

(MEREDITH *exits up* C)

CARLA. You understand, don't you, just what I want done?

JUSTIN. (*crossing to* R) You want to reconstruct in your mind's eye what happened here sixteen years ago. You want each witness in turn to describe the scene in which they participated. Much of it may be trivial and irrelevant, but you want it in full. (*He moves to her*) Their recollections, of course, will not be exact. In a scene where more than one witness was present, the two accounts may not agree.

CARLA. That might be helpful.

JUSTIN. (*doubtfully*) It might—but you must not build too much on it. People do recollect things differently. (*He moves up stage and looks around*)

CARLA. What I'm going to do is to make believe I *see* it all happening. I shall imagine my mother and my father . . . (*She suddenly breaks off*) You know, I think my father must have been great fun.

JUSTIN. (*moving behind Carla*) What?

CARLA. I think I should have liked him a lot.

JUSTIN. (*turning and peering off down* L; *dryly*) Women usually did.

CARLA. It's odd—I feel sorry for Elsa. In that picture in there she looks so young and alive—and now—there's no life left in her. I think it died when my father died.

JUSTIN. (*sitting below Carla on the bench*) Are you casting her as Juliet?

CARLA. You don't?

JUSTIN. No. (*He smiles*) I'm your mother's man.

CARLA. You're very faithful, aren't you? Too faithful, maybe.

(JUSTIN *looks at Carla*)

JUSTIN. (*after a pause*) I don't really quite know what we're talking about.

CARLA. (*rising; matter-of-fact*) Let's get back to business. Your part is to look hard for discrepancies—flaws—you've got to be very legal and astute.

JUSTIN. Yes, ma'am.

(*Voices of the others arriving can be heard off up* C, *with* MEREDITH *greeting them*)

(*He rises*) Here they are.

CARLA. I'll go and meet them.

(CARLA *goes into the room and exits* C. *The lights slowly dim to* BLACK-OUT, JUSTIN *moves down* L, *then a spotlight comes up revealing his face. He acts as compere*)

JUSTIN. Now, are we all ready? I will just impress on you once more why we are all here. We want to reconstruct, as far as we can, the happenings of sixteen years ago. We shall endeavour to do this, by asking each person or persons to recount in turn their own part in what went on, and what they saw, or overheard. This should make an almost continuous picture. Sixteen years ago. We shall start on the afternoon of the sixteenth of August, the day before the tragedy took place, with a conversation that Mr. Meredith Blake had with Caroline Crale in the garden room. Out here on the terrace, Elsa Greer was posing for Amyas Crale who was painting her. From that we shall go on to Elsa Greer's narrative, to the arrival of Philip Blake, and so on. Mr. Meredith Blake, will you begin?

(*The spotlight fades.* MEREDITH'S *voice can be heard in the darkness*)

MEREDITH. It was the afternoon of the sixteenth of August, did you say? Yes, yes, it was. I came over to Alderbury. Stopped in on my way to Framley Abbott. Really to see if I could pick any of them up later to give them a lift —they were coming over to me for tea. Caroline had been cutting roses, and when I opened the door into the garden room ...

(*The* LIGHTS *come up. It is a glorious, hot summer's day.*
CAROLINE CRALE *is standing in the french windows
looking on to the terrace. She carries a trug with roses,
etc., and wears gardening gloves. On the terrace,* ELSA
poses on the bench, facing C. *She wears a yellow shirt
and black shorts.* AMYAS CRALE *is seated on a stool* C,
facing L, *before his easel, painting Elsa. His paintbox is
on the ground below him. He is a big, handsome man,
wearing an old shirt and paint-stained slacks. There is
a trolley* L *of the terrace with various bottles and glasses,
including a bottle of beer in an ice-bucket. In the room,
a landscape now hangs in place of the portrait.* MERE-
DITH *enters up* C)

Hullo, Caroline.

CAROLINE. (*turning*) Merry! (*She crosses to the stool, puts
the trug on it, removes her gloves and puts them in the
trug*)

MEREDITH. (*closing the door*) How's the picture going?
(*He crosses to the french windows and looks out*) It's
a nice pose. (*He moves to* L *of the stool and takes a rose
from the trug*) What have we here? "Ena Harkness."
(*He smells the rose*) My word, what a beauty.

CAROLINE. Merry, do you think Amyas really cares for that
girl?

MEREDITH. No, no, he's just interested in painting her. You
know what Amyas is.

CAROLINE. (*sitting in the armchair* R) This time I'm afraid,
Merry. I'm nearly thirty, you know. We've been married
over six years, and in looks, I can't hold a candle to
Elsa.

MEREDITH. (*replacing the rose in the trug and moving above
the stool to* L *of Caroline*) That's absurd, Caroline. You
know that Amyas is really devoted to you and always will
be.

CAROLINE. Does one ever know with men?

MEREDITH. (*close to her and bending over her*) I'm still devoted to you, Caroline.

CAROLINE. (*affectionately*) Dear Merry. (*She touches his
cheek*) You're so sweet.

(*There is a pause*)

I long to take a hatchet to that girl. She's just helping herself to my husband in the coolest manner in the world.

MEREDITH. My dear Caroline, the child probably doesn't realize in the least what she's doing. She's got an enormous admiration and hero worship for Amyas and she probably doesn't understand at all that he's maybe falling in love with her.

(CAROLINE *looks pityingly at him*)

CAROLINE. So there really are people who can believe six impossible things before breakfast.

MEREDITH. I don't understand.

CAROLINE. (*rising and crossing to L of the stool*) You live in a nice world all your own, Merry, where everybody is just as nice as you are. (*She looks at the roses. Cheerfully*) My "Erythina Christo Galli" is in wonderful bloom this year. (*She crosses to the french windows and goes on to the terrace*)

(MEREDITH *follows Caroline on to the terrace*)

Come and see it before you go into Framley Abbott. (*She crosses to the upstage end of the pergola*)

MEREDITH. Just you wait till you see my "Tecoma Grandiflora." (*He moves to Caroline*) It's magnificent.

(CAROLINE *puts her fingers to her lips to quieten Meredith*)

CAROLINE. Ssh!

MEREDITH. What? (*He looks through one of the arches of the pergola at Elsa and Amyas*) Oh, man at work.

(CAROLINE *and* MEREDITH *exit by the upstage end of the pergola*)

ELSA. (*stretching herself*) I *must* have a break.

AMYAS. No—no, wait. There—oh, well, if you must.

(ELSA *rises*)

(*He takes a cigarette from a packet in the paintbox, and lights it*) Can't you stay still for more than five minutes?

ELSA. Five minutes! Half an hour. (*She moves down L*) Anyway, I've got to change.

AMYAS. Change? Change what?

ELSA. Change out of this. (*She crosses above Amyas and stands behind him*) We're going out to tea, don't you remember? With Meredith Blake.

AMYAS. (*irritably*) What a damned nuisance. Always something.

ELSA. (*leaning over Amyas and putting her arms around his neck*) Aren't you sociable!

AMYAS. (*looking up at her*) My tastes are simple. (*As though quoting*) A pot of paint, a brush and thou beside me, not able to sit still for five minutes . . .

(*They both laugh.* ELSA *snatches Amyas' cigarette and straightens up*)

ELSA. (*drawing on the cigarette*) Have you thought about what I said?

AMYAS. (*resuming painting*) What did you say?

ELSA. About Caroline. Telling her about us.

AMYAS. (*easily*) Oh, I shouldn't worry your head about that just yet.

ELSA. But, Amyas . . .

(CAROLINE *enters down* L)

CAROLINE. Merry's gone into Framley Abbott for something, but he's coming back here. (*She crosses below the bench towards the french windows*) I must change.

AMYAS. (*without looking at her*) You look all right.

CAROLINE. I must do something about my hands, they're filthy. I've been gardening. Are you going to change, Elsa?

(ELSA *returns the cigarette to Amyas*)

ELSA. (*insolently*) Yes. (*She moves to the french windows*)

(PHILIP *enters up* C)

CAROLINE. (*moving into the room*) Philip! The train must have been on time for once.

(ELSA *comes into the room*)

This is Meredith's brother Philip—Miss Greer.

ELSA. Hullo. I'm off to change.

(ELSA *crosses and exits up* C)

CAROLINE. Well, Philip, good journey? (*She kisses him*)

PHILIP. Not too bad. How are you all?

CAROLINE. Oh—fine. (*She gestures towards the terrace*) Amyas is out there on the terrace. I must clean up, forgive me. We're going over to Merry's to tea.

(CAROLINE *smiles and exits up* C. PHILIP *closes the door after her, then wanders on to the terrace and stands in front of the bench*)

AMYAS. (*looking up and smiling*) Hullo, Phil. Good to see you. What a summer. Best we've had for years.

PHILIP. (*crossing below Amyas to* R) Can I look?

AMYAS. Yes. I'm on the last lap.

PHILIP. (*looking at the painting*) Wow!

AMYAS. (*stubbing out his cigarette*) Like it? Not that you're any judge, you old Philistine.

PHILIP. I buy pictures quite often.

AMYAS. (*looking up at him*) As an investment? To get in on the ground floor? Because somebody tells you So-and-so is an up-and-coming man? (*He grins*) I know you, you old money hog. Anyway, you can't buy this. It's not for sale.

PHILIP. She's quite something.

AMYAS. (*looking at the portrait*) She certainly is. (*Suddenly serious*) Sometimes I wish I'd never seen her.

PHILIP. (*taking a cigarette from his case*) D'you remember when you first told me you were painting her? "No personal interest in her," you said. Remember what I said? (*He grins*) "Tell that to the Marines."

AMYAS. (*overlapping*) "Tell that to the Marines." All right—all right. So you were clever, you cold-blooded old fish. (*He rises, crosses to the trolley, takes the bottle of beer from the ice-bucket, and opens it*) Why don't *you* get yourself a woman? (*He pours the beer*)

PHILIP. No time for 'em. (*He lights his cigarette*) And if I were you, Amyas, I wouldn't get tied up with any more.

AMYAS. It's all very well for you to talk. I just can't leave women alone. (*He grins suddenly*)

PHILIP. How about Caroline? Is she cutting up rough?

AMYAS. What do you think? (*He takes his glass, crosses to the bench and sits on the downstage end*) Thank the Lord you've turned up, Phil. Living in this house with four women on your neck is enough to drive any man to the loony bin.

PHILIP. Four?

AMYAS. There's Caroline being bloody to Elsa in a well-bred, polite sort of way. Elsa, being just plain bloody to Caroline.

(PHILIP *sits on the easel stool*)

There's Angela, hating my guts because at last I've persuaded Caroline to send her to boarding-school. She ought to have gone years ago. She's a nice kid, really, but Caroline spoils her, and she's inclined to run wild. She put a hedgehog in my bed last week.

(PHILIP *laughs*)

Oh, yes, very funny—but you wait till *you* ram your feet down on a lot of ruddy prickles. And then lastly, but not leastly, there's the governess. Hates me like poison. Sits there at meals with her lips set together, oozing disapproval.

MISS WILLIAMS. (*off; down* L) Angela, you must get changed.

ANGELA. (*off*) Oh, I'm all right.

PHILIP. They seem to have got you down a bit.

MISS WILLIAMS. (*off*) You're not all right. You can't go out to tea with Mr. Blake in those jeans.

AMYAS. *Nil desperandum!* (*He drinks*)

(ANGELA *enters down* L)

ANGELA. (*as she enters*) Merry wouldn't mind. (*She crosses to Philip and pulls him to his feet*) Hullo, Philip.

(MISS WILLIAMS *enters down* L *and crosses above the bench to the french windows*)

MISS WILLIAMS. Good afternoon, Mr. Blake. I hope you had a good journey down from London?

PHILIP. Quite good, thank you.

(MISS WILLIAMS *goes into the room, sees the trug on the stool, picks it up, returns to the terrace and exits by the garden door up* L)

ANGELA. (*crossing to* L *of Amyas*) You've got paint on your ear.

AMYAS. (*rubbing a painty hand on his other ear*) Eh?

ANGELA. (*delighted*) Now you've got paint on both ears. He can't go out to tea like that, can he?

AMYAS. I'll go out to tea with ass's ears if I like.

ANGELA. (*putting her arms around Amyas's neck from behind and mocking him*) Amyas is an ass! Amyas is an ass!

AMYAS. (*chanting*) Amyas is an ass!

(MISS WILLIAMS *enters up* L *and moves to the french windows*)

MISS WILLIAMS. Come along, Angela.

(ANGELA *jumps over the bench and runs to the easel*)

ANGELA. You and your stupid painting. (*Vindictively*) I'm going to write "Amyas is an ass" all over your picture in scarlet paint. (*She bends down, grabs a brush and proceeds to rub it in the red paint on the palette*)

(AMYAS *rises quickly, puts his glass downstage of the bench, crosses to* ANGELA *and grabs her hand before she has time to damage the picture*)

AMYAS. If you ever tamper with any picture of mine— (*seriously*) I'll kill you. Remember that. (*He picks up a piece of rag and cleans the brush*)

ANGELA. You're just like Caroline—she's always saying, "I'll kill you" to people—but she never does, why, she won't even kill wasps. (*Sulkily*) I wish you'd hurry up and finish painting Elsa—then she'd go away.

PHILIP. Don't you like her?

ANGELA. (*snappily*) No. I think she's a terrible bore. (*She crosses to* L *and turns*) I can't imagine why Amyas has her here.

(PHILIP *and* AMYAS *exchange looks.* AMYAS *crosses to Angela*)

I suppose she's paying you a terrible lot of money for painting her, is she, Amyas?

AMYAS. (*putting his arm around Angela's shoulders and guiding her towards the french windows*) Go and finish your packing. Four-fifteen train tomorrow, and good riddance. (*He gives her a playful shove and turns down stage*)

(ANGELA *hits* AMYAS *on the back. He turns and collapses on the bench, and she pommels his chest*)

ANGELA. I hate you—I hate you. Caroline would never have sent me away to school if it wasn't for you.

PHILIP. Mind the beer. (*He crosses to the bench, picks up the glass and puts it on the trolley*)

ANGELA. You just want to get rid of me. You wait—I'll get even with you—I'll—I'll . . .

MISS WILLIAMS. (*with sharp authority*) Angela! Angela, come along.

ANGELA. (*near to tears; sulkily*) Oh, all right. (*She runs into the room*)

(MISS WILLIAMS *follows Angela into the room.* ELSA *enters up* C. *She has changed into a dress and looks ravishing.* ANGELA *gives* ELSA *a venomous look and runs out up* C. MISS WILLIAMS *follows Angela off, and closes the door*)

AMYAS. (*sitting up*) Wham! Why didn't you stand up for me? I'm black and blue.

PHILIP. (*leaning against the downstage end of the pergola*) Black and blue? You're all the colours of the rainbow.

(ELSA *wanders on to the terrace and moves down* C, *beside the easel*)

You've got enough paint on you to . . . (*He breaks off as he sees Elsa*)

AMYAS. Hullo, Elsa. All dolled up? You'll knock poor old Merry all of a heap.

PHILIP. (*dryly*) Yes—I—I've been admiring the picture. (*He crosses below the easel to* R *of it and looks at the portrait*)

ELSA. I shall be glad when it's finished. I *loathe* having to sit still. Amyas grunts and sweats and bites his brushes and doesn't hear you when you speak to him.

AMYAS. (*playfully*) All models should have their tongues cut out.

(ELSA *crosses and sits below Amyas on the bench*)

(*He looks appraisingly at her*) Anyway, you can't walk across the fields to Merry's in those shoes.

ELSA. (*turning her foot this way and that; demurely*) I shan't need to. He's coming to fetch me in his car.

AMYAS. Preferential treatment, eh? (*He grins*) You've certainly got old Merry going. How do you do it, you little devil?

ELSA. (*playfully*) I don't know what you mean.

(AMYAS *and* ELSA *are immersed in each other.* PHILIP *crosses to the french windows*)

PHILIP. (*as he passes them*) I'll go and have a wash.
AMYAS. (*not hearing Philip; to Elsa*) Yes, you do. You know damn well what I mean. (*He moves to kiss Elsa's ear, realizes Philip has said something and turns to him*) What?
PHILIP. (*quietly*) A wash.

(PHILIP *goes into the room and exits up* C, *closing the door behind him*)

AMYAS. (*laughing*) Good old Phil.
ELSA. (*rising and crossing below the easel to* R) You're very fond of him, aren't you?
AMYAS. Known him all my life. He's a great guy.
ELSA. (*turning and looking at the portrait*) I don't think it's a bit like me.
AMYAS. Don't pretend you've any artistic judgement, Elsa. (*He rises*) You know nothing at all.
ELSA. (*quite pleased*) How rude you are. Are you going out to tea with all that paint on your face?

(AMYAS *crosses to the paintbox, takes up a piece of rag and moves to Elsa*)

AMYAS. Here, clean me off a bit.

(ELSA *takes the rag and rubs his face*)

Don't put the turps in my eye.
ELSA. Well, hold still. (*After a second she puts both her arms around his waist*) Who do you love?
AMYAS. (*not moving; quietly*) Caroline's room faces this way —so does Angela's.
ELSA. I want to talk to you about Caroline.
AMYAS. (*taking the rag and sitting on the stool*) Not now. I'm not in the mood.
ELSA. It's no good putting it off. She's got to know *sometime*, hasn't she?
AMYAS. (*grinning*) We could go off Victorian fashion and leave a note on her pin-cushion.
ELSA. (*moving between Amyas and the easel*) I believe that's just what you'd like to do. But we've got to be absolutely fair and aboveboard about the whole thing.

AMYAS. Hoity-toity!

ELSA. Oh, do be serious.

AMYAS. I *am* serious. I don't want a lot of fuss and scenes and hysterics. Now, mind yourself. (*He pushes her gently aside*)

ELSA. (*moving* R) I don't see why there should be scenes and hysterics. Caroline should have too much dignity and pride for that. (*She pivots around*)

AMYAS. (*absorbed in painting*) Should she? You don't know Caroline.

ELSA. When a marriage has gone wrong, it's only sensible to face the fact calmly.

AMYAS. (*turning to look at her*) Advice from our marriage counsellor. Caroline loves me and she'll kick up the hell of a row.

ELSA. (*moving down* R) If she *really* loved you, she'd want you to be happy.

AMYAS. (*grinning*) With somebody else? She'll probably poison you and stick a knife into me.

ELSA. Don't be ridiculous!

AMYAS. (*wiping his hands and nodding at the picture*) Well, that's that. Nothing doing until tomorrow morning. (*He drops the rag, rises and moves to Elsa*) Lovely, lovely Elsa. (*He takes her face in his hands*) What a lot of bloody nonsense you talk. (*He kisses her*)

(ANGELA *rushes in up* C, *runs on to the terrace and exits down* L. ELSA *and* AMYAS *break apart.* MISS WILLIAMS *enters up* C, *goes on to the terrace and looks off* L)

MISS WILLIAMS. (*calling*) Angela!

AMYAS. (*crossing down* L) She went this-a-way. Shall I catch her for you?

MISS WILLIAMS. (*moving down* LC) No, it's all right. She'll come back of her own accord as soon as she sees nobody is paying any attention to her.

(ELSA *goes into the room, picks up a magazine from the sofa and sits in the armchair* R)

AMYAS. There's something in that.

MISS WILLIAMS. She's young for her age, you know. Growing up is a difficult business. Angela is at the prickly stage.

AMYAS. (*moving up* L) Don't talk to me of prickles. Reminds me too much of that ruddy hedgehog.

MISS WILLIAMS. That was very naughty of Angela.

AMYAS. (*moving to the french windows*) Sometimes I wonder how you can stick her.

MISS WILLIAMS. (*turning to face Amyas*) I can see ahead. Angela will be a fine woman one day, and a distinguished one.

AMYAS. I still say Caroline spoils her. (*He goes into the room and crosses to C of it*)

(MISS WILLIAMS *moves to the french windows and listens*)

ELSA. (*in a whisper*) Did she see us?

AMYAS. Who can say? I suppose I've got lipstick on my face now as well as paint.

(AMYAS *glances off* L *and exits quickly up* C. MISS WILLIAMS *comes into the room and moves above the stool, uncertain whether to go or not. She decides to stay*)

MISS WILLIAMS. You haven't been over to Mr. Blake's house yet, have you, Miss Greer?

ELSA. (*flatly*) No.

MISS WILLIAMS. It's a delightful walk there. You can go by the shore or through the woods.

(CAROLINE *and* PHILIP *enter up* C. CAROLINE *glances around the room, then goes to the french windows and looks on to the terrace.* PHILIP *closes the door and looks at the carved head on the table up* LC)

CAROLINE. Are we all ready? Amyas has gone to clean the paint off himself.

ELSA. He needn't. Artists aren't like other people.

(CAROLINE *pays no attention to Elsa*)

CAROLINE. (*moving to the armchair* L; *to Philip*) You haven't been down here since Merry started on his lily pond, have you, Phil? (*She sits*)

PHILIP. Don't think so.

ELSA. People in the country talk of nothing but their gardens.

(*There is a pause.* CAROLINE *takes her spectacles from her handbag and puts them on.* PHILIP *looks at Elsa, and then sits on the stool facing the head*)

CAROLINE. (*to Miss Williams*) Did you ring up the vet about Toby?

MISS WILLIAMS. Yes, Mrs. Crale. He'll come first thing to-
    morrow.

CAROLINE. (to Philip) Do you like that head, Phil? Amyas
    bought it last month.

PHILIP. Yes. It's good.

CAROLINE. (searching in her handbag for her cigarettes) It's
    the work of a young Norwegian sculptor. Amyas thinks
    very highly of him. We're thinking of going over to
    Norway next year to visit him.

ELSA. That doesn't seem to me very likely.

CAROLINE. Doesn't it, Elsa? Why?

ELSA. You know very well.

CAROLINE. (lightly) How very cryptic. Miss Williams, would
    you mind—my cigarette case—(she indicates the table
    RC) it's on that little table.

(MISS WILLIAMS goes to the table RC, picks up the cigarette
    case, opens it and offers a cigarette to Caroline. PHILIP
    takes out his cigarettes, rises and offers them to Caro-
    line)

    (She takes a cigarette from her own case) I prefer
    these—do you mind?

(MISS WILLIAMS moves to the table up LC and puts the case
    on it. PHILIP lights Caroline's cigarette, then takes one
    of his own and lights it)

ELSA. (rising and moving below the stool) This would be
    quite a good room if it was properly fixed. All this litter
    of old-fashioned stuff cleared out.

    (There is a pause. PHILIP looks at Elsa)

CAROLINE. We like it as it is. It holds a lot of memories.

ELSA. (loudly and aggressively) When I'm living here I shall
    throw all this rubbish out.

    (PHILIP crosses to Elsa and offers her a cigarette)

No, thank you.

    (PHILIP crosses to R)

Flame-coloured curtains, I think—and one of those
French wallpapers. (To Philip) Don't you think that
would be rather striking?

CAROLINE. (*evenly*) Are you thinking of buying Alderbury, Elsa?

ELSA. It won't be necessary for me to buy it.

CAROLINE. What do you mean?

ELSA. Must we pretend? (*She moves* C) Come now, Caroline, you know perfectly well what I mean.

CAROLINE. I assure you I've no idea.

ELSA. (*aggressively*) Oh, don't be such an ostrich, burying your head in the sand and pretending you don't know all about it. (*She turns, moves to* R *of the stool, tosses the magazine on to the armchair* R *and moves up* R) Amyas and I love each other. It's his house, not yours.

(ANGELA *runs down* L, *crosses to the french windows, stops outside and listens.* PHILIP *and* MISS WILLIAMS *are frozen*)

And after we're married I shall live here with him.

CAROLINE. (*angrily*) I think you must be crazy.

ELSA. Oh, no, I'm not. (*She sits on the sofa at the left end*) It will be much simpler if we're honest about it. There's only one decent thing for you to do—give him his freedom.

CAROLINE. Don't talk nonsense!

ELSA. Nonsense, is it? Ask *him*.

(AMYAS *enters up* C. ANGELA, *unseen, exits by the door up* L)

CAROLINE. I will. Amyas, Elsa says you want to marry her. Is it true?

AMYAS. (*after a slight pause; to Elsa*) Why the devil couldn't you hold your tongue?

CAROLINE. Is it true?

(AMYAS, *leaving the door open, crosses to the armchair* R, *picks up the magazine and sits*)

AMYAS. We don't have to talk about it now. (*He looks at the magazine*)

CAROLINE. But we *are* going to talk about it now.

ELSA. It's only fair to Caroline to tell her the truth.

CAROLINE. (*icily*) I don't think you need bother about being fair to me. (*She rises and crosses to Amyas*) Is it true, Amyas?

(AMYAS *looks hunted and glances from Elsa to Caroline*)

AMYAS. (*to Philip*) Women.

CAROLINE. (*furiously*) Is it true?

AMYAS. (*defiantly*) All right. It's true enough.

(ELSA *rises, triumphant*)

But I don't want to talk about it now.

ELSA. You see? It's no good your adopting a dog-in-the-manger attitude. These things happen. It's nobody's fault. One just has to be rational about it. (*She sits on the stool, facing up stage*) You and Amyas will always be good friends, I hope.

CAROLINE. (*crossing to the door up* C) Good friends! Over his dead body.

ELSA. What do you mean?

CAROLINE. (*turning in the open doorway*) I mean that I'd kill Amyas before I'd give him up to you.

(CAROLINE *exits up* C. *There is a frozen silence.* MISS WILLIAMS *sees Caroline's bag on the armchair* L, *picks it up and exits hurriedly up* C)

AMYAS. (*rising and crossing to the french windows*) Now you've done it. We'll have scenes and ructions and God knows what.

ELSA. (*rising*) She had to know some time.

AMYAS. (*moving on to the terrace*) She needn't have known till the picture was finished.

(ELSA *moves to the french windows*)

(*He stands behind the bench*) How the hell can a man paint with a lot of women buzzing about his ears like wasps.

ELSA. You think nothing's important but your painting.

AMYAS. (*shouting*) Nothing is to me.

ELSA. Well, I think it matters to be honest about things.

(ELSA *rushes angrily out up* C. AMYAS *comes into the room*)

AMYAS. Give me a cigarette, Phil.

(PHILIP *offers his cigarettes and* AMYAS *takes one*)

(*He sits astride the stool*) Women are all alike. Revel in scenes. Why the devil couldn't she hold her tongue? I've got to finish that picture, Phil. It's the best thing I've ever done. And a couple of damn women want to muck it up between them. (*He takes out his matches and lights his cigarette*)

PHILIP. Suppose she refuses to give you a divorce?

AMYAS. (*abstracted*) What?

PHILIP. I said—suppose Caroline refuses to divorce you. Suppose she digs her toes in.

AMYAS. Oh, that. Caroline would never be vindictive. (*He tosses the spent match out of the french windows*) You don't understand, old boy.

PHILIP. And the child. There's the child to consider.

AMYAS. Look, Phil, I know you mean well, but don't go on croaking like a raven, I can manage my own affairs. Everything will turn out all right, you'll see.

PHILIP. Optimist!

(MEREDITH *enters up* C, *closing the door behind him*)

MEREDITH. (*cheerily*) Hullo, Phil. Just got down from London? (*To Amyas*) Hope you haven't forgotten you're all coming over to me this afternoon. I've got the car here. I thought Caroline and Elsa might prefer it to walking this hot weather. (*He crosses to* LC)

AMYAS. (*rising*) Not Caroline *and* Elsa. If Caroline drives Elsa will walk, and if Elsa rides, Caroline will walk. Take your pick. (*He goes on to the terrace, sits on the stool and busies himself with painting*)

MEREDITH. (*startled*) What's the matter with him? Something happened?

PHILIP. It's just come out.

MEREDITH. What?

PHILIP. Elsa broke the news to Caroline that she and Amyas planned to marry. (*Maliciously*) Quite a shock for Caroline.

MEREDITH. No! You're joking!

(PHILIP *shrugs, moves to the armchair* R, *picks up the magazine, sits and reads*)

(*He goes on to the terrace and turns to Amyas*) Amyas! You—this—it can't be true?

AMYAS. I don't know yet what you're talking about. What can't be true?

MEREDITH. You and Elsa. Caroline . . .

AMYAS. (*cleaning his brush*) Oh, that.

MEREDITH. Look here, Amyas, you can't just for the sake of a

sudden infatuation, break up your whole married life.
I know Elsa's very attractive . . .

AMYAS. (*grinning*) So you've noticed that, have you?

MEREDITH. (*crossing below Amyas to* R; *much concerned*) I
can quite understand a girl like Elsa bowling any man
over, yes, but think of *her*—she's very young, you know.
She might regret it bitterly later on. Can't you pull
yourself together? For little Carla's sake? Make a clean
break here and now, and go back to your wife.

(AMYAS *looks up thoughtfully*)

(*He crosses to the bench and turns*) Believe me, it's
the right thing. I know it.

AMYAS. (*after a pause; quietly*) You're a good chap, Merry.
But you're too sentimental.

MEREDITH. Look at the position you've put Caroline in by
having the girl down here.

AMYAS. Well, I wanted to paint her.

MEREDITH. (*angrily*) Oh, damn your pictures!

AMYAS. (*hotly*) All the neurotic women in England can't do
that.

MEREDITH. (*sitting on the bench*) It's disgraceful the way
you've always treated Caroline. She's had a miserable
life with you.

AMYAS. I know—I know. I've given Caroline one hell of a
life—and she's been a saint about it. (*He rises and
moves down* R) But she always knew what she was
letting herself in for. Right from the start I told her
what an egotistic loose-living bastard I was. (*He turns*)
But this is different.

MEREDITH. (*quickly*) This is the first time you've brought a
woman into the house and flaunted her in Caroline's
face.

AMYAS. (*crossing to the trolley*) What you don't seem to
understand, Meredith, is that when I'm painting, nothing else matters—least of all a pair of jealous, quarrelling
women. (*He turns to the trolley and picks up the glass
of beer*)

(ANGELA *enters by the door up* L *and moves slowly to easel.
She is now clean and tidy, in a cotton frock*)

Don't worry, Merry, everything's going to be all right,
you'll see. (*He sips the beer*) Oh, it's warm. (*He turns*

and sees Angela) Hullo, Angy, you're looking remarkably clean and tidy.

ANGELA. (*abstracted*) Oh—yes. (*She crosses to Amyas*) Amyas, why does Elsa say she's going to marry you? She couldn't. People can't have two wives. It's bigamy. (*Confidentially*) You can go to prison for it.

(AMYAS *glances at Meredith, puts his glass on the trolley, puts an arm around Angela's shoulder and leads her to* RC)

AMYAS. Now, where did you hear that?

ANGELA. I was out here. I heard it through the window.

AMYAS. (*sitting on the stool by the easel*) Then it's time you got out of the habit of eavesdropping.

(ELSA *enters up* C *with her bag and gloves, which she puts on the table up* LC)

ANGELA. (*hurt and indignant*) I wasn't—I couldn't *help* hearing. Why did Elsa say that?

AMYAS. It was a kind of joke, darling.

(CAROLINE *enters by the door up* L *and moves down* L)

CAROLINE. It's time we started. Those of us who are going to walk.

MEREDITH. (*rising*) I'll drive you.

CAROLINE. I'd rather walk.

(ELSA *comes on to the terrace*)

Take Elsa in the car. (*She crosses below Amyas to Angela*)

ELSA. (*moving to* R *of Meredith*) Don't you grow herbs and all sorts of exciting things?

CAROLINE. (*to Angela*) That's better. You won't be able to wear jeans at school, you know.

ANGELA. (*crossing angrily down* L) School! I wish you wouldn't keep on about *school*.

MEREDITH. (*continuing to Elsa*) I make cordials and potions. I have my own little laboratory.

ELSA. It sounds fascinating. You must show me.

(CAROLINE *crosses to Angela, looking at Elsa on the way. She straightens Angela's pig-tails*)

MEREDITH. I shall probably deliver a lecture. I'm terribly enthusiastic about my hobby.

ELSA. Doesn't one pick certain herbs by the light of the moon?

CAROLINE. (*to Angela*) You'll like school, you know, once you get there.

MEREDITH. (*to Elsa*) That was the old-fashioned superstition.

ELSA. You don't go as far as that?

MEREDITH. No.

ELSA. Are they *dangerous*?

MEREDITH. Some of them are.

CAROLINE. (*turning*) Sudden death in a little bottle. Belladonna. Hemlock.

(ANGELA *runs between Elsa and Meredith and puts her arms around his waist*)

ANGELA. You read us something once—about Socrates—and how he died.

MEREDITH. Yes, conine—the active principle of hemlock.

ANGELA. It was wonderful. It made me want to learn Greek.

(*They all laugh.* AMYAS *rises and picks up his paintbox*)

AMYAS. We've talked enough. Let's get started. (*He moves towards the door up* L) Where's Phil? (*He glances in the french windows and calls*) Phil.

PHILIP. Coming.

(AMYAS *exits by the door up* L. PHILIP *rises and puts down the magazine.* ELSA *goes into the room and collects her gloves and bag*)

ANGELA. (*moving to* R *of Caroline*) Caroline—(*she whispers anxiously*) it isn't possible, is it, for Elsa to marry Amyas?

(CAROLINE *replies calmly, overheard only by* MEREDITH)

CAROLINE. Amyas will only marry Elsa after I am dead.

ANGELA. Good. It *was* a joke.

(ANGELA *runs off down* L)

MEREDITH. (*moving to* R *of Caroline*) Caroline—my dear—I can't tell you . . .

CAROLINE. Don't . . . Everything's finished—I'm finished . . .

(PHILIP *comes on to the terrace*)

PHILIP. The lady's waiting to be driven.

MEREDITH. (*slightly at a loss*) Oh.

(MEREDITH *goes into the room and escorts* ELSA *off up* C. MISS WILLIAMS *enters up* C *and looks off after Meredith and Elsa. She stands in the room, uncertain for a moment, then goes to the french windows and overhears the last of the conversation between Philip and Caroline*)

CAROLINE. (*to Philip; brightly*) We'll go by the wood path, shall we?

PHILIP. (*moving to* R *of* CAROLINE) Caroline—is it in order for me to offer my condolences?

CAROLINE. Don't.

PHILIP. Perhaps you realize, now, that you made a mistake.

CAROLINE. When I married him?

PHILIP. Yes.

CAROLINE. (*looking Philip straight in the eye*) However it may turn out—I made no mistake. (*She resumes her light manner*) Let's go.

(CAROLINE *exits down* L. PHILIP *follows her off.* MISS WILLIAMS *comes on to the terrace*)

MISS WILLIAMS. (*calling*) Mrs. Crale. (*She moves below the bench*) Mrs. Crale.

(CAROLINE *re-enters down* L)

CAROLINE. Yes, Miss Williams?

MISS WILLIAMS. I'm going into the village. Shall I post the letters that are on your desk?

CAROLINE. (*turning to go*) Oh, yes, please. I forgot them.

MISS WILLIAMS. Mrs. Crale——

(CAROLINE *turns*)

—if I could do anything—anything at all to help . . .

CAROLINE. (*quickly*) Please. We must go on as usual—just behave as usual.

MISS WILLIAMS. (*fervently*) I think you're wonderful.

CAROLINE. Oh, no, I'm not. (*She moves to* L *of Miss Williams*) Dear Miss Williams. (*She kisses her*) You've been such a comfort to me.

(CAROLINE *exits quickly down* L. MISS WILLIAMS *looks after her, then sees the empty beer bottle and glass on the trolley. She picks up the bottle, looks at it for a moment, and then looks off after Caroline. She puts the bottle in the ice-bucket, picks up the ice-bucket and glass and crosses below the bench to the french windows. As she does so, the lights slowly dim to* BLACK-OUT. *A spotlight comes up on Justin down* L)

JUSTIN. We come now to the next morning, the morning of the seventeenth. Miss Williams?

(*The spotlight fades,* MISS WILLIAMS' *voice can be heard in the darkness*)

MISS WILLIAMS. I'd been going through Angela's school list with Mrs. Crale. She looked tired and unhappy but she was very composed. The telephone rang, and I went into the garden room to answer it.

(*The* LIGHTS *come up. A clean glass and a fresh bottle of beer, not in an ice-bucket, are on the trolley.* PHILIP *is seated on the bench on the terrace reading a Sunday paper. The telephone rings.* MISS WILLIAMS *enters up* C, *goes to the telephone and lifts the receiver. She carries a school list.* CAROLINE *follows Miss Williams on, with her spectacles in her hand. She looks towards the telephone, then crosses wearily above the stool to the armchair* R *and sits*)

(*Into the telephone*) Yes? . . . Oh, good morning, Mr. Blake . . . Yes, he's here. (*She looks through the french windows to Philip and calls*) Mr. Blake, it's your brother, he'd like to have a word with you. (*She holds out the receiver*)

(PHILIP *rises, folds his paper, tucks it under his arm, comes into the room and takes the receiver*)

PHILIP. (*into the telephone*) Hullo, Philip here . . .
MISS WILLIAMS. (*crossing above the stool to* R *of it; to Caroline*) That completes the school list, Mrs. Crale. I wonder if you would like to give it a final check? (*She sits on the right end of the stool*)
CAROLINE. (*taking the list*) Let me see. (*She puts on her spectacles and studies the list*)
PHILIP. (*into the telephone*) What? . . . What do you say? . . . Good Lord—are you sure? . . . (*He looks round at Caroline and Miss Williams*) Well, I can't talk now . . . Yes, better come along here. I'll meet you . . . Yes —we'll talk it over—discuss what's best to be done . . .

CAROLINE. (*to Miss Williams*) What about these?

MISS WILLIAMS. (*looking at the list*) Those items are optional.

PHILIP. (*into the telephone*) No, I can't, now—it's difficult . . . You are sure? Yes, but you're a bit vague sometimes. It could have got mislaid . . . All right—if you're sure . . . Be seeing you. (*He replaces the receiver, gives a worried look at the others, goes on to the terrace and paces up and down*)

CAROLINE. (*giving the list to Miss Williams*) I do hope I'm doing the right thing about Angela. (*She removes her spectacles*)

MISS WILLIAMS. I think you can be quite certain of that, Mrs. Crale.

CAROLINE. I want so terribly to do what's best for her. You know why.

MISS WILLIAMS. Believe me, you have nothing to reproach yourself with where Angela is concerned.

CAROLINE. I—disfigured her for life. She'll always have that scar.

(PHILIP *looks off* L *through the pergola*)

MISS WILLIAMS. One cannot alter the past.

(PHILIP *exits up* L, *above the pergola*)

CAROLINE. No. It taught me what a wicked temper I have. I've been on my guard ever since. But you *do* see, don't you, why I've always spoilt her a little?

MISS WILLIAMS. School life will suit her. She needs the contacts of other minds—minds of her own age. (*She rises*) You're doing the right thing—I'm sure of that. (*In a business-like way*) I'd better get on with her packing— I don't know whether she wants to take any books with her.

(MISS WILLIAMS *exits up* C, *closing the door behind her.* CAROLINE *sinks wearily back into her chair.* PHILIP *enters down* L *and stands looking off* L. AMYAS *enters by the door up* L, *carrying his paintbox*)

AMYAS. (*to Philip; irritably*) Where is that girl? (*He moves to his stool*) Why can't she get up in the morning?

(PHILIP, *looking off* L, *does not answer*)

(*He sits, puts his paintbox on the ground beside him
and arranges his gear*) Have you seen her, Phil? What's
the matter with you? Has nobody given you any breakfast?

PHILIP. (*turning*) Eh? Oh, yes, of course. I—I'm waiting for
Merry. He's coming over. (*He looks at his watch*) I
wonder which way he'll come—I forgot to ask him.
Upper or lower path. I could go along and meet him.

AMYAS. Lower path's the shorter one. (*He rises and goes into
the room*) Where the devil is that girl? (*To Caroline*)
Have you seen Elsa? (*He goes to the door up* C)

CAROLINE. I don't think she's up yet.

(AMYAS *is about to open the door*)

Amyas, come here, I want to talk to you.

AMYAS. (*opening the door*) Not now.

CAROLINE. (*firmly*) Yes, now.

(AMYAS *looks sheepish, but closes the door.* PHILIP *moves
below the bench.* ELSA *enters down* L, *dressed in shorts
and shirt*)

PHILIP. (*to Elsa*) You're late on parade. You look on top of
the world this morning.

ELSA. (*radiant*) Do I? I feel it.

(PHILIP *exits down* L. ELSA *goes to the bench and sits facing
the pergola, basking in the sun*)

AMYAS. (*moving above the stool*) Caroline, I've told you I
don't want to discuss this. I'm sorry Elsa blew her top.
I told her not to.

CAROLINE. You didn't want a scene until you'd finished your
picture, is that it?

AMYAS. (*moving to Caroline*) Thank the Lord you understand.

CAROLINE. I understand you very well.

(ELSA *swings her legs over the bench and faces front. After
a moment she hears raised voices, rises and goes to the
french windows to listen*)

AMYAS. Good. (*He bends down to kiss Caroline*)

(CAROLINE *ducks aside, rises and crosses below Amyas to the
stool*)

CAROLINE. I may understand, but that doesn't mean that I'm taking this lying down. (*She turns to him*) Do you really mean you want to marry this girl?

AMYAS. (*moving to her*) Darling, I'm very fond of you—and of the child. You know that. I always shall be. (*Roughly*) But you've got to understand this. I'm damned well going to marry Elsa and nothing shall stop me.

CAROLINE. (*facing front*) I wonder.

AMYAS. (*moving up* R *of the stool*) If you won't divorce me, we'll live together and she can take the name of Crale by deed poll.

(PHILIP *enters down* L, *sees* ELSA *listening, and unseen, lounges against the downstage pillar of the pergola*)

CAROLINE. You've thought it all out, haven't you?

AMYAS. (*moving* R) I love Elsa—and I mean to have her.

CAROLINE. (*trembling*) Do as you please—I'm warning you.

AMYAS. (*turning*) What do you mean by that?

CAROLINE. (*turning suddenly on him*) I mean you're mine—and I don't mean to let you go.

(AMYAS *moves to Caroline*)

Sooner than let you go to that girl, I'll . . .

AMYAS. Caroline, don't be a fool.

CAROLINE. (*near to tears*) You and your women! You don't deserve to live.

AMYAS. (*trying to embrace her*) Caroline . . .

CAROLINE. I mean it. (*She pushes him away*) Don't touch me. (*She crosses to the door down* R *in tears*) It's too cruel—it's too cruel.

AMYAS. Caroline . . .

(CAROLINE *exits down* R. AMYAS *gives a hopeless gesture, turns and crosses towards the french windows.* ELSA *turns quickly away, sees Philip and quickly looks nonchalant*)

(*He goes on the terrace*) Oh, there you are at last. (*He moves to his stool and sits*) What do you mean by wasting half the morning? Get into the pose.

ELSA. (*looking at Amyas over the top of the easel*) I'll have to get a pullover. It's quite a chilly wind.

AMYAS. Oh, no, you don't. It'll change all the tones of the skin.

ELSA. I've got a yellow one like this shirt—and, anyway, you're painting my hands this morning, you said so.

(ELSA *pouts and runs off by the door up* L)

AMYAS. (*shouting after Elsa*) You don't know what I'm painting. Only *I* know that. Oh, hell! (*He squeezes paint from a tube on to his palette and mixes the paint*)

PHILIP. Trouble with Caroline?

AMYAS. (*looking up*) Heard some of it, did you?

(PHILIP *crosses below Amyas to* R)

I knew just what would happen. Elsa had to open her big mouth. Caroline gets hysterical and won't listen to reason.

PHILIP. (*turning*) Poor Caroline! (*He does not say it with pity, instead there is trace of satisfaction in his tone*)

(AMYAS *looks sharply at Philip*)

AMYAS. Caroline is all right. Don't waste your pity on her.

PHILIP. (*crossing to* LC) Amyas, you're incredible. I don't know that I'd really blame Caroline if she took a hatchet to you.

AMYAS. (*irritably*) Do stop pacing, Phil. You're putting me off. I thought you were going to meet Merry.

PHILIP. (*moving to the upstage end of the pergola*) I was afraid of missing him.

AMYAS. What's the big hurry? You saw him yesterday.

PHILIP. (*crossly*) Since I seem to annoy you, I'll take myself off.

(PHILIP *exits up* L, *above the pergola.* ELSA *enters by the door up* L, *with a pullover draped over her arm*)

AMYAS. (*looking up*) At last! Now, get me some beer, will you, I'm thirsty. What on earth you want with a pullover on a day like this I don't know. I'm boiling. You'll be wanting snow boots next, and a hot-water bottle to sit on.

(ELSA *drops her pullover on the bench, goes to the trolley and pours a glass of beer*)

(*He rises, goes down* R, *turns and looks at his painting*) This is the best thing I've ever done. (*He moves to the painting and bends down to it*) Do you think Da Vinci knew what he'd done when he'd finished La Giaconda?

(ELSA *crosses with the glass of beer and holds it out over the easel*)

ELSA. La—what?

AMYAS. (*taking the glass*) La Gia—the Mona Lisa, you ignorant bitch—oh, never mind. (*He drinks*) Pah! It's warm. Isn't there a bucket of ice?

ELSA. (*sitting on the bench*) No. (*She takes up her pose*)

AMYAS. Somebody's always forgetting something. (*He crosses above the bench and looks off* L) I loathe hot beer. (*He calls*) Hi, Angela!

ANGELA. (*off* L; *calling*) What?

AMYAS. Go and get me a bottle of beer from the refrigerator.

(ANGELA *enters down* L)

ANGELA. Why should I?

AMYAS. Common humanity. (*He crosses to his stool*) Come on, now, be a sport.

ANGELA. Oh, all right.

(ANGELA *sticks her tongue out at Amyas and runs off by the door up* L)

AMYAS. Charming little girl. (*He sits on his stool*) Your left hand's wrong—up a bit.

(ELSA *moves her left hand*)

That's better. (*He sips some beer*)

(MISS WILLIAMS *enters up* C *and goes on to the terrace*)

MISS WILLIAMS. (*to Amyas*) Have you seen Angela?

AMYAS. She's just gone into the house to get me some beer. (*He paints*)

MISS WILLIAMS. Oh.

(MISS WILLIAMS *seems surprised. She turns and exits quickly by the door up* L. AMYAS *whistles as he works*)

ELSA. (*after a few moments*) Must you whistle?

AMYAS. Why not?

ELSA. That particular tune?

AMYAS. (*not understanding*) What? (*He sings*) "When we are married, why what shall we do?" (*He grins*) Not very tactful.

(CAROLINE *enters by the door up* L, *carrying a bottle of beer*)

CAROLINE. (*moving down* C; *coldly*) Here's your beer. I'm sorry the ice was forgotten.

AMYAS. Oh, thank you, Caroline. Open it for me, will you? (*He holds out his glass*)

(CAROLINE *takes the glass, crosses to the trolley, and with her back to the audience, opens the bottle and pours the beer.* AMYAS *begins to whistle the same tune, realizes this, and checks himself.* CAROLINE *takes the bottle and the glass of beer to* AMYAS)

CAROLINE. Here's your beer.

AMYAS. (*taking the glass*) And you hope it chokes me. (*He grins*) Here's to hoping! (*He drinks*) Phew, this tastes worse than the other. Still, it is cold.

(CAROLINE *places the bottle beside the paintbox, goes into the room and exits up* C. AMYAS *resumes painting.* MEREDITH *enters breathlessly down* L)

MEREDITH. Is Phil about?

AMYAS. He went to meet you.

MEREDITH. Which path?

AMYAS. Lower one.

MEREDITH. I came by the other.

AMYAS. Well, you can't go on chasing each other. Better hang on and wait.

MEREDITH. (*taking out his handkerchief and wiping his brow*) I'm hot. I'll go inside. It's cooler. (*He crosses to the french windows*)

AMYAS. Get yourself a cold drink. Get one of the women to get it for you.

(MEREDITH *goes into the room, and hesitates, uncertain what to do*)

(*He looks at Elsa*) You've wonderful eyes, Elsa. (*He pauses*) I'll leave the hands—concentrate on the eyes. I haven't quite got them.

(MEREDITH *moves to the french windows and looks out to the terrace*)

Move your hands as much as you like—I'm getting it. Now for God's sake don't move or talk.

(MEREDITH *turns and crosses in the room to* RC)

ELSA. I don't want to talk.

AMYAS. That's a change.

(ANGELA *enters up* C, *carrying a tray with a jug of iced lemonade and two glasses, which she places on the table* R)

ANGELA. Refreshments!

MEREDITH. Oh, thank you, Angela. (*He moves to the tray and pours a glass of lemonade*)

ANGELA. (*crossing to the french windows*) We aim to please. (*She goes on to the terrace. To Amyas*) Did you get your beer all right?

AMYAS. Sure I did, You're a great gal.

ANGELA. (*laughing*) Very kind, aren't I? Ha, ha. You wait and see.

(ANGELA *runs into the room and exits up* C, *closing the door behind her.* MEREDITH *sips his lemonade*)

AMYAS. (*suspicious*) That kid's up to something. (*He rubs his right shoulder*) That's funny.

ELSA. What's the matter?

AMYAS. I'm very stiff this morning. Rheumatism, I suppose.

ELSA. (*mocking*) Poor creaking old man.

(PHILIP *enters down* L)

AMYAS. (*chuckling*) Creaking with age. Hullo, Phil. Merry's inside waiting for you.

PHILIP. Good. (*He crosses and goes into the room*)

(MEREDITH *puts his glass on the tray and meets* PHILIP *at* C. AMYAS *resumes painting*)

MEREDITH. Thank goodness you've come. I didn't know what to do.

PHILIP. What is all this? Caroline and the governess were in the room when you rang up.

MEREDITH. (*in a low voice*) There's a bottle missing from my lab.

PHILIP. So you told me. But what's in it?

MEREDITH. Conine.

PHILIP. Hemlock?

MEREDITH. Yes, conine's the pure alkaloid.

PHILIP. Dangerous?

MEREDITH. Very.

PHILIP. And you've no idea whatsoever who could have taken it?

MEREDITH. No. I always keep the door locked.

PHILIP. You locked it yesterday?

MEREDITH. You know I did. You saw me.

PHILIP. You're sure about this—you haven't just mislaid the bottle—shoved it away somewhere? (*He crosses to* R)

MEREDITH. I showed it them all yesterday. And then I put it back in its place on the shelf.

PHILIP. (*turning; sharply*) Who came out of the room last?

MEREDITH. (*unwillingly*) Caroline—I waited for her.

PHILIP. But you weren't watching her?

MEREDITH. No.

PHILIP. (*with decision*) Well, then Caroline took it.

MEREDITH. You really think so?

PHILIP. (*crossing above Meredith to* L) So do you, or you wouldn't be in such a state.

MEREDITH. That's what she had in mind yesterday—when she said everything was finished for her. She meant to do away with herself. (*He sinks on to the stool, and faces up stage*)

PHILIP. Well, cheer up, she hasn't done away with herself yet.

MEREDITH. You've seen her this morning. Is she all right?

PHILIP. Seems just the same as usual to me.

MEREDITH. What are we going to do?

PHILIP. You'd better tackle her.

MEREDITH. I don't know—how shall I go about it?

PHILIP. I should just say straight out—"You pinched my conine yesterday. Hand it back, please."

MEREDITH. (*doubtfully*) Like that?

PHILIP. (*crossing above Meredith to* R) Well, what do you want to say ?

MEREDITH. I don't know. (*He brightens*) We've got plenty of time, I imagine. She wouldn't take the stuff until she goes to bed, would she?

PHILIP. (*dryly*) Probably not. If she means to take it at all.

MEREDITH. You think she doesn't?

PHILIP. (*crossing below Meredith to* L) She may want it to make a theatrical scene with Amyas. Give up that girl or I'll swallow this and kill myself.

MEREDITH. That wouldn't be like Caroline.

PHILIP. Well—you know her best. (*He moves up* LC)

MEREDITH. You're always bitter about Caroline. You used to be crazy about her once—don't you remember? (*He rises*)

PHILIP. (*turning; annoyed*) A brief attack of calf love. It wasn't serious.

MEREDITH. And then—you turned against her.

PHILIP. (*exasperated*) Let's stick to the present, shall we?

MEREDITH. Yes. Yes, of course.

(CAROLINE *enters up* C)

CAROLINE. Hullo, Merry, stay to lunch, won't you? It'll be ready in a moment. (*She moves to the french windows*)

MEREDITH. Well, thanks.

(CAROLINE *goes on to the terrace and stands by the easel, looking at Amyas*)

ELSA. (*to Amyas; as Caroline comes out*) I shall have a break.

AMYAS. (*rather indistinctly*) Stop where you are, damn you.

MEREDITH. (*to Philip*) After lunch, I'll take Caroline out in the garden and tackle her. All right?

(PHILIP *nods, closes the door up* C *and moves to the french windows.* ELSA *rises and stretches.* MEREDITH *moves to the table* R *and picks up his half-finished lemonade*)

CAROLINE. (*urgently*) Amyas ...

PHILIP. (*moving on to the terrace*) You seem very preoccupied this morning, Caroline.

CAROLINE. (*to Philip; over her shoulder*) I? Oh, yes, I'm very busy getting Angela off. (*To Amyas. Very urgently*) You will do it, Amyas. You *must*. This afternoon.

(PHILIP *moves above the bench.* AMYAS *passes his hand over his forehead. He has lost control of clear speech*)

AMYAS. All ri-right! I'll see—her packing ...

CAROLINE. (*turning to the french windows*) We—we do want Angela to get off without too much fuss. (*She goes into the room and stands above the stool*)

(PHILIP *crosses to the french windows.* ELSA *sits on the bench.* AMYAS *shakes his head to try and clear his brain*)

PHILIP. (*to Caroline*) You spoil that brat.

CAROLINE. (*plumping cushions on the sofa*) We shall miss
her terribly when she's gone.

PHILIP. (*stepping into the room*) Where's little Carla?

(MEREDITH *crosses to the armchair* L *with his drink, and sits*)

CAROLINE. She's gone to stay with her godmother for a week.
She'll be home the day after tomorrow.

MEREDITH. What's Miss Williams going to do with herself
when Angela's gone?

CAROLINE. She's got a post at the Belgian Embassy. I shall
miss her.

(*A dinner gong sounds off in the hall*)

Lunch.

(ANGELA *bursts in up* C)

ANGELA. (*as she enters*) I'm starving. (*She runs on to the
terrace. To Elsa and Amyas*) Lunch, you two.

(MISS WILLIAMS *appears in the doorway up* C. CAROLINE
crosses to the table RC *and picks up her cigarette case*)

ELSA. (*rising and picking up her pullover*) Coming.

(ANGELA *goes into the room*)

(*To Amyas*) Lunch?

AMYAS. I—ah!

MISS WILLIAMS. Do try not to shout so, Angela, it really isn't
necessary.

ANGELA. I'm not shouting.

(ANGELA *exits up* C. MISS WILLIAMS *follows her off*)

CAROLINE. (*moving to the door up* C; *to Meredith*) I should
bring that in with you.

(MEREDITH *rises*)

PHILIP. (*looking at Meredith*) What—lemonade?

CAROLINE. (*to Philip*) For you, we've got a lovely bottle
of . . .

PHILIP. Château Neuf du Pape? Good! Hasn't Amyas finished it yet?

CAROLINE. (*to Meredith*) What a nice surprise to see you.

MEREDITH. I really came over to see Philip, but I'm always
happy to stay to lunch.

(CAROLINE *and* PHILIP *exit up* C. ELSA *comes into the room*)

(*He turns to Elsa*) Amyas?

ELSA. (*crossing to the door up* C) There's something he wants to finish.

(ELSA *exits up* C. MEREDITH *follows her off*)

ANGELA. (*off*) He hates stopping for lunch.

(*The paintbrush drops from* AMYAS' *hand. The* LIGHTS *slowly dim to* BLACK-OUT. *A spotlight comes up on Justin down* L)

JUSTIN. They all went in to lunch, leaving Amyas painting on the terrace. After lunch, Miss Williams and Mrs. Crale went out with coffee. Miss Williams?

(*The spotlight fades.* MISS WILLIAMS' *voice can be heard in the darkness*)

MISS WILLIAMS. Mr. Crale often refused lunch and went on painting. It was nothing out of the ordinary. He liked a cup of coffee brought to him, though. I poured it and Mrs. Crale took it out to him, and I followed. At the trial I told what we found. But there was something else —something I have not told anyone. I think it right that I should tell it now.

(*The* LIGHTS *come up.* AMYAS *lies prostrate on the ground below the easel.* CAROLINE *and* MISS WILLIAMS *are in the room, standing at the stool, on which there is a tray of coffee.* MISS WILLIAMS *is* R *of the stool, pouring out a cup of coffee, which she gives to Caroline.* CAROLINE *takes the coffee on to the terrace*)

CAROLINE. (*as she goes on to the terrace*) Amyas. (*She sees Amyas on the ground. Horrified*) Amyas! (*She stands for a moment, puts the coffee-cup on the bench, rushes to Amyas, kneels beside him and picks up his hand*)

(MISS WILLIAMS *comes quickly on to the terrace and moves to* L *of Caroline*)

He's—I think he's dead. (*She is distracted*) Well, go on. Quick. Telephone for a doctor or something.

(MISS WILLIAMS *goes quickly into the room. As soon as Miss Williams reaches the french windows,* CAROLINE *gives a furtive look round, takes out her handkerchief, picks up the beer bottle, wipes it, then presses Amyas' hand round it.* MEREDITH *enters up* C)

MISS WILLIAMS. (*to Meredith*) Get Dr. Fawcett, quickly. It's Mr. Crale. He's been taken ill.

(MEREDITH *stares at Miss Williams for a moment, then moves to the telephone and lifts the receiver.* MISS WILLIAMS *goes on to the terrace in time to see Caroline pressing Amyas' fingers round the bottle.* MISS WILLIAMS *freezes.* CAROLINE *rises, crosses quickly to the trolley, puts the bottle on it, then stands facing* L. MISS WILLIAMS *turns slowly and goes into the room*)

MEREDITH. (*into the telephone*) Four-two, please . . . Dr. Fawcett? . . . This is Alderbury . . . Can you come at once? Mr. Crale has been taken seriously ill . . .

MISS WILLIAMS. He's . . .

MEREDITH. (*to Miss Williams*) What? (*Into the telephone*) Just a moment. (*To Miss Williams*) What did you say?

(ELSA *enters up* C. PHILIP *follows her on. They are laughing and joking*)

MISS WILLIAMS. (*in a clear voice*) I said he's dead.

(MEREDITH *replaces the receiver*)

ELSA. (*staring at Miss Williams*) What did you say? Dead? Amyas? (*She rushes on to the terrace and stares down at Amyas*) Amyas! (*She draws in her breath, runs and kneels above Amyas and touches his head*)

(CAROLINE *turns. The others are motionless*)

(*Quietly*) Amyas!

(*There is a pause.* PHILIP *runs on to the terrace and stands below the bench.* MISS WILLIAMS *comes on to the terrace and stands below the french windows.* MEREDITH *follows her on and stands up* L *of the bench*)

(*She looks up at Caroline*) You've killed him. You said you'd kill him, and you've done it. Sooner than let me have him, you've killed him. (*She jumps up and goes to throw herself at Caroline*)

(PHILIP *moves quickly, stops Elsa and propels her round to Miss Williams.* ELSA *is hysterical and screams.* ANGELA *enters up* C *and stands beside the sofa*)

MISS WILLIAMS. Be quiet. Control yourself.
ELSA. (*in a frenzy*) She killed him. She killed him.
PHILIP. Take her inside—get her to lie down.

(MEREDITH *takes Elsa into the room*)

CAROLINE. Miss Williams, don't let Angela come—don't let her see.

(MEREDITH *takes* ELSA *off up* C. MISS WILLIAMS *looks at Caroline for a moment, then sets her lips firmly and goes into the room.* PHILIP *kneels beside Amyas and feels his pulse*)

ANGELA. Miss Williams, what is it? What's happened?
MISS WILLIAMS. Come to your room, Angela. There's been an accident.

(MISS WILLIAMS *and* ANGELA *exit up* C)

PHILIP. (*looking at Caroline*) It's murder.
CAROLINE. (*shrinking back; suddenly indecisive*) No. No—he did it himself.
PHILIP. (*quietly*) You can tell that story—to the police.

(*The* LIGHTS *slowly dim to* BLACK-OUT. *A spotlight comes up on Justin down* L)

JUSTIN. In due course the police arrived. They found the missing phial of conine in a drawer in Caroline's room. It was empty. She admitted taking it—but denied using it and swore she had no idea *why* it should be empty. No fingerprints but Meredith's and her own were found on it. On the terrace, a small eye-dropper was found crushed underfoot. It contained traces of conine and shows how the poison was introduced into the beer. Angela Warren told how she got a fresh bottle of beer from the refrigerator. Miss Williams took it from her and Caroline took it from Miss Williams, opened it and gave it to Amyas, as you have just heard. Neither Meredith nor Philip Blake touched it or went near it.

A week later Caroline Crale was arrested on a charge of murder.

(*The spotlight fades. After a moment, the* LIGHTS *come up showing the scene as it was at the beginning of the Act. The coffee, lemonade, trolley, easel, etc., have been removed. The picture on the wall is again that of Elsa.* PHILIP *stands* R *of the sofa.* MEREDITH *is seated on the sofa at the left end.* ANGELA *is seated on the left arm of the sofa.* ELSA *stands in front of the door up* C. MISS WILLIAMS *is seated on the right end of the stool.* CARLA *is seated in the armchair* R. JUSTIN *is just inside the french windows with a notebook in his hand. They are all dressed for outdoors with coats and hats.* ELSA *is in mink. She appears excited.* MEREDITH *is crushed and miserable.* PHILIP *is aggressive.* MISS WILLIAMS *sits with lips set firm.* ANGELA *is upright, interested and thoughtful*)

PHILIP. (*irritably*) Well, we've been through this extraordinary performance which must have been most painful to some of us. (*He crosses above the stool to* R *of Justin*) And what have we learnt? Nothing that we did not know before. (*He glares at Justin*)

(JUSTIN *smiles.* PHILIP *goes on to the terrace, stands by the bench and lights a cigarette.* MISS WILLIAMS *rises and moves* R)

JUSTIN. (*thoughtfully*) I wouldn't say that.
MEREDITH. It's brought it all back—just as though it happened yesterday. Most painful.
ELSA. (*crossing to the sofa and sitting on it,* R *of Meredith*) Yes, it brought it all back. It brought *him* back.
ANGELA. (*to Justin*) What have you learned that you did not know before?
JUSTIN. We shall go into that.

(PHILIP *comes into the room and crosses to* C)

PHILIP. May I point out something that does not seem to be recognized by anybody? (*He moves to* R *of Justin*) What we have been listening to—and supplying—can only be recollections, and probably faulty ones at that.
JUSTIN. As you say.
PHILIP. And therefore quite useless as evidence. (*He turns*

away up LC) We haven't heard *facts* at all, only people's vague recollections of facts.

JUSTIN. (*moving to* L *of Philip*) What we have heard has no evidential value as such—but it *has* a value, you know.

PHILIP. In what way?

JUSTIN. Shall we say, in what people choose to remember? Or, alternatively, choose to forget.

PHILIP. Very clever—but fanciful.

ANGELA. (*to Philip*) I don't agree. I . . .

PHILIP. (*overriding Angela*) And I will point out something else. (*He crosses below the stool and stands between Miss Williams and Elsa*) It's not just a question of what people remember, or do not remember. It might be a question of deliberate lying.

JUSTIN. Of course.

ANGELA. That's just the point, I rather imagine. (*She rises and moves* C) Or am I wrong?

JUSTIN. You are thinking on the right lines, Miss Warren.

(ANGELA *crosses to the armchair* L)

PHILIP. (*exasperated*) Look here, what is all this? If somebody is deliberately lying—why then . . .

ANGELA. (*sitting in the armchair* L) Exactly.

PHILIP. (*crossing to Justin; angrily*) Do you mean you have got us here with the idea—the preposterous idea, that one of us could be guilty of murder?

ANGELA. Of course he has. Have you only just realized it?

PHILIP. I never heard such offensive nonsense in my life.

ANGELA. If Amyas didn't kill himself, and if his wife didn't murder him, then one of us must have done so.

PHILIP. But it has already been made perfectly clear, in the course of what we've heard, that nobody but Caroline *could* have killed him.

JUSTIN. I don't think we can be as certain as all that.

PHILIP. (*crossing below the stool to* R) Oh, God!

JUSTIN. (*not heeding*) There is the question you yourself raised, the question of lying.

(*There is a slight pause.* PHILIP *sits on the right end of the stool, with his back to the audience*)

When one person's evidence is corroborated or acquiesced in by another person—(*he moves down* C) then it can be regarded as checked. But some of what we have heard is vouched for by only one person. *(He crosses below the stool and moves up* C) For instance, at the very beginning, we had to rely solely on Mr. Meredith Blake here for what passed between him and Caroline Crale.

MEREDITH. *(indignantly)* But, really . . .

JUSTIN. *(quickly)* Oh, I'm not disputing the authenticity of what you told us. I only point out that the conversation *could* have been an entirely different one.

MEREDITH. *(rising)* It was as accurate as anything could be after a lapse of sixteen years.

JUSTIN. Quite. *(He crosses to the french windows and goes on to the terrace)* But remember the fine weather and the open windows. This means that most of the conversations, even those that were apparently *tête-à-têtes*, could be and probably were, overheard from either inside or outside the room. *(He comes into the room and stands up* LC) But that is not so for all of them.

MEREDITH. *(moving* L) Are you getting at me?

(There is a pause. JUSTIN *looks at his notebook)*

JUSTIN. Not necessarily. I singled you out because you started the ball rolling.

MISS WILLIAMS. *(moving to* R *of the stool)* I would like to state here and now that any account I have given of *my* part in the affair is true. There is no witness who saw what I saw—Caroline Crale wiping fingerprints off that bottle, but I solemnly swear that is exactly what I saw her do. *(She turns to Carla)* I am sorry, for Carla's sake, I have to tell you this, but Carla is, I hope, courageous enough to face the truth.

ANGELA. Truth is what she asked for.

JUSTIN. And truth is what will help her. *(He crosses below the stool to Miss Williams)* What you don't realize, Miss Williams, is that what you have told us goes a long way towards proving Caroline Crale's *innocence*, not her guilt.

(There are general exclamations from the others. PHILIP *rises and moves to* L *of the stool)*

MISS WILLIAMS. What do you mean?

JUSTIN. You say you saw Caroline Crale take a handkerchief,

wipe the beer bottle, and then press her husband's fingers on it?

MISS WILLIAMS. Yes.

JUSTIN. (*after a pause; quietly*) The beer *bottle*?

MISS WILLIAMS. Certainly. The bottle.

JUSTIN. But the poison, Miss Williams, was not found in the bottle—not a trace of it. The conine was in the *glass*.

(*There are general exclamations from the others*)

ANGELA. You mean . . . ?

JUSTIN. (*moving up* C) I mean that if Caroline wiped the bottle, she thought the conine had been in the bottle. But if she had been the poisoner, she would have *known* where the conine was. (*He turns to Carla*)

(MISS WILLIAMS *moves to the sofa.* MEREDITH, *bewildered, moves* R)

CARLA. (*on a very soft sigh*) Of course.

(*There is a pause*)

JUSTIN. (*moving to Carla*) We all came here today to satisfy one person. Amyas Crale's daughter. Are you satisfied, Carla?

(*There is a pause.* CARLA *rises and moves above the stool.* JUSTIN *sits in the armchair* R)

CARLA. Yes. I'm satisfied. I know now—oh, I know now such a lot of things.

PHILIP. What things?

CARLA. (*moving* LC) I know that you, Philip Blake, fell violently in love with my mother, and that when she turned you down and married Amyas, you never forgave her. (*To Meredith*) You thought you still loved my mother—but really it was Elsa you loved.

(MEREDITH *looks at* ELSA, *who smiles triumphantly*)

But all that doesn't matter—what does matter is that I know now what made my mother behave so oddly at her trial.

(MISS WILLIAMS *sits on the sofa at the left end*)

I know what she was trying to hide. (*She crosses above the stool to Justin*) And I know just why she wiped those fingerprints off the bottle. Justin, do you know what I mean?

JUSTIN. I'm not quite sure.

CARLA. There's only one person Caroline would have tried to shield—(*she turns to Angela*) you.

ANGELA. (*sitting up*) Me?

CARLA. (*crossing to Angela*) Yes. It's all so clear. You'd played tricks on Amyas, you were angry with him— vindictive because you blamed him for sending you to school.

ANGELA. He was quite right.

CARLA. But you didn't think so at the time. You were angry. It was you who went and fetched a bottle of beer for him, although it was my mother who took it to him. And, remember, you'd tampered with his beer once before. (*She moves above the stool and kneels upon it*) When Caroline found him dead with the beer bottle and glass beside him, all that flashed into her mind.

ANGELA. She thought I'd murdered him?

CARLA. She didn't think you meant to. She thought you'd just played a trick, that you meant to make him sick, but that you had miscalculated the dose. Whatever you'd done, you'd killed him and she had to save you from the consequences. Oh, don't you see, it all fits in? The way she got you hustled off to Switzerland, the pains she took to keep you from hearing about the arrest and the trial.

ANGELA. She must have been mad.

CARLA. She had a guilt complex about you, because of what she'd done to you as a child. So, in her way, she paid her debt.

ELSA. (*rising and crossing below the stool to Angela*) So, it was you.

ANGELA. Don't be absurd. Of course it wasn't. Do you mean to say you believe this ridiculous story?

CARLA. Caroline believed it.

JUSTIN. Yes, Caroline believed it. It explains so much.

ANGELA. (*rising and crossing below the stool to Carla*) And you, Carla? Do you believe it?

CARLA. (*after a pause*) No.

ANGELA. Ah! (*She moves to the sofa and sits on it at the right end*)

CARLA. But then, there's no other solution.

(ELSA *sits in the armchair* L)

JUSTIN. Oh, yes, I think there might be. (*He rises and crosses to* LC) Tell me, Miss Williams, would it be natural or likely for Amyas Crale to have helped Angela by packing her clothes for her?

MISS WILLIAMS. Certainly not. He'd never dream of doing such a thing.

JUSTIN. And yet you, Mr. Philip Blake, overheard Amyas Crale say, "I'll see to her packing." I think you were wrong.

PHILIP. Now look here, Fogg, have you got the nerve to insinuate that I was lying?

(*The* LIGHTS *dim to* BLACK-OUT)

JUSTIN. I'm not insinuating anything. But let me remind you that the picture we now have is built up from remembered conversations.

(*The spotlight comes up on Justin down* L)

Memory is the only thread that hangs this picture together—it is a fragile thread and uncertain. I suggest one conversation we've heard about went quite differently. Let's suppose it went something like this.

(*The spotlight fades and after a moment the* LIGHTS *come up to reveal the house and terrace as it was sixteen years previously.* CAROLINE *is seated in the armchair* R, *and* AMYAS *is about to open the door up* C *to go out. Instead he turns towards Caroline*)

AMYAS. I've told you, Caroline, I don't want to discuss this.

CAROLINE. You didn't want a scene until you'd finished your picture. That's it, isn't it?

(AMYAS *crosses and leans over Caroline*)

Oh, I understand you very well.

(AMYAS *is about to kiss her*)

(*She rises quickly and crosses to* L) And what you're
doing is monstrous. You're going to treat this girl the
same way as you've treated all the others. You were in love
with her, but you're not now. All you want is to string
her along so that you can finish that picture.

AMYAS. (*smiling*) All right, then. That picture matters.

CAROLINE. So does she.

AMYAS. She'll get over it.

CAROLINE. (*partly pleading*) Oh, you! You've got to tell her.
Now—today. You can't go on like this, it's too cruel.

AMYAS. (*crossing to Caroline*) All right, I'll send her packing.
But the picture . . .

CAROLINE. Damn the picture! You and your women. You
don't deserve to live.

AMYAS. Caroline. (*He tries to embrace her*)

CAROLINE. I mean it. No, don't touch me. (*She crosses down*
R) It's too cruel—it's too cruel.

AMYAS. Caroline!

(CAROLINE *exits down* R. *The* LIGHTS *dim to* BLACK-OUT. *The*
spotlight comes up on Justin down L)

JUSTIN. Yes, that's how that conversation went. Caroline
pleaded, but not for herself. Philip Blake didn't hear
Amyas say, "I'll see to her packing"—what he in fact
heard was the voice of a dying man struggling to say,
"I'll *send* her packing."

(*The spotlight fades on Justin. The* LIGHTS *come up. Every-*
one is back in the same positions as they were before
the BLACK-OUT)

A phrase he'd no doubt used before of other mistresses,
but this time he spoke of you—(*he turns to Elsa*) didn't
he, Lady Melksham? The shock of that conversation
was terrific, wasn't it? And straight away you acted.
You'd seen Caroline take that phial of conine the day
before. You found it at once when you went upstairs
for a pullover. You handled it carefully, filled an eye-
dropper from it, came down again, and when Amyas
asked you for beer, you poured it into the glass, added
the conine, and brought the beer to him. You resumed
your pose. You watched him as he drank. Watched him
feel the first twinges, the stiffness of the limbs, and the

slow paralysis of the speech. You sat there and watched him die. (*He gestures to the portrait*) That's the portrait of a woman who watched the man she loved die.

(ELSA *rises quickly and stands looking at the portrait*)

And the man who painted it didn't know what was happening to him. But it's there, you know—in the eyes.

ELSA. (*in a hard voice*) He deserved to die. (*She looks at Justin*) You're a clever man, Mr. Fogg. (*She moves to the door up c and opens it*) But there isn't a damn thing you can do about it.

(ELSA *exits up c. There is a stunned silence, then gradually everyone starts to speak together.* CARLA *goes on to the terrace and stands below the bench*)

PHILIP. There—there must be *something* we can do.

MEREDITH. I can't believe it, I simply can't believe it.

ANGELA. (*rising*) It stares one in the face—how blind we've been.

PHILIP. What can we do, Fogg—what the hell can we do?

JUSTIN. In law, I'm afraid, nothing.

PHILIP. Nothing—what do you mean—nothing? (*He goes to the door up c*) Why the woman practically admitted . . . I'm not so sure you're right about that.

(PHILIP *exits up c*)

ANGELA. (*moving to the door up c*) It's ridiculous, but true.

(ANGELA *exits up c*)

MISS WILLIAMS. (*moving to the door up c*) It's incredible, it's incredible! I can't believe it.

(MISS WILLIAMS *exits up c.* PHILIP *re-enters up c*)

PHILIP. (*to Justin*) I'm not so sure you're right about that. I'll get my fellow on to it in the morning.

(PHILIP *exits up c*)

MEREDITH. (*moving to the door up c*) Elsa of all people, it seems absolutely impossible. Caroline's dead, Amyas is dead, there's no-one to bear witness—(*he turns in the doorway*) is there?

(MEREDITH *shakes his head and exits up* C. *The babel dies down.* CARLA *sits on the upstage end of the bench.* JUSTIN *looks out of the french windows for a moment at Carla, then goes on to the terrace.*)

JUSTIN. What do you want done, Carla?

CARLA. (*quietly*) Nothing. She's been sentenced already, hasn't she?

JUSTIN. (*puzzled*) Sentenced?

CARLA. To life imprisonment—inside herself. (*She looks at him*) Thank you.

JUSTIN. (*crossing above the bench to* L; *embarrassed*) You'll go back to Canada, now, and get married. There's no legal proof, of course, but we can satisfy your Jeff. (*He crosses below Carla to* C *and looks at his notes*)

CARLA. We don't need to satisfy him. I'm not going to marry him. I've already told him so.

JUSTIN. (*looking up*) But—why?

CARLA. (*thoughtfully*) I think I've—well—grown out of him. And I'm not going back to Canada. After all, I do belong here.

JUSTIN. You may be—lonely.

CARLA. (*with a mischievous smile*) Not if I marry an English husband. (*Gravely*) Now, if I could induce *you* to fall in love with me . . .

JUSTIN. (*turning to her*) *Induce* me? Why the devil do you think I've done all this?

CARLA. (*rising*) You've been mixing me up with my mother. But I'm Amyas' daughter, too. I've got a lot of the devil in me. I want you to be in love with *me*.

JUSTIN. Don't worry. (*He smiles, moves to her and takes her in his arms*)

CARLA. (*laughing*) I don't.

(*They kiss.* MEREDITH *enters up* C)

MEREDITH. (*as he enters*) May I suggest a drink at my house before . . . (*He realizes the room is empty, goes to the french windows and looks out*) Oh! (*He smiles*) My word!

MEREDITH *exits up* C *and the* LIGHTS *dim to* BLACK-OUT *as—*

the CURTAIN *falls*

ABOUT THE AUTHOR

AGATHA CHRISTIE, the great mystery writer, was born in England. After the publication of her first mystery in 1922, she wrote over sixty books. She was one of the few writers of detective and mystery fiction whose books consistently appeared on bestseller lists. In addition to her fiction, she also wrote successful plays, including *The Mousetrap* and *Witness for the Prosecution*. Many of her books and plays have been made into movies.